"Son of Man"

Volume 1
EARLY JEWISH LITERATURE

"Son of Man"

Volume 1
EARLY JEWISH LITERATURE

RICHARD BAUCKHAM

WILLIAM B. EERDMANS PUBLISHING COMPANY
GRAND RAPIDS, MICHIGAN

Wm. B. Eerdmans Publishing Co.
4035 Park East Court SE, Grand Rapids, Michigan 49546
www.eerdmans.com

© 2023 Richard Bauckham
All rights reserved
Published 2023
Printed in the United States of America

29 28 27 26 25 24 23   1 2 3 4 5 6 7

ISBN 978-0-8028-8326-1

Library of Congress Cataloging-in-Publication Data

A catalog record for this book is available from the Library of Congress.

Contents

List of Tables vii

Preface ix

List of Abbreviations xi

Introduction 1

PART 1: THE PARABLES OF ENOCH 5

1.1 Introduction to the Parables of Enoch 7

1.2 The Messianic Figure ("Son of Man") in the Parables of Enoch 17

1.3 The Messianic Figure in the Eschatological Narrative of the Parables of Enoch 58

1.4 The Identity of "That Son of Man" 80

1.5 Conclusions on the Messianic Figure in the Parables of Enoch 109

1.6 The Date of the Parables of Enoch: A Preliminary Discussion 112

1.7 The Place of Composition of the Parables of Enoch 119

Part 2: Interpretation of Daniel 7 in Second Temple–Period Judaism — 133

2.1 Introduction to Jewish Interpretations of Daniel 7 — 135

2.2 The Greek Versions of Daniel 7 — 142

2.3 The Oldest Interpretation of Daniel 7: 4Q246 (4QAramaic Apocalypse) — 173

2.4 Interpretation of Daniel 7 in Sibylline Oracles Book 5 — 201

2.5 Interpretation of Daniel 7 in the Apocalypse of Ezra (4 Ezra) — 221

2.6 A Messiah from the Past in Rabbinic Traditions — 260

2.7 A Context for the Parables of Enoch — 267

2.8 Interpretation of Daniel 7 in the Syriac Apocalypse of Baruch (2 Baruch) — 293

2.9 Rabbi Aqiva on Daniel 7 — 314

2.10 The Significant Absence of Daniel 7 in the Works of Josephus — 328

2.11 Conclusions on Jewish Interpretations of Daniel 7 — 370

Bibliography — 377

Index of Authors — 397

Index of Themes and Subjects — 402

Index of Ancient People and Places — 408

Index of Ancient Literature — 412

Tables

CHAPTER 1.2

1	Designations of the Messianic Figure and references to a throne of glory	51
2	Biblical allusions in Parables 2 and 3	53
3	Proposed translations of "throne of glory"	57

CHAPTER 1.4

1	Expressions and objects of "worship"	107

CHAPTER 2.2

1	"The abomination of desolation"	167
2	Daniel 7:13–14: the versions	168
3	Daniel 7:27: the versions	171

CHAPTER 2.3

1	Allusions to Daniel in 4Q246	195
2	4Q246 i 9–ii 1 with parallels	196
3	Scriptural allusions in 4Q246	198
4	The Messianic Figure in 4Q246: sources and themes	199
5	Exegetical sources for the Messianic Figure: 4Q246 and the Parables of Enoch compared	200

Chapter 2.4

1	Four oracles in Sibylline Oracles 5:52–434	219
2	Biblical allusions in Sibylline Oracles 5:414–433	220

Chapter 2.5

1	The Messiah in 4 Ezra	256
2	Biblical allusions in 4 Ezra 11–13	257
3	"Those who have not tasted death"	258

Chapter 2.7

1	Scriptural sources of the Messianic Figure: 4 Ezra and the Parables of Enoch compared	286
2	1 Enoch 56:5–8 with scriptural sources	287
3	Kings from the east	288
4	Resurrection	290
5	The number of the righteous dead	291

Chapter 2.8

1	Allusions to Daniel 7 in 2 Baruch	307
2	Biblical background to 2 Baruch 36–37	308
3	Biblical background to 2 Baruch 53	310
4	Isaianic background to 2 Baruch 72–74	312
5	Exegetical sources of the Messianic Figure: 2 Baruch, 4 Ezra, and the Parables of Enoch compared	313

Preface

This book (comprising both the present volume and volume 2) has been my pandemic project. I began work on it shortly before the Covid-19 pandemic began and have continued writing it throughout the pandemic. Just as the pandemic went on and on, far longer than anyone at first expected, so this book grew longer and longer, far beyond what I originally intended. It is almost by accident that it has become the largest book I have written. At every stage I realized that the content required more extensive examination and discussion than I had thought. It was only at the beginning of 2022 that I realized both that it needed to become two volumes and that what I had written fell neatly into two roughly equal halves: one volume on the Jewish literature, the other on the Gospels and Jesus. What convinced me that such an extensive discussion of this topic was worthwhile was that, as I entered into more detailed study of every part of it, I frequently found, not only that I was coming up with new observations and conclusions, but also that these were unexpected and surprising to me. I hope there will be many surprises for readers too.

I have no competence in Ethiopic, and so I was delighted that Darrell Hannah, who has himself worked extensively on the Ethiopic text of the Parables of Enoch, was willing to read the whole of my treatment of the Parables and made many helpful comments. Others who gave me assistance or suggestions on particular matters within this volume are Simon Gathercole, Loren Stuckenbruck, and Grant Macaskill.

When I was installed as Professor of New Testament Studies at the University of St. Andrews, thirty years ago, I was presented with a book to mark the occasion. I asked for it to be Matthew Black's commentary on 1 Enoch (1985), a landmark contribution to the study of the Enoch literature. I thought this appropriate because Black was a very distinguished predecessor in biblical studies at St. Andrews (Professor of Biblical Criticism 1954–1978) and also because it symbolized my commitment to studying the New Testament in its context in late Second Temple Judaism. I had long been interested in the Jewish apocalypses, and first read 1 Enoch around 1973. But at the time of my induction as professor, I certainly did not expect that I would myself write extensively about the Parables of Enoch, the most enigmatic component of 1 Enoch. Only while I was finishing the present volume did I realize that my choice of Matthew Black's book in 1992 has turned out to be even more appropriate than I thought at the time.

Abbreviations

Abbreviations of ancient works generally follow those listed in *The SBL Handbook of Style*, 2nd ed. (Atlanta: SBL Press, 2014).

AB	Anchor Bible
ABD	*Anchor Bible Dictionary*. Edited by David Noel Freedman. 6 vols. New York: Doubleday, 1992
AGJU	Arbeiten zur Geschichte des antiken Judentums und des Urchristentums
ArBib	The Aramaic Bible
ASV	American Standard Version
BAGD	Bauer, Walter, William F. Arndt, F. Wilbur Gingrich, and Frederick W. Danker. *Greek-English Lexicon of the New Testament and Other Early Christian Literature*. 2nd ed. Chicago: University of Chicago Press, 1979
Bib	*Biblica*
BibOr	Biblica et orientalia
CBQMS	Catholic Biblical Quarterly Monograph Series
cod.	codex
DSD	*Dead Sea Discoveries*
DSS	Dead Sea Scrolls
EJL	Early Judaism and Its Literature
frag.	fragment
GAP	Guides to Apocrypha and Pseudepigrapha
HSS	Harvard Semitic Studies
ICC	International Critical Commentary

JBL	*Journal of Biblical Literature*
JCT	Jewish and Christian Texts in Contexts and Related Studies
JJS	*Journal of Jewish Studies*
JSJ	*Journal for the Study of Judaism in the Persian, Hellenistic, and Roman Periods*
JSJSup	Supplements to the Journal for the Study of Judaism
JSP	*Journal for the Study of the Pseudepigrapha*
JSPSup	Journal for the Study of the Pseudepigrapha Supplement Series
JTS	*Journal of Theological Studies*
KJV	King James Version
LNTS	Library of New Testament Studies
LXX	Septuagint
MT	Masoretic Text
NASB	New American Standard Bible
NETS	*A New English Translation of the Septuagint*. Edited by Albert Pietersma and Benjamin G. Wright. New York: Oxford University Press, 2007
NIGTC	New International Greek Testament Commentary
NIV	New International Version
NJB	New Jerusalem Bible
NRSV	New Revised Standard Version
NTS	*New Testament Studies*
OTP	*The Old Testament Pseudepigrapha*. Vol. 1. Edited by James H. Charlesworth. London: Darton, Longman & Todd, 1983
OG	Old Greek
OTPMNS	*Old Testament Pseudepigrapha: More Noncanonical Scriptures*. Vol. 1. Edited by Richard Bauckham, James R. Davila, and Alexander Panayotov. Grand Rapids: Eerdmans, 2013
pap.	papyrus
par.	parallel
REB	Revised English Bible
RNJB	Revised New Jerusalem Bible
RSV	Revised Standard Version
RQ	*Revue de Qumrân*
SDSSRL	Studies in the Dead Sea Scrolls and Related Literature
SJ	Studia Judaica
SNTSMS	Society for New Testament Studies Monograph Series
StPB	Studia Post-biblica
SVTP	Studia in Veteris Testamenti Pseudepigrapha

Abbreviations

TDNT	*Theological Dictionary of the New Testament.* Edited by Gerhard Kittel and Gerhard Friedrich. Translated by Geoffrey W. Bromiley. 10 vols. Grand Rapids, 1964–1976
Tg.	Targum
Th	Theodotion
TSAJ	Texte und Studien zum antiken Judentum
VTSup	Supplements to Vetus Testamentum
WBC	Word Biblical Commentary
WUNT	Wissenschaftliche Untersuchungen zum Neuen Testament
[ ]	Scriptural references printed thus give the chapter and/or verse reference in Hebrew or Greek Bibles where their numbering differs from that in English translations.

Introduction

The phrase "the Son of Man" occurs about eighty times in the four Gospels in the New Testament but only once in the rest of the New Testament (Acts 7:56). It occurs almost exclusively on the lips of Jesus, and most readers readily recognize that Jesus uses it to refer to himself. But the meaning and significance of the phrase is never explained in the Gospels and is by no means obvious. In the history of the church it has been variously understood, and since the beginnings of modern New Testament scholarship in the early nineteenth century, it has been extensively studied and debated. After two hundred years it has to be said that that often professed goal of biblical scholars—a scholarly consensus—remains as elusive as ever.

The whole history of interpretation has been impressively recounted by Mogens Müller. His book plots the fortunes of all the major and many minor lines of interpretation.[1] The briefer survey by Delbert Burkett is also helpful in setting out the main issues and proposals.[2] Among the complexities of the debate is the question of authenticity. If not all of the "Son of Man" sayings in the Gospels are authentic sayings of Jesus, it might be that Jesus used the phrase in one way but tradents of the sayings or the evangelists used it in another way. If Jesus used the phrase originally in Aramaic, its significance might have been different from that of its Greek translation in the context of our Gospels. Then again, perhaps the significance of the expression in John's Gospel differs from

---

1. Mogens Müller, *The Expression "Son of Man" and the Development of Christology: A History of Interpretation* (London: Equinox, 2008).

2. Delbert Burkett, *The Son of Man Debate: A History and Evaluation*, SNTSMS 107 (Cambridge: Cambridge University Press, 1999).

that in the Synoptic Gospels. All these questions require close study of all the evidence in the Gospels, which I will undertake, in volume 2 (part 3) of this work, more thoroughly than has been done thus far in the history of scholarship. In connection with that study of the Gospels, I will address the question of what Jesus meant by the phrase in Aramaic. At that point I will discuss the claim that Jesus used an existing Aramaic idiom. (The evidence adduced for that claim is not found in the Jewish literature of the Second Temple period, and so it will not be considered in volume 1.)

Since the phrase "the Son of Man" appears without explanation in the Gospels, it is not surprising that many scholars have postulated a history of usage in Jewish religious tradition before Jesus (or before the Gospels). It has very often been argued that Jesus used the expression with reference to the figure in Daniel's vision in Daniel 7:13, which describes "one like a son of man," especially as a few of the sayings of Jesus undoubtedly allude to that text (Mark 13:26; 14:62; Matt 24:30; 26:64).[3] Jesus, it is argued, used the expression "the Son of Man" as a title referring to the figure of Daniel 7:13, identifying himself with that figure. But the fact that the phrase is not itself used as a title in Daniel has led to the theory that a Son of Man tradition existed in Second Temple Judaism, in which "the Son of Man" was known as the title of a messianic figure, arguably a transcendent Messiah from heaven, distinguished from the earthly Son of David. Daniel 7:13 itself would have been understood within such a tradition.

Central to this discussion has been the Parables (or Similitudes) of Enoch, since in the whole of Second Temple Jewish literature the phrase "son of man" is used with reference to a messianic figure only in this work. Many aspects of the Parables of Enoch are debatable: its original language (since it is now extant only in Ethiopic), its date and provenance, and, crucially for our purposes, the nature and identity of the messianic figure who is prominent in it. It has been dated both before the time of Jesus and after the writing of the Gospels. While it has often been taken as evidence of a wider Son of Man tradition within which it belongs, some have argued that the Parables of Enoch itself was a source known to Jesus or to the early Christians, thus dispensing with the need to postulate a wider tradition in order to explain the usage in the Gospels. But there are also serious questions to be addressed as to the way the phrase "son of man" is used in the Parables of Enoch. Is it used as a messianic

---

3. In general, scripture quotations, unless otherwise indicated, are from the NRSV. However, when I quote or allude to Dan 7:13, I use the translation "one like a son of man," which is the marginal reading in NRSV.

title that could be taken out of its literary context in the Parables and used independently as a self-explanatory title? It is because of the unresolved nature of so many key questions about the Parables of Enoch, as well as the fact that it has played a unique role in the debate about "the Son of Man" in the Gospels, that the first of the three parts of the present work is devoted to the Parables. It contains, in fact, the fullest study yet published of the messianic figure in the Parables of Enoch.

Besides the Parables of Enoch, the aspect of Second Temple Jewish literature that is most relevant as possible background or context for the use of "Son of Man" in the Gospels is the interpretation of Daniel 7. Whether or not there was a Son of Man tradition, there was certainly Jewish interpretation of the figure described in Daniel 7:13. So part 2 is devoted to Jewish interpretation of Daniel 7, including the two Greek translations of the text. The full range of texts from this period that draw on Daniel 7:13 has never been adequately studied before. The conclusions of this study are among the most novel results of the research embodied in this volume.

Finally, a note is required on my own use of "Son of Man" in the title of this work and throughout it. Like most people writing English today, I long ago gave up the use of masculine terms to refer to humans of both genders. I would not normally use "man" or even "mankind" in the generic sense, preferring "humanity" or "humans." But in the context of this book the phrase "Son of Man" is technical. I continue to use it because it is the term that has always been used in English and continues, almost universally, to be used. No alternative has established itself. The most recent translations of the Gospels still use "Son of Man." To break with this usage would have seemed unnecessarily strange. Even though I argue that the term is never used as a title, I capitalize "Son" and "Man" to signal that it is a technical usage.

PART 1

The Parables of Enoch

CHAPTER 1.1

Introduction to the Parables of Enoch

The Parables of Enoch (also known as the Similitudes of Enoch) is an early Jewish work that is now extant only in classical Ethiopic (Ge'ez). It forms part of the book known in Ethiopia as the Book of the Prophet Enoch, which belongs to the scriptures of the Ethiopian Orthodox Tewahedu church.[1] This is the book that in western biblical scholarship has become known as Ethiopic Enoch or 1 Enoch.[2] It is a compilation of several ancient works ascribed to or associated with the biblical figure of Enoch. It is usually divided into five major works and two short appendices: the Book of Watchers (chapters 1–36), the Book of the Parables of Enoch (37–71), the Astronomical Book (or Book of the Luminaries) (72–82), the Dream Visions of Enoch (83–90), the Epistle of Enoch (91–105), the Birth of Noah (106–107), and the Final Book of Enoch (108). The five major works were originally all distinct, composed at various times in the Second Temple period, but none has survived entirely in the original language. All were composed in a Semitic language (Aramaic in most cases, possibly Hebrew in the case of the Parables),[3] translated into Greek, and then translated from Greek into Ethiopic. The Ethiopic version remains the only complete version of any of them, but there are substantial Greek sections of the Book of Watchers, the Dream Visions, and the Epistle of Enoch (repre-

---

1. For an overview of its place in the Ethiopian Christian tradition, see Bruk Ayele Asale, *1 Enoch as Christian Scripture* (Eugene, OR: Pickwick, 2020) chapters 5–6.

2. These titles distinguish it from Slavonic Enoch or 2 Enoch.

3. But for a possible indication that the Parables was composed in Greek, using the Greek version of the Book of Watchers, see Loren Stuckenbruck, "The Parables of Enoch According to George Nickelsburg and Michael Knibb," in *Enoch and the Messiah Son of Man: Revisiting the Book of Parables*, ed. Gabriele Boccaccini (Grand Rapids: Eerdmans, 2007) 65–71, here 69–71.

senting more than one Greek version). Many Aramaic fragments of the Book of Watchers, the Book of the Luminaries, the Dream Visions, and the Epistle (including chapters 106–107) were found at Qumran. Some Greek fragments that may be from a manuscript of the Epistle of Enoch were also found in the Qumran caves.[4] In addition, Aramaic fragments of another work in which Enoch features, the Book of Giants, were found in Cave 4. But no fragment of the Parables of Enoch has been identified among the Qumran scrolls.

The significance of the absence of the Parables from the Dead Sea Scrolls is not easy to assess. It always needs to be stressed that absence of evidence is not evidence of absence. Even if the Parables was not in the Qumran library, that would not necessitate that it did not exist at the time. The Qumran library was not an exhaustive collection of all Jewish writings extant in that period. Those who collected and used the library were evidently interested in Enoch literature, but there could be a variety of reasons why the Parables was not in their collection. After all, the compilation of Enochic literature we know as 1 Enoch does not include the Book of Giants, which undoubtedly existed when this compilation was finalized.

But do we really know that the Parables of Enoch was not in the Qumran library? The Aramaic fragments of the Enoch literature (excluding the Book of Giants) derive from twelve distinct manuscripts.[5] At least some of these contained more than one of the three works the Book of Watchers, the Dream Visions, and the Epistle of Enoch.[6] Those three were evidently already a collection. It is unlikely (though it cannot be excluded) that any of these manuscripts also contained the Parables. But the Book of the Luminaries, a very long work, is found only in distinct manuscripts (4Q208, 209, 210, 211). The Book of Giants, a work closely related to the Book of Watchers and evidently popular at

---

4. For details of the Greek fragments, see Michaël Langlois, *Le premier manuscrit du Livre d'Hénoch: Étude épigraphique et philologique des fragments araméens de 4Q201 à Qumrân*, Lectio Divina (Paris: Cerf, 2008) 55; Michael A. Knibb, "The Book of Enoch or Books of Enoch? The Textual Evidence for 1 Enoch," in *The Early Enoch Literature*, ed. Gabriele Boccaccini and John J. Collins, JSJSup 121 (Leiden: Brill, 2007) 21–40, here 35. The identification has been questioned by George Nickelsburg, "The Greek Fragments of 1 Enoch from Qumran Cave 7: An Unproven Identification," *RQ* 21 (2004) 361–63; Peter W. Flint, "Papyri from Qumran Cave 7," in *Dictionary of Early Judaism*, ed. John J. Collins and Daniel C. Harlow (Grand Rapids: Eerdmans, 2010) 1026–27, here 1027.

5. Eleven have long been recognized: 4Q201(En^a), 4Q202(En^b), 4Q204(En^c), 4Q205(En^d), 4Q206(En^e), 4Q207(En^f), 4Q208(Enastr^a), 4Q209(Enastr^b), 4Q210(Enastr^c), 4Q211(Enastr^d), 4Q212(En^g). Esther Eshel and Hanan Eshel, "New Fragments from Qumran: 4QGenf, 4QIsa^b, 4Q226, 8QGen, and XQpapEnoch," *DSD* 12 (2005) 134–57, identified a fragment of another manuscript (unlike the others, papyrus).

6. For the contents of each manuscript, see Langlois, *Le premier manuscrit*, 51–59.

Qumran, is also found only in distinct manuscripts (1Q23, 1Q24, 2Q26, 4Q203, 530, 531, 532, 533, 6Q8). So it remains a possibility that one or more manuscripts containing the Parables, a relatively long text, existed, although no fragments have been identified. A very large number of very small fragments, containing too little text to be identifiable, were found in Cave 4,[7] not to mention other caves, from which only a handful of identifiable texts were recovered. A fragment of the Book of Giants on papyrus (6Q8) is among the only twenty identifiable fragments from Cave 6. The very small papyrus fragments of the Epistle of Enoch in Greek (7Q 4, 8, 11–14), if they are correctly identified as such, were among the very few identifiable fragments from Cave 7. Moreover, only in 2004 was a small fragment of a papyrus that contained the Book of Watchers (XQpapEnoch) identified by Esther and Hanan Eshel.[8] (It could not be assigned to any of the known caves.) So the possibility undoubtedly remains that fragments of the Parables of Enoch might still be identified.

It would be hazardous to conclude anything from the absence of the Parables among the Scrolls. It may have been in the Qumran library, though not identifiable in any surviving fragments. If it was not in the library, it may have been preserved by other Jewish groups during the period when the Qumran library was in use. Or it may not have been written at the time when that collection was being made. But whereas the Qumran Aramaic fragments of the other Enochic works give us significant (though far from complete) access to those works in their original language, and also help us to date them, in the case of the Parables Qumran is hardly any help at all. After the discoveries at Qumran, we still lack any fragment of the Parables in a language other than Ethiopic, and the question of its date is as open as it ever was. Later in this book I shall argue, on other grounds, that the Parables was probably written in the late first century or early second century CE, but I do not treat its absence from Qumran as evidence for this. Nor do I think we can be as confident about its date as we can about those components of 1 Enoch that have been found at Qumran.

7. James H. Charlesworth, "The Date and Provenience of the *Parables of Enoch*," in *Parables of Enoch: A Paradigm Shift*, ed. Darrell L. Bock and James H. Charlesworth, JCT 11 (London: Bloomsbury, 2013) 37–57, here 44, says: "hundreds of thousands of fragments," which may be an exaggeration.

8. Esther Eshel and Hanan Eshel, "New Fragments from Qumran: 4QGen[f], 4QIsa[b], 4Q226, 8QGen, and XQpapEnoch," *DSD* 12 (2005) 134–57. They first published the identification in *Tarbiz* 73 (2004) 171–79. See also Loren Stuckenbruck, "The Early Traditions Related to 1 Enoch from the Dead Sea Scrolls: An Overview and Assessment," in *The Early Enoch Literature*, ed. Boccaccini and Collins, 41–63, here 54–56. (Since writing this, I have been alerted to the fact that this fragment has been shown to be probably a modern forgery: see Kipp Davis et al., "Nine Dubious 'Dead Sea Scrolls' Fragments from the Twenty-First Century," *DSD* 24 [2017] 189–228.)

However, there is one respect in which the Qumran Aramaic fragments should affect the study of the Ethiopic version of the Parables, still the only version in which the Parables are extant. Of these Aramaic fragments of other parts of 1 Enoch, Loren Stuckenbruck writes, "Taken together, they may reflect a text for some parts of 1 Enoch that is longer than what is extant from the later versions of 1 Enoch. . . . Moreover, they provide evidence for a different text or perhaps even recensions of books which do not strictly correspond to the later Greek and Ethiopic recensions."[9] Michael Knibb suggests that "the relationship between the Ethiopic and Greek on the one hand and the Aramaic on the other is not that of straight translation, but is rather comparable to that between the Hebrew of the Massoretic Text of Jeremiah and the Hebrew text that served as the *Vorlage* of the Old Greek of Jeremiah."[10]

Since the Ethiopic version of the Parables was translated, along with the other parts of 1 Enoch, from Greek, itself derived from an Aramaic or possibly Hebrew original,[11] these observations suggest that in the case of the Parables also we are not dealing with a "straight translation." There may have been more than one recension of the original Semitic text, and the Ethiopic may be based on a Greek version that was not in every respect faithful to its Semitic *Vorlage*. The surviving Greek texts of parts of 1 Enoch certainly attest more than one recension of the Greek.[12] So in studying the Parables of Enoch, we must reckon not only with the character of the Ethiopic as a translation of a translation, which itself entails errors of translation as well as accidental errors

---

9. Stuckenbruck, "The Early Traditions," 63. For detailed examples of differences between the Aramaic, Greek, and Ethiopic, see Knibb, "The Book of Enoch," 21–25.

10. Knibb, "The Book of Enoch," 29.

11. Suggestions that the Ethiopic is a direct translation of the Aramaic or Hebrew, or that it is a translation from Greek that also reflects knowledge of the Aramaic, have been generally rejected in recent scholarship: see George W. E. Nickelsburg, *1 Enoch 1: A Commentary on the Book of 1 Enoch Chapters 1–36; 81–108*, ed. Klaus Baltzer, Hermeneia (Minneapolis: Fortress, 2001) 15–16; George W. E. Nickelsburg and James C. VanderKam, *1 Enoch 2: A Commentary on the Book of 1 Enoch Chapters 37–82*, ed. Klaus Baltzer, Hermeneia (Minneapolis: Fortress, 2012) 30–34. (Within the latter volume, Nickelsburg is author of the commentary on chapters 37–71 [the Parables] and VanderKam of the commentary on chapters 72–82 [the Book of the Luminaries]. In the rest of this book, Nickelsburg's work in this volume will be cited as Nickelsburg, *1 Enoch 2*.) Michael A. Knibb, *The Ethiopic Book of Enoch: A New Edition in the Light of the Aramaic Dead Sea Fragments* (Oxford: Clarendon, 1978) 2:44–46, offers evidence that the Ethiopic version sometimes agrees with the Aramaic against the extant Greek texts, but this could be explained by the hypothesis of different recensions of the Greek text.

12. For a suggested stemma, relating the Aramaic to the two recensions of the Greek, and the Ethiopic to one of these recensions, see Langlois, *Le premier manuscrit*, 486.

of transmission, but also with editorial interventions in the text, especially in the Greek version that was translated into Ethiopic.

This obviously makes study of the Parables as a work of Second Temple–period Judaism a hazardous, perhaps even questionable enterprise. I undertake such an enterprise in the first part of this book, both because some form of a Second Temple–period Jewish work undoubtedly has come down to us in Ethiopic,[13] and because so many scholars have already made use of the Parables of Enoch either in order to throw light on the use of the phrase "son of man" by Jesus in the Gospels or for the sake of its perceived relevance to early Christology more generally. I take the view that we must make the best of the evidence we have, while acknowledging that all our conclusions carry more than the usual degree of uncertainty that necessarily attaches to the interpretation of an ancient text of which we know little other than the text itself. Occasionally it will be appropriate to suspect some errors underlying the readings of the Ethiopic manuscripts available. Occasionally it will be appropriate to propose emendations. Sometimes dislocations of the text seem very likely to have occurred. Finally, it is a well-recognized characteristic of the Ethiopic version of the Parables that it contains substantial interpolations that cannot be part of the original work.[14] This recognition is based on the content of these passages and their discontinuity with the surrounding context.

These are commonly known as Noachic passages, because, although Enoch does appear in them, they are narrated in the first person by Noah. They have been generally thought to derive from a book of Noah that bore some relationship to the Enoch literature, perhaps especially to the Parables. The following can be safely identified as interpolations: 54:7–55:2; 60:1–10, 24–25; 65:1–69:25. (The last passage probably consists of a number of distinct fragments.) It is also clear that a portion of the original text of the Parables has been omitted between 64:2 and 65:26 and replaced by the interpolated material in 65:1–69:25.[15] (This will be discussed in chapter 1.3.) For our present purposes we can disre-

---

13. József T. Milik, *The Books of Enoch: Aramaic Fragments of Qumrân Cave 4* (Oxford: Clarendon, 1976) 89–98, famously argued that the Parables is a Christian work of the third century CE, but I am unaware of any contemporary scholar who doubts that it derives from late Second Temple–period Judaism. But cf. Ida Frölich, "The Parables of Enoch and Qumran Literature," in *Enoch and the Messiah*, ed. Boccaccini, 343–51, here 351: "I think we should not even rule out the possibility that the authors of the Parables might have been Jewish Christians."

14. On dislocations and interpolations, see George W. E. Nickelsburg, "Discerning the Structure(s) of the Enochic Book of Parables," in *Enoch and the Messiah*, ed. Boccaccini, 23–47.

15. Nickelsburg, *1 Enoch 2*, 20; Nickelsburg, "Discerning the Structure(s)," 45–46.

gard these interpolations, though we must take account of the fact that some original text is missing between 64:2 and 69:26. There is no strong reason for regarding any other passages as secondary additions to the original form of the Parables.[16] Many scholars have thought that chapters 70–71 (or 70:3–71:17), in which "that Son of Man" is identified as Enoch, must be a later addition to a work that did not originally make this identification. Others have thought that the identification with Enoch was intended originally, and in chapter 1.4 I shall offer evidence that there are deliberate hints of this identification throughout the Parables. There is no good reason to consider chapters 70–71 secondary.

It is assumed that the whole of Ethiopic Enoch (the collection now known as 1 Enoch) was translated from Greek to Ethiopic along with the rest of the Old and New Testaments sometime between the fourth century, when the Christian faith was introduced into Ethiopia, and the end of the sixth century.[17] This particular collection of Enochic works must therefore have existed in Greek, but we do not know when it was assembled. Although it contains five major works, there is no reason to suppose that it was ever regarded as an Enochic "Pentateuch," comparable with the Mosaic one. The Parables could have been translated into Greek independently of other Enochic works and come to form part of the collection only in Greek. Presently we have no means of determining these issues.[18]

The superscription to the Book of Parables in Ethiopic begins, "The second vision that he saw," but these words were likely added when the Parables was incorporated into the larger collection, placed after the Book of Watchers, and refer back to 1:2.[19] They treat the Book of Watchers as Enoch's first vision and the Parables as his second. Neither book is really a single vision. George Nickelsburg regards the words "another vision" in 39:4 as also a gloss that was added when the collection was made,[20] but it is possible that the vision in this case is being related not to the whole of the Book of Watchers but to the series of visions Enoch sees in chapters 17–36. In that case, 39:4 is describing the vision in chapter 39 as another of the same kind. Others follow in the rest

---

16. Whether chapter 42 is original or a secondary addition is debated; cf. Stuckenbruck, "The Parables of Enoch," 68.

17. Knibb, *The Ethiopic Book of Enoch*, 2:22; Asale, *1 Enoch*, 10–11.

18. A good discussion of the issue of Enochic collections, stressing how little we know, is in Eibert J. C. Tigchelaar, "Remarks on Transmission and Traditions in the Parables of Enoch: A Response to James VanderKam," in *Enoch and the Messiah*, ed. Boccaccini, 100–109, here 102–4.

19. Nickelsburg, *1 Enoch 2*, 85, textual note.

20. Nickelsburg, *1 Enoch 2*, 111, note 4a.

of the Book of Parables. This interpretation coheres with the fact that 39:1–2 is a brief summary of the narrative part of the Book of Watchers (6–16). This would suggest that the Book of Parables was designed to be a sequel to the Book of Watchers, consisting of a series of cosmic journeys and visions similar to those of chapters 17–36. Its place as the second work in the collection is therefore very appropriate, but this does not mean that it was written to be part of that collection or even that it originally circulated attached to the Book of Watchers.

How does the Parables of Enoch relate to the rest of the Enoch literature that we know as part of 1 Enoch and of which Aramaic fragments have been preserved at Qumran? There is now broad agreement about the dates of those works. The Astronomical Book is probably the oldest Enochic work. Both it and the Book of Watchers date from the third century BCE. The historical allegory in the Animal Apocalypse (1 En. 85–90) indicates a fairly precise date for the Book of the Dream Visions (1 En. 83–90) between 164 and 160 BCE. The Epistle of Enoch (incorporating the Apocalypse of Weeks) is usually dated somewhat earlier, before the Maccabean revolt. Thus the major Enochic works found at Qumran all date from before the middle of the second century BCE.[21] They undoubtedly form a literary tradition, sharing a number of key themes and interests associated with the figure of Enoch. It is likely that the authors of the later works were all familiar with the earlier ones. However, each of the works is significantly different from the others. Each is a novel and distinctive contribution to the corpus.

Whether this literary tradition developed within a specific social context—groups of Jews for whom the Enoch literature was central and defined their form of Judaism—is much less certain. It has become common to postulate an "Enochic Judaism" that produced this literature and may have formed the older milieu from which the Qumran community sprang.[22] Specific social contexts for individual parts of the literature are proposed. But extrapolating groups from texts that have very little to say about the social context in which they were written and to which they were designed to speak is a highly speculative enterprise. (Similar attempts to reconstruct the settings and audiences

---

21. The date of the Book of Giants is uncertain.
22. For examples of scholars who are doubtful about the existence of "Enochic Judaism," see Frölich, "The Parables of Enoch," 350–51; Patrick Tiller, "The Sociological Settings of the Components of 1 Enoch," in *The Early Enoch Literature*, ed. Boccaccini and Collins, 237–55; Pierluigi Piovanelli, "'Sitting by the Waters of Dan,' or the 'Tricky Business' of Tracing the Social Profile of the Communities That Produced the Earliest Enochic Texts," in *The Early Enoch Literature*, ed. Boccaccini and Collins, 257–83.

of the Gospels have suffered setbacks in recent decades.)[23] We cannot assume that those who read the Enochic literature all belonged to the same specific groups or that they did not also read other literature such as the Mosaic Torah. Nor can we assume that the continuity of the Enochic literary tradition was matched by a sociological continuity of its writers and readers. Even if the literary works did emerge from something we could call "Enochic Judaism," they were undoubtedly read later by other Jews, such as the Qumran community and early Christians (the Book of Watchers is cited in Jude 14), who probably gave them only an ancillary role in the understanding and practice of their religion.

The book of the Parables of Enoch certainly stands in a strong literary connection with the Book of Watchers.[24] It is so closely modeled on that book that Nickelsburg can call it, with some exaggeration, "a kind of elaboration" of the Book of Watchers.[25] But, since the earliest date that scholars now assign to it is the late first century BCE, it is temporally separated from that work by at least two centuries. The author may have known the other early Enochic writings, but there is no really strong evidence of that.[26] Probably for this author the Book of Watchers, at least, was authoritative scripture, but from the plentiful allusions to many parts of the Hebrew Bible, it is clear that the Torah, the Latter Prophets, Daniel, and the Psalms were also inspired authorities. It is implausible to connect this author either to a chain of teachers in continuity with the authors of the early Enoch literature or to some Jewish group in sociological continuity with those who particularly valued that literature in the third and second centuries BCE. All we can really say is that the author of the Parables studied the Book of Watchers and was inspired to write something like a new version of it, extending its themes in a novel direction. The relationship of the Parables of Enoch to the older Enoch literature is perhaps more like that of the Wisdom of Solomon to the older Solomon wisdom tradition than it is like the relationship of the early Enochic works to each other.

---

23. Richard Bauckham, ed., *The Gospels for All Christians: Rethinking the Gospel Audiences* (Grand Rapids: Eerdmans, 1998); Edward W. Klink, ed., *The Audience of the Gospels: The Origin and Function of the Gospels in Early Christianity*, LNTS 353 (New York: T&T Clark, 2010).

24. James C. VanderKam, "The Book of Parables within the Enoch Tradition," in *Enoch and the Messiah*, ed. Boccaccini, 81–99, here 84–91.

25. Nickelsburg, *1 Enoch 2*, 3.

26. VanderKam, "The Book of Parables," 91–98, discusses connections between the Parables and the Astronomical Book, concluding that "they show no clear evidence of a *literary* relationship" (98).

The Parables of Enoch is composed of three "parables" (38:1–44:1; 45:1–57:3; 58:1–69:29) preceded by a prologue (37:1–5) and followed by an epilogue (70:1–71:14). The divisions are clearly marked (37:5; 38:1; 45:1; 57:3b; 58:1; 69:29b). The word "parable" (*messālē*) seems to be taken from the opening of the Book of Watchers (1:2, 3) and is also used in the Epistle of Enoch (93:1, 3). The fuller phrase "he took up his/my discourse" (1:2, 3; 37:5; 93:1, 3) shows that the term imitates the way the oracles of Balaam are introduced in Numbers 23:7, 18; 24:3, 15, 20, 21. In the Parables of Enoch the term bears little if any trace of the meaning "comparison" (the basic sense of משל).[27] Depending on its use in 1:2, 3, to refer to the prophecy of 1:3b–5:9, the author of the Parables probably uses it to mean something like "eschatological oracle" or "prophecy of the final judgment." (Balaam's oracles were commonly understood as prophecies of the events of the end times in Second Temple Judaism.) This accords with the way the book itself classifies the contents of the second and third parables (45:1; 58:1), referring to the destinies in store for the righteous and the wicked at the time of the judgment.

It is true that the cosmic tours on which Enoch is taken by the angels in the Parables include revelations of secrets of the cosmos as well as visions and prophecies of the eschatological future. But the latter predominate. The author of the Parables has taken over the genre of cosmic tour from chapters 17–36 and adopts a good deal of the subject matter of Enoch's visions from those chapters, with creative variation. But he also adopts the genre of prophetic oracle from the introductory section of the Book of Watchers (chapters 1–5), beginning with the first passage of the First Parable (38:1–6). Like the opening section of the Book of Watchers (1:3b–5:9), this prophecy predicts the contrasting futures of the righteous and the wicked when the time of judgment arrives.

The Parables continues to follow the structure of the Book of Watchers, since what follows this prophecy is a short summary of the narrative section of the Book of Watchers (chapters 6–16). The cosmic tours follow, corresponding to chapters 17–36 of the Book of Watchers. Each of the two other parables also begins with a prophetic oracle (45:1–6; 58:1–6) before resuming the narrative of the visions Enoch saw on his travels around the heavens and the ends of the earth. There is a significant difference, however, between the narratives of Enoch's visions in the Book of Watchers and those in the Parables. There is considerable eschatological content to the former, but whereas they include prophecies of the judgment in the form of interpretations by the angels of what Enoch sees in various parts of the cosmos, they do not include prophetic

---

27. In this respect I am not convinced by the discussion in Nickelsburg, *1 Enoch 2*, 92–94.

oracles by Enoch himself. In the Parables there are major passages of prophecy spoken by Enoch (e.g., 48:4–51:5; 62:3–63:12).[28] The literary form of vision seems constantly to morph into that of prophetic oracle. Thus, whereas the eschatological content of the cosmic tours in the Book of Watchers is restricted to interpretation of what Enoch sees, the lavish use of predictive prophecy in the Book of Parables enables it to tell what amounts to a narrative of the eschatological events. Enoch sees some of these events in vision (e.g., 47:3), but frequently he merely narrates them in the future tense.

The theme of eschatological judgment dominates the Enoch literature. Even the narrative of the watchers in the Book of Watchers (6–16) functions typologically to refer to the eschatological judgment. But the Parables represents a novel development. While formally imitating the Book of Watchers, such that it forms a kind of new version of that book, the Book of Parables intensifies the focus on the coming judgment. It does not do so by means of a historical review that leads up to the judgment, as in the earlier Enoch apocalypses (the Apocalypse of Weeks and the Animal Apocalypse), nor does it address the righteous and the wicked at length as the Epistle of Enoch does. Rather, it adapts the genre of the cosmic tour, so that the revelations of cosmological secrets become a framework for visions of the end time, modeled in part on Daniel 7, and prophetic discourses that resemble the oracles of Daniel and the biblical prophets as well as that of Enoch in the introduction to the Book of Watchers. With this goes another development: outside of 1:3b–9, the eschatological passages in the Book of Watchers rarely allude to biblical prophecy. Those in the Parables constantly do so.

The new focus on eschatological prophecy drawing on Daniel and the biblical prophets enables the author of the Parables to introduce a major new element into the eschatological expectation: the introduction of a Messianic Figure (variously called "that Son of Man," "the Chosen One," and "the Anointed One") as God's agent in executing the final judgment. This may indeed have been the author's overriding aim. It is the aspect of the Parables with which the following chapters will be concerned.[29]

---

28. On these, see Nickelsburg, *1 Enoch 2*, 24–25.
29. Readers who would like an overview of the contents of the Parables before turning to the detail of the text will find a short one in Daniel M. Gurtner, *Introducing the Pseudepigrapha of Second Temple Judaism* (Grand Rapids: Baker Academic, 2020) 36–40, or a longer one in Nickelsburg, *1 Enoch 2*, 10–19.

CHAPTER 1.2

The Messianic Figure ("Son of Man") in the Parables of Enoch

In my early work on early Jewish monotheism and early Christology, I treated the "Son of Man" (as I then called him) in the Parables of Enoch as an exception among the various prominent angels and exalted patriarchs who feature in early Jewish literature. My argument was that the heavenly throne of God was a crucially important symbol of Jewish monotheistic faith. It was the throne from which God ruled the whole of the created cosmos, and so it symbolized the uniquely divine sovereignty over all things, which, along with the uniquely divine role of creating all things, entailed an absolute distinction between the one God and all other things. In the literature, I argued, only God himself sits on that throne. In a few texts the personified figure of Wisdom sits beside him as his counselor, but Wisdom was precisely God's own wisdom, not something or someone other than God but integral to God's unique divine identity. From this perspective the very early Christian belief that God had exalted Jesus of Nazareth to sit beside him on his cosmic throne (expressed in language borrowed from Ps 110:1) is a strikingly novel development. It meant, in effect, that Jesus shared in the unique divine identity of YHWH. The worship of Jesus, another innovation in the earliest Christian movement, belonged very intelligibly with the exaltation of Jesus to God's throne. In Jewish practice, worship was restricted to the one God of Israel, because he was the sole creator of all things and the sole sovereign ruler of all things. The early Christians included Jesus in the worship of God because he shared the divine throne.

However, I shared with most other scholars the view that in the Parables of Enoch the "Son of Man," as the eschatological judge, sits on God's own throne and receives worship:

17

PART 1 · THE PARABLES OF ENOCH

There is one exception which proves the rule. In the *Parables of Enoch*, the Son of Man will in the future, at the eschatological day of judgment, be placed by God on God's own throne to execute judgment on God's behalf. He will also be worshipped. Here we have a sole example of an angelic figure or exalted patriarch who has been included in the divine identity: he participates in the unique divine sovereignty and therefore, in recognition of his exercise of the divine sovereignty he receives worship. His inclusion in the divine identity is partial, since he plays no part in the work of creation or indeed in the divine sovereignty until the future day of judgment, and therefore his inclusion in the divine identity remains equivocal. But he is the only such equivocal case, who shows, by contrast, the absence in other cases of any of the criteria by which Second Temple Jews would consider a heavenly figure to share the divine identity.[1]

This idea of an "exception which proves the rule" has been variously received. Andrew Chester says that "to have even one such exception is potentially deeply damaging for the absolute distinction Bauckham wants to draw."[2] I do not accept that it is "deeply damaging" because, with the literature at our disposal, no one could claim that anything was characteristic of early Judaism *without exception*. On any issue whatever, there could have been Jews who took a different approach that has left no trace in the surviving evidence. My aim was to establish what was generally true of early Judaism, so far as we can tell, and to show that the early Christian view of Jesus's exaltation to the throne of God was a major innovation in that general context, an innovation that requires explanation. If the Parables of Enoch offer a partial parallel to such an innovation, this would seem an eccentric example by comparison with the rest of Jewish literature, and it too would require explanation, not as an example of a broad trend, but as an exceptional case. In this book I shall not find it necessary to offer such an explanation, because I shall argue that I was mistaken about the Parables of Enoch and that it is not, in fact, an exception.

Chris Tilling, on the other hand, while accepting that the Son of Man's occupation of the divine throne is a unique exception in Second Temple–period Jewish literature, suggests that the worship of the "Son of Man"

---

1. Richard Bauckham, *Jesus and the Identity of God*: God Crucified *and Other Studies on the New Testament's Christology of Divine Identity* (Grand Rapids: Eerdmans, 2008) 16. There is a fuller treatment in *Jesus and the Identity of God*, 169–72.

2. Andrew Chester, *Messiah and Exaltation: Jewish Messianic and Visionary Traditions and New Testament Christology*, WUNT 207 (Tübingen: Mohr Siebeck, 2007) 22–23.

need not imply the significance Bauckham has ascribed to it. It is so significant for Bauckham because of the divine throne in his divinity identity scheme, and because this Son of Man sits on it. But the language in these passages [46:4–5; 48:5; 62:6–7, 9], especially the first and last, sound very much like an earthly or military rout, the political submission of one king to another more mighty.... These Enochic passages likely do not portray the worship of the Son of Man in the way only God should be worshipped.[3]

Crispin Fletcher-Louis responds differently to my argument: he largely accepts my account of the "Son of Man" in the Parables but denies that these features are unique in early Jewish literature.[4] In what follows I shall find myself agreeing with Tilling on this point, but without severing the close connection I see between the divine throne and worship.

The need for the detailed study that follows in this essay arose initially out of the remarkable renaissance of studies on the Parables of Enoch that has taken place in the last fifteen years. The Enoch Seminar devoted its third biennial meeting in 2005 to "Enoch and the Messiah Son of Man: Revisiting the Book of Parables," and the published volume of papers is a very important collection of essays and discussion by many of the leading scholars in the field of the Enoch literature.[5] A few years later James Charlesworth and Darrell Bock organized a colloquium, focused more specifically on the relationship between the Book of Parables and early Christianity, with a greater representation of New Testament scholars included. The published essays are significantly titled *Parables of Enoch: A Paradigm Shift*.[6] Around the same time two doctoral dissertations on the relationship of the Parables of Enoch to the Gospel of Matthew and to the Pauline Letters were published.[7] Perhaps the

---

3. Chris Tilling, *Paul's Divine Christology*, 2nd ed. (Grand Rapids: Eerdmans, 2012) 215–16. For the same understanding of the "worship" of the "Son of Man," but without reference to my work, see Larry W. Hurtado, *Lord Jesus Christ: Devotion to Jesus in Earliest Christianity* (Grand Rapids: Eerdmans, 2003) 38–39.

4. Crispin Fletcher-Louis, *Jesus Monotheism*, vol. 1, *Christological Origins: The Emerging Consensus and Beyond* (Eugene, OR: Cascade, 2015) 182–86. He thinks it "unwise to speak of an 'inclusion' in the divine identity (even a '*partial*' inclusion).... The messiah figure *expresses* and *partially shares* in the divine identity" (185). He finds the same features in Dan 7 and the Life of Adam and Eve.

5. Gabriele Boccaccini, ed., *Enoch and the Messiah Son of Man: Revisiting the Book of Parables* (Grand Rapids: Eerdmans, 2007).

6. Darrell L. Bock and James H. Charlesworth, eds., *Parables of Enoch: A Paradigm Shift*, JCT 11 (London: Bloomsbury, 2013).

7. Leslie W. Walck, *The Son of Man in the Parables of Enoch and in Matthew*, JCT 9 (Lon-

most important of all the recent studies of the Parables is George Nickelsburg's commentary on 1 Enoch 37–71 in volume 2 of the Hermeneia commentary on 1 Enoch.[8] This is now an invaluable and indispensable source and guide for all who would engage with the Parables of Enoch in a more than superficial way. I should also mention important individual essays and articles by Darrell Hannah, Daniel Olson, and Ted Erho, published in the last decade.[9] We also now have two excellent new English translations of 1 Enoch,[10] which can be used in addition to the older translations by Michael Knibb and Matthew Black. Access to the text of the Parables of Enoch in Ethiopic for those who are not proficient in the language has never been better, though it is set to improve even more when Loren Stuckenbruck's work of assembling a much larger Ethiopic manuscript base bears fruit in a new edition.[11]

While some of this new interest in the Parables of Enoch is primarily concerned with understanding the place of the work in early Judaism, much of it is also driven by its possible influence on early Christology or even on Jesus himself. There was a time, in the first half of the last century, when the Parables were widely thought to be important for the study of Christian origins. Writing of the history of religions school in Germany, Mogens Müller comments, "It became nearly an *opinio communis* that Early Judaism knew of a specific apocalyptic expectation of a heavenly and universal Son of Man in the

---

don: T&T Clark, 2011); James A. Waddell, *The Messiah: A Comparative Study of the Enochic Son of Man and the Pauline Kyrios*, JCT 10 (London: T&T Clark, 2011).

8. George W. Nickelsburg and James C. VanderKam, *1 Enoch 2: A Commentary on the Book of 1 Enoch Chapters 37–82*, Hermeneia (Minneapolis: Fortress, 2012).

9. Darrell D. Hannah, "The Chosen Son of Man of the *Parables of Enoch*," in *"Who Is This Son of Man?" The Latest Scholarship on a Puzzling Expression of the Historical Jesus*, ed. Larry W. Hurtado and Paul L. Owen, LNTS 390 (London: T&T Clark, 2011) 130–58; Daniel C. Olson, "Enoch and the Son of Man in the Epilogue of the Parables," *JSP* 9 (1998) 27–38; Olson, "'Enoch and the Son of Man' Revisited: Further Reflections on the Text and Translation of 1 Enoch 70:1," *JSP* 18 (2009) 233–40; Ted M. Erho, "Historical-Allusional Dating and the Similitudes of Enoch," *JBL* 130 (2011) 493–511; Erho, "Internal Dating Methodologies and the Problem Posed by the Similitudes of Enoch," *JSP* 20 (2010) 83–103; Erho, "The Ahistorical Nature of *1 Enoch* 56:5–8 and Its Ramifications upon the *Opinio Communis* on the Dating of the *Similitudes of Enoch*," *JSJ* 40 (2009) 23–54.

10. George W. E. Nickelsburg and James C. VanderKam, *1 Enoch: The Hermeneia Translation*, 2nd ed. (Minneapolis: Fortress, 2012); Daniel C. Olson, *Enoch: A New Translation* (North Richland Hills, TX: BIBAL Press, 2004).

11. Loren T. Stuckenbruck with Ted M. Erho, "The Book of Enoch and the Ethiopian Manuscript Tradition: New Data," in *"Go Out and Study the Land" (Judges 18:2): Archaeological, Historical and Textual Studies in Honor of Hanan Eshel*, ed. Aren M. Maeir, Jodi Magness, and Lawrence H. Schiffman, JSJSup 148 (Leiden: Brill, 2012) 257–67.

The Messianic Figure ("Son of Man") in the Parables of Enoch · 1.2

centuries around the beginning of the Common Era as a sort of alternative to the more nationalistic and particularistic Messiah."[12] The Parables of Enoch was essential to that *opinio communis*. The work was generally regarded as pre-Christian in date and therefore treated as uniquely illuminating background to early Christology.

This situation changed markedly from about 1970 onward, for two main reasons. First, while manuscript fragments of the texts of all the other major parts of 1 Enoch and most of the individual chapters were found among the Dead Sea Scrolls at Qumran, the Parables of Enoch (chapters 37–71) were notable for their complete absence. Many scholars concluded that they were therefore probably of later date.[13] Józef Milik, who edited the Qumran fragments of the Enochic books, argued that the Parables are a Christian work dating from the late third century.[14] Not many scholars actually followed Milik's lead.[15] Most continued to think it a non-Christian Jewish work, but some inclined to date the work to the late first century or early second century CE,[16] while others, who did not think the absence of the Parables from Qumran necessarily excluded an earlier date for the Parables, continued to date the work to the pre-70 CE period or as early as the reign of Herod the Great.[17] Despite the persistence of that view, New Testament scholars generally became very cautious about appealing to the Parables in their work on early Christology and the Gospels.[18] David Suter wrote in 1981, "There seems to be a basic consensus that the Similitudes does not antedate the origins of the Christian

---

12. Mogens Müller, *The Expression "Son of Man" and the Development of Christology: A History of Interpretation* (London: Equinox, 2008) 418.

13. Delbert Burkett, *The Son of Man Debate: A History and Evaluation*, SNTSMS 107 (Cambridge: Cambridge University Press, 1999) 70–72.

14. Józef T. Milik, "Problèmes de la littérature Hénochique à la lumière des fragments araméens de Qumran," *Harvard Theological Review* 64 (1971) 333–78; Milik, *The Books of Enoch: Aramaic Fragments of Qumrân Cave 4* (Oxford: Clarendon, 1976) 89–100.

15. See Müller, *The Expression*, 338 n. 53.

16. Müller, *The Expression*, 338 nn. 54–55.

17. Müller, *The Expression*, 338 nn. 56–57. Müller calls a date around the beginning of the Common Era "more and more the *opinio communis*" (338).

18. E.g., James D. G. Dunn, *Christology in the Making: An Inquiry into the Origins of the Doctrine of the Incarnation* (London: SCM, 1980) 75–78, concluding, "*There is nothing in 1 Enoch 37–71 to suggest that there was a pre-Christian Jewish tradition concerning the Son of Man as a heavenly individual* (whether redeemer or judge), nothing to suggest that the early Christian Son of Man tradition knew or was influenced by the Similitudes, and what other evidence there is points toward a post-AD 70 date at the earliest for the Similitudes themselves" (78, italics original).

movement and therefore does not provide *direct* evidence for a pre-Christian Jewish Son of Man."[19]

The second reason for the decline of interest in the Parables of Enoch by Gospels scholars, in particular, was the increasing popularity of the view that the expression "son of man" in the Aramaic sayings of Jesus was not a title but an idiomatic form of self-reference. This view (in itself an old proposal)[20] was brought to prominence by the work of Geza Vermes, beginning in 1967,[21] and Maurice Casey, beginning in 1976.[22] (Their differing understandings of the Aramaic idiom are not important in the present context.)[23] For scholars who followed this approach, the fact that "the Son of Man" appears to become a title in the Gospels was due to the translation of the phrase that Jesus used into Greek and the use of Daniel 7:13 as a source of Christology. A pre-Christian Son of Man title or Son of Man concept became redundant in understanding the sayings of Jesus and the Gospels. Casey, who continued to see the Parables of Enoch as pre-Christian in date, argued that there was no Son of Man title or Son of Man concept in the Parables of Enoch either—a view with which I now find myself in agreement (it will be argued in detail in what follows).

The new wave of interest in the Parables of Enoch, beginning with the Enoch Seminar of 2005, has swept aside those developments. There has been a strong trend to date the Parables before the time of Jesus, around the turn of the eras, and this early Roman-period date is now being claimed as a "consensus." Many of the scholars contributing to the renaissance are not merely reviving the view that the Parables of Enoch witnesses to a pre-Christian Jewish "concept" of the Son of Man, with the phrase once again regarded as a title, but incline to think the Parables of Enoch stands in some kind of direct relationship with the early Christian movement in Jewish Palestine and may even have been known to Jesus himself. At the same time—and differing to a large extent from the earlier twentieth-century consensus—is a trend toward

---

19. David W. Suter, "Weighed in the Balance: The Similitudes of Enoch in Recent Discussion," *Religious Studies Review* 7 (1981) 217–21, here 218, quoted in Burkett, *The Son of Man Debate*, 73 (italics original).

20. Burkett, *The Son of Man Debate*, 82–85.

21. Geza Vermes, "Appendix E: The Use of בר נש/בר נשא in Jewish Aramaic," in Matthew Black, *An Aramaic Approach to the Gospels and Acts*, 3rd ed. (Oxford: Clarendon, 1967) 310–30.

22. Maurice Casey, "The Use of the Term 'Son of Man' in the Similitudes of Enoch," *JSJ* 7 (1976) 11–29.

23. The work of Vermes and Casey will be discussed in part 3 (vol. 2).

the view that the identification of "the Son of Man" with Enoch in the last chapter of the Parables is not a result of secondary editing but was integral to the book all along.

Darrell Bock and James Charlesworth are confident in advocating what they call a "new paradigm" and explain it thus: "[The Parables of Enoch] is certainly Jewish, with a celebration of Enoch as 'that Son of Man.' It is also most likely contemporaneous with Jesus or slightly earlier. Most importantly, evidence is mounting to indicate that the provenience of the *Parables of Enoch* lies in Galilee."[24] They claim that certain messianic themes occur uniquely in the Parables and the sayings of Jesus in the Gospels and appear "to point to some influence of" the Parables on Jesus.[25] We can see here how, despite the rather more cautious and open approach to the Parables and Jesus by various other contributors earlier in this volume, the editors are most interested in the opportunity the early dating provides for making the Parables of Enoch a source for study of the historical Jesus.

But the recent development that impacts most closely my own previous treatment of the Parables of Enoch as an "exception" to the rule that in early Judaism no human or angelic figure sits on the divine throne and receives worship is the work of Daniel Boyarin. Boyarin essentially takes over Larry Hurtado's understanding of early Christology as a "binitarian" mutation in Jewish monotheism and my own idea of the "inclusion" of Jesus in the unique identity of God, and retrojects these ideas into early Judaism, with the Parables of Enoch as the indispensable key evidence. For Boyarin, the "Son of Man" in the Parables is unequivocally a divine figure: "This figure is a part of God; as a second or junior divinity, he may even be considered a Son alongside the Ancient of Days, whom we might begin to think of as the Father Almighty. . . . It is hard to escape the conclusion that the Son of Man is in fact a second person, as it were, of God. . . . Enoch becomes the Son of Man—he becomes God."[26] In Boyarin's view, this is not just a peculiarity of the Parables of Enoch.

---

24. Darrell L. Bock and James H. Charlesworth, "Conclusion," in *Parables of Enoch*, ed. Bock and Charlesworth, 364–72, here 371.

25. Charlesworth and Bock, "Conclusion," 372.

26. Daniel Boyarin, *The Jewish Gospels: The Story of the Jewish Christ* (New York: New Press, 2012) 77, 81, 82. Cf. the rather more sober statement in Boyarin, "How Enoch Can Teach Us about Jesus," *Early Christianity* 2 (2011) 51–76, here 74: "All the elements of Christology are essentially in place then in the Parables." The Christian doctrinal language he uses in *The Jewish Gospels* may be deliberately adopted for addressing readers of that relatively popular book.

The Parables was just "part of a more general Jewish world of thought and writing."[27] "Son of Man speculation and expectation seem . . . to have been a widespread form of Jewish belief at the end of the Second Temple period."[28]

On the basis also of the "two powers in heaven" traditions in rabbinic literature (all later than the first century CE), Boyarin thinks that "in the first century many—perhaps most—Jews held a binitarian doctrine of God."[29] Not surprisingly, therefore, Boyarin finds "incomprehensible" my "claim to some absolute uniqueness to Christology in the Jesus version."

> It should be emphasized that accepting Bauckham's premise, which seems compelling, that there are not a series of semi-divine mediator figures within Second Temple Judaism to which Jesus can have been assimilated forces us to recognize that Daniel 7:13–14 already assumes that the Son of Man shares in God's divinity. . . . The Similitudes and the Gospels represent two developments out of the Danielic tradition.[30]

Thus the Parables of Enoch and their interpretation are central and indispensable to Boyarin's construction of a widespread "binitarian" Judaism in the first century CE.

The most recent study I shall cite here is the first volume of Crispin Fletcher-Louis's *Jesus Monotheism*, a major study of the origins of divine Christology, in which there is a chapter on the Parables of Enoch.[31] Referring to Larry Hurtado's work and mine, Fletcher-Louis considers that "the lack of interest in the Jewish Son of Man texts [the Parables of Enoch and 4 Ezra] among those championing the early high Christology emerging consensus is striking."[32] He thinks the Parables and 4 Ezra both envisage "a pre-existent Son of Man figure who is at the least heavenly or 'transcendent,' if not actually 'divine' in some sense."[33] High Christology developed through the identification of Jesus with this preexistent, heavenly Son of Man figure.[34]

Fletcher-Louis thinks the need for advocates of early high Christology to

---

27. Boyarin, *The Jewish Gospels*, 77.
28. Boyarin, *The Jewish Gospels*, 77.
29. Daniel Boyarin, "Two Powers in Heaven; or, the Making of a Heresy," in *The Idea of Biblical Interpretation: Essays in Honor of James L. Kugel*, ed. Hindy Najman and Judith H. Newman, JSJSup 83 (Leiden: Brill, 2003) 331–70, here 334.
30. Boyarin, *The Jewish Gospels*, 178 n. 27.
31. Fletcher-Louis, *Jesus Monotheism*, 171–201.
32. Fletcher-Louis, *Jesus Monotheism*, 173.
33. Fletcher-Louis, *Jesus Monotheism*, 172.
34. Fletcher-Louis, *Jesus Monotheism*, 173.

engage with the Parables of Enoch is clear in the light of what I have called the renaissance in study of the Parables. He sees in the work of the Enoch Seminar in 2005 "a rehabilitation of the *Similitudes* as an important Jewish text . . . most likely written before Jesus' ministry."[35] He speaks of the "new consensus that the *Similitudes* are pre-Christian."[36] Against any view that the Parables of Enoch represents merely a partial *parallel* to early high Christology, he insists that, according to the *communis opinio* of the Enoch Seminar, "there is some kind of *genetic* relationship between the *Similitudes* and NT Christology."[37] Coming rather close to Boyarin's view, he suggests, while leaving the question open, that "*1 Enoch* and the *Similitudes* reflect mainstream and broadly shared messianic beliefs," which would make the relationship of "Jesus Son of Man" to the "Enochic Son of Man" more intelligible than if the Parables were a narrowly sectarian text.[38] In many ways, Fletcher-Louis has reverted to the view that was common in the earlier part of the twentieth century, but with a refined view of how the "Son of Man" in the Parables of Enoch is related to God, a view that is indebted to my own way of conceptualizing "the unique divine identity" of early Judaism and early Christianity:

> In the *Similitudes of Enoch*, the Son of Man-Messiah *expresses* and *participates* in the divine identity. There are good reasons for thinking that this fascinating text represents mainstream first-century Jewish beliefs.[39]

> The Jesus of the Gospels and of other NT texts is clearly more than the Son of Man of the Similitudes . . . but there is much in this Jewish material that anticipates aspects of "Christological monotheism."[40]

The challenge he puts out to other scholars is for Gabriele Boccaccini and his colleagues in the Enoch Seminar to engage more with the "Christological monotheism" of the New Testament, and for "Hurtado and Bauckham and their colleagues" to engage with the findings of the Enoch Seminar.[41] In the

---

35. Fletcher-Louis, *Jesus Monotheism*, 175. The volume edited by Charlesworth and Bock appears in his bibliography, but he does not refer to it in this chapter, which I presume was written before it was available to him.
36. Fletcher-Louis, *Jesus Monotheism*, 177.
37. Fletcher-Louis, *Jesus Monotheism*, 189.
38. Fletcher-Louis, *Jesus Monotheism*, 193. He develops this point more fully on pp. 201-2.
39. Fletcher-Louis, *Jesus Monotheism*, 203.
40. Fletcher-Louis, *Jesus Monotheism*, 173.
41. Fletcher-Louis, *Jesus Monotheism*, 176-77.

sad absence of Larry Hurtado, who passed away in 2019, this book is my own response to that challenge.

The Messianic Figure and the Scriptures

I use the term "Messianic Figure" for the figure to whom the Parables refers in three ways: as the Chosen One (or Elect One), as "son of man" (usually "that son of man"), and as the Anointed One (or Messiah) (used only twice). Many scholars consider that there is also a fourth term (used in 38:2; 53:6), "the Righteous One," but I am not convinced. This term is found in some manuscripts at 38:2, where the alternative reading "righteousness" seems to me more plausible.[42] In 53:6 "Righteous" is not a separate title but expands "the Chosen One" into "the Righteous and Chosen One."

It is very clear that the three designations all refer to the same figure, but, as table 1 shows, the two frequent ones, "the Chosen One" and "that son of man," occur in distinct blocks of text. "Son of man" is used only in 46:2–48:2 and 62:5–71:14, while neither "the Chosen One" nor "the Anointed One" occurs within these two sections of text. "The Chosen One" is used in chapters 39–45, before the term "son of man" is introduced in 46:2, and in the section of the text between the two "son of man" sequences (49:2–62:1). The two occurrences of "the Anointed One" are placed just before (at 48:10) and within (52:4) this "Chosen One" section. The alternation of sections in which "the Chosen One" is used and sections in which "the son of man" is used is certainly not due to distinct sources from which the Parables has been composed (as has sometimes been suggested), but, as we shall see, these alternating sections do correspond roughly to the different biblical sources on which the author has drawn in these passages.

The author of the Parables was a learned scriptural exegete. We should not be misled by the fact that he represents the content of his work as heavenly disclosures made to Enoch. That belongs to the apocalyptic genre. The author did not see the visions he ascribes to Enoch; rather, they are a vehicle for what he has learned from his study of the scriptures. In particular, the revelations about the Messianic Figure and his role in the eschatological judgment depend

---

42. If "the Righteous One" is the correct reading, then this would be the first appearance of the Messianic Figure in the Parables. It seems odd that on this first appearance he should be designated in a way that is never used again in the book. "Righteousness" in the sense of justice for the righteous, revealed at the judgment, seems more appropriate to the context and forms a better parallel to "light appears" later in the verse.

closely on scriptural exegesis. Though there are some biblical allusions in other parts of the Parables, the passages about the Messianic Figure are peculiarly dense with such allusions (see table 2). In other parts of the Parables, the author often depends on the Book of Watchers (1 En. 1–36),[43] including the introductory chapters 1–5, which deal with the eschatological judgment. But the Messianic Figure is this author's novel contribution to the Enoch tradition, and for sources he has turned to biblical prophecies.

His main biblical sources are three, and they correspond to the three designations he uses for the Messianic Figure. The title "Chosen One" comes from Isaiah 42:1 ("my chosen, in whom my soul delights"), an inference that is confirmed by the more precise allusion to that text when he is called by God "my Chosen One" (1 En. 45:3, 5; 51:5; 55:4) and by the fuller allusion in 1 Enoch 49:4 ("the Chosen One . . . according to his good pleasure"). It is notable that the Parables does not use the term "servant of the Lord," which is the more common designation for this figure in the servant passages of Isaiah. The reason may well be that the author has selected the title that links this figure with one of his designations for the people of God: "the chosen ones" or "the righteous and chosen ones," a term he probably derived from 1 Enoch 1:1, 8.[44] It is notable that the designation "the Chosen One" frequently occurs in close connection with reference to "the chosen ones" (39:6-7; 40:5; 45:3-5; 51:3-5; 61:4-5; 62:1, 7, 8, 11, 12, 13, 15). This close connection is established for the reader by the first two references to "the Chosen One" in the Parables (39:6-7; 40:5). The principal significance of the title would therefore seem to be that "the Chosen One" is the heavenly representative of "the righteous and chosen ones." When he judges the wicked, it is on their behalf, and their destiny, after death and in the new creation, is to be with him in paradise. It is appropriate therefore that the archangel Raphael pronounces blessing on both him and them: "blessing the Chosen One and the chosen ones who depend on the Lord of Spirits" (40:5). Their destiny is inseparable.

Doubtless the author will have noticed that the servant of the Lord in Isaiah functions as a representative of Israel. In one of the passages on which he has drawn in his depiction of the Messianic Figure, the servant is addressed by God as "Israel" (Isa 49:3). The two passages about the servant on which the Parables depend are Isaiah 42:1-7 and 49:1-7, passages in which all readers recognize one and the same figure. What may seem surprising from a modern perspective is that he treats Isaiah 11:2-5 as another description of the same

---

43. Nickelsburg, *1 Enoch 2*, 55–57.
44. On this term, see Nickelsburg, *1 Enoch 2*, 99–100.

figure. But from an ancient Jewish exegetical perspective this is not surprising. Both Isaiah 11:2–5 and Isaiah 42:1–7 describe an eschatological judge endowed with the divine Spirit and judging justly:

> The spirit of the LORD shall rest on him.
> ....
> With righteousness he shall judge the poor,
>   and decide with equity for the meek of the earth. (11:2, 4)

> I have put my spirit upon him;
>   he will bring forth justice to the nations. (42:1)

There is also a striking link between Isaiah 11:2–5 and Isaiah 49:1–7:

> He shall strike the earth with the rod of his mouth. (11:4)

> He made my mouth like a sharp sword. (49:2)

These are the kinds of verbal, as well as thematic, links that told an ancient Jewish exegete that different biblical passages should be interpreted in connection with each other. Notably, this author ignores Isaiah 11:1, which rather clearly depicts the figure described in 11:2–5 as a descendant of David.

The Parables may allude to one other Isaianic passage about the servant of the Lord (Isa 52:13–15), though the evidence is less decisive (see 1 En. 62:5 with Isa 52:13). An echo of Isaiah 52:13 in 1 Enoch 70:1–2 would make sense if, as I shall argue, the Messianic Figure in the Parables is Enoch. If the Parables does allude to Isaiah 52:13–15, the author evidently saw this passage as unconnected with chapter 53, of which the Parables shows no trace. But George Nickelsburg makes the interesting suggestion that in the Parables it is the righteous and chosen on earth who are the suffering servant, while the Messianic Figure is their heavenly patron or representative.[45]

The term "son of man" (which, as I shall explain in due course, should not be regarded as a title) derives, of course, from Daniel 7:13, as is very clear from 1 Enoch 46:1–2. The distinctive divine title "the Head of Days," which occurs in the Parables only in connection with "that son of man," derives from Daniel 7:9 ("the Ancient of Days"), and the less common divine designation

---

45. Nickelsburg, *1 Enoch 2*, 44.

The Messianic Figure ("Son of Man") in the Parables of Enoch · 1.2

"the Most High" probably also derives from Daniel (7:22, 25, 27).[46] The whole passage in Daniel on which the author draws for his account of "that son of man" is Daniel 7:9-27. As table 2 makes clear, apart from the allusions to Daniel 7:9 in 1 Enoch 40:1 (referring to the myriad angels) and to Daniel 7:13 in 1 Enoch 52:9, allusions to Daniel 7 occur exclusively in the sections of the text that use the term "son of man" to refer to the Messianic Figure (1 En. 46:1-48:2; 62:5-71:17).[47] Allusions to the Isaianic passages (Isa 11:2-5; 42:1-7; 49:1-7) are not so exclusively limited to the "Chosen One" sections of the text. There are some within the "son of man" sections. But they are especially concentrated in 49:1-62:3. The fact that they also occur within "son of man" sections serves to bind the two types of passage together as referring to only one Messianic Figure under two designations. It is notable that, immediately after the term "the son of man" has been introduced, it is said of the figure so designated that "the Lord of spirits has chosen him" (1 En. 46:3). This serves to identify him with the figure already known to readers as "the Chosen One."

Besides these Isaianic and Danielic sources, the author has drawn on two psalms for his account of the Messianic Figure. One of these, Psalm 2, accounts for the third of the designations for this figure: the Anointed One (Messiah). The word occurs in Psalm 2:2. Both occurrences of the title in the Parables (48:10; 52:4) are associated with further allusions to this psalm. (In 48:8 the phrase "the kings of the earth," as in Ps 2:2, occurs only here in the Parables. In 52:4 the "authority" of the Anointed One "on earth" alludes to Ps 2:8.) We should also note that the phrase "a rod of iron" in Psalm 2:9 provides an exegetical link with the Isaianic texts (Isa 11:4; 49:2). Moreover, in both cases the actual phrase is "his Anointed One," as in Psalm 2:2. So this is not a term that has become independent of a specific scriptural context from which it derived.

What characterizes all three of these biblical sources, in the author's interpretation, and explains why he has privileged them over other biblical passages that others read with reference to a Messianic Figure is that they all concern a figure who executes God's eschatological judgment on the powerful oppressors of the people of God, thereby also saving the "chosen and righteous ones." If there is a difference of emphasis, it is that the Chosen One judges on behalf of the chosen ones,

---

46. In the Parables it occurs only in 46:7; 59:22; 62:7, and once in a "Noachic" interpolation indebted to Dan 7 (60:1).

47. I exclude allusions within the "Noachic" interpolations: 60:1-2 (Dan 7:9-10, 25). Maurice Casey, *Son of Man: The Interpretation and Influence of Daniel 7* (London: SPCK, 1979) 107, gives a longer list of possible Danielic allusions, but he himself finds some of them unlikely.

while "that son of man" brings judgment to bear on their enemies (1 En. 46:4–6; 62:5–9; 63:11), as does "his Anointed One" (48:10). But these are two sides of the same coin and the distinction of usage is not absolute (cf. 48:7; 62:1).

In the biblical literature, exercising just judgment is a key function of a king, and so, as we shall see, the Messianic Figure in the Parables has a throne on which to sit for judgment (as he does not explicitly have in any of these biblical prophecies). But the author is remarkably uninterested in any other royal function of this figure. He is a judge, but not, in any broader sense, a king, and is never called one. This focus on his role as judge also accounts for the strong emphasis on "righteousness" (or "justice") in descriptions of him (39:6; 46:3; 49:2–3; 62:2–3; 71:14, 16), which corresponds with the biblical sources (Isa 11:2–5; 42:6; cf. Jer 23:5–6; 33:15–16).

One other biblical source should be mentioned, though it does not, like the three we have discussed, supply a designation for the Messianic Figure. This is Psalm 72, a psalm about the ideal king who executes just judgment.[48] There is a clear link with Isaiah 11:2–5:

> May he judge your people with righteousness,
>   and your poor with justice. (Ps 72:2)

> With righteousness he shall judge the poor,
>   and decide with equity for the meek of the earth. (Isa 11:4)

The allusions to this psalm in 1 Enoch 48:2–6 will be discussed later.

How did the author of the Parables infer from Daniel 7 that the role of "the son of man" was to execute eschatological judgment? He will have noted, as other Jewish and Christian exegetes did, that in Daniel 7:9 Daniel saw "thrones," only one of which belongs to the Ancient of Days. Since the "one like a son of man" is the only other notable figure in the context, it would be easy to suppose that there were two thrones, one for the Ancient of Days and one for the humanlike figure. According to Daniel, the latter arrives in the presence of the Ancient of Days and is given "dominion and glory and kingship" (7:13–14), which could naturally be thought to entail a throne. Yet the author of the Parables, as we have already noted, seems not to be interested in

---

48. From 1 En. 39:7 it would seem that the author also read Ps 61 as describing the Messianic Figure. But I am not convinced by Pierpaolo Bertalotto, "The Enochic Son of Man, Psalm 45, and the *Book of Watchers*," JSP 19 (2010) 195–216, that the Parables reflect Ps 45. There are no clear allusions.

"that son of man" as a ruler.[49] For him the role of "that son of man" is to judge and his throne is a judgment seat. This interpretation is exegetically enabled especially by connecting Daniel 7:13-14 with Isaiah 11:1-5, a passage that is strongly echoed in 1 Enoch 62:2.[50] Though evidently a descendant of David (Isa 11:1), a feature the author of the Parables ignores, the messianic figure in Isaiah 11 is not actually said to rule, in a general sense, but only to judge. He exercises an ideal form of judgment, in which the sentence he pronounces actually effects the death of the criminals, so that no other action is required in order to execute the punishment the judge decrees (Isa 11:4).

A judge must be presumed to have a judgment seat. The fact that 1 Enoch 62:2 is based entirely on Isaiah 11:2-5 explains why God is there called the Lord of Spirits (the regular divine title in the Parables), not the Head of Days, while the messianic judge is called the Chosen One (1 En. 62:1), not "that son of man" (cf. similarly 49:4; 61:8).

A later passage, describing the judgment by "that son of man" more briefly and probably also alluding to Isaiah 11:4, puts it in this way:

> And he [that son of man] sat on the throne of his glory,
> and the whole judgment was given to the son of man,
> and he will make sinners vanish and perish from
> the face of the earth. (1 En. 69:27)

It may be that the second line reflects Daniel 7:22: "judgment was given for the holy ones of the Most High" (ודינא יהב לקדישי עליונין). The obvious meaning of these words in Daniel is that judgment was given in favor of the holy ones, and the words have already been echoed, with that meaning, in 1 Enoch 47:2. But it was quite possible for a Jewish exegete to derive two interpretations from the same scriptural words. Daniel's words could be taken to mean that authority to judge was given to the holy ones of the Most High. (An interpretation of Dan 7:22 in this sense is found in 4QpHab v 4-5.) It may be that the author thought that "the son of man," as heavenly patron of the people of God, executes the authority to judge that, according to Daniel 7:22, was given to them. (A similar interpretation of Dan 7:22 may lie behind John 5:27 and Rev 20:4.)[51]

---

49. Only in 62:6 is he said to rule, and the originality of the text at that point is suspect, as will be shown later. Otherwise the role of king is reserved for God (63:4). In 51:4 the mountains of minerals are said to "serve the authority of his Anointed One, so that he may be powerful and mighty on the earth." This will enable him to abolish weapons.

50. Note also Isa 42:1: "he will bring forth justice to the nations."

51. Cf. John Nolland, *The Gospel of Matthew*, NIGTC (Grand Rapids: Eerdmans, 2005) 800.

The Term "Son of Man"

Undoubtedly, the phrase "son of man," one of the two principal ways in which the Parables refers to the Messianic Figure, derives from Daniel 7:13, where Daniel sees "one like a son of man" (כבר אנש) coming to "the Ancient of Days," as God is called there. Most commentators now have no doubt that in Daniel the phrase means no more than that the figure resembled a human being. It is an example of the Semitic idiom, found in both Aramaic and Hebrew, according to which "a son of man" is a way of saying "a human." The disputed issue, with regard to the usage of the Parables, is whether here the expression has acquired the status of something like a title.

We need first to observe how the phrase is first used in the Parables. In 46:1 Enoch sees two figures in heaven:

> There I saw one who had a head of days,
> and his head was like white wool.
> And with him was another, whose face was
>   like the appearance of a man;
> and his face was full of graciousness like one of the holy angels.

These are clearly the two figures described in Daniel 7:9 ("the Ancient of Days") and 7:13 ("one like a son of man"). The first is subsequently called "the Head of Days" (1 En. 46:2; 47:3; 48:2; 71:10, 12, 13, 14). Enoch evidently does not need to be told that this figure is God. But he asks his interpreting angel about the other figure, referring to him as "that son of man" (46:2). The same phrase, with some variation, recurs many times thereafter.

However, the matter is complicated by the fact that the phrase "son of man" in English translations of the Parables actually renders three different expressions in Ethiopic (Geʻez): *walda sabʼ* (46:2, 3, 4; 48:2), *walda beʼesi* (62:5; 69:29 [*bis*]; 71:14), and *walda ʼegwala ʼemaḥeyāw* (62:7, 9, 14; 63:11; 69:26, 27; 70:1; 71:17).[52] Although some attempts have been made to regard these as translating different terms in the Greek and/or Semitic *Vorlage*[53] or as reflecting deliberate distinctions made by the Ethiopian scribes,[54] they are usually re-

---

52. There are some variant readings in a few of these verses. 1 En. 60:10 (which has *walda sabʼ*) is omitted here because it is part of the interpolated Noachic material.

53. Helge S. Kvanvig, "The Son of Man in the Parables of Enoch," in *Enoch and the Messiah*, ed. Boccaccini, 179-227. Against his argument, see Nickelsburg, *1 Enoch 2*, 114-15.

54. Klaus Koch, "Questions Regarding the So-Called Son of Man in the Parables of Enoch: A Response to Sabino Chialà and Helge Kvanvig," in *Enoch and the Messiah*, ed.

garded as merely translation variants of the same Greek phrase in the putative Greek version ([ὁ] υἱὸς [τοῦ] ἀνθρώπου), which in turn rendered an Aramaic (בר [א]נש[א]) or Hebrew (בן [ה]אדם) original.⁵⁵

Ethiopic has no definite article or emphatic state, but in all but four of the sixteen occurrences of these Ethiopic phrases for "son of man," the phrase is accompanied by a demonstrative: "that son of man" (*zekku*: 46:2; 48:2; 62:5, 9, 14; 63:11; *we'etu*: 69:26, 29 [*bis*]; 70:1; 71:17) or, in one case, "this son of man" (*zentu*: 46:4). In two other cases it is clear that a demonstrative is not needed because instead there is a qualifying phrase: "This is the son of man who has righteousness" (46:3); "You are the son of man who was born for righteousness" (71:14).⁵⁶ In only two cases is there neither a demonstrative nor other qualifier (62:7; 69:27).

The Ethiopic demonstrative could be a way of rendering the Greek definite article, but, as Maurice Casey points out, in the eleven relevant instances of "the Chosen One" the demonstrative is never used.⁵⁷ It would be odd if the Greek definite article with "son of man" were regularly rendered with an Ethiopic demonstrative but the Greek definite article with "Chosen One" were never so rendered.

Nickelsburg argues that the Ethiopic demonstratives with "son of man" translate Greek demonstratives, which were used because all the instances of this phrase point back to the figure described in 46:1. The English translation should therefore be "that son of man" in most cases, "this son of man" in 46:4, "the son of man who has righteousness" in 46:3, and "that son of man who was born for righteousness"⁵⁸ in 71:14. Only in 62:7 and 69:27, where there is no qualifier in the Ethiopic, does Nickelsburg's translation have "the son of man."⁵⁹ It is arguable that in these two cases proximity to occurrences of "that

---

Boccaccini, 228–37, here 234. Against his argument, see Hannah, "The Chosen Son of Man," 139–40.

55. Hannah, "The Chosen Son of Man," 141; Nickelsburg, *1 Enoch 2*, 114.
56. There is a useful tabulation of this data in Walck, *The Son of Man*, 71.
57. Casey, "The Use," 14. Casey refers to twelve instances, but he appears to be mistaken in including 51:5 ("my Chosen One"), which is not relevant. The eleven instances are 39:6; 40:5; 49:2, 4; 51:3; 52:6, 9; 61:5, 8, 10; 62:1. Other instances are 45:3, 5; 51:5; 55:4 ("my Chosen One"); 53:6 ("the Righteous and Chosen One").
58. In this case there may not be a demonstrative in the Ethiopic, but supplying it in English makes the sense clear in the context.
59. Matthew Black, *The Book of Enoch or 1 Enoch*, SVTP 7 (Leiden: Brill, 1985) 207, thinks that in these cases and 71:14 the term has "already become a title." But in 71:14 there is a qualifier ("who was born for righteousness") that functions in place of the demonstrative. In 62:7 and 69:27 the phrase occurs in the contexts where "that son of man" occurs immediately

son of man" both before and after "the son of man" sufficiently makes clear that the reference is to the same figure.

Similarly, Daniel Olson's translation has "that Son of Man" in all cases except 46:4 ("this Son of Man"), two cases where "the Son of Man" has a qualifier (46:3; 71:14), one exceptional case of "the Son of Man" where the Ethiopic has neither demonstrative nor other qualifier (62:7),[60] and the first occurrence of the phrase (46:2), where Olson gives a very literal rendering: "the one who was born of men."

It follows from this usage that "son of man" is not a title. Daniel Boyarin makes a fundamental mistake when he argues that in 46:2-3 there is a transition from Enoch's expression "that son of man" to the angel's "the son of man": "We find already the angel using the term in a fully technical sense; this is *the* son of man. We can thus observe the actual linguistic/literary means by which Daniel's 'One like a Son of Man' is transformed into the titular 'Son of Man.'"[61] Boyarin's mistake is to ignore the qualifying phrase "who has righteousness." The phrase is not additional information about someone called "the son of man." It explains *which* "son of man" the figure Enoch has seen is. The angel's words mean, not "This is the Man, who has righteousness," but "This is the man who has righteousness."[62] If this were not the case, it would be inexplicable that Enoch continues to refer to "that son of man" in almost all instances in the rest of the book.

Nickelsburg says that "although the Parables employ 'Son of Man' as a designator for the messianic . . . judge and they allude to a figure known from Daniel 7, they do not employ the expression as a formal messianic title nor do they indicate that 'Son of Man' was a traditional messianic title."[63] That "son of man" in the Parables is not a title was already argued in detail by Sjöberg[64]

---

before. They scarcely attest a title that could be taken out of this literary context and carry its own significance. Speculatively, one might wonder whether the two anomalous cases in 62:7 and 69:27 are the result of changes made in the transmission of the text in Ethiopic, since scribes would be familiar with the quasi-titular use of "the Son of Man" in the Gospels.

60. The fact that Olson has "that Son of Man" in 69:27 is anomalous.
61. Boyarin, "How Enoch Can Teach Us," 59.
62. Casey, *Son of Man*, 102-3.
63. Nickelsburg, *1 Enoch 2*, 116.
64. Erik Sjöberg, *Der Menschensohn im äthiopischen Henochsbuch* (Lund: Gleerup, 1946) 40-60. Sjöberg thinks it is a "fixed term" and on the way to becoming a title, but this judgment is probably influenced by the view that the Gospels are evidence that it did become a title. The view of Black, *The Book of Enoch*, 207, that the phrase has "already become a title" in the instances where the Ethiopic lacks a demonstrative (62:7; 69:27; 71:14) is implausible. As Walck, *The Son of Man*, 72, observes, "It is unlikely . . . that the author would use the term as

and is maintained also by Vermes,[65] Casey,[66] Lindars,[67] Hannah,[68] Walck,[69] and now Nickelsburg.[70] In this respect "son of man" differs from "the Chosen One," which is more like a title, introduced without explanation (39:6), and so I prefer to use lowercase letters: "the son of man."

I also put the phrase in quotation marks whenever I use it because an accurate translation would be "man" or "human." As is very well known, the expression "son of man," both in Ethiopic (all three versions) and in the Semitic original of the Parables, whether Hebrew or Aramaic, is an idiomatic way of saying "man" or "human."[71] Thus in 46:2-3 Enoch asks the angel about "that man" and is told, "This is the man who has righteousness." Wherever the Ethiopic has (literally rendered) "that son of man," the meaning is simply "that man"—the man Enoch saw in his vision (46:1). The term "son of man" itself is no more technical than when it is used, in the plural, meaning "humans" in the First Parable (1 En. 39:1, 5; 42:2), and frequently in the Book of Watchers,[72] or when Enoch (or Noah?) is addressed as "son of man" in 1 Enoch 60:10. (This verse is part of a "Noachic" interpolation, which does not belong to its current context in the Parables but nevertheless uses some of the distinctive terminology of the Parables, such as "the Head of Days" [60:2].)

Would Enoch or the angel have referred to the second figure in 46:1 in so ordinary a way as "that man"? In view of his appearance along with the Head of Days, there can be no doubt that that figure ("whose face was like the appearance of a man") is the figure more briefly described in Daniel 7:13 (כבר אנש,

---

a title in so few instances, intermingled with non-titular uses." Earlier scholars who denied that "son of man" in the Parables is a title include Hans Lietzmann (1896), Gustaf Dalman (1898), Julius Wellhausen (1899), and Ragnar Leivestad (1968 and 1871/2): see Müller, *The Expression*, 194, 198, 200, 357.

65. Geza Vermes, *Jesus the Jew: A Historian's Reading of the Gospels*, 2nd ed. (London: Collins, 1976) 175.

66. Casey, "The Use," 14.

67. Barnabas Lindars, *Jesus Son of Man: A Fresh Examination of the Son of Man Sayings in the Gospels in the Light of Recent Research* (London: SPCK, 1983) 9-10.

68. Hannah, "The Chosen Son of Man," 143.

69. Walck, *The Son of Man*, 70-72.

70. Nickelsburg, *1 Enoch 2*, 116.

71. For a survey of the usage in the Hebrew Bible, see Morna D. Hooker, *The Son of Man in Mark: A Study of the Background of the Term "Son of Man" and Its Use in St Mark's Gospel* (London: SPCK, 1967) 30-32. For a survey of the usage in LXX, see Larry W. Hurtado, "Summary and Concluding Observations," in *"Who Is This Son of Man?,"* ed. Hurtado and Owen, 159-77, here 160-62.

72. 1 En. 10:21; 11:1; 12:1; 15:12; cf. also 93:11; 101:1.

"one like a human being"), but the description is actually closer to that of the angel Gabriel in Daniel 8:15 (כמראה גבר, "one having the appearance of a man") and 10:18 (כמראה אדם, "one having the appearance of a human").[73] Gabriel can be described as "the man Gabriel" (9:21: האיש גבריאל), and the glorious angel Daniel sees in 10:5-6, probably also Gabriel, is also described as "a man" (איש). So the angelic appearance of the figure Enoch sees would not have deterred him from calling it "that man." The fact that to say this he chooses the phrase "son of man" serves the writer's purpose by alluding to the terminology of Daniel 7:13, which in this respect 1 Enoch 46:1 does not. In connection with the phrase "whose face was like the appearance of a man," many scholars refer to Ezekiel 1:26, where the prophet sees, seated on the divine throne, "a likeness like the appearance of a human being" (דמות כמראה אדם).[74] But since 1 Enoch 46:1 goes on to say that the figure's face was "like one of the holy angels," Daniel 8:15 or 10:18 is a much more likely source for the expression "like the appearance of a man" than is Ezekiel 1:26. There is nothing in the description in 46:1 to suggest that the figure is "divine,"[75] and therefore there is no reason why Enoch's phrase "that son of man" should be thought to carry any greater significance than the straightforward meaning "that man."

Is the figure actually a human or an angel? The description itself cannot decide this, since it says that his face is both "like the appearance of a man" and "like one of the holy angels." But we should note that an *exalted* human, a human taken up into the divine presence in heaven, would be expected to look just like an angel. Readers of the Parables already know that after the judgment the wicked "will not be able to look at the face of the holy, for the light of the Lord of Spirits will have appeared on the face of the holy, righteous and chosen" (38:4; cf. 39:14; 50:1).[76] If the figure is in fact Enoch himself, as I shall argue later, then Enoch's transformation in 71:11 fully accounts for his angelic appearance in 46:1.

73. This may account for the fact that the Ethiopic does not, as we might expect if it were merely following Dan 7:13, have "son of man" (*walda sab'*) in 46:1, but just "man" (*sab*).

74. E.g., Crispin Fletcher-Louis, "The Worship of Divine Humanity as God's Image and the Worship of Jesus," in *The Jewish Roots of Christological Monotheism: Papers from the St. Andrews Conference on the Historical Origins of the Worship of Jesus*, ed. Carey C. Newman, James R. Davila, and Gladys S. Lewis, JSJSup 63 (Leiden: Brill, 1999) 112–28, here 114; Fletcher-Louis, *Jesus Monotheism*, 184–85; Charles A. Gieschen, "The Name of the Son of Man in the Parables of Enoch," in *Enoch and the Messiah*, ed. Boccaccini, 238–49, here 240; Waddell, *The Messiah*, 61, 81–82.

75. Against, e.g., Nickelsburg, *1 Enoch 2*, 157: "The deity is accompanied by another divine figure."

76. See also Acts 6:15, where Stephen's face is said to be "like the face of an angel."

The Messianic Figure ("Son of Man") in the Parables of Enoch · 1.2

In further support of the contention that the expression "that son of man" in the Parables means simply "that man," we may compare the way that reference is made to the figure in Daniel 7:13 in other literature of the period, excluding the contentious territory of the Gospels:

- In Revelation 1:13 and 14:14 there is a literal Greek rendering of the Aramaic phrase used in Daniel 7:13: "one like a son of man" (ὅμοιον υἱὸν ἀνθρώπου).[77]
- Another literal echo of the phrase in Daniel 7:13, this time following the Septuagint, is in words Justin attributes to his Jewish interlocutor Trypho: "a glorious and great one, like a son of man [ὡς υἱὸν ἀνθρώπου], who receives from the Ancient of Days the eternal kingdom" (*Dial.* 32.1, my translation).
- Sibylline Oracles 5:414–16: "For a blessed man [ἀνὴρ μακαρίτης] came from the expanses of heaven / with a scepter in his hands which God gave him, / and he gained sway over all things well."[78] This and the following texts reflect the interpretation of Daniel 7:13 according to which the humanlike figure comes from heaven to earth.
- In 1 Corinthians 15:47–49 Paul probably refers to the figure in Daniel 7:13.[79] Contrasted with the first man, Adam, who was from the dust, "the second man [is] from heaven" (ὁ δεύτερος ἄνθρωπος ἐξ οὐρανοῦ).[80] He goes on to call him "the heavenly one" (ὁ ἐπουράνιος).
- 2 Baruch 39:7–40:3 is probably dependent on Daniel 7, but its messianic figure is called "my Anointed One" (cf. Ps 2:2).
- Of greatest interest for comparison with the Parables is the vision of a man from the sea in 4 Ezra 13, since it is an extended vision of a messianic figure who acts as the eschatological judge. It is clearly modeled on Daniel 7. Ezra sees "something like the figure of a man" coming out of the sea.[81] As he looks, "that man [*ipse homo*] flew with the clouds of heaven" (13:3). Then he is called "the man who came up out of the sea" (13:5). Later he is identified

---

77. In my view, the author of Revelation does not normally depend on the Old Greek/Septuagint but translates directly from the Hebrew Bible. Note that in 14:14 this figure is seated on a cloud.

78. Translation by John J. Collins in *OTP* 1:403. On this passage as alluding to Dan 7:13, see William Horbury, *Messianism among Jews and Christians: Twelve Biblical and Historical Studies* (London: T&T Clark, 2003) 140, 142, and the full discussion in chapter 2.4 below.

79. Charles Kingsley Barrett, *A Commentary on the First Epistle to the Corinthians*, Black's New Testament Commentary (London: Black, 1968) 375–76.

80. Cf. 1 Thess 1:10; Phil 3:20.

81. The sea derives from Dan 7:3. The author has supposed that, like the four beasts, the humanlike figure of Dan 7:13 came up from the sea.

again as "that man" (*ipsum hominem*) (13:12). When the angel interprets Ezra's vision for him, he explains the man thus: "This is he whom the Most High has been keeping for many ages, through whom he will deliver his creation" (13:26).[82] Subsequently the figure is called "my son" (or "my servant") (13:32, 37).[83] The references back to the figure in the vision as "that man" (13:3, 12) are strikingly like "that son of man" in the Parables. Perhaps the putative Semitic original of 4 Ezra also used the Semitic idiom "son of man," but in that case the versions correctly translated it as "man."

In none of these texts do we find the expression "the Son of Man." None of the ways in which Daniel's phrase "one like a son of man" is echoed in these texts could be used outside these textual contexts and still be understood as a reference to that figure.[84] Whether, in the Gospels, the Greek phrase "the son of man" (ὁ υἱὸς τοῦ ἀνθρώπου) is used as a title, as is commonly asserted, is a question that will be discussed in part 3 of this book.[85] But that it existed as a title outside the Gospels cannot be supported from the Parables of Enoch or from any other early allusions to the figure of Daniel 7:13.

The notion that "Son of Man" is a title in the Parables is an example of the way study of the Parables has been distorted by letting an issue in the study of the Gospels determine the reading of the Parables. It was because the term was generally regarded as a title in the Gospels that scholars thought there must be Jewish precedent for such a usage and found it in the Parables of Enoch.[86]

James Charlesworth writes, "Perhaps too much discussion has been directed to prove that the Son of Man is not a title in Judaism before Jesus from Nazareth and too little towards developing a method by which to distinguish

---

82. Cf. 12:32, which makes clear that 4 Ezra thought of a descendant of David who has been reserved by God for the end time.

83. Translation from Michael Edward Stone, *Fourth Ezra*, Hermeneia (Minneapolis: Fortress, 1990) 381–82, 392–93, but whereas Stone translates *ipse homo* as "that man" in 13:3, but "the same man" in 13:12, I have translated both as "that man." The Latin text lacks the first part of 13:3 (including "something like the figure of a man"), which has to be supplied from the other versions.

84. Paul's phrase ὁ ἐπουράνιος (1 Cor 15:48–49) has perhaps the potential to be a title, but he does not actually use it outside these verses, where it is contrasted with ὁ χοϊκός.

85. On this I am in broad agreement with Hurtado, "Summary and Concluding Observations," 163–76. This essay is reprinted in Larry W. Hurtado, *Ancient Jewish Monotheism and Early Christian Jesus-Devotion: The Context and Character of Early Christian Faith*, Library of Early Christology (Waco: Baylor University Press, 2017) 389–406.

86. Cf. Maurice Casey, *The Solution to the "Son of Man" Problem*, LNTS 343 (London: T&T Clark, 2007) 92–93.

a term from 'a title,' and upon why such a distinction is appropriate and meaningful in antiquity."[87] Given that "title" can sometimes be used loosely and ambiguously, I take the term to signify that the expression "the son of man" could on its own have been understood as referring to a known messianic figure or, more specifically, to the figure described in Daniel 7:13. Charlesworth claims that, whereas in Daniel and Ezekiel "the son of man" is "an open-ended image," by the time these words are used in the Parables of Enoch "they introduce a recognizable character."[88] This character seems to consist in the function of judgment on the oppressors at the eschaton.[89] But this is a misreading of the way the phrase is used in the Parables. In the first place, allusion to Daniel 7:13 is carefully established in 1 Enoch 46:2 and all occurrences of the phrase "son of man" (usually "that son of man") refer back to the figure there depicted. This usage does not allow us to suppose that the phrase "the son of man" could, just by itself, bring to mind the figure in Daniel 7:13. Secondly, the "recognizable character" is constructed by the Parables of Enoch itself.

Charlesworth also speaks of "the concept 'Son of Man,'" claiming that this concept "is attractively ambiguous."[90] He means that the phrase conveyed the idea of an eschatological judge while leaving other features of the figure open. Others have considered the "concept" of the Son of Man a particular kind of messianic expectation: a "transcendent" figure, of heavenly rather than human origin. But the Parables of Enoch cannot be used to support the existence of such a concept. It constructs a picture of its Messianic Figure by drawing on a range of biblical sources, in Isaiah and the Psalms as well as Daniel, and refers to this figure as "the Chosen One" almost as often as it refers to him as "that son of man." His function as judge is created from an exegetical fusion of Isaiah 11:2–5; 42:1 and Daniel 7. From comparison with 4 Ezra 13 we may infer that the author of the Parables was not wholly original in bringing those two passages together and making them the key to his depiction of a Messianic Figure. He may well have worked within an exegetical tradition on which 4 Ezra 13 is also dependent.[91] But this was an exegetical tradition, not a fixed messianic "concept." Jewish messianic expectations were largely

---

87. James H. Charlesworth, "Did Jesus Know the Traditions in the *Parables of Enoch*? ΤΙΣ ΕΣΤΙΝ ΟΥΤΟΣ Ο ΥΙΟΣ ΤΟΥ ΑΝΘΡΩΠΟΥ; (Jn 12:34)," in *Parables of Enoch*, ed. Bock and Charlesworth, 201.
88. Charlesworth, "Did Jesus Know," 201.
89. Charlesworth, "Did Jesus Know," 201–2.
90. Charlesworth, "Did Jesus Know," 202.
91. In chapter 2.8 I shall offer some arguments for thinking that the Parables of Enoch is dependent on 4 Ezra.

traditions of exegesis. Different selections and combinations of biblical texts account for a range of variation in characterizing an eschatological agent of God. So depictions of such figures were always flexible. Each one overlapped others, sharing some characteristics, lacking others. They cannot be classified into distinct "concepts."

In conclusion, "son of man" in the Parables of Enoch (i.e., "that son of man," "this son of man," "the son of man who . . . ," and "the son of man") is used strictly contextually to refer to the figure Enoch sees in his vision in 46:1. Only by virtue of that contextual allusion to 46:1 does it also function as an allusion to Daniel 7:13. Moreover, it is only one of several ways of referring to the Messianic Figure of the Parables, just as Daniel 7 is one of several key biblical sources from which the picture of the Messianic Figure is constructed. In the Parables, "the son of man" is neither a title nor a concept.

The Term "Throne of Glory"

Another recurrent term (which, like "son of man," is used only in the Second and Third Parables) is "throne of glory" (*manbara sebḥat*), which sometimes appears with a possessive suffix: "throne of his glory" (*manbara sebḥatihu*). Three linguistic observations are important: (1) Ethiopic has no definite article, and so *manbara sebḥat* can be translated as "a throne of glory" or "the throne of glory."[92] (2) The expression is a Semitic idiom: the second noun, in the construct position, takes the place of an adjective. Thus the expression would be more idiomatically translated "glorious throne."[93] (3) With the pronominal suffix the phrase means "his glorious throne." I shall use these idiomatic translations, which avoid the misunderstanding that "the throne of glory" is the throne on which "Glory" (as a periphrasis for the divine presence) sits.[94]

Most scholars suppose that there is only one throne of glory—the divine throne in heaven—on which both God and the Messianic Figure, at different

---

92. Darrell D. Hannah, "The Throne of His Glory: The Divine Throne and Heavenly Mediators in Revelation and the Similitudes of Enoch," *Zeitschrift für die alttestamentliche Wissenschaft* 94 (2003) 68–96, here 82–83: "It is at least theoretically possible that the phrase in question could be rendered 'a glorious throne' rather than 'the throne of glory.'"

93. Compare some similar expressions: "the throne of his holiness" (כסא קדשו) = his holy throne (Ps 47:9); "the name of his glory" (שם כבודו) = his glorious name (Ps 72:19; cf. Neh 9:5); "the eyes of his glory" (עני כבודו) = his glorious presence (Isa 3:8).

94. Olson's translation "the throne of Glory" appears to misunderstand the phrase in this way. He may be influenced by 1 En. 14:20: "the Great Glory sat upon it" (the throne in heaven).

The Messianic Figure ("Son of Man") in the Parables of Enoch · 1.2

places in the Parables, sit.[95] But, as Matthew Black points out,[96] this is problematic, because the expression "his glorious throne" (*manbara sebḥatihu*) is used with reference both to God and to the Messianic Figure. In 1 Enoch 47:3, 60:2,[97] and 71:7 the Head of Days sits "on his glorious throne." But in other texts the Chosen One sits "on his glorious throne" (62:3) and "that son of man" sits "on his glorious throne" (62:5;[98] 69:27, 29). While we could envisage the Messianic Figure sitting with God on God's throne (as the ascended Jesus does in the New Testament), it is not plausible that God's throne could be called the Messianic Figure's own throne, however exalted we might imagine this figure to be. The possessive suffixes serve precisely to distinguish at least two thrones, one belonging to God, the other to the Messianic Figure.[99] In addition to these texts, there are two occasions on which the Messianic Figure sits on "a/the glorious throne" (45:3; 55:4[100]) and one occasion on which God seats the Messianic Figure on "a/the glorious throne" (61:8).[101] These should be translated as indefinite. In 45:3 no glorious throne has been previously mentioned, and so the natural meaning is "my Chosen One will sit on a glorious throne." In 55:4, which is in the Second Parable and a different visionary context, where no throne has hitherto been mentioned, the appropriate translation is "my

---

95. Scholars who think the Messianic Figure has his own throne, distinct from God's, include Andrei A. Orlov, "Roles and Titles of the Seventh Antediluvian Hero in the Parables of Enoch: A Departure from the Traditional Pattern?," in *Enoch and the Messiah*, ed. Boccaccini, 110–36, here 127; Hurtado, *Lord Jesus Christ*, 39 n. 38; John J. Collins in Adela Yarbro Collins and John J. Collins, *King and Messiah as Son of God: Divine, Human, and Angelic Messianic Figures in Biblical and Related Literature* (Grand Rapids: Eerdmans, 2008) 94.

96. Black, *The Book of Enoch*, 214, 220.

97. 1 En. 60:2 belongs to a "Noachic" interpolation.

98. The first edition of the translation by Nickelsburg and VanderKam has "the throne of glory" in 62:5, but this is a mistake (George W. E. Nickelsburg and James C. VanderKam, *1 Enoch: A New Translation; Based on the Hermeneia Commentary* [Minneapolis: Fortress, 2004]). Other translations and Nickelsburg, *1 Enoch 2*, 255, have "the throne of his glory."

99. I therefore find it very puzzling that Hannah, "The Throne," 86, writes: "So the precise phrase 'the throne of his glory' is used both for the Son of Man and for the Lord of Spirits, without any indication that a different reality is intended. One cannot help concluding that our author speaks of one reality, the one throne of glory." The fact that this precise phrase (with the possessive suffix) is used both for the Son of Man and for the Lord of Spirits surely does indicate that two different realities are intended, one belonging to each.

100. Some manuscripts have "the throne of my glory" ("my glorious throne") (*manbara sebḥateya*). On this textual issue, see Walck, *The Son of Man*, 124 n. 186. Nickelsburg and Olson prefer the reading "the throne of glory." Since God is speaking, it is understandable that scribes might add the possessive suffix.

101. Some manuscripts have "the throne of his glory" ("his glorious throne").

Chosen One . . . will sit on a glorious throne." In 61:8 the scene is in heaven, arguably not the location of the Chosen One's throne in 55:4, and so once again we can render it as "a glorious throne."

There are two somewhat problematic texts. First Enoch 51:3 is the only case where a throne on which God or the Messianic Figure sits is not called "glorious." Moreover, there are variant readings: "the Chosen One, in those days, will sit on my throne" (the reading of the group of manuscripts known as Eth I or α) or "the Chosen One, in those days, will sit on his throne" (the reading of the group of manuscripts known as Eth II or β). Since the Eth I group is generally regarded as preserving an older form of the text, it is understandable that its reading is preferred by Nickelsburg and Olson, though not by Black[102] or Knibb.[103] On the other hand, the scribes seem to have been uncertain whether God was speaking in 51:1-3: there is variation between "the Chosen One" and "my Chosen One" in both 51:3 and 51:5. The readings "my Chosen One" and "my throne" probably reflect an understanding that God's speech in 50:5 continues through the following verses.[104] But 51:3b ("for the Lord of Spirits has given [them] to him and glorified him") shows that understanding to be incorrect. It is plausible that "his throne" is original.[105] Given the current state of uncertainty that surrounds the Ethiopic text of 1 Enoch, it would seem reasonable to allow general considerations of the context to influence our decision on the better reading in this place. As we have seen, the Parables elsewhere seem to attribute his own throne to the Messianic Figure. It is also surprising that only here (among references to the throne of God or of the Messianic Figure) all manuscripts have simply "throne" rather than "throne of glory." This might point to an early corruption of the text.[106]

The other problematic text is 62:2, where all manuscripts have "And the Lord of Spirits sat down on the throne of his glory." It is generally agreed that the text must be corrupt,[107] since what follows undoubtedly refers to the Messianic Figure, drawing on Isaiah 11:2-4. Whereas Black corrects the

---

102. Black, *The Book of Enoch*, 51, 214.
103. Michael A. Knibb, *The Ethiopic Book of Enoch: A New Edition in the Light of the Aramaic Dead Sea Fragments* (Oxford: Clarendon, 1978) 2:135.
104. Thus Olson places closing quotation marks between 51:3a and 51:3b.
105. Walck, *The Son of Man*, 124, evidently accepts this, though without discussion.
106. Note also that the text seem to be disordered: Nickelsburg and Olson move 51:5a to precede 51:2.
107. Among the English translations, only Isaac retains the reading of the manuscripts without correction: see Ephraim Isaac, "1 (Ethiopic Apocalypse of) Enoch," *OTP* 1:5-89, here 43.

The Messianic Figure ("Son of Man") in the Parables of Enoch · 1.2

text to "And the Chosen One sat on the throne of his glory," others prefer the simpler correction, "And the Lord of Spirits seated him upon the throne of his glory." The Chosen One has been mentioned in the preceding verse, and the statement resembles 61:8: "And the Lord of Spirits seated the Chosen One on a throne of glory." In that case, "his glorious throne" is at first sight ambiguous: the possessive could refer either to the Lord of Spirits or to the Chosen One. But the ambiguity is resolved by the next verse, where the Chosen One sits "on his glorious throne." (For a summary of my proposed translations of the phrase "throne of Glory" in its various occurrences in the Parables, see table 3.)

We must now consider the arguments that have been advanced for the view that in the Parables of Enoch there is only one "throne of glory," which is the one and only heavenly throne of God:

(1) I have argued that there must be more than one because the phrase "his glorious throne" (*manbara sebḥatihu*) is used with reference both to God and to the Messianic Figure. But Johannes Theisohn argues that the third-person-singular suffix in this Ethiopic phrase is a feature only of the Ethiopic translation. Since Ethiopic lacks a definite article, the possessive suffix represents the Greek definite article in a Greek *Vorlage* that had ἐπὶ τοῦ θρόνου τῆς δόξης.[108] Theisohn thinks that originally the Parables spoke of only one throne, God's heavenly throne, called "the throne of glory." We might wonder why, in that case, the Ethiopic Parables sometimes has "throne of glory" without the possessive suffix (four times out of twelve), but the Ethiopic translator(s) cannot necessarily be relied on to be consistent in such matters. More important is the evidence that other occurrences of the phrase "throne of glory" with reference to God's throne in the Hebrew Bible and in Second Temple–period Jewish literature almost all have a second- or third-person-singular possessive suffix or pronoun:[109]

---

108. Johannes Theisohn, *Der Auserwählter Richter*, Studien zur Umwelt des Neuen Testaments 12 (Göttingen: Vandenhoeck & Ruprecht, 1975) 64–66. Theisohn's argument is discussed by Matthew Black, "The Messianism of the Parables of Enoch: Their Date and Contributions to Christological Origins," in *The Messiah: Developments in Earliest Judaism and Christianity*, ed. James H. Charlesworth (Minneapolis: Fortress, 1992) 145–68, here 154. Against Black's earlier position, here he leans toward agreeing with Theisohn. He is perhaps influenced by Theisohn's argument that Ps 110:1 lies behind all the texts about the throne in the Parables.

109. I have not included in this list OG-Dan 3:54, where the variant reading θρόνου δόξης τῆς βασιλείας is probably not original (though it has a close parallel in 4Q405 23 i 3: "the thrones of the glory of his kingdom"), or T. Levi 5:1, since we cannot be sure that our text dates to the Second Temple period. One group of manuscripts has "I saw the holy temple and the Most High upon a [or "the"?] throne of glory (θρόνου δόξης)." I have also

- Jeremiah 14:21: "Do not dishonor your glorious throne [כסא כבודך]" (OG: θρόνον δόξης σου).
- Jeremiah 17:12: "A glorious throne [כסא כבוד], exalted from the beginning, is the place of our sanctuary" (NIV)[110] (OG: θρόνος δόξης).
- Wisdom 9:10: "from the throne of your glory [ἀπὸ θρόνον δόξης σου] send her [Wisdom]."
- 1 Enoch 9:4: "and the throne of your glory (exists) for every generation of the generations that are from of old." The phrase "the throne of your glory" appears in the Aramaic and the versions thus: Aramaic (4QEn[b] 1 iii 15): כורס]א יקרך; Greek: ὁ θρόνον δόξης σου; Ethiopic: "the throne of your glory."[111] This example shows the Ethiopic possessive suffix representing the Greek possessive pronoun, which translates the Aramaic possessive suffix. If the Ethiopic Parables derive from a Semitic original via a Greek version, this example provides a good parallel for what we can presume to be the background of the Ethiopic phrase "his glorious throne" in the Parables. But 1 Enoch 9:4 is also important because the author of the Parables was deeply indebted to the Book of Watchers, and it is highly likely that his use of the expression "throne of glory" derives from 1 Enoch 9:4.
- 11Q17 (Songs of the Sabbath Sacrifice) x 7: The angels praise God "for his glorious thrones" (לכסאי כבודו).[112] The phrase is the first item in a list of the objects in the heavenly temple, which moves from the center outward and continues: "and for his footstool, and for all his majestic chariots, and for his holy debirim [. . .] and for the portals of the entrance of [. . .]." The plural "thrones" may be a plural of majesty, referring to only one divine throne, or a plurality of divine thrones may be envisaged (perhaps owing to the plural in Dan 7:9).[113] It is also worth noticing that in another part of the Songs of the Sabbath Sacrifice (4Q405 20–21–22 ii 9) there is a reference to "the seat of his glory" (מושב כבודו),[114] apparently referring to the "throne" of Ezekiel 1:26.[115]

---

excluded Lad. Jac. 2:5, which appears to refer to God's throne as "the fiery throne of glory," but where the meaning of the Slavonic text is uncertain.

110. REB: "A glorious throne, exalted from the beginning, is the site of our sanctuary." NRSV: "O glorious throne, exalted from the beginning, shrine of our sanctuary!"

111. This is the reading of a few manuscripts; most have "the throne of his glory."

112. Text and translation from Carol Newsom, *Songs of the Sabbath Sacrifice: A Critical Edition*, HSS 27 (Atlanta: Scholars Press, 1985) 374.

113. Newsom, *Songs*, 376–77.

114. Newsom, *Songs*, 303, 306.

115. Cf. 4Q405 20–21–22 ii 2: "a seat like the throne of his kingdom" (מושב ככסא מלכותו). The word מושב is probably preferred to כסא because it is part of the chariot.

Thus, in five examples, the phrase "throne of glory," referring to God's throne, is in three cases qualified by the possessive "your" and once by the possessive "his," while in the remaining case (if we follow the NIV and REB translations of Jer 17:12) the phrase is indefinite but qualified in the context. So it would seem that in this period the phrase "the throne of glory" had not yet become a technical expression for the heavenly divine throne, as it later became in rabbinic literature.[116] This evidence leads to the conclusion that in the phrase "the throne of his glory," in the Parables of Enoch, the possessive suffix is not a feature merely of the Ethiopic version but reflects the putative Greek and/or Semitic *Vorlage*. We may also conclude that in the Parables the term "throne of glory" is not a technical expression for the one heavenly throne of God, since in the majority of cases it appears in the form "the throne of his glory" (where "his" refers in some cases to God and in others to the Messianic Figure), while in others it can be translated "a throne of glory."

(2) A second argument for the view that there is only one "throne of glory" in the Parables is stated by Darrell Hannah, who writes of "the unlikelihood of there being more than one throne of glory in a heavenly context."[117] In a general sense this is right: in most Jewish literature there is only one heavenly throne, from which God alone rules the cosmos. But for the author of the Parables, one of his key texts is Daniel 7:9-10, which refers to "thrones" in the plural but then describes only one throne, on which the Ancient of Days takes his seat. The author of the Parables could well have thought that there were two thrones,[118] the other being reserved for the "one like a son of man" (Dan 7:13), whose authority is described in 7:14 in terms that seem to require a throne. Most early readers of Daniel evidently took this scene of judgment in Daniel 7:9-10 to be set on earth, but, as we shall see below, the author of the Parables understood it to be located in heaven. He had a good exegetical basis, then, for envisaging two glorious thrones in heaven.

(3) Leslie Walck writes, "Nowhere in *Par. En.* is the throne in heaven spoken of in the plural. . . . Nowhere in *Par. En.* is the heavenly court depicted as having more than one throne. The foundational vision in Dan. 7:9-14 depicts

---

116. Beata Ego, quoted in Hannah, "The Throne," 83 n. 63, called it a "Terminus Technicus für den Thron Gottes." According to Hannah, "The Throne," 83, "In Rabbinic literature both the indefinite כסא כבוד and the definite כסא הכבוד are only ever used for the divine throne, although to be sure the latter greatly outnumber the former."

117. Hannah, "The Throne," 83. In n. 61 he correctly claims a heavenly context for 47:1-4 and 61:8, but does not discuss whether the context in chapter 62 is heavenly or earthly. We shall take up this issue below.

118. As some of the rabbis later supposed (b. Hag. 14a). See chapter 2.9 below.

thrones in the plural set in place, but *Par. En.* is vague on that question."[119] But if there is only one throne, the Parables is also remarkably vague on how God and the Messianic Figure are supposed to share it. It does not say that God sets the Messianic Figure beside him on the throne ("at his right hand," as we might have expected him to say if he were inspired by Ps 110, as some scholars think), but nor does it say that God vacates the throne to make way for the Messianic Figure. In this respect, it is certainly no more difficult to read the Parables as envisaging more than one throne than it is to read it as depicting God and the Messianic Figure occupying the same throne.

(4) Hannah refers to 1 Enoch 62:3, where, in Nickelsburg's translation, the kings and the mighty "will see and recognize that he [the Chosen One] sits on the throne of his glory." Hannah renders this as "will see him and recognize him, because he sits on the throne of his glory." What, he asks, could this "possibly mean if two different thrones of glory were in view? The kings and the mighty will recognise in the Son of Man the Lord of Spirit's agent of eschatological judgment, precisely because he sits on that throne usually reserved for the Lord of Spirits himself."[120]

I suggest there is at least one other possible meaning. In 62:1 the Lord of Spirits addresses the kings and the mighty: "Open your eyes and lift up your horns, if you are able to recognize the Chosen One." He then seats the Chosen One on his (the Chosen One's) throne of glory (62:2). They then see the Chosen One and recognize him as a specific human person, Enoch, now glorified and seated on a glorious throne so that he can pronounce divine judgment on them. The scene is parallel to Wisdom 4:16–5:13, which describes how the righteous person who appears to have died (cf. 3:2; 4:10–11; the figure is modeled on Enoch) will condemn the oppressors who are living (4:16):[121]

> Then the righteous man will stand with great confidence
> in the presence of those who have oppressed him. . . .
> When they see him, they will be shaken with dreadful fear,
> and they will be amazed at the unexpected salvation
>   (of the righteous man).

---

119. Walck, *The Son of Man*, 126.
120. Hannah, "The Throne," 86.
121. See the detailed comparison of 1 En. 62–63 with Isa 52:13–53:12 and Wis 4:18–5:13 in Nickelsburg, *1 Enoch 2*, 258–59, summarizing his discussion in George W. E. Nickelsburg, *Resurrection, Immortality, and Eternal Life in Intertestamental Judaism*, Harvard Theological Studies 26 (Cambridge, MA: Harvard University Press, 1972) 83–107.

They will speak to one another in repentance,
and in anguish of spirit they will groan, and say,
"This is the man we once held in derision. . . .
Why is he numbered among the sons of God
and why is his lot among the holy ones?" (Wis 5:1–5)[122]

Probably, as Nickelsburg argues, in 1 Enoch 62:1–7 "the text suggests that the kings and the mighty recognize the Chosen One as a previously known entity—that is, that they recognize in the Chosen One the chosen ones whom they have been persecuting, or, more generally, that they recognize him to be the heavenly patron and vindicator of the chosen ones."[123] What matters with regard to the throne on which he sits is that it is a throne of judgment on which God has placed him. There is no need for it to be God's own throne.

In positive support of the view that there is more than one glorious throne in the Parables, we need now to take account of the occurrences of the phrase in the Hebrew Bible and early Jewish literature where it does *not* refer to the throne of God:[124]

- 1 Samuel 2:8: God makes the poor "sit with princes and inherit a glorious throne [כסא כבוד]" (my translation) (OG: θρόνον δόξης).
- Isaiah 22:23: Eliakim "will become a glorious throne [לכסא כבוד] for the house of his father" (my translation) (OG: θρόνον δόξης).
- Sirach 47:11 (Greek): God gave David "a covenant of kingship and a glorious throne [θρόνον δόξης] in Israel." The extant Hebrew text (from the Cairo Genizah) omits "of glory." It dates from a time when "the throne of glory" had become a technical term for the heavenly throne of God and would have been thought an unsuitable description of David's throne.[125]
- Aramaic Levi 93: People will "enthrone" the wise man "on a throne of glory

---

122. This translation is my modification of the NRSV, which, like other modern translations, turns the singular "righteous man" (ὁ δίκαιος) into plurals ("the righteous"). The translators do so because they recognize that "the righteous man" is a representative figure and they wish to avoid gendered language, but they obscure the fact that a specific individual (the same individual as in 2:10–20, where the NRSV uses the singular "righteous man") is being taken as representative. He is probably a combination of Enoch and the suffering servant of Isa 52:13–15.

123. Nickelsburg, *1 Enoch 2*, 260.

124. All translations in this list are my own.

125. Hannah, "The Throne," 84.

[כורסי ייקר] in order to hear his words of wisdom."[126] The meaning in context is that they will treat him like a king.[127]

- Psalms of Solomon 2:19: "Her [Jerusalem's] beauty was dragged down from a/the glorious throne [ἀπὸ θρόνου δόξης]." While Hannah suggests that this is a metaphorical reference to God's throne,[128] I think it is much more likely that Jerusalem is here depicted as a queen who has been dragged from her glorious throne (cf. Isa 47:1). It is an example of an ordinary usage of the phrase for a royal throne, as in the other examples just listed.
- 4QpIsa[a](4Q161) 8–10 iii 20: "a glorious throne [כס[א כבוד]], a holy crown, and multi-coloured garments." This fragment (the words on either side of it are lost)[129] is from the Qumran pesher (commentary) on Isaiah, specifically from the passage of comment on Isaiah 11:1–5, which we have seen is also one of the most important biblical sources for the delineation of the Messianic Figure in the Parables of Enoch. In the pesher the "Shoot of David" is described as king and judge over all the nations. The three items in the list in line 20 are obviously his accoutrements of office. Like the author of the Parables, the writer of this pesher assumes that a figure of the kind described in this biblical passage must have a throne. As in the case of the four preceding examples of "throne of glory," there is no question here of the throne being God's. Like the others, this text belongs to the period when "a glorious throne" was simply the kind of throne a king would have.
- Matthew 19:28: "at the regeneration of all things, when the Son of Man takes his seat on his glorious throne [ἐπὶ θρόνου δόξης αὐτοῦ]" (my translation); Matthew 25:31: "When the Son of Man comes in his glory [ἐν τῇ δόξῃ αὐτοῦ] and all the angels with him, then he will take his seat on his glorious throne [ἐπὶ θρόνου δόξης αὐτοῦ]." Like the translators of the Old Greek and of Ben Sira, Matthew has preserved the Semitic idiom "throne of

---

126. Translation from the Cambridge manuscript in James R. Davila, "Aramaic Levi: A New Translation and Introduction," *OTPMNS* 1:121–42, here 141. I have consulted the Aramaic text in Robert A. Kugler, *From Patriarch to Priest: The Levi Priestly Tradition from Aramaic Levi to Testament of Levi*, EJL 9 (Atlanta: Scholars Press, 1996) 119. The latter part of the line ("in order to hear his words of wisdom") is also preserved in 4QLevi[a] ar (4Q213) 6 i 18.

127. Cf. T. Levi 13:9: "he will be enthroned with kings" (σύνθρονος ἔσται βασιλέων). Testament of Levi is a later work, in a Christian redaction, based on Aramaic Levi. Here it is interesting evidence of how Aramaic Levi 93 was understood.

128. Hannah, "The Throne," 84.

129. Maurya P. Horgan, *Pesharim: Qumran Interpretations of Biblical Books*, CBQMS 8 (Washington, DC: Catholic Biblical Association of America, 1979) 76, 86, tentatively but plausibly restores "And God gave him" before the fragment.

glory"[130] but comes even closer to the Parables of Enoch insofar as he uses the phrase with a third-person possessive pronoun: "the throne of his glory." (The phrase is uniquely Matthean among the Gospels and is paralleled nowhere else.)[131] We need not discuss here the issue of a literary relationship between Matthew and the Parables (it will be discussed in chapter 3.8). What is notable is that in the Matthean texts "his" cannot conceivably refer to God. This is the Son of Man's own throne.[132] In 25:31, as in the Parables, it is a judgment seat, though in 19:28 it seems to be the throne from which he will rule the messianic kingdom.[133] Moreover, it is located on earth, since the "coming" of the "Son of Man" (Matt 25:31) must be his return to earth for judgment (cf. 16:27; 24:27, 30). It may be that Matthew associates the glory of the coming "Son of Man" with the glory of God (cf. 16:27: "the Son of Man is going to come in the glory of his Father with his angels" [my translation]).[134] He participates in the glory of God, and this may be why, in Matthew's usage, his throne is "glorious." But it is undoubtedly his own throne, a judgment seat on earth, distinguished from God's heavenly throne (5:34; 23:22).[135]

From these examples we can conclude that in the Hebrew Bible and Second Temple–period Jewish literature a "throne of glory" certainly need not be God's. In fact, the usage is evenly balanced: in the Hebrew Bible (and OG) there are two examples where the throne is God's, two where it is not; in later Jewish literature there are three examples where the throne is God's (always "throne of your glory"), four where the throne is not (or six, if we include the texts in Matthew). All we can say is that thrones, whether God's or those of earthly kings, including the Messiah, are sometimes described as "glorious." This is what we should expect, since "glory" was regularly associated with kings

---

130. This kind of Semitic idiom is frequently echoed in Jewish Greek, including the New Testament.

131. The association of "glory" with the parousia is also found in Mark (8:38; 10:37; 13:26) and Luke (9:26; 21:27). Matthew extends this by adding "the throne of his glory" and thereby emphasizing the role of judging.

132. Consistently with his reading of the Parables of Enoch, Hannah, "The Throne," 85, thinks Matthew means that "Christ will sit on the divine throne."

133. See the discussion in chapter 3.7.

134. For Matthew, as for the Hebrew Bible, "glory" characterizes earthly rulers (4:8; 6:29) as well as God.

135. In T. Ab. B8:5 Adam sits on "a throne of great glory." I have not included this text in my list of examples because I do not think we can safely treat the Testament of Abraham as a Second Temple–period Jewish work.

(e.g., Ps 21:5; 45:3; Isa 8:7; 11:10; 13:19; 14:18; Jer 13:18; Dan 2:37; 4:30, 36; 5:18, 20; Matt 4:8; 6:29; Luke 4:6). This evidence entitles us to take seriously the language of the Parables of Enoch when it assigns to God "the throne of his glory" and to the Messianic Figure "the throne of his glory." There are two thrones. The Messianic Figure does not sit on God's throne; still less is he "divine."

It has not infrequently been claimed that Psalm 110:1 lies behind the enthronement of the Messianic Figure in the Parables.[136] But there is no allusion to Psalm 110 in the Parables, by contrast with the New Testament, where the remarkably frequent allusions to Psalm 110:1 are clearly signaled by statements that the exalted Jesus is seated "at the right hand" of God.[137] In early Christian usage, this usually means that he sits beside God on God's own throne. We have seen that this is not the case in the Parables of Enoch. Psalm 110:1 could be taken to mean that the Messiah sits on a throne next to God's throne. But the Parables do not say even that. When God seats the Messianic Figure on that figure's throne (1 En. 61:8; 62:2), there is no indication that God himself is seated. There is no interest at all in the location of the Messianic Figure's throne in relation to God's. The Messianic Figure does not gain his authority from God by virtue of being seated beside God, but simply by virtue of being placed by God on a throne.

The terms "son of man" and "throne of glory" have been the source of much misunderstanding of the Parables of Enoch. Translated literally in English, they have the appearance of titular or technical terms. If they are translated idiomatically and correctly as "that man" and "glorious throne," these misperceptions lose much of their power.

---

136. E.g., Theisohn, *Der Auserwälter Richter*, 94–95; Black, "The Messianism," 152-55; Grant Macaskill, "Matthew and the *Parables of Enoch*," in *Parables of Enoch*, ed. Charlesworth and Bock, 218–30, here 226–27.

137. There are twenty-one such allusions, listed in Richard Bauckham, *Jesus and the God of Israel: God Crucified and Other Studies on the New Testament's Christology of Divine Identity* (Grand Rapids: Eerdmans, 2008) 21 n. 39.

TABLE 1. *Designations of the Messianic Figure and references to a throne of glory*

	Elect One	"Son of Man"	Righteous One?	Messiah	Throne of glory	Head of Days	Throne of glory
38:2			✓?				
39:6	✓?						
40:5	✓						
45:3	✓				✓		
45:4	✓						
46:2		✓				✓	
46:3		✓					
46:4		✓					
47:3						✓	✓his
48:2		✓				✓	
48:10				✓			
49:2	✓						
49:4	✓						
51:3	✓				(✓)*		(✓)*
51:5	✓						
52:4				✓			
52:6	✓						
52:9	✓						
53:6	✓†		✓†				
(55:1)**						✓	
55:4	✓				✓		
(60:2)**						✓	✓his
61:5	✓						
61:8	✓				✓		
61:10	✓						
62:1	✓				✓his		
62:2					✓his		

51

62:3					✓		
62:5	✓				✓		
62:7	✓						
62:9	✓						
62:14	✓						
63:11	✓						
69:26	✓						
69:27	✓				✓his		
69:29	✓				✓his		
69:29	✓						
70:1	✓						
71:7							✓his
71:10						✓	
71:12						✓	
71:13						✓	
71:14	✓					✓	
71:17	✓						

*my/his throne   **Noachic passages   †the Righteous and Elect One

TABLE 2. *Biblical allusions in Parables 2 and 3*

Parable 2

45:1		
45:2		
45:3	Chosen One	
45:4	Chosen One	Isa 65:17; 66:22
45:5		
45:6		
46:1	(Head of Days), (Son of Man)	Ps 16:11
46:2	Son of Man, Head of Days	Dan 7:9, 13; 8:15
46:3	Son of Man	Dan 7:16
46:4	Son of Man	Isa 11:5; 32:16; 42:1
46:5		Isa 49:7; Ps 3:7
46:6		Dan 5:20–21; 4:25, 32
46:7	Most High	
47:1		Dan 7:23; 8:10
47:2		
47:3	Head of Days	Deut 32:43; **Dan 7:22**
47:4		Dan 7:9–10
48:1		Ps 9:12
48:2	Son of Man, Head of Days	Isa 55:1
48:3		
48:4		Ps 72:17; Isa 49:1?
48:5		Ps 72:4?; Isa 49:6?
48:6		Ps 72:11; Isa 49:7
48:7		
48:8		Ps 72:17?; Isa 49:6, 8?
48:9		*Ps 2:2*
48:10	*Messiah*	Exod 15:7, 10
49:1		*Ps 2:2*

49:2	Chosen One	
49:3		Job 14:2; **Dan 7:13–14**
49:4	Chosen One	Isa 11:2
		Isa 11:4; 42:1
51:2		
51:3	Chosen One	
51:4		**Dan 7:14**
51:5	Chosen One	Ps 114:4
52:1–3		Dan 12:1?
52:4	*Messiah*	
52:5		*Ps 2:8*
52:6	Chosen One	
52:7		Mic 1:4; 1 En. 1:6
52:8		Zeph 1:18
52:9	Chosen One	
		Dan 7:13
56:2		
56:7a		Jer 51:11
56:7b		Zech 12:2–4
57:1		Ezek 38:21
		Isa 66:20

Parable 3

59:22	**Most High**	
60:1	**Most High**	
60:2	**Head of Days**	**Dan 7:25, 9–10**
		Dan 7:9
62:1	Chosen One	
62:2		
62:3		Isa 11:2–4
62:4		Isa 49:7

62:5	Son of Man	Isa 13:8
62:6		Isa 13:8; 52:15
62:7	Son of Man, Most High	Dan 7:14?
62:8		Isa 49:2
62:9	Son of Man	
62:10–11		Isa 49:7
62:12		
		Isa 66:24
62:13		Isa 34:5–6; Jer 46:10
62:14	Son of Man	Isa 41:12; Exod 14:13
62:15		Zeph 3:13
62:16		Isa 60:1–2
63:1–10		Isa 52:1–2
63:11	Son of Man	
63:12		Gen 3:23–24
69:26	Son of Man	
69:27	Son of Man	
69:28		Dan 7:14, 22
69:29	Son of Man (× 2)	

(Conclusion)

70:1	Son of Man	
70:2		Isa 52:13
71:1		Isa 52:13; 2 Kgs 2:11–12
71:2–4		Gen 5:24
71:5		
71:6–7		Gen 5:24
71:8		
71:9		Dan 7:9
71:10	Head of Days	

71:11		**Dan 7:9**
71:12	**Head of Days**	
71:13	**Head of Days**	
71:14	**Son of Man, Head of Days**	**Dan 7:9**
71:15		
71:16		
71:17	**Son of Man**	

Note: Allusions to Daniel 7 are in bold; allusions to Isaiah 11:2–5, 42:1–7, and 49:1–7 are underlined; allusions to Psalm 2 are italicized.

TABLE 3. *Proposed translations of "throne of glory"*

45:3	My Chosen One will sit on a glorious throne
47:3	The Head of Days took his seat on his glorious throne
51:3	The Chosen One will sit on his throne
55:4	My Chosen One will sit on a glorious throne
61:8	The Lord of Spirits seated the Chosen One on a glorious throne
62:2	The Lord of Spirits seated him [the Chosen One] on his glorious throne
62:3	[The Chosen One] is sitting on his glorious throne
62:5	That son of man sitting on his glorious throne
69:27	[That son of man] sat on his glorious throne
69:29	[That son of man] sat down on his glorious throne
71:7	[Angels] guard his [the Head of Days'] glorious throne

CHAPTER 1.3

The Messianic Figure in the Eschatological Narrative of the Parables of Enoch

The Eschatological Narrative Sequence

The content of the Parables of Enoch (excluding the Noachic interpolations) can be quite easily divided between Enoch's travels to various parts of the cosmos, where secrets of the cosmos are revealed to him, and his visions of the time of the end: the coming judgment of the wicked and the new world in which the righteous will live afterward. Since our interest is in the Messianic Figure, we can largely ignore the cosmic travels. At first sight the parts of the book concerned with the events of the end time seem to lack coherent organization, partly because the judgment and the life after the judgment are so often foreseen in vision and predicted in oracles. In fact, there is a definite narrative sequence of future events that unfolds in the sections 39:3–41:9 (in the First Parable), 45:1–51:5 (in the Second Parable), and 61:6–63:12 (in the Third Parable), followed by a summary in 69:27-29. We shall see that between 63:12 and 69:27 a significant stage of the narrative has been lost and has been replaced by interpolated material.

The first of these sequences (39:3–41:9) begins with a vision in which Enoch sees the righteous dead in heaven or paradise, interceding for humans on earth (39:4-5). This is the first stage of the eschatological events, because, as we later learn (47:1-2), the prayers are for judgment to deliver and avenge the righteous who are suffering and dying at the hands of the oppressors. We are then introduced to the Chosen One who is with the chosen ones in heaven. Finally, there is a vision of the judgment (41:1-2, 9),[1] the first of several in the

1. George W. E. Nickelsburg and James C. VanderKam, *1 Enoch 2: A Commentary on*

book. Humanity is divided into the chosen ones and the sinners, who are allotted different destinies. Notably, "the judge" here (41:9) is presumably the Lord of Spirits. The role of the Chosen One in the judgment is not disclosed until the Second Parable (45:3).

The narrative sequence in the Second Parable (45:1–51:5) is framed by an *inclusio*: two parallel accounts of the Messianic Figure's judgment of the wicked and the consequent paradisal future of the righteous (45:3–6; 51:2–5). In both passages the Messianic Figure is called the Chosen One. He is said to sit on the throne. In the first passage, the judgment of sinners is said to be near (45:3), while in the second passage, the other side of the same coin is stated: salvation for the chosen ones is near (51:2). In both passages it is said that the chosen ones will dwell on the renewed earth (45:5; 51:5). In the first passage, the formula "On that day" is used twice (45:3, 4), dividing the passage into a section about the judgment and a section about the new world after the judgment. In the second passage, the corresponding division is marked by the repeated formula "In those days" (51:5b, 4).[2] Other details in the two passages vary around this core of common structure and elements. A key difference is that the first passage describes the Chosen One's sitting on the throne and judgment as destruction for the wicked (45:3, 6b),[3] while the second passage describes it as liberation for the righteous (51:2). These are complementary aspects of the same event.

Between these two enclosing passages, Enoch sees a sequence of events in which the eschatological judgment is unfolded. These events lead up to the key moment when the Messianic Figure takes his seat on a glorious throne to implement the divine judgment. In other words, they lead up to the event that is narrated twice, at the beginning and the end of the whole section (45:3–6; 51:2–5). The sequence of events is accompanied by commentary that looks backward and forward, but once the events themselves are distinguished, most of the other material in the section falls into place intelligibly around them. The sequence is based on Daniel 7:9–14, and the key events are as follows:

1. Enoch sees the Head of Days and a humanlike figure together before the beginning of the judgment (46:1).

---

the Book of 1 Enoch Chapters 37–82, ed. Klaus Baltzer, Hermeneia (Minneapolis: Fortress, 2012) 135, is probably right to argue that the text of chapters 41–44 is disordered and that 41:3–9 should follow 42:3.

2. Here I accept Nickelsburg's and Olson's rearrangement of the text, transferring v. 5a to precede v. 2. Comparison with 45:3–6 strengthens the case for this rearrangement.

3. 1 En. 45:3 is problematic and may not refer to the wicked.

2. The prayers of the righteous are answered when the Head of Days takes his seat on his throne and the books are opened (47:1–4) (= Dan 7:9b–10).
3. The Messianic Figure is summoned by name into the presence of God (48:2).
4. The Messianic Figure stands in the presence of God (49:1–4) (= Dan 7:13–14).
5. The Messianic Figure takes his seat on his throne to implement the judgment (45:3, 6b; 51:5a, 2–3).
6. God renews the world for the chosen ones to dwell there (45:4–6a; 51:4, 5b).

In this sequence, within the Second Parable, event (5)—judgment by the Messianic Figure on his throne—appears as a single event, but in the Third Parable it is expanded into a sequence of three events:

(5a) The Messianic Figure sits on a throne to judge the holy ones in heaven (61:8–13).
(5b) The Messianic Figure sits on his throne to judge the kings and the mighty (62:1–12).
(5c) The Messianic Figure judges the fallen angels (the account of this is missing; cf. 55:4; 69:28).

Following (5b) there is an account of event (6) (62:13–16), and then a kind of appendix to (5b), in which the kings and the mighty appeal to God for mercy, over the head of the Messianic Figure, and God confirms their sentence (63:1–12).

With this sequence in chapters 62–63 there are two problems. The Messianic Figure's judgment of the holy ones (the angels) is a surprising element, since they appear to have done nothing wrong and are not condemned. Instead, they react by praising God. I suggest that the author has included this event because he is reliant on Isaiah 24:21:[4]

> On that day the Lord will punish [יפקד]
> the host [צבא] of heaven [המרום] in heaven [במרום],
> and on earth the kings of the earth.

(Note that the phrase "the kings of the earth" connects this verse with Ps 2:2 and is echoed in 1 En. 48:8, with allusion to Ps 2:2 in 48:10.) A more literal

---

4. David W. Suter, *Tradition and Composition in the Parables of Enoch*, Society of Biblical Literature Dissertation Series 47 (Missoula: Scholars Press, 1979), argues that the Parables are based on a "midrash" on Isa 24:17–23, but he does not see the connection I discuss here. I do not find his general thesis convincing.

translation of the first line of Isaiah 24:21 would be: "On that day YHWH will visit [their sins] upon the host of the heights [of heaven] in the heights [of heaven]." The words צבא and מרום are echoed in 1 Enoch 61:8, "the works of all the holy ones in the heights of heaven,"[5] and 61:10, "all the host of heaven and all the holy ones in the heights, and the host of the Lord."[6] But the author of the Parables could not envisage that God would punish the host of heaven in the heights of heaven. (The fallen angels are to be punished, but not in heaven.) So he understood the verb פקד in Isaiah 24:21 to mean "to visit" with the purpose of testing the works of those visited, as in Psalm 17:3 and Job 7:18.[7] The angels pass the test, but the kings do not. So he paraphrases the first line of Isaiah 24:21 thus:

> He will judge all the works of the holy ones in the heights
>   of heaven,
> and in the balance he will weigh their deeds. (1 En. 61:8b)

For this purpose the Messianic Figure is seated by God on a glorious throne in heaven (61:8). But if my account of the author's dependence here on Isaiah 24:21 is correct, then it follows that, when God seats the Messianic Figure on a glorious throne to judge the kings (62:1–2), the throne must be *on earth*. The Messianic Figure's throne is located in heaven in chapter 61, on earth in chapter 62. This makes good sense. There is no reason to suppose that the kings and the mighty are transported to heaven in order to be judged and punished.

Thus, whereas the sequence of events in the Second Parable was based on Daniel 7, the sequence of events in the Third Parable is based on Isaiah 24:21. This explains the paucity of allusion to Daniel in the Third Parable. Daniel 7 itself did not suggest to this author that the Messianic Figure was to perform more than one act of judgment, but Isaiah 24:21 did, and so in the Third Parable the Messianic Figure's judgment is subdivided.

The second problem in the sequence of eschatological events in chapters 62–63 as I outlined it above is that there is no account of (5c) in the extant text of the Parables. During his journeys to distant parts of the earth in the Second Parable, Enoch sees the burning pit where the fallen angels are going to be thrown when they are judged (54:1–6), and he hears God predict:

---

5. Cf. 47:2; 71:8.
6. Cf. 47:3.
7. For the sake of this meaning, he has had to ignore the על before the two nouns.

> Mighty kings who dwell on the earth, you will have to witness my Chosen One, how he will sit on the throne of glory and judge Azazel and all his associates and all his host in the name of the Lord of Spirits. (55:4)

This suggests that there was once an account of the judgment of the fallen angels closely associated with the judgment of the kings and the mighty in chapter 62. Perhaps 64:1-2 was the beginning of that account. Certainly 65:1–69:25 is an interpolation, probably from more than one source, and it is clear from 69:26 (where "they" has no antecedent) that material now lost originally preceded it.[8] It is notable that 69:2-5 is about the fallen angels. Perhaps it was originally inserted alongside the lost account of their judgment.

In 69:27-29 the whole course of the judgment is summarized in the following sequence:

(A) 69:29a: The "son of man" appears[9]
(B) 69:27a–b, 29b: He sits on his throne and the judgment is given to him
(C) 69:27c: He judges sinners and destroys them
(D) 69:28:   The fallen angels are judged and punished
(E) 69:29a–b: Everything corruptible and everything evil disappears

This summary begins with the appearance of the Messianic Figure on earth and so does not include the preceding events in heaven, which I have numbered (1)–(5a).

In the following sections we shall look in detail at these key stages in the eschatological narrative: (1), (2), (3), (4), and (5b).

Enoch's Vision of Two Heavenly Figures (46:1-8)

The interpretation of Daniel begins at 46:1:

> There I saw one who had a head of days,
> and his head was like white wool.
> And with him was another, whose face was like the appearance
>   of a man;
> and his face was full of graciousness like one of the holy angels.

---

8. Nickelsburg, *1 Enoch 2*, 311–12.
9. This probably means that he appears in the world (cf. 2 Bar. 29:3).

These are clearly the two figures described in Daniel 7:9 ("the Ancient of Days") and 7:13 ("one like a son of man"). But there is no reference to the throne on which the Ancient of Days sits in Daniel 7:9. Enoch sees them before the Ancient of Days sits down on the throne (Dan 7:9; cf. 1 En. 47:3) and before the "one like a son of man" is presented before him (Dan 7:13; cf. 1 En. 49:2–4; 52:9; 69:29). In Daniel the identity of the "one like a son of man" is not explained. When Daniel asks one of the attendant angels about the meaning of his vision, he is told whom the four beasts represent, but not who the "one like a son of man" is. Some modern interpreters take the view that he is a symbol for "the holy ones of the Most High" (Dan 7:16–18), but ancient interpreters, including the author of the Parables of Enoch, did not.[10] From the Parables as a whole, we can infer that he thought the Chosen One or "son of man" was the heavenly patron of the people of God, but not a mere symbol for them.

So, unlike Daniel, Enoch asks his interpreting angel a question directly about the figure "whose face was like the appearance of a man":

> And I asked the angel of peace, who went with me and showed me all the hidden things, about that son of man. Who was he? Where did he come from? Why did he accompany the Head of Days? (1 En. 46:2)[11]

This is the first occurrence in the book of the phrase "that son of man" (i.e., "that man"), and it is clear that it functions contextually as a way of referring to the humanlike figure Enoch saw in his vision. All later occurrences of the phrase similarly refer back to this figure in the vision. As I have argued earlier, it is not a title that could stand outside this particular literary context.

Enoch's three questions about "that son of man" (who, whence, why) set the agenda for the rest of the narrative about him and are not fully answered until the closing section, when Enoch is told that he himself is "that son of man" (71:14). To the question "Who was he?" he receives a preliminary answer in 46:3: "This is the son of man who has righteousness, and righteousness dwells with him." Righteousness is his key characteristic, which qualifies him to be God's agent of judgment. But this is not an adequate answer, since the question "Who is he?" surely requires that his personal name be revealed. So the adequate answer comes only in 71:14, when 46:3 is echoed and Enoch is told, "You are that son of man who is born for righteousness, and righteousness dwells on you." (We shall discuss Enoch's

---

10. See part 2.
11. The first half of this verse is Nickelsburg's translation; the second half is Olson's. The series of three questions is clearer in the latter.

identity as "that son of man" later.) For the time being Enoch's angel ignores the question "Where did he come from?" Later Enoch learns that he was "hidden" in the presence of God in heaven (62:7), a somewhat enigmatic answer that is also more fully explicated only in the conclusion to the Parables (70:1–2).

Most of the angel's immediate enlightenment of Enoch about "that son of man" consists in the prediction that he is to be the eschatological judge of "the kings and the mighty" who oppress the righteous (46:4–8). This is probably to be understood as an answer to the question "Why did he accompany the Head of Days?": they are on their way to the thrones on which they will sit to judge (47:3; 51:2). In this stage of the answer, only the negative aspect of judgment—the condemnation of the wicked—is depicted.

THE HEAD OF DAYS TAKES HIS SEAT FOR JUDGMENT (47:1–4)

Here the prayers of the persecuted and murdered righteous and the prayers of the angels who plead their cause in heaven are answered when the Head of Days takes his seat on his glorious throne. The scene in 47:3 plainly reproduces Daniel 7:9–10:

> In those days I saw the Head of Days as he took his seat on the throne of his glory, and the books of the living were opened in his presence, and all his host, which was in the heights of heaven, and his court, were standing in his presence. (1 En. 47:3)

The significance of this act is that now the righteous will be vindicated and their murder avenged. The wicked who murdered them are obviously in mind, but it is notable that in this passage they are never explicitly mentioned. The focus is entirely on judgment as judgment *for* the righteous and oppressed. In accordance with this focus, the phrase "the books were opened" (Dan 7:10) is interpreted as "the books of the living" (1 En. 47:3). The Danielic phrase could refer to books in which the deeds, good and bad, of all people are recorded, but the author of the Parables has interpreted it in the light of Daniel 12:1 ("at that time your people shall be delivered, everyone who is found written in the book") and with a phrase, "the book of the living" or "the book of life," that elsewhere in the Hebrew Bible refers to a book containing the names of the righteous who will be spared the judgment that condemns and destroys their persecutors (Ps 69:28; Isa 4:3; cf. Mal 3:16–18; 1 En. 104:1).[12]

---

12. In 2 Bar. 24:1, also alluding to Dan 7:9, the books are those "in which are written the

Another variation from Daniel 7:10 is highly significant. In Daniel, while the myriads of angels stand in attendance on the Ancient of Days, "the court sat in judgment" (דינא יתב). In the Parables, "all his host . . . and his court were standing in his presence" (1 En. 47:3). The members of the court do not judge; they are assimilated to the angels, servants who always stand in the presence of God. The other throne that is implied by the plural "thrones" in Daniel 7:9 is reserved for "that son of man," who, when he sits on it, "will choose the righteous and holy from among them" (51:2). In other words, he will read out the names in "the book of the living." The author of the Parables has read the description of what happens in Daniel 7:9-10 in a minimal sense. The Head of Days sits on his throne and the books of the living are opened, but he does not go on to pronounce judgment. That is the role of "that son of man," when, as Daniel 7:13 depicts, he appears in the presence of the Head of Days.[13] So chapter 47 ends with rejoicing because what has happened so far indicates that the process of judgment is beginning. The prayer of the righteous has been heard; they know that they are about to be vindicated; but the verdict has not yet been announced.

In addition to interpreting Daniel 7:9-10, this passage also alludes to Daniel 7:21-22, as the words "that judgment might be executed for" the righteous (1 En. 47:2) shows:

> As I looked, this horn made war with the holy ones and was prevailing over them, until the Ancient One came; then judgment was given for the holy ones of the Most High, and the time arrived when the holy ones gained possession of the kingdom. (Dan 7:21-22)

The author of the Parables changes Daniel's terminology, since for him "the holy ones" are frequently angels, while the people of God are "the righteous" or "the chosen ones." Daniel's horn is, for him, "the kings and the mighty."[14] Daniel's references to "the kingdom" he seems to have chosen to ignore. In the Parables neither the Messianic Figure nor the righteous reign. Perhaps the author's hatred of the despotic and oppressive rule of the earthly kings was such that he did not wish to suggest that the Messianic Figure or his people would supplant them and play the same role. Only God can be trusted with absolute power.

---

sins of all those who have sinned." At the same time the "treasuries" of the good deeds of the righteous will be opened.

13. This point is made by Sabino Chialà, "The Son of Man: The Evolution of an Expression," in *Enoch and the Messiah Son of Man: Revisiting the Book of Parables*, ed. Gabriele Boccaccini (Grand Rapids: Eerdmans, 2007) 153-78, here 161.

14. Daniel's image of the horn is perhaps echoed in 62:1.

But another phrase in Daniel 7:22 is of interest: "the Ancient One came." This evidently means that he came to wherever his throne was and sat down on it, as 7:9 says. Neither for Daniel nor for the author of the Parables is this throne the one from which God continuously rules the cosmos, or, at least for the author of the Parables, that is not its function here. It is the seat of judgment. But in order to sit on it, does the Head of Days come from heaven to earth or from somewhere in heaven to somewhere else in heaven?

It seems clear that the scene in this chapter of the Parables takes place in heaven. The prayer of the righteous ascends from the earth into the presence of God (1 En. 47:1), where the angels "who dwell in the heights of heaven" take up their cause (47:2). There is no movement from heaven to earth indicated when the Head of Days takes his seat (47:3).[15] Most commentators take it for granted that the throne is in heaven and that this is unproblematic. But it is not obvious that the throne in Daniel 7:9–10 is in heaven, and we need to explain why the author of the Parables evidently thought it was.

Modern commentators on Daniel are divided on whether the judgment scene in Daniel 7:9–10 takes place in heaven[16] or on earth[17] or "simply in mythic space."[18] A good case can certainly be made for locating the scene on earth, which is where other scenes of divine judgment in the Hebrew Bible take place (Joel 3:2; Ps 50:1–6; 96:10–13; and note especially Jer 49:38: "I will set my throne in Elam").[19] The thrones are "set in place," and the Ancient of Days takes his (Dan 7:9). This cannot be the heavenly throne from which God continuously rules the cosmos. It must be a throne set in place specifically for the purpose of judgment. The preceding vision of the four beasts (7:1–8) takes place on the earth (to which they come from the sea), and there is no indication of a change of scene in 7:9. That the humanlike figure comes "with the clouds of heaven"

---

15. If 48:1 belongs in its present position, it confirms that the location in the preceding verses is heaven.

16. E.g., Louis F. Hartman and Alexander A. Di Lella, *The Book of Daniel*, AB 23 (New York: Doubleday, 1978) 217. The only reason they give is the reference to "the clouds of heaven" in 7:13. See also Timo Eskola, *Messiah and the Throne: Jewish Merkabah Mysticism and Early Christian Exaltation Discourse*, WUNT 2/142 (Tübingen: Mohr Siebeck, 2001) 69; Christopher Rowland, *The Open Heaven: A Study of Apocalyptic in Judaism and Early Christianity* (London: SPCK, 1982) 179.

17. E.g., John Goldingay, *Daniel*, WBC 30 (Dallas: Word, 1989) 164–65; Maurice Casey, *Son of Man: The Interpretation and Influence of Daniel 7* (London: SPCK, 1979) 22; Paul Owen, "Aramaic and Greek Representations of the 'Son of Man' and the Importance of the Parables of Enoch," in *Parables of Enoch*, ed. Charlesworth and Bock, 114–23, here 114–15.

18. John J. Collins, *Daniel*, Hermeneia (Minneapolis: Fortress, 1993) 303.

19. See also 1 En. 1:3–9.

The Messianic Figure in the Eschatological Narrative · 1.3

need not mean that the scene takes place in heaven. He could come with (or "on," as in OG) the clouds from heaven to earth. Indeed, this is likely the sense, because the figure "like a son of man" is thereby contrasted with the four beasts: they come up from the sea onto the earth (7:2), whereas he comes down from heaven to the earth. Finally, the impression that the Ancient of Days has come from heaven to take his seat on a throne on earth is confirmed by 7:22, according to which the horn was prevailing against the holy ones "until the Ancient One came; then judgment was given for the holy ones of the Most High."

We should also take account of three texts within the Enoch literature, which may well have been known to the author of the Parables, and which envisage a scene very like Daniel 7:9–10 taking place on earth:

- 1 Enoch 25:3: "This high mountain that you [Enoch] saw,[20] whose peak is like the throne of God, is the seat where the Great Holy One, the Lord of glory, the King of eternity, will sit, when he descends to visit the earth in goodness." This use of the verb "to visit" is traditional in Jewish literature with reference to judgment, while "in goodness" characterizes the judgment as it appears to the righteous, for whom it will be deliverance from their enemies. The next verse speaks of "the great judgment, in which there will be vengeance on all and a consummation forever" (25:4).
- 1 Enoch 90:20: "And I saw until a throne was constructed in the pleasant land and the Lord of the sheep sat upon it, and he took all the sealed books and opened those books before the Lord of the sheep." The so-called Animal Apocalypse or Second Dream Vision (1 En. 85–90) dates from around the same time as Daniel and may be dependent on it. In any case, the close correspondence would easily be recognized by anyone who knew both texts. (Note that the description of the land of Israel as "the pleasant land" also occurs in Dan 8:9; 11:16, 41.)
- 4QEnGiants[b] (4Q530) ii 16–19: "Be]hold, the ruler of the heavens descended to the earth, and thrones were erected, and the Great Holy One s[at down. A hundred hun]dreds were serving him; a thousand thousands [were worshiping?] him; [a]ll were standing [b]efore him. And behold, [book]s were opened and judgment was spoken; and the judgment of [the Great One] was [wr]itten [in a book] and sealed in an inscription."[21] This passage describes

---

20. The mountain is described in 18:8: "And the middle one of them reached to heaven like the throne of God—of antimony; and the top of the throne was of lapis lazuli."
21. Translation from Loren T. Stuckenbruck, *The Book of Giants from Qumran: Texts, Translation, and Commentary*, TSAJ 63 (Tübingen: Mohr Siebeck, 1997) 120.

the judgment of the giants before the Flood, but clearly it is very closely related to Daniel 7:9–10. I think it is very probably dependent on Daniel, but Loren Stuckenbruck argues that the two texts share common tradition.[22] In either case, this passage is good evidence that the scene depicted in Daniel 7:9–10 could be understood as located on earth.

All three of these texts refer to a throne on earth as God's judgment seat. In addition, 1 Enoch 1:3–9 speaks of God coming from his dwelling place to earth in order to execute judgment on all the wicked, and 1 Enoch 102:3 probably also locates the final judgment on earth.

So why, given that there are such good reasons to think that the judgment in Daniel 7:9–10 takes place on earth, and given that other writers in the Enoch tradition evidently read it in that way, did the author of the Parables think differently? A likely reason is that he observed the similarities between Daniel 7:9–10 and the description of the heavenly throne of God in the Book of Watchers (1 En. 14:18–23). Modern scholars recognize the resemblance and discuss which of the two passages is dependent on the other. This would not have been an issue for the author of the Parables, but the similarities between the two descriptions would have been, especially as he himself, in 71:5–8, modeled his own description of the heavenly throne of God on both Daniel 7:9–10 and 1 Enoch 14. However, while locating the scene in Daniel 7:9–10 in heaven, he did not contradict the strong tradition that eschatological judgment will take place on earth, where the sinners who are to be judged are. For 1 Enoch 47 understands Daniel 7:9–10 as only the beginning of the process of judgment. The Head of Days inaugurates the judgment in heaven, but in the Second Parable the location of the Messianic Figure's throne of judgment is left unspecified (45:3; 51:2–3). In the Third Parable it will become clear that his judgment of the kings and the mighty takes place, as we should expect, on earth (chapter 62).

"That Son of Man" Is Summoned (48:2–10)

The next event in the sequence of eschatological occurrences is this:

> And in that hour that son of man was named in the presence of
>   the Lord of Spirits,
> and his name, before the Head of Days. (1 En. 48:2)

22. Stuckenbruck, *The Book of Giants*, 120–23.

We should take seriously the distinctive expression "in that hour." While "in those days" and "on that day" occur frequently in the Parables, "in that hour" is unique. It indicates that this "naming" of "that son of man" occurs immediately after the Head of Days has taken his seat on his throne. The Messianic Figure is now required to carry out the judgment, and he is summoned to fulfill this, his appointed role. By whom is he "named"? Although the phrase "in the presence of the Lord of Spirits" is common in the Parables and usually carries a literal sense (39:12, 13; 45:6; 47:1, 2, 3; 49:2, 4; 50:4; 62:16; 63:11; 70:1; cf. "before the Lord of Spirits" in 52:9; 58:6), it is possible that in this case it is a reverential periphrasis, indicating that God himself calls the Messianic Figure (cf. 39:8–9). Alternatively, we are to think of an angel issuing the summons on God's behalf. The Ethiopic verb ṣawweʿa, which in 48:2, where it is used in the passive (taṣawweʿa), most of the English translations render "was named,"[23] means "to call, to name, to summon," reflecting the Greek καλέω and the Hebrew or Aramaic קרא.[24] We could translate the verse:

> And in that hour that son of man was called in
>   the presence of the Lord of Spirits,
> and his name [was called], before the Head of Days.

He is called by his name, much like Cyrus in Isaiah 45:4 ("I call you by your name" [אקרא בשמך]). In both cases, it is a matter of being summoned to carry out the task God has given him. We should note that "his name" cannot be intended metaphorically, but must refer to the personal name of "that son of man," though the author at this point refrains from revealing it to the readers.

The summoning of "that son of ʿman" forms a bridge, in the author's interpretation of Daniel 7, between 7:10 and 7:13.[25] He could not suppose that "that son of man" just happened to turn up in the presence of God. He appears at the moment when he is needed for his task, and he does so because God summons him. The next time he appears in the eschatological narrative sequence, he is "in the presence of the Lord of Spirits" (1 En. 49:2, 4).

We should not attempt to synchronize the "naming" in 48:2 and the "naming" in 48:3.[26] They are distinct events. To my knowledge, only one scholar has correctly recognized the scriptural basis for 48:3:

23. Isaac combines it with the noun "name" and translates: "was given a name." This is certainly wrong. See Ephraim Isaac, "1 (Ethiopic Apocalypse of) Enoch," *OTP* 1:5–89, here 35.
24. Nickelsburg, *1 Enoch 2*, 593.
25. Nickelsburg, *1 Enoch 2*, 169, sees it as an interpretation of Dan 7:14.
26. Nickelsburg, *1 Enoch 2*, 169–70, rightly argues for two different chronological references.

> Even before the sun and the constellations were created,
> before the stars of heaven were made,
> his name was named before the Lord of Spirits.

James Kugel points out the similarity with Psalm 72:17a, which he translates thus:

> May his name be forever;
> his name bursts forth **before the sun**.[27]

He explains, "The highlighted phrase, in Hebrew [לפני] as in English, is ambiguous: 'before' can mean both 'in front of' and 'preceding in time.' If the latter, then the words of this psalm might be interpreted as meaning that even before the sun was created, the name of the messiah bursts forth."[28] This account of the biblical source of 1 Enoch 48:3 explains why specifically the sun and the stars are mentioned there. Since the heavenly bodies were created on the fourth day of creation (Gen 1:14–18), reference to them is not an obvious way of saying "before the creation of the world."

In 48:3 there may be an additional, but secondary allusion to Isaiah (49:1b):

> The LORD called me [קראני] from the womb,
> from the belly of my mother he named my name [הזכיר שמי].
> (my translation)

Only if read in conjunction with Psalm 72:17a could this suggest a "calling by name" before the heavenly bodies were created.

Psalm 72 probably also lies behind 1 Enoch 48:5a: "All who dwell on the earth shall fall down and worship before him." Compare Psalm 72:11:

---

27. NRSV: "May his name endure forever, / his fame continue as long as the sun." The verb ינון (Qal imperfect of נון or נין?), which Kugel translates as "bursts forth" and the NRSV "continue," is a *hapax legomenon*. Translators suppose it is cognate with the noun נין (offspring) and look for a metaphorical sense in which a name can have offspring. But the author of the Parables may have known the variant reading כון, meaning "be established." In 1 En. 39:8, Enoch says, "There [in the presence of God] my portion has been from the first, for thus it has been established concerning me in the presence of the Lord of Spirits."

28. James Kugel, *Traditions of the Bible: A Guide to the Bible As It Was at the Start of the Common Era* (Cambridge, MA: Harvard University Press, 1998) 59–60. He says that "this tradition was common in rabbinic Judaism." Ps 72:17 is quoted in this sense in the parallel passages b. Pesah. 54a; b. Ned. 39b. See also Ephraim E. Urbach, *The Sages: Their Concepts and Beliefs*, trans. Israel Abrahams (Jerusalem: Magnes, 1979) 684.

> May all kings fall down before him,
> all nations give him service.

This is closer to the Enochian text than Isaiah 49:7. It has both verbs ("fall down" and "give him service") and refers to "all nations," not just kings.[29]

The author of the Parables probably noticed the resemblances between Psalm 72:17a and Isaiah 49:1b, and between Psalm 72:11 and Isaiah 49:7. In 1 Enoch 48:3-7 he has woven together allusions to the psalm and to Isaiah 49:

1 En. 48:3	Ps 72:17a	Isa 49:1b
1 En. 48:4a	Ps 72:4?	Isa 49:6a?
1 En. 48:4b		Isa 49:6b
1 En. 48:5a	Ps 72:11	Isa 49:7b
1 En. 48:6[30]	Ps 72:17a	
1 En. 48:7c	Ps 72:13?	Isa 49:6?

We must return to the connection between 48:2 and 48:3, between the calling of the Messianic Figure in the last days and his calling before the sun and the stars were created. Nickelsburg puts it succinctly: "At the critical hour in the eschaton God calls into action the one whom God designated for the task already before the cosmos was created."[31] First Enoch 48:4-10 then expands on what the vocation is for which he was designated before the stars were created and which he is now called upon to carry out. It is parallel to 46:4-8, but gives priority to the positive, salvific aspect of this role.

In view of 48:3, 6, we need to discuss the disputed issue of the preexistence of "that son of man."

Preexistence?

Do the Parables of Enoch portray the Messianic Figure as personally preexistent before creation (or at least at the outset of creation)? The judgment that they do is widely thought to be inconsistent with the identification

---

29. Craig C. Broyles, "The Redeeming King: Psalm 72's Contribution to the Messianic Ideal," in *Eschatology, Messianism and the Dead Sea Scrolls* (Grand Rapids: Eerdmans, 1997) 23-40, argues for allusions to Ps 72 in the Psalms of Solomon and in Matt 2:11 but does not discuss 1 En. 48.

30. The influence of Isa 49:2 is often seen in the phrase "hidden in his presence," but the next section will show why I disagree with that judgment.

31. Nickelsburg, *1 Enoch 2*, 170, and see his fuller discussion of the issue there.

of Enoch with "that son of man" in chapter 71.[32] It is probably the major obstacle to supposing that that identification is not a secondary addition to the Parables but the climax to which the whole work was always designed to lead. Among those who hold that the identification of Enoch with "that son of man" belongs to the original design of the Parables there are those who think that in 48:3, 6; 62:7 only his foreordination in the mind of God is intended[33] and others who think that "that son of man" is a kind of heavenly counterpart of Enoch, existing before Enoch's birth, and that Enoch is somehow fused with him in 71:14[34] or even that the heavenly figure is "incarnated" in Enoch.[35]

The primordial "naming" of "that son of man" in 48:3 certainly need not imply that he already existed then.[36] It means only that God pre-ordained him for the role of eschatological judge, just as he appointed Jeremiah for his

---

32. E.g., John J. Collins, *The Scepter and the Star: The Messiahs of the Dead Sea Scrolls and Other Ancient Literature* (New York: Doubleday, 1996) 180–81; Darrell D. Hannah, "The Chosen Son of Man of the *Parables of Enoch*," in *"Who Is This Son of Man?" The Latest Scholarship on a Puzzling Expression of the Historical Jesus*, ed. Larry W. Hurtado and Paul L. Owen, LNTS 390 (London: T&T Clark, 2011) 148–58.

33. Morna D. Hooker, *The Son of Man in Mark: A Study of the Background of the Term "Son of Man" and Its Use in St Mark's Gospel* (London: SPCK, 1967) 42–43; James C. VanderKam, "Righteous One, Messiah, Chosen One, and Son of Man in 1 Enoch 37–71," in *The Messiah: Developments in Earliest Judaism and Christianity*, ed. James H. Charlesworth (Minneapolis: Fortress, 1992) 169–91, here 180–82; Rowland, *The Open Heaven*, 185; Leslie W. Walck, *The Son of Man in the Parables of Enoch and in Matthew*, JCT 9 (London: T&T Clark, 2011) 97–99.

34. Michael A. Knibb, *Essays on the Book of Enoch and Other Early Jewish Texts and Traditions*, SVTP 22 (Leiden: Brill, 2009) 321–22; Andrei A. Orlov, *The Glory of the Invisible God: Two Powers in Heaven Traditions and Early Christology*, JCT 31 (London: T&T Clark, 2019) 21–22.

35. Daniel Boyarin, *The Jewish Gospels: The Story of the Jewish Christ* (New York: New Press, 2012) 75: "A particular divine-human Redeemer figure eventually incarnated in the figure of Enoch." Helge S. Kvanvig, "The Son of Man in the Parables of Enoch," in *Enoch and the Messiah*, ed. Boccaccini, 202–6, thinks that Enoch was preexistent in the form of Wisdom before his life on earth (cf. 1 En. 42:1–2).

36. In b. Pesah. 54a; b. Ned. 39b, "the name of the Messiah" is one of the "seven things created before the creation of the world." Joseph Klausner, *The Messianic Idea in Israel from Its Beginnings to the Completion of the Mishnah*, trans. W. F. Stinespring (London: Allen & Unwin, 1956) 460–61, takes this to mean "the idea of the Messiah," and similarly Hannah, "The Chosen Son of Man," 149, thinks it refers to the Messiah's "identity" in the mind of God. In view of rabbinic speculation about the name of the Messiah, I am more inclined to think the "name" is intended literally, but with the implication that a name names someone's identity. See also Tg. Mic 5:1; Zech 4:7.

prophetic vocation before his birth (Jer 1:5). The claim that "that son of man" ontologically preexisted creation rests on only two verses, the first of which is evidently developing the thought expressed in 48:3:

> For this (reason) he was chosen and hidden in his presence
>   before the world was created and forever.
> And the wisdom of the Lord of Spirits has revealed him to the holy
>   and the righteous;
> for he has preserved the lot of the righteous. (48:6–7a)

> For from the beginning the son of man was hidden,
>   and the Most High preserved him in the presence of his might,[37]
>   and revealed him to the chosen. (62:7)

The two passages have obvious similarities, and so it is quite possible that the textual tradition of one has affected the textual tradition of the other. There is a difficulty in the extant text of 48:6. While it makes sense to say that "that son of man" was chosen "before the world was created and forever," to say that he was also "hidden in [God's] presence" "before the world was created *and forever*" is not at all consistent with what we learn from chapter 62. There he is hidden only *until* he sits on his throne and is seen by the kings and the mighty. I suggest that "hidden in his presence" in 48:6 is a gloss introduced by a scribe who recalled 62:7. (A Christian scribe, believing this figure to be Jesus Christ, would, of course, assume that he preexisted creation, not only in God's intention but also in ontological reality.)[38] If we remove that phrase from 48:6, we find that the two passages are thematically distinct, despite their similarities. First Enoch 48:6–7a is about the chosenness of the Messianic Figure, whereas 62:7 is about his hiddenness. The distinction is appropriate to these passages' respective contexts: the former (48:4–7) concerns the vocation of the Messi-

---

37. Hannah, "The Chosen Son of Man," 150, plausibly argues that this should be translated "in the presence of his host," meaning the angelic host (as in 61:10–11). The implication is important: "The reference to the angelic host rules out merely an idea in the mind of God; such could not be preserved *with* or *in the presence of* the angelic host" (150).

38. For the identification of the "son of man" in the Parables of Enoch with Jesus Christ in the Ethiopian Christian tradition, see Daniel Assefa, "The Identity of the Son of Man in the Traditional Ethiopian Commentaries on 1 Enoch," in *Wisdom Poured Out like Water: Studies on Jewish and Christian Antiquity in Honor of Gabriele Boccaccini*, ed. J. Harold Ellens et al., Deuterocanonical and Cognate Literature Studies 38 (Berlin: de Gruyter, 2018) 24–31, here 26.

anic Figure, while 62:1–7 is about the effect on the kings and the mighty when the one who has previously been hidden with God in heaven appears before them on his throne of judgment.

Without the phrase "hidden in his presence," 48:6 can be read without difficulty as asserting that God chose "that son of man" for his task before the creation of the world and before he existed ontologically. This could be said of Enoch. Moreover, if we distinguish the themes of the two passages, we can also give due weight to the fact that he is not said, in 62:7, to have been hidden before the creation of the world, but "from the beginning" (*ʾem-qedm*).[39] Assuming a Greek *Vorlage*, it would have had ἀπ' ἀρχῆς,[40] which would plausibly be a translation of Hebrew or Aramaic מקדם, as it is in OG Micah 5:2[1]. (This text may well be actually the biblical source behind 1 En. 62:7.) מקדם means "from ancient times," "from of old."[41] From the perspective of the kings and the mighty at the time of the eschatological judgment, Enoch had been hidden "from ancient times"—that is, since his translation to heaven. If Enoch is "the son of man," the statement is entirely appropriate. (Compare the reference to Enoch's contemporaries as "ancients" in 1:2.)

There is a close parallel to 1 Enoch 62:7 in 4 Ezra 13:26. Speaking of the "man from the sea" whom Ezra has seen in his vision and who, like the Messianic Figure in the Parables, is based on Daniel 7:13, Isaiah 11:2–5, and Psalm 2, the interpreting angel says: "This is he whom the Most High has been keeping for many ages [*ipse est quem conservat Altissimus multis temporibus*], through whom he will deliver his creation."[42] Strikingly, the parallel extends even to the designation used for God: "the Most High" (common in 4 Ezra, very rare in the Parables).[43] I do not think the author of 4 Ezra thought this figure was Enoch, but he did think he was a human person born in the distant past, taken up to heaven and preserved there by God in preparation for his role as Messiah at the end of history. He seems to have thought of a descendant of David, born

---

39. VanderKam, "Righteous One," 181, argues that *ʾem-qedm* need mean no more than "beforehand" (i.e., before the kings and the mighty saw him), but does not discuss the possible Greek or Semitic *Vorlage*.

40. Knibb, *Essays*, 314, notes that *ʾem-qedm* translates ἀπ' ἀρχῆς in 1 John 1:1.

41. Casey, *The Solution*, 103–4, reconstructs the Aramaic as מן עלמא, with the same meaning ("from of old").

42. This is Stone's translation in Michael Edward Stone, *Fourth Ezra*, Hermeneia (Minneapolis: Fortress, 1990) 392. NRSV has, following the Latin, "who will himself deliver his creation," whereas, for these words, Stone follows the other versions.

43. 1 En. 46:7; 60:1, 22; 62:7. Of these, 60:1, 22 occur in a "Noachic" interpolation. In all cases, the title seems drawn from Dan 7:22, 25, 27, which may also be the case in 4 Ezra 13:26.

to the royal line in biblical times, and removed to heaven after his birth, as a tale later told by some of the rabbis relates.[44] In another messianic vision he sees "the Messiah whom the Most High has kept until the end of days, who will arise from the offspring of David" (4 Ezra 12:32 NRSV).[45]

Clearly 4 Ezra and the Parables have drawn on common tradition, as in other parts of the vision in 4 Ezra 13.[46] The application to a Davidide must surely be the more original version, since Isaiah 11:2–5, drawn on very similarly by the two works, is so obviously Davidic and it is odd that the Parables ignores that aspect of the passage. It looks as though a tradition in which the eschatological judge is to be a descendant of David, born in the distant past, has been appropriated in the Parables to Enoch, born in the even more distant past. But in neither case is there any idea of premundane existence or more than human origin. Both take seriously that the figure in Daniel 7:13 is "like a human being" and suppose he must be someone who once lived as a human on earth and has in the meantime been kept by God in heaven, ready for his eschatological moment.

In the Parables of Enoch, "that son of man" is said to have been "hidden" by God. Rather similarly, in 4 Ezra, when Ezra asks why he saw "the man coming up from the heart of the sea," he is told, "Just as no one can explore or know what is in the depths of the sea, so no one on earth can see my son or those who are with him, except in the time of his day" (13:52).[47] In 4 Ezra, "those who are with him" are others who have been taken up to heaven without dying (cf. 6:25; 7:28; 14:9), no doubt including Enoch, though it may be by design that 4 Ezra makes no explicit reference to the figure of Enoch. But in the Parables of Enoch, the notion that the Messianic Figure was "hidden" applies very readily to Enoch. Probably the author was inspired in this respect, as in many others, by the Book of Watchers, here specifically by 1 Enoch 12:1: "Enoch was taken, and no human being knew where he had been taken, or where he was, or what had happened to him." Though, in its context, this

---

44. Y. Ber. 2:4, 5a; Lam. Rab. 1:51 (on 1:16); Num. Rab. 13:5. See the discussion in Martin Hengel, *The Zealots*, trans. D. Smith (Edinburgh: T&T Clark, 1989) 295–96; Martha Himmelfarb, "The Mother of the Messiah in the Talmud Yerushalmi and Sefer Zerubbabel," in *The Talmud Yerushalmi and Graeco-Roman Culture*, vol. 3, ed. Peter Schäfer, TSAJ 93 (Tübingen: Mohr Siebeck, 2002) 369–89.

45. 4 Ezra envisages a plurality of people, not limited to Enoch and Elijah, who were taken up to heaven without dying and will appear on earth again at the end (6:26). They include the Messiah (7:28; cf. 13:52; 14:9).

46. In chapter 2.7 I shall suggest that the Parables of Enoch is dependent on 4 Ezra.

47. Translation from Stone, *Fourth Ezra*, 394 (I have changed "my servant" to "my son").

statement refers to Enoch's absence from the earth at an earlier period of his life, before his final ascension, the author of the Parables could easily suppose it would also be true of the latter.

A difference between 4 Ezra and the Parables is that, whereas the identity of the Messianic Figure in 4 Ezra remains hidden from the readers (apart from the information that he is a Davidide), in the Parables his identity is eventually disclosed to the readers, when they learn that he is Enoch.

The Chosen One Appears in the Presence of the Lord of Spirits (49:1–4)

The result of the summoning of the Messianic Figure (1 En. 48:2) is that he "has taken his stand in the presence of the Lord of Spirits" (49:2),[48] alluding to Daniel 7:13. The passage continues with a probable allusion to Daniel 7:14:

> To him was given dominion and glory and kingship,
> that all peoples, nations, and languages should serve him.
> His dominion is an everlasting dominion that shall not pass away,
> and his kingdom is one that shall never be destroyed. (NRSV)

The Book of Parables consistently avoids using language of kingship and rule in connection with the Messianic Figure, and so Daniel 7:14 is transmuted in 1 Enoch 49:2 thus:

> and his glory is forever and ever,
> and his might for all generations.

(There is a rather similar avoidance of kingship language in 1 Enoch 52:4: "the authority of his Anointed One, so that he may be powerful and mighty on the earth." This alludes to Ps 2:2, 9, but avoids echoing the psalm's description of the Lord's Anointed One as his "king" [2:6].)

Although the moment described in 1 Enoch 49:2b corresponds to Daniel 7:13, the terms "Lord of Spirits" and "Chosen One" are used rather than "Head of Days" and "that son of man." This is probably because the passage continues with a strong echo of Isaiah 11:2–3 (1 En. 49:3–4a) and concludes with an allusion to Isaiah 42:1 (1 En. 49:4b). The Messianic Figure is not a king, but he is preeminently a judge. Daniel does not say so, but Isaiah does.

---

48. The same phrase is used of angels standing in the presence of God in 39:12–40:1.

So his appearance before the Lord of Spirits is accompanied by a description of his endowment with qualities of the Spirit (1 En. 49:3, alluding to Isa 11:2) that enable him, unlike any other judge, to see into the hearts of those he assesses (1 En. 49:4a, probably based on Isa 11:3b). Since Isaiah 42:1b also links the Messianic Figure's endowment with divine spirit and his delivering of justice, this section of the Parables of Enoch appropriately ends with allusion to Isaiah 42:1a. This passage is an instructive example of the way this author constructs his Messianic Figure by combining features of Daniel 7, Isaiah 11, and Isaiah 42.

Probably there is a similar combination of allusions to Isaiah 11:2-4 and Daniel 7:14 in 1 Enoch 51:3b:

> And all the secrets of *wisdom* will go forth from the *counsel* of
> *his mouth*,
> for the Lord of Spirits has given (them) to him and glorified him.

The italicized words allude to Isaiah 11:2 and 4b, while "glorified him" echoes Daniel 7:14 ("to him was given . . . glory").

THE JUDGMENT OF THE KINGS AND THE MIGHTY (62:1-12)

We have already seen that the Messianic Figure's task of pronouncing judgment, to which the Second Parable refers in general terms (1 En. 45:3-6; 51:2-3), is unpacked, in the Third Parable and under the influence of Isaiah 24:21, as consisting in three stages: the judgment of the holy angels, the judgment of the kings and the powerful ones, and the judgment of the rebellious angels. The third stage we have to suppose (on the basis of 55:4 and 69:28) was in a section of the text that has been lost between 64:2 and 69:26. The judgment of the holy angels takes place, following Isaiah 24:21, in heaven. The Lord of Spirits seats the Chosen One on a throne of glory for that purpose (61:8). The judgment of "the kings and the mighty and the exalted and those who possess the earth" (62:1) takes place, I have suggested, on the earth (again in accordance with Isa 24:21). For this purpose the Lord of Spirits seats the Chosen One on the Chosen One's "glorious throne" on earth (62:2). His throne of judgment has been transferred from heaven to earth for that purpose. The judgment of the fallen angels probably also takes place on earth (cf. 55:4).

Here I need to substantiate in more detail the claim that the throne from which the Messianic Figure delivers judicial sentence on the kings, resulting in their destruction, is understood to be situated on earth. The main reason that scholars have generally assumed it is located in heaven[49] is that they think there is only one "throne of glory" in the Parables, which is God's heavenly throne. If the throne in 62:2 is, as I have argued, the Messianic Figure's own glorious throne, then a strong reason for locating the scene in heaven disappears. It is surely to be expected that, just as the Messianic Figure judges the angels "in the heights of heaven" (61:8) where they are ordinarily to be found, so he judges "the kings and the mighty and the exalted and those who possess the earth" (62:1, cf. 3, 6; 63:1) or "those who rule the earth" (62:9) on earth, where they are to be found. Elsewhere it is said that he "will make sinners vanish and perish from the face of the earth" (69:27; cf. 45:6).

The closest parallels to this scene of judgment outside the Parables of Enoch are in 4 Ezra and 2 Baruch, where similarly the Messianic Figure judges the oppressive rulers of the earth (identified in both works as Daniel's fourth kingdom and understood as the Roman Empire). In 4 Ezra, as in the Parables, the key texts of the Hebrew Bible on which this narrative of judgment depends are Daniel 7, Isaiah 11:2-5, and Psalm 2. In 2 Baruch the dependence on Daniel 7 and Psalm 2 is clear, on Isaiah 11:2-5 less so.[50] In these accounts the judgment takes place on Mount Zion, the location suggested by Psalm 2:6 (4 Ezra 13:35; 2 Bar. 40:1). The Messianic Figure (who in 4 Ezra 13 is clearly the "humanlike one" of Dan 7:13 and in 2 Bar. 39-40 "my Anointed One" of Ps 2:2) pronounces judicial sentence on the rulers of the empire (4 Ezra 12:32-33), the nations who attack Jerusalem (4 Ezra 13:9-11, 27-38), or the "last ruler" of the fourth kingdom (2 Bar. 40:1). In 4 Ezra 13:37-38 this pronouncing of judgment itself destroys the wicked, as in 1 Enoch 62:2; both passages derive this idea from Isaiah 11:4. Scholars discussing the Parables of Enoch have not always noticed that 4 Ezra and 2 Baruch portray the Messianic Figure as a judge, but their use of judicial language makes this quite clear. They do not explicitly envisage him sitting on a throne of judgment, but 4 Ezra 12:32-33 comes close to it:

---

49. E.g., Nickelsburg, *1 Enoch 2*, 239.

50. See 2 Bar. 39:3-5 (the four kingdoms of Dan 7); 39:7; 40:1 ("my Anointed One" on "Mount Zion," as in Ps 2:2, 6). In "The Messianic Interpretation of Isaiah 10:34," in Richard Bauckham, *The Jewish World around the New Testament: Collected Essays I*, WUNT 233 (Tübingen: Mohr Siebeck, 2008; repr., Grand Rapids: Baker Academic, 2010) 193-205, here 197-200, I have argued that 2 Bar. 36-40 reflects a messianic interpretation of Isa 10:34 in conjunction with Isa 11:1-5. The relationship of 2 Baruch to Dan 7 will be discussed further in chapter 2.8 below.

He will denounce them[51] for their ungodliness and for their wickedness and will cast up before them their contemptuous dealings. For first he will set them living in judgment, and when he has reproved them, then he will destroy them.[52]

The Latin that Stone here translates as "For first he will set them living in judgment" is *Statuet enim eos primum in iudicium vivos*. The phrase *in iudicium* is a technical term meaning "before a court of law." A literal translation would be "For first he will stand them, alive, before the court." The NRSV's translation, "For first he will bring them alive before his judgment seat," is a paraphrase, but not, as Stone alleges, a misleading one.[53] The Messiah is the judge, and he can be presumed to have a judgment seat.

The importance of these parallels for our present purposes is that they very clearly locate *on earth* the judgment of the oppressive rulers by a Messianic Figure who resembles that of the Parables. This figure comes to earth, confronts the oppressors, pronounces their legal condemnation, and thus destroys them. There seems to be no example in Jewish literature of a Messianic Figure who judges earthly kings or powers in heaven.

---

51. It is not quite clear who "they" are, but presumably they are the rulers of the empire.
52. Translation from Stone, *Fourth Ezra*, 360.
53. Stone, *Fourth Ezra*, 360 n. j.

CHAPTER 1.4

The Identity of "That Son of Man"

REVEALING THE IDENTITY OF "THAT SON OF MAN"

It is now generally agreed that in 71:14 Enoch is told that he himself is the "son of man" he has seen in his visions. But to most scholars this seems like a complete surprise for which the rest of the book has in no way prepared. For this and other reasons, chapter 71 has been widely regarded as a later addition to the Book of the Parables, introducing an identification of the "son of man" with Enoch that the rest of the book had not envisaged. On the other hand, it is entirely possible that chapter 71 is an original and integral part of the book and that the revelation of the identity of the "son of man" was intended to surprise readers, like the solution to a murder mystery revealed at the end of a modern detective novel. But, to press that analogy, we should not in that case expect the solution to come as a *complete* surprise. Clues to the solution would have been planted by the author along the way, so that when the solution is revealed, readers would be able to recognize it as appropriate and to see that it makes sense of aspects of the earlier narrative. Some readers may well be able, on the strength of the clues, to guess the solution before it is formally uncovered at the end.

In my view, the Book of the Parables contains a number of such clues, which means that for an appropriately informed reader the revelation that the "son of man" of Enoch's visions is in fact Enoch himself would not come as a complete surprise. Some of these may be more convincing than others, but there seems to me to be a good cumulative case for supposing that the identification of the "son of man" with Enoch was envisaged in the composition of the book from the start.[1]

---

1. Scholars who think that the identification of the "son of man" with Enoch belongs

1 Enoch 37:1

The opening of the Book of Parables introduces Enoch by reciting his genealogy in six generations back to Adam. This might be intended merely to emphasize his antiquity or his special status as "the seventh from Adam" (as in Jude 14), but James VanderKam comments:

> It is intriguing that two of the names in the genealogy offer a suggestive idea. Since *walda* ["son"] is used before each name, one twice reads expressions that in the original language meant literally "son of man": Enoch is *walda hēnos* (son of Enosh = son of man) and *walda 'adām* (son of Adam = son of man). It is not impossible that the writer is indulging in a sort of wordplay which prepares the reader, however obliquely, for Enoch's identification of[2] son of man in 71:14.[3]

The phrase *walda 'adām* is not one of the Ethiopic expressions used for "son of man" in the Parables. So, if the wordplay suggested by VanderKam was intended in the original version of the Parables, it would seem that the Ethiopic translator did not recognize it.

---

to the original form of the Book of Parables include Morna D. Hooker, *The Son of Man in Mark: A Study of the Background of the Term "Son of Man" and Its Use in St Mark's Gospel* (London: SPCK, 1967) 41–43; James C. VanderKam, "Righteous One, Messiah, Chosen One, and Son of Man in 1 Enoch 37–71," in *The Messiah: Developments in Earliest Judaism and Christianity*, ed. James H. Charlesworth (Minneapolis: Fortress, 1992) 182–85; Maurice Casey, *Son of Man: The Interpretation and Influence of Daniel 7* (London: SPCK, 1979) 102–7; Helge S. Kvanvig, "The Son of Man in the Parables of Enoch," in *Enoch and the Messiah Son of Man: Revisiting the Book of Parables*, ed. Gabriele Boccaccini (Grand Rapids: Eerdmans, 2007); Leslie W. Walck, *The Son of Man in the Parables of Enoch and in Matthew*, JCT 9 (London: T&T Clark, 2011) 5–7; Matthew Black, *The Book of Enoch or 1 Enoch*, SVTP 7 (Leiden: Brill, 1985) 187–89; Loren T. Stuckenbruck, "The Building Blocks of Enoch as the Son of Man in the Early Enoch Tradition," in *Parables of Enoch: A Paradigm Shift*, ed. Darrell L. Bock and James H. Charlesworth, JCT 11 (London: Bloomsbury, 2013) 315–28; Andrei A. Orlov, *The Enoch-Metatron Tradition*, TSAJ 107 (Tübingen: Mohr Siebeck, 2005) 82–84; Orlov, *The Glory of the Invisible God: Two Powers in Heaven Traditions and Early Christology*, JCT 31 (London: T&T Clark, 2019) 21–24; James A. Waddell, *The Messiah: A Comparative Study of the Enochic Son of Man and the Pauline Kyrios*, JCT 10 (London: T&T Clark, 2011) 51–60.

2. I presume "of" should be "as."
3. VanderKam, "Righteous One," 178–79.

1 Enoch 39:6–8

In 39:3 Enoch's first vision in the Book of Parables begins and includes his first sight of the Messianic Figure (whom he next sees in the Danielic vision of 46:1). The vision is set in heaven, where he sees "the dwellings of the holy ones, and the resting places of the righteous" (39:4). He sees them interceding for "the sons of men" (39:5). These are the intercessory prayers that in 47:1 begin to be answered when the Head of Days takes his seat on the throne of judgment. So Enoch does not see heaven as it was in his own, antediluvian times, but in the future, probably the time of the real author and his readers. After these deceased righteous people, Enoch sees the Chosen One:

> And in that place my eyes saw the Chosen One[4] of righteousness
>   and faith,
> and righteousness will be [in][5] his days,
> and the righteous and chosen will be without number before him
>   forever and ever.
> And I saw his dwelling beneath the wings of the Lord of Spirits,
> and all the righteous and chosen were mighty before him like
>   fiery lights,
> and their mouths were full of blessing,
> and their lips praised the name of the Lord of Spirits.
> And righteousness did not fail before him,
> nor did truth fail before him.
> There I wished to dwell,
> and my spirit longed for that dwelling.
> There my lot had been from before,[6]
> for thus it has been established concerning me in the presence
>   of the Lord of Spirits. (39:6–8)

---

4. Some manuscripts read: "the place of the chosen."

5. The word "in" is accidentally omitted in George W. E. Nickelsburg and James C. VanderKam, *1 Enoch: The Hermeneia Translation*, 2nd ed. (Minneapolis: Fortress, 2012).

6. In the first edition of Nickelsburg and VanderKam's translation, this line was translated: "There my portion has been from the first" (George W. E. Nickelsburg and James C. VanderKam, *1 Enoch: A New Translation; Based on the Hermeneia Commentary* [Minneapolis: Fortress, 2004]). Ethiopic *qedma* has a range of meanings, including "from the first" or "at first," but also "before," "formerly," "beforehand," "previously."

No doubt Enoch's wish (which echoes Ps 84:1–2) is, in his own mind at this point, a longing to be with the Chosen One in heaven, a destiny he knows has been determined for him already (cf. 1 En. 37:4). But, with readerly hindsight, from the perspective of the continuation and especially the end of the book, his wish looks very much like a wish *to be* the Chosen One. He longs for "that dwelling." The righteous have their own dwellings (39:4). What Enoch desires is the Chosen One's own dwelling. The description of the Chosen One here—"righteousness will not fail before him" (39:7)—is echoed in the angel's words to Enoch, when he has been told that he is "that son of man": "the righteousness of the Head of Days will not forsake you" (71:14). (The promise is repeated in 71:16.) In relation to the righteous, Enoch there steps into precisely the role the Chosen One has in 39:6–7. From that perspective his assurance that his "lot" has been in "that dwelling" "from before, for thus it has been established concerning me in the presence of the Lord of Spirits" (39:8), is reminiscent of the "naming" of "that son of man" "before the Lord of Spirits" before the heavenly bodies were created (48:3).

The text is very far from an unambiguous identification of Enoch with the Chosen One, but it seems to have been written so that it is open to such a reading. A further hint may be given in the next verse, where Enoch joins the righteous in heaven in praising God, "for he has established me for his blessing and praise according to the good pleasure of the Lord of Spirits" (39:9). Virtually the same phrase, "according to the good pleasure of the Lord of Spirits," was used of Enoch's exceptional reception of wisdom in the prologue to the book (37:4). It recurs with reference to the Chosen One in 49:4: "he is the Chosen One in the presence of the Lord of Spirits according to his good pleasure."[7] In 1 Enoch 1:8, God's "good pleasure" (εὐδοκίαν) is given to all the righteous, though Charles and Knibb suggest that εὐδοκίαν here was a mistake for εὐοδίαν ("prosperity").[8] In any case, in the Parables the phrase (with minor variations) occurs only in the three passages just quoted—with reference to Enoch and the Chosen One. In 49:4 it certainly reflects Isaiah 42:1 ("my chosen one, in whom my soul takes pleasure [רצתה]"). This verb (רצה) and its cognate noun (רצון) are not common in the Hebrew Bible in this sense of God's favor to

---

7. There is a small difference in the wording: in 37:4 and 49:4 the verb *faqada*, "to desire," is used, while 39:9 has the noun *faqād* (accusative *faqāda*) ([good] pleasure). I am grateful to Darrell Hannah for clarifying this point.
8. See Michael A. Knibb, *The Ethiopic Book of Enoch: A New Edition in the Light of the Aramaic Dead Sea Fragments* (Oxford: Clarendon, 1978) 1:4, who cites Charles.

a specific human,[9] though they are more common with reference to his favor to God's people or to righteous people.[10] The use of this term in the Parables with reference specifically to Enoch and to the Chosen One is striking.

To the identification of the Messianic Figure with Enoch, it is sometimes objected that Enoch, situated on earth, can hardly be seeing himself in heaven and, moreover, not recognize himself. The answer is that all Enoch's visions of the Messianic Figure relate to the future, after he has ascended to heaven and has been transformed into the appearance of a heavenly being.

1 Enoch 46:1

In Enoch's initial vision of "that son of man" in 46:1, he is described thus:

> whose face was like the appearance of a man,
> and his face was full of graciousness like one of the holy angels.

Although clearly alluding to Daniel 7:13, none of this description is actually taken from that verse. The first description of his face draws on Daniel 8:15 (כמראה גבר: "one having the appearance of a man") and 10:18 (כמראה אדם: "one having the appearance of a human"). Since in Daniel these refer to an angel, it is not surprising that Enoch also describes the figure's face as "like one of the holy angels." But "full of graciousness" seems to be an entirely original element. Nickelsburg comments, "The expression 'full of grace' (*melu' ṣagā*) is not used here theologically but denotes a physical characteristic. The noun *ṣagā* presumably translates Gk. χάρις, which in turn would reflect Aram. חנא (*ḥinā*), Heb. חן (*ḥēn*). The basic meaning of the Semitic root *ḥnn* is 'grace.'" The noun, like the Greek χάρις, refers in the first place to beauty or physical attractiveness. "Thus the figure here described is characterized by a humanlike face, which, however, is surpassingly beautiful and graceful like the countenance of the angels."[11] It is not surprising that the face of an angel should be very beautiful, but the observation is hard to parallel in the literature of this period.[12]

---

9. In prayers: Ps 30:7, 10; 106:4.

10. Righteous people, Israel, Jerusalem: Deut 33:23; Job 33:26; Ps 5:12; 51:18; 89:17; 147:11 ("the Lord takes pleasure in those who fear him"); 149:4 ("the Lord takes pleasure in his people"); Prov 8:35; 11:20; 12:2, 22; 18:22; Isa 60:10.

11. George W. E. Nickelsburg and James C. VanderKam, *1 Enoch 2: A Commentary on the Book of 1 Enoch Chapters 37–82*, ed. Klaus Baltzer, Hermeneia (Minneapolis: Fortress, 2012) 157.

12. The closest seems to be the description of Polycarp before his martyrdom (τὸ

The Identity of "That Son of Man" · 1.4

It is possible that the phrase appealed to the author as a pun on the name Enoch (חנוך). There are many examples of wordplay on names in Genesis, including the name of Enoch's great-grandson Noah (Gen 5:29), while the Book of Watchers has, in close connection, puns on the names of Enoch's father Jared and of Mount Hermon. It associates Jared with the Hebrew ירד, "to descend," and Hermon with the Hebrew חרם, "curse." The Watchers "descended in the days of Jared onto the peak of Mount Hermon. And they called the mountain 'Hermon' because they swore and bound themselves with a curse on it" (1 En. 6:6). In the Enochic fragment about the birth of Noah (1 En. 106–107), the narrative seems to be constructed around etymologies of the names of Enoch and his relatives Jared, Methuselah, Lamech, and Noah.[13] In addition to such parallels in Genesis and the Enoch literature, Philo attests an etymology of the name Enoch that connects it with "grace" (χάρις).[14] More precisely, he says the name means "your grace" or "your gift" (χάρις σου), evidently reading the name as composed of the Hebrew noun חן and the possessive suffix ך.[15] The author of the Parables could have known this etymology or, with the precedents of wordplay on related names in Genesis and the Book of Watchers in mind, could have come up with the same etymology himself.

1 Enoch 46:3

When Enoch asks his guiding angel about "that son of man," he is told

> This is the son of man who has righteousness,
> and righteousness dwells with him. (46:3)

There is a clear echo of this when Enoch is told that he himself is "the son of man":

πρόσωπον αὐτοῦ χάριτος ἐπληροῦτο) (Mart. Pol. 12.1). 2 Macc 3:26 describes two angels as "gloriously beautiful."

13. James C. VanderKam, *Enoch: A Man for All Generations* (Columbia: University of South Carolina Press, 1995) 97–101. He suggests that in the case of Enoch, the wordplay may depend on connecting the name either with חן, "grace, favor," or with חנך, "to train (a child)" (97). There may also be an allusion to the etymology that connects the name with חן, "grace, favor," in the Genesis Apocryphon (1QapGen ii 20): see Joseph A. Fitzmyer, *The Genesis Apocryphon of Qumran Cave 1 (1Q20): A Commentary*, 3rd ed., BibOr 18/B (Rome: Pontifical Biblical Institute, 2004) 135.

14. Philo, *Abr.* 17; *Post.* 35; 41; *Conf.* 123.

15. See VanderKam, *Enoch*, 148. The same etymology of Enoch was known to Origen.

> You are that son of man who was born for righteousness,
> and righteousness dwells on you. (71:14)

The correspondence between these two passages is the decisive evidence that in the closing section of the book Enoch is identified not merely as "a man" who was born for righteousness[16] but as "the man" he had seen in his visions.[17] At the same time, the use of the verb "was born" in the second passage adapts the formula so that it refers unambiguously to a human being. This is appropriate at the point where the figure's identity as Enoch is revealed, whereas in 46:2 the author will have wanted to maintain the mystery around the identity of "that son of man" by leaving open the question whether he is human or some other kind of heavenly being.

Righteousness is here described as the defining characteristic of "that son of man" (see also 39:6–7; 53:6; 62:2–3). The Book of Watchers introduced Enoch as "Enoch, a righteous man" (1:2), and subsequently uses the word almost formulaically to describe him (12:4; 15:1; see also Jub. 10:17). Of course, the word also applies to all of those whom the Parables often call "the righteous and chosen ones." But there is force in Casey's claim that "to a member of the Enoch circles the simple description of a single, otherwise unidentified, man as 'the man who has righteousness, with whom righteousness dwells' [46:3] could hardly mean anyone but Enoch himself."[18] This may be somewhat overstated, but, to a reader who shared the author's adulation of Enoch, the description in 46:3 might already suggest the possibility that this heavenly man is Enoch himself.

1 Enoch 70:1–2

There is a textual problem in 70:1 that has been much discussed.[19] The textual variant is in itself small: the presence or absence of the prepositional phrase "to

---

16. John J. Collins, *The Scepter and the Star: The Messiahs of the Dead Sea Scrolls and Other Ancient Literature* (New York: Doubleday, 1996) 180–81.

17. This argument is made in detail by Walck, *The Son of Man*, 152–54.

18. Casey, *Son of Man*, 103.

19. Maurice Casey, "The Use of the Term 'Son of Man' in the Similitudes of Enoch," *JSJ* 7 (1976) 25–27; VanderKam, "Righteous One," 183–84; Daniel C. Olson, "Enoch and the Son of Man in the Epilogue of the Parables," *JSP* 9 (1998) 27–38; Michael A. Knibb, "The Translation of *1 Enoch* 70:1: Some Methodological Issues," in *Essays on the Book of Enoch and Other Early Jewish Texts and Traditions*, SVTP 22 (Leiden: Brill, 2009) 161–75 (this essay was first published in 2001); Daniel C. Olson, "'Enoch and the Son of Man' Revisited: Further

the presence of" (*ba-xabēhu*) before "that son of man" (*la-weʾetu walda ʾegwāla ʾemma-ḥeyāw*). Until recently the shorter reading was known only in two late manuscripts and one early manuscript (Abb 55) known to be prone to omissions. Most scholars therefore preferred the longer reading. But recently, considerably more support for the shorter reading has come to light in newly available manuscripts,[20] so that Loren Stuckenbruck calls it "the increasingly defensible reading."[21] Leslie Walck has made a good text-critical case for the shorter reading, even while taking no account of the new manuscript evidence.[22] The details cannot be discussed here, but it seems to me that the case for the shorter reading is the more probable, although it cannot be considered conclusive. Although the variation concerns the presence or absence of only one phrase, the difference of meaning is considerable. According to the longer reading, the subject of the sentence is "his name," presumably Enoch's, and Enoch is distinguished from "that son of man," while according to the shorter reading, the subject of the sentence is "the name of that son of man," referring presumably to Enoch.

Thus Nickelsburg's translation, based on the longer reading, is

> And after this, while he was living, his name was lifted up
> > into the presence of that Son of Man
> > and into the presence of the Lord of Spirits
> > from among those who dwell on the earth.[23]

Translations based on the shorter reading vary:

> Afterwards it came to pass that the living name of that Son of Man was exalted by the Lord of Spirits above all those who dwell on earth. (Olson)[24]

> Afterwards it happened that the living name of the Son of Man was exalted in the presence of the Lord of Spirits above all those who live on dry land. (Stuckenbruck)[25]

Reflections on the Text and Translation of *1 Enoch* 70:1," *JSP* 18 (2009) 233–40; Walck, *The Son of Man*, 130–35; Nickelsburg, *1 Enoch 2*, 315–19; Stuckenbruck, "Building Blocks," 318.

20. Olson, "Enoch and the Son of Man," 30–31; Stuckenbruck, "Building Blocks," 318.
21. Stuckenbruck, "Building Blocks," 318.
22. Walck, *The Son of Man*, 132–35.
23. Nickelsburg, *1 Enoch 2*, 315.
24. Olson, "'Enoch and the Son of Man' Revisited," 236. Olson's translation is adopted by Casey, *The Solution*, 107.
25. Stuckenbruck, "Building Blocks," 318.

> And it came to pass after this the name of that Son of Man was raised, while alive, to the presence of the Lord of Spirits from those who dwell on earth. (Walck)[26]

If the shorter reading is preferred, the interpretative choice is between a reference to Enoch's translation to heaven (Walck) and a statement that Enoch's name was exalted above all earthly names. But, whichever choice is made, it is clear that "that son of man" refers to Enoch.

First Enoch 70:1 follows the subscript "This is the third parable of Enoch" (69:29). The conclusion to the book (70:1–71:17) corresponds to the introduction (37:1-5). It follows the subscript to the Third Parable just as the introduction precedes the superscript to the First Parable (37:6). We should therefore expect 70:1 to refer to Enoch, as the continuation in 70:2 unmistakably does. Since "that son of man" means no more than "that man," this is intelligible, though unprecedented within the Book of Parables. (In 60:10, an angel addresses Enoch as "son of man," but this belongs to the "Noachic" interpolation in 60:1-25.) But the phrase "the name of that son of man" has been used only a few verses previously, in the concluding section of the third Parable (69:26). So the effect of reading this phrase in 70:1 could well be ambiguous: it must refer to Enoch but at the same time recalls the figure in Enoch's visions. Readers, we may suppose, are being prepared for the revelation that comes at 71:14.

The Name of "That Son of Man"

The Parables of Enoch refers to "the name of that son of man" four times (48:2, 3; 69:26; 70:1; cf. 70:2). In 70:1 there is a textual problem that we have discussed above. If we follow the shorter reading and read "the name of that son of man" in this verse, then it would seem that "his name" in 70:2 must also refer to this same name of "that son of man." Of course, many scholars accept only three references to this name (48:2, 3; 69:26).

There have been two ways of explaining the term. Steven Scott,[27] Charles Gieschen,[28] and James Waddell[29] have argued that this name is the divine

---

26. Walck, *The Son of Man*, 132.
27. Steven Richard Scott, "The Binitarian Nature of the *Book of Similitudes*," *JSP* 18 (2008) 55–78, here 62–73.
28. Charles A. Gieschen, "The Name of the Son of Man in the Parables of Enoch," in *Enoch and the Messiah*, ed. Boccaccini, 238–49.
29. Waddell, *The Messiah*, 72–75, 168–69. He was aware of Gieschen's work, but apparently not of Scott's. Cf. also Crispin Fletcher-Louis, "*The Similitudes of Enoch* (1 Enoch

name, the Tetragrammaton (YHWH), the same name to which the Parables often refers to as "the name of the Lord of Spirits."[30] But the claim is based on misunderstandings of relevant texts. These writers understand 48:2–3 to mean that, before the creation of the world, "the son of man" was given a name by God, or more precisely he was given *the* name, so that the divine name is now also his name. But, as we have seen, these verses do not mean that "that son of man" was given a name but that he was called by his name. Gieschen connects the reference to "the name of that son of man" in 69:26 with the preceding passage about the cosmic oath, which is probably the divine name (69:13–25).[31] But the connection between this passage and 69:26 in the extant text of the Parables is artificial, as is clear from the fact that "they" in 69:26 has no antecedent. This is widely recognized.[32] Finally, all three writers read 48:5 as a case of synonymous parallelism, so that "fall down and worship before him [that son of man]" is equivalent to "glorify and bless and sing hymns to the name of the Lord of Spirits." In other words, here "the son of man" is actually called "the name of the Lord of Spirits."[33] But, as we shall see in the next section, the Book of Parables makes a careful distinction between obeisance ("fall down and worship"), which is here given to "that son of man," and cultic worship, which is here given to the Lord of Spirits. The poetry of the Parables frequently contains couplets in which the second line adds something new to what is said in the first line. There is no reason at all to read this verse as synonymous parallelism.

If these scholars' interpretation of 48:5 were correct, then we should expect "the name of the Lord of Spirits" to refer to "the son of man" in other cases. Scott and Waddell attempt to carry through this idea in exegesis of some other passages,[34] but their attempt is not convincing. In many cases it would be

---

37–71): The Son of Man, Apocalyptic Messianism and Political Theology," in *The Open Mind: Essays in Honour of Christopher Rowland*, ed. Jonathan Knight and Kevin Sullivan, LNTS 522 (London: Bloomsbury, 2015) 58–79, here 73–74, referring to Gieschen's and Waddell's work, but not Scott's. Fletcher-Louis proposes that the background is the association of the high priest with the divine name.

30. 1 En. 39:7, 9; 40:6; 41:2; 43:4; 45:1, 2, 3 ("my glorious name"); 46:6, 7, 8; 47:2; 48:5, 7, 10; 50:2, 3; 53:6; 55:4; 60:6 ("his name"); 61:3, 9, 11, 12 ("your blessed name," "your name"), 13; 67:8; 69:24; 71:17. God's name is also called "the name of the Lord" (39:13; 41:8; 67:3); "the name of the Lord of the kings" (63:7); "his great name" (referring to the Head of Days) (55:2); "the name of the eternal Lord" (58:4).

31. Gieschen, "The Name," 241–42; cf. Scott, "The Binitarian Nature," 71–72.

32. Nickelsburg, *1 Enoch 2*, 313–14.

33. Scott, "The Binitarian Nature," 70; Gieschen, "The Name," 240; Waddell, *The Messiah*, 73–74.

34. Scott, "The Binitarian Nature," 70–73; Waddell, *The Messiah*, 74.

impossible to take "the name of the Lord of Spirits" to be a reference to "the son of man," and so there is insufficient reason to suppose that it is in just a few cases. For example, compare these references to the wicked:

- "those who have denied the Lord of Spirits" (38:2)
- "the sinners who deny the name of the Lord of Spirits" (41:2)
- "the sinners who have denied the name of the Lord of Spirits" (45:2)
- "they deny the name of the Lord of Spirits" (46:7)
- "they have denied the Lord of Spirits and his Anointed One" (48:10)

It is evident that "deny the Lord of Spirits" and "deny the name of the Lord of Spirits" are equivalent phrases. The "name of the Lord of Spirits" is used as a periphrasis for "the Lord of Spirits," not for "the son of man." In 48:10, alluding to Psalm 2:2, the author has added "his Anointed One" to the standard phrase.

This point about the equivalence between "the Lord of Spirits" and "the name of the Lord of Spirits" leads to the second way in which scholars have explained "the name of that son of man." The argument is that, just as in the Hebrew Bible and the Parables of Enoch, referring to the name of God can simply be a way of referring to God himself, so "the name of that son of man" is a way of designating his person. In Walck's words, "The name of the person represents the power and authority of that figure."[35] But this will not do. God's name can stand for God himself or his authority only because God does actually have a personal name. In Isaiah 45:4 and 49:1, passages often cited to explain 1 Enoch 48:2–3, the person whom God calls by name has a personal name that God presumably uses: Cyrus in one case (Isa 45:1) and Israel in the other (Isa 49:3). The calling to a task involves calling them by their personal names.

We may recall that, on first seeing "that son of man," the first of Enoch's questions about him was "who he was" (1 En. 46:2). Such a question would normally expect a name or at least a title in answer to it. The term "son of man" is certainly not an answer to the question, since Enoch already uses it in asking this question. The term "Chosen One" seems more like a title, but it is a title Enoch has already used himself for a figure he sees in vision in 39:6. It is true that, when the angel responds to Enoch's questions, his initial response includes the information that "the Lord of Spirits has chosen him" (46:3), and no doubt this does serve to identify the figure Enoch has just seen with the figure he already knows as the Chosen One. But it is presented not specifically as the answer to the question "Who is he?" but only as part of a

---

35. Walck, *The Son of Man*, 123.

broader description of "that son of man." This broader description serves as an initial indication of who he is, but it cannot be an adequate answer to Enoch's question, since in biblical and Jewish thought a personal being, heavenly or human, is usually assumed to have a name, even if the name is secret. In the context of Daniel's visions, where the important angels Gabriel and Michael are named, and where the Ancient of Days is, of course, assumed to have the sacred name, an exegete might well ask of the "one like a son of man" (7:13) what his name was.

In 62:7 we learn that, while "that son of man" was hidden in the presence of the Most High, he "revealed him to the chosen" (see also 48:7). In 69:26, a verse that evidently lacks its original preceding context, we are told that

> they had great joy,
> and they blessed and glorified and exalted,
> because the name of that son of man had been revealed to them.

In the former case, Walck is probably correct in supposing that the revelation was made through the Book of the Parables of Enoch itself.[36] The expected readers of Enoch's visions live in the time before the revelation of the Messianic Figure to the world and to the kings and the mighty, but they have privileged knowledge of him through the Book of the Parables. But these readers cannot be the subject of the verbs in 69:26, who are figures within Enoch's visions.

First Enoch 69:26 leads into 69:27–29 ("he" at the beginning of 69:27 refers to "that son of man" in 69:26). The scene, now lost, that formed the preceding context to 69:26 probably coincided with the "appearance" of "that son of man" to which 69:29 refers, since both are followed by his sitting down on his glorious throne (69:27, 29). A plausible reconstruction is that "that son of man" appeared on earth, his name was revealed to the chosen ones alive at that time, and then he sat down on his glorious throne, as already described in 62:2. The subjects ("they") of 69:26 are "all the chosen" who "stand in his presence on that day" (62:8).

At that time what is revealed to those chosen ones is not merely the Messianic Figure as an unknown heavenly figure but "his name," his identity. They recognize him as someone whose name they know. It is unlikely that in the lost passage preceding 69:26 this name was made explicit to the readers of the Parables (and therefore also to Enoch within the vision), because that would preempt the climax in 71:14, where it finally becomes unambiguously clear

---

36. Walck, *The Son of Man*, 123.

that he is Enoch. But perhaps the indications that the name is Enoch were sufficiently strong to motivate the omission of this passage in the Ethiopian transmission of the text of the Parables, in a context where "that son of man" was understood to be Jesus Christ.

At 71:14 the identification of Enoch himself with "that son of man" is made in such a way as to indicate that this is the answer to his inquiry as to the identity of "that son of man" in 46:2. In 46:3 ("This is the son of man who has righteousness, and righteousness dwells with him") the angel began to answer the question, but not fully, because the name and therefore the actual identity of the figure were not disclosed. In 71:14 the same angel ("that angel") reminds Enoch of his initial answer ("that son of man who was born for righteousness, and righteousness dwells on you") and now completes the answer by identifying Enoch himself as "that son of man."

At the beginning of 71:14 the manuscripts vary between "And he" and "And that angel."[37] Nickelsburg comments, "If 'that angel' is original, the text is vague as to which angel is speaking to Enoch,"[38] while Walck judges that the reading "that angel" is "problematic because the demonstrative has no antecedent."[39] Both have missed the reference back to 46:2–3. Just as "that son of man" always refers back to 46:2, so here "that angel" also refers back to 46:2. He comes to "greet" Enoch because they are already well acquainted.[40] The same angel Enoch originally asked about the identity of "that son of man" now answers the question with the words, "You are that son of man who was born for righteousness."

Finally, the actual occurrence of the name Enoch in 71:5 should not escape our attention. Since most of the Book of Parables is narrated in the first person by Enoch, it is not surprising that his name appears only rarely:[41] in the title of the book (37:1), in a brief passage that speaks about Enoch in the third person (39:2), in the subscription to the Third Parable (69:29), and in 71:5, where Enoch interrupts his first-person narration in order to identify himself: "And he took my spirit—even me, Enoch—to the heaven of heavens." This kind of self-identification occurs also in the Book of Watchers (12:3; 19:3), and so there is no reason to doubt its originality. Its function here is to remind readers of

---

37. In the first edition of Nickelsburg and VanderKam, *1 Enoch* (2004), they opt for "And that angel," but in the second edition (2012) they opt for "And he," in accordance with Nickelsburg, *1 Enoch 2*, 320.

38. Nickelsburg, *1 Enoch 2*, 328.

39. Walck, *The Son of Man*, 147.

40. He appears also in 52:3, 5; 53:4; 54:4; 56:2; 61:2; 64:2.

41. In the Book of Watchers, Enoch is sometimes addressed by name (12:4; 13:1; 14:24; 15:1), but this does not happen in the Book of Parables.

Enoch's name just before Enoch is identified as "that son of man" (71:14), making it unmistakable that "the name of that son of man" is Enoch.[42]

Is the Messianic Figure "Worshiped"?

The Book of Parables frequently depicts the cultic worship of God in heaven. We can properly call this "cultic" worship because, as in Second Temple–period literature generally, heaven is conceived as a space that is both the throne room of God, whence he governs the cosmos, and a temple in which he is continuously worshiped by the hosts of his angels. A series of verbs are used, usually in combinations of three or four, to describe this heavenly cult. As can be seen from table 1, the most common are "bless," "praise," "exalt," and "glorify." In some cases the words of praise are recorded:

Blessed be he, and may he be blessed from the beginning and forever. (39:10)

Holy, holy, holy is the Lord of Spirits, he fills the earth with spirits. (39:12)[43]

Blessed are you, and blessed is the name of the Lord forever and ever. (39:13)

Blessed (is he), and blessed be the name of the Lord of Spirits forever and ever. (61:11)[44]

The righteous dead in paradise also praise God (39:7; 61:12), while on two occasions Enoch himself joins in the heavenly worship (39:9–10; 71:11–12). As well as the angels and the righteous humans in heaven, the sun and the moon are said to give praise and glory to God (41:7), while in one expansive description "every spirit of light" and "all flesh" bless and glorify God (61:12).[45]

Besides the verbs that describe this cultic worship (bless, praise, exalt, glorify, sing hymns, sanctify), another expression is used always separately: "fall down and worship" (57:3; 63:1). This never describes what angels or the righteous dead do, and it never takes place in heaven. It is used to describe

42. This is also the view of Barnabas Lindars, "Re-enter the Apocalyptic Son of Man," in *The Son of Man Problem: Critical Readings*, ed. Benjamin E. Reynolds (London: T&T Clark, 2018) 377–98, here 384.

43. Based on Isa 6:3.

44. See also 48:1.

45. See also 69:22–24, a passage that may be a displaced section of the original text of the Book of Parables.

submission to the sovereignty of God by humans at the end time. In 57:3 the subjects seem to be the gentile nations who will come from the four corners of the earth to Zion, bringing with them the exiles of Israel (57:1-2; cf. Isa 60:4, 9; 43:5-6). The Second Parable thus ends on a climactic note: the universal acknowledgment of the supremacy of the Lord of Spirits: "they all fell down and worshiped the Lord of Spirits" (57:3). There may be an echo of Isaiah 66:23: "all flesh shall come to worship [השתחות] before me, says the LORD."[46]

In 1 Enoch 63:1 the kings and the mighty ones, who, after the judgment, have been delivered to the angels of punishment, beg for the opportunity to "fall down and worship in the presence of the Lord of Spirits, and that they might confess their sins in his presence." In this context they also offer cultic worship: they "will bless and glorify the Lord of Spirits" (63:2). Their hymn of praise to the Lord "who reigns over all kings" is quoted at length (63:2-4). Then their request for the opportunity to repent is repeated, this time in the language of cultic worship: "that we might glorify and praise and make confession" (63:6). It is clear here that cultic worship and submission to the divine sovereignty go together, but that is because they are rebellious earthly rulers, who need to acknowledge the divine supremacy as well as to praise the divine glory.

We may now turn to passages that seem to depict worship of the Messianic Figure. Only one of these is located in the context of the cultic worship in heaven.[47] In 40:2-7 Enoch sees the four archangels and hears their voices. The first voice (Michael) "blesses the Lord of Spirits forever and ever" (40:4). The second voice (Raphael) he hears "blessing the Chosen One and the chosen ones who depend on the Lord of Spirits" (40:5). This passage is one of the clearest that associates "the Chosen One" and "the chosen ones," suggesting that he is a kind of heavenly representative or patron of the righteous people. Although the word "bless" is used in both these cases, its significance is clearly different. Raphael is not offering cultic worship to the Chosen One and his chosen ones. Rather, he is invoking God's blessing on them.

This is the only case, apart from the debatable instance of 62:6, which will be discussed shortly, in which any of the verbs of cultic blessing are applied to the Messianic Figure.[48] He is not the object of worship in heaven. This is espe-

---

46. Cf. Ps 86:9.

47. For a definition of cultic worship, see Larry W. Hurtado, *Lord Jesus Christ: Devotion to Jesus in Earliest Christianity* (Grand Rapids: Eerdmans, 2003) 31 n. 10: "devotion offered in a specifically worship (liturgical) setting and expressive of the thanksgiving, praise, communion, and petition that directly represent, manifest, and reinforce the relationship of the worshipers with the deity."

48. I do not think 46:5 is such a case. Based on Dan 5:20-21, the text means that the kings do not exalt or praise God or acknowledge that their kingdom was given them by God

cially clear in chapter 61. Here the Lord of Spirits seats the Chosen One on his glorious throne in heaven so that he may assess the deeds of the angels. Here if anywhere we should expect a scene in which the Messianic Figure is worshiped by the hosts of angels along with the Lord of Spirits. But the worship that is then described extremely fulsomely (61:9b-12) is directed exclusively to God. The Chosen One joins all the heavenly hosts in worshiping the Lord of Spirits (61:10).[49] It is instructive to compare the strikingly similar scene in Revelation 5, where the Lamb appears to occupy the divine throne in heaven and all the heavenly host worship him. As in 1 Enoch 61, the worshiping circle expands to include every creature in the cosmos, who sing, "To the one seated on the throne and to the Lamb be blessing and honor and glory and might forever and ever!" (Rev 5:13). The terms of worship closely parallel those in 1 Enoch, but the contrast is therefore all the more significant: the Lamb on the throne is included in the cultic worship of God, whereas the Chosen One is not.

There is also a contrast with chapter 14 of 3 Enoch, the medieval Hekhalot text that some think must be in some way dependent on the Parables of Enoch.[50] In 3 Enoch, Enoch, transported to heaven, is transformed into Metatron, installed as God's vicegerent on "a throne like the throne of glory" (10:1), given the name "the lesser YHWH" (12:4-5), and crowned with a crown on which the four letters of the divine name are written (13:1-2). As a result, all the hosts of heaven, high and low, tremble before him (14:1-2) and the eighteen named angels who control the cosmos "fell prostrate when they saw me" (14:4-5).[51] This is a scene of universal obeisance in the heavenly world that resembles Revelation 5 much more than it does 1 Enoch 61. It highlights again the fact that, although the Messianic Figure in the latter passage is installed on a glorious throne in heaven, he receives no worship of any kind, whether praise or obeisance. The key difference is that, whereas Metatron-Enoch becomes second only to God in his rule over the whole cosmos from his throne

---

(Nickelsburg, *1 Enoch 2*, 159). While 61:6-7 is obscure (apparently having lost a preceding context), I think the object of praise is likely to be God. (One would expect praise of the Chosen One to follow his enthronement in 61:8, not to precede it.) Other evidence cited by Waddell, *The Messiah*, 99 n. 113, of language of worship applied to the Messianic Figure is based on misunderstandings of the texts. That the Lord of Spirits "glorified" the Chosen One (51:3) is hardly evidence that he receives praise or glory from humans!

49. The grammar of this verse is problematic: see Nickelsburg, *1 Enoch 2*, 247. But however it is understood, it is entirely clear that the Chosen One is not worshiped.

50. James R. Davila, *The Provenance of the Pseudepigrapha: Jewish, Christian, or Other?*, JSJSup 105 (Leiden: Brill, 2005) 133, 135; Crispin Fletcher-Louis, *Jesus Monotheism*, vol. 1, *Christological Origins: The Emerging Consensus and Beyond* (Eugene, OR: Cascade, 2015) 200.

51. Philip S. Alexander, "3 Enoch," OTP 1:263-67.

in heaven, the Messianic Figure in the Parables has only one heavenly function for which he is seated in heaven in the last days: to conduct an assessment of the deeds of the angelic powers. Their response is not to worship him but to join with him in the praise of God, the only kind of worship that happens in heaven according to the Parables.

Another passage that similarly, in a heavenly context, excludes the Messianic Figure from the cultic worship offered to God is in the vision in which Enoch first sees the Messianic Figure in heaven:

> And I saw his [the Chosen One's] dwelling beneath the wings of
>   the Lord of Spirits,
> and all the righteous and chosen were mighty before him like
>   fiery lights.
> And their mouths were full of blessing,
>   and their lips praised the name of the Lord of Spirits.
>   (1 En. 39:7)

The righteous and chosen are here the companions of the Chosen One, not his worshipers. If it were appropriate for them to offer him worship, surely this would be the place for it to be mentioned. In fact, there is reference only to their praise of the Lord of Spirits.

The two cases in the Parables in which the Messianic Figure is the object of the expression "fall down and worship" are located on earth and resemble those in which God is the object. According to 48:5:

> All who dwell on the earth will fall down and worship before him,
> and they will glorify and bless and sing hymns to the name of the
>   Lord of Spirits.

The first line is based on Isaiah 49:7 (following the allusion to Isa 49:6 in 1 En. 48:4): "Kings shall see and stand up, princes, and they shall prostrate themselves [וישתחוו]." The implication in this text in Isaiah is undoubtedly that the rulers will prostrate themselves before the servant of the Lord, to whom these words are addressed. In 1 Enoch 48:5 we see the same combination of submission to authority and cultic worship as we saw in 63:1-6, where the Lord of Spirits is the object of both. Here the submission is made to the Messianic Figure, but the cultic worship is directed to the Lord of Spirits. That only the obeisance is made to the Messianic Figure is surely significant.[52]

---

52. The Ethiopic verb *sagada/sagda*, which appears in both 48:5 and 62:6, and which

In 62:9, also based on Isaiah 49:7, it is the kings and the mighty who fall prostrate before the Messianic Figure, just as they wish to do before God in 63:1:

> And all the kings and the mighty and the exalted and those who rule the land[53] will fall on their faces in his presence [i.e., of "the son of man"];
> and they will worship and set their hope on that Son of Man,
> and they will supplicate and petition for mercy from him.

Here the kings, facing judgment, do more than submit. They also hope and beg for mercy from the Messianic Figure. But the language of cultic worship does not appear, as it does when the prostration is before God in 63:1–6.

It looks like a rule that "to fall down and worship" can apply either to God or to the Messianic Figure, when the latter is seated on his throne to judge, but that the language of cultic worship applies only to God. However, there is an apparent exception earlier in the narrative of how the kings and the mighty react to seeing the Messianic Figure on his glorious throne:

> And the kings and the mighty and all who possess the land
> will bless and glorify and exalt him who rules over all,
> who was hidden. (62:6)

According to the extant text of this verse, "him who rules over all" would seem to be "that son of man," who is mentioned in the previous verse, sitting on his glorious throne, and who in the following verse is said to have been hidden. However, as we have observed before, elsewhere in the Parables the Messianic Figure is not said to rule, still less to rule "over all," whereas the Lord of Spirits is described (by these very kings and mighty ones) as "him who reigns over all kings" (63:4).[54] If 62:6 referred to the Messianic Figure, it would be a unique instance both of cultic worship being offered to him and of kingly rule being ascribed to him. I suggest that the difficulty can be dispelled by treating "who was hidden" as a gloss. An Ethiopian scribe, who of course believed that Jesus Christ, the Son of Man, ruled over all and should be accorded cultic worship, wanted to clarify the verse in this sense and so borrowed the word "hidden"

Nickelsburg renders "worship," need mean nothing more than prostration. (I owe this observation to Darrell Hannah.)

53. The translation "earth" is in my view more probable, here and in other passages quoted below.

54. It is, of course, a commonplace in Jewish literature that God rules over all things.

from the next verse ("from the beginning the son of man was hidden"). Without the phrase "who was hidden" in 62:6, the sense would be that the kings and the mighty, when they see that the Lord of Spirits has seated the Messianic Figure on his glorious throne (62:2), first offer cultic praise to the Lord of Spirits, who had addressed them in 62:1. Their next act is to fall down and worship the Messianic Figure (62:9). The passage would then conform to the pattern in 48:4: cultic worship of God along with obeisance to the Messianic Figure.

In support of this interpretation of 62:6, we should also notice the parallelism between 61:6–13 (judgment of the holy angels) and 62:1–63:12 (judgment of the kings and the mighty).[55] In both cases God seats the Messianic Figure (here in both cases called the Chosen One) on a glorious throne (61:8; 62:2), the Messianic Figure passes judgment (61:8–9; 62:2), those being judged "bless and glorify and exalt" (61:9b; 62:6), and they either receive God's mercy (61:13) or do not receive it (62:9–11; 63:1–12). Within this parallelism, 61:9b and 62:6 are parallel:

> They [the angels] will all speak with one voice,
> and bless and glorify and exalt
> and sanctify the name of the Lord of Spirits. (61:9b)

> And the kings and the mighty and all who possess the land
> will bless and glorify and exalt him who rules over all,
> who was hidden. (62:6)

The parallel suggests that in 62:6, as throughout the rest of the book, the verbs "bless and glorify and exalt" are used for the cultic worship of the Lord of Spirits. In the light of this otherwise clear parallelism, only the phrase "who was hidden" raises a problem. The problem is easily resolved if we conjecture that the phrase is a gloss.

If this minor textual emendation is justified, the Parables presents a very clear picture with regard to cultic worship and what we might call political obeisance. (It is important to note that this is *not* a distinction between religious and nonreligious.) In heaven there is cultic worship, vocally expressed and directed to God. There is no obeisance in heaven[56] and the Messianic Figure is not "worshiped" in heaven in either sense. When the Messianic Figure appears on earth at the end of the history of this world, he receives the obeisance of

---

55. Nickelsburg, *1 Enoch 2*, 257.
56. In some other accounts of heaven, obeisance does take place—e.g., 4Q405 20-21-22 ii 6-9; Rev 4:10.

all people, including the earthly rulers on whom he pronounces judgment. At the same time, God himself receives the obeisance of all the nations, as well as cultic worship from the hitherto rebellious kings and mighty ones.

The expression "to fall down and worship" requires closer attention. The Ethiopic verb *sagada/sagda*, which appears in both 48:5 and 62:6, and which Nickelsburg renders "worship," need mean nothing more than prostration. This verb was doubtless προσκυνέω in Greek and either Hebrew השתחוה (Hitpalel of שחה) or Aramaic סגד[57] in the Semitic original of the Parables. All these verbs (with or without an additional verb meaning "to fall down") refer to the physical act of prostration on the ground before someone. Essentially the gesture was a strong expression of respect for a social superior. As such, it was highly appropriate as an expression of reverence for God or a divine being, and in the Hebrew Bible in a majority of instances the object of reverence is the true God or other gods or their images. In such instances, English translations usually render the verb as "worship." But in other instances, where the object is a human superior, modern English versions usually translate it as "bow down." There are about sixty occasions in the Hebrew Bible where the object is a human superior. The English translation "worship" is not helpful because in modern English this verb refers almost exclusively to activities expressing reverence and devotion to God or divine beings, by no means necessarily entailing prostration.

In Jewish usage, in the Hellenistic and Roman periods, the cults of divine rulers made many Jews careful about the use of this gesture. They might refuse to prostrate themselves before a ruler who claimed divinity (OG Add Esth C 5–7; Philo, *Legat*. 114–116) or before a heavenly being who might be confused with God (Rev 22:8–9). But context was everything, and in the right context the gesture was an acceptable expression of high respect for a human superior (Jdt 10:23; 14:7; 11QT[a] 39:6; 1 En. 90:30; Rev 3:9).[58]

It seems that the Parables of Enoch carefully distinguishes between, on the one hand, the cultic worship of which God is the only appropriate object and, on the other hand, the obeisance that should be given both to God himself as

---

57. This verb occurs twelve times in Daniel: 2:46; 3:5, 6, 7, 10, 11, 12, 14, 15 (*bis*), 18, 28. Ethiopic *sagada/sagda* is cognate with Aramaic סגד.

58. On the distinction between obeisance (προσκυνέω) and cultic worship, see Larry W. Hurtado, "The Binitarian Shape of Early Christian Worship," in *The Jewish Roots of Christological Monotheism: Papers from the St. Andrews Conference on the Historical Origins of the Worship of Jesus*, ed. Carey C. Newman, James R. Davila, and Gladys S. Lewis, JSJSup 63 (Leiden: Brill, 1999) 187–213, here 187–91. The use of προσκυνέω requires special study; see now Ray M. Lozano, *The* Proskynesis *of Jesus in the New Testament: A Study on the Significance of Jesus as an Object of* προσκυνέω *in the New Testament Writings*, LNTS 609 (London: T&T Clark, 2020).

the universal sovereign and to the Messianic Figure who implements God's sovereignty in judgment at the end. We should note again the clear distinction made in 48:5:

> All who dwell on the earth will fall down and worship before him ["that son of man"],
> and they will glorify and bless and sing hymns to the name of the Lord of Spirits.

We should also notice that, whereas in the Hebrew Bible the gesture of obeisance, when directed to God, is sometimes accompanied by praise and hymns and other expressions of cultic worship (e.g., Gen 24:48; 2 Chr 29:28–30; Ps 66:4; 86:9; 99:5, 9; 138:1–2), the Parables keeps them distinct.

It is also important to take account of the exegetical basis for obeisance to the Messianic Figure in the Parables.[59] It is undoubtedly based on Isaiah 49:7, but we should notice both that the servant of the Lord in that chapter is explicitly representative of Israel (49:3) and that in Isaiah 45:14 God promises that the nations will "bow down" (ישתחוו) to Israel, while acknowledging that their God is the only true God.[60] The Messianic Figure in the Parables is a kind of heavenly representative of "the righteous and the chosen" people, and the author, careful exegete that he was, would have noticed the parallel between Isaiah 49:7 and Isaiah 45:14. Also relevant may be the indications in Daniel 7 both that all nations are going to "serve" (יפלחון)[61] the humanlike figure (7:14) and that all kingdoms will "serve" (יפלחון) the people of the saints of the Most High (7:27). So it would be as representing his people that the Messianic Figure in the Parables receives the obeisance of the nations and the kings. The author would also have noticed that God himself is predicted to receive the obeisance of all the nations at the end (Isa 66:23), and so have concluded that this gesture is appropriately given to both God and the Messianic Figure. He had no such exegetical warrant for extending the cultic worship of God to the

---

59. Fletcher-Louis, "*The Similitudes*," 76, claims that there are no allusions to "biblical texts that might have offered inspiration for worshipful *proskynesis* to the Son of Man *as king*." This is true, but his inference that therefore the "Son of Man" is portrayed as a high priest is unwarranted, since there is very probable allusion to Isa 49:7, where the servant of the Lord is not a high priest. Fletcher-Louis's interpretation depends on the highly debatable contention that the figure in Dan 7:13 is a high priest.

60. This passage is probably echoed in 1 En. 90:30.

61. The Aramaic verb פלח can mean to serve a human or a divine overlord.

Messianic Figure, and doubtless understood that to be the exclusively divine worship of the one God.

We should not obscure this key distinction by speaking generally of the "worship" of the Messianic Figure. It would be better to distinguish between cultic worship and obeisance, and not to call the latter "worship." Obeisance is not as such divine worship. With this more precise terminology, it turns out that the Messianic Figure in the Parables of Enoch is not worshiped.

In my early work on Jewish monotheism and divine-identity Christology, I treated the Parables of Enoch as a unique exception to the rule that in Second Temple–period Jewish literature no figure extrinsic to the divine identity (i.e., other than God himself and his Wisdom) ever sits on the cosmic throne of God or receives worship.[62] Detailed study of the Parables has convinced me that I was wrong. If the Messianic Figure sat on God's own throne, it would not be surprising if he received divine worship, since the throne represents God's unique sovereignty and Jewish monotheistic worship was recognition of that sovereignty. But I now see that the Messianic Figure sits on his own throne, not God's, and that the "worship" he receives is obeisance on earth, not cultic worship in heaven or on earth.

Why Enoch?

What led the author of the Parables of Enoch to identify Daniel's humanlike figure and Isaiah's "chosen one" with Enoch? No trace of this identification is found anywhere else in the Enoch literature (or elsewhere). It is this author's original and distinctive contribution, a contribution that apparently did not make a sufficiently favorable impression to be taken up by any later writers whose work has survived. So what led the author to this unexpected idea? The question can hardly be answered conclusively, but I think we can guess his thinking to a limited extent.

Our author undoubtedly knew Genesis 5, which lay at the root of all later literary developments of the Enoch legend. There Enoch is exceptional among the antediluvian patriarchs because the paragraph about him (5:21–24) departs uniquely and significantly from the stereotyped formulae that are used to summarize the lives of all the other persons in this genealogy. Enoch is said to have "walked with God" (a phrase later used of Noah in 6:9, but of no one else in Genesis), and, in place of the verb "he died" that ends the account of

---

62. Richard Bauckham, *Jesus and the God of Israel: God Crucified and Other Studies on the New Testament's Christology of Divine Identity* (Grand Rapids: Eerdmans, 2008) 16, 169–171.

every other person in the genealogy, of Enoch it is said that he "was no more, because God took him" (ואיננו כי־לקח אתו אלהים) (5:24).

In the early Enoch literature the statement in Genesis that "Enoch walked with God" (ויתהלך חנוך את־האלהים) was understood to mean that he "walked with the heavenly beings," the angels.[63] For a period in his life prior to his final departure from the earth, Enoch was absent from the earth in the company of the angels, who took him on the tours of the cosmos in which he was given the revelations recorded in the Astronomical Book (1 En. 72–82) and the latter parts of the Book of Watchers (1 En. 17–36). He was subsequently returned to earth. But these Enochic works had nothing to say about what happened to Enoch after his final departure in the 365th year of his life. Other Enoch literature apart from the Parables had something, but not much, to say. According to the Animal Apocalypse in the Dream Visions (1 En. 85–90), three angels took him up to a "tower high above the earth" (87:3), from where he would be able to see all the subsequent events on earth. (Here the statement that "God took him" in Gen 5:24 is taken to mean that "heavenly beings" took him.) At the time of the final judgment the same three angels bring him back to earth (90:31), but he is not given any role in the final events of the history of this age. In the story of the birth of Noah (1 En. 106–107), Enoch after his final departure was "with the angels" (106:7), "at the ends of the earth" (106:8), where his son Methuselah sought him out in order to consult him.[64] Only in the book of Jubilees do we find the tradition that Enoch was taken to the Garden of Eden, where he is "writing condemnation and righteousness of the world, and all the evils of the children of men" (4:23). Here Enoch has an important role throughout history until the day of judgment, when presumably his record of all the deeds of humans will be used for the purpose of judging them (cf. 4:24). This tradition is taken up in the Testament of Abraham (B11:2–10), in the context of a different kind of eschatology. Interestingly, in that context it is insisted that Enoch only writes; he leaves judgment to God.[65] This is

---

63. VanderKam, *Enoch*, 19, 32, 43.

64. Although the chronology appears to differ from Gen 5, it seems clear that this incident takes place after Enoch's final removal from the earth; see George W. E. Nickelsburg, *1 Enoch 1: A Commentary on the Book of 1 Enoch Chapters 1–36; 81–108*, ed. Klaus Baltzer, Hermeneia (Minneapolis: Fortress, 2001) 544–45. The same story appears in the Genesis Apocryphon (1QapGen ii 1–26), where Enoch is said to be in "the land of Parvaim," probably here a term for the land in which the Garden of Eden was located (cf. 2 Chr 3:6).

65. On this tradition here and in later texts, see John C. Reeves and Annette Yoshiko Reed, *Enoch from Antiquity to the Middle Ages*, vol. 1, *Sources from Judaism, Christianity, and Islam* (Oxford: Oxford University Press, 2018) 46–48, 244–47. The epithet "the scribe of righteousness" (T. Ab. B11:3) is evidently borrowed from 1 En. 12:4, where its significance is different.

therefore a role very different from that of the Messianic Figure in the Parables of Enoch, who never writes, but executes God's judgment.[66]

The author of the Parables of Enoch either did not know or ignored the idea of Enoch as the scribe who records human deeds. Without it, Enoch's biography must have seemed seriously incomplete. Why was Enoch spared from death and taken to be with the angels? By treating him in this unique way, the author of the Parables may well have thought that surely God must have intended to preserve him for some important role in God's purposes. The only other figure in the Hebrew Bible who was taken from the earth without dying was Elijah (2 Kgs 2:9-12). Already in the prophet Malachi is found the expectation that Elijah will return to earth and play an important part in the events of the last days (Mal 4:5-6). By the first century CE it was evidently a widespread view that Elijah would return in the last days to perform a role of preparing Israel for the judgment (Sir 48:10-11; Mark 9:12; LAB 48:1; cf. Luke 1:17; 4Q588 i 2:4).[67] If Elijah was taken up without dying so that he could return in the last days, might not the same be the case for Enoch? The author of the Parables likely thought Enoch a more eminent figure than Elijah, and so he gives him an even more important role: the one who, on behalf of God, will execute the final judgment on the oppressors of Israel and the fallen angels.

So a major purpose of the Parables of Enoch is to add a new and final chapter to the story of Enoch: his future destiny. From this point of view it is surely significant that the first vision in which the Messianic Figure appears

---

66. Stuckenbruck, "Building Blocks," 325-27, argues that the figure of a "man" tasked with observing and recording the evil deeds of the seventy "shepherds" in the Animal Apocalypse (1 En. 89:61-64, 70-71, 76-77; 90:14-20) formed a kind of bridge between the Enoch of the earlier Enoch literature and the "Son of Man" who executes judgment in the Parables of Enoch, since that figure's record brings about the judgment of the "shepherds." But the figure is clearly an angel (in this apocalypse angels are called "men" and humans are depicted as animals), one of the seven angels (90:22) who first appear in 87:2, who include the four principal angels (Sariel, Raphael, Gabriel, and Michael). See Patrick A. Tiller, *A Commentary on the Animal Apocalypse of* 1 Enoch, EJL 4 (Atlanta: Scholars Press, 1993) 246. I do not think it is plausible that the author of the Parables took this figure to be Enoch, especially as Enoch speaks of himself in the first person in the course of this narrative (90:31). Moreover, the Messianic Figure in the Parables of Enoch does not record deeds. He is not a scribe. There is no bridge from Enoch the scribe whose record is the basis of judgment to "that son of man" who executes judgment.

67. For a full study see Richard Bauckham, "The Restoration of Israel in Luke-Acts," in *The Jewish World around the New Testament: Collected Essays I*, WUNT 233 (Tübingen: Mohr Siebeck, 2008) 325-70, here 329-37.

picks up the story of Enoch at precisely the point where other Enoch literature left him: with the angels in paradise (1 En. 39:4–8). The repetition of the word "dwelling" throughout this passage may perhaps be an echo of 1 Enoch 106:7: "his dwelling is with the angels."

The Parables of Enoch owes much to the Book of Watchers, including its eschatology. Like the Book of Watchers, its dominant expectation of the future is for a great day of judgment, when God will intervene, condemn the wicked for eternity, thus delivering the righteous people of God from their oppression, and bestow on the righteous eternal light, joy, and peace. These themes are prominent in the opening section of the Book of Watchers (1:4–5:9), in which, unusually, Enoch speaks as a prophet, echoing the biblical prophets, as Enoch often does in the Parables. Given such an eschatology, the obvious major role that could be given to Enoch "the righteous" would be that of God's agent in the final judgment. But the author did not have to invent such a role. He found it in the prophecies of the Hebrew Bible, especially in two anonymous figures: the humanlike figure of Daniel 7:13 and God's "chosen one" of Isaiah 42:1. Identifying these figures with Enoch solved a serious exegetical problem: Who are these anonymous but evidently very important figures?

As we shall see in part 2 of this book, Jewish exegetes seem to have been agreed that the figure in Daniel 7:13 is a human being. They did not think the figure was either simply a symbol for the "people of the saints of the Most High" or an angel. Both these views were theoretically possible, but there is no evidence that they were entertained in the Second Temple period. Instead, it was assumed the figure must be a human who had at some time in the past lived on earth and was being preserved by God for his eschatological role. As we shall see, there were a number of opinions as to the identity of this figure. There is no evidence that he was ever identified as Elijah, but we should note that, as someone who had not died, Elijah would have been a good candidate for identification with this figure, had his eschatological role not been defined in other ways. But Elijah's theoretical suitability for this role can alert us to the fact that, to the author of the Parables, surely Enoch, as the other biblical figure who escaped death, must seem the most suitable candidate for the role of "one like a son of man" in Daniel 7:13–14. The two questions—Why did God exempt Enoch from death and preserve him thereafter in paradise? and Who is the "one like a son of man" who is given exceptional authority over the nations?—answer each other. If Enoch was a figure in search of an eschatological role and Daniel's "one like a son of man" was a figure in search of an identity, they could easily be seen as a perfect match.

We have already seen that in the Parables Daniel 7:14 and 7:21–22 are understood as indicating that God gives authority to judge to the "one like a son of man." Probably, the author of the Parables was drawn to the figure of God's "servant" in Isaiah 42–43 because of the way he is first introduced in 42:1:

> Here is my servant, whom I uphold,
>   my chosen [one], in whom my soul delights;
> I have put my spirit upon him;
>   he will bring forth justice [משפט] to the nations.

The main function of this anonymous figure appears to be judgment, like the humanlike figure of Daniel in the Parables' interpretation. Identifying him with the latter and with Enoch would easily follow. The Parables of Enoch never uses the term "servant" for its Messianic Figure, but "the chosen one" or "my chosen one" is frequent. The author probably preferred this designation because it highlighted his solidarity with the righteous people of God, already known as "the chosen ones" in the Book of Watchers (1:8; 5:7) and frequently so called in the Parables. But there may be another reason too.

The fragmentary Aramaic text of 1 Enoch 92:1 (4QEn^g ii 22–23), which is the opening verse of the Epistle of Enoch, differs from the Ethiopic and includes the words "wisest of men and chosen of the sons of..." ([וח]כימי אנושא ובחיר[בני]) (but the letters בני are uncertain). Black reconstructed this portion of text as "wisest of men and the chosen of the sons of men."[68] This seems plausible. The word "chosen" at least is here definitely used of Enoch. In what sense might Enoch be "chosen"? Perhaps as the one who uniquely was exempted from death. It is possible that the author of the Parables of Enoch found here a connection with "my chosen one" in Isaiah 42:1, which suggested that the latter was Enoch.

In conclusion we may observe how the narrative of chapters 70–71 situates itself in the known story of Enoch. At the time of his ascension Enoch is taken first to paradise (70:3–4),[69] which is where he was already known to have been after his removal from the earth (1 En. 106:7–8; Jub. 4:23). Only at an undisclosed time after that sojourn in the Garden of Eden does Michael take him up to heaven, viewing all manner of cosmic secrets on the way (1 En. 71:1–4). The scene in heaven resembles in many ways Enoch's first vision (39:3–40:10). Then he had seen heaven in a vision of the future. Now he is in heaven in his

---

68. Black, *The Book of Enoch*, 84. The more ambitious reconstruction in Józef T. Milik, *The Books of Enoch: Aramaic Fragments of Qumrân Cave 4* (Oxford: Clarendon, 1976) 260, is very uncertain.

69. There is a reference back here to his vision in 61:1–5.

own present existence. Then he had seen the dwelling of the Chosen One and longed to dwell there himself (39:7–8). Now he does so. Thus, as well as the way that 71:14–15 picks up 46:1–3 (the first passage about "that son of man"), the conclusion also relates back to Enoch's earlier vision of the Chosen One with the righteous in heaven (39:3–40:10; cf. 71:16–17). At the end of Enoch's story readers are taken back to the beginning of the story of the Messianic Figure as he had seen it in vision. They can now read it again with the knowledge that that figure is Enoch himself, after his ascension to heaven.

TABLE 1. *Expressions and objects of "worship"*

	bless	praise	exalt	glorify	hymns	sanc-tify	pros-trate	wor-ship	con-fess
		God/Lord of Spirits
39:7	*	*							
39:9	*	*	*						
39:10	*	*							
39:12	*	*	*			(*)			
39:13	*								
40:3		*							
40:4	*								
41:7		*		*					
46:5		*	*						
47:2	*	*		*					
48:5	*			*	*				
57:3							*	*	
61:7	*		*	*					
61:9	*		*	*		*			
61:11	*		*	*					
61:12	*		*	*		*			
63:1							*	*	*
63:2	*			*					
63:4	*			*					
63:5		*		*					*
63:7				*					*
69:26	*	*	*						
71:11	*	*	*						

	bless	praise	exalt	glorify	hymns	sanc-tify	pros-trate	wor-ship	con-fess
				Chosen One/"Son of Man"					
40:5	*								
48:5							*	*	
62:9							*	*	
				(Ambiguous)					
62:6	*	*	*						

Note: References in bold: the subjects of the verbs are the kings and the mighty.

CHAPTER 1.5

Conclusions on the Messianic Figure in the Parables of Enoch

The key results of the investigation conducted in the preceding chapters can be summed up:

(1) The term "son of man" is not a title, a conventional expression, or a technical term. It is an ordinary way of saying "man" or "human" in Semitic languages and is undoubtedly used in the Book of Parables in the plural to mean no more than "humans" (1 En. 39:1, 5; 42:2). As applied to the Messianic Figure, it is almost always accompanied by a demonstrative ("that son of man" or "this son of man") or other qualifying expression ("the son of man who..."). In every case it is a way of referring back to the humanlike figure Enoch saw in his vision in 46:1. It means simply "that man," "this man," or "the man who..." Doubtless it deliberately coincides with the language of Daniel 7:13 ("like a son of man" or "like a human"), but it cannot by itself constitute an allusion to that text. Only by way of reference back to 46:1, where the two figures Enoch sees are obviously those of Daniel 7:9, 13, can it make a connection with Daniel 7:13. Since the phrase "that son of man" (and variations) always refers back to 46:1, it is inseparable from its literary context in the Parables of Enoch. It could not be taken out of that context and used independently as a way of referring to a Messianic Figure. Not only is it not a title, conventional expression, or technical term within the Parables of Enoch; the Parables of Enoch provides no basis for it to become such.

(2) There is no *concept* of "the son of man" in the Parables of Enoch. The Messianic Figure, described as the Chosen One, the Anointed One, and "that son of man," is constructed from the interpretation of a particular selection of biblical texts that are understood all to describe such a figure: Isaiah 11:2–5; 42:1–7; 49:1–7; Daniel 7:9–27; Psalms 2 and 72. A special feature of the inter-

pretation is that the Figure is not said to rule and is not descended from David (these aspects of the texts are ignored). His function is focused on his role as eschatological judge. The depiction of a Messianic Figure elsewhere in early Jewish literature that comes closest to that in the Parables of Enoch is in 4 Ezra 11–13, in which the biblical sources are Genesis 49:9-10, Isaiah 11:1-5, Daniel 7, and Psalm 2.[1] Fourth Ezra shares with the Parables the idea that this figure is a man who comes from heaven, where he has been kept by God for the role of judge at the end, but in 4 Ezra the figure is a Davidide. Nevertheless, as in the Parables, 4 Ezra 11–13 makes no reference to his kingship or rule, focusing purely on his role as the judge who will condemn and destroy the forces of oppression. Like the Messianic Figure in the Parables, in the vision of 4 Ezra 13 he is called "that man" (13:3b, 5, 12), referring back to the humanlike figure Ezra first saw in his vision (13:3a). So the Messianic Figures of the Parables of Enoch and 4 Ezra 11–13 have much in common. They are variations on a common theme, but there is no justification for calling this a "son of man concept."[2]

(3) The term "throne of glory" was not yet, in the late Second Temple period, a technical term for the cosmic throne of God. It is a Semitic expression meaning "glorious throne" and could refer to royal thrones or the throne of the Messiah on earth as well as to God's heavenly throne. In the Parables of Enoch, the fact that the phrase "his glorious throne" is used both with God as the referent of "his" and with the Messianic Figure as the referent of "his" shows that the Messianic Figure does not sit on God's throne. He has his own throne, a seat of judgment, on which he sits, first in heaven, to judge the angels, and then on earth, to judge the kings and the mighty.

(4) There is nothing "divine" about the Messianic Figure. The phrase in 46:1 that has sometimes been taken as an allusion to Ezekiel 1:26 is much more plausibly based on Daniel 8:15 and 10:18. He did not exist ontologically before the creation of the world, but only in God's intention. He is described as "that man" ("that son of man") because he is human, an eminently righteous human being who has been hidden by God in heaven from ancient times, transformed to resemble the angels.[3] He is qualified to be the eschatological judge by his excep-

---

1. If the translation "my servant" were correct in 13:32, 37, it would be an allusion to Isa 42:1. But since he stands on mount Zion (13:35), I think the allusion is to Ps 2:6-7 and we should translate "my son." See the fuller discussion of the biblical sources of 4 Ezra 13 in chapter 2.5 below.

2. Delbert Burkett, *The Son of Man Debate: A History and Evaluation*, SNTSMS 107 (Cambridge: Cambridge University Press, 1999) 120, makes a similar point.

3. Some scholars would use the word "divine" to describe any heavenly being, including angels, but this is a misleadingly loose usage with respect to late Second Temple–period

tional righteousness, and also because he is a kind of representative or patron of the righteous people of God and can execute judgment on their oppressors on their behalf. In the new creation, he will be their companion in paradise.

(5) The Messianic Figure is Enoch. The identification of "that son of man" with Enoch is not the invention of a later editor who added chapters 70–71 to the book. Those chapters are an epilogue that belongs integrally to the design of the book. The author, whose estimation of the figure of Enoch derives from his familiarity with the Book of Watchers, intended all along that his Messianic Figure should be Enoch, and designed his work so that the identity of the Messianic Figure should be a mystery until the revelation at the end of the book that he is Enoch. Probably, however, there are some hints of this at earlier points in the book. The "name of that son of man," of which readers learn before they are told what it is, is Enoch.

(6) The Book of Parables makes a clear distinction between obeisance, the gesture of bowing down before a person of superior status, divine or human, and cultic worship, which is expressed verbally in praise and limited to God. In heaven there is only cultic worship of God, and such worship is very evidently not offered to the Messianic Figure, even when he sits on a glorious throne (not God's) in heaven. There is no obeisance in heaven. On earth, both God and the Messianic Figure receive obeisance, and God also receives cultic worship. When he appears on earth as the eschatological judge, the Messianic Figure receives the obeisance of all people and of the rebellious kings and powerful ones. This is based on Isaiah 49:7 and probably also on Isaiah 45:14, indicating that it is on behalf of the people of God that he receives the obeisance of those who have oppressed them.

Judaism, which distinguished between the one God, creator and ruler of all things, and angels, who are created by God and servants of God.

CHAPTER 1.6

The Date of the Parables of Enoch: A Preliminary Discussion

The argument of the preceding chapters is not affected by decisions about the date and place of origin of the Parables of Enoch, though it does presume that the book was written sometime during the late Second Temple period (generally understood as extending to the early second century CE). Hardly any scholars now doubt this. Józef Milik's argument for Christian provenance in the third century CE never had much support from experts (though it sowed some doubt about the Jewish provenance of the Parables among scholars who did not engage with the text themselves) and can safely be said to have no support today. There is also a general consensus that the Parables fits most plausibly into the Roman period, ruling out R. H. Charles's view that the book belongs to the Hasmonean period. Finally, the view that the absence of any fragments of the Book of Parables from the Dead Sea Scrolls has a bearing on its date is now generally seen to be invalid.

That leaves us with a possible range of dates between 50 BCE and 150 CE. Ted Erho, arguing against more specific proposals, has suggested that, on the basis of such consensus as exists, we can be reasonably certain that the book was written within the period 50 BCE to 100 CE.[1] I am not so sure that we can rule out the early second century. If a range of two hundred years seems unsatisfactorily vague, it is not in fact so exceptional in the case of ancient Jewish writings that lack any specific historical references by which to date them or clear evidence of their dependence on or use by other writings. At the 2005 Enoch Seminar, devoted to the Parables, Michael Stone observed:

---

1. Ted W. Erho, "Historical-Allusional Dating and the Similitudes of Enoch," *JBL* 130 (2011) 493–511, here 509–10.

The first thought that occurs to me is that the dating of the Parables is such a central issue for only one reason: the title Son of Man and its occurrence in the Gospels. . . . I wonder how we would approach this question if the title had not been used in the Gospels or, alternatively, if the Gospels were not the canonical writings of Christianity. Naturally the transformation of the Hebrew/Aramaic expression and its application to a redeemer figure is a totally legitimate object of scholarly investigation. Yet, perhaps few would zealously attempt to reach chronological precision with such meager evidence had the title not occurred in the Gospels. Such intellectual energy is not expended on the dating of the Testament of Job, the Paralipomena of Jeremiah, or the Greek Baruch.[2]

This observation is, if anything, even more true of the volume of essays edited by Bock and Charlesworth proclaiming a "new paradigm" that hinges entirely on dating the Parables around the turn of the era, in the reign of Herod the Great, and so, crucially, "before the beginning of Jesus' ministry."[3] The editors claim that "archaeologists, philologists, specialists on the Pseudepigrapha and the Dead Sea Scrolls, as well as New Testament scholars, are coming to a consensus: it is possible that the Parables of Enoch helped to shape Jesus' mind and influenced aspects of the Evangelists' theology. . . . How could Jesus not have known the Parables of Enoch, if it was composed about Jesus' time and in areas of Galilee that he frequented?"[4]

Leaving aside for the moment the issue of place of composition, the answer to the question might be that Jesus knew of it but was not in the least interested in it. Why should he pay much attention to a work that revealed Enoch to be the eschatological judge? The alleged "consensus" is surely greatly exaggerated unless it means only that the Parables *may* have been written before Jesus's time and that therefore "it is *possible* that the Parables of Enoch helped to

---

2. Michael Stone, "Enoch's Date in Limbo; or, Some Considerations on David Suter's Analysis of the Book of Parables," in *Enoch and the Messiah Son of Man: Revisiting the Book of Parables*, ed. Gabriele Boccaccini (Grand Rapids: Eerdmans, 2007) 444-49, here 445. When Leslie W. Walck, "The Son of Man in the Parables of Enoch and the Gospels," in *Enoch and the Messiah*, ed. Boccaccini, 298-337, here 299, opines that "the dating of the Parables, while tentative, is important," he means that the question of the possibility that the Parables influenced the Gospels hangs on it.

3. James H. Charlesworth and Darrell L. Bock, "Conclusion," in *Parables of Enoch: A Paradigm Shift*, ed. Darrell L. Bock and James H. Charlesworth, JCT 11 (London: Bloomsbury, 2013) 364-72, here 371.

4. Charlesworth and Bock, "Conclusion," 372.

shape Jesus' mind" (italics added). A lot of scholars might agree with that who would not be at all certain of the date of the Parables owing to the serious lack of strong evidence. Much as New Testament scholars would like to know whether the Parables could have influenced the early Palestinian Christian movement, if not Jesus himself, it is important that, in the question of date as in other respects, we do not allow the concerns of the study of the Gospels to exert undue influence on the study of the Parables of Enoch.

To return, first, to the 2005 Enoch Seminar, it seems to me that Paolo Sacchi exaggerates the degree of consensus at the seminar, when he concludes, "We may observe that those scholars who have directly addressed the problem of dating the Parables all agree on a date around the time of Herod."[5] This neglects the fact that some of those scholars reach conclusions with extreme caution. David Suter concludes his essay: "While . . . a clear majority of specialists argues for a date at the turn of the era, I maintain that we are not yet in a position to rule out a date after the destruction of Jerusalem. The nature of the evidence and the existence of divergent methodologies for its assessment are such that the appropriate date and context of the Parables *continue to elude us.*"[6]

Michael Stone's conclusion, responding to Suter, is this: "The date of the Parables may remain in limbo, then, *as Suter rightly remarks,* but in my judgment we shall not be far wrong if we put it in the latter part of the first century B.C.E., or somewhat later."[7] Stone's own judgment is based on a "relative typology" of Son of Man messianism, in which the "treatment of the Son of Man in the interpretation of 4 Ezra is typologically later than the Parables and the Gospels." But he then immediately admits that "typologically later" is not the same as chronologically later: "Is this difference to be explained chronologically, assuming a more or less direct genetic relation, or is it to be explained by social (or even geographical) differences?"[8] In any case, Stone's typology depends on the notion of a Son of Man concept that was clear to readers of the Parables but no longer so to the readers of 4 Ezra, a notion that is certainly disputable.

---

5. Paolo Sacchi, "The 2005 Camaldoli Seminar on the Parables of Enoch: Summary and Prospects for Future Research," in *Enoch and the Messiah,* ed. Boccaccini, 499–512, here 510.

6. David W. Suter, "Enoch in Sheol: Updating the Dating of the Book of Parables," in *Enoch and the Messiah,* ed. Boccaccini, 415–43, here 443 (italics added). Suter's essay surveys the scholarly discussion, since about 1980, of issues relevant to the dating of the book. In the course of it, he recognizes the strength of arguments tending in different directions.

7. Stone, "Enoch's Date," 449 (italics added).

8. Stone, "Enoch's Date," 449.

Apparently most scholars at the 2005 Enoch Seminar were inclined to date the Parables in the reign of Herod, but this may well have been, as Sacchi remarks, because those who explicitly addressed the question of date inclined to such a date (though not all conclusively). He explains:

> It is interesting that those who have not accepted a date around the turn of the era do not propose any alternative date but instead focus on the many possibilities and uncertainties in dating this text. In fact, no specific date other than the turn of the era was proposed at the conference. This lack of specificity on the part of some seems to have resulted in a scholarly impasse, since the two positions represented at the conference are basically asymmetrical. Those offering concrete proposals on the date of the Parables are unable to assess the alternative hypotheses that lack concrete elements for evaluation. . . . The burden of proof has shifted to those who disagree with the Herodian date. It is now their responsibility to provide evidence that would reopen the discussion.[9]

There seem to me to be two problems with this conclusion. One is that it is an entirely defensible position to think that the evidence offered for the Herodian date is weak and that the question of date should be left open. It is quite possible, even probable, that, given the nature of the Parables of Enoch, we simply do not have enough evidence to be so specific about the date. Specificity does not have to be opposed with alternative specificity; it can be opposed with rejection of specificity. This is in effect what Ted Erho does in three significant (though overlapping) articles written in the light of the 2005 Enoch Seminar's published volume.[10] He argues cogently that the only two passages that can be adduced as historical allusions (56:5-8; 67:8-10) cannot in fact, for a variety of reasons, yield historical specificity, and that tradition-historical arguments (such as Stone's reported above) based on a reconstructed history of the development of ideas can at best only delimit a broad time frame.[11] This responds to the specificity of the "consensus" at the Enoch seminar by arguing that, in the

---

9. Sacchi, "The 2005 Camaldoli Seminar," 510-11.
10. Ted M. Erho, "The Ahistorical Nature of 1 Enoch 56:5-8 and Its Ramifications upon the *Opinio Communis* on the Dating of the *Similitudes of Enoch*," *JSJ* 40 (2009) 23-54; Erho, "Internal Dating Methodologies and the Problem Posed by the *Similitudes of Enoch*," *JSP* 20 (2010) 83-103; Erho, "Historical-Allusional Dating."
11. The former point is made in all three articles, the latter in "Internal Dating Methodologies," 102-3.

nature of this case, it is impossible to be so specific. He suggests we be content with a date in the period 50 BCE to 100 CE.[12]

The second problem with Sacchi's conclusion is that it ignores at least one good argument for a date in the late first century, which, if not actually advocated within the volume, is at least reported in David Suter's survey. This is the affinity between the Parables, on the one hand, and Jewish and Christian writings of the period after 70 CE: 2 Baruch, 4 Ezra, and Revelation.[13] Michael Knibb's argument to this effect, though brief, should not be ignored, especially since it follows a critical assessment of the arguments for an earlier date.[14] As a response to the challenge posed at the end of Sacchi's conclusion, I shall briefly sketch a more precise form of this argument, which my present study of the Parables has made possible.

The portrayal of the Messianic Figure in the Parables has a distinctive resemblance to the portrayals of such a figure in three apocalypses from the late first century: 4 Ezra, 2 Baruch, and the book of Revelation.[15] At the core of this resemblance is a particular set of biblical sources: Daniel 7, Isaiah 11:1–5, and Psalm 2. These messianic passages are common to all four works, and the combination is distinctive. Other portrayals of the Messianic Figure in early Jewish and Christian works depend at most on only two of these sources. While it can reasonably be claimed that these three texts are of central importance for all four apocalypses, each also draws on other biblical sources to a greater or lesser extent,[16] such as Isaiah 42:1–7 and 47:1–7 in the Parables of Enoch, Genesis 49:9–12 in 4 Ezra, and Genesis 49:9–12 and Isaiah 53 and other texts in Revelation (which draws on a particularly wide range of biblical sources for its portrayal of Jesus Christ). The selection of messianic texts from the Hebrew Bible is a key element in the production of differing portrayals of the Messiah, but these four works also share a particular interpretative framework that enables them to bring Daniel 7:13–14 together with the other two texts. This is the notion that Daniel 7:13 portrays a human figure who had previously lived on earth and was exalted to heaven, where he awaits the time

12. Erho, "Historical-Allusional Dating," 509–10.
13. Suter, "Enoch in Sheol," 431, 440.
14. Michael A. Knibb, "The Date of the Parables of Enoch: A Critical Review," NTS 25 (1978–79) 345–59, reprinted in Knibb, *Essays on the Book of Enoch and Other Early Jewish Texts and Traditions*, SVTP 22 (Leiden: Brill, 2009) 143–60. See also Knibb, *Essays*, 312–13.
15. In my view 2 Baruch is dependent on 4 Ezra, but neither of these works has a direct literary relationship with Revelation.
16. See the discussion of 4 Ezra in chapter 2.5 and the discussion of 2 Baruch in chapter 2.8.

when he will come to earth as the eschatological judge.[17] They also share the view that the Messiah will overthrow the oppressive powers, not by warfare, but by his word of judicial condemnation (echoing Isa 11:4).

It would seem that the four works share an exegetical tradition, but with considerable flexibility that is partly determined by the parts or aspects of the three biblical sources that each of these four works draws out and develops, and partly also by the other biblical sources that each text brings into the mix. In three of the four works the Messianic Figure is a descendant of David, but in the Parables of Enoch he is Enoch. This is remarkable because, of the three sources, Isaiah 11:1-5 is explicit about the Messiah's descent from David, while Psalm 2 is most naturally read as referring to a Davidic king. (It is notable that, whereas the other three works echo Ps 2:6 ["I have set my king on Zion, my holy hill"] by referring to Mount Zion, the Parables do not.) This strongly suggests that the Parables of Enoch have refunctioned an exegetical tradition that related to the Davidic Messiah, applying it to Enoch instead. This makes the Parables, in its use of this exegetical tradition, typologically subsequent to the other works. This need not mean that it is chronologically later, but does suggest that it is chronologically not too much earlier than the late first century, given that the exegetical tradition is not evidenced in other works earlier than that time.

One other consideration arises from the comparison of these works. In all of them the idea of a messianic war, in which the Messiah leads an army that defeats the oppressor in battle, is absent. Instead, the Messiah alone effects the defeat of the oppressors by a powerful word of judicial condemnation. The common dependence on Isaiah 11:4 at this point is impressive. In 4 Ezra 13 there is considerable stress on this nonmilitary role of the Messianic Figure (13:37-38), while the nine northern tribes, who in an earlier tradition had probably played the role of a messianic army, are repeatedly described as "peaceable" (13:12, 39, 47). In Revelation, while the Messiah is portrayed as a warrior who conquers in battle (19:11-21), the image is reinterpreted so that he comes as "the word of God" (19:13) and his weapon is "a sharp sword" coming from his mouth (19:15), an allusion to Isaiah 11:4. His army (19:14) consists of the martyrs who have "conquered" by their faithful witness to death (12:11, etc.), following, in that respect, their leader (14:1). Similarly, in the Parables, "the word of his mouth will slay all sinners" (1 En. 61:2), and the scene is purely judicial. There is no hint of a military victory, and "the righteous and

---

17. This is not explicit in 2 Baruch, but I think it can be argued (especially if, as I think, 2 Baruch is dependent on 4 Ezra) that it is implicit.

chosen," despite the Messianic Figure's solidarity with them, do not form an army. Second Baruch is less clear on this point (39:7–40:2), but makes clear that it is by a judicial process that the Lord's Anointed One deals with "the last ruler" (40:1–2).

Clearly the book of Revelation, which transmutes the images of a messianic war into victory through martyrdom as well as through judicial conviction, pursues a specifically Christian approach. But the avoidance of the idea of a messianic war in the three Jewish works would be very intelligible after the failure of the first Jewish revolt against Rome. This could very well have been understood as signifying that the liberation of God's people from their pagan oppressors was not to take place through an ordinary human leading a human army (even with angelic assistance, as in the Qumran War Rule). It would be accomplished by a man sent from heaven, acting alone and by judicial, not military, means. The Parables of Enoch fits well into such a scenario.

This evidence is not conclusive. But it is evidence that should be thrown in the balance against the reasons for an earlier dating of the Parables that evidently prevailed at the Enoch Seminar in 2005 and at the colloquium subsequently convened by Charlesworth and Bock. It is certainly too early to speak of a consensus on the date of the Parables. This question will be taken up again at the end of part 2 of this book, when we have studied in detail the interpretation of Daniel 7 in other Jewish literature of the Second Temple period.

CHAPTER 1.7

The Place of Composition of the Parables of Enoch

Most scholars assume that the Parables of Enoch, presumed to have been written originally in either Hebrew or Aramaic, was composed somewhere in Jewish Palestine, but have not attempted to be more specific. To my knowledge only two scholars, James Charlesworth (who has recently lived in Galilee) and Galilean archaeologist Mordechai Aviam, have argued for a more specific location: in Galilee and, even more specifically, in Magdala.[1]

Before proceeding to their arguments, we must note Charlesworth's claim: "The *Parables of Enoch* were most likely composed somewhere in Galilee before the Roman destruction of 67 CE; this position is now a consensus among Enoch specialists."[2] Charlesworth is prone to use the word "consensus" loosely and optimistically, but this statement is especially remarkable. I am not aware

---

1. They both refer to this place as Migdal, but this is an error. It is the name of the modern Israeli town near to the ancient site and would have been the Hebrew name of the ancient town if it were known by a Hebrew name. But none of the extant sources attribute the Hebrew name Migdal to it. As well as the Greek name Taricheae, two Aramaic names are attested: Migdal (or Magdal) Nunayya ("the Tower of the Fish") and Migdal (or Magdal) Ṣabʿayya ("the Tower of the Dyers"). Migdal or Magdal in these composite names is not the Hebrew word *migdal* but the construct form of the Aramaic, which can only be used with a following connected noun. So the short form of the name was Magdala ("the Tower"). There is no reason to think it was ever called Migdal. See Richard Bauckham, "Magdala As We Now Know It: An Overview," in *Magdala of Galilee: A Jewish City in the Hellenistic and Roman Period*, ed. Richard Bauckham (Waco: Baylor University Press, 2018) 1–67, here 5–7.

2. James H. Charlesworth, "Did Jesus Know the Traditions in the *Parables of Enoch*? ΤΙΣ ΕΣΤΙΝ ΟΥΤΟΣ Ο ΥΙΟΣ ΤΟΥ ΑΝΘΡΩΠΟΥ; (JN 12:34)," in *Parables of Enoch: A Paradigm Shift*, ed. Darrell L. Bock and James H. Charlesworth, JCT 11 (London: Bloomsbury, 2013) 173–217, here 186.

PART 1 · THE PARABLES OF ENOCH

of any scholar apart from Charlesworth and Aviam (who is not an Enoch specialist) who has expressed the view in published work that the Parables was written in Galilee. The sentence just quoted from Charlesworth is followed by a footnote number (42), but readers will search in vain at the bottom of this page or the next for a footnote 42. Footnote 43 follows footnote 41 immediately. This is disconcerting if one wishes for even a modicum of evidence for Charlesworth's claim to report "a consensus among Enoch specialists." Readers wanting this will be similarly frustrated at an earlier point in this volume, where Charlesworth writes, "If the *Parables of Enoch* is the latest composition in the corpus defined by *1 Enoch* and was composed in Galilee, as now seems evident to many Enoch specialists (see the following). . . ."[3] But if we read on in the following pages, looking for some reference to any Enoch specialists other than Charlesworth who think the Parables was written in Galilee, we shall again be disappointed. All that we find are Charlesworth's own arguments about the geographical location of the Parables.[4] Perhaps he has had conversations with Enoch specialists in which they have told him that they support his view on this point,[5] but if so, he should have told us. To assert a consensus of Enoch specialists or even the view of "many" Enoch specialists without giving any evidence at all for such a claim is seriously misleading.

I note that George Nickelsburg, a preeminent Enoch specialist, writing in 2012, just one year before the quoted comments of Charlesworth were published, knows nothing of any such consensus:

> The geographical provenance of the Parables is unknown. Composition in Hebrew or Aramaic around the turn of the era suggests Palestine. The references to Upper Galilee in the Book of Watchers . . . taken together with the Son of Man theology in the early Jesus movement are suggestive, but it needs to be emphasized that there are no such references in the Parables; the only real (as opposed to mythic) geographical references in the Parables are to Jerusalem (56:7) and, probably, Kallirrhoë (though not by name) on

---

3. James H. Charlesworth, "The Date and Provenience of the Parables of Enoch," in *Parables of Enoch*, ed. Charlesworth and Bock, 37–57, here 45–46.

4. Charlesworth, "The Date," 48–54.

5. Is this what is meant when he and Bock (James H. Charlesworth and Darrell L. Bock, "Conclusion," in *Parables of Enoch*, ed. Charlesworth and Bock, 371) claim that "these insights" (i.e., that the Parables are Jewish, identify Enoch as "that Son of Man," are contemporaneous with Jesus or slightly earlier, and derived from Galilee) are "a virtual consensus among those who attend the biennial sessions of the Enoch Seminar"?

The Place of Composition of the Parables of Enoch · 1.7

the eastern shore of the Dead Sea.... Thus, the text's communal and geographical provenance remain a mystery.[6]

Another Enoch specialist, Michael Knibb, wrote in 2010 that it is "likely that the *Parables* come from Jerusalem or the surrounding area."[7]

In the volume deriving from the 2005 Enoch Seminar (which unfortunately has no indices), as far as I can see, only two of its many contributors comment on the geographical provenance of the Parables. Pierluigi Piovanelli merely points out that the references to locations in Upper Galilee in the Book of Watchers are part of the tradition that did not survive into the Book of Parables.[8] The other opinion on this matter in the volume is Charlesworth's own: he previews the argument about dry land and swamps that he develops further in his later work (see below).[9] Incidentally, here he argues for the Hulah Valley as "the best location" for the Parables,[10] writing before he became convinced of Aviam's argument for locating the composition of the work in Magdala.

The "consensus" in favor of a Galilean location seems to be entirely imaginary. But this does not mean that Charlesworth's and Aviam's arguments for it may not be convincing. They need to be examined in their own right.

The first argument for a Galilean provenance of the Parables of Enoch, made by both writers, is based on the geographical references in the Book of Watchers to Mount Hermon and the "waters of Dan" (1 En. 6:6; 13:7).[11] There is also a reference to the nearby place Abel-Mayyin in 13:9.[12] Although neither

---

6. George W. E. Nickelsburg and James C. VanderKam, *1 Enoch 2: A Commentary on the Book of 1 Enoch Chapters 37–82*, ed. Klaus Baltzer, Hermeneia (Minneapolis: Fortress, 2012) 66.

7. Michael A. Knibb, "Enoch, Similitudes of (1 Enoch 37–71)," in *Dictionary of Early Judaism*, ed. John J. Collins and Daniel C. Harlow (Grand Rapids: Eerdmans, 2010) 585–87, here 587.

8. Pierluigi Piovanelli, "'A Testimony for the Kings and the Mighty Who Possess the Earth': The Thirst for Justice and Peace in the Parables of Enoch," in *Enoch and the Messiah Son of Man: Revisiting the Book of Parables*, ed. Gabriele Boccaccini (Grand Rapids: Eerdmans, 2007) 377–78.

9. James H. Charlesworth, "Can We Discern the Composition Date of the Parables of Enoch?," in *Enoch and the Messiah*, ed. Boccaccini, 450–68, here 460–61, 465.

10. Charlesworth, "Can We Discern," 465.

11. Mordechai Aviam, "The Book of Enoch and the Galilean Archaeology and Landscape," in *Parables of Enoch*, ed. Bock and Charlesworth, 159–69, here 159–61; Charlesworth, "Did Jesus Know," 184.

12. On the reading Abel-Mayya here (cf. T. Levi 2:8; 4QLevi[b] ar), see George W. E. Nickelsburg, *1 Enoch 1: A Commentary on the Book of 1 Enoch Chapters 1–36; 81–108*, ed. Klaus Baltzer, Hermeneia (Minneapolis: Fortress, 2001) 248.

author points it out, an argument for connecting the Book of Watchers with Upper Galilee, on the basis of these references, was already made by George Nickelsburg in 1981.[13] The argument was updated in 2001 in the first volume of his commentary on 1 Enoch,[14] where he rehearses the extensive evidence, literary and archaeological, for the fact that the area around Mount Hermon was treated as sacred territory for more than three millennia. He also points out that in Testament of Levi 2–7 Levi's visionary ascent to heaven is located in the same area (Abel-Mayyin),[15] and that in Matthew Jesus's commissioning of Peter is located in the same area (Caesarea Philippi) (Matt 16:13–19). He concludes that "parallels between 1 Enoch 13 and *Testament of Levi* 2–7 must be taken seriously as attestations of Jewish religious, indeed, revelatory activity in this area during the Hellenistic period."[16]

I am dubious about this conclusion. Nickelsburg agrees with the scholarly consensus that the Enochic Book of Watchers (1 En. 1–36), or at least chapters 6–16, was written prior to the book of Daniel, thus in the early second or the third century BCE.[17] There were no Jews living in Upper Galilee at that period or in most of the rest of Galilee. Settlement of Jews from Judea in Galilee began in the Hasmonean period in the late second century,[18] as Aviam himself points out, on the basis of the archaeology, in this very essay![19] I said "most of the rest of Galilee" because Aviam, unlike some archaeologists,[20] thinks (on the basis of 1 Macc 5:14–24) that "there was a small weak minority of Jewish survivors in the western Lower Galilee [around Nazareth and Sepphoris], surrounded by gentiles."[21] This is hardly a basis for supposing that there was Jewish religious activity in the area of Dan.

It seems to me much more likely that, as well as the pun on the name Hermon (1 En. 6:6) that connects it with the curse of the fallen angels, the reason

---

13. George W. E. Nickelsburg, "Enoch, Levi, and Peter: Recipients of Revelation in Upper Galilee," *JBL* 100 (1981) 575–600.

14. Nickelsburg, *1 Enoch 1*, 238–47.

15. The name is preserved in 4QLevi[b] ar: see James R. Davila, "Aramaic Levi," *OTPMNS* 1:121–42, here 134.

16. Nickelsburg, *1 Enoch 1*, 247.

17. Nickelsburg, *1 Enoch 1*, 119.

18. Bauckham, "Magdala," 13–14.

19. Aviam, "The Book of Enoch," 163–64.

20. Notably, Uzi Leibner, *Settlement and History in Hellenistic, Roman, and Byzantine Galilee: An Archaeological Survey of the Eastern Galilee*, TSAJ 127 (Tübingen: Mohr Siebeck, 2009) 219–29.

21. Mordechai Aviam, *Jews, Pagans and Christians in the Galilee: 25 Years of Archaeological Excavations and Surveys; Hellenistic to Byzantine Periods* (Rochester, NY: University of Rochester Press, 2004) 43.

this part of the Book of Watchers was set in that vicinity is its connection with the fallen angels (6:6; 13:9). In the Enoch tradition, these rebellious angels (called Watchers) were the origin of all evils on earth, including idolatrous religion. The northern Israelite cult center at Dan, where King Jeroboam set up the statue of a golden calf, is roundly condemned in the books of Kings as idolatrous, in a narrative that associates the calf with the golden calf made by Aaron in the wilderness, Israel's first act of apostasy (1 Kgs 12:25–33). There is no reason to suppose the author of the Book of Watchers would have thought otherwise. The site was still a cult center in the Hellenistic period, and an inscription in Greek and Aramaic from around 200 BCE reads: "To the god who is in Dan [or "among the Danites"] Zoilos made a vow."[22] But Zoilos and his fellow worshipers are very unlikely to have been Jews. They were pagans worshiping the local god, once called YHWH, now "the god who is in Dan." Moreover, also by 200 BCE, the famous shrine of the god Pan was already established at the nearby Paneas (modern Banias).[23]

The fallen Watchers were the first apostates, who abandoned their place and offices in heaven (see 1 En. 15:1–16:4), and became on earth the source of all human apostasy from the true God and his ways. The author of the Book of Watchers made Dan the place of their apostasy in order to recall and associate with it the apostasy of Israel in the time of Jeroboam (1 Kgs 12:25–33). This apostasy is described later in the Enochic Animal Apocalypse as the source of all the evil ways that led to the downfall of both Israelite kingdoms (1 En. 89:51, 54–58). So the author had very good reasons to locate the fall of the Watchers in the area of Dan, quite irrespective of where he lived. In addition, the fact that Mount Hermon was the highest mountain in Israel's vicinity made it obviously suitable as the place to which angels descending from heaven would come.

Nickelsburg, who thinks that chapters 6–16 of 1 Enoch *may* have been written in Upper Galilee, points out that the "presence of the Enochic texts at Qumran attests knowledge of them in Judea."[24] (The Parables, of course, has not been found at Qumran.) Even if chapters 6–16 were written in Upper Galilee (for which I think there is no good evidence), they were later read in other places. There is no reason to suppose that the other Enochic works were written in the same place as the Book of Watchers. In particular, the Parables is generally agreed to be the latest of the collection of Enochic works we know as 1 Enoch. It was written at least two centuries later than the Book of Watchers. Whatever we think about other Enochic works, there is unlikely to have

---

22. Nickelsburg, *1 Enoch 1*, 244.
23. Nickelsburg, *1 Enoch 1*, 244.
24. Nickelsburg, *1 Enoch 1*, 65.

been any sociological continuity between the contexts in which the Book of Watchers and the Parables were written. Unlike other Enochic works, the Parables does not work with a distinction between the righteous and the wicked within the people of God. Arguably it is a nonsectarian work concerned with the sufferings of Jews as such under the oppression of the ruling class.[25]

The author of the Parables undoubtedly thought highly of the Book of Watchers and made its hero, Enoch, his own. But by his time the Book of Watchers was well known. It was read by early Christians (Jude 14–15) and may already have been translated into Greek. There is no reason to suppose that, wherever the Book of Watchers was written, the author of the Book of Parables lived in the same place. So the geographical references in the Book of Watchers are completely irrelevant to the location in which the Book of Parables was written.[26]

At this point we should notice that Aviam supposes that "the latest parts of the *Parables of Enoch* and the final editing of the *Books of Enoch* took place in Galilee,"[27] a view that is apparently shared by Charlesworth.[28] We need to be clear that the compilation we know as 1 Enoch exists only in Ethiopic. When or where the Parables, the second component of this collection of Enochic works, was incorporated into such a collection is a matter for speculation. There is no good reason to think that the creation of this collection was connected with the composition of the Parables itself. The interpolation of sections of an (otherwise lost) Noah apocryphon into the text of the Parables could suggest that the Book of Parables originally circulated along with this apocryphon of Noah.[29] We do not know!

The second argument for a Galilean origin of the Parables that I shall address is made by Charlesworth. He focuses on the repeated use in the Parables of phrases like "the kings and the mighty and the exalted and those who possess the earth/land" (62:3), and argues that the powerful elite to whom

---

25. Piovanelli, "'A Testimony,'" 363–79; Daniel Boyarin, "Was the Book of Parables a Sectarian Document? A Brief Brief in Support of Pierluigi Piovanelli," in *Enoch and the Messiah*, ed. Boccaccini, 380–85. But for a different view, see Lester L. Grabbe, "The Parables of Enoch in Second Temple Jewish Society," in *Enoch and the Messiah*, ed. Boccaccini, 386–402, here 398.

26. Charlesworth, "Did Jesus Know," 185, makes the extraordinarily lame argument that the fallen Watchers also appear in the Parables, which describes the place of their punishment (56:1–4). I fail to see how this is an argument for locating the Parables in Galilee.

27. Aviam, "The Book of Enoch," 169.

28. Charlesworth, "Did Jesus Know," 191.

29. I think there are sufficient resemblances to suggest that both may have been the work of the same author.

the Parables is opposed includes not only political rulers but also rich gentile landowners who have taken over the land that traditionally belonged to Jewish families. More specifically, however, he points out that the Ethiopic word means "dry ground," and takes this to refer to dry ground as opposed to swamps and marshland that was of no agricultural use. This refers most plausibly, he thinks, to ancient Galilee, where the swamp that filled the Hulah Valley stretched from Capernaum north to Paneas. The Parables reflects a situation where the fertile "dry ground" is owned by the powerful landowners, leaving the Jews in possession only of the unproductive swamp.[30] An initial observation is that, if this were the case, would we not expect some reference to the marshland in the Parables? There is no such reference.

However, the fatal weakness of Charlesworth's proposal is philological. He does not tell us that the Ethiopic word meaning "dry ground" is one of the *two* words translated "earth" or "land" in the Parables, and he does not investigate the general usage of these two words in the Parables. Instead, he makes only this comment: "The Ethiopic word for 'dry ground' can mean the division of the cosmos into the waters and the earth (or dry ground), but every good translator of the Ethiopic knows that one must keep in mind that the Ethiopic itself is a translation, and the underlying Aramaic (or Hebrew) is not always accurately represented."[31] This appears to mean that, whereas the Ethiopic word is ambiguous, the underlying Hebrew or Aramaic would have clearly referred to "dry ground" in the specific sense of dry ground as opposed to wetlands. But he does not suggest what such an Aramaic or Hebrew word would have been. This makes it impossible to assess his claim.

Fortunately, two scholars, George Nickelsburg[32] and Shizuka Uemura,[33] have investigated carefully the usage of the Ethiopic words *medr* and *yabs* in the Parables of Enoch. They seem to differ on only one significant point. Uemura supposes that *medr* ("earth") translates Aramaic 'ara' (ארע), because it does in other parts of 1 Enoch where the Aramaic survives, and that *yabs* ("dry land"), which is not used in the Ethiopic of 1 Enoch outside the Parables, translates the Hebrew *yabbāšâ* (יבשה), which means "dry land" (Nickelsburg adds the Aramaic equivalent *yabbîš* [יביש]).[34] Nickelsburg, on the other hand,

30. Charlesworth, "The Date," 48–50.
31. Charlesworth, "The Date," 49.
32. Nickelsburg, *1 Enoch 2*, 89–90.
33. Shizuka Uemura, *Land or Earth: A Terminological Study of Hebrew 'ereṣ and Aramaic 'ara' in the Graeco-Roman Period*, Library of Second Temple Studies 84 (London: T&T Clark [Continuum], 2012) 145–53.
34. The Hebrew word יבשה occurs fourteen times in the Hebrew Bible and five in DSS. It

concludes that the difference "may reflect stylistic variations by the Ethiopian translators, or a fluctuation between γῆ and οἰκουμένη and ξήρα in the Greek *Vorlage*. This latter in turn could reflect a variety of nouns in the original."[35] He gives possibilities such as Aramaic ארע and תבל, or Hebrew אדמה, ארץ, and תבל, but it is impossible to be sure which words were used in the original, and he does not think the two Ethiopic words can consistently be translations of two corresponding Aramaic or Hebrew words.

However, much more important is that the two scholars, working independently, agree that the two Ethiopic words *medr* and *yabs* (which occur, respectively, forty-three and forty-two times) are used largely synonymously and interchangeably.[36] For example, the expression "the face of the earth" occurs six times with *medr*[37] and twice with *yabs*.[38] The expression "those who dwell on the earth" occurs twenty-four times with *yabs*[39] and once with *medr*.[40] These usages are explicable if the Ethiopic translator thought of *yabs* as meaning all the dry ground in the world, as opposed to sea or the waters in general (as it does in 1 En. 53:1; 60:9; 61:10; cf. Gen 1:9–10), but not if he thought it meant dry ground as opposed to wetlands.

The most decisive evidence is the usage in the phrase "those who possess the earth/land" (or similar). Here we find that *yabs* is used five times and *medr* four, thus:

- "the kings of the earth [*medr*] and the strong who possess the earth/land [*yabs*]" (48:8)
- "all the kings and the mighty and the exalted and those who rule the earth/land [*yabs*]" (62:9)
- "the mighty and the kings and those who possess the earth/land [*yabs*]" (63:1)

---

can refer to the dry land of the world as a whole, contrasted with the sea or the waters (Gen 1:9; Ps 66:6; Jon 1:9). In Gen 1:9–10 God creates "the dry land" and calls it "earth" (ארץ). The word יבשה is also used for the dry ground on which the Israelites walk through the sea (Exod 14:16, 22, 29; 15:19; Neh 9:11) and through the river Jordan (Josh 4:22). It also refers to dry ground in Isa 44:3 (where the sense is of ground dried up and in need of moisture), Exod 4:9, and (opposed to sea) Jon 2:10.

35. Nickelsburg, *1 Enoch 2*, 89.
36. Uemura, *Land or Earth*, 148.
37. 1 En. 39:3; 45:6; 52:9; 53:2; 69:27, 28.
38. 1 En. 38:1; 67:3.
39. 1 En. 37:2, 5; 38:2; 40:6, 7; 43:4; 48:5; 54:6, 9; 53:9; 55:1, 2, 4; 59:2; 60:5, 22; 65:6, 12; 66:1; 67:7, 8; 69:1, 7; 70:1.
40. 1 En. 62:1.

- "the mighty and the kings and the exalted and those who possess the earth/land [*yabs*]" (63:12)
- "the kings and the mighty who possess the earth/land [*yabs*]" (67:12)
- "the mighty and exalted who possess the earth/land [*medr*]" (38:4)
- "the kings and the mighty and the exalted and those who possess the earth/land [*medr*]" (62:1)
- "the kings and the mighty and the exalted and those who possess the earth/land [*medr*]" (62:3)
- "the kings and the mighty and all who possess the earth/land [*medr*]" (62:6)

With this evidence before us, it is impossible to see significance in the fact that the Ethiopic word *yabs* means specifically "dry ground." The two Ethiopic words are used interchangeably, and, if they do represent different words in the underlying Aramaic or Hebrew, those words also were used interchangeably. There is room for discussion as to whether the translation should be the universal "the earth" or the local "the land." Nickelsburg prefers the latter in these phrases.[41] This leaves open the question whether, if the translation "land" is preferred, the meaning of "those who possess the land" is that they have political control over it or have seized agricultural land from its traditional owners. In the latter case, Charlesworth would be partially correct. But the contrast of dry land and swampy land is certainly not envisaged.

So the argument from particular Galilean geographical conditions fails. I am inclined to think that these phrases, like "the kings of the earth," which Charlesworth agrees with other scholars refers to the Roman emperors,[42] have universal possession of "the earth" in view, rather than specifically local conditions. But it is hard to be sure. The important point, in our present context, is that, supposing that the reference is to land-grabbing by gentile landowners, there is no reason why this should be limited to Galilee. The evidence Charlesworth provides for this phenomenon under Herod and his dynasty applies to Judea as much as to Galilee.[43] Wherever specifically the author lived, he would be referring to a phenomenon common to Jewish Palestine.

A third argument for locating the Parables in Galilee is made by Aviam, who proposes a specific connection with the city of Magdala. The argument concerns the well-known and remarkable decorated stone block that was found in the synagogue in Magdala when it was excavated. Aviam and I are the

---

41. Nickelsburg, *1 Enoch 2*, 104.
42. Charlesworth, "The Date," 48.
43. Charlesworth, "The Date," 51.

PART 1 · THE PARABLES OF ENOCH

joint authors of a chapter on the stone in the volume on Magdala that I edited.[44] The chapter shows a large measure of agreement between us, as well as some significant disagreements, including over the difficult issue of the function of the stone. We agree in general that the designs on the five faces of the stone all relate in some way to the Jerusalem temple, and there is in fact a large measure of agreement by other scholars too on this point, even though we do not all agree about the exact significance of all the designs. Aviam's argument in the present contexts focuses on one of the two short sides of the object. Here is the whole of his argument for a connection with the Parables of Enoch:

> The back side represents, in my view, a clear hint of the divine presence inside the Holy of Holies. The two wheels certainly represent the divine chariot, and the six triangles below each may represent flames. These two elements appear in the famous descriptions of the divine chariot in Daniel and Zachariah as well as in *1 Enoch* 114:18 [*sic*]:[45] "and I saw therein a lofty throne: its appearance was as crystal, and *the wheels* thereof as the shining sun.... And from underneath the throne came *streams of flaming fire*."... Thus we seem to have found the provenience of the *Parables of Enoch*; and certainly, as Enoch specialists concur, the author knew the earlier Enoch compositions.[46]

I agree with Aviam that this facade of the stone probably depicts the divine presence in the holy of holies in the Jerusalem temple. But, before proceeding further, I have to correct one of his biblical references. Zechariah's vision in 6:1–6 has nothing at all to do with the divine chariot. The four chariots Zechariah sees in the vision are four patrols sent out by God in the four directions to patrol the earth.[47] There is no fire in the vision. The divine throne in Daniel 7:9 certainly does have wheels, and both the throne and the wheels are made of fire. But we should note that it is not located in the temple. Enoch's vision of the divine throne in the Book of Watchers (1 En. 14:18–19) is located in the divine throne room in heaven, to which Enoch has ascended in vision. Perhaps surprisingly, Aviam does not mention that, in the Book of Parables itself, Enoch ascends to heaven and sees the divine throne (71:7). Here the walls of

---

44. Mordechai Aviam and Richard Bauckham, "The Synagogue Stone," in *Magdala of Galilee*, ed. Bauckham, 135–59.
45. This is a mistake for 14:18.
46. Aviam, "The Book of Enoch," 167 (italics original).
47. Zech 6:5 seems to identify them with the four winds.

the heavenly temple emit fire (71:6), but the throne itself is not explicitly linked with fire. The wheels do appear, but in a novel way:

> And around it [the glorious throne] (were) Seraphin and Cherubin, and Ophannin,
> and these are they who sleep not,
> but guard the throne of his glory. (71:7)[48]

The Ophannin (Aramaic אופנין, Hebrew אופנים, "wheels"), who appear also in 61:10, are the "wheels" of Ezekiel's vision of the divine chariot, where, as here, they are closely associated with the cherubim (Ezek 1:15–21). The connection with the cherubim, as well as the word used (in Dan 7:9 a different Aramaic word is used for "wheels"), makes it clear that the text reflects Ezekiel's vision. The way the wheels are depicted there (they move apparently of their own volition) led later Jewish interpreters to think of them as angelic beings (while remaining wheels).[49] This is an interesting difference between the Book of Watchers, which seems not to be dependent on Ezekiel, and the Book of Parables, which is.[50]

However, the important point is that the chariot thrones in Daniel and Enoch are not located in the temple, whereas the chariot depicted on the synagogue stone is. This means that its scriptural connection is not with Daniel or Enoch but with Ezekiel. Ezekiel describes the chariot throne at extraordinary length in his inaugural vision (Ezek 1:4–28). Later he sees it in vision within the Jerusalem temple (10:1–8), and he sees it depart from the temple (10:9–22), in anticipation of God's judgment of the temple and its destruction. But much later in his book, in the context of his elaborate description of the new temple (chapter 40–47), he sees the divine glory return to the temple (43:1–9). Once again God resides on his throne in the temple. This, surely, is the source of the depiction of the fiery chariot on the synagogue stone in Magdala.[51] Those who

---

48. Nickelsburg, *1 Enoch 1*, 320.

49. Saul M. Olyan, *A Thousand Thousands Served Him: Exegesis and the Naming of Angels in Ancient Judaism*, TSAJ 36 (Tübingen: Mohr Siebeck, 1993) 34–41; David J. Halperin, *The Faces of the Chariot: Early Jewish Responses to Ezekiel's Vision*, TSAJ 16 (Tübingen: Mohr Siebeck, 1988) 45–47, 85–86, 448–49.

50. Since the Ophannin do not appear elsewhere in Second Temple–period Jewish literature (unless 2 En. 20:1 dates from that period), but do appear in rabbinic literature, their appearance in the Parables of Enoch may be a minor indication of the relatively late date of that work.

51. I made this point in Aviam and Bauckham, "The Synagogue Stone," 141–42.

commissioned and fashioned it believed that the divine presence had returned to the temple that was built after the exile, as Ezekiel had predicted.

The Enochic books, the Book of Watchers and the Parables, do not refer to the divine presence in the earthly temple at all. (Of course, whatever these authors thought about the Jerusalem temple, it did not exist in the antediluvian times in which their books are set.) From the depiction of the divine presence in the holy of holies on the synagogue stone, there is no reason to suppose that those who commissioned it and fashioned it knew the books of Enoch at all. The depiction on the stone is much more adequately explained from the book of Ezekiel.

Aviam claims that the synagogue stone "sheds a very important light, maybe for the first time as an archaeological object, on Jewish mysticism in a Jewish, Galilean society and inside a synagogue."[52] He also speaks of it as "archaeological evidence for mystical, eschatological, and apocalyptic symbolism."[53] This is quite unwarranted. The stone depicts the Jerusalem temple and the divine presence in its holy of holies, as Aviam himself maintains. *Merkavah* mysticism (of which perhaps we have early evidence in the Songs of the Sabbath Sacrifice from Qumran) entailed ascent to the heavenly throne of God. Of course, the heavenly and earthly temples were thought to correspond and be connected, but this does not mean that a depiction of God's presence in the Jerusalem temple is connected with *Merkavah* mysticism—or, indeed, with eschatology. The priests and citizens of Magdala who ministered in or visited the temple were not mystics. They were attending, with sacrifices and prayers, to the very near presence of God in Jerusalem.

These are the substantial arguments for locating the origin of the Parables of Enoch in Galilee. We need not discuss Aviam's arguments from agriculture and botany, because they relate only to the Book of Watchers (10:19; 24:4; 31:2; 32:4).[54] It is crucially important to stress that, wherever the Book of Watchers was written (and I do not think the arguments for Galilee are in fact cogent), there is no reason to think that two centuries later (and this is according to the early Herodian date for the Parables advocated by Charlesworth) the author of the Parables of Enoch was living in the same place.

---

52. Aviam, "The Book of Enoch," 167.
53. Aviam, "The Book of Enoch," 169.
54. Aviam, "The Book of Enoch," 161. In fact, nothing in these references is peculiar to Galilee.

Finally, Charlesworth points to the influence of Babylonian astronomy on the Parables of Enoch,[55] pointing out that Galilee had close connections with the East. But so did Jerusalem. We have to conclude, quite simply, that we do not know where the Parables of Enoch were written and, in the nature of the case, we are unlikely ever to know. Literature of this kind does not often disclose its place of origin. It is noteworthy that few scholars feel the need to identify a precise place of origin. In Charlesworth's work this need obviously arises from the desire to make a connection with Jesus. From the archaeological point of view, it would be gratifying, on the basis of the archaeology, to be able to relate specific literary works to specific sites and discoveries, but (except when the discoveries include texts) this is very rarely possible.

---

55. Charlesworth, "The Date," 185.

PART 2

Interpretation of Daniel 7 in Second Temple–Period Judaism

CHAPTER 2.1

Introduction to Jewish Interpretations of Daniel 7

This part of the book offers a detailed investigation of the interpretation of Daniel 7 in the extant Jewish literature of the late Second Temple period, with special attention to the interpretation of Daniel 7:13–14.[1] Some readers might expect that such an investigation would start with an exegesis of the text of Daniel 7 itself, but I have deliberately decided not to offer one. Beginning with such an exegesis, of the kind that modern historical-critical scholarship can provide, could too easily prejudice the study of later Jewish interpretation of the text by privileging one example of exegesis as though this "original meaning" is some kind of standard against which Jewish interpretations are to be measured. With historical-critical interpretations in mind, we may too easily assume that such interpretations were available to ancient exegetes.

We need to be aware that ancient interpreters of Daniel approached the text in ways that diverge considerably from the approach of modern scholars. They all assumed that the whole book was written by the historical Daniel in the period of the Babylonian and Persian Empires. They did not treat any of the book's predictions as *vaticinia ex eventu*, nor did they imagine that any of these inspired prophecies could be mistaken. They did not treat the events of the crisis in the reign of Antiochus Epiphanes as the key to understanding most of Daniel's prophecies. Though they would have seen some references to those events (foreseen by Daniel centuries before), they understood the prophesied course of events to reach down to their own time and beyond. In particular, they usually "actualized" the text by finding in it references, often

---

1. A history of the interpretation of the whole book of Daniel in this period would be of great interest but cannot be undertaken here. In the following chapters, the interpretation of other parts of the book is studied where it is relevant to the interpretation of chapter 7.

precise, to events and circumstances of their own time. Once the Romans came to dominate the Near East, they took it for granted that the fourth world empire in the succession predicted by Daniel was the Roman Empire. This would have seemed simply obvious.

The background in Canaanite mythology that many modern scholars bring to their interpretation of Daniel 7[2] would have been very largely unknown to these ancient exegetes and in any case not considered relevant. Much more relevant were the rest of the Hebrew scriptures. They expected Daniel's prophecies, especially those relating to the end times, to cohere with those of other prophets. They were generally less interested than modern scholars in what is distinctive about the book of Daniel, more interested in Daniel's contribution, often a major one, to a picture indebted to many scriptures.

In the rest of this introductory chapter we shall consider briefly some literature from the period that is indebted to the book of Daniel and in which we might have expected to find evidence of interpretation of chapter 7, but which actually offers no or hardly any such evidence. The scrolls from Qumran are especially disappointing in this respect.

Daniel at Qumran

The book of Daniel was highly regarded in the community whose library was preserved in the caves at Qumran, and this was evidently the case from the earliest days of the community. The scrolls include the remains of no less than eight separate manuscripts of the book of Daniel, though one of these may have contained only Daniel's prayer from chapter 9 (4QDan^e).[3] These manuscripts are closer in time to their autograph than the surviving manuscripts of any other book of the Hebrew Bible. The earliest was copied in the late second or early first century BCE, the latest around the middle of the first century CE, spanning the whole history of the Qumran community.[4]

---

2. E.g., André Lacocque, "Allusions to Creation in Daniel 7," in *The Book of Daniel: Composition and Reception*, vol. 1, ed. John J. Collins and Peter W. Flint, VTSup 83 (Leiden: Brill, 2001) 114-31; John J. Collins, *Daniel*, Hermeneia (Minneapolis: Fortress, 1993) 286-94.

3. For details see Peter W. Flint, "The Daniel Tradition at Qumran," in *Eschatology, Messianism, and the Dead Sea Scrolls*, ed. Craig A. Evans and Peter W. Flint, SDSSRL (Grand Rapids: Eerdmans, 1997) 41-60, here 41-45; Eugene Ulrich, "The Text of Daniel in the Qumran Scrolls," in *The Book of Daniel: Composition and Reception*, vol. 2, ed. John J. Collins and Peter W. Flint, VTSup 83 (Leiden: Brill, 2001) 573-85. Every chapter of Daniel (MT) is represented in these manuscripts except chapter 12. It is clear that the form of the book known at Qumran was the one preserved in the MT. The so-called Greek Additions to Daniel are not included.

4. For the dates, see Ulrich, "The Text," 574; Peter W. Flint, "The Daniel Tradition at Qumran," in *The Book of Daniel*, vol. 2, ed. Collins and Flint, 329-67, here 330. Confusingly,

Introduction to Jewish Interpretations of Daniel 7 · 2.1

Another indication of the significance of Daniel for the community is in 4QFlorilegium, the pesher on a collection of scriptural texts that are interpreted as referring to the events of the last days and the community's own role in them. One of these texts is quoted from "the book of Daniel the prophet" and is a conflated version of Daniel 12:10 and 11:32 (4QFlor 1–3 ii 3–4c). This puts Daniel in the same category as "the book of Isaiah the prophet" and "the book of Ezekiel the prophet," cited elsewhere in this composition. It also shows what we should in any case have guessed: that the importance of Daniel for the community lay in its predictions of the crucial period in which they understood themselves to be living and playing a central role.

In addition to the manuscripts of the book of Daniel that now forms part of the Hebrew canon, there are, by Peter Flint's reckoning, nine other manuscripts found at Qumran, all in Aramaic and most very fragmentary, that contain works relating in some way to Daniel, either because the figure of Daniel appears in them or because their content resembles that of the book of Daniel. These nine manuscripts preserve seven distinct compositions (none of them known outside the Qumran library).[5] One of the manuscripts is 4Q246, which will be the subject of chapter 2.3. It is the only one that provides good evidence of the use and interpretation of Daniel 7.

Another that may have done so, if more of the text were available, is 4Q243–244 (4QpsDan[a, b] ar).[6] This apocalypse, attributed to Daniel at the court of King Belshazzar, is an outline of world history from before the flood until the last days. However, in the surviving fragments of the text, no clear allusions to the book of Daniel are evident.[7] References to "kingdoms of the peoples" and "the holy kingdom,"[8] in the context of God's saving intervention on behalf of his people in the last days, are certainly reminiscent of Daniel 7 but are not precise allusions and give little indication of how the author may have understood Daniel 7.

Another apocalypse in which Daniel is probably the seer is 4Q552–553 (4QFour Kingdoms[a, b] ar). Again the surviving text is very fragmentary. Four

---

Flint published two different (though related) essays with the same title. In these notes they will be distinguished by date.

5. Flint, "The Daniel Tradition" (2001) 331–32.

6. 4Q245 (4QpsDan[c] ar) has often been thought to belong to the same document, but, according to Flint, "The Daniel Tradition" (2001) 338, "this is manifestly not the case."

7. This is the judgment of Flint, "The Daniel Tradition" (2001) 339–40, in the light of his reconstruction of the text from all the fragments (341–49). Collins, *Daniel*, 76, following Milik's earlier and less complete reconstruction, does find borrowings from Daniel.

8. Lines 81–82 in Flint's reconstruction ("The Daniel Tradition" [2001] 346–47). But see his detailed comments on these lines: Flint, "The Daniel Tradition" (2001) 351.

trees represent four kingdoms, beginning with Persia (governed from Babylon). But the identity of the others is not clear. The fourth might be Rome, or it might be the eschatological kingdom of God.[9] The vision seems to be inspired by Daniel 7, but the way the author interpreted Daniel 7 is not clear. Neither of these two apocalypses, in the fragments of them we have, offers any clue at all as to how the figure of "one like a son of man" was understood.[10]

These Danielic compositions may or may not have been produced by the Qumran covenanters themselves, but there is no doubt as to the group's authorship of the War Rule (1QM). In the introduction to this work (i 1–17; cf. xv 1) the framework of events is clearly derived from Daniel 11:29–12:1, and the role of Michael (xvii 6–7) very likely reflects Daniel 12:1. References to Israel's eternal kingdom (xii 16; xix 8) may reflect Daniel 7:18 and/or 27, but an allusion to the distinctive phrase "the people of the holy ones of the Most High" (Dan 7:27) in 1QM xii 8 is uncertain. In the words עם קדושים, עם could be read either as the noun "people" ("the people of the holy ones") or as the preposition "with" ("with the holy ones"). But in x 10 "the people of the holy ones of the covenant" (עם קדושי ברית) must be the correct translation and in context refers to the people of Israel. There are similar phrases in vi 6; xii 5; xvi 1. It seems that the community did think of itself as "the people of the holy ones," perhaps on the basis of Daniel 7:27. Whether the "holy ones" are the angels, as is usually the case in 1QM and other Qumran compositions, or the people themselves is unclear.[11]

The importance of the book of Daniel for the community's expectations of the eschatological events in which they expected to play a key role is evident in the War Rule,[12] but we cannot tell from it what they made of Daniel 7:13–14.

Another text that refers explicitly to Daniel is 11QMelchizedek (11Q13), which introduces a quotation with the words "as Dan[iel][13] said" (ii 18). Unfortunately, the quotation itself has not survived in the manuscript, but part of Daniel 9:25 ("until an anointed one, a prince, seven weeks" [my translation]) suits the context and has been widely accepted as likely.[14] The only other

---

9. Flint, "The Daniel Tradition" (2001) 362–63.

10. Another Aramaic apocalypse, not associated with Daniel, which seems to draw on Dan 11:30–35, as well as the 490-years prophecy of Dan 9:20–27, is the Apocryphon of Jeremiah C (4Q383–390: but it is debatable which of these fragmentary manuscripts belong to the same work): see Bennie H. Reynolds, "Adjusting the Apocalypse: How the *Apocryphon of Jeremiah C* Updates the Book of Daniel," in *The Dead Sea Scrolls in Context*, vol. 1, ed. Armin Lange, Emanuel Tov, and Matthias Weigold, VTSup 140 (Leiden: Brill, 2011) 279–94.

11. Collins, *Daniel*, 315–16.

12. Collins, *Daniel*, 73–74.

13. Only the letter ד can be read with certainty, and נ is very probably the next letter. The reconstruction דניאל is very plausible and has been generally accepted.

14. See the discussion in Michael Flowers, "The Two Messiahs and Melchizedek in

possible allusion to Daniel resembles the phrase just discussed in 1QM xii 8: עם קדושי אל (ii 9). It could mean "the people of the holy ones of God" or "with the holy ones of God." In the first case, the "people" would be identical to Melchizedek's "hosts" (צבאים), which are certainly his armies of angels. Perhaps the author read Daniel 7:27 in that sense, but it is unlikely. He is referring to the armies with which Melchizedek carries out judgment on "the peoples" (ii 11), not to the kingdom that will follow. It seems better to read "with the holy ones of God" in ii 9.

The identity of Melchizedek has been extensively discussed. The argument that Melchizedek is another name[15] for the angelic "great prince" Michael (Dan 12:1) is quite strong.[16] Some scholars have tried to detect a connection between Melchizedek and the "one like a son of man" of Daniel 7:13, but the arguments are weak, resting on general resemblances.[17] It is possible that the Qumran community identified the figure in Daniel 7:13 with the principal good angel in their worldview, known as Michael, Melchizedek, or the Prince of Light. But the extant literature offers no hint of this.

It is important to remember that we do not have the complete text of any of the works discussed in this section and that there were undoubtedly many documents in the Qumran library that have not survived at all. So Maurice

---

11QMelchizedek," *Journal of Ancient Judaism* 7 (2016) 194–227, here 197–202. Flowers argues that this is the royal Messiah. In addition, there may be an allusion to Dan 9:24 in 11QMelch ii 7–8: see Roger T. Beckwith, "The Significance of the Calendar for Interpreting Essene Chronology and Eschatology," *RQ* 10 (1980) 167–202, here 171–72.

15. Melchizedek should perhaps be described as a title rather than a name. In 11QMelch it is written as two words, מלכי צדק, "king of righteousness."

16. Paul J. Kobelski, *Melchizedek and Melchirešaʿ*, CBQMS 19 (Washington, DC: Catholic Biblical Association of America, 1981) 71–74; Flowers, "The Two Messiahs," 209–13; James R. Davila, "Melchizedek, Michael, and War in Heaven," Old Testament Pseudepigrapha, University of St. Andrews, https://otp.wp.st-andrews.ac.uk/divine-mediator-figures-course/melchizedek-michael-and-war-in-heaven/ (accessed January 18, 2022). For Melchizedek's appearance as an angelic priest in fragments of the *Songs of the Sabbath Sacrifice*, see Aleksander R. Michalak, *Angels as Warriors in Late Second Temple Jewish Literature*, WUNT 2/230 (Tübingen: Mohr Siebeck, 2012) 186–89.

17. Pierpaolo Bertalotto, "Qumran Messianism, Melchizedek, and the Son of Man," in *The Dead Sea Scrolls in Context*, vol. 1, ed. Lange, Tov, and Weigold, 325–39, here 332, thinks that "even without any explicit citations, the Danielic background of such speculations is perfectly perceivable." See also David Flusser, "Melchizedek and the Son of Man," in *Judaism and the Origins of Christianity* (Jerusalem: Magnes, 1988) 186–92; J. Harold Ellens, "The Dead Sea Scrolls and the Son of Man in Daniel, 1 Enoch, and the New Testament Gospels: An Assessment of 11QMelch (11Q13)," in *The Dead Sea Scrolls in Context*, vol. 1, ed. Lange, Tov, and Weigold, 341–63.

Casey's judgment that Daniel 7 "was not of specially fundamental importance to the sect"[18] may be going a little too far.

SIBYLLINE ORACLES 3:388-400

This passage was apparently not part of the main corpus of the third book of the Sibyllines, which was written in Egypt and is dated by John Collins to the period 163-145 BCE.[19] Lines 388-400 seem to be an independent oracle that was added, along with others, to the main corpus.[20] If Maurice Casey is correct in dating it around 140 BCE,[21] it was incorporated in the third book at an early date. Certainly it dates from before the Roman conquest of the East.

Beginning with a prophecy of Alexander the Great (lines 388-394), it appears then to focus on Alexander's Seleucid successors in an obscure passage that certainly echoes Daniel 7:7-8. While Casey's attempt to identify in this passage the history of the Seleucid rulers following Antiochus IV Epiphanes may not be entirely correct (he admits that it entails guesswork),[22] it is reasonably clear that it does reflect events in the period immediately after the book of Daniel itself was written, during the reign of Antiochus Epiphanes. It reinterprets Daniel 7:7-8 to include these later events. What is of most interest is that Daniel's fourth beast is here understood to be the Macedonians (Alexander and his successors). The interpretation of the fourth beast as Rome, which is found in the later Jewish literature to be studied in the following chapters, has at this date yet to be developed.

Unfortunately, the oracle ends with the last horn of Daniel's vision reigning (line 400; cf. Dan 7:8). It does not go on to prophesy the divine judgment of the horn (the whole oracle makes no reference to God), and so there is no clue at all to the way the author may have understood Daniel 7:13-14.

TESTAMENT OF MOSES

The Testament of Moses (sometimes called the Assumption of Moses), a composition that is most often dated to the early first century CE,[23] survives in only one

---

18. Maurice Casey, *Son of Man: The Interpretation and Influence of Daniel 7* (London: SPCK, 1979) 115.

19. John J. Collins, "Sibylline Oracles," *OTP* 1:317-472, here 355.

20. Collins, "Sibylline Oracles," 359.

21. Casey, *Son of Man*, 119.

22. Casey, *Son of Man*, 117-19. See also James A. Montgomery, *A Critical and Exegetical Commentary on the Book of Daniel*, ICC (Edinburgh: T&T Clark, 1927) 292, for a similar, though much less detailed, interpretation.

23. In my view, a good case can also be made for a post-70 date.

incomplete and badly preserved manuscript in Latin. Much of the surviving text contains a long prophecy attributed to Moses, speaking to Joshua at the end of his life. He foretells the history of Israel down to the end time. Daniel himself appears anonymously in the narrative, praying for the people during the exile (T. Mos. 4:1-5; cf. Dan 9:1-19), but there is not much evidence for the influence of Daniel's prophecies. There is probably an allusion to Daniel 12:1 in 8:1, and the "messenger" (*nuntius*) who is going to avenge Israel on her enemies (10:2) may well be Michael, picking up the reference to him in Daniel 12:1.[24] The association of Israel with the stars of heaven (10:9) probably reflects Daniel 12:3. This group of allusions suggests that the author read Daniel 11:40-12:3 as predicting the final, unprecedented persecution of the Jewish people and their eschatological deliverance.

However, there is no evidence of influence from Daniel 7. The "kingdom" that appears throughout creation at the decisive eschatological moment (T. Mos. 10:1) is simply the kingdom of God, not a kingdom given to the "one like a son of man" or to "the holy ones of the Most High," as in Daniel 7:14, 18, 22, 27. Klaus Koch's suggestion that "the heavenly one" (*caelestis*) (10:3) might be the "one like a son of man" is not plausible.[25] The principal allusion here is to Micah 1:3, and "the heavenly one" must be identical to "the Most High God" in 10:7. Elsewhere in the Testament of Moses, God is called "the heavenly God" (2:4: *Deus caelestis*) and "heavenly Lord" (4:4: *Domine caelestis*).

---

24. Darrell D. Hannah, *Michael and Christ: Michael Traditions and Angel Christology in Early Christianity*, WUNT 2/109 (Tübingen: Mohr Siebeck, 1999) 37-38. The Latin word *nuntius* does not mean "angel." But it is very plausibly a translation of ἄγγελος, which means "messenger" or "angel." The phrase "then the hands of the messenger will be filled" (*tunc implebuntur manus nuntii*) is difficult. The expression "to fill the hands" is a circumlocution for priestly ordination, but, although Michael was sometimes regarded as the heavenly high priest, it is strange that he should be ordained to that office at this point and in order to perform a function that is hardly priestly. It may be that "hands will be filled" has a different significance here. Cf. Rev 16:1-2. Johannes Tromp, *The Assumption of Moses*, SVTP 10 (Leiden: Brill, 1993) 229-31, argues that the *nuntius* is Taxo, whose story is told in chapter 9, but the text gives insufficient basis for making this connection.

25. Klaus Koch, "Stages in the Canonization of the Book of Daniel," in *The Book of Daniel*, vol. 2, ed. Collins and Flint, 421-46, here 433 ("God? The Son of Man?").

CHAPTER 2.2

The Greek Versions of Daniel 7

The Two Greek Versions of Daniel

Among the books of the Jewish scriptures, the book of Daniel is unusual in that we have the complete texts of two Greek versions, known as the Old Greek and Theodotion. The Old Greek (also known as the Septuagint) has survived in only two copies because in Christian usage it was replaced at an early date by Theodotion's version, which is found in almost all manuscripts of the Greek Bible. One of the manuscripts of the Old Greek is Codex Chisianus 88 (once owned by the Chigi family), which dates from sometime in the ninth to eleventh centuries. The text it attests is not the original Old Greek but that in Origen's Hexapla (marked with Origen's text-critical symbols). Its value for reconstructing the "original" Old Greek is compromised by Origen's tendency to emend the text, especially to conform to the Hebrew text he knew.[1] The Hexaplaric text is also attested in a very literal Syriac version, known as the Syrohexapla, which was made in 615–617 CE. A second copy of the Old Greek is found in Papyrus 967, though it is fragmentary in places, and dates from the second or early third century CE.[2] The reason it fell out of use is probably that, as Jerome put it, "it differs widely from the original"[3]—that is, from the Hebrew and Aramaic version of Daniel (the Proto-Masoretic) that Jerome knew and translated into Latin.

---

1. Sharon Pace Jeansonne, *The Old Greek Translation of Daniel 7–12*, CBQMS 19 (Washington, DC: Catholic Biblical Association of America, 1988) 8–10.
2. For details, see John J. Collins, *Daniel*, Hermeneia (Minneapolis: Fortress, 1993) 4–5; Alexander A. Di Lella, "The Textual History of Septuagint-Daniel and Theodotion-Daniel," in *The Book of Daniel: Composition and Reception*, vol. 2, ed. John J. Collins and Peter W. Flint, VTSup 83 (Leiden: Brill, 2001) 586–607, here 586–87, 590.
3. Jerome, *Preface to Daniel*, quoted in Collins, *Daniel*, 4.

The so-called Theodotion version that supplanted the Old Greek was associated in Christian tradition with a second-century Jewish Bible translator of that name, but it is now widely thought that this version has earlier origins and the attachment of the name Theodotion to it may well be entirely misleading.[4] It is retained as the traditional designation.[5] In the rest of this chapter the two versions will be called OG-Daniel and Th-Daniel. The Masoretic Hebrew/Aramaic text of Daniel will be called MT-Daniel and used as evidence of the "Proto-Masoretic" version that was known in this period. It should be noted that the Qumran fragments of Daniel[6] diverge only in insignificant ways (such as orthography and morphology) from the Masoretic text. So we are justified in the working assumption that the extant Masoretic text is usually as near as we can get to the "Proto-Masoretic" version that was known in this period (MT-Daniel) and, indeed, that it is not much different.[7]

The relationship between these two Greek versions and the relationships of each to MT-Daniel, as well as to other hypothetical Semitic *Vorlagen*, has been extensively investigated and debated, but unfortunately, as Alexander Di Lella observed in 2001, "there is scholarly consensus on relatively few issues regarding the textual history of OG-Dan and Th-Dan."[8] The present chapter aims only to clarify these issues so far as possible in a short discussion and to the extent that is necessary for the study specifically of chapter 7 in the two versions.

THE DATE OF THE OLD GREEK VERSION

The Old Greek version is generally said to date from the late second or early first century BCE,[9] but in fact there is little firm evidence for its date. Sev-

---

4. It is common to speak of a "proto-Theodotionic" version of other biblical books, but the Theodotionic Daniel does not seem to be related to this version of other books. Nor should it be associated with the so-called *kaige* recension of other biblical books, although this has been proposed: see Amanda M. Davis Bledsoe, "The Relationship of the Different Editions of Daniel: A History of Scholarship," *Currents in Biblical Research* 13 (2015) 175–90, here 180.

5. Cf. Di Lella, "The Textual History," 596: "Though the expression 'Th-Dan' is a misnomer, it seems best to keep this designation to avoid creating further confusion."

6. See chapter 2.1.

7. Cf. Collins, *Daniel*, 3: "On the whole, the Qumran discoveries provide powerful evidence of the antiquity of the textual tradition of the MT." He notes a few cases of variance from the MT.

8. Di Lella, "The Textual History," 604. For the history of scholarship, see Collins, *Daniel*, 4–11; Davis Bledsoe, "The Relationship"; Pace Jeansonne, *The Old Greek*, 24–31.

9. E.g., Di Lella, "The Textual History," 590; Collins, *Daniel*, 8; Davis Bledsoe, "The Relationship," 177.

eral short passages in 1 Maccabees have been cited as dependent on it.[10] The Hebrew original of 1 Maccabees (not extant) was composed around the end of the second century BCE, but unfortunately we do not know when our Greek version of it was made. The statement by Hartman and Di Lella that, since the Greek version of 1 Maccabees is "no earlier than 100 B.C., we may safely conclude that LXX-Daniel originated about that time,"[11] is singularly lacking in logic. That Josephus knew the Greek 1 Maccabees in the late first century CE[12] seems to provide the only firm *terminus ad quem* for it, though it would certainly have been an appropriate work to translate during the Hasmonean period.

But is 1 Maccabees dependent on OG-Daniel? Sharon Pace Jeansonne has argued that the points of contact are not sufficient to show dependence, and her case is a good one in at least three of the four alleged instances.[13] But the fourth case is not so clear. It is the phrase βδέλυγμα ἐρημώσεως ("abomination of desolation") in 1 Maccabees 1:54. According to this verse, people carrying out orders from Antiochus Epiphanes "erected an abomination of desolation [ᾠκοδόμησεν βδέλυγμα ἐρημώσεως] on the altar of burnt offering"[14] in the temple. This appears to echo Daniel 11:31, where, in the Old Greek, agents of the king who in the prophecy represents Antiochus Epiphanes "will give an abomination of desolation" (δώσουσι βδέλυγμα ἐρημώσεως).[15] The context of defiling the sanctuary and putting an end to the sacrifices is the same in both passages (1 Macc 1:45–46; Dan 11:31), and it is plausible that 1 Maccabees intends to record the fulfillment of Daniel's prophecy. If so, it is likely that the Hebrew original of 1 Maccabees echoes the Hebrew text of Daniel. The issue is whether the translator's use of the Greek phrase βδέλυγμα ἐρημώσεως is dependent on the Old Greek of Daniel. It is by no means the only possible translation of the Hebrew phrase, as the different translation in Th-Daniel 11:31 shows (see table 1).[16] But James Montgomery, who appears to think the other

---

10. James A. Montgomery, *A Critical and Exegetical Commentary on the Book of Daniel*, ICC (Edinburgh: T&T Clark, 1927) 38; Louis F. Hartman and Alexander A. Di Lella, *The Book of Daniel*, AB 23 (New York: Doubleday, 1978) 78.

11. Hartman and Di Lella, *The Book of Daniel*, 78.

12. John R. Bartlett, *1 Maccabees*, GAP (Sheffield: Sheffield Academic, 1998) 16–17.

13. Pace Jeansonne, *The Old Greek*, 16–18. The three cases are 1 Macc 1:9 (cf. Dan 12:4); 1:18 (cf. Dan 11:26); 4:41, 43 (cf. Dan 8:14). It should also be noted that the relevant words in Daniel in two cases (11:26; 8:14) are identical in OG-Dan and Th-Dan.

14. NRSV altered.

15. The curious use of "give" (δώσουσι, also in Th-Dan) is an overly literal translation of the Hebrew נתן, which here means "to set up."

16. The use of ἀφανίζω and ἀφανισμός to render the Hebrew root שמם is characteris-

three alleged cases of 1 Maccabees' dependence on OG-Daniel convincing, says of this phrase that it may have arisen contemporaneously with Antiochus's sacrilege.[17] Pace Jeansonne claims that the "phrase appears to have been a slogan or rallying cry by which the community understood their plight," and "may well have been the typical way by which pious Jews referred to the altar or statue which Antiochus had set up in the Temple."[18] But it can be questioned whether "pious Jews" at this date would have used a Greek phrase for this purpose.

If the Greek phrase were standard and well known, we should expect it to be the same in all its occurrences in the Old Greek (Dan 9:27; 11:31; 12:11). As table 1 shows, it is not. The underlying Hebrew phrase also varies in the three instances. What is particularly notable is that the Old Greek varies the phrase between 9:27 and the other two cases in a way that seems to be responding to the very strange Hebrew phrase שקוצים משמם. As André Lacocque observes, this is a linguistic "impossibility." The first word is in the plural, but the predicate is in the singular. (Lacocque suggests that the plural "abominations" is a substitute for the Hebrew אלהים, a plural form that governs a singular verb or predicate.)[19] The translator of OG-Daniel seems to have dealt with the problem by reversing the singular and plural, producing the Greek phrase βδέλυγμα τῶν ἐρημώσεων ("an abomination of the desolations"), different from the phrase he uses in 11:31 and 12:11, where βδέλυγμα ἐρημώσεως renders the Hebrew of those verses more or less literally. If this phrase were, as Pace Jeansonne supposes, "a slogan or rallying cry," he would also have used it in 9:27, in place of the virtually meaningless phrase he uses there to translate the peculiar Hebrew. (βδέλυγμα ἐρημώσεως is usually taken to mean an abomination that desolates or causes desolation, but what could βδέλυγμα τῶν ἐρημώσεων mean?)

It seems likely, therefore, that the Greek phrase βδέλυγμα ἐρημώσεως was invented by the translator of OG-Daniel to render the Hebrew phrase in Daniel 11:31, and the translator of 1 Maccabees used it either because he was familiar with its use in OG-Daniel or because it had gained currency as a result of its use in OG-Daniel. (The phrase also occurs in Th-Dan 12:11 but not

---

tic of Th-Dan: cf. 9:18, 26, and Montgomery, *A Critical and Exegetical Commentary*, 403. The phrase βδέλυγμα ἠφανισμένον (11:31) appears to mean something like "an obliterated abomination" (NETS).

17. Montgomery, *A Critical and Exegetical Commentary*, 38.
18. Pace Jeansonne, *The Old Greek*, 18.
19. André Lacocque, *The Book of Daniel*, trans. David Pellauer (London: SPCK, 1979) 199.

Th-Dan 11:31.[20] So it is less likely, though not impossible, that the translator of 1 Maccabees knew Th-Daniel.)[21]

This investigation leads us to the conclusion that OG-Daniel antedates the Greek version of 1 Maccabees, but since the date of the latter cannot be determined at all precisely, neither, on this evidence, can that of OG-Daniel. Stronger, but rather late, evidence of dependence on OG-Daniel can be found in New Testament writings and in Josephus. Though the allusions to Daniel in New Testament writings require more careful analysis than has been done or can be done here (see the next section of this chapter), the use of OG-Daniel is clear at least in the Gospel of Matthew. Thus, in 24:30 and 26:64 Matthew revises the allusions to Daniel 7:13 in Mark 13:26 and 14:62 to conform them closely to OG-Daniel, while Matthew 28:18b–20 is closely dependent on OG-Daniel 7:13 and 27.[22] As for Josephus, in the *Antiquities* his allusions to Daniel conform more often to OG-Daniel than to Th-Daniel where there are differences between the two versions. This may indicate that Josephus employed a "mixed" text of Daniel or perhaps that where he departs from the wording of OG-Daniel he was working directly from the Hebrew.[23]

The Date of the Th-Daniel

It is now generally recognized that Th-Daniel is substantially a version that existed prior to the Theodotion of the second century CE, though some would explain the traditional connection with Theodotion by supposing that he revised

---

20. Pace Jeansonne, *The Old Greek*, 17–18, is mistaken on this point.

21. It is possible that, since Th-Dan and OG-Dan differ at 11:31, the agreement at 12:11 is due to later textual corruption. This is proposed by R. Timothy McLay, *The OG and Th Versions of Daniel*, Septuagint and Cognate Studies 43 (Atlanta: Scholars Press, 1996) 194, but it goes against his general thesis that OG-Daniel was revised in the direction of MT-Daniel and Th-Daniel. In favor of the originality of βδέλυγμα ἐρημώσεως in Th-Dan 12:11 is the fact that the phrase occurs in Mark 13:14. Mark does not otherwise show signs of dependence on OG-Daniel except at 13:4 (cf. OG-Dan 12:7, but the phrase is a literal version of the Hebrew). In Mark 13:1–27, Mark is working with Dan 12:1–11 (and 7:13), not Dan 11, and so he derives the phrase βδέλυγμα ἐρημώσεως from 12:11, not 11:31 (see chapter 3.4 and table 6 of that chapter). So he could have known it in Th-Dan 12:13 rather than the OG.

22. See chapter 3.7 and table 7 of that chapter.

23. Geza Vermes, "Josephus' Treatment of the Book of Daniel," *JJS* 42 (1991) 149–66, here 161; Christopher T. Begg and Paul Spilsbury, trans. and eds., *Flavius Josephus: Judean Antiquities Books 8–10*, vol. 5 of *Flavius Josephus: Translation and Commentary*, ed. Steve Mason (Leiden: Brill, 2005) 266.

this "proto-Theodotion." A date in the first century CE for the translation of Th-Daniel is usually supported by the claim that New Testament writers and some other early Christian writers show dependence on it, along with the deuterocanonical book of Baruch (sometimes called 1 Baruch to distinguish it from 2 Baruch, the Syriac apocalypse).[24] Unfortunately, as far as it concerns New Testament writers, this claim is problematic because it assumes that their knowledge or use of the book of Daniel was exclusively dependent on one or more existing Greek versions. This may be true in some cases, such as Hebrews, which makes a clear allusion to Th-Daniel 6:22 in 11:33 (Montgomery calls this "the closest correspondence" although it covers only three words in Th-Daniel).[25] But, since Th-Daniel is generally close to MT-Daniel and often uses Greek equivalents for Hebrew words that were standardly used in Jewish translations of the Hebrew scriptures (as does OG-Daniel, but to a notably lesser extent), it would not be surprising if authors writing in Greek while having in mind the Aramaic/Hebrew text of Daniel often produced renderings that coincide with Th-Daniel.[26]

I think this is certainly the case in the book of Revelation, whose author habitually works directly from the Hebrew text of the Jewish scriptures, even if occasionally he echoes an existing Greek version. Two examples will suffice. In Revelation 11:7 the words "will make war with them and conquer them" (ποιήσει μετ' αὐτῶν πόλεμον καὶ νικήσει αὐτούς) correspond closely to the Aramaic text of MT-Daniel 7:21. The allusion is closer to Th-Daniel (ἐποίει πόλεμον μετὰ τῶν ἁγιῶν καὶ ἴσχυσεν πρὸς αὐτούς) than to OG-Daniel (πόλεμον συνιστάμενον πρὸς τοὺς ἁγίους καὶ τροπούμενον αὐτούς), but the explanation is that both Revelation and Th-Daniel are initially very close to the Aramaic (עברה קרב עם־קדישׁין) but then diverge in their respective choices for translating ויכלה (Revelation: νικήσει; Th-Daniel: ἴσχυσεν). By contrast with both, OG-Daniel is somewhat paraphrastic, as is often the case. There is no reason to suppose that the author of Revelation has either Greek version in mind at this point.

---

24. Montgomery, *A Critical and Exegetical Commentary*, 47–50; Di Lella, "The Textual History," 593–94. On Justin, Hermas, and the Epistle of Barnabas, see also Pierre Grelot, "Les Versions Grecques de Daniel," *Bib* 47 (1966) 381–402, here 383–85.

25. Montgomery, *A Critical and Exegetical Commentary*, 49. There is no corresponding matter in OG-Daniel.

26. Cf. McLay, *The OG*, 13, critiques "a basic but misleading assumption that scholars have made, i. e. that common readings prove dependence." The same argument that he applies to the relationship of OG-Daniel and Th-Daniel I am applying to the relationship of Th-Daniel and the New Testament.

Revelation 9:20 corresponds quite extensively to MT-Daniel 5:23, though not without divergence (for περιπατεῖν cf. rather Wis 15:15). The vocabulary, but not the syntax, resembles Th-Daniel 5:23, but comparison of the texts will show that all the words in common are obvious, even necessary, translations of the Aramaic. The correspondence is much as we would expect of two Greek writers independently following MT-Daniel 5:23, whereas OG-Daniel here diverges widely from MT-Daniel. These two examples illustrate how, once we allow that the author of Revelation was a close reader of the Hebrew/Aramaic texts of the Jewish scriptures, his dependence on any Greek version can be shown only by examples where he is unlikely to have produced the same Greek translation independently. I do not think this is the case with Th-Daniel. When we recall that the book of Revelation supplies a very large majority of the alleged cases of dependence on Th-Daniel in the New Testament,[27] the general case for the New Testament writings as evidence for the date of Th-Daniel looks much weaker than has conventionally been supposed. The whole issue requires a fresh and detailed investigation, which should extend also to second-century Christian literature.

However, according to Montgomery, "the most striking parallelism in an early Gr[eek] document with Θ [Theodotion] of Dan[iel] is found in the Epistle of Baruch, the date of which is now commonly placed about A.D. 70."[28] Di Lella states that the translation of Baruch occurred "probably around CE 70,"[29] but both are dependent on an article by John Gwynn, published in 1887.[30] The date 70 CE reflects the view that the last section of this composite work (Bar 4:5–5:9) was written in the light of the fall of Jerusalem to the Romans. But this, like almost everything else concerning the sources, composition, date(s), and translation of this book is debated.[31] It is generally agreed that most of the book, at least, was composed in Hebrew and translated into Greek (the only version now extant). The relationship with Th-Daniel concerns the section 1:15–3:8, a long prayer that is undoubtedly related to the prayer in Dan-

---

27. Twelve out of seventeen in the list given by Davis Bledsoe, "The Relationship," 179.
28. Montgomery, *A Critical and Exegetical Commentary*, 49.
29. Di Lella, "The Textual History," 594.
30. John Gwynn, "Theodotion," in *Dictionary of Christian Biography*, ed. W. Smith and H. Wace (London: Murray, 1877) 4:970–79.
31. See Doron Mendels, "Baruch, Book of," *ABD* 1:618–20; Carey A. Moore, *Daniel, Esther and Jeremiah: The Additions*, AB 44 (New York: Doubleday, 1977) 258–61. Moore dates the "final compilation" (in Hebrew) to the early second century BCE, though the last section (4:5–5:9) may be an addition from the first century BCE.

iel 9:4–19. Scholars do not all agree that the relationship is one of dependence by Baruch on Daniel, but in any case the issue of dependence on Th-Daniel concerns not the original Hebrew composition but its Greek translation. As in the case of 1 Maccabees and OG-Daniel, the question is whether the translator was influenced by Th-Daniel in translating a Hebrew text that was itself verbally close to MT-Daniel. We need to ask the same question as we did of Revelation: Is this a case of dependence or of two translators independently producing similar translations? Montgomery points out instances where Baruch agrees with the Hebrew of Daniel 9 rather than Th-Daniel.[32] The issue needs fresh investigation. It is irresponsible simply to repeat the conclusions of a scholar who wrote 150 years ago when much work has been done on Baruch and on Th-Daniel since his time. But since the date of the translation of Baruch into Greek, like the date of the translation of 1 Maccabees, is likely to remain uncertain,[33] a fresh investigation probably will not throw much light on the issue of the date of Th-Daniel.

The disappointing conclusion is that so far we lack strong evidence of the date of Th-Daniel within the first century, though it seems to me likely that a few New Testament passages (probably including Mark 13:2–27[34] and Heb 11:33) are evidence of at least some form of the version we know as Th-Daniel.

The Relationships between OG-Daniel, Th-Daniel, and MT-Daniel

In this complex issue there are two main questions: (1) Is Th-Daniel a revision of OG-Daniel or an independent translation? (2) Does OG-Daniel or part of it translate a different Semitic *Vorlage* rather than MT-Daniel?

An important fact is that in chapters 4–6 OG-Daniel differs much more widely from MT-Daniel and Th-Daniel than in the other chapters. This has frequently been explained by the hypothesis that in these chapters OG-Daniel had a different *Vorlage* and perhaps also a different translator.[35] A different *Vorlage* for these chapters is accepted by scholars such as Tim McLay who

---

32. Montgomery, *A Critical and Exegetical Commentary*, 50. His own view is that "Ur-Theodotion" was a kind of Hellenistic oral targum, which the translator knew well but could correct from his knowledge of the Hebrew of Daniel.

33. A promising clue may be Emanuel Tov's argument that the translator who revised the OG version of Jer 29–52 also revised Bar 1:1–3:8 (see Mendels, "Baruch," 619).

34. See chapter 3.4.

35. McLay, *The OG*, 212, agrees with Rainer Albertz that OG-Dan 4–6 is the work of a different translator.

do not think the remaining chapters of OG-Daniel reflect a *Vorlage* different from MT-Daniel.[36] A recent article by Andrew Daniel, proposing a different methodology for distinguishing use of a different *Vorlage* from a translator's own rewriting and expansion of the text, concludes, from examples in chapters 4–6, that OG-Daniel as a whole does not depend on a *Vorlage* different from MT-Daniel but is a rewritten version of Daniel and, as such, "categorically different from Theodotion."[37] Since our concern in this chapter focuses on chapter 7 of Daniel, we can leave aside the dispute over chapters 4–6, but we must still attend to the possible reasons why OG-Daniel in the other chapters diverges more from MT-Daniel than Th-Daniel does.

It is often said that Th-Daniel is a more "literal" and OG-Daniel a more "free" translation of MT-Daniel, but these terms are too loose to be very helpful. Pace Jeansonne characterizes the translation technique of the translator of OG-Daniel 7–12 thus:

> In the attempt to translate, the OG translator was most concerned with conveying an accurate rendering in Greek of the Semitic text available. If, on occasion, this required that an antecedent be expressed, a phrase in apposition be added, a paraphrase be used, or that one particular connotation of a word be emphasized, the translator felt free to do so. . . . The OG translator was more concerned with providing an interesting and readable Greek style than a consistent, standardized translation. A variety of syntactical and grammatical usages, a wide vocabulary, and picturesque speech characterize the work. These features are most notable when compared with the recension of [Theodotion].[38]

Pace Jeansonne regards Th-Daniel as a revision of OG-Daniel in a more "literal" direction.

McLay, who thinks OG-Daniel and Th-Daniel are independent translations, characterizes their different translation techniques as, respectively, dynamic and formal equivalence: "TH could be characterized as exhibiting formal equivalence to the source text, whereas OG could be understood as more dynamic or functional in its approach."[39] As a result of his detailed study,

---

36. McLay, *The OG*, 10–12. For others who take this view, see Davis Bledsoe, "The Relationship," 183.

37. Andrew Glen Daniel, "The Translator's Tell: Translation Technique, Verbal Syntax, and the Myth of Old Greek Daniel's Alternative Semitic Vorlage," *JBL* 140 (2021) 723–49.

38. Pace Jeansonne, *The Old Greek*, 132–33.

39. R. Timothy McLay, "Daniel: To the Reader," in *A New English Translation of the*

McLay concludes that the "most consistent characteristic of OG's dynamic approach was variety in the choice of lexical equivalents." OG-Daniel also "employs various methods to avoid excessive parataxis," and makes additions or slight changes to make the implicit explicit. Like Pace Jeansonne, McLay maintains that most changes are attempts to be faithful to "the content and intention of the *Vorlage*."[40] We shall return to the issue of whether the OG translator also interprets the text to an extent that goes beyond this.

According to McLay, the translator of Th-Daniel generally follows a pattern of formal equivalence that includes staying close to the word order of the source text and translating word-for-word. However, he does deviate from this pattern of formal equivalence when clarity and the demands of the Greek language require. He tends to employ standard Greek equivalents for Hebrew and Aramaic words, but not when the semantic range of the former does not overlap with the meaning of the latter in particular contexts. His basic technique of formal equivalence shows his "reverence for the text," but he attempts to "translate faithfully the meaning of the parent text."[41]

Th-Daniel has most often been regarded as a revision of OG-Daniel, designed to bring the text into closer alignment with MT-Daniel,[42] but McLay argues that it is an independent translation. The fact that there is a high degree of verbal agreement between the two versions, "at times as high as 50% through most of chapters 1–3 and 7–12," does not necessarily prove dependence, because most of the common readings "exhibit the typical formal equivalence to the MT that is found throughout the LXX." To prove Th-Daniel's dependence on OG-Daniel, there would need to be a significant number of distinctive agreements. But the picture is confused because, McLay argues, the textual tradition of OG-Daniel (available to us only in three witnesses) has been corrupted by the influence of Th-Daniel. This is only to be expected since the two versions coexisted. "It is impossible to know," argues McLay, how "much of the OG has been irretrievably lost through successive revisions toward MT and Th." So distinctive agreements between the two Greek versions are less likely to be due to Th-Daniel's knowledge of OG-Daniel than to Th-Daniel's influence on the textual tradition of OG-Daniel.[43] One indication that Th-Daniel was not revising OG-Daniel is the respective ways in which the two versions deal with

---

Septuagint, ed. Albert Pietersma and Benjamin G. Wright (New York: Oxford University Press, 2007) 991–94, here 993.

40. McLay, *The OG*, 211–12.
41. McLay, *The OG*, 212–13.
42. E.g., Pace Jeansonne, *The Old Greek*, 22.
43. McLay, *The OG*, 214–15.

texts they had trouble understanding. While OG-Daniel offers a translation based on the context, Th-Daniel sometimes resorts to transliteration of unknown words. In such cases Th-Daniel is clearly not revising OG-Daniel.[44]

McLay does not rule out the possibility that Th-Daniel knew OG-Daniel and occasionally borrowed from it, but he finds evidence of such borrowing scarce.[45] Di Lella's view could be seen as a mediating one. He thinks that the Th-Daniel translator thought OG-Daniel insufficiently accurate and so translated Daniel anew from MT-Daniel, but "with an eye" on OG-Daniel.[46] There seems to be some convergence on the view that Th-Daniel is essentially an independent translation, whose base text was MT-Daniel, even if it was influenced to some degree by OG-Daniel. The difficulty or impossibility of reconstructing the original text of OG-Daniel from the meagre surviving witnesses seems bound to leave us with some uncertainty about the true relationship between the two versions, including their relative dates.

There seems also to be convergence on the view that, outside OG-Daniel 4–6, neither version provides evidence for a Semitic *Vorlage* significantly different from MT-Daniel. However, at this point we must return to the question whether the OG translator interprets the text to an extent that goes beyond faithful translation. A hard line between translation and interpretation cannot be drawn. All translation entails interpretation. A translator often has to resolve a degree of ambiguity in the source text, especially when the semantic range of a word in the source text's language does not match the semantic range of the words that could be used to translate it. For this reason a formal equivalence translation technique that usually employs the same Greek word to translate a particular Hebrew or Aramaic word may be less faithful to the meaning of the source text than a "freer" translation that varies the vocabulary or even paraphrases. The difference between the formal equivalence technique of Th-Daniel and the dynamic equivalence technique of OG-Daniel does not itself mean that the latter is a less faithful translation, but the latter may reveal rather more to us of the way the translator understood his source text.

Often a potential ambiguity in a text may be resolved by clues provided in the context, but it is possible for a translator to overlook those clues or read them differently, resulting in what we, but not the translator, would regard as a misinterpretation of the text. A translator may also expand a text in order to make clearer what he or she takes to be its meaning. In none of these cases are

44. McLay, "Daniel," 992–93.
45. McLay, *The OG*, 216.
46. Di Lella, "The Textual History," 596; also Hartman and Di Lella, *The Book of Daniel*, 82.

we dealing with deliberate theological interpretation of the text, though the translator's choices may reveal how he or she reads the text and may in effect bring the text closer to their own ideological approach where this differs from that of the original author.

Interpretation that goes beyond merely rendering the meaning of a source text, in the intention of the translator, can take the form of deliberately changing the sense of the text, when the translator finds the apparent meaning unacceptable. But it can also take the form of paraphrases and additions that extend or develop what the translator sees in the text. In effect this is a form of commentary embedded in the translation. It is what happens in the Targums and in some forms of what are loosely called "rewritten Bible" texts of the Second Temple period. In a work like the *Biblical Antiquities* of Pseudo-Philo, for example, the text may sometimes stay close to the source text in the Hebrew Bible, while in other passages there may be paraphrases and additions in the manner of the Targums, and in yet other and frequent passages the source text is replaced by extensive new composition. In the case of OG-Daniel, Andrew Daniel concludes from his study of its divergences from MT-Daniel in chapters 4–6 that the OG translator "is not merely translating"[47] but has produced a version of Daniel that belongs with the "rewritten Bible" texts of the Second Temple period.[48] On the other hand, Tim McLay, who thinks that in chapters 4–6 OG-Daniel is dependent on a *Vorlage* different from MT-Daniel, concludes that the translator of OG-Daniel is a faithful translator using the dynamic equivalence technique.[49] But it is possible to envisage a translator who treated the narrative material of chapters 4–6 differently from the prophetic visions of chapters 7–12 (and the dream in chapter 2). He could have regarded the latter as divine revelation that he was not free to rewrite, while using the dynamic equivalence technique to render it faithfully. In our study of passages in chapter 7 we shall have to examine the case for theologically motivated rewriting by the OG. (McLay's selective study does not include chapter 7.)

OG-DANIEL 7:13–14

The OG translation of Daniel 7:13 is potentially of considerable significance for our purpose in part 2 of this book. The interest scholars have shown in OG-Daniel's version of this verse is of course closely related to the attempt

---

47. Daniel, "The Translator's Tell," 748.
48. Daniel, "The Translator's Tell," 747–48.
49. McLay, *The OG*, 212–13.

to reconstruct a Son of Man tradition in which the figure in Daniel 7:13 was understood as a heavenly or even divine figure, closely related to God. If not a witness to a more original, Hebrew form of Daniel 7:13 than the Aramaic of MT-Daniel, as Johan Lust argues,[50] it might constitute the earliest interpretation of Daniel 7:13 and have influenced the interpretation of that verse to be found in the Gospels.[51] Crispin Fletcher-Louis aligns it closely with the interpretation of Daniel 7:13 in the Parables of Enoch, as he understands it: they evidence a common tradition of a Son of Man figure who has some kind of divine identity and is worshiped.[52]

Table 2 displays the extant texts of Daniel 7:13–14: MT-Daniel (Aramaic), Th-Daniel, and the readings of the two Greek manuscripts that are our only witnesses for OG-Daniel. The translations are as literal as possible, keeping the word order of the originals as far as possible, in order to show how far the Greek versions retain the word order of the Aramaic. For ease of discussion, in every case both verses are divided into four verselets (a, b, c, d), a division that conforms to the syntax of the texts.

We should recall that Papyrus 967 dates from the second or early third century CE and Codex 88 from the ninth to the eleventh century CE. The latter is the text of Origen's Hexapla, for which we also have the Syriac version that agrees closely with Codex 88. This is meagre evidence for making an accurate reconstruction of the original text of OG-Daniel,[53] to be dated earlier than the New Testament writings. The differences between Papyrus 967 and Codex 88 show that we do not have an entirely stable text. The word βασιλική (7:14a), present in Papyrus 967 but not in Codex 88, seems almost certain to be original, since it makes this version of Daniel 7:14a a plausible paraphrase of the Aramaic. Its absence from Codex 88 is presumably due to scribal error, since there is no good reason why it should have been deliberately edited out. But the relatively early date of Papyrus 967 does not mean we can rule out the possibility of textual corruption there, since it is the only manuscript we have from the early period.

The differences between Th-Daniel and OG-Daniel in these two verses largely reflect the different translation techniques of the two versions. Th-Daniel is a

---

50. Johan Lust, "Daniel 7,13 and the Septuagint," in *The Son of Man Problem: Critical Readings*, ed. Benjamin E. Reynolds (London: Bloomsbury T&T Clark, 2015) 490–96. This essay was first published in *Expository Times* 54 (1978) 62–69.

51. See Benjamin E. Reynolds, "Introduction to Part 4," in *The Son of Man Problem*, ed. Reynolds, 485–89, here 488–89.

52. Crispin Fletcher-Louis, *Jesus Monotheism*, vol. 1, *Christological Origins: The Emerging Consensus and Beyond* (Eugene, OR: Cascade, 2015) 195–99.The issue of worship relates to Dan 7:14 and will be discussed separately below.

53. See the discussion in Pace Jeansonne, *The Old Greek*, 80.

word-for-word translation, reproducing even the word order of the Aramaic exactly. OG-Daniel (both witnesses) employs dynamic equivalence, resulting in a "freer" but not necessarily less accurate translation for the most part. For example, in 7:14a, the three terms in the Aramaic ("dominion and glory and kingdom") are summed up in the phrase "royal authority" (Pap. 967). But OG-Daniel's differences from MT-Daniel in 7:13b–c require more discussion, since a number of scholars have seen them as theologically motivated changes to MT-Daniel. It will be useful to begin the discussion with 7:13c. I should explain that the translations of ὡς παλαιὸς ἡμερῶν παρῆν (7:13c in Pap. 967 and Cod. 88) given in table 2 are those I judge to be correct, but, as we shall see, there are other proposals.

In MT-Daniel 7:13b, כבר אנש ("like a son of man") functions as the subject of the verbal phrase אתה הוה ("was coming") and so is usually rendered "one like a son of man." Th-Daniel translates this Semitism literally, so that ὡς υἱὸς ἀνθρώπου functions as the subject of the verbal phrase ἐρχόμενος ἦν. The OG also translates the phrase literally, but in the next verselet (13c) there follows a similar phrase, ὡς παλαιὸς ἡμερῶν, where Th-Daniel has a literal translation of the Aramaic: ἕως τοῦ παλαιοῦ τῶν ἡμερῶν.

To explain the phrase ὡς παλαιὸς ἡμερῶν in OG-Daniel 7:13c, an obvious possibility is textual corruption. An original εως was miscopied by a scribe as ως. This explanation, which has been adopted by a number of scholars,[54] has been developed and justified most fully by Pace Jeansonne.[55] She argues that the text of OG-Daniel 7:13c–d was corrupted in three stages. In the first stage ως replaced εως. The case for postulating such an error is strongly supported by the fact that in two other places in OG-Daniel the two manuscripts, Papyrus 967 and Codex 88, vary between ως and εως (Dan 2:43; 4:33[30]).[56] In the second stage of corruption a scribe realized that ως should be followed by the nominative, not the genitive case, and so "corrected" παλαιου to παλαιος. A third stage affected 7:13d, where Papyrus 967 has προσηγαγον but Codex 88 has παρῆσαν. Pace Jeansonne argues that the former is more original and the latter reading arose through scribal error, influenced by the use of the verb πάρειμι in 7:13c (παρην).[57] This third stage is not essential to the argument: the difference might be explained in other ways. But the first two stages seem a

---

54. Montgomery, *A Critical and Exegetical Commentary*, 304; Collins, *Daniel*, 319; Maurice Casey, *Son of Man: The Interpretation and Influence of Daniel 7* (London: SPCK, 1979) 132; Adela Yarbro Collins, "The 'Son of Man' Tradition and the Book of Revelation," in *The Messiah: Developments in Earliest Judaism and Christianity*, ed. James H. Charlesworth (Minneapolis: Fortress, 1992) 571–97, here 553–55.

55. Pace Jeansonne, *The Old Greek*, 96–99.

56. Pace Jeansonne, *The Old Greek*, 98.

57. Pace Jeansonne, *The Old Greek*, 98.

very plausible explanation of the peculiar reading of OG-Daniel 7:13c, around which so much discussion has taken place.

As Adela Yarbro Collins points out, "It is better to explain variants as mechanical errors when such an explanation is credible."[58] But Loren Stuckenbruck has raised two objections to Pace Jeansonne's reconstruction of textual history. He claims that it does not explain παρῆν in 7:13c, because an original reading ἕως παλαιοῦ ἡμερῶν παρῆν would not make sense. But this is based on the presumption that the verb πάρειμι can only mean "to be present."[59] In fact, παρῆν could properly be translated "came," as in, for example, Acts 12:20: παρῆσαν πρὸς αὐτὸν (NRSV: "they came to him").[60]

Stuckenbruck's second objection to Pace Jeansonne's case is that it is hard to believe that a scribe (at the second stage of corruption) made the grammatical correction of παλαιου to παλαιος without realizing the theological significance of the resulting phrase ὡς παλαιὸς ἡμερῶν.[61] But this presupposes Stuckenbruck's own understanding of the meaning of OG-Daniel 7:13b–c—that is, that the phrase ὡς παλαιὸς ἡμερῶν describes "one like a son of man." In that case, the theological significance is remarkable, if also obscure. But if, as I shall argue, the phrase would most naturally be understood to mean "one like an ancient of days" (see the OG translations in table 2), Stuckenbruck's objection does not hold. There is nothing theologically very remarkable about OG-Daniel 7:13b–c if it means "one like a son of man came and one like an ancient of days was present."

Although it is very plausible that the extant text of OG-Daniel 7:13 resulted from a process of textual corruption, it is nonetheless still relevant to ask how the extant text would have been understood by scribes who continued to copy it and readers who read it. For this purpose we can examine the arguments of those scholars who contend that the extant text is a deliberate theological revision of MT-Daniel as well those who examine the meaning of the extant text regardless of how it may have come about.

Most such scholars regard the phrase ὡς παλαιὸς ἡμερῶν as describing the

---

58. Collins, "The 'Son of Man' Tradition," 555. By contrast, Fletcher-Louis, *Jesus Monotheism*, 196–99, fails even to mention the possibility of textual corruption.

59. Loren T. Stuckenbruck, "'One like a Son of Man as the Ancient of Days' in the Old Greek Recension of Daniel 7:13: Scribal Error or Theological Translation?," in *The Son of Man Problem*, ed. Reynolds, 497–507, here 501.

60. Other examples are given in BAGD 773; Otfried Hofius, "The Septuagint Version of Daniel 7:13–14: Deliberations on Form and Substance," in *The Son of Man Problem*, ed. Reynolds, 508–22, here 512 n. 21.

61. Stuckenbruck, "'One like a Son of Man,'" 502.

same figure as the "one like a son of man," usually without argument. They take the phrase to mean either "like the Ancient of Days," comparing the "one like a son of man" with the Ancient of Days, or "as the Ancient of Days," in some sense identifying him with the Ancient of Days. But it is not clear how this works syntactically. Martin Hengel and Seyoon Kim propose the translation "he came like a son of man and was present like an ancient of days [or "as the Ancient of Days"]."[62] But this cannot be correct, because "he" would be without an antecedent. The phrase ὡς υἱὸς ἀνθρώπου must function as the subject of the verb (ἤρχετο) in 7:13b, just as the equivalent phrases do in MT-Daniel and Th-Daniel.[63]

Accepting this argument, other scholars translate the text along these lines: "one like a son of man came and he was present as/like the Ancient of Days."[64] The "one like a son of man" is said either to resemble the Ancient of Days ("like") or to be present in the same way as the Ancient of Days ("as"). These scholars have then debated the sense in which either of these claims is intended.[65] A problem with this view is that the two closely similar phrases, ὡς υἱὸς ἀνθρώπου and ὡς παλαιὸς ἡμερῶν, are understood to have different meanings: the first functions as a substantive ("one like . . ."), the second as an adverbial phrase ("as/like . . ."). Would not readers have been likely to understand them as strictly parallel? The great merit of Gotfried Hosius's quite different interpretation of the text (which I have adopted in table 2) is that it does justice to the parallelism:

> And see, one came on the clouds of the heavens who looked
> > like a man
> and the one who looked like an Ancient of Days was present.[66]

---

62. Martin Hengel, *Studies in Early Christology* (Edinburgh: T&T Clark, 1995) 183; Seyoon Kim, *"The Son of Man" as the Son of God*, WUNT 30 (Tübingen: Mohr Siebeck, 1983) 23.

63. Stuckenbruck, "'One like a Son of Man,'" 498 n. 4; Hofius, "The Septuagint Version," 517.

64. Cf. Benjamin E. Reynolds, "The 'One Like a Son of Man' According to the Old Greek of Daniel 7:13," in *The Son of Man Problem*, ed. Reynolds, 523-34, here 525; Stuckenbruck, "'One like a Son of Man,'" 498 n. 4.

65. E.g., Stuckenbruck, "'One like a Son of Man,'" 506 (functionally identified with God); Reynolds, "The 'One Like a Son of Man,'" 526 (similar to but not identical with the Ancient of Days); Christopher Rowland, *The Open Heaven: A Study of Apocalyptic in Judaism and Early Christianity* (London: SPCK, 1982) 98 ("the son of man is the embodiment of the person of the Ancient of Days").

66. Hofius, "The Septuagint Version," 520.

PART 2 · INTERPRETATION OF DANIEL 7 IN SECOND TEMPLE-PERIOD JUDAISM

The same translation has been independently offered by Timothy Meadowcroft:

> On the clouds of heaven one like a son of man came
> and one like an ancient of days was nearby.[67]

It is surprising that this rather obvious possibility for interpreting the text has not occurred to other scholars. As Hofius says, the structural parallelism of these two verselets indicates that just as ὡς υἱὸς ἀνθρώπου is the subject of ἤρχετο, so ὡς παλαιὸς ἡμερῶν is the subject of παρῆν.[68] This is the most natural reading of the text and gives a more straightforward sense than the attempt to make ὡς υἱὸς ἀνθρώπου the subject of παρῆν.[69]

The use of ὡς with a noun in this manner (representing Hebrew or Aramaic כ + noun) is a Semitic idiom used in visionary literature with the sense "something like...." It signals that what is seen is vision, not mundane reality. The idiom occurs elsewhere in OG-Daniel in 8:14; 10:16, 18.[70] Similar expressions are used throughout Ezekiel's inaugural vision (OG 1:4, 5, 13, 22, 26, 27, 28). Scribes and readers of OG-Daniel would be familiar with the idiom and not be at all surprised to find it used in the expression ὡς παλαιὸς ἡμερῶν. It could even be seen to correct the impression that God actually is an aged human, which might be obtained from a literal reading of 7:9.

"On the Clouds of Heaven"

Although Meadowcroft does not think the phrase ὡς παλαιὸς ἡμερῶν compares the humanlike figure with the Ancient of Days, there is another feature of OG-Daniel 7:13 that he, like some other scholars,[71] thinks is indicative of the divinity of the "one like a son of man."[72] The Aramaic phrase עִם־עֲנָנֵי שְׁמַיָּא ("with the clouds of heaven") is translated in Th-Daniel in the most obviously

---

67. T. J. Meadowcroft, *Aramaic Daniel and Greek Daniel: A Literary Comparison*, Journal for the Study of the Old Testament Supplement Series 198 (Sheffield: Sheffield Academic, 1995) 224.

68. Hofius, "The Septuagint Version," 518.

69. The objections to Hofius's proposal raised by Reynolds, "The 'One Like a Son of Man,'" 526-27, could only have any force if OG-Dan 7:13 were a free composition, not if the phrase ὡς παλαιὸς ἡμερῶν resulted in the first place from a scribal error. Reynolds argues that 7:13b-c is an example of poetic parallelism, in which both lines refer to the same figure, said to be "like a son of man" and "like the Ancient of Days." But the passage is not poetry.

70. It is also used in 4 Ezra 11:37; Rev 4:5; 8:8; 9:7; 15:2; cf. 19:1, 6.

71. Lust, "Daniel 7,13," 495; Reynolds, "The 'One Like a Son of Man,'" 528-29.

72. Meadowcroft, *Aramaic Daniel*, 224-28.

literal way as μετὰ τῶν νεφελῶν τοῦ οὐρανοῦ, but in OG-Daniel as ἐπὶ τῶν νεφελῶν τοῦ οὐρανοῦ ("on the clouds of heaven"). Some scholars think the difference of prepositions is insignificant.[73] Pace Jeansonne points out that, whereas Th-Daniel tries consistently to match each Aramaic preposition with a Greek equivalent, OG-Daniel characteristically varies the Greek prepositions. For the OG, she writes, "επι is the most frequently used preposition, found for אל, על, -ב, לפני, and עד. The OG may have used it for עם as well, if this were indeed in the *Vorlage*."[74] Expanding the last phrase, she argues that there was much confusion in the copying of prepositions from one Hebrew or Aramaic manuscript to another and in the Greek translation of such prepositions. Thus the OG translator could have found a preposition other than עם in Daniel 7:13, or have misread עם as עד or על.[75] These are, of course, real possibilities.

However, Meadowcroft, in a more detailed examination of the evidence, shows that, specifically with reference to the prepositions עם and על, there is "a remarkable consistency" in the way the OG translator represents them in Daniel 2–7.[76] The translation of עם in its fifteen occurrences varies considerably, but in each case except 7:13, the translation is "an attempt at a particular portion of its semantic range. Such is clearly not the case" at 7:13. Conversely, among the fifty-six occurrences of ἐπί in these chapters of OG-Daniel, it corresponds to עם only in 7:13.[77] Meadowcroft reaches this conclusion: "The point of all this is to suggest that the [OG] translator does distinguish between עם and על. From whatever angle the rendering of prepositions from Aramaic into Greek is examined, the distinction is observed except at 7:13." He explains this by postulating that the Aramaic *Vorlage* had על at 7:13.[78]

So it would appear that, whether the use of ἐπί is to be attributed to the OG's *Vorlage* or seen as a deliberate modification of the sense of MT-Daniel by the OG translator, there must be some significance in its difference from MT-Daniel. Along with a number of other scholars,[79] Meadowcroft explains this difference from the usage of the Hebrew Bible where clouds are associated with God. There are, of course, many texts that in a variety of ways associate God with clouds. He is often said to be hidden in or appears in a cloud or

---

73. John Goldingay, *Daniel*, WBC 30 (Dallas: Word, 1989) 145; R. B. Y. Scott, "Behold, He Cometh with Clouds," *NTS* 5 (1958–59) 127–32.
74. Pace Jeansonne, *The Old Greek*, 112.
75. Pace Jeansonne, *The Old Greek*, 113.
76. Meadowcroft, *Aramaic Daniel*, 225.
77. Meadowcroft, *Aramaic Daniel*, 225.
78. Meadowcroft, *Aramaic Daniel*, 226.
79. Cf. Montgomery, *Daniel*, 303.

clouds (e.g., Exod 13:21–22; 40:34–35; Lev 16:2; 1 Kgs 8:10–11; Lam 3:44; Ps 97:2; cf. 2 Macc 2:8). The clouds in such cases function to hide the otherwise unbearable glory of the Lord's presence. So it is, not surprisingly, rare for God to be said to be "on" a cloud or clouds, in which case he would presumably not be hidden. There are only two examples in the Hebrew Bible. In Isaiah 19:1 it is said that "YHWH is riding on a swift cloud [רכב על־עב קל] and comes to Egypt." Here the OG uses the preposition ἐπὶ (κάθεται ἐπὶ νεφέλης κούφης). The other example is in Psalm 68:4[5], where God is described as "him who rides upon the clouds" (לרכב בערבות).[80] Here the preposition -ב is used rather than על. The OG has ἐπὶ but no clouds: "him who rides upon the sunset" (τῷ ἐπιβεβηκότι ἐπὶ δυσμῶν). The third example is in Psalm 104:3: "who makes the clouds his chariot, who rides on the wings of the wind" (my translation). In this example it is not so clear that God is "on" the clouds. Rather, he sits in the chariot of clouds and rides on the wings of the wind, as also happens in Psalm 18:10–11[11–12], where he rides on the wings of the wind and the clouds function, not to transport him, but to hide him. The OG here (Ps 103:3 [104:3]) has "who makes the clouds what he steps on [ὁ τιθεὶς νέφη τὴν ἐπίβασιν αὐτοῦ], who walks on wings of winds."[81] It should be noted that the only text in the Hebrew Bible that uses either על or, in the OG, ἐπί to describe God as "on" a cloud or clouds is Isaiah 19:1.

On the basis of these texts, Meadowcroft concludes that "the figure in v.13 who arrives 'on' (ἐπί) the clouds is likely to be divine. The same cannot necessarily be said of the one who arrives 'with' (עם) the clouds."[82] On the other hand, Pace Jeansonne thinks there is not enough evidence to warrant such a conclusion.[83]

What the discussions of this issue seem to neglect is the function of the cloud(s). In most cases in which God is associated with clouds, they function to conceal his glory while indicating his presence in the clouds. They are not a means of transport. This is clear in Psalm 18:10–11, where the clouds conceal his presence and the winds are his means of transport. The distinction makes meteorological sense and should not be fudged.[84] In Isaiah 19:1, on the other

---

80. This description parallels a common epithet of Baal in Ugaritic literature: "rider of the clouds" (Pace Jeansonne, *The Old Greek*, 111–12). While this Canaanite usage may lie in the background to Ps 68 itself, it is unlikely to have been known to Jewish writers in the late Second Temple period.

81. I have modified the NETS translation.

82. Meadowcroft, *Aramaic Daniel*, 228. Cf. Fletcher-Louis, *Jesus Monotheism*, 197: "The man figure has a specifically divine prerogative in his travelling on clouds."

83. Pace Jeansonne, *The Old Greek*, 112.

84. Note also 1 En. 14:8, where various meteorological phenomena are associated with Enoch's ascent to heaven. Clouds summon him, but winds carry him up to heaven.

hand, the cloud is clearly the means of transport, a means of transport appropriate to a heavenly figure associated with the sky. This provides the obvious reason why OG-Daniel 7:13 makes the humanlike figure come "on (ἐπί) the clouds of heaven." Whether the humanlike figure is understood to be coming from earth to God's throne in heaven or from heaven to God's throne on earth or from one part of heaven to another, the clouds are obviously his mode of transport in the heavenly sphere.[85]

If the OG translator found עִם in his *Vorlage*, as in MT-Daniel, he probably wished to clarify the function of the clouds by making clear that they are the vehicle that bears the humanlike figure to the throne of God. Their function in the Aramaic is unclear.[86] Th-Daniel translates עִם literally as μετά, leaving the function unclear. The translator of OG-Daniel, on the other hand, is characteristically concerned to clarify the meaning of his source text. Ἐπί is not a good translation of עִם, and so OG-Daniel does not render עִם as ἐπί anywhere else. But in this case the translator felt the need to explain his source text by clarifying the function of the clouds. To suppose that he did so because, on the basis of one or two texts in the Hebrew Bible, clouds are God's means of transport is entirely unnecessary. He uses ἐπί not to give the humanlike figure an aura of divinity but simply to clarify what the clouds are doing in the text: they carry the humanlike figure from place to place.

The "Worship" of the "One like a Son of Man"

There is a third feature of OG-Daniel 7:13–14 that is alleged to indicate the "divinity" of the "one like a son of man": the word λατρεύουσα (7:14b). Th-Daniel here has δουλεύσουσιν. Both are plausible renderings of the Aramaic verb פלח, which, like the Hebrew עבד, has the broad meaning of "to work" or "to serve (someone as a slave)" but can also be used of the cultic service of God or gods. In Daniel it has the latter sense in at least seven of its nine occurrences (3:12, 14, 17, 18, 28; 6:17, 21). The remaining two, which require discussion here, are in 7:14, 27. The Greek verb λατρεύω, though it had a broader usage in nonbiblical Greek, is used in biblical Greek (as also in the New Testament)

---

85. Hofius, "The Septuagint Version," 517, recognizes that ἐπί gives the clouds the function of transport, but he unnecessarily specifies this as movement from earth to heaven.

86. See especially Goldingay, *Daniel*, 167. Arguing that the throne of God and the court are located on earth, he sees the phrase "among the clouds of heaven" as intended to indicate that the "one like a son of man" is coming to earth from heaven.

exclusively for the cultic service of God or gods,[87] whereas δουλεύω, though it can be used in this sense, also has a broader semantic range, referring to service to a human master or superior.

OG-Daniel translates פלח with λατρεύω on seven of its nine occurrences (3:12, 14, 18, 28[95]; 6:17, 21; 7:14). The OG translator's tendency to vary vocabulary accounts for the use of φοβέω rather than λατρεύω at 3:17. More notable is the OG's use of ὑποτάσσω to translate פלח in 7:27 (see table 3). In addition to the seven cases where λατρεύω represents פלח, OG-Daniel also uses λατρεύω twice where there is no corresponding word in MT-Daniel (4:34; 6:27).

Th-Daniel agrees with OG-Daniel in most of these cases. It translates פלח with λατρεύω on seven occasions (3:12, 14, 17, 18, 28[95]; 6:17, 21). As we might expect of Th-Daniel, this use is somewhat more consistent than OG-Daniel's, since it includes 3:17, but it is less consistent in that Th-Daniel uses δουλεύω to translate פלח in both 7:14 and 7:27. It looks as though in 7:14, where "all the peoples, tribes, and languages" serve the "one like a son of man," the Th-Daniel translator thought λατρεύω, given its strong association with the worship of divinities, not appropriate, and preferred the more general word δουλεύω, which could refer unproblematically to serving a human person. In Th-Daniel 7:27, however, the object of service is "the Most High" (ὑψίστου),[88] and so we might expect the translator to revert to translating פלח with λατρεύω. If the use of δουλεύω here is more than an unreflective continuation of the use in 7:14, the reason for choosing δουλεύω may be that it seemed more appropriate for use in combination with ὑπακούω ("they will serve and pay heed to him").

It is striking that, whereas at 7:14 Th-Daniel diverges from its previous practice in translating פלח, OG-Daniel does not. The translator must have thought λατρεύω an appropriate word to use for the service given by "all the nations of the earth" and "every glory" to the "one like a son of man," after he was given "royal authority." Before considering the significance of this, we should also note that OG-Daniel does diverge from its previous practice in translating פלח at 7:27, where the verb ὑποτάσσω ("to be subjected to") is used. In OG-Daniel, different in this respect from Th-Daniel, the object of the verb may be "the holy people" (λαῷ ἁγίῳ) rather than "the Most High" (ὑψίστου). In that case, the OG translator may have thought that the "one like a son of man" was an appropriate object of λατρεύω but the people of Israel were not.

---

87. Meadowcroft, *Aramaic Daniel*, 107–8; Takamitsu Muraoka, *A Greek-English Lexicon of the Septuagint* (Leuven: Peeters, 2009) 426.

88. This is the only available antecedent for αὐτῷ.

But it is perhaps more likely that, as I have suggested in the case of Th-Daniel, he thought that in the combination of two verbs ("will be subjected to him and obey him") the sense was better conveyed by ὑποτάσσω.

Th-Daniel's use of δουλεύω rather than λατρεύω in 7:14 very likely reflects a monotheistic restriction of worship to the Ancient of Days. Evidently the OG translator did not feel this restraint. Two other features of 7:14 in OG-Daniel should be noted. First, the "royal authority" is *given* to the "one like a son of man" by (it is implied) the Ancient of Days. It does not belong to him inherently. It is only as a consequence of this investiture with authority that he receives the service of all the nations. Second, the emphatic description of the eternity of the authority of the "one like a son of man" in 7:14c–d strongly echoes the description of the kingdom that God will set up in the future according to OG-Daniel 2:44, but also resembles the description of God's eternal authority in OG-Daniel 4:34. OG-Daniel lacks the descriptions of God's eternal rule in MT-Daniel 4:3 and 6:26, but it is nevertheless clear that it is God's eternal rule that is delegated to the humanlike figure in 7:14.[89] No doubt this is why the OG translator thought λατρεύω the appropriate rendering of פלח here. It is God's sovereignty, exercised by the humanlike one, that the nations will serve. This is the limited sense in which OG-Daniel uses "divine" language about the "one like a son of man."[90]

There is a resemblance here to the passages in the Parables of Enoch in which "the kings and the mighty" do obeisance not only to God but also to the Messianic Figure.[91] As in Daniel 7:14, this represents the subjection of the rebellious powers to the eschatological reign of God, and the Messianic Figure receives this obeisance as the one who carries out God's judgment at that time. The difference between OG-Daniel and the Parables of Enoch, in this respect, is that the latter makes a clear terminological distinction between the cultic worship of God, given only to God, and the political obeisance that is offered to both God and the Messianic Figure. Th-Daniel also makes such a distinction (distinguishing λατρεύω and δουλεύω). In OG-Daniel, on the other hand, λατρεύω is used for both the cultic worship of God and the polit-

---

89. It is also universal rule, in the sense of being exercised over all nations, but we should note that, according to OG-Daniel, the fourth kingdom also rules over the whole earth (7:23), while Nebuchadnezzar's subjects are all nations and peoples and languages (4:34b). Such language indicates universal earthly rule, not cosmic rule.

90. So Fletcher-Louis, *Jesus Monotheism*, 197, exaggerates considerably when he claims, "He is worshipped *because he manifests and expresses the divine identity, and because he possesses (delegated) divine prerogatives*" (italics original).

91. See chapter 1.4.

ical subjection of the nations to the "one like a son of man" when he receives the kingdom. But it is nevertheless true that in OG-Daniel 7:14 λατρεύω refers at least primarily to political subjection.

OG-Daniel 7:8b

At the end of 7:8 OG-Daniel has six words that have no parallel in MT-Daniel or Th-Daniel: "And it [the little horn] made war against the holy ones" (καὶ ἐποίει πόλεμον πρὸς τοὺς ἁγίους). These words are best explained, not as a translation of OG-Daniel's *Vorlage*,[92] but as an addition, an example of the OG translator's tendency to explain and interpret the source text. In MT-Daniel there is no mention of "the holy ones" or of the action taken against them by the "little horn" in Daniel's dream itself (7:2–14), but in the interpretation of the dream he is told that "this horn made war with the holy ones and was prevailing over them" (7:21). The OG translator evidently thought that the dream itself ought to contain something to which this element in the interpretation would relate. So, borrowing the words from 7:22, he added 7:8b. At 7:21 his preference for varying the language explains his somewhat different translation: "And I was observing that horn preparing for war against the holy ones and routing them" (καὶ κατενόουν τὸ κέρας ἐκεῖνο πόλεμον συνιστάμενον πρὸς τοὺς ἁγίους καὶ τροπούμενον αὐτούς).

Modern interpreters of Daniel 7 have often argued that the "one like a son of man" is a symbol for the "the holy ones of the Most High," supporting this with the observation that the "holy ones" appear in the interpretation of the dream but not in the dream itself, while the "one like a son of man" appears in the dream but not in the interpretation. The words that OG-Daniel adds at the end of 7:8 show that this translator did not share that view. He clearly thought that the "one like a son of man" was an individual distinct from the "holy ones."[93] He surely did not make the addition *in order* to clarify this point, but the addition shows that he took it for granted. This is of considerable interest for the history of interpretation of Daniel 7 in the late Second Temple period and aligns OG-Daniel in this respect with our other evidence of the way the humanlike figure of Daniel 7 was understood.

---

92. As Meadowcroft, *Aramaic Daniel*, 216, thinks.
93. This point is made by Benjamin Reynolds, "The 'One Like a Son of Man,'" 533.

CONCLUSION

About the origins and relationship of the two Greek versions of Daniel, much remains obscure. OG-Daniel probably originated prior to the Greek version of 1 Maccabees, Matthew's Gospel, and the *Antiquities* of Josephus, but the evidence is not sufficient for us to be more precise. Much of the evidence commonly cited to date Th-Daniel prior to the late first century is not persuasive, but it remains likely that it existed before the New Testament writings. Recent research seems to indicate that Th-Daniel is not a revision of OG-Daniel but an independent translation, perhaps made with some reference to OG-Daniel. Arguments for the view that OG-Daniel is a translation of a *Vorlage* different from MT-Daniel are unpersuasive, at least for most of the book, though it is possible that chapters 4–5, where OG-Daniel differs widely from MT-Daniel, reflect a different *Vorlage*.

The two versions are characterized by different translation techniques, with Th-Daniel aiming at formal equivalence and OG-Daniel at dynamic equivalence. These entail different notions of what accurate translation would be. In order to convey the sense of the source text as he understood it (which might not, of course, be the original author's intention), the OG translator used a wide vocabulary, made additions to clarify the meaning, and on occasion paraphrased. In narrative he might also be concerned to tell the story in a lively and appealing manner. All translation entails interpretation, but OG-Daniel's translation technique reveals more of how the translator understood the source text than Th-Daniel's does. Whether the OG translator deliberately suppressed what he understood to be the meaning of the source text, replacing it with a theologically more acceptable text, cannot easily be demonstrated, though it cannot be ruled out. Even the translator of Th-Daniel, with its generally word-for-word equivalence, had to make interpretative choices in deciding how to translate the source text.

In the context of this book, interest attaches especially to the translations of Daniel 7:13–14 and the question whether the versions embody a particular interpretation of the "one like a son of man." In OG-Daniel some scholars have argued that the phrase ὡς παλαιὸς ἡμερῶν implies the divinity of the humanlike figure, expressing his resemblance to or even identity with the Ancient of Days. It is likely that the reading developed originally from a scribal error (ὡς for ἕως). When copied and read in the manuscript tradition, its obvious meaning would have been "one like an ancient of days," construed as the subject of the verb ("one like an ancient of days was there"). It says nothing about the "one like a son of man." Nor does OG-Daniel's use of the preposition ἐπί in the phrase "coming on the clouds of heaven" imply anything about the divinity of this figure. It is a clarificatory translation, typical of OG-Daniel, making clear that the function of the clouds is to transport the "one like a son of man." The claim that traveling on clouds was a divine prerogative is not adequately based on evidence.

Of more theological consequence is the difference between Th-Daniel and OG-Daniel in translating the Aramaic verb פלח in 7:14b. Th-Daniel's use of δουλεύω, departing from its previous use of λατρεύω, must be based on a monotheistic conviction that cultic service, implied by λατρεύω, should not be offered to any figure other than the one God. OG-Daniel, however, continues its regular practice of using λατρεύω to render פלח, doubtless because the royal authority delegated to the humanlike figure is the eternal sovereignty of God. Unlike Th-Daniel and the Parables of Enoch, the OG translator was evidently not concerned to distinguish terminologically between the cultic worship of God and the political obeisance that is due not only to God but also to his eschatological deputy. But such obeisance is appropriately given to the "one like a son of man" only after he has been given royal authority (7:14a). It does not require OG-Daniel to depict the humanlike figure as already some kind of divinity in 7:13.

Finally, the additional content of OG-Daniel at 7:8 is also significant for the translator's understanding of the "one like a son of man." It shows that he could not have understood the latter to be a mere symbol of the holy ones of the Most High, as many modern scholars do. In OG-Daniel both the holy ones and the humanlike figure appear in Daniel's dream. The latter must be an individual distinct from the holy ones. OG-Daniel here agrees with other examples of Jewish understanding of this figure in the late Second Temple period.

TABLE 1. *"The abomination of desolation"*

Daniel 8:13	MT	וְהַפֶּשַׁע שֹׁמֵם
	OG	ἡ ἁμαρτία ἐρημώσεως
	Th	ἡ ἁμαρτία ἐρημώσεως
Daniel 9:27	MT	שִׁקּוּצִים מְשֹׁמֵם
	OG	βδέλυγμα τῶν ἐρημώσεων
	Th	βδέλυγμα τῶν ἐρημώσεων
Daniel 11:31	MT	הַשִּׁקּוּץ מְשׁוֹמֵם
	OG	βδέλυγμα ἐρημώσεως
	Th	βδέλυγμα ἠφανισμένον
Daniel 12:11	MT	שִׁקּוּץ שֹׁמֵם
	OG	τὸ βδέλυγμα τῆς ἐρημώσεως
	Th	βδέλυγμα ἐρημώσεως
1 Maccabees 1:54		βδέλυγμα ἐρημώσεως
Mark 13:14		τὸ βδέλυγμα τῆς ἐρημώσεως
Matthew 24:15		τὸ βδέλυγμα τῆς ἐρημώσεως

TABLE 2. *Daniel 7:13–14: the versions*

Aramaic (MT)

חָזֵה הֲוֵית בְּחֶזְוֵי לֵילְיָא	13a
וַאֲרוּ עִם־עֲנָנֵי שְׁמַיָּא כְּבַר אֱנָשׁ אָתֵה הֲוָה	b
וְעַד־עַתִּיק יוֹמַיָּא מְטָה	c
הַקְרְבוּהִי׃ וּקְדָמוֹהִי	d
וְלֵהּ יְהִיב שָׁלְטָן וִיקָר וּמַלְכוּ	14a
וְכֹל עַמְמַיָּא אֻמַּיָּא וְלִשָּׁנַיָּא לֵהּ יִפְלְחוּן שָׁלְטָנֵהּ	b
שָׁלְטָן עָלַם דִּי־לָא יֶעְדֵּה	c
וּמַלְכוּתֵהּ דִּי־לָא תִתְחַבַּל	d

13 a I saw in the night visions
    b and behold! with the clouds of heaven one like a son of man was coming,
    c to the Ancient of Days he came
    d and before him he was presented.
14 a And to him was given dominion and glory and kingdom,
    b that all peoples, nations, and languages should serve him.
    c His dominion is an everlasting dominion that shall not pass away,
    d and his kingdom one that shall not be destroyed.

Theodotion

13a ἐθεώρουν ἐν ὁράματι τῆς νυκτὸς
  b καὶ ἰδοὺ μετὰ τῶν νεφελῶν τοῦ οὐρανοῦ ὡς υἱὸς ἀνθρώπου ἐρχόμενος ἦν
  c καὶ ἕως τοῦ παλαιοῦ τῶν ἡμερῶν ἔφθασεν
  d καὶ ἐνώπιον αὐτοῦ προσηνέχθη.
14a καὶ αὐτῷ ἐδόθη ἡ ἀρχὴ καὶ ἡ τιμὴ καὶ ἡ βασιλεία,
  b καὶ πάντες οἱ λαοί, φυλαί, γλῶσσαι αὐτῷ δουλεύσουσιν·
  c ἡ ἐξουσία αὐτοῦ ἐξουσία αἰώνιος, ἥτις οὐ παρελεύσεται,
  d καὶ ἡ βασιλεία αὐτοῦ οὐ διαφθαρήσεται.

13a I was watching in the night visions
  b and behold! with the clouds of heaven one like a son of man was coming,
  c and to the Ancient of Days he came
  d and before him was presented.
14a And to him was given the dominion and the honor and the kingdom,

b   and all the peoples, tribes, and languages were serving him.
c   His authority is an everlasting authority that shall never pass away,
d   and his kingdom will never perish.

Papyrus 967

13a ἐθεώρουν ἐν ὁράματι τῆς νυκτὸς
b   καὶ ἰδοὺ ἐπὶ τῶν νεφελῶν τοῦ οὐρανοῦ ἤρχετο ὡς υἱὸς ἀνθρώπου,
c   καὶ ὡς παλαιὸς ἡμερῶ(ν) παρῆν,
d   καὶ οἱ παρεστηκότες προσήγαγον αὐτῷ.
14a καὶ ἐδόθη αὐτῷ ἐξουσία βασιλική,
b   καὶ πάντα τὰ ἔθνη τῆς γῆς κατὰ γένη καὶ πᾶσα δόξα λατρεύουσα αὐτῷ
c   καὶ ἡ ἐξουσία αὐτοῦ ἐξουσία αἰώνιος, ἥτις οὐ μὴ ἀρθῇ,
d   καὶ ἡ βασιλεία αὐτοῦ, ἥτις οὐ μὴ φθαρῇ.

13a I was watching in the night visions
b   and behold! on the clouds of heaven came one like a son of man,
c   and one like an ancient of days was present,
d   and the bystanders approached him.
14a And there was given to him royal authority,
b   and all the nations of the earth according to their lineage and every glory was serving him,
c   and his authority is an eternal authority that shall never be removed,
d   and his kingdom one that shall never perish.

Codex 88 (supported by the Syro-Hexaplar)

13a ἐθεώρουν ἐν ὁράματι τῆς νυκτὸς
b   καὶ ἰδοὺ ἐπὶ τῶν νεφελῶν τοῦ οὐρανοῦ ὡς υἱὸς ἀνθρώπου ἤρχετο,
c   καὶ ὡς παλαιὸς ἡμερῶν παρῆν,
d   καὶ οἱ παρεστηκότες παρῆσαν αὐτῷ.
14a καὶ ἐδόθη αὐτῷ ἐξουσία,
b   καὶ πάντα τὰ ἔθνη τῆς γῆς κατὰ γένη καὶ πᾶσα δόξα αὐτῷ λατρεύουσα
c   καὶ ἡ ἐξουσία αὐτοῦ ἐξουσία αἰώνιος, ἥτις οὐ μὴ ἀρθῇ,
d   καὶ ἡ βασιλεία αὐτοῦ, ἥτις οὐ μὴ φθαρῇ.

13a I was watching in the night visions
b   and behold! on the clouds of heaven one like a son of man came,

c	and one like an ancient of days was present,
d	and the bystanders were present with him.
14a	And there was given to him authority,
b	and all the nations of the earth according to their lineage and every glory was serving him,
c	and his authority is an eternal authority that shall never be removed,
d	and his kingdom one that shall never perish.

TABLE 3. *Daniel 7:27: the versions*

Aramaic (MT)

וּמַלְכוּתָה וְשָׁלְטָנָא וּרְבוּתָא דִּי מַלְכְוָת
תְּחוֹת כָּל־שְׁמַיָּא
יְהִיבַת לְעַם קַדִּישֵׁי עֶלְיוֹנִין
מַלְכוּתֵהּ מַלְכוּת עָלַם
וְכֹל שָׁלְטָנַיָּא לֵהּ יִפְלְחוּן וְיִשְׁתַּמְּעוּן:

> The kingship and the dominion and the greatness of the kingdoms under the whole heaven
> will be given to the people of the holy ones of the Most High,
> and his/their kingdom shall be an everlasting kingdom
> and all dominions shall serve and obey him/them.

Theodotion

> καὶ ἡ βασιλεία καὶ ἡ ἐξουσία καὶ ἡ μεγαλωσύνη τῶν βασιλέων τῶν ὑποκάτω παντὸς τοῦ οὐρανοῦ ἐδόθη ἁγίοις ὑψίστου, καὶ ἡ βασιλεία αὐτοῦ βασιλεία αἰώνιος, καὶ πᾶσαι αἱ ἀρχαὶ αὐτῷ δουλεύσουσιν καὶ ὑπακούσονται. ἕως ὧδε τὸ πέρας τοῦ λόγου.

> And the kingdom and the authority and the greatness of the kings
>   who are under the whole heaven was given to the holy ones
>   of the Most High,
> and his kingdom is an everlasting kingdom,
> and all dominions will serve and pay heed to him.
> Here the account ends.

Papyrus 967

> καὶ τὴν ἐξουσίαν καὶ τὴν βασιλείαν καὶ τὴν μεγαλειότητα πάντων καὶ τὴν ἀρχὴν πασῶν τῶν ὑπὸ τὸν οὐρανὸν βασιλειῶν ἔδωκα λαῷ ἁγίῳ ὑψίστου βασιλεῦσαι βασιλείαν αἰώνιον, καὶ πᾶσαι ἐξουσίαι ὑποταγήσονται αὐτῷ καὶ πειθαρχήσουσιν.

> And the authority and the kingdom and the greatness of all and
>   the dominion of all the kingdoms that are under heaven
> he gave to holy people of the Most High

to reign over an everlasting kingdom,
and every authority will be subject to him/them and will obey
    him/them.

Codex 88

καὶ τὴν βασιλείαν καὶ τὴν ἐξουσίαν καὶ τὴν μεγαλειότητα αὐτῶν καὶ τὴν ἀρχὴν πασῶν τῶν ὑπὸ τῶν οὐρανῶν βασιλειῶν ἔδωκε λαῷ ἁγίῳ ὑψίστῳ βασιλεῦσαι βασιλείαν αἰώνιον, καὶ πᾶσαι ἐξουσίαι αὐτῷ ὑποταγήσονται καὶ πειθαρχήσουσιν αὐτῷ ἕως καταστροφῆς τοῦ λόγου.

And the kingdom and the authority and the greatness of them and
    the dominion of all the kingdoms that are under heaven
he gave to holy people of the Most High
to reign over an everlasting kingdom,
and every authority will be subject to him/it and will obey
    him/them.

CHAPTER 2.3

The Oldest Interpretation of Daniel 7: 4Q246 (4QAramaic Apocalypse)

This Aramaic text, which has also been called the Daniel Apocryphon and the "Son of God" text, survives in fragmentary form in a manuscript from Qumran Cave 4, which is dated on paleographic grounds to circa 25 BCE.[1] The fragment comprises two columns of nine lines each, but, while the whole of the second column has survived, only the ends of the lines of the first column are preserved. More of the document, both before and after these two columns, certainly existed, but there is no way of knowing how long the document as a whole was. The text has attracted considerable scholarly attention and dispute, mainly because of its reference to a figure who "will be called son of God" (ii 1). The translation I provide in table 1 is based on that in *The Dead Sea Scrolls Study Edition*,[2] but I have modified it in the light of other translations, the scholarly discussions, and my own judgments.

Like other Aramaic manuscripts from Qumran, this text is unlikely to have been composed within the Qumran community itself,[3] and this copy from the Qumran library will not have been the original. So its composition could date from any time between the writing of the book of Daniel (c. 162 BCE), on which it is very likely dependent,[4] and the date of the Qumran manuscript

---

1. Émile Puech, "4QApocryphe de Daniel ar (Planche XI)," in *Qumran Cave 4: Parabiblical Texts, Part 3*, by George Brooke, John Collins, Torleif Elgvin, et al., Discoveries in the Judaean Desert 22 (Oxford: Clarendon, 1996) 165-84, here 166.

2. Florentino García Martínez and Eibert J. C. Tigchelaar, eds., *The Dead Sea Scrolls Study Edition*, vol. 1 (Leiden: Brill, 1997) 493, 495.

3. See especially Sharon Lea Mattila, "Two Contrasting Eschatologies at Qumran," *Bib* 75 (1994) 518-38.

4. But Puech, "4QApocryphe de Daniel," 183, thinks it may be contemporary with Daniel.

(c. 25 BCE). The reference to kings of Assyria and Egypt (i 6), which are plausibly understood as ciphers for the Seleucid kings of Assyria and the Ptolemaic kings of Egypt, suggests a date before the Roman period.

Obscure and debated though this text is, it is important for our purposes because it may well be the earliest evidence of interpretation of Daniel 7, and, although it makes no allusion to Daniel 7:13, it may be possible to detect how its author understood the "one like a son of man" of that verse. In the present context it will not be possible to discuss every aspect of 4Q246 or to argue in detail against all alternative views of it. I shall focus on the issues that are relevant to the understanding of Daniel 7:13 that may be implied.

4Q246 AND THE BOOK OF DANIEL

It has been widely recognized that 4Q246 has close affinities with the book of Daniel. Since the relevant portions of Daniel are in Aramaic, it is possible to detect some close verbal resemblances to Daniel. The most striking are to Daniel 7: the two assertions of eternal rule (ii 5: "his kingdom will be an eternal kingdom"; ii 9: "his rule will be an eternal rule") occur respectively in Daniel 7:27 and 7:14, though they also occur respectively in Daniel 3:33 [4:3] and 4:31[34]. (In the latter two cases they describe God's eternal kingdom and so may be less close to the usage in 4Q246 than the occurrences in Dan 7 are.) In addition, the use of the verb דוש ("to trample") twice in 4Q246 ii 3 is reminiscent of the use of that verb in Daniel 7:23, where it describes the destructive effect of the fourth kingdom on the whole earth. However, table 3 shows that these are by no means the only verbal connections with Daniel. The other verbal connections indicated there may not all be intentional allusions, but they show at least that the author of 4Q246 was well acquainted with chapters 2–7 of Daniel, easily able to echo their terminology. Although it cannot be demonstrated, it is not unlikely that the figure to whom the opening of the fragment refers is in fact Daniel, represented as a wise man who can interpret a pagan king's vision of future history, just as Daniel does in Daniel 2–6. 4Q246 may well be an apocryphal Daniel text, comparable with the Aramaic Daniel apocrypha preserved in other fragments in Cave 4 (4Q242–245).[5]

The opening lines of the fragment enable us to infer that the literary genre of the whole was a story like that in Daniel 2. An account of the king's vision, like that of Nebuchadnezzar's dream, must have preceded the extant

---

5. On these see Peter W. Flint, "The Daniel Tradition at Qumran," in *Eschatology, Messianism, and the Dead Sea Scrolls*, ed. Craig A. Evans and Peter W. Flint, SDSSRL (Grand Rapids: Eerdmans, 1997) 41–60

text, though we cannot tell whether the king himself narrated the vision, like Nebuchadnezzar in Daniel 4, or the wise interpreter told the king what he had seen in the vision, as Daniel does in Daniel 2. The vision must have been a symbolic one, which, like Nebuchadnezzar's in Daniel 2, encoded a prediction of future history, including the end of the pagan kingdoms and the establishment of an eternal kingdom by God. The only part of the content of the vision that we know is the "shooting stars" (ii 1–2). The word could also be translated as "sparks" or "comets." Perhaps in the vision they were seen setting fire to the earth, symbolizing the destruction and chaos that the kingdom they symbolize will cause, according to the interpretation of them in ii 2–3. The whole of the interpreter's speech in i 4–ii 9 should be understood as interpretation of the vision, other elements of which were presumably referenced in the missing parts of the text in column i.

In modeling his work on Daniel 2 and also drawing on Daniel 7, the author has recognized that these two chapters are quite closely connected. Both describe the succession of the pagan kingdoms, featuring especially the destructive activity of the fourth and last of them, and their replacement by a kingdom that God will establish and which will endure forever. To describe this kingdom, the author of 4Q246 has drawn on the descriptions of the kingdom of the "one like a son of man" in Daniel 7:13 (ii 9: "his rule will be an eternal rule") and of the kingdom given to the people of God in Daniel 7:27 (ii 5: "his kingdom will be an eternal kingdom"). However, it is also notable that in ii 4, a sentence that the scribe has highlighted by leaving spaces at the beginning and the end of the line, there is a probable allusion to Daniel 2:44. The scribe has set line ii 4 apart because it is the turning point of future history, the point of divine intervention to establish the eternal kingdom. In this respect it corresponds to Daniel 2:44, which twice uses the verb קום ("to arise, to stand"): "in the days of those kings the God of heaven will set up [יקים] a kingdom that shall never be destroyed.... It shall stand [תקום] forever." The verb is picked up in 4Q246 ii 4: "Until he raises up [יקים] the people of God."[6]

The theme of the coming supersession of the pagan kingdom by the eternal kingdom is the main theme of 4Q246 and derives primarily from Daniel 2 and 7. But in its account of how the eternal kingdom overcomes the pagan powers and of the character of the kingdom, 4Q246 does not owe much to Daniel 7. It draws, as we shall see, on other scriptural sources, especially those that were understood to refer to the Davidic Messiah and promised that his kingdom would be characterized above all by peace.

---

6. See the detailed discussion below.

Who Is "the Son of God"?

Two major interpretative issues have featured in the discussion of 4Q246. The first concerns the figure to whom i 9–ii 1 refers. Is he a pagan king who claims divine titles for himself (such as a Seleucid king at the time of writing), or is he some kind of messianic figure (angelic or human) who is entitled to be called the son of God?[7] Probably the strongest argument in favor of the former view is that, if the whole passage is understood as a continuous narrative of future history, then the figure called the son of God evidently belongs to the period in which the forces of evil are dominant, which comes to an end only at ii 4. In my view Tucker Ferda, in one of the most recent studies of 4Q246, has cogently argued that, since the passage is interpreting the king's vision, it need not be understood as a single sequential narrative.[8] Rather, the speaker will be explaining different elements of the vision one by one. The sentence that begins at the end of ii 1 ("Like the shooting stars of the vision...") indicates that the speaker here moves on to explicate a different element of the vision, the shooting stars and their activity. (There are similar transitions in Dan 2:41, 43; 4:23[20].) The third person plurals of line ii 2 ("their kingdom... they will rule") do not have an antecedent in the preceding passage but must have made sense as interpretation of the vision. (There are similar unexplained uses of "they" in Dan 2:43 and 4:26[23]). So the fact that the "son of God" figure is introduced in the vision interpretation before the period of rule of the "shooting stars" is described need not mean that, chronologically, he is to precede that period.

Ferda also argues that the first three verbs of naming in i 9–ii 1 (יתקרא, יתאמר, יתכנה), although they could be read as reflexive ("he will call himself"), are more plausibly understood as divine passives, indicating that it is God who names this figure. Biblical parallels are found in Genesis 32:29; Isaiah 4:3; 9:6; 61:6; 62:4; and Zechariah 8:3. Ferda concludes from these parallels that 4Q246 here adopts a "rhetoric of divine naming" familiar from the Hebrew Bible.[9] He goes on to argue for a "messianic naming tradition," in which the Messiah is given his name by God.[10] In this tradition he places Luke 1:32–33, which, as many studies of 4Q246 have noted,[11] strongly resembles 4Q246

---

7. There is an up-to-date survey of the various ways in which scholars have understood this figure in Tucker S. Ferda, "Naming the Messiah: A Contribution to the 4Q246 'Son of God' Debate," *DSD* 21 (2014) 150–75, here 153–56.
8. Ferda, "Naming the Messiah," 160–63.
9. This is a summary of the detailed argument in Ferda, "Naming the Messiah," 164–71.
10. Ferda, "Naming the Messiah," 172–75.
11. Beginning with Joseph A. Fitzmyer, "The Contribution of Qumran Aramaic to the Study of the New Testament," *NTS* 20 (1973–74) 382–407, here 391–94.

i 9–ii 1. Here too the verb "will be called" should be understood as a divine passive, parallel to the explicitly divine act in the following clause ("will give to him").

It is worth examining more closely this parallel between 4Q246 and Luke 1:32-33 (see table 2). It is generally agreed that the Lukan passage is based on passages in the Hebrew Bible (the indebtedness to these sources is independent of the OG) that were in this period understood in a messianic sense.[12] These certainly include 2 Samuel 7:9-16 and Isaiah 9:5-6[6-7], and perhaps also Micah 5:4[3] and Psalm 2:7. The comparison of these texts in table 2 shows that the resemblances between 4Q246 and Luke 1:32-33 are the result of common dependence on 2 Samuel 7:9, 14a, along with one or two of the other passages. The two authors have followed the common Jewish exegetical practice of bringing together passages understood to be messianic, especially when they share common vocabulary. (In this case the common vocabulary is "great" [2 Sam 7:9; Mic 5:4(3)][13] and "son" [2 Sam 7:14; Isa 9:6(5);[14] Ps 2:7].) To explain the resemblance between 4Q246 and Luke a common exegetical practice of bringing 2 Samuel 7:9-16 together with other messianic passages almost entirely suffices. All that this does not explain is the use of the divine title "the Most High," which is found in both 4Q246 and Luke but not in the biblical passages. But this coincidence is unremarkable, since "the Most High" is common in the book of Daniel and so is an example of the dependence of 4Q246 on Danielic terminology (Dan 4:17, 24, 25, 32, 34; 7:18, 22, 25 [bis], 27; cf. 3:26; 4:2 [3:32]; also 4QPrNab [4Q242] frag. 1–3),[15] while the title is also used a number of times in Luke's writings (Luke 1:35, 76; 6:35; Acts 7:48), including the closely similar Luke 1:76 (he "will be called the prophet of the Most High"). Both authors required a divine title to place in poetic parallelism to "God"/"Lord God." It is not surprising that they both chose "the Most High," which for the author of 4Q246 had a strongly Danielic resonance and for Luke a more generally biblical one.[16]

---

12. E.g., I. Howard Marshall, *The Gospel of Luke*, NIGTC (Exeter: Paternoster, 1978) 66-68; Joseph A. Fitzmyer, *The Gospel According to Luke (I–IX)*, AB 28A (New York: Doubleday, 1981) 338-39; John Nolland, *Luke 1–9:20*, WBC 35A (Dallas: Word, 1989) 51-52.

13. The dependence of 4Q246 on Mic 5:3 is very likely in view of the earlier parallel in 4Q246 i 7; see table 3.

14. Since Isa 9:6[5] does not specify *whose* son was given, it was possible to infer from comparison with 2 Sam 7:14 that he is *God's* son.

15. While Daniel uses the Aramaic word עליא, 4Q246 prefers the Hebrew עליון, as it does for all divine designations.

16. On the divine designation "the Most High" in Second Temple-period Jewish literature, see Richard Bauckham, "The 'Most High' God and the Nature of Early Jewish

The comparison of the texts in table 2 also highlights a very interesting feature. Luke's echo of the passage in 2 Samuel 7 picks up not only the notion that the Davidic Messiah will be called Son of God but also the claim that his kingdom will last forever, and this especially creates the link with Isaiah 9:5–6, with which Luke 1:32–33 has close verbal parallels. By contrast, 4Q246 i 9–ii 1 does not allude to an eternal kingdom, but, as we have already noted, this is a strongly emphasized theme in the latter part of this text (ii 5, 9). If 4Q246 i 9–ii 1 refers to the Davidic Messiah, depending on 2 Samuel 7 and Isaiah 9, then it is not surprising that the author goes on to speak of his eternal kingdom, this time with allusion to Daniel 7. We can now see that, just as this author has brought together Daniel 2 and Daniel 7 because of their common climax in the eternal kingdom to come, so he has also selected for allusion messianic passages that refer to the eternal kingdom of the Davidic Messiah. What holds together the whole passage is the prediction of a Davidic Messiah to whom God will give an eternal kingdom. As so often in the Jewish literature of the Second Temple period, the key to understanding this text lies in identifying its biblical sources and recognizing the exegetical work behind the text that explains why these specific passages have been chosen and combined.

Who Is the Subject in 4Q246 ii 4–9?

The translation in table 1 assumes that (apart from God) there is a singular male subject in these lines. But it is possible that the third-person masculine suffixes have the masculine noun עַם (ii 4: "the people") as their antecedent, in which case we should have to translate them in English as "it" or, more idiomatically, "they." Here are the relevant lines (ii 4–9) with the alternative translations indicated:

> *vacat* Until he raises up the people of God [*or* until the people of
>   God arise] and everyone will rest from the sword. *vacat*
> His/its kingdom will be an eternal kingdom, and all his/its paths in
>   righteousness. He/it will jud[ge]
> the earth in righteousness and all will make peace. The sword will
>   cease from the earth,
> and all the provinces will bow down to him/it. The great God is
>   his/its strength,

Monotheism," in *Jesus and the God of Israel: God Crucified and Other Studies on the New Testament's Christology of Divine Identity* (Grand Rapids: Eerdmans, 2008) 107–26.

he will wage war for him/it; he will give the peoples into his/its
hand and
he will throw them all down before him/it. His/its rule will be an
eternal rule, and all the deeps of [. . .]

James Dunn has argued for the translation "it" or "they," referring to the people of God, throughout lines 5–9.[17] His argument depends on the way that line 5 ("his/its kingdom will be an eternal kingdom") and line 9 ("his/its rule will be an eternal rule") echo, respectively, Daniel 7:27 and Daniel 7:14. He argues that in Daniel 7:27 the masculine singular pronominal suffix refers to "the people of the holy ones of the Most High," suggesting that this must also be the meaning of the same words as they appear in 4Q246 ii 5. In Daniel 7:14, on the other hand, in the words echoed by 4Q246 ii 9, the masculine singular pronominal suffix refers to the figure "like a son of man" of Daniel 7:13. According to Dunn, this shows that the author of 4Q246 understood Daniel's "one like a son of man" to be a symbol of "the people of the holy ones of the Most High," interpreting Daniel 7 in the way that Dunn himself, along with many modern scholars, thinks was the original meaning of the text.[18]

A serious flaw in this argument is that Dunn takes it for granted that an ancient reader of Daniel 7:27 would read it in the way that many modern English translations understand it, translating it thus:

The kingship and dominion and the greatness of the kingdom under the whole heaven shall be given to the people of the holy ones of the Most High; their kingdom shall be an everlasting kingdom, and all dominions shall serve and obey them. (NRSV)[19]

---

17. James D. G. Dunn, "'Son of God' as 'Son of Man' in the Dead Sea Scrolls? A Response to John J. Collins on 4Q246," in *The Scrolls and the Scriptures: Qumran Fifty Years After*, ed. Stanley E. Porter and Craig A. Evans, JSPSup 26, Roehampton Institute London Papers 3 (Sheffield: Sheffield Academic, 1997) 198–210. Cf. also Michael Segal, "Who is the 'Son of God' in 4Q246? An Overlooked Example of Early Biblical Interpretation," *DSD* 21 (2004) 289–312. I am not at all convinced by Segal's argument for allusion to Ps 82:6 in 4Q246.

18. Dunn, "'Son of God,'" 205–9.

19. RSV, REB also translate the verse in this way. This interpretation is taken for granted in modern commentaries on Daniel: R. H. Charles, *A Critical and Exegetical Commentary on the Book of Daniel* (Oxford: Clarendon, 1929) 195; Louis F. Hartman and Alexander A. Di Lella, *The Book of Daniel*, AB 23 (New York: Doubleday, 1978) 207; John E. Goldingay, *Daniel*, WBC 30 (Dallas: Word, 1989) 143; John J. Collins, *Daniel*, Hermeneia (Minneapolis: Fortress, 1993) 322 ("The most natural antecedent is the singular עם rather than עליונין").

But the verse can be translated otherwise, as it was in the King James Version:

> And the kingdom and dominion, and the greatness of the kingdom under the whole heaven, shall be given to the people of the saints of the most High, whose kingdom is an everlasting kingdom, and all dominions shall serve and obey him.

The New International Version, among others, represents the same interpretative choice of translation today:

> Then the sovereignty, power and greatness of all the kingdoms under heaven will be handed over to the holy people of the Most High. His kingdom will be an everlasting kingdom, and all rulers will worship and obey him.

These translations[20] take the antecedent of the masculine singular pronominal suffixes in the second half of the verse to be, not "the people," but "the Most High."[21]

Which translation represents the original meaning of the text is not important for our purposes. We need only observe that the interpretative judgment the KJV and NIV translators made could also have been made by an ancient reader of the text, such as the author of 4Q246. Evidence of this is found in the ancient Greek versions. The Old Greek (LXX) seems to go with the line of interpretation represented by the NRSV while retaining some of the ambiguity of the Aramaic:

> And he shall give the authority and the kingdom and the magnitude of all the kingdoms, which are under heaven, to the holy people [λαῷ] of the Most High, to reign over an everlasting kingdom, and all authorities will be subjected to him [αὐτῷ] and obey him [αὐτῷ]. (NETS)

This translation of the Old Greek takes the antecedent of the two occurrences of αὐτῷ to be "the Most High," but they could presumably be understood to refer back to "the people." Theodotion's version, on the other hand, represents

---

20. ASV, NASB, NJB also translate the verse in this way. RNJB preserves the ambiguity of the Aramaic.

21. The Aramaic word עליונין is plural, like the Hebrew אלהים, and is generally taken to be a plural of majesty, but, like אלהים, it is treated as grammatically singular. So there is no difficulty in seeing it as the antecedent of the pronominal suffixes.

unequivocally the line of interpretation represented in English versions by the KJV and the NIV:

> And the kingdom and the authority and the greatness of the kings, which are under the whole heaven, was given to the holy ones of the Most High, and his [αὐτοῦ] kingdom is an everlasting kingdom, and all dominions shall serve and heed him [αὐτῷ]. (NETS, modified)

Thus the author of 4Q246 could have read the words he has taken from Daniel 7:27 to refer to God's kingdom, especially since the same words refer to God's kingdom in Daniel 4:3 [3:33]. He could have transferred them to a messianic kingdom, on the principle that the kingdom over which the Messiah will rule eternally is God's eternal kingdom. In taking this approach, he could also have been influenced by Daniel 7:14, from which he quotes the parallel expression (ii 5), if he understood the "one like a son of man" to be an individual, not a symbol for the people of the holy ones. But, finally, he could even have taken the antecedent of the pronominal suffixes in the second half of Daniel 7:27 to be neither the people nor the Most High but the figure described in Daniel 7:13–14. It may have seemed natural to him that this passage in Daniel, having spoken of the transfer of the kingdom to the people of God, should then revert to speaking of the messianic ruler of the people of God who, in his view, had been introduced in Daniel 7:13–14. Such arguments cannot be conclusive, but they should at least show that there is no good reason why the author of 4Q246 should have read Daniel 7:27 in the way Dunn does. Other readings were available to him.

I propose in what follows a fresh approach to the identity of the subject in ii 4–9 by looking more closely at the rest of the content of this section.

The Exegetical Background of 4Q246 II 4–9

Righteous Judgment

A key role of the subject of ii 4–9 is righteous judgment (ii 5–6). The key word that occurs twice in these two lines (קשוט, קשט) has usually been translated as "truth." For example, the *Dead Sea Scrolls Study Edition* has: "all his paths in truth. He will judge the earth in truth."[22] But this noun, from the root קשט, "to straighten," means literally "straightness" and is used to mean both "truth" and

---

22. García Martínez and Tigchelaar, *The Dead Sea Scrolls*, 495.

"righteousness." It clearly means "truth" in Daniel 2:47 and perhaps for that reason is often translated "truth" in Daniel 4:37[34], where Nebuchadnezzar says of God, "the King of heaven,"

> All his works are truth [קשט],
> and his ways [ארחתה] are justice [דין].

But here, in parallel with דין, the translation "right" (RSV, NIV) is more appropriate, though it is likely to be read as an adjective, whereas the Aramaic word is a noun. These are the only two occurrences in Daniel (and in biblical Aramaic), but the meaning "right" or "righteousness" is attested elsewhere (e.g., 4QTob[b] [4Q197] 4 ii 2).

It seems to have escaped the attention of most scholars working on 4Q246 that the words "all his/its paths in righteousness" (בקשוט ארחתה כל) in ii 5 are an allusion to Daniel 4:37[34].[23] There they refer to God. The author of 4Q246 has transferred them to either a Messianic Figure or the people of God, presumably because he/they exercise God's righteous judgment.[24]

The following words in 4Q246 ii 5–6 ("he/it will judge the earth in righteousness") are especially helpful in resolving that choice between a Messianic Figure and the people of God. John Collins points out that here "the people is an unlikely antecedent," since in the Hebrew Bible and early Jewish literature it is always God himself or a king who exercises judgment.[25] But we can go further and suggest that here 4Q246 is actually alluding to passages in the Hebrew Bible that were interpreted as referring to the Davidic Messiah:

> With righteousness he shall judge the poor,
> and decide with equity [במישד] for the meek of the earth.
> (Isa 11:4a)
>
> May he judge your people with righteousness
> and your poor with justice. (Ps 72:2)

---

23. The parallel is noted by Puech, "4QApocryphe de Daniel," 175.

24. In Aramaic Levi (4QLevi[b] ar) 1 i 12, Levi prays to God, "Grant me all the paths of truth" (כל ארחת קשט). Here, in a striking parallel to 4Q246, קשט could be perhaps better translated as "righteousness," since Levi continues, "Remove far from me, Lord, the spirit of injustice and evil thought and fornication."

25. John J. Collins, *The Scepter and the Star: The Messiahs of the Dead Sea Scrolls and Other Ancient Literature* (New York: Doubleday, 1996) 159.

The Hebrew word מישר that the NRSV translates as "equity" in Isaiah 11:4 is a close Hebrew equivalent to the Aramaic word קשט in 4Q246 ii 6, since the root ישר means "to straighten."[26]

The three words of "he will judge the world in righteousness" (ידי[ן] ארעא בקשט) in 4Q246 are all taken, in translation, from Isaiah 11:4a and form a summarizing interpretation of it, thus:

> With righteousness he shall **judge** [שפט] the poor,
> and decide **with equity** [במישר] for the meek of **the earth** [ארץ].
> (Isa 11:4a)

Isaiah 11:1–5 was one of the passages of the Hebrew Bible on which expectations of the Davidic Messiah most commonly drew.[27] It was understood to mean that he would judge and rule all the peoples of the earth (4QpIsa[a] 8–10 iii 21–22; Pss. Sol. 17:29, 35; cf. 1QSb v 24–28). It is likely that the allusion to it in 4Q246 would be readily recognized.

Peace

4Q246 emphasizes that the coming kingdom will be characterized by peace, by contrast with a preceding period of war and internecine strife.[28] When the people of God are raised up, "everyone will rest from the sword" (ii 4), presumably meaning that the people of God themselves will abandon weapons. In the following passage peace is portrayed as a consequence of either the Messiah's or the people's eternal rule and his/their judgment of the earth in righteousness:

> His/its kingdom will be an eternal kingdom, and all his/its paths in righteousness. He/it will jud[ge] the earth in righteousness and all will make peace. The sword will cease from the earth. (ii 5–6)

Here the peace is universal.[29]

---

26. The word קשט itself makes only a very rare appearance in biblical Hebrew (Prov 22:21; possibly Ps 60:6), though it is more common in rabbinic Hebrew.

27. Collins, *The Scepter*, 65–66.

28. This emphasis is noted by Mattila, "Two Contrasting Eschatologies," 518–38, especially 527–28.

29. In 1 Macc 9:73 the expression "the sword ceased from Israel" means that they were safe from attack and invasion by enemies.

There is no reference to peace in Daniel 7, but it is a common feature of the eschatological hope of the prophets. Sometimes it occurs without reference to a messianic figure (Isa 2:4 = Mic 4:3; Hos 2:18[20]), but more often it is portrayed as the consequence and characteristic of the rule of the Davidic Messiah (Ps 72:7; Isa 9:6–7[5–6]; 11:6–9; Mic 5:5; Zech 9:10). In that context, it is sometimes said to be eternal, like the messianic ruler's kingdom (Isa 9:6[5]; Ps 72:7). If we distinguish two stages of pacification—the abolition of weapons first among the people of God and then universally—we find both stages explicit only in Zechariah 9:10. The second part of line 6 ("*the sword* will cease *from the earth*") sounds like an echo specifically of Hosea 2:18[20]: "I will abolish the bow, *the sword*, and war *from the land/earth*"). Peace is never said to be the consequence of rule by the people of God.

The association that we find in 4Q246 between righteous rule, peace, and the eternal kingdom can be seen in Isaiah 9:6–7[5–6] and in Psalm 72:2, 5, 7, 17. It is strongly suggestive of Davidic messianism. If the author of 4Q246 drew on Hosea 2:18[20], as the verbal similarity suggests, then he is likely to have related that verse to those where it is the Davidic Messiah who establishes peace both in Israel and in the world (Ps 72:7; Isa 9:6–7[5–6]; Zech 9:10).

Homage

Associated with the abolition of "the sword" is the prophecy that "all the provinces will bow down to him/it" (4Q246 ii 7). If these words apply to the people rather than the Messiah, Isaiah 45:14, 49:23, and 60:14 are possible sources of the idea.[30] But a more plausible source is Psalm 72:7–11, because it shares with 4Q246 ii 5–7 the same sequence of righteousness, peace, and homage paid by all:

> In his days may righteousness flourish
>   and peace abound, till the moon is no more.
> . . . .
> May his foes *bow down before him*,
>   and his enemies lick the dust.
> . . . .
> May all kings *fall down before him*,
>   all nations give him service.

---

30. 1 En. 90:30 is probably based on these passages.

This psalm about the ideal Davidic king was read messianically in the Second Temple period.

God Wages War

We turn next to this passage:

> The great God[31] is his/its strength,[32]
> he will wage war for him/it; he will give the peoples into his/its hand and
> he will throw them all down before him/it. (4Q246 ii 7–9)

Again, this is a theme that does not derive from Daniel 7, where there is no mention of war waged by God or even by the people of God. We need to look elsewhere for 4Q246's exegetical sources.

The view that the pronominal suffixes refer to the people rather than the Messiah could appeal to some scriptural passages, especially Zechariah 9:13–15, where YHWH leads his people in battle against their enemies, and Isaiah 11:14, where the people returning from exile subjugate the neighboring nations. But, following the repeated reference to the abolition of "the sword" (ii 4, 6), it is likely that we should understand the war in ii 8–9 as not merely assisted by God but carried out only by God. Moreover, it seems to result, not in the destruction of the enemies, but in their surrender and submission.

The clear scriptural echoes in this passage are of the Song of Moses at the Sea (Exod 15:1–18). The words "the great God is his/its strength" reflect a key verse of the song:

> The LORD is my strength and my might
> and he has become my salvation. (Exod 15:2)

This is echoed in Psalms 28:7, 118:14, and Isaiah 12:2b, the last in the context of a kind of eschatological version of the Song at the Sea, to be sung by the exiles at the time of their new exodus. It is relevant to note that in Jewish Aramaic literature the divine name is not used and the word "God" is commonly used as a substitute. Here the term "the great God" serves to specify the God of Israel, as it does in Daniel 2:45–47.

---

31. This phrase (אל רבא) may derive from Dan 2:45 (אלה רב). 4Q246 uses the Hebrew terms for God (here and elsewhere), whereas Daniel has the Aramaic.

32. On the rare word איל, see Puech, "4QApocryphe de Daniel," 177 n. 29.

A further key echo of the Song at the Sea is in the words "he will throw them all down [ירמה]" before him/it," which correspond verbally to the opening verse of the Song:

> I will sing to the Lord, for he has triumphed gloriously;
> horse and rider he has thrown [רמה] into the sea. (Exod 15:1)

This verse is repeated as the Song of Miriam in Exodus 15:21. These two verses in fact contain the only uses of the verb רמה in this sense in the Hebrew Bible. Since the same root is also used in Aramaic, the author of 4Q246 has been able to make a precise verbal allusion to this distinctive usage in the Hebrew of the Song.

The Song at the Sea also contains the claim "the Lord is a man of war" (Exod 15:3 KJV), to which 4Q246's words "he will wage war for him/it" correspond. But the closer link here is with the narrative before the Song, in which Moses says to the people, "The Lord will fight for you [plural], and you have only to keep still" (Exod 14:14). In the Exodus narrative the victory over the Egyptians is won by God alone, while his people take no part and Moses does nothing but stretch out his hand. A victory achieved by God alone seems to be what is also envisaged in 4Q246.

The Song at the Sea ends with the words "The Lord will reign forever and ever" (Exod 15:18), which were later read as a prophecy of the eschatological, eternal kingdom. Correspondingly, this passage of 4Q246 is followed immediately by the words taken from Daniel 7:14: "His rule will be an eternal rule." The new exodus will issue in the eternal kingdom—but is this the kingdom of God, or the people, or the Messiah?

At the crossing of the sea in Exodus, God waged war for his people, and so such an allusion to that event in 4Q246 would be possible if the pronominal suffixes refer to the people rather than the Messiah. The precise allusions are somewhat ambiguous in this respect. In the Song, Moses says in the first-person singular, "The Lord is my strength and my might," and so the corresponding words of 4Q246, "the great God is his/its strength," may similarly apply to the leader of God's people rather than the people itself. On the other hand, "The Lord will fight for you" is spoken by Moses to the people, and so the words of 4Q246, "he will wage war for him/it," may similarly refer to the people rather than their leader.

A more decisive indication will emerge if we turn to the only words of 4Q246 ii 7–9 for which we have not yet identified a scriptural source: "he will give the peoples into his/its hand." The common expression "to give X into Y's hand" can mean to hand over X into Y's power so that X must serve Y (e.g., Isa 47:6; Dan 1:2). It may be that these words also allude, like the reference to the eternal kingdom, to Daniel 7:14:

> *To him was given* dominion
>   and glory and kingship,
> that all *peoples*, nations, and languages
>   *should serve him*.[33]
> **His dominion is an everlasting dominion.**

The beginning of this verse employs a divine passive, meaning "God gave to him." 4Q246 picks up the words in italics and creates, as we have seen in other cases, a summarizing paraphrase of the first half of the verse: "he will give the peoples into his hand." The words in bold are those cited verbatim in 4Q246.

If this is correct, then, in these last three lines of column ii, the author has brought together allusions to the exodus (Exod 14–15) and allusions to Daniel 7:14, in both cases combining precise verbal citation with somewhat more paraphrastic allusion. He must have taken the leader of the people in the new exodus (playing Moses's role) to be identical with the singular figure of Daniel 7:13–14, the "one like a son of man," who in his view is presumably not a symbol of "the people of the holy ones of the Most High" but their messianic ruler. That 4Q246 does not use the phrase "one like a son of man" is only to be expected, for he is a figure in Daniel's vision, like the four beasts. The king's vision in 4Q246 must have comprised a different set of symbolic images, one of which will have stood for the Messiah.

All the Deeps

Our fragmentary text of this work ends with the words "and all the deeps of" (וכל תהומי). We can only guess what followed, although, since תהומי is the construct form of the word, we can be sure that it was followed by another noun. There must have been a phrase such as "deeps of the earth" (as in Ps 71:20) or "deeps of the waters" (as in 4QJubª ii 11). Probably the text went on to say that these deeps were subject to him or obedient to him. I will make two necessarily tentative suggestions as to the exegetical source of such an idea. First, the word "deeps" (תהמת) occurs twice in the Song at the Sea

---

33. פלח can mean to worship a deity, but also to work for or to serve a human being.

187

(Exod 15:5, 8), and so there may be a continuation of the new exodus theme. Second, the idea that the deeps are subject to the Messiah may come from Psalm 89:25, where God says to the Davidic ruler:

> I will set his hand on the sea [בים]
> and his right hand on the rivers.

This means that he will be given power over the sea and the rivers, and so could easily be understood to mean that even the watery deeps of creation will be subject to the Davidic Messiah. Unfortunately, we shall probably never know whether either of these suggestions is correct, but at least we can say that these last words of our text can be understood as coherent with the interpretation of the preceding lines that has been propounded here.

Raising the People

Having clarified most of this passage (4Q246 ii 4–9), we are now in a better position to discuss the opening four words (עד יקים עם אל), which I have translated "Until he raises up the people of God," but which others have construed as "Until the people of God arises." But before discussing that issue, it is worth noting that the scribe has left a space before writing these words, setting them off from what precedes, and also the special significance of the first word "until" (עד). Émile Puech has pointed out how, in a series of texts, this word marks out the decisive turning point in the sequence of eschatological events, when God or the Messiah takes action to bring about salvation.[34]

The most interesting example occurs in a fragmentary commentary on Genesis from Qumran Cave 4, since here too the scribe has left a space before the word עד:

> Until the messiah of righteousness comes, the branch of David. For to him and to his descendants has been given the covenant and the kingship of his people for everlasting generations. (4QCommGenA [4Q252] v 3–4)

As in 4Q246, the turning point is here linked to the eternal kingdom. The passage is actually part of an interpretation of Genesis 49:10, which probably had special prestige as a messianic prophecy since it was the oldest prophecy

---

34. Puech, "4QApocryphe de Daniel," 174.

of a ruler to come from the tribe of Judah. The commentary has picked up the word עד from that biblical text:

> The scepter shall not depart from Judah
>   nor the ruler's staff from between his feet,
> until [עד כי] he comes to whom it belongs[35]
>   and the obedience of the peoples is his. (Gen 49:10
>   NRSV margin)

It is not unlikely that 4Q246 also picks up the word עד from Genesis, in which case the following word would have the Messiah as its subject. But it is also possible that the use of עד in 4Q246 reflects Daniel 7:21–22, where the little horn is said have been prevailing over "the holy ones . . . until [עד די] the Ancient of Days came" (NRSV margin).

The second word in this line can be read as either יקים (Haphel of קום) or יקום (Pael of קום). (The letters *yod* and *vav* are indistinguishable here.) In the former case the first four words mean "Until he raises up the people of God"; in the latter case, "Until the people of God arises."[36] In the latter case it would be possible, probably even necessary, to understand "the people of God" as the main subject in the lines that follow. But we have seen strong reasons to suppose that the main subject is the Messiah, and so it seems that the other translation ("Until he raises up the people of God") is preferable and that it is the Messiah who raises up the people. If the subject were God, we should expect "he will raise up his people."

We have seen that all or most of lines 4–9 has an exegetical background, and since the first words of line 4 have the special significance of describing the decisive intervention in the course of events, we should expect there to be an exegetical source here too. It is likely to be Daniel 2:44:

> And in the days of those kings the God of heaven shall set up [יקים] a kingdom that shall never be destroyed, nor shall this kingdom be left to another people [עם]. It shall crush all these kingdoms and bring them to an end, and it shall stand [תקום] forever.

---

35. This line is a famous crux. This translation depends on reading שלה ("belonging to him") for שילה, which seems to have been how the LXX translator read it and how it was understood by the author of 4Q252.

36. See the full discussion in Puech, "4QApocryphe de Daniel," 174–75.

Like so many of the exegetical sources of 4Q246 ii 4–9, this text relates to the eternal kingdom. In 4Q246 ii 4–9 the process of setting up this kingdom begins with the setting up of the people of God, in which the Messiah acts as God's agent. But the role of the Messiah may well reflect Isaiah 49:6, where God addresses the servant:

> It is too light a thing that you should be my servant
> to raise up [להקים] the tribes of Jacob
> and to restore the survivors of Israel;
> I will give you as a light to the nations,
> that my salvation may reach to the ends of the earth.

The Hebrew Hiphil of קום here is equivalent to the Aramaic Haphel in Daniel 2:44 and 4Q246 ii 4.

We do not have to choose between these two possible sources of 4Q246. Rather, we may well have here an example of the Jewish exegetical practice of bringing together two texts that share significant vocabulary and allowing each to interpret the other.[37] The author has inferred from Isaiah 49:6 that the *raising up* of the eternal kingdom to which Daniel refers must begin with the *raising up* of the people of God.

Summary of the Exegetical Background of 4Q246 ii 4–9

Table 3 summarizes the exegetical sources of this passage. We can now see that, in addition to the two verbatim citations from Daniel 7:14 and 7:27, which have been widely recognized, there are other strong verbal allusions to Daniel 4:34, Isaiah 11:4, and Exodus 15:2, as well as echoes that pick up one or two key words from the source in the case of Daniel 2:44, Isaiah 49:6, Hosea 2:18[20], Psalm 72:11, and Exodus 15:1. There are also parallels that are more thematic than verbal. Even though not all these allusions are equally probable, it is clear that the passage derives from close study of many of the key eschatological prophecies (as they were understood in this period) in the Hebrew Bible. Along with Daniel 7, the Song at the Sea (Exod 15:1–18) and prophecies of the rule of the future Davidic king seem especially influential.

---

37. This is the technique called Gezerah Shavah II in David Instone Brewer, *Techniques and Assumptions in Jewish Exegesis before 70 CE*, TSAJ 30 (Tübingen: Mohr Siebeck, 1992) 18. It is widely evidenced in Second Temple–period Jewish literature and in the New Testament.

Table 4 plots the exegetical sources of the main themes of the passage. The sources here are extended to include those on which the account of the Messiah in i 7–ii 2 depends (2 Sam 7:13–14; Mic 5:4[3]; Isa 9:6[5]). The exegetical sources indicated in this table are in many cases not just the single verse to which 4Q246 alludes but the wider context of which the author would have been aware. This enables us to see how the key themes of 4Q246 recur in many of these contexts. So, for example, we can see that, in the case of the theme of the eternal kingdom, 4Q246 draws explicitly only on Daniel 7:14 and 27, but many of the other exegetical sources of 4Q246 also refer to the eternal kingdom. The occurrence of this theme must have been one of the principles that led the author to associate these texts with each other and with Daniel 7. Only one other of the five themes appears in Daniel 7. This is the eternal kingdom's dominance over all the nations (especially in Dan 7:14, to which 4Q246 ii 8 alludes). These two themes—the eternal kingdom and its rule over all the nations—serve to draw into the range of the author's sources almost all the other passages to which he alludes. This brings the other three themes into an interpretative relationship with Daniel 7. The other passages make clear that the one who presides over the eternal kingdom is the Messiah of David and that his rule is characterized by peace and justice.

It is certainly the case that some of 4Q246's allusions are more probable than others. But even if several of the biblical passages listed in the table are discounted, the general picture will remain the same. In particular, it is clear that the key actor (besides God) in this eschatological scenario is the future Davidic king. This author must have understood the figure to whom Daniel 7:13–14 refers as the same figure who appears in such key texts of Davidic messianism as Isaiah 11, Micah 5, and the promise to David in 2 Samuel 7.

It is important to realize that interpreters of the Hebrew Bible in the Second Temple period did not think analytically, like modern biblical scholars. They did not compare Daniel 7 and the major prophecies of a new David, observe that they do not have much in common, and see them as offering different eschatological scenarios or different kinds of messianic figure. Rather, they thought synthetically. They brought such passages together in such a way that they complemented and interpreted each other.

This is why there is no Son of Man figure in early Judaism, a kind of eschatological savior from heaven conceived as an alternative to the Davidic ruler of earthly origin. When Jewish writers took note of Daniel 7:13–14, they naturally sought to relate those verses to other scriptural expectations of the coming of God's kingdom. Many did expect an eschatological priest and an eschatological prophet as well as the messianic king, but if Daniel 7:13–14 were to fit that scheme, it obviously referred to the king, not the priest or the prophet. It is also relevant and important to remember that Jewish theology was pervasively exegetical. There were no "messianic concepts" that subsisted independently of the scriptural texts. There were varying descriptions of the Messiah, but the variety was dependent on the emphasis and interpretation given to specific scriptural sources. So, for example, the emphasis on peace in 4Q246 is relatively distinctive, but it is not just an idea that the author wants to expound. It is a feature of scriptural prophecies to which he gives emphasis.

General Conclusion

As far as we can tell from our incomplete text, the main interest of the author of 4Q246 was in the eternal kingdom that will bring peace to the world by contrast with the devastating wars that characterized the present time. Writing in the tradition of works about or ascribed to Daniel, he focuses on the theme of the eternal kingdom in chapters 2 and 7 of Daniel. He also draws extensively on other biblical sources that connect the eternal kingdom to come with justice and peace. In most of these passages the kingdom is ruled, on God's behalf, by a king from the line of David, who will judge and rule the nations with justice and inaugurate the eternal peace for God's people and the world. According to 4Q246, alluding to 2 Samuel 7:14, this ruler will be called the Son of God, and, by implication, he is also identified with the figure described in vision in Daniel 7:13–14. His victory over the nations opposed to God and God's people will not be achieved by human military force. Rather, victory will be won for him by God in a new exodus event, which 4Q246 depicts by echoing the Song at the Sea (Exod 15:1–18). While it is not entirely clear whether the hostile nations will be destroyed or merely brought into submission to the rule of God and his Son, the strong emphasis on peace in the whole account suggests the latter.

This detailed study of 4Q246 has been necessary in order to demonstrate a conclusion that is important for our study. This undoubtedly pre-Christian text identifies the humanlike figure of Daniel 7:13–14 with the Davidic Messiah.[38]

38. Daniel Stökl Ben Ezra, "Messianic Figures in the Aramaic Texts from Qumran," in *Aramaica Qumranica*, ed. Katell Berthelot and Daniel Stökl Ben Ezra, Studies on the Texts of the Desert of Judah 94 (Leiden: Brill, 2010) 515–44, here 537, thinks the absence of allusion to Dan 7:13, in the context of allusions to 7:22 and 7:27, remarkable, and thinks that the author of 4Q246 may have known a version of Dan 7 that lacked verses 9–10 and 13–14. But he fails to notice that 4Q246 has many allusions to Davidic messianic texts as well as to Dan 7. If the author identified the humanlike figure of Dan 7:13–14 with the Davidic Messiah of Isa

As we shall see, the same identification is made in other texts of the Second Temple period in which we find an interpretation of Daniel 7:13–14 (4 Ezra, 2 Baruch) as well as in rabbinic traditions.

Unfortunately, we do not know how the author of 4Q246 understood more precisely the scene depicted in Daniel 7:13. Since this author, who himself had created a symbolic vision that is then interpreted in our part of his work, understood that visions of this kind deal in symbols, not literal depictions, he could have understood the scene in Daniel 7:13 to refer symbolically to God's appointment of the Davidic Messiah to rule his eternal kingdom. He need not have thought of a literal journey on clouds to appear before the divine throne (whether on earth or in heaven). Alternatively, he may have thought, as some later interpreters of Daniel 7 evidently did, of a descendant of David, born on earth in the past but taken up to heaven until the time arrived for his rule on earth.

Comparison with the Parables of Enoch

The Messianic Figures in 4Q246 and the Parables of Enoch are in many respects significantly different. In 4Q246 the Messianic Figure is called "the Son of God." In the Parables of Enoch, the Messianic Figure is called "the Chosen One," "that son of man," and "(God's) Anointed One." In 4Q246 the main functions of the Messianic Figure are to achieve and to rule the eternal kingdom. In the Parables the main function of the Messianic Figure is to pronounce judgment on the oppressors and to vindicate the righteous. Afterward he will be with the righteous in paradise, but he is not said to rule and there is no interest in an eternal kingdom. However, in both works the Messianic Figure receives the obeisance of all people. In 4Q246 the Messianic Figure and his kingdom are characterized by justice and peace, whereas in the Parables the Messianic Figure is just in his judgments, but there is little interest in the theme of peace. (Only in 52:6–9 is the abolition of all weapons described.) In 4Q246 the Messianic Figure appears to be a descendant of David, whereas in the Parables the Messianic Figure is Enoch, though some Davidic prophecies contribute to the portrait of him.

Behind these overlapping but different messianic profiles lie not only the specific concerns of each writer but also the exegetical sources from which they have constructed their Messianic Figures. Table 5 provides a comparative

9:5–7 and 11:1–4, among other passages, he would not necessarily have made verbal allusion to Dan 7:13. The case is similar to 2 Bar. 36–40 (see chapter 2.8 below).

table of these. Daniel 7 is prominent in both, although the Parables takes up explicitly Daniel's vision of the humanlike figure in Daniel 7:13, along with his relationship to the Ancient of Days, whereas Daniel 7:14 is clearly cited in 4Q246 and reference to Daniel 7:13 is only implicit (in the extant text). In its use of Daniel 7, 4Q246 is primarily interested in the eternal kingdom, relating it also to the same theme in Daniel 2, whereas in the Parables the presence of "that son of man" in heaven and his role as judge are highlighted (though the latter mainly from other sources).

Despite these differences, it is very striking that both works, in constructing their Messianic Figure, combine allusion to Daniel 7 with allusions to prophecies of the Davidic Messiah and of the Isaianic servant of the Lord. 4Q246 draws on a wide range of passages understood to refer to the Davidic Messiah and in such a way that its Messianic Figure appears as indubitably a descendant of David. (It would be very hard to understand 2 Sam 7:13–14 or Isa 9:5–6 in any other way.) The Book of Parables, on the other hand, draws on only a few such passages and, by identifying the Messiah of those passages with Enoch, evidently detaches them from the expectation of a literal descendant of David. 4Q246 gathers references to the eternal kingdom and the peace that will characterize it, whereas the Parables focuses on prophecies of the eschatological judge. But in both works the Messianic Figure's role relates both to the people of God and to the nations, with allusions to Isaiah 49:6 probably to be found in both. Finally, the allusions to the exodus event and the Song at the Sea in both works are a striking point of convergence.

The most important point of commonality is that both works construct their profile of the Messianic Figure by combining Daniel's humanlike figure, the Davidic king, and the servant of the Lord in Isaiah. While modern scholars tend to distinguish sharply between these three categories of eschatological figures, both the works we have studied bring them all together. These works must stand in an exegetical tradition to which they are both indebted while developing rather different profiles of the Messianic Figure. The differences arise from the selection and the interpretation of the texts they drew from the common fund of scriptural material. It seems very likely that the Parables of Enoch is the more innovatory in identifying Enoch as the Messianic Figure to whom material from all three categories of scriptural prophecies apply. Its strong allusions, nonetheless, to some Davidic prophecies probably shows that in the exegetical tradition behind the Parables the three categories were understood as all relating to a distinctly Davidic Messiah. In this respect at least, 4Q246 seems to offer a more traditional messianic profile.

TABLE 1. *Allusions to Daniel in 4Q246*

4Q246

Col. I ¹[. . .] settled [up]on him and he fell before the throne ²[. . . k]ing (live) **forever**! You are angry, and **have changed**	Dan 2:4; 3:9; 5:10; 6:21/ Dan 5:6
³[. . .] . . . your vision, and everything that shall come forever. ⁴[. . . mi]ghty ones, oppression will come upon the earth ⁵[. . .] and great slaughter in the provinces ⁶[. . .] king of Assyria [and E]gypt ⁷[. . .] and he will be great over the earth	
⁸[. . .] they [will d]o, and all **will serve**	Dan 7:10 (cf. 14)
⁹[. . . gr]eat will he be called and he will be designated by his name. Col. II ¹He will be called son of God, and they will call him son of the Most High. Like the shooting stars ²of the vision, so will their kingdom be; they will rule (several) year[s] over	
³**the earth** and **trample** on everything; a people will **trample** on another people, and a province another provi[n]ce.	Dan 7:23 Dan 2:41
⁴ *vacat* Until he **raises up** the people of God and everyone will rest from the sword. *vacat*	Dan 2:44
⁵**His kingdom will be an eternal kingdom**, and **all his paths in righteousness**. He will jud[ge]	Dan 3:33; 7:27 Dan 4:34
⁶the earth in righteousness and all will make peace. The sword will cease from the earth,	
⁷and all the provinces will **bow down to him**. **The great God** is his strength,	Dan 2:46/ Dan 2:45
⁸he will wage war for him; **he will give the peoples** into his hand and	Dan 7:14
⁹he will throw them all down before him. **His rule will be an eternal rule**, and all the deeps of	Dan 4:31; 7:14

Note: Words printed in bold are in verbatim or near-verbatim correspondence to Daniel.

TABLE 2. *4Q246 i 9–ii 1 with parallels*

4Q246 i 9–ii 1	2 Samuel 7:9, 13–14a, 16[a]	Luke 1:32–33
great he will be called, and he will be designated by his name. He **will be called son** of God, and they will call him **son of** <u>the Most High</u>.	I will make for you a *great* name, like the name of the *great* ones of the earth. . . . He shall build a house for my name, and I will establish the throne of *his kingdom forever.* I will be his father and *he shall be my son.* . . . Your house and your kingdom shall be made sure *forever* before me; *your throne* shall be established *forever.* Isaiah 9:6–7[5–6] For a child has been born for us, a *son* given to us; . . . *his name will be called* Wonderful Counselor, Mighty God, Everlasting Father, Prince of Peace. Of the increase *of his government* and of peace *there will be no end*, for *the throne of David* and his kingdom. He will establish and uphold it with justice and with righteousness from this time forward and *forevermore.*	*He will be great,* and *will be called the Son of* <u>the Most High</u>, and the Lord God will give to him *the throne of his ancestor David.* He will reign over the house of Jacob *forever,* and *of his kingdom there will be no end.*

4Q246 i 7	Micah 5:4[3]	Luke 1:32–33
he will be great over **the earth**	*He shall be great* to the ends of **the earth**	*He will be great,*
	Psalm 2:7	and *will be called the Son of* <u>the Most High</u>,
	He said to me, "You are my son; today I have begotten you."	and the Lord God will give to him *the throne of his ancestor David.* He will reign over the house of Jacob *forever,* and *of his kingdom there will be no end.*

Note: Parallels between 4Q246 and the Hebrew Bible are in bold; those between Luke and the Hebrew Bible are in italics. The parallel between 4Q246 and Luke that does not correspond to the biblical passages is underlined.

[a]The translations of biblical passages in this column are from NRSV but modified to reflect the Hebrew more literally.

TABLE 3. *Scriptural allusions in 4Q246*

4Q246

Col. i ¹[. . .] settled [up]on him and he fell before the throne	
²[. . . k]ing (live) **forever!**	Dan 2:4; 3:9; 5:10; 6:21
You are angry, and **have changed**	Dan 5:6
³[. . .] . . . your vision, and everything that shall come forever.	
⁴[. . . mi]ghty ones, oppression will come upon the earth	
⁵[. . .] and great slaughter in the provinces	
⁶[. . .] king of Assyria [and E]gypt	
⁷[. . .] and **he will be great** over **the earth**	Mic 5:3
⁸[. . .] they [will d]o, and all will serve	
⁹[. . . gr]eat will he be called	<u>2 Sam 7:9</u>; Mic 5:3
and he will be designated by his name.	
Col. ii ¹**He will be called son** of God,	Isa 9:5; <u>2 Sam 7:14</u>
and they will call him **son** of the Most High.	
Like the shooting stars ²of the vision, so will their kingdom be;	
they will rule (several) year[s] over	
³**the earth** and **trample** on everything;	Dan 7:23
a people will **trample** on another people,	
and a province on another provi[n]ce.	
⁴*vacat* Until he **raises up** the people of God	Dan 2:44; Isa 49:6
and everyone will rest from **the sword.** *vacat*	Zech 9:10
⁵**His kingdom will be an eternal kingdom,**	Dan 3:33; 7:27
and **all his paths in righteousness.**	Dan 4:34
He will jud[ge] ⁶**the earth in righteousness**	Isa 11:4
and all will make **peace.** The **sword** will cease **from the earth,**	Isa 2:4; <u>9:6</u>; Hos 2:20
⁷and **all the provinces will bow down to him.**	Ps 72:11
The great God is his **strength,**	Dan 2:45; Exod 15:2
⁸**he will wage war for** him;	Exod 14:13; 15:3
he will give the peoples into his hand	Dan 7:14
and ⁹he **will throw** them all **down** before him.	Exod 15:1
His rule will be an eternal rule,	Dan 4:31; 7:14
and all the deeps of	<u>Ps 89:26</u>?

Note: Words printed in bold are in verbatim or close correspondence to the language of the texts in the Hebrew Bible. Texts underlined refer to the Messiah of David.

TABLE 4. *The Messianic Figure in 4Q246: sources and themes*

	Eternal kingdom	Messiah of David	Peace	Justice	Rule over nations
Dan 7:9–27	✓				✓
Exod 15:1–18	✓				
2 Sam 7:13–14	✓	✓			
Ps 72:1–11	✓	✓	✓	✓	✓
Ps 89:20–29	✓	✓			
Isa 2:4 (= Mic 4:3)			✓	✓	✓
Isa 9:6–7[5–6]	✓	✓	✓	✓	
Isa 11:1–9		✓	✓	✓	✓
Isa 49:6					✓
Dan 2:44–45	✓				✓
Dan 4:34–37[31–34]	✓			✓	
Hos 2:18–19[20–21]			✓	✓	
Mic 5:4–5[3–4]		✓	✓		
Zech 9:9–10		✓	✓		✓

TABLE 5. *Exegetical sources for the Messianic Figure: 4Q246 and the Parables of Enoch compared*

4Q246	Parables of Enoch
\multicolumn{2}{c}{Daniel}	
Dan 2:44–45	
Dan 4:34	
Dan 7:13–27	Dan 7:9–22
	Dan 8:15
\multicolumn{2}{c}{Davidic ruler}	
2 Sam 7:13–14	
	Ps 2:2, 8
Ps 72:1–11	Ps 72:1–17
Ps 89:26	
Isa 9:5–6	
Isa 11:4	Isa 11:2–5
Mic 5:3–4[2–3]	
Zech 9:10	
\multicolumn{2}{c}{Isaianic servant}	
	Isa 41:11–12
	Isa 42:1–7
Isa 49:6	Isa 49:1–8
	Isa 52:13, 15
\multicolumn{2}{c}{Non-messianic passages}	
	Gen 3:23–24
	2 Kgs 2:11–12
	Ps 3:7
Isa 2:4 (= Mic 4:3)	
	Isa 13:8
	Isa 24:21
Hos 2:20–22	
	Mic 1:4
	Zeph 1:18
	Zeph 3:13
\multicolumn{2}{c}{Exodus 14–15}	
Exod 14:14	Exod 14:13
Exod 15:1–3	Exod 15:1, 7, 10

CHAPTER 2.4

Interpretation of Daniel 7 in Sibylline Oracles Book 5

Book 5 of the Sibylline Oracles has been relatively neglected in studies of early Jewish messianism, perhaps because, unlike the other texts we have studied, it derives from the diaspora, specifically from Egypt.[1] Written in the late first or early second century CE,[2] it has the special interest that it probably expresses the kind of ideology that inspired the Jewish diaspora revolts of 115–117 CE.[3] Our interest, however, will be primarily in the interpretation of Daniel to which it bears witness. Its background in Daniel 7 has not been sufficiently recognized. This may be partly because the Sibyllines, a distinct literary genre from the Jewish apocalypses, are prone to contrived obscurity and allude to scriptural sources less often and less obviously. (Verbatim allusions are in any case difficult within the constraints of hexameter verse.) The passages that are of most relevance to the subject of this book are unusual in the density of

---

1. Thus, for example, it does not appear in Antti Laato, *A Star Is Rising: The Historical Development of the Old Testament Royal Ideology and the Rise of the Jewish Messianic Expectations* (Atlanta: Scholars Press, 1997), which limits its field to Palestinian Judaism. But there is extensive and valuable discussion of Sib. Or. 5 in Andrew Chester, *Messiah and Exaltation: Jewish Messianic and Visionary Traditions and New Testament Christology*, WUNT 207 (Tübingen: Mohr Siebeck, 2007) 399–405, 471–96.

2. In line 397 the Roman destruction of the temple is said to have taken place πάλαι. The word does not necessarily mean "long ago." The meaning could be simply "some time ago." The time of writing seems very likely to be before the diaspora revolts of 115–117 CE.

3. William Horbury, *Jewish War under Trajan and Hadrian* (Cambridge: Cambridge University Press, 2014) 32: "In this Jewish Greek verse composition the Sibyl is almost the prophetess of the diaspora revolt." See also John M. G. Barclay, *Jews in the Mediterranean Diaspora: From Alexander to Trajan (323 BCE–117 CE)* (Edinburgh: T&T Clark, 1996) 226–28.

their biblical allusions, though even here, as we shall see, they are paraphrastic rather than verbal.

John Collins has helpfully analyzed the central part of the book (lines 52–434) as consisting of four oracles that display a common pattern. Each of them contains four elements: (1) oracles of judgment against various nations (especially Egypt and Rome); (2) the return of the emperor Nero as an eschatological adversary;[4] (3) the advent of a savior figure (usually from heaven); (4) a destruction (usually by fire).[5] Even if this scheme is slightly too neat, it highlights well what is distinctive in the eschatological scenario of the book. Whether the four oracles all derive from the same author is not of primary importance for our present purposes, but clearly they do all conform to a common pattern and must have originated in the literary connection in which they now appear. It seems to me very plausible that one author designed the four oracles as a way of developing his eschatological vision in varying but complementary ways. Especially in relation to the Messianic Figure, there is a progression from his brief appearance in the first oracle (lines 108–109) to the fullest account in lines 414–434.

Relationship with Daniel 7

Table 1 highlights the key passages in each of the four oracles for our present purposes: those about Nero and especially those about the Messianic Figure. But it also notes the allusions to Daniel 7. The most unmistakable of these is probably the allusion to Daniel 7:8 in lines 222–223 (Oracle C):

> For, first of all, cutting off[6] the roots from three heads
> mightily with a blow, he will give them to others to eat.[7]

---

4. On the belief that Nero was not dead but hidden and would return, see Richard Bauckham, *The Climax of Prophecy: Studies on the Book of Revelation* (Edinburgh: T&T Clark, 1993) 407–23.

5. John J. Collins, "Sibylline Oracles," *OTP* 1:317–472, here 390; also Collins, *The Apocalyptic Imagination: An Introduction to the Jewish Matrix of Christianity* (New York: Crossroad, 1984) 187–88.

6. Collins here translates Rzach's correction of the text to σχισσάμενος.

7. All quotations are based on the translation by Collins, "Sibylline Oracles," 393–495, but I have frequently modified that translation. I have consulted these editions of the Greek text: Aloisius Rzach, *ΧΡΗΣΜΟΙ ΣΙΒΥΛΛΙΑΚΟΙ: Oracula Sibyllina* (Leipzig: Freytag, 1891) 104–29; Johannes Geffcken, *Die Oracula Sibyllina*, Die griechischen christlichen Schriftsteller der ersten [drei] Jahrhunderte 8 (Leipzig: Hinrichs, 1902) 103–29; Alfons Kurfess, *Sibyllinische Weissagungen* (Berlin: Heimeran, 1951) 120–50.

Compare Daniel's vision of the fourth beast, with its ten horns:

> And many designs were in its horns, and lo, one horn grew up among them, a little one among its horns, and three of the earlier horns were removed by it. (Dan 7:8a OG, NETS; see also 7:20)

> I was considering its horns, and lo, another little horn came up among them, and three of the horns of those that preceded it were uprooted from before it. (Dan 7:8a Theod, NETS)

This allusion situates the returning Nero within the eschatological scenario of Daniel 7, as the last and most arrogant of the Roman emperors. (As in other early Jewish and Christian texts, the fourth beast is understood to be the Roman Empire.) According to Daniel 7:8, the little horn has "a mouth speaking great things," and this characteristic is picked up in the denunciation of arrogance that follows in the Sibylline text (lines 228–237).[8]

This rather clear allusion to Daniel 7 makes it plausible that there is another allusion, also casting the returning Nero in the role of Daniel's little horn, in lines 106–107:

> But when he attains a powerful height and odious audacity,
> he will also come, wishing to destroy the city of the blessed ones.

Compare

> ... and that horn had eyes and a mouth speaking great things, and its looks surpassed the others, and I was observing that horn preparing for war against the holy ones and routing them. (Dan 7:20b–21 OG, NETS)

> ... which had eyes and a mouth speaking great things. And its appearance was greater than the rest. I kept watching and that horn made war with the holy ones and prevailed over them. (Dan 7:20b–21 Theod, NETS)[9]

In Daniel the little horn prevails over "the holy ones" until the Ancient of Days comes and gives judgment for them. Then royal authority is removed from the

---

8. Sib. Or. 3:396–400 is also based on Dan 7:7–8. The author of Sib. Or. 5 doubtless knew this passage and has updated the political application.

9. See also Dan 8:23–25.

little horn and given to "the holy ones" (Dan 7:22, 26–27). In the Sibylline text, these events are paraphrased and interpreted. A king sent by God carries out God's judgment on Nero and his entourage:

> And then a certain king sent from God against him
> will destroy all the great kings and noble men.
> Thus there will be judgment on people by the imperishable One.
> (lines 108–110)

The reference to divine judgment in line 110 shows that the author is in touch with the Danielic text, where it is God who judges the little horn (Dan 7:22, 26). The reference to "all the great kings" likely reflects the universal language of Daniel 7:27. In this interpretative context, we should probably conclude that the king sent by God is the humanlike figure of Daniel 7:13.

In Oracle B, the returning Nero is apparently described as attacking the Jewish people (line 149).[10] The next event, the appearance of a great star that will destroy the whole earth, is said to occur "after the fourth year" (line 155). This surprisingly precise chronological note is probably based on Daniel 7:25, which predicts that the people of God will be given into the hands of the little horn "for a time and times and half a time" (cf. also Dan 12:7). Interpreters of Daniel took this to mean three and a half years (see Rev 12:14 compared with 11:2).

In Oracles C and D, the Messianic Figure is said to come "from the sky" (line 256) or "from the vault of heaven" (line 414). These must be allusions to Daniel 7:13 and will be discussed in more detail below. The two references to (the) "holy ones" (ἁγίων: lines 401, 432), referring to the people of God, are more significant than might be supposed. In biblical and early Jewish literature the term usually denotes angels, but in its six occurrences in Daniel 7 it has usually been understood to refer to the human people of God. Book 5 of the Sibyllines uses a variety of other ways of describing the people of God. The "holy ones" occurs only in these two lines.

It is striking that there is at least one allusion to Daniel 7 in each of the four oracles (whether or not this was deliberately designed by the author). It shows that this passage came to mind whenever the author thought about the returning Nero and the Messianic Figure. Daniel 7 supplied the template for the eschatological narratives he tells. These two key protagonists he understood to be the littler horn and the humanlike figure of Daniel's vision.

---

10. Lines 150–155 refer to what Nero did before his alleged death and flight to the east.

The Messianic Figure in Oracle A

> And then a certain king sent from God [θεόθεν] against him
> [Nero]
> will destroy all the great kings and noble men. (lines 108–109)

This first reference to a Messianic Figure is the briefest. His description will be further developed in the three subsequent references to him. Although this account is short, it is distinctive. In Jewish literature, angels and prophets are sent by or from God, but not usually kings. It is likely that the author has adopted this description from the earlier Sibyl of Egyptian Judaism, book 3. There an ideal king of the future is depicted thus:

> And then God will send a King from the sun
> who will stop the entire earth from evil war,
> killing some, imposing oaths of loyalty on others. (lines 652–654)[11]

Whatever "from the sun" may originally have meant here,[12] it is possible that the author of book 5 took it to mean "from the sky," which is what he says of the Messianic Figure in later references (lines 158, 256, 414).

A king sent by God need not come from heaven, but a "king sent *from* God" (Sib. Or. 5:108: θεόθεν) must surely come from the heavenly presence of God. This phrase is in this way more precise than the statement in 3:652 that "God will send a king." It therefore prepares the way for the more explicit indications that the Messianic Figure comes from heaven in the later oracles of book 5. As I have already suggested, the identification of the returning Nero with the little horn of Daniel 7 makes it likely that the king sent from God is the humanlike figure of Daniel 7:13. This figure, though not called a king in Daniel 7, is given by God universal rule over all the nations of earth (Dan 7:14), and so it would make sense if the author of this Sibylline text supposed that God will send him to earth to establish his kingdom, destroying all opponents.

The phrase "a certain king" (line 108: τις ... βασιλεύς) is an example of a formula that occurs several times in books 3 and 5 of the Sibylline Oracles.

---

11. Quotations of Sib. Or. 3 are taken from the translation by Collins, "Sibylline Oracles," 362–80.
12. See Chester, *Messiah and Exaltation*, 348–50, 402 n. 12, 475–76, for discussion of Collins's view that it refers to an Egyptian king. My own view is that line 652 is probably based on Jer 23:5, where the word "branch" (צמח), referring to the coming Davidic king, is rendered in OG as ἀνατολή, which is most commonly used to mean "the rising of the sun."

It is an example of the cryptic style of the oracles, a way of indicating a personage (or group) who would be well known to readers, but without divulging their identity directly. In most cases the name of the person (or group) could be expected to be known to readers. These are the seven occurrences of the formula:

1. 3:288: "There is a certain royal tribe [τις φυλὴ βασιλήιος] whose race will never stumble." In context this is an unmistakable reference to the tribe of Judah.
2. 3:419: "Then there will be a certain false writer [τις ψευδογράφος], an old man." The following lines make it abundantly clear that this is Homer.
3. 5:36: "Then will come a certain [τις] great destroyer of pious men." In the following line he is identified by gematria as the emperor Vespasian.
4. 5:108: "And then a certain king sent from God against him."
5. 5:237: "By you [Arrogance] a certain king [τις βασιλεύς], cast down, destroyed his august life." This occurs within an elaborate denunciation of Arrogance. The reference is almost certainly to Nebuchadnezzar, who for his overweening pride was cast down from his throne and lived like a beast of the field, according to Daniel 4.
6. 5:256: "Then there will be a certain person [εἷς δὲ τις] from the sky, an exceptional man." I shall argue below that this is Joshua.
7. 5:408: "But now a certain insignificant and impious king [τις ... βασιλεύς]." The emperor Titus, who destroyed the temple in Jerusalem, is clearly meant here.

All of these figures would be known by name to readers (provided my explanation of 5:256 is correct) with the apparent exception of the king in 5:108. If the usage here is consistent with the others, then readers may not be familiar with the king's name at this point in the poem but will learn who he is when he appears with a different description in lines 256, 258–259. Alternatively, readers are not in this case expected to know the king's name, but they are expected to be able to identify him with a specific, known figure, who could be either the king who is similarly described in Sibylline Oracles 3:652–654 or the figure called "one like a son of man" in Daniel 7:13.

The Messianic Figure in Oracle B

> But when after the fourth year a great star shines
> which alone will destroy the whole earth, because of

> the honor which they first gave to Poseidon of the sea,
> a great star will come from heaven [οὐρανόθεν] to
> > the wondrous sea
> and will burn the deep sea and Babylon itself. (lines 155–159)

The first of these lines (155) probably alludes to Sibylline Oracles 3:334, which describes a comet that heralds destruction. But the second "great star," which comes from heaven (line 158), corresponds to the role of the Messianic Figure in the three other oracles (two of which portray him as coming from heaven) and so must be understood as a metaphor for a human person.

Probably the image derives from the famous oracle of Balaam in Numbers 24:17,[13] which in the Septuagint reads:

> A star shall dawn out of Jacob,
> and a human [ἄνθρωπος] shall rise up out of Israel. (Num 24:17b NETS, modified)

In this translation the poetic parallelism equates the star with a human being.[14] The text does not obviously provide a basis for speaking of a star coming "from heaven," but it poses a problem: stars are to be seen in the sky and do not arise out of nations. The Sibylline text may be a subtle interpretation of Balaam's oracle, solving the problem by postulating a figure who did come from the nation of Israel on earth but is now in heaven and will in the future return to earth from heaven. (Such an interpretation could have been assisted by Dan 12:3, which compares the righteous after death to the stars of heaven.) We shall see that another of the messianic passages in this Sibylline book does seem to envisage such a figure: a famous Israelite of the past who will come again to earth from heaven.

---

13. For the importance of this passage in Jewish messianism, see John J. Collins, *The Scepter and the Star: The Messiahs of the Dead Sea Scrolls and Other Ancient Literature* (New York: Doubleday, 1995) 65–66, 202; William Horbury, *Messianism among Jews and Christians: Twelve Biblical and Historical Studies* (London: T&T Clark, 2003) 144–47; Horbury, *Jewish Messianism and the Cult of Christ* (London: SCM, 1998) 50.

14. I cannot see how this makes ἄνθρωπος (here and in 24:7) a "messianic title," as Horbury, *Messianism*, 144–45, claims. In his whole discussion (144–51) Horbury seems to confuse the use of "a man" to refer to a Messianic Figure with the use of the word as a title. There seems to me nothing remarkable in the use of "a man" to refer to a Messianic Figure who was human in contexts where his messianic role or status is indicated in other ways, as is the case in Num 24:17 LXX.

This account of the Messianic Figure focuses exclusively on his destructive effect, which may reflect the continuation of Balaam's prophecy in Numbers 24:17c–24. It is a major emphasis in book 5 of the Sibyllines.

The Messianic Figure in Oracle D

The difficult text of Oracle C will be more easily understood after examining the clearer depiction of the Messianic Figure that forms the climactic conclusion to Oracle D (lines 414–433). A translation is given in table 2. The use of the past tense, instead of the future that has been used in all the previous accounts of the Messianic Figure, expresses the certainty with which the readers are to view this prophecy. These still-future events are no less bound to occur than those described in lines 397–413, which readers would know had already been fulfilled. The Sibyl in prophetic vision has seen them happen, just as though they already had (line 388).

The figure who comes from heaven (line 414) is unequivocally a man (ἀνήρ). Like the Parables of Enoch, this author understood the "one like a son of man" in Daniel 7:13 to be a human being exalted to heaven. Previous scholarship has failed to notice the significance of the word "blessed," which here translates μακαρίτης. Unlike the much more common word μακάριος, which is usually rendered "blessed" or "happy" in English, μακαρίτης generally refers to the blessed dead, those who have departed this life and are happy in the afterlife.[15] Its application to the man from heaven here should be taken seriously. He is a man who after departing life on earth (whether by dying or, like Enoch, leaving this world without dying) now enjoys a blessed life in heaven.

The "scepter" (σκῆπτρον), which God has conferred on him, is the symbol of the royal authority with which, according to Daniel 7:14, God invested the "one like a son of man." It might also allude to Numbers 24:17, which in the Hebrew text reads:

> A star shall come out of Jacob
> and a scepter shall rise out of Israel.

---

15. See the references in Franco Montanari, *The Brill Dictionary of Ancient Greek*, ed. Madeleine Goh and Chad Schroeder (Leiden: Brill, 2015) s.v. μακαρίτης: Aristophanes, Aeschylus, Menander, Plutarch, Athenaeus, Lucian; and add Alciphron 2.35; 3.14; Lucian, *Luct.* 24; *Philops.* 27. In later Christian usage it came to mean "Saint" (equivalent to Latin *beatus*). In the Sibylline Oracles it occurs only here.

In the Septuagint, as we have seen, the word "scepter" has been replaced by "human." But this prophecy was so well known that the Sibylline author may well have had access to a source that reflected the Hebrew more closely. In that case he has taken up Balaam's image of the "star" in Oracle B and that of the "scepter" here in Oracle D. The word "all" (πάντας) in line 416 alludes to the universal dominion over all peoples that is given to the "one like a son of man" in Daniel 7:14.[16]

Another possible allusion is to Psalm 2:8–9, where God addresses the messianic king:

> Ask of me, and I shall give you nations as your heritage,
> and as your possession the ends of the earth.
> You shall shepherd them with an iron rod [ῥάβδῳ]
> and like a potter's vessel you shall shatter them. (NETS)

Whereas the scepter is a symbol of royal authority, the "iron rod" seems to be more an instrument of rule, but the two could have been assimilated.

The burning of cities and nations (lines 418–419) might allude to Daniel 7:11, where the body of the beast is "given over to burning with fire" (NETS).[17] But burning a city down is an obvious way to destroy it, and destruction by burning is a common phenomenon in book 5 of the Sibyllines (lines 118, 159, 177, 211–213, 274, 369, 377–378, 399). Since the Jerusalem temple is said to have been "soaked in fire by an impious hand" (line 399), the Messianic Figure's actions of burning down all cities and burning evil nations may be understood as divine vengeance.

Lines 420–427 describe a very distinctive role for this Messianic Figure. The new Jerusalem and the new temple are well attested elements of the Jewish eschatological hope, but they are not usually expected to be built by the Messianic Figure.[18] There seem to be only two biblical texts that could have been

---

16. In lines 415–416 there may well also be an echo of Sib. Or. 3:49–50: "For a holy prince will come to gain sway [κρατήσων] over the scepters of the whole earth [πάσης γῆς σκῆπτρα] forever." Lines 1–96 of Sib. Or. 3 are generally considered not originally part of book 3 but to have been part of another collection. There is no reason, however, why they should not have been known to the author of Sib. Or. 5, as this correspondence between 3:49–50 and 5:415–16 suggests.

17. Horbury, *Messianism*, 140, sees a reference to Isa 11:4 here, but "the breath of his lips" is interpreted as fire only in 4 Ezra 13:10.

18. See Chester, *Messiah and Exaltation*, 480–86.

understood to predict such an event.[19] One is 2 Samuel (OG 2 Kgdms) 7:13: "He shall build a house for my name." This dynastic oracle was widely understood in a messianic sense and, as we have seen, probably explains the messianic application of the designation "Son of God" in 4Q246. The other text is Zechariah 6:12–13, where it is promised that the temple will be built by "a man, Shoot [Ἀνατολή] is his name" (6:12 NETS). The word ἀνατολή is used here, as in Zechariah 3:8 and Jeremiah 23:5, to translate צמח, which means "branch." But the Greek word, meaning literally "rising," is more commonly used to refer to the rising of the sun or the dawn. It is possible that the Sibylline author connected this messianic title with the king God will send from the sun (Sib. Or. 3:652) and with the man "from heaven."[20]

These biblical texts, understood messianically, would suggest that it is the Davidic Messiah who will build the new temple. This is obviously the case in 2 Samuel 7, and, although for an ancient reader Zechariah 6:12–13 might not be as clearly Davidic as it seems to a modern scholar (who will connect it with Zerubbabel's Davidic descent), the fact that the same messianic title is used in Jeremiah 23:5, where the messianic king is explicitly a descendant of David, makes it unlikely that the Sibylline author would have missed the Davidic character of the temple-builder in Zechariah. If so, then here we have the same phenomenon of prophecies of the Messiah of David associated with Daniel 7:13–14 that we find in the Parables of Enoch, 4Q246, and 4 Ezra. However, we know from the Parables of Enoch that this association of messianic texts need not oblige an author to think that the Messianic Figure would actually be a descendant of David.

The Messianic Figure in Oracle C

> Then[21] there will be[22] a certain person from the sky,
> an exceptional man,
> (εἷς δὲ τις ἔσσεται αὖθις ἀπ' αἰθέρος ἔξοχος ἀνήρ)
> [whose hands he stretched out on the fruitful wood]

---

19. Horbury, *Messianism*, 149, also mentions Ezek 37:24–28, which associates "David" with the new temple but does not make him its builder.
20. Note also Luke 1:78–79.
21. Αὖθις here must mean "thereafter" or "next," as in Sib. Or. 3:419, 573, not "back" or "again."
22. Some editors amend ἔσσεται to ἔξεται, but that ἔσσεται is correct is suggested by the parallels in Sib. Or. 3:419, 573.

the best of the Hebrews, who once made the sun stand still[23]
by crying out with noble speech and holy lips. (lines 256–259)

Almost all scholars agree that line 257 is a Christian gloss referring to the crucifixion of Jesus and associating the cross with the tree of life, a common theme in patristic writers.[24] John O'Neill argued ingeniously that all four lines are Jewish and not Christian and refer to the return of a great Jewish teacher who had been crucified.[25] It seems much more plausible that a Christian scribe, recognizing the reference to Joshua in lines 258–259, assumed that Joshua here is a type of his namesake Jesus of Nazareth, and made this clear by adding line 257. It seems to be the only Christian gloss in the manuscripts of book 5 of the Sibylline Oracles,[26] but it could be that this passage offered an exceptional opportunity to identify the figure of Jesus in this much respected prophecy.

Some scholars have considered all four lines to be a Christian insertion,[27] a contention that is best answered by making good sense of them (without line 257) as original to the text and coherent with the other passages about the Messianic Figure in this book. The pattern that is common to the four oracles A–D requires that there should be a messianic passage in Oracle C, just as there is a passage about the returning Nero (see table 1).

---

23. Collins's translation, "who will one day cause the sun to stand," is based on a correction of the text from στῆσεν (past) to στήσει (future). But there is no other evidence that a sun-stopping miracle was expected in the future, in the time of the coming Messianic Figure, whereas the text as it stands makes good sense as a reference to Joshua's miracle in the past.

24. References in John C. O'Neill, "The Man from Heaven: SibOr 5.256–259," JSP 9 (1991) 87–102, here 92.

25. O'Neill, "The Man from Heaven," 87–102. David C. Mitchell, *Messiah ben Joseph* (Newton Mearns: Campbell, 2016) 76–78, also defends the originality of all four lines. He argues that they refer to the Messiah ben Joseph (or Messiah ben Ephraim) who in later Jewish tradition is expected to fight against the forces of Gog and die in battle. He does not see the connection between lines 256–259 and lines 414–419. I do not find Mitchell's argument that the Messiah ben Joseph tradition can be traced as far back as the Hebrew Bible convincing, and the evidence for it even within the late Second Temple period is tenuous at best. It is tempting to think that the idea of the returning Joshua in Sib. Or. 5 may have some connection with the origin of the tradition, since Joshua was from the tribe of Ephraim. In Tg. Ps.-J. Exod 40:11 the Messiah ben Ephraim is said to be a descendant of Joshua.

26. Similarly, there may be only one Christian gloss in Sib. Or. 3 (line 776).

27. E.g., Johannes Geffcken, *Komposition und Entstehungszeit der Oracula Sibyllina*, Texte und Untersuchungen zur Geschichte der altchristlichen Literatur, neuen Folge 8.1 (1902; repr., Leipzig: Hinrichs, 1967) 29. Others are listed in Chester, *Messiah and Exaltation*, 399 n. 7.

Line 256 appears to be rather closely modeled on Sibylline Oracles 3:419 (referring to Homer):

> Then there will be a certain false writer, an old man.
> (καί τις ψευδογράφος πρέσβυς βροτός ἔσσεται αὖτις) (3:419)

> Then there will be a certain person from the sky,
>   an exceptional man.
> (εἷς δὲ τις ἔσσεται αὖθις ἀπ' αἰθέρος ἔξοχος ἀνήρ) (5:256)

The parallel shows that αὖθις should not be rendered "again" (as in Collins's translation of both passages), which would be quite inappropriate in the case of Homer, but "then." Another parallel, referring to a people rather than a person, is 3:573: "Then there will be [ἔσσεται αὖτις] a holy race of pious men." But this lacks the expression "a certain . . ."

We have already seen, in our discussion of Oracle A, that the expression "a certain (τις) . . . ," which is used in this way seven times in books 3 and 5, is an example of the cryptic nature of Sibylline prophecy, indicating a specific person who would be known to the readers, but without explicitly identifying him. In most cases, this known person has a name familiar to the readers, but that appears not to be the case in 5:108 (the first reference in this book to the Messianic Figure). In the closest parallel to 5:256, which is 3:419 (quoted above), the intended person was very well known by name, and this suggests that this is likely to be the case also in 5:256. Indeed, just as the lines following 3:419 make it unmistakably clear that the person in question is Homer, so the lines following 5:256 (lines 258–259) make it clear that the person in question is Joshua, the only man who ever stopped the sun.

Lines 258–259 are a clear reference to the narrative in Joshua 10:12–14, which reads in the Old Greek:

> Then Iesous spoke to the Lord, on the day when God delivered the Amorrite into the control of Israel, when he shattered them at Gabaon, and they were shattered before the sons of Israel, and Iesous said,
>
> > "Let the sun stand at Gabaon,
> >   and the moon at the ravine of Ailon."
>
> And the sun stood still, and the moon was in position until God avenged himself on their enemies, and the sun stood in midheaven; it did not go

forward to set until the end of one day. And there was not such a day either before or after so that a god heeded a human being, because the Lord fought alongside Israel. (NETS)

Joshua's words were the means of securing this unparalleled event, and so it is understandable that the Sibylline text speaks of his "noble speech and holy lips." The biblical text stresses the utterly unique character of this occasion when "a god heeded a human being," explaining how the Sibylline text can call Joshua "an exceptional [ἔξοχος] man," even "the best [ὁ ἄριστος] of the Hebrews."

It is important to recall what this miracle achieved. Five kings of the Amorites had combined forces to attack Israel. Joshua's army defeated them, and he hanged the five kings. On the same, miraculously extended day,[28] he went on to capture, one by one, seven major cities, to put their kings to death, and to slaughter all the inhabitants of the cities, in accordance with the practice of holy war:

> And Iesous smote all the land of the hill country and the Nageb and the plain and Asedoth and its kings; they did not leave any of them who survived, and they utterly destroyed everything that breathed with life, as the Lord, the God of Israel commanded. (Josh 10:40 NETS)

The following chapter describes an equally devastating victory over another alliance of Canaanite kings, with the total elimination of all the inhabitants of all the cities of their lands. After narrating other campaigns, chapter 12 lists by name the twenty-nine kings of the Amorites whom Joshua and the Israelites slew. These campaigns, which put the greater part of the promised land into the possession of the Israelites, made Joshua, in the eyes of the author of the Sibylline text, "the best of the Hebrews," presumably surpassing even the achievements of Moses, who merely led the people to the promised land and commanded them to do what Joshua actually accomplished.

So who better than Joshua to return from heaven and accomplish what "the blessed man from the vault of heaven" (line 414) will do? Of the latter it is said:

> He destroyed every city from its foundation with much fire
> and burned nations of mortals who were formerly evildoers.
>   (lines 418–419)

---

28. In OG it is clearer than in MT that all this happens on the same day, because OG omits 10:15 and 43.

Several scholars have supposed that lines 256 and 257–259 portray Joshua as a type of the "man from the sky" to come. But the passage does not say that there will be a man like the one who stopped the sun. It says that a certain man, an exceptional man, the best of the Hebrews, who made the sun stand still, will be there (coming) from the sky. John Collins translates our passage thus:

> There will again be one exceptional man from the sky,
> the best of the Hebrews, who will one day cause the sun to stand,
> speaking with fair speech and holy lips. (lines 256, 258–259)

The translation "will . . . cause the sun to stand" is based on a correction of the text from στῆσεν (past) to στήσει (future). This is a correction of the text made in Geffcken's edition but not in those of Rzach and Kurfess. It has no manuscript support. The effect is to make the whole of lines 256 and 258–259 refer to what the coming man from the sky will do. There is then no direct reference to Joshua at all. Rather, the Messianic Figure will repeat the miracle that Joshua performed in the past. But as John O'Neill says, this correction creates "a new unheard-of eschatological miracle." As he observes, "the eclipse of the sun at the end of history is a frequent theme" (Sib. Or. 3:801–802; 5:349, 477–478), but the standing still of the sun is unparalleled.[29] O'Neill himself thinks that the recently crucified Jewish teacher (not Jesus), who is in his view the "exceptional man," had once stopped the sun.[30] But postulating such an unparalleled historical event is surely no more satisfactory than postulating an otherwise unattested eschatological event. The only plausible reading of the text is that it refers to the actual miracle performed by Joshua in the days of the conquest of the promised land.

If these lines speak of the actual return from heaven of the historical Joshua, then the possibility that they could be Christian is ruled out. Someone who thought the historical Joshua was a type of Jesus, as a Christian might, could have misread the lines in that sense (and thus be inspired to add line 257), but they could not have written them.

Ancient exegetes of Daniel 7 who took the "one like a son of man" to be indeed a man, not a god or an angel but a human being, born on earth and exalted to heaven, must have asked themselves the question: Who could this "exceptional man" be? The author of the Parables of Enoch, both because of his veneration for Enoch and because Enoch was believed not to have died,

---

29. O'Neill, "The Man from Heaven," 90.
30. O'Neill, "The Man from Heaven," 100.

thought that the exceptional man must be Enoch. The author of book 5 of the Sibylline Oracles, for different reasons, came to the conclusion that the exceptional man must be Joshua. For him, the most essential role of the Messianic Figure depicted in Daniel 7:13–14 was to establish his universal kingdom by destroying all the enemies of Israel. No figure in Israel's past succeeded in destroying the enemies of God's people more comprehensively than Joshua did.

This Sibylline author's view that the "man from heaven" will be Joshua returning to earth may not be entirely unique in our evidence. Sometime in the 50s CE, a man known only as "the Egyptian" is said by Josephus to have called himself a prophet and led an army to the Mount of Olives, where he told his followers that the walls of Jerusalem would fall down at his command. In the event, the Romans took effective action against them.[31] As many have observed, it looks very much as though this man intended to reenact Joshua's miraculous capture of the city of Jericho, which was the beginning of his campaign to conquer the promised land (Josh 6). Presumably, the Egyptian expected, having conquered Jerusalem, to go on to reconquer the rest of the land from its Roman occupiers.

We do not know whether this rebel leader actually claimed to be Joshua, returned to earth.[32] Perhaps it was because he did and used no other name that people who did not want to credit his claim called him simply "the Egyptian." His self-description as a prophet would be consistent with such a claim, since Joshua, like Moses, was known as a prophet (Sir 46:1). A prophet in this sense was a leader of God's people, appointed and inspired by God. Perhaps he claimed only to be the one who would follow Joshua's example and recover the land for the people. In any case, it is intriguing that as an Egyptian he was a native of the place where, a few decades later, the author of book 5 of the Sibylline Oracles wrote. There may be some continuity of tradition between them. In the time of the Sibylline author, after the Roman capture and destruction of Jerusalem and its temple, the need for a reconquest of the land, treating the gentile occupiers as Joshua did the Amorites, must have seemed even more necessary.

---

31. Josephus, *War* 2.261–262; *Ant.* 20.169–171. On the inconsistencies between these two accounts in Josephus, see Rebecca Gray, *Prophetic Figures in Late Second Temple Jewish Palestine: The Evidence from Josephus* (New York: Oxford University Press, 1993) 116–18. See also Acts 21:38.

32. The fact that Joshua had unquestionably died and been buried (Josh 24:30–31) was not necessarily an impediment to popular belief in such a claim. Cf. 2 Macc 15:12–16; Mark 8:28; Matt 16:14.

Finally, there may be another trace of the Joshua narratives in Sibylline Oracles 5:96–97, where the returning Nero is described, for the first time in the book, as

> a savage-minded mighty man, much-bloodied, raving nonsense,
> with a full host numerous as sand, bringing destruction
>   on you [Rome].³³

According to Joshua 11:4, the great army assembled by King Jabin against Joshua was "as the sand of the sea in multitude." The same phrase is also used to describe the camels of the Midianites and Amalekites (Judg 7:12) and the army of the Philistines (1 Sam [1 Kgdms] 13:5), but the parallel in Joshua is the closest.³⁴ We might think it no more than a common phrase, were it not that it associates Nero with the army of nations defeated by Joshua in the process of his conquest of the promised land.

Conclusion

This book of the Sibylline Oracles, written against the background of the Roman destruction of Jerusalem and its temple, portrays the key events of the future as the return of the emperor Nero, who will destroy Rome, massacre the greater part of humanity, and attack the Jewish people, and the advent of the Messianic Figure, who will defeat Nero and destroy all the enemies of God and his people, including whole nations of evildoers. The author finds these two mutual adversaries and the outcome of their conflict in Daniel 7. Nero is the last ruler of the Roman Empire, which is depicted in Daniel 7 as the fourth beast. He is the little horn who makes war on the "holy ones," the Jewish people. The Messianic Figure is the "one like a son of man" to whom God has given universal sovereignty and who comes from heaven to implement that sovereignty by destroying all the godless rulers and their peoples. In this way he carries out the judgment of God on the fourth beast and the little horn and the judgment of God in favor of the "holy ones."

Just as Nero is a figure from history who, after hiding out in the east, returns, so the Messianic Figure is a figure from history who, after living in

---

33. Collins, "Sibylline Oracles," 395 n. a2, takes the city that is addressed to be Alexandria, in view of the explicit address to Alexandria in line 88. But it is more likely that a new addressee is introduced in line 98 as "most prosperous of cities," which would apply most aptly to Rome. This would also make good sense of the description of Asia in lines 99–100. The returning Nero was commonly expected to march on Rome (cf. line 367).

34. In Rev 20:8 it describes the nations gathered by Gog and Magog for battle.

heaven, returns. The author presumes that the "one like a son of man" is a man, not a god or an angel, and, since he is in heaven, he must have lived on earth in the past. The ideal figure for the task of defeating the Romans, eliminating all the ungodly nations, and restoring God's people is Joshua, who defeated the Amorites, eliminated most of the Canaanite population, and established the people of Israel in their land. He is the man who will return from heaven and, single-handedly this time, destroy the ungodly rulers, cities, and nations. This extraordinary feat can be expected of him because, in the period of the conquest, he performed the exceptional act of commanding the sun to stand still. Whereas in 4Q246 the historical model for the future event of salvation is the crossing of the Red Sea, for book 5 of the Sibyllines it is the destruction of the Amorites on the day when Joshua stopped the sun.

In the first three oracles the role of the Messianic Figure, portrayed as the king sent from God, as the star that falls from the sky, and as Joshua returning from heaven, is entirely destructive.[35] Only in the fourth oracle is the positive sequel to his holy war against all enemies of God and his people portrayed. He will transform Jerusalem and build the glorious new temple. A future of justice and peace ensues, for righteous gentiles as well as the people of God. (There are passages referring to this final paradisal state of affairs also outside the passages about the Messianic Figure, such as lines 381–385.)

Apart from Daniel 7 and Joshua 10, not many biblical prophecies contribute to the portrayal of the Messianic Figure. A messianic understanding of the star in Numbers 24:17 lies behind lines 158–160, and perhaps the "scepter" in line 415 alludes to the same verse. The unusual depiction of the Messianic Figure as builder of the new temple probably depends on 2 Samuel (2 Kgdms) 7:13 and/or Zechariah 6:12–13. This may be the only point at which Davidic messianic texts are drawn on. (The Messianic Figure of Num 24:17 is an Israelite but not necessarily Davidic.) Additionally, there may be an allusion to Psalm 2:8–9 in lines 415–416, but it is not possible to be sure.

Comparison with the Parables of Enoch

The Messianic Figures of the Parables of Enoch and book 5 of the Sibylline Oracles are different in many respects. The Messianic Figure of the Parables

---

35. It is not clear whether the idyllic picture of Judea and Jerusalem in lines 260–270 is to be understood as the consequence of the advent of the Messianic Figure in lines 256, 258–259. There are reasons to think the text of the whole section 238–285 has been somehow disordered. Lines 244–245 repeat lines 229–230.

of Enoch is a judge who delivers the chosen ones from the oppression of the kings and the mighty by his powerful condemnation. He does not rule. The Messianic Figure of the fifth Sibylline is a king who destroys the kings and the nations opposed to God's people (though apparently not with an army). He builds the new Jerusalem and the new temple, which are not mentioned in the Parables.

For both writers the Messianic Figure is the "one like a son of man" of Daniel 7:13, but in other respects they draw on rather different aspects of Daniel 7. In the Parables the profile of the Messianic Figure is drawn from a wide range of scriptural prophecies, including those of an ideal Davidic king and those about the servant of the Lord in Isaiah. In the fifth Sibylline there is no allusion to the servant in Isaiah (though the Isaianic prophecies of the restored Jerusalem are echoed) and the appropriation of Davidic expectations is very limited. There is reference to Numbers 24:17, which is ignored in the Parables of Enoch. Apart from Daniel 7, there are no scriptural sources about a Messianic Figure that the two works have in common, with the possible exception of Psalm 2. But there is far less allusion to scriptural passages in Sibylline Oracles book 5 than there is in the Parables of Enoch.

In one very significant way they agree in their understanding of Daniel 7:13. For both writers the "one like a son of man" is a human being who had previously lived on earth and had been exalted to heaven. He is not a being of heavenly origin, a god or an angel, though he is a very remarkable, even unique, man. In one case this man is Enoch, in the other Joshua.

TABLE 1. *Four oracles in Sibylline Oracles 5:52–434*

Oracle A: 5:52–110

Allusions to Persons
Nero (vv. 93–107)
Messianic Figure (vv. 108–109)

Allusions to Other Scripture Passages
Dan 7:20 (v. 106)
Josh 11:4 (v. 7)

Oracle B: (5:111–178)

Allusions to Persons
Nero (vv. 137–154)
Messianic Figure (vv. 155–161)

Allusions to Other Scripture Passages
Dan 7:25 (v. 155)
Numbers 24:17 (vv. 155, 158)

Oracle C: 5:179–285

Allusions to Persons
Nero (vv. 214–227)

Allusions to Other Scripture Passages
Dan 7:8 (vv. 222–223)
Dan 7:13 (v. 256)
Josh 10:12–14 (256, 258–259)

Oracle D: 5:286–434

Allusions to Persons
Nero (vv. 361–374)

Allusions to Other Scripture Passages
Dan 7:13–14 (vv. 414–415)
Dan 7:11 (vv. 418–419)?
Dan 7:8, 18, 21–22, 25, 27 (vv. 401, 432)
Num 24:17 (v.415?)

TABLE 2. *Biblical allusions in Sibylline Oracles 5:414–433*

⁴¹⁴For a blessed **man** [ἀνὴρ μακαρίτης] came from the vault of **heaven**	Dan 7:13
⁴¹⁵with a **scepter** in his hands which God **gave** him,	Dan 7:14; Num 24:17?; Ps 2:8–9?
and he gained sway over **all** well, and gave back the wealth to all the good, which previous men had taken.	
He destroyed every city from its foundation with much **fire**	Dan 7:11?
and **burned** nations of mortals who were formerly evildoers.	
⁴²⁰And the city which God desired, this he made more brilliant than stars and sun and moon,	Isa 60:19–20
and he provided ornament and made a holy **house**,	2 Kgdms [2 Sam] 7:13; Zech 6:12–13
exceedingly beautiful in its fair shrine, and he fashioned a great and immense tower over many stadia	
⁴²⁵touching even the clouds and visible to all,	Isa 2:2–3
so that all faithful and all righteous people could see the glory of eternal God, a form desired.	Isa 60:1
East and West sang out the glory of God.	Isa 59:19
For terrible things no longer happen to wretched mortals, ⁴³⁰no adulteries or illicit love of boys,	
no murder, or din of battle, but competition is fair among all.	Isa 60:17–18
It is the last time of the **holy people** when God, who thunders on high,	Dan 7:8, 18, 21–22, 25, 27
founder of the greatest temple, accomplishes these things.	

CHAPTER 2.5

Interpretation of Daniel 7 in the Apocalypse of Ezra (4 Ezra)

The work that modern scholars call 4 Ezra is part of the Latin text traditionally known in English as 2 Esdras. Since the sixteenth century, 2 Esdras has formed part of the Apocrypha in English, though unlike most other books in the Apocrypha it never appears in manuscripts of the Old Greek Bible. Therefore 2 Esdras is not one of the deuterocanonical books in the biblical canon recognized by the Roman Catholic Church, but it does appear in an appendix in editions of the Vulgate (Latin) Bible. The Jewish apocalypse known as 4 Ezra comprises chapters 3–14 of 2 Esdras. Chapters 1–2 (known to scholars as 5 Ezra) and chapters 15–16 (known as 6 Ezra) are later additions by Christian writers.[1]

Most scholars are agreed that 4 Ezra was originally written in Hebrew and then translated into Greek. Unfortunately it has not survived in either of these languages (other than a few short quotations of the Greek in patristic literature). We can access the text only in versions made from the Greek. But the situation is better than that of the Parables of Enoch because more than one such version is known. The most important are the Latin and the Syriac, which are closely related.[2] Most modern English translations are based primarily on them, but Michael Stone's version in his commentary[3] also takes appropriate account of the Ethiopic and the Georgian versions, which seem to reflect a reworked form

---

1. For a good brief account of 4 Ezra that also includes a chapter on 5 and 6 Ezra, see Bruce W. Longenecker, *2 Esdras*, GAP 7 (Sheffield: Sheffield Academic, 1995).

2. For a detailed account of the versions, see Michael E. Stone, *Fourth Ezra*, Hermeneia (Minneapolis: Fortress, 1990) 1–9.

3. Stone, *Fourth Ezra*.

of the Greek. (Quotations from 4 Ezra in this chapter will usually be in Stone's translation.) The complex textual situation means that there are places where it is difficult to be at all sure of the original sense. One such case is the most common designation for the Messiah in 4 Ezra, which may have originally been either "my son" or "my servant." This will be discussed in due course.

Something that is not in doubt is the overall structure of 4 Ezra, which is generally agreed to comprise a series of seven self-contained episodes (sometimes called "visions"). They are (1) 3:1–5:20; (2) 5:21–6:34; (3) 6:35–9:26; (4) 9:27–10:59; (5) 11:1–12:51; (6) 13:1–58; (7) 14:1–48. (See also table 1.)

The Place of Daniel 7 in the Argument of 4 Ezra

Fourth Ezra is a sustained and profound reflection on the justice and mercy of God in relation to his people Israel, in the light of the destruction of Jerusalem by the Romans in 70 CE. The fictional setting, according to which Ezra, in Babylon in the thirtieth year of the Babylonian exile (3:1), is in severe distress and theological bewilderment over the fall of Jerusalem to the Babylonians (3:2–3), is plainly meant to be read as typological of the situation of the real author and the readers at the end of the first century CE (whether or not precisely in 100 CE, as the dating to the thirtieth year of the Babylonian exile might indicate). The theological journey Ezra undertakes in 4 Ezra finds its starting point in the apparent fact that, if the fall of Jerusalem is understood as God's judgment on Israel's sin, as much of the Hebrew Bible would suggest, then God must be understood to treat even his own covenant people with merciless justice. How can this be consistent with the merciful character of God portrayed in Israel's scriptures and with the covenant God made with Abraham and his descendants? How can it be that the gentile nations flourish, despite their total disregard for God's commandments, whereas Israel, which has at least observed the law much better than they, is punished for their sins?

Recent studies of 4 Ezra agree that the book plots a journey of understanding, in which Ezra moves from this starting point to a kind of resolution of the problems it presents. Ezra begins with a kind of inclusive covenantalism, in which God's covenant with his people requires him to treat the nation as a whole, not with strict justice, but with mercy. Ezra cannot accept that Israel's sin can explain God's abandonment of his people to their enemies. As I see it, this is the view that the book assumes that its readers are likely to hold. The book is designed to take them with Ezra on the journey of understanding that is possible only through the revelations from God that Ezra, said to be the only one worthy to receive them, is granted. In the early dialogues with the angel Uriel, Ezra resists the angel's insistence on a sharp distinction between the few righteous and the many sinners. According to Uriel, God cares only for those who succeed in keeping his law, difficult though that is. If sinners flourish while the righteous do not, that is because God "made this world [or age] for the sake of many, but the world [or age] to come for the sake of only a few" (8:1). He struggles to persuade Ezra that Ezra himself is one of the few.

Only when the dialogues give way to visions (from 9:27 onward) does Ezra undergo a kind of conversion to Uriel's view (which is, of course, God's). He becomes open to the fuller understanding that the three eschatological visions of chapters 9–13, with the interpretations of them given to him by God, open up for him. At the end of this experience he is finally able to praise God for the way he governs the course of history (13:57–58). I do not share the view that Ezra's problems, voiced in the dialogues, are overcome by the visions only in a psychologically or existentially, rather than rationally, satisfying way.[4] At the end of the last vision Ezra finds that what has been revealed to him in them resolves the problems with which his journey of understanding began.[5]

The key to appreciating this is to observe that the visions take up traditional material, grounded in scriptural prophecies, but at the same time give Ezra a deeper or fuller understanding of it. This is particularly true of the last two visions, which build especially on Daniel's vision in Daniel 7. They each develop a different aspect of it. The vision in 11:1–12:51 (Episode 5) takes up Daniel's vision of the fourth beast. It even makes this explicit: "the fourth kingdom that appeared in a vision to your brother Daniel" (12:11). The vision in chapter 13 (Episode 6) takes up the figure of the "one like a son of man" in Daniel 7:13. Each of these two visions also appropriates other key scriptural texts, as we shall see. But it is notable that it is to Daniel 7 that this author primarily turns in order to seek resolution of the problem presented by the fall of Jerusalem to the Romans. In the earlier part of the book there is only one allusion to Daniel 7 (4 Ezra 6:20; cf. Dan 7:10), but in the last two visions Daniel 7 is hugely influential. Fourth Ezra draws on Daniel 7 to resolve Ezra's problem, but it explicitly claims revelation that goes further than was revealed to Daniel. Following the explicit reference to the fourth kingdom in Daniel's vision (4 Ezra 12:11), God continues, "But it was not explained to him as I now

---

4. Stone, *Fourth Ezra*, 32–33.

5. For a fuller account of the overall argument of 4 Ezra, see Richard Bauckham, "Covenant, Law and Salvation in the Jewish Apocalypses," in *The Jewish World around the New Testament: Collected Essays I*, WUNT 233 (Tübingen: Mohr Siebeck, 2008) 268–323, here 294–309.

explain to you or have explained it" (12:12). Ezra is privileged to understand more than Daniel did.

The Messiah in Episode 1

It has often been claimed that the Messianic Figure in 4 Ezra plays only a rather limited role, but this is to neglect the way in which the revelations that Ezra receives progress over the course of the book and reach a climax in Episode 6. There the figure of "the man from the sea" (clearly based on the figure in Dan 7:13) takes center stage. He is evidently key to the resolution of Ezra's disturbing problem about the faithfulness of God. When earlier references to the Messianic Figure are considered as a series, it is clear that Ezra is given a progressive understanding of this figure and his role. The profile of this book's Messianic Figure is built up step by step, such that only in Episode 6 does his identification as Daniel's "one like a son of man" complete the profile.

Table 1 shows that the Messiah appears in some form in five of the seven episodes.[6] The references to the Messiah in Episodes 3, 5, 6, and 7 are clear and universally recognized, but the appearance of the Messiah in Episode 2 has not been recognized by other scholars and will have to be argued. Whether the Messiah appears in Episode 1, as has been claimed, will be discussed shortly, but shown to be unlikely.

Each of the first three Episodes contains a passage of eschatological predictions (5:1–13; 6:18–28; 7:26–44). These are designed to be complementary rather than repetitive. We need to consider each in turn in order to appreciate how the Messiah appears in them. The first is prefaced by a significant dialogue between Ezra and the angel Uriel. Ezra asks, "Do you think that I shall live until those days? Or what will take place in those days?" (4:51).[7] In the first of these two questions, Ezra takes up Uriel's earlier hint that perhaps Ezra will live to see the salvific events that will put to rights the intolerable situation of the present (4:26). He is also emboldened to ask by the revelation that the greater part of the history of this age has already passed (4:44–50). But Uriel can make no promises on that score:

> Concerning the signs about which you ask me, I can tell you in part; but I was not sent to tell you concerning your life, for I do not know. (4:52)

---

6. The suggestion that the son of the woman in the vision in Episode 4 is the Messiah is clearly ruled out by 10:41–48, which identifies the son as the Jerusalem temple.

7. Quotations from 4 Ezra are from Stone's translation unless otherwise indicated.

Although Ezra's first question, about his own future, does not receive an answer until Episode 7 (14:9), it is kept alive in the speech of Uriel that follows (5:4). Evidently, for the author, it has some importance.

Uriel begins to answer Ezra's second question in the passage about "signs" that follows. These predictions paint a very dark picture in which righteousness has disappeared from the world and nature is in chaos. This world in the period leading up to the end is in a far worse state than that in which Ezra is living (5:2). It is important to notice that the predictions are made from the perspective of "those who dwell on earth" (5:1) or "the many" (5:7). These phrases refer to the wicked mass of humanity, on whom divine justice rightly falls, and among whom Ezra, at this stage of the narrative, counts himself (4:39). He has not yet learned about "the few," the righteous remnant, to whom salvation is promised. So in this first passage of eschatological predictions, the inhabitants of the earth, observing the "signs," are terrified and uncomprehending (5:1, 12). In fact, this is only to be expected, given Uriel's earlier dictum, that

> those who dwell upon the earth can understand only what is on the earth, and he who is above the heavens can understand what is above the height of the heavens. (4:21)

At this stage Ezra himself can understand only earthly things. He has not yet been privileged to understand the divine purpose.

The nearest this passage comes to anything positive is this:

> And the region that you now see ruling
> shall be waste and untrodden
> and men shall see the land desolate. (5:3)

Although commentators say that this is the Roman Empire,[8] for Ezra it must be Babylon on the Euphrates. When he does have a vision of the Roman Empire and its fall (in Episode 5), identified for him as Daniel's fourth beast, it is for him a future reality, unlike Babylon (see especially 14:18). I do not think "the region that you now see ruling" here functions even typologically as Rome. The prediction echoes Isaiah 13:15–22, which prophesies the total devastation of the city of Babylon:

---

8. E.g., Stone, *Fourth Ezra*, 110: "This verse refers to the destruction of the Roman Empire."

> It will never be inhabited
> > or lived in for all generations;
> Arabs will not pitch their tents there,
> > shepherds will not make their flocks lie down there. (Isa 13:20)

Elaborate prophecies of the destruction of Babylon on the Euphrates are found in the third and fifth books of the Sibylline Oracles (3:300–313; 5:434–446), the latter more or less contemporary with 4 Ezra. Jewish writers of this period did not think that the most evil city of biblical times had yet been sufficiently punished. Though it had been reduced to insignificance when the inhabitants were transferred to the new capital, Seleucia, in the late third century BCE, it could not yet be said to be as completely devastated as Isaiah predicted.

A reference to the fall of Rome at the very beginning of the eschatological predictions in 4 Ezra would be quite inappropriate, but a prediction of the total desertion of Babylon is very appropriate. It connects Ezra's own time with the future and assures him that the evil empire that has triumphed over God's people will in the end come to nothing. Its total devastation will match the enormity of its evil as Ezra perceived it. For Ezra, it must be the only positive element in the whole passage, but it is not connected with any corresponding prophecy of the flourishing of God's people. Moreover, it is not even presented as divine judgment, since it is seen from the perspective of the inhabitants of the earth who recognize nothing of God's purpose in the events predicted.

The section of the predictions in Episode 1 that may be open to a messianic interpretation is this:

> And one shall reign whom those who dwell on earth
> > do not expect,
> and the birds shall fly away,
> and the sea of Sodom shall cast up fish;
> and one whom the many do not know shall make his voice heard
> > by night, and all shall hear his voice. (5:6–7a)

The birds and the fish are portents,[9] like others listed in this passage (5:4–5, 7b–9a), but the two references to a person that precede and follow these two portents may have more significance. The king has usually been thought to be an "antichrist" figure, an evil ruler of the last days, like the "little horn" of Daniel (7:8, 20–21; 8:23–25), and, while some scholars think the voice is un-

---

9. For the birds, cf. Jer 4:25.

connected, others suppose that it is the voice of this king.[10] On the other hand, Jonathan Moo has made a good case for thinking that the one who reigns and the one whose voice is heard are both the Messiah.[11] He points out that a final wicked king is not to be found in chapters 11–12, where we would expect to find him if he were part of 4 Ezra's eschatological scenario. Perhaps more significantly, he points to the parallel between what is said about the voice in 5:7 and the description of the Messiah's voice in 13:4, 33.

However, a reference to the Messiah, even as seen by "those who dwell on earth" (5:6) and heard by "the many" (5:7), seems inappropriate at this stage of 4 Ezra's eschatological predictions. In 13:33 the Messiah's voice prompts the gathering of the nations to fight against him, and his destruction of them follows (7:28; 12:34). These events mark the great turning point in the events of the last days. They would be out of place in 5:1–13. So the unexpected king and the voice heard by all the world are probably to be understood as portents like others in this catalogue and need not be mutually connected, especially as they are separated by two other such portents. What makes them portents is that they are strange, unlike the regular course of the world. The king is perhaps a deliberately vague reference to a Roman emperor who comes to power unexpectedly. (The returning Nero would fit the description well but seems to have no place in 4 Ezra's expectation as it is presented in Episodes 5 and 6.) The unknown voice can be paralleled in the context of portents of divine judgments in the Sibylline Oracles:

> And God will speak, with a great voice
> to the entire ignorant empty-minded people. (Sib. Or. 3:669–670)[12]

> The whole world will hear a roaring sound and a powerful voice.
> (Sib. Or. 4:175, my translation)

The Messiah will come after the portents, not during the course of them.

THE MESSIAH IN EPISODE 2

Before considering the continuation of the predictions of signs, we must give some attention to 5:56–6:10. In 5:56 Ezra asks God to show him "through

---

10. E.g., Stone, *Fourth Ezra*, 112.
11. Jonathan Moo, "A Messiah Whom 'the Many Do Not Know'? Rereading 4 Ezra 5:6–7," *JTS* 58 (2007) 525–36.
12. Translation from John J. Collins, "Sibylline Oracles," *OTP* 1:317–472, here 377.

whom" he will visit his creation—that is, in judgment. In Stone's translation the answer comes thus:

> And he said to me, "The beginning is through man and the end is through myself. For before the circle of the earth existed . . . [a poetic passage describing features of creation follows, ending with the following] . . . then I planned these things, and they came into being through me and not through another." (6:1–6)

Stone's translation of 6:1 and 6:6 follows the text of all the versions (including Syriac, Ethiopic, and Georgian) except the Latin, which omits part of 6:1 and has an addition to 6:6:

> He said to me, "At the beginning of the circle of the earth . . . then I planned these things, and they were made through me alone and not through another; just as the end shall come through me alone and not through another." (NRSV)

The difference is of considerable importance. In the majority of the versions, as rendered by Stone, God's judgment is to take place in two stages: the beginning of the judgment will be "through humankind," but the end will be through God alone, just as creation was. According to the Latin version, the judgment, like creation, will take place through God alone.

Stone is surely right to prefer the other versions, representing both main text types, to the Latin in this instance. The Latin presumably arose through accidental omission of words in 6:1. With that omission, the whole passage, 6:1–6, refers to creation and does not reply to Ezra's question in 5:56 ("Through whom will you visit your creation?"). So the additional words at 6:6 would have been added to make the point that in this respect the end will be the same as creation.

The majority text makes very good sense. According to 4 Ezra as a whole, there are two stages of judgment, separated by the four hundred years of the paradisal age over which the Messiah will preside (7:28; 12:34). At the first stage, before the messianic age, the evil rulers and nations will be judged by the Messiah (12:31–33; 13:25–38). But the dead will not be judged until the resurrection and the last judgment, which will take place after the four hundred years, at the time of the new creation (7:31–44, 70). At this judgment God alone will be the judge. So the beginning of God's "visitation" of his creation in judgment will be through human agency, but the end of it will be accomplished by God alone, as the creation was. The emphasis on creation in 6:2–6 is explicable because the last judgment is part of the new creation of the world (7:30–33). Creation and new creation are both the unaided work of God alone. The judgment of rulers and nations by the agency of the Messiah, on the other hand, is more like the many acts of divine judgment in the history of Israel, when God acted to deliver his people through the agency of some leader of the people. That this is the meaning of this passage is confirmed by 9:1–6, which, near the end of Episode 3, sums up the significance of the eschatological predictions of the first three episodes.[13]

Ezra's question in 5:56 (NRSV: "show your servant through whom you will visit your creation") may be intended to pose an issue that was debated among Jewish interpreters of scripture. Some prophecies seem to depict the final, decisive intervention of God as the activity of God alone, but in others a Messianic Figure acts as his agent. This difference is reflected in late Second Temple–period literature. For example, the book of Jubilees, much of the Enoch literature, and the Testament of Moses make no reference to a Messianic Figure, whereas the Psalms of Solomon and the Parables of Enoch have a strong focus on the agency of a Messianic Figure.

The author of 4 Ezra seems to have wanted to resolve this issue by means of a clear distinction between what will happen within the history of this world, when the evil empires will be succeeded by a time of prosperity for the people of God, and what will happen when God, through a newly creative act, comparable with the original creation, accomplishes a radical transformation of the creation (7:30–31). In the former case, the Messiah is central to God's purpose and activity on behalf of his people, but he plays no part at all in the new creation. The point is made emphatically by the statement that, at the end of the four hundred years, when this whole creation is dissolved, the Messiah himself will die along with all other humans alive at that time (7:29).

In 6:1 the Syriac and Ethiopic both have the expression "the son of man." Stone is probably right to take this as generic: "man" (or better: "humankind"). The contrast is between human agency and purely divine agency. A reference to a specific individual, "the man," would not at this point be appropriate, since it is not until Episode 3 that the Messiah is explicitly introduced into the eschatological predictions. The human agency implied is that of the Messiah, but for the time being this is left implicit. However, it is worth noticing that the use of "humankind" here, distinguished from God, implies that the Messiah is a human figure, distinguished from God.

The focus on judgment in 5:56–6:6 leads into the second passage of eschatological predictions (6:18–28), which is a considerable advance on the first. Whereas the unnatural events of the first passage were not explicitly said to

---

13. Cf. also 13:26: the Messiah "through whom he will deliver his creation."

be portents of judgment and were not so understood by the inhabitants of the earth, the second series of predictions begins with the awe-inspiring voice of God himself declaring that, when the time for him to visit the earth draws near, he will show signs. The first of these is as follows:

> The books shall be opened before the firmament,
> and all shall see it together. (6:20b)

This is a clear allusion to Daniel 7:10 ("the books were opened").[14] Fourth Ezra has turned what Daniel saw in vision into a sign that apparently appears in the sky so that all the inhabitants of the earth can see it. This rather odd notion is an example of the notion of signs portending judgment appearing for all to see (Sib. Or. 4:173–174; 3:672–674; 2:34–38), just as there were expected to be noises that all would be able to hear (Sib. Or. 4:175; Apoc. Ab. 30:8). The fact that the present series of signs begins with the opened books shows unequivocally that judgment is now at hand.

This allusion to Daniel 7, the only such outside Episodes 5 and 6, is of special interest because it shows that the author of 4 Ezra understood the judgment described in Daniel 7 to be, not the judgment of the dead that follows the resurrection, but the judgment on the powers and peoples who are alive in the last generation of history, before the four-hundred-year messianic age. This is how Daniel 7 is understood also in Episodes 5 and 6, when it becomes clear that the Messiah, identified with the figure of Daniel 7:13, is the one through whom God executes this judgment. For the time being the sign of the opened books is the only indication that the rest of the events of Daniel 7 are due to unfold. An informed reader might expect a Messianic Figure to appear in the subsequent verses and may not be disappointed.

At 6:25 the eschatological predictions shift to the perspective of the "survivors"—the righteous remnant who will not be impacted by the judgments but survive to witness salvation. This is Ezra's first introduction to a category of people who will be important in the rest of the book. They will "see my salvation and the end of my world" (6:25), but very little about the actual events they will witness is disclosed here. Much is deliberately held back until the visions of Episodes 4–6, in which Ezra receives revelations of the eschatological

---

14. The same phrase from Dan 7:10 is echoed in 2 Bar. 24:1; 1 En. 47:3; Rev 20:12. All of these writers are well acquainted with Dan 7 and will have been aware of the source of the words. They would not have regarded them merely as a stock expression.

events that will be of most concern to him. At this point, what the survivors actually see is limited to this:

> And they shall see the people who were taken up, who from their birth have not tasted death. (6:26a)[15]

Why these people, who must presumably include Enoch and Elijah, are important enough to be highlighted here and to be mentioned four more times in the book (7:28; 13:52; 14:9, 50) will be discussed in the next section. There I shall argue that they include the Messiah. In that case, the reference to them here is precisely equivalent to their appearance in the third sequence of eschatological events (7:26–44):

> My Messiah shall be revealed with those who are with him. (7:28)

These two formulations interpret each other. From 6:26 we know that those who are with the Messiah in 7:28 are the people who had not died. From 7:28 we know, retrospectively, that the Messiah himself is one of those who had been taken up without tasting death.

So in Episode 2 the Messiah is being introduced implicitly—both in 6:1 and in 6:26. Readers are being led along with Ezra himself on a journey of progressive understanding of God's purpose for the eschatological future. The disclosure that will deal with the problem Ezra poses at the beginning of the book is not made all at once, but in gradual steps, so that Ezra can recognize and digest each stage one by one. The Messiah will turn out, in Episodes 5 and 6, to be of central and indispensable importance, but this is not clear from the beginning. In Episode 3 he will appear for the first time explicitly, but with only part of his significance revealed. In Episode 2 he appears only anonymously so that, when these implicit references to him are recognized retrospectively, he can be seen to have been in mind all along. There have been carefully designed preparations for the prominence that he gradually assumes in Episodes 3, 5, and 6.

Within the predictions in 6:18–28, those who have not tasted death do not appear to have any function unless it is they who are responsible for the phenomenon that follows:

---

15. I have changed "men" to "people."

The heart of the earth's inhabitants shall be changed and converted to a different spirit. (6:26b).

This would be consistent with the traditional role of the returning Elijah (Mal 4:5–6 [3:23–24]), but the language is closer to Ezekiel 11:19 and 36:26–27, except that Ezekiel's prophecies refer only to Israel. This is the only point at which 4 Ezra implies any hope for the world beyond Israel.

Fourth Ezra 6:27–28 forms an *inclusio* with 5:1–2 and so provides an eschatological resolution to the state of affairs described in 5:1–2 (and further in 5:9–11). The evil state of the world will be reversed. What has not been disclosed as yet is how this will happen. So Ezra is given, in these two passages of prediction that focus on signs, a sketch that further revelations must fill out. The revelations so far leave him deeply unsatisfied.

Those Who Have Not Tasted Death

In table 3, all five of the references to these people in 4 Ezra are printed along with, for comparison, passages in the *Biblical Antiquities* of Pseudo-Philo (LAB) and in 2 Baruch that also refer to them. In 2 Baruch only Baruch himself is actually said to belong to this category, but the references would be more intelligible if readers are expected to know of others (such as Enoch and Elijah) who are like Baruch in this respect. These three roughly contemporary works share significant resemblances, especially in eschatological terms and concepts.

The passage in LAB 48:1 needs some explanation. Aaron's grandson Phinehas, whose death is not recorded in scripture, is here supposed to be the same person as Elijah the prophet. Instead of dying, Phinehas was hidden and provisioned by God in a remote location, until the time when he reappeared in the world as Elijah, a figure to whose ancestry the Hebrew Bible rather oddly never refers, calling him simply "the Tishbite." The identification of Phinehas and Elijah was thus a deduction from the silence of scripture: Phinehas apparently did not die, and Elijah apparently had no father. The identification of the two figures would have been facilitated by the "zeal" that both famously displayed in putting flagrant transgressors of God's law to death.[16] The identification

---

16. Phinehas: Num 25:11–13; cf. Sir 45:23; 1 Macc 2:26, 54; 4 Macc 18:12; LAB 47:1; Elijah: 1 Kgs 19:10; cf. Sir 48:2; Phinehas and Elijah identified: Pirqe R. El. 29. Another factor in the identification of Phinehas and Elijah must have been the parallel between the eternal "covenant of peace" made by God with Phinehas (Num 25:12; Sir 45:24) and Mal 2:4–7, which refers to God's covenant of peace with Levi and describes "the priest" as a "messenger of YHWH of hosts." This links Phinehas with "the messenger of the covenant" (Mal 3:1), who

of Phinehas with Elijah explains those Jewish traditions in which Elijah was expected to return, not as a prophet, but as the eschatological high priest.[17] As Phinehas, he was a direct successor to Aaron.

The passage in LAB then refers to Elijah's translation (2 Kgs 2:9–12) in the significant words "You will be raised up [*elevaberis*] to the place where those who were before you were raised up." There must be more people in this category than Enoch, though it is not easy to guess who could be in mind.[18] (As we shall see, rabbinic tradition later had some suggestions.) Neither Baruch nor Ezra lived before Elijah. But the idea that there were more people in this category than just the two obvious biblical examples, Enoch and Elijah, makes good sense of the references in 4 Ezra too. LAB refers to "the place where those who were before you were raised up, and you will be there until I remember the world." None of these three works actually identifies the place where these people await their eschatological return to the world. It could be heaven but is more plausibly paradise, which is where Enoch was located in the Enoch traditions (Jub. 4:23; cf. 1 En. 103:8).

Finally, LAB 48:1 explains that both Phinehas-Elijah and the others who have been "lifted up" will in the end die. While this is not attested in other Jewish traditions about Enoch or Elijah,[19] it coheres well with the eschatological program in 4 Ezra 7:28–30. At the end of the four hundred years of rejoicing, "all who draw human breath" will die, including the Messiah (7:29), and "no one shall be left" (7:30). The whole of this creation must dissolve back into its primordial state before the new creation can come to be (7:30–31). From this

---

is Elijah, and the covenant of peace with Elijah's eschatological ministry of reconciliation (Mal 4:6 [3:23]).

17. Tg. Ps.-J. Exod 4:13; 6:18; 40:10; Deut 30:4; cf. Num 25:12. See Martin Hengel, *The Zealots*, trans. D. Smith (Edinburgh: T&T Clark, 1989) chapter IV.B, for a fuller study of the evidence; and Robert Hayward, "Phinehas—the Same Is Elijah," *JJS* 29 (1978) 22–34, for a theory that links the origins of this identification with John Hyrcanus.

18. Those whose deaths are explicitly recorded in LAB are presumably excluded. They include Noah (5:8), Moses (19:16), Joshua (24:5–6), Kenaz (28:10), and Deborah (33:6). In the case of 4 Ezra, Moses is excluded by 7:129. Of the names of those who entered the Garden of Eden alive, given in Der. Er. Zut. 1:20 (see below), the following lived before Elijah: Eliezer the servant of Abraham, Jabez, Bithiah the daughter of Pharaoh, and Serah the daughter of Asher.

19. See Richard Bauckham, "The Martyrdom of Enoch and Elijah: Jewish or Christian?," in *The Jewish World*, 3–25. The death of Phinehas-Elijah and others like him in LAB and 4 Ezra must be distinguished from the *martyrdom* of Enoch and Elijah (when they return to earth), which became a common feature of Christian expectations of the last days (on the basis of Rev 11:3–13).

we could have deduced that those who are with the Messiah, those who had not tasted death, will at this point die. LAB 48:1 makes the point explicitly. No doubt the Messiah and those with him will then be raised to new life, along with all the dead (4 Ezra 7:31–32).

One reason why this group of people is important in 4 Ezra is that Ezra himself is one of them. Since they accompany the Messiah to earth, they are the only people from the past who are privileged to see God's "wonders" (7:27; 13:50)—the extraordinary blessings of the paradisal age. Otherwise only survivors of the generation alive at the time will witness the events that vindicate and fulfill God's purpose and his covenant with Israel. Early in the book, the question of whether Ezra would live to see the eschatological events was raised but left open (4:26, 51).[20] Only in Episode 7 is it answered, when Ezra is told that he will be one of those who will not die but return with the Messiah (14:9). This disclosure at the end of the book is rather like the revelation to Enoch that he himself is "that son of man" (1 En. 71:14). Similarly Ezra discovers that he himself is one of a privileged group of people who have featured in the eschatological events as they have been disclosed to him. In both cases, this retrospective identification is possible because the seer does not die but survives to reappear in the world at the end. Ezra's future identity is rather less momentous than Enoch's, but there is a real parallel and perhaps a literary connection.

However, this personal privilege of Ezra does not sufficiently explain the prominence of those who did not taste death in 4 Ezra. In three of their five appearances they are depicted as companions of the Messiah. It is in this capacity that they return to earth and are "revealed" along with him (7:28; 13:52). Moreover, 14:9 implies that, already at the time of Ezra's translation, they and the Messiah are together in the place where they await the time of the end. This close association of those who had not died with the Messiah is the clue to understanding the otherwise puzzling information about the Messiah in the interpretation of Ezra's vision of the eagle in Episode 5:

> This is the Messiah whom the Most High has kept until the end of days, who will arise from the posterity of David, and will come and speak to them. (12:32)

---

20. Also relevant is 13:14–20, where Ezra ponders whether it is better to die before the last days and never see God's wonders or to survive and endure the peril of the last days and see God's wonders. It turns out that Ezra himself will fall into neither category. He is destined for the privilege of seeing the wonders of the last days without having to live through the distress.

How can the Messiah who already exists in heaven or paradise before he is "revealed" at the climax of history be descended from David? The answer is now obvious: he was born into the line of David in the past and, like his companions, was taken up without dying, preserved by God for the time of the end.[21] He is actually one of "the people who were taken up, who from their birth have not tasted death" (6:26), preeminent among them but not essentially different from them. It is worth noticing that the statement that "God has kept [the Messiah] until the end of days" is paralleled by what is repeatedly said of Baruch in 2 Baruch (13:3; 25:1).

We can now also understand correctly the description of the Messiah in Episode 6, in the interpretation of Ezra's last vision: "he whom the Most High has been keeping for many ages [*multis temporibus*]" (13:26). This does not mean that he was preexistent from eternity or before the creation of the world, only that his life on earth took place long ago. As Stone observes,[22] this coheres with the perception of time elsewhere in 4 Ezra: the Roman Empire has dominated the earth for "so long" or "for so many ages" (*tot temporibus*) (11:40), while truth has been without fruit in the world for "so long" or "such long ages" (*tantis temporibus*) (6:28).[23] The claim in 4 Ezra that God has been preserving the Messiah "for many ages" could be an echo of Micah 5:2 ("whose origin is from of old, from ancient days").

Derekh Eretz Zuta

A remarkable later trace of the idea that the Messiah, having lived on earth, is now in paradise with the others who have not tasted death is found at the end of the first chapter of Derekh Eretz Zuta, one of the Minor (or "Extracanonical") Tractates of the Babylonian Talmud. Following a list of seven patriarchs with whom a covenant was made and a list of seven patriarchs whose bodies

---

21. Stone, *Fourth Ezra*, 210, recognizes this but compares the Messiah in this respect with Melchizedek in 2 En. 71–72, rather than noticing the more obvious parallel with Enoch, Elijah, and all of those described in 6:26. On the other hand, Antii Laato, *A Star Is Rising: The Historical Development of the Old Testament Royal Ideology and the Rise of the Jewish Messianic Expectations* (Atlanta: Scholars Press, 1997) 363, seems to think that the Messiah in 4 Ezra was preexistent before his birth into the line of David, like Jesus in New Testament Christology. This is not credible. Kenneth E. Pomykala, *The Davidic Dynasty Tradition in Early Judaism*, EJL 7 (Atlanta: Scholars Press, 1995) 219–20, draws attention to the "fusion of a cosmic figure with a davidic descendant," but concludes merely that the "contradiction perceived by modern interpreters was presumably not understood as such by the author."

22. Stone, *Fourth Ezra*, 401.

23. Here the other versions have "years."

have not decayed in the tomb, there is a list of nine who entered paradise without dying:

> There were nine who entered the Garden of Eden alive. And they are: Enoch, Elijah, the Messiah, Eliezer the servant of Abraham, Hiram the king of Tyre, Ebed-melech the Cushite, Jabez the grandson of Rabbi Judah ha-Nasi [*read:* the offspring of Judah],[24] Bithiah the daughter of Pharaoh, and Serah the daughter of Asher. And some say: "also Rabbi Joshua ben Levi." [*Another reading:* Some say: "Hiram the king of Tyre was expelled and in his place entered Rabbi Joshua ben Levi." *Or:* Some say: "Omit Hiram the king of Tyre and include Rabbi Joshua ben Levi in his place."] (Der. Er. Zut. 1:20)[25]

It is not easy to date the origin of this tradition. Derekh Eretz Zuta is a compilation of several collections of sayings. The collection in chapters 1–3 "roughly dates back to Tannaitic times," though "the final editing did not take place until Gaonic times"[26]—that is, after the final redaction of the Babylonian Talmud. The three numerical sayings at the end of chapter 1 (1:18–20) are missing in some manuscripts of Derekh Eretz Zuta, and so it is possible that they were added at an early stage of the development of the text,[27] but this is not necessarily the case. They do not connect at all obviously with the preceding material in this chapter, but the lists of those whose bodies have not decayed and those who did not die relate to the theme of "the way of the earth" since they constitute exceptions to what normally happens to people (they die, their bodies decay). In any case, the date of their inclusion in Derekh Eretz Zuta does not determine the date of the traditions themselves. Nor is the reference to Joshua ben Levi in 1:20 any help in dating the tradition of the nine who entered paradise alive.[28]

---

24. The reference must be to Jabez, who appears among the descendants of the patriarch Judah in 1 Chr 4:9–10. The identification of Judah as Rabbi Judah ha-Nasi is a scribal mistake.

25. Translation from Marcus van Loopik, *The Ways of the Sages and the Way of the World: The Minor Tractates of the Babylonian Talmud; Derekh 'Eretz Rabbah, Derekh 'Eretz Zuta, Pereq ha-Shalom*, TSAJ 26 (Tübingen: Mohr Siebeck, 1991) 205. I have adjusted the spelling of the names to their regular English forms. Similar lists (some longer) in later Jewish literature, such as the Alphabet of Ben Sira, are probably dependent on this text in Derekh Eretz Zuta (van Loopik, *The Ways*, 206–7).

26. Van Loopik, *The Ways*, 9, cf. 14.

27. Van Loopik, *The Ways*, 202.

28. Van Loopik, *The Ways*, 14, is surprisingly mistaken when he says, "At the ending of *Derekh 'Eretz Zuta* I there is mention of the grandson of Rabbi Jehoshua ben Levi, a much later tradent than those mentioned in other parts of the *Derekh 'Eretz*." The reference is in

The tradition that Joshua ben Levi entered the Garden of Eden alive dates from Talmudic times (b. Ketub. 77b), but it is clear that the list of nine already existed before some said that he should be added to the list or substituted for Hiram.

Attempts have been made to date the tradition by means of its reference to Enoch. Louis Ginzberg argues that because "the older rabbinic literature is not particularly favorably inclined toward Enoch," the list of those who entered paradise alive must date from "the time when Enoch came to be honored again"—"hardly earlier than the end of the tenth century C.E."[29] On the other hand, Kaufmann Kohler draws the opposite conclusion from the same observation about Enoch in rabbinic tradition: "The very fact that [in this tradition] *Henoch* is, contrary to the later Rabbinical opinions . . . , extolled as immortal, evidences the antiquity of this tradition."[30] For evidence of the early rabbinic hostility to Enoch, both scholars depend on a passage in Genesis Rabbah (25:1) that collects the sayings of four rabbis unfavorable to Enoch.[31] According to Rabbi Ḥama ben Rabbi Hoshaya (third century) Enoch was wicked, while according to Rabbi Aibu (fourth century) he was a hypocrite, righteous sometimes but wicked at other times. Then two rabbis are cited as arguing, in different ways, that Genesis 5:24 does not mean that Enoch did not die. Rabbi Abbahu (third century) makes this point in argument with *minim* (heretics) who asserted that Enoch did not die, while Rabbi Yose (mid-second century) makes it in argument with a matrona (a Roman lady) who also asserted that Enoch's death is not recorded in scripture.[32]

---

fact to the grandson of Rabbi Judah ha-Nasi, but this is clearly a confusion of an original reference to Judah the patriarch, as van Loopik himself accepts. The reference to Rabbi Joshua ben Levi (not his grandson) is also plainly an addition to the original tradition.

29. Louis Ginzberg, *The Legends of the Jews*, 7 vols. (Philadelphia: Jewish Publication Society, 1909–1946) 5:96 n. 68.

30. Kaufmann Kohler, "The Pre-Talmudic Haggada I," *Jewish Quarterly Review* 5 (1893) 399–419, here 417. Writing long before the discovery of the Dead Sea Scrolls, Kohler attributed this and many other haggadic traditions to the Essenes.

31. On this passage, see Peter Schäfer, *Two Gods in Heaven: Jewish Concepts of God in Antiquity*, trans. Allison Brown (Princeton, NJ: Princeton University Press, 2020) 102–4; James C. VanderKam, *Enoch: A Man for All Generations* (Columbia: University of South Carolina Press, 1995) 163–64.

32. This is one of a large group of traditions in which Rabbi Yose answers the (heretical) questions of a matrona: see Rosalie Gershenzon and Elieser Slomovic, "A Second Century Jewish-Gnostic Debate: Rabbi Jose ben Halafta and the Matrona," *JSJ* 16 (1985) 1–41. They argue that the matrona voices a coherent set of gnostic beliefs, which are represented in Jewish midrashic terminology. However, Gen. Rab. 25:1 does not fit well into their argument. There is no evidence of gnostic interest in Enoch. It is likely that Yose's debates with a matrona became a literary convention.

Peter Schäfer argues that these *minim* were "Christianized heretics," but, while it is true that Christian writers of the first, second, and third centuries did read Genesis 5:24 to mean that Enoch was translated without dying,[33] it is hard to believe that Enoch was important enough in Christian belief and apologetic to merit this rabbinic repudiation of the reading of Genesis 5:24 that (so far as we know) was universal among Jews and Christians before Rabbi Yose. In our literature the highest exaltation of Enoch, prior to 3 Enoch and the identification of Enoch with Metatron, occurs in the Parables of Enoch. Christians did not, as the Parables do, identify Enoch with the humanlike figure of Daniel 7:13 or portray him as eschatological judge in place of the Messiah ben David. It seems likely, therefore, that the *minim* who provoked the rabbinic "degradation" of Enoch[34] were Jews who valued the Enoch literature, including the Parables, and associated themselves with an Enoch who was presently living in paradise, awaiting the time when he would come to liberate them from their oppressors. The surest way to pull the rug from under all these speculations about Enoch was to demonstrate from scripture that actually Enoch died.

It follows that there may well have been Jewish groups who, in spite of these rabbinic refutations and despite the fact that Enoch is simply ignored in almost all rabbinic literature,[35] continued to read Genesis 5:24 in the way that had hitherto been universal and revere the figure of Enoch as he was portrayed in the Enoch literature. This is supported by the variety of interpretations of Genesis 5:24 in the Targums.[36] According to Targum Onqelos, "he was no more, for the Lord had caused him to die," but in some manuscripts this is corrected to "the Lord did not cause him to die."[37] According to Targum Neofiti, "it is not known where he is, because he was withdrawn by a command from before the Lord." But a marginal gloss at Genesis 5:23 reads, "and he died and was gathered from the midst of the world," while another adds to the version of verse 24 given above: "and behold he was not."[38] While these words come from the Hebrew text of Genesis 5:24, they are doubtless intended by this gloss to endorse Rabbi Yose's view that they mean that Enoch died. Finally, Targum

---

33. Schäfer, *Two Gods*, 104–7. Van Loopik, *The Ways*, 209, also thinks the assertion that Enoch died is anti-Christian polemic.
34. The term is used by Schäfer, *Two Gods*, 102.
35. VanderKam, *Enoch*, 162.
36. VanderKam, *Enoch*, 165–67.
37. Bernard Grossfeld, *The Targum Onqelos to Genesis*, ArBib 6 (Edinburgh: T&T Clark, 1988) 51 n. 3.
38. Martin McNamara, *Targum Neofiti 1: Genesis*, ArBib 1A (Edinburgh: T&T Clark, 1992) 70–71.

Pseudo-Jonathan attests the view (elsewhere found in 3 Enoch) that Enoch, translated to heaven, was transformed into the angel Metatron: "Behold he was not with the inhabitants of the earth because he was taken away and he ascended to the firmament at the command of the Lord, and he was called Metatron, the Great Scribe."[39]

It is clear that the attempts of the rabbis (or some of them) to suppress the idea that Enoch entered paradise alive did not entirely succeed. The list of nine people who did not die was probably, before its adoption into Derekh Eretz Zuta, handed down by tradents outside the mainstream rabbinic tradition. It could have survived from a very early date. That this is likely appears when we consider, not just Enoch, but the first three persons in the list: Enoch, Elijah, the Messiah. The list obviously begins with the two examples well attested in scripture, but the inclusion of the Messiah in the list has seemed anomalous to scribes and scholars.[40] In the context of the list, it cannot refer to the destiny of the Messiah in the future, following his eschatological appearance on earth, and it cannot refer to a preexistent Messiah who may be currently in paradise but has not entered it alive, in the sense of not dying. The only parallel that makes sense of the appearance of the Messiah in this list is the idea we have identified in 4 Ezra: that the Davidic Messiah lived on earth at some time in the past, was taken up to paradise without dying, where he is in the company of others who had similarly not tasted of death, and will come to earth with them in the future. The list cannot be dependent on 4 Ezra, because Ezra himself is not included in it, but preserves a traditional notion that the author of 4 Ezra also deployed. The fact that the list goes on to put six other biblical persons in the same category also helps to explain the impression given by Pseudo-Philo's *Biblical Antiquities*, as well as 4 Ezra and 2 Baruch, that there were more people than just Enoch and Elijah who were thought not to have died. Of course, the list may have developed over time and we cannot tell which people already belonged to it in the late Second Temple period, but in the case of at least some of them we can see how exegetical ingenuity could have inferred from the biblical text that they did not die.[41]

---

39. Michael Maher, *Targum Pseudo-Jonathan: Genesis*, ArBib 1B (Edinburgh: T&T Clark, 1992) 36–37.

40. One manuscript of Derekh Eretz Zuta omits משיח, while another has משה (Moses), which could be a scribe's attempt to correct the text. Kohler, "The Pre-Talmudic Haggadah," 417, brackets the word in his version of the text and ignores it in his discussion. Van Loopik, *The Ways*, 211, discusses but fails to account for the idea that the Messiah has *already* entered paradise alive.

41. Hiram king of Tyre (Ezek 28:13), Jabez (1 Chr 4:10), Ebed-melech (Jer 39:15–18). (On

THE MESSIAH IN EPISODE 3

The third passage of eschatological predictions (4 Ezra 7:26–44) focuses initially on the survivors, who were briefly introduced in 6:25, and on the Messiah, who for the first time in the book makes an unequivocal appearance. His role as judge of the evil rulers and nations is not mentioned, which is not a problem if we remember that the various eschatological revelations made to Ezra are complementary and progressive. Both the identity and the role of the Messiah are unveiled in stages, in a process that comes to its climax in the vision and its interpretation in Episode 6. In Episode 3 the Messiah's role in judgment is withheld with a view to its extensive treatment in Episodes 5 and 6. Instead, the focus here is on the Messiah's positive significance for the survivors.

He will inaugurate what studies of 4 Ezra commonly call the messianic kingdom, but would be more appropriately called the messianic age, since he is not said (here or anywhere in 4 Ezra) to rule. In fact, all we are told about it is that "he shall make those who remain rejoice [*jocundabit*] for four hundred years" (7:28). But there is more to this brief statement than meets the eye, since the exegesis behind it becomes explicit in rabbinic traditions.[42] It results from bringing together two scriptural texts, one of which is

> Make us glad as many days as you have afflicted us,
> and as many years as we have seen evil. (Ps 90:15)

The other text is Genesis 15:13, where God tells Abraham that his descendants "shall be aliens in a land that is not theirs [i.e., Egypt], and shall be slaves there, and they shall be oppressed for four hundred years." A literal reading of the psalm requires that the four hundred years of suffering in Egypt should be matched by an equal period of rejoicing. (It is also relevant that Ps 90 is the only psalm ascribed to Moses.)

It is worth noticing that this combination of texts and the conclusion drawn from it are variously ascribed to Rabbi Dosa ben Arḥinos (b. Sanh. 99a) and to Rabbi Eliezer ben Hyrcanus (Pesiq. Rab. 1), both of whom were second-generation Tannaim and so contemporaries of the author of 4 Ezra. But probably more important is the fact that the six rabbis to whom the Bavli attributes various exegetical opinions on the length of "the days of the Messiah,"

---

the basis of the fact that the same promise was made to Ebed-melech and to Baruch [Jer 45:5], they are considered in rabbinic literature to be the same person.)

42. See especially George H. Box, *The Ezra-Apocalypse* (London: Pitman, 1912) 115–16.

including this one, all belong to that same generation (b. Sanh. 99a). While the attribution of rabbinic sayings to individual rabbis cannot be uncritically accepted, there seems to be evidence here that the question of the length of the messianic age was discussed as an exegetical issue in the period when 4 Ezra was written.

In fact, a background in Genesis 15:13 and Psalm 90:15 illuminates our passage in other ways too. This account of eschatological events begins with a somewhat enigmatic prediction:

> The city which now is not seen will appear
> and the land which now is hidden will be disclosed. (4 Ezra 7:26b)

The city is the heavenly Jerusalem, not built by human hands, which Ezra will see in the first of his three visions (10:25–27, 53–55). The hidden land is the promised land as it will be in the messianic age (9:8; 12:34; 13:48). It is the land in which the survivors will rejoice for four hundred years (12:34). But it is also, like the time period, a kind of recompense for the years of oppression, which were spent as "aliens in a land that is not theirs" (Gen 15:13). In the messianic age they will be at home within God's borders (4 Ezra 13:48) in the land he has given them.

Psalm 90 continues, after the verse just quoted:

> Let your work be manifest to your servants,
>   and your glorious power to their children. (90:16)

This is surely echoed in 4 Ezra's promise that the survivors "shall see my wonders" (7:27; cf. 13:50). They are the miracles of the new exodus.

After this brief but suggestive account of the messianic age, the passage goes on to stress its temporary nature, for the Messiah, his companions, and the survivors must all die in the general dissolution of creation that must precede the new creation, the resurrection, and the last judgment. The last judgment becomes the dominant theme both of this passage of predictions and of the rest of this long episode. It is given this full treatment before being left aside completely in the rest of the book. The three visions that follow in Episodes 4–6 focus instead on what the survivors will witness in the transition to the messianic age. These are the eschatological events that readers of 4 Ezra are encouraged to think are imminent and that are of the greatest interest to Ezra himself as he seeks resolution to his bewilderment as to the justice, mercy, and especially the faithfulness of God.

My Son or My Servant?

In 4 Ezra the Messiah is called by two titles. One, "the Messiah," occurs three times (7:28, 29; 12:32), and the textual evidence is relatively clear that this is the correct reading in all three cases. But in the case of the other title, which occurs six times (7:28, 29; 13:32, 37, 52; 14:9), the complex textual situation makes it very difficult to be sure whether it was originally "my Son" or "my Servant." (In every case it occurs in words of God.) Most editors and translators have opted for "my Son," which is the consistent reading of the Latin and Syriac versions, but there is considerable variation in the other versions, none of which have a word meaning unambiguously "son." In many cases they have words meaning "young man"/"child" or "servant."[43] Stone therefore argues that most probably the Greek used the word παῖς in the sense of "servant" and based on the Hebrew עבד. The Greek παῖς can mean "child," "servant," and "son," and so (Stone argues) some Christian translators, rather naturally, understood God to be calling the Messiah "my Son." Others opted for "young man" or "servant."[44] Stone's main argument is that the range of renderings in the versions is explicable if they derive from παῖς in the Greek:

> Had any Christian translator (and all the translators can be assumed to be Christian) had the word "son" before him, referring to the Messiah or the Christ, it is hard to assume he would change it for some other word. However, if he had a word before him that could mean "son" but could also mean "child" or "servant," he might have translated it by a word that was unambiguously "son" in some cases, while retaining a translation of it as "young man" or "servant" in others.[45]

However, I think there is another possible explanation of the textual evidence. While we can assume that the translators of the extant versions were Christians, it is likely that the translator of the Greek version from the original Hebrew was Jewish, and that manuscripts of the Greek version circulated among Jews as well as (later?) among Christians. The Greek version could have originally had υἱός, translating Hebrew בן, but this usage would have become

---

43. The complete textual evidence is set out in tabular form in Stone, *Fourth Ezra*, 209.
44. Michael E. Stone, *Features of the Eschatology of IV Ezra*, HSS 35 (Atlanta: Scholars Press, 1989) 71–75; Stone, *Fourth Ezra*, 207–8.
45. Stone, *Fourth Ezra*, 207.

unacceptable to Jews because of the Christian use of "Son of God" for Jesus and the high christological sense that Christians gave it. Therefore, *Jewish* scribes copying the Greek version of 4 Ezra might simply omit ὁ υἱός μου (as in some of the extant versions at 7:28) or substitute ὁ παῖς μου, using the word that in the Septuagint is used for the servant of the Lord in Isaiah. This would result in variety in the Greek manuscripts, accounting for the variation in the extant versions.

Stone also argues that, although it is possible that "Son of God" was in Jewish use as a messianic title based on Psalm 2:7 in the late Second Temple period, there is no actual evidence of this. He dismisses the allusion to Psalm 2:7 in Psalms of Solomon 17:26 as not relevant (since there is no actual allusion to "my Son" in 2:7) and ignores the application of 2 Samuel 7:14 ("I will be his father, and he will be my son" [NIV]) in 4Q174.[46] But, crucially, he wrote before the publication of 4Q246, which we have seen provides good evidence of the titular use of "Son of God" for a Messianic Figure (see chapter 2.3).

There are no allusions in 4 Ezra to the "servant of the Lord" passages in Isaiah. If the original text did refer to "my Servant" rather than "my Son," the best explanation would be that it depends on the description of David as a "servant" (*servum*) of God in 3:23, following ample biblical precedent.[47] In particular, the description of the new David, the Messiah, as "my servant David" in Ezekiel 34:23–24 and 37:24–25, is relevant, though in these passages the Septuagint translates עבדי as ὁ δοῦλος μου. However, it is much more likely that "my Son" was used, with allusion to Psalm 2:7, since there is substantial dependence on other elements of Psalm 2 in 4 Ezra 13, as we shall see.[48]

It is noteworthy that in Episode 5 God calls the Messiah "the Messiah" (12:32), not "my Son," but adopts the latter terminology in Episode 6 (13:32, 37, 52; see also 14:9), where Psalm 2 is a major source of the vision. In 7:28–29 the best reading is probably "my Son the Messiah," though it is possible that

---

46. Stone, *Fourth Ezra*, 208.

47. E.g., 2 Sam 3:18; 7:5, 8; Ps 89:3, 20; Jer 33:21–22, 26; Ps 132:10 ("my servant David" in all these cases). Note also Zech 3:8: "my servant the Branch"; 2 Bar. 70:9: "my servant the Messiah." See also Nathan C. Johnson, "Rendering David a Servant in *Psalm of Solomon* 17.21," *JSP* 26 (2017) 235–50.

48. John J. Collins, *The Scepter and the Star: The Messiahs of the Dead Sea Scrolls and Other Ancient Literature* (New York: Doubleday, 1995) 165, also disagrees with Stone for this reason: "The Latin and Syriac reading, 'my son' should be accepted as a faithful rendering of the original, at least in chapter 13." But he offers no explanation of the textual evidence, which for Stone was decisive.

in 7:28 "my Messiah" was the original text.[49] In any case, whether in both these verses or in one of them, the author introduces the term "my Son" by coupling it with "Messiah." This may indicate that it was a somewhat unusual term for the Messiah (as our other evidence would also suggest), and so the author establishes its reference to the Messiah initially in 7:28–29 before using it without "Messiah" in Episodes 6–7. His reason for using this unusual, though not unprecedented, title for the Messiah will have been precisely because of its occurrence in Psalm 2. Since Psalm 2 speaks of the Messiah both as "his [the Lord's] anointed" (2:2) and as "my son" (2:7), the double description "my Son the Messiah" (4 Ezra 7:28–29) can also be regarded as alluding to Psalm 2.

The Messiah in Episode 5

As far as relationship to Daniel 7 is concerned, there is a kind of symmetry between the two visions in Episodes 5 and 6. In Episode 5 the portrayal of the enemies of God is an interpretation of their portrayal as the "fourth beast" in Daniel 7, but the portrayal of the Messiah draws on other scriptural sources. In Episode 6 the portrayal of the enemies of God is based on other scriptural sources, but the portrayal of the Messiah is an interpretation of the "one like a son of man" (Dan 7:13), though drawing on other scriptural sources too.

The long and complex description of the eagle and its interpretation (4 Ezra 11:1–35; 12:11–30) has been much discussed. There is no doubt that the eagle represents the Roman Empire and its wings and heads represent the Roman emperors. Exactly how they match the history of the emperors is a debatable issue that need not detain us here.[50] We need only note that Ezra is explicitly told that the eagle "is the fourth kingdom which appeared in a vision to your brother Daniel. But it was not explained to him as I now explain it to you" (12:11–12). The point is presumably that Ezra, unlike Daniel, is privileged to know the details of the fourth kingdom's history.[51]

The lion as an image of the Davidic Messiah derives from Genesis 49:9 and appears also in 1QSb v 29 and Revelation 5:5. It is a natural image of

---

49. This is Stone's judgment.

50. See Stone, *Fourth Ezra*, 362–65; Emil Schürer, *The History of the Jewish People in the Age of Jesus Christ (175 BC–AD 135)*, vol. 3/1, rev. and ed. Geza Vermes, Fergus Millar, and Martin Goodman (Edinburgh: T&T Clark, 1986) 297–300; Lorenzo DiTommaso, "Dating the Eagle Vision of *4 Ezra*: A New Look at an Old Theory," *JSP* 20 (1999) 3–38. DiTommaso argues that the text was updated by an editor in 218 CE.

51. For the differences from Daniel, see Maurice Casey, *Son of Man: The Interpretation and Influence of Daniel 7* (London: SPCK, 1979) 123.

destructive power and used as such quite often in the Hebrew Bible.[52] This aspect is emphasized in 1QSb 5:29, which alludes also to the image of the lion in prophecies of Israel conquering other nations (Num 23:24; Mic 5:8). The lion is also an image of royalty and, in view of the proximity to 49:10, it is easy to see that Genesis 49:9 should be understood to refer to the royal line from the tribe of Judah and so to the expected Messiah of David. But in 4 Ezra 11–12 the connotation of military conquest is completely absent. The Messiah does destroy the enemy, but by judicial sentence and execution, not warfare. The explicit statement that he "will arise from the posterity [literally, "seed"] of David" (12:32) echoes 2 Samuel 7:12 and would ordinarily indicate that he is a king. But the only royal role he performs is that of judge. By condemning and destroying the enemy, he liberates the people of God, but, as in 4 Ezra 7:28, he is not said to rule them but to "make them joyful until the end come" (12:34). The description of his judgment of the eagle does not make any verbal allusion to a scriptural source of this idea, but it is likely that Isaiah 11:4 lies behind it, as it certainly does in chapter 13.

THE MESSIAH IN EPISODE 6

Ezra's vision in this episode begins with the appearance of the Messiah (4 Ezra 13:3) and only subsequently depicts the "innumerable multitude . . . gathered together from the four winds of heaven to make war" against him (13:5). Although both Episode 5 and Episode 6 are concerned with the Messiah's destruction of the enemies of God and his people, in Episode 5 the focus is on the enemy (the eagle), while in Episode 6 the focus moves to the Messiah himself. Moreover, along with Daniel 7, other scriptural sources now make a major contribution: Psalm 2, Daniel 2:31-45 (like 4Q246, 4 Ezra develops the parallel between these two Danielic visions), and Isaiah 11 (see table 2). The main function of the Messiah, as in Episode 5, is to destroy the enemy by judicial condemnation. This is now depicted by an image of battle, albeit one in which the Messiah wields no weapon other than "the rod of his mouth" and "the breath of his lips" (Isa 11:4).[53]

Ezra sees "something like the figure of a man come up out of the heart of the sea" (4 Ezra 13:3). Unfortunately, these words have been accidentally omitted,

---

52. Richard Bauckham, *The Climax of Prophecy: Studies on the Book of Revelation* (Edinburgh: T&T Clark, 1993) 181–82.
53. Against the view of Stone and others that the author of 4 Ezra did not compose the vision himself but took it over from a source, see Casey, *Son of Man*, 126–28.

by *homoioteleuton*, in the Latin version. Stone's translation ("something like the figure of a man") is of the Syriac (*'ayk dmuta' dbarnasha'*). The Ethiopic and the Armenian have "something like a man"; Arabic 2 has "the figure of a man." It is not possible to be sure what expression was used in the Greek or the putative Hebrew original.[54] But it seems likely that the Hebrew was כמראה גבר ("one like the appearance of a man"), as in Daniel 8:15, or כמראה אדם ("one like the appearance of a human"), as in Daniel 10:18, or perhaps כמראה בן אדם ("one like the appearance of a son of man").[55] If the latter expression was used in the Hebrew original, then either the Greek correctly translated "son of man" as ἄνθρωπος or the Greek translated the phrase literally as υἱὸν ἀνθρώπου and the Latin correctly translated this as *homo*. Whichever phrase was in the Greek, the Syriac would be a correct translation, since *barnasha'* is a common term for "man" in Syriac.

There is no doubt that the reference in 4 Ezra 13:3 is to the "one like a son of man" (Aramaic כבר אנש) in Daniel 7:13, but the use of the fuller expression, "something like the figure of a man," to describe him is strikingly parallel to 1 Enoch 46:1, where that figure, on his first appearance in the book, is called "another, whose face was like the appearance of a man," probably reflecting Daniel 8:15 or 10:18. While in 1 Enoch the identity of this figure as the "one like a son of man" of Daniel 7:13 is made unmistakably clear by the description of God that precedes (echoing Dan 7:9), in 4 Ezra it is made equally clear by the information that he "flew with the clouds of heaven" (4 Ezra 13:3).

Another remarkably close correspondence with the Parables of Enoch is the fact that, having introduced the figure as "something like the figure of a man," Ezra, describing his vision, then refers to him as "that man" (*ipse homo*): "that man flew with the clouds of heaven" (13:3). Then he calls him "the man who came up out of the sea" (13:5). Later he identifies him again as "that man" (*ipsum hominem*) (13:12).[56] This is very like the way the Parables of Enoch refers back to the figure described in 46:1 as "that son of man" (1 En. 46:2; 48:2; 62:5, 9, 14; 63:11; 69:26, 29; 70:1; 71:17). Also in the interpretation of the vision, the figure is never indicated just by "the man" but always with an accompanying phrase that makes clear that the man Ezra saw in his vision is the man in question (4 Ezra 13:25, 32, 51). These instances resemble 1 Enoch 46:3 and 71:14. In both 1 Enoch and 4 Ezra, these linguistic features are necessary because neither "son of man" nor "man" in 4 Ezra is a title. So, in both cases,

---

54. See the discussions in Casey, *Son of Man*, 124-25; Collins, *The Scepter*, 183.

55. It may well be that, because the author of 4 Ezra was writing in Hebrew, he preferred the expressions used in Dan 8:15; 10:18, to the Aramaic expression in Dan 7:13.

56. Here Stone translates the Latin as "the same man."

some defining element (such as a demonstrative or an adjectival phrase) is needed to make it clear that the reference is to the human figure that the seer has seen in his vision.

It is especially important to note that, in the interpretation of Ezra's vision, the man who came up from the sea is treated only as a symbolic figure in the vision (13:25, 32), just as the lion was in the previous vision. The person who is symbolized in the vision by the man is never himself called "the man" in the interpretation. Rather, he is "my Son" (13:32, 37), alluding to Psalm 2:7. God says, "my Son will be revealed, whom you saw as a man coming up from the sea" (13:32). For the author of 4 Ezra, Daniel 7:13 is visionary imagery, whereas Psalm 2:7 is real-world truth. As Maurice Casey comments, this author "had a clear appreciation of the difference between visionary symbolism and actual reality, not in any way inconsistent with his great love of the former, and it is unfortunate that this clear appreciation has been largely obscured by scholars."[57]

So it is clear that for this author "the man" (even if in the Hebrew original it was "the son of man") was not a title.[58] Nor would he have taken the expression out of its visionary context in chapter 13 and used it as a way of referring to Daniel 7:13 or to the Messiah. It is only a visionary image, "something like the figure of a man" (13:3), just as "something like a lion" (11:37) is in the previous vision. Both are visionary symbols for the Messiah, not terms that could be used to refer to the Messiah. This usage is very different from the use of "the Son of Man" in the Gospels.

The way that the symbols representing the Messiah are initially explained to Ezra in the two vision interpretations is parallel:

> And as for the lion whom you saw rousing up out of the forest . . . this is the Messiah whom the Most High has kept until the end of days, who will arise from the posterity of David. (12:31–32)

> As for seeing a man come up from the heart of the sea, this is he whom the Most High has been keeping for many ages, through whom he will deliver his creation. (13:25–26)

In the latter passage we might have expected "this is the Son of the Most High whom he . . . ," but 4 Ezra only uses the word "son" for the Messiah in the possessive form: "my Son." This shows that the term is a direct allusion to Psalm 2:7 ("you are my son").

---

57. Casey, *Son of Man*, 124.
58. Casey, *Son of Man*, 125–26, puts the case very well.

In Daniel 7 the four beasts come up from the sea (7:3), but it is not said where the "one like a son of man" comes from. In 4 Ezra both the eagle (11:1) and "the man" come up from the sea, but the latter from "the heart of the sea" (13:2). There is no reason to think that the sea in 4 Ezra retains the mythological significance (as the primordial chaos) it may have had originally in Daniel 7. It is part of the visionary scene setting, like the wind in 13:2, also borrowed from Daniel (7:2). Ezra does not see "the man" with God in a scene like Daniel 7:13 and 1 Enoch 46:1, but as arriving on earth to implement the divine judgment that has already taken place for all to see (6:20). So coming up from the sea would seem to be just a way of saying that he arrives on the earthly scene. The explanation in 13:52 spells that significance out rather more explicitly: "No one can see my Son or those who are with him, except in the time of his day." It is characteristic of Ezra's visions, unlike Enoch's, that he never sees into heaven or paradise or even the remote parts of the earth. What he sees with his eyes is what people on earth see or will see. The fact that an element of the vision that appears early in the description of the vision is not interpreted until the end of the long interpretation of the vision is not a sign of redactional addition to the text. It has been placed at this point to give it special emphasis.[59] The Messiah will be revealed in his time, not before. The introduction of "those who are with" the Messiah (13:52), who were not symbolized in the vision or mentioned in the interpretation up to this point, is to prepare for the revelation to Ezra, in 14:9, that he will be one of them.

Some scholars argue that the characteristics of "the man" in 4 Ezra 13:3–4, 10–11 echo biblical theophany language (especially of God as Warrior) and so make him a "divine" figure.[60] We need to take these features one by one:

- That he "flew with the clouds of heaven" (13:3) has been compared with Isaiah 19:1, where God rides on a cloud.[61] But "with the clouds of heaven" is a verbatim citation of Daniel 7:13.[62] It is gratuitous to postulate any other source.

---

59. Casey, *Son of Man*, 126.

60. Michael E. Stone, "The Question of the Messiah in 4 Ezra," in *Judaisms and Their Messiahs at the Turn of the Christian Era*, ed. Jacob Neusner, William S. Green, and Ernest Frerichs (Cambridge: Cambridge University Press, 1987) 213; Longenecker, *2 Esdras*, 79; Crispin Fletcher-Louis, *Jesus Monotheism*, vol. 1, *Christological Origins: The Emerging Consensus and Beyond* (Eugene, OR: Cascade, 2015) 182, 187. But Stone comments: "All of these elements had been freed from the concept of God as Warrior before the time of 4 Ezra, and they are attributes of the man in the symbolic dream" (213).

61. Box, *The Ezra-Apocalypse*, 283. Box thinks the vision comes from a source that was not dependent on Daniel 7. See Stone, "The Question," 221 n. 17, for many other references to clouds associated with theophanies.

62. It is notable that in the Aramaic, Dan 7:13 reads, "came with [עם] the clouds," The-

- According to 13:3, "wherever he turned his face to look, everything under his gaze trembled." This resembles Habakkuk 3:6: "he looked and made the nations tremble." (Cf. Ps 104:32: God "looks on the earth and it trembles.")
- According to 13:4, "wherever the voice of his mouth issued forth, all who heard his voice melted as wax melts when it feels the fire." The simile is used several times in the Hebrew Bible to describe what happens to people or mountains in the presence of God (Ps 68:2 [the wicked]; 97:5 [mountains]; Mic 1:4 [mountains]), but only the first of these has "before the fire." In no case does it refer to the effect of God's voice. In Judith 16:15 rocks melt before God's glance (with no reference to fire); in 1 Enoch 1:6 (in a passage modeled on biblical theophany accounts) the high hills "melt like wax before the fire." First Enoch 52:6, most likely in dependence on 1 Enoch 1:6, says that the seven mountains Enoch sees "will be before the Chosen One like wax before the fire." This is the only text, other than 4 Ezra 13:4, where the simile is used with reference to a Messianic Figure, rather than God. The simile itself is thus a standard one, which 4 Ezra has used innovatively with reference to the voice of the Messiah.
- According to 4 Ezra 13:10, the Messiah "sent forth from his mouth a stream of fire, and from his lips a flaming breath, and from his tongue he shot forth a storm of fiery coals." The combined force of these burned up the innumerable multitude (13:11). Fire is a common means or image of God's judgment, as is the notion that God's word or breath destroys the wicked. Psalm 18:8[9] (par. 2 Sam 22:9) is particularly close to this passage about the Messiah in 4 Ezra: "Smoke went up from his nostrils, and devouring fire from his mouth, glowing coals flamed forth from him." Isaiah 66:15–16 describes God's judgment by fire, including "his rebuke in flames of fire" (66:15; cf. Isa 30:27).

It is often claimed, as evidence that the author of 4 Ezra took over the vision from a source and added his own interpretation to it, that these "divine" characteristics of the Messiah in the vision are ignored in the interpretation or, in the case of the last, interpreted in such a way as to be consistent with a purely human Messiah, as the Messiah in 4 Ezra elsewhere is. However, the way in which 13:10–11 is interpreted in 13:36–37 may suggest a better understanding of these so-called divine characteristics. We need to recall Isaiah 11:4, that favorite messianic text:

---

odotion's version also has "with [μετὰ]," but OG has "on [ἐπὶ] the clouds." 4 Ezra's paraphrase of the Aramaic, "flew with the clouds of heaven," is understandable: since he rode on the clouds, he must have flown with them. By contrast, in Isa 19:1 God rides on (עַל) a cloud.

> He shall strike the earth with the rod of his mouth
> and with the breath of his lips he shall kill the wicked. (11:4b)

The image is of spoken words that not only pronounce but effect judgment. The text is also understood in this way in 1 Enoch 62:2 and Psalms of Solomon 17:24, 35.

In 4 Ezra 13:10, Isaiah's reference, in parallel, to "mouth" and "lips" is expanded to a threefold parallelism: "mouth," "lips," and "tongue," each of which produces some form of fire. Since fire is a common image of destructive judgment, this is quite an obvious way to imagine the words of the Messiah judging and destroying the wicked. But in the exegetical work behind the text of 4 Ezra, there seems to be also an association of biblical texts. Isaiah 11:4b has been brought together with other texts, especially Psalm 18:8[9] and Isaiah 66:15, where fire from the mouth of God represents his judgment. If the Messiah kills with breath from his mouth (Isa 11:4b) this must be because he pronounces the judgment of God that issues from God's mouth like fire.

In the interpretation of the vision, the three forms of fire are explained thus:

> And he, my Son, will reprove the assembled nations for their ungodliness (this was symbolized by the storm), and will reproach them to their face with their evil deeds and the torments with which they are to be tortured (which were symbolized by the flames), and will destroy them without effort by the law (which is symbolized by the fire). (4 Ezra 13:37–38)

This means that the Messiah pronounces *God's* condemnation and destroys by *God's* law. That makes him, not divine, but a human agent of God, and it probably explains the two "divine" characteristics in 13:3b–4. His look conveys the divine anger, and so everything trembles (13:3). His voice announces the divine judgment, and all who hear it melt like wax before the fire (13:4). These echoes of biblical language used of God characterize his mission from God as that of the one who executes the divine condemnation of the enemies. This is why they receive no specific comment in the interpretation.

So we should not think of the Messiah's appearance as a theophany. Some language has been drawn from biblical passages that depict the terrifying and destructive impact of God on the world, but the imagery is understood to describe God's judgment on sinners, and it therefore depicts the Messiah as the one who comes to execute God's judgment. It does not mean that he is understood to be divine or even angelic, and so does not conflict with the rest of the book's portrayal of the Messiah.

The idea that the Messiah defeats and destroys the enemy by his word and not by weapons belongs to a tradition, dependent on Isaiah 11:4, that can also be seen in the Psalms of Solomon (17:22–25) as well as in the Parables of Enoch and in Revelation (19:11, 15).[63] (4Q246 is different in that there God defeats the enemy for him.) The motif is emphasized in 4 Ezra by the "multitude" of the returning northern tribes, which might have served as his army but instead are emphatically described as "peaceable" (13:12, 39, 47). Thus, although his gathering of them (13:12, 39, 47) reflects Isaiah 11:12, the military role that Isaiah 11:14 gives them is rejected. There was probably a tradition in which the nine and a half tribes, on their return from exile, were known as a highly militant force, destroying the hostile nations and arriving in Jerusalem in time to deliver the city from the last great assault on it.[64] In that case, 4 Ezra radically refunctions them.

The long account of them (13:39–47) is necessary to explain this new function. It depicts them as migrating to an uninhabited region so that there they could keep the Mosaic law faithfully. Without the risk of influence and contamination from gentiles living around them, they succeed in keeping the law in a way that only a few of those in the land of Israel managed to do. In this way they function, in Ezra's journey of understanding, to resolve finally his initial bewilderment about the faithfulness of God in the light of the destruction of Jerusalem. He has gradually come to accept Uriel's argument that God must maintain the strictest standard of justice. The majority of Israelites in the land rightly perish under his judgment, leaving only the "survivors," the faithful few. But he nevertheless remains faithful to his promise in his covenant with the patriarchs, that he would bless and not forsake the multitude of their descendants, because the nine and a half tribes, in their hidden remoteness, have remained faithful to the Torah as very few of the Israelites in the land or in the later diaspora had done.[65] This is why the interpretation of the vision devotes so much attention to them even though their role in the action seems minimal. The important thing is that they exist and arrive. They are the rabbit the author of 4 Ezra finally pulls out of his hat to resolve the dilemma with which the book began.

In Episode 6, as in Episode 5, the Messiah's role focuses on his judicial condemnation and destruction of the enemies of Israel, who seem to be all the

---

63. Revelation and 4 Ezra both interpret the idea of a messianic war in purely forensic terms, but in somewhat different ways.

64. See Richard Bauckham, "The Nine and a Half Tribes," *OTPMNS* 1:346–59.

65. Richard Bauckham, "Apocalypses," in *Justification and Variegated Nomism*, vol. 1, *The Complexities of Second Temple Judaism*, ed. Donald A. Carson, Peter T. O'Brien, and Mark A. Seifrid, WUNT 2/140 (Tübingen: Mohr Siebeck, 2001) 166–69.

nations. By doing this he proves to be the one "through whom [the Most High] will deliver his creation" (13:26, cf. 48), an important reference back to 5:56–6:1. There God's response to Ezra's request that he show him "through whom thou dost visit thy creation" was the vague statement "The beginning [of the visitation] is through man." Now at last Ezra's question is answered more precisely.

The key functions of the Messiah, as they have now emerged in this final vision, are to destroy the hostile nations by judicial implementation of God's law, to liberate the survivors, and to summon the nine and a half tribes from their hidden location. As for other roles, according to 13:26, the Messiah will "direct [*disponet*] those who are left." Stone's translation "direct"[66] is potentially misleading if it suggests an ongoing activity. The Greek verb was very likely διατάσσω,[67] which, with an accusative, means "to set in order, to arrange" something or someone. Perhaps the meaning is that the Messiah will make the survivors into an orderly society, or perhaps it is that he will settle them on the land in an orderly arrangement according to their tribes (as in Ezek 48:23–29; Pss. Sol. 17:28). While the exact meaning is obscure, the general sense must be that he will set the people in order.[68] Importantly, it does not mean that he rules them.

More easily intelligible is the statement in 13:49–50 where we learn that "he will defend the people who remain. And then he will show them very many wonders." The "wonders" in this case must refer to the fabulous state of nature described in 2 Baruch 29:3–8.[69] (The close relationship between the texts of 4 Ezra and 2 Baruch at this point can be inferred from the fact that, immediately before this passage, at 29:2, 2 Baruch has a close parallel to 4 Ezra 13:48–49: "For at that time I will protect only those who are found in those very days in this land" [cf. 2 Bar. 40:2].) The enjoyment of these paradisal wonders is probably the meaning of the statement that the Messiah will make the survivors "rejoice" (4 Ezra 7:28), so that the content of what is said about

---

66. This is also the NRSV's translation.

67. The Syriac has "he will lead (the survivors) across" (*n'br*), presumably rendering διάξῃ ("he will lead across," from διάγω), whereas the Latin "he will set in order" (*disponet*) plausibly renders διατάξῃ ("he will set in order," from διατάσσω). The latter is more likely the original, while διάξῃ is explicable as a scribal error for διατάξῃ.

68. Cf. Jacob M. Myers, *I and II Esdras*, AB 42 (New York: Doubleday, 1972) 310: "As the text now stands it appears to mean that the messiah will arrange or create the new order for those who survive."

69. Note the word "wonders" in 29:6. Note also the correspondence between 4 Ezra 6:52 (God has preserved Leviathan and Behemoth "to be eaten by whom you wish, when you wish") and 2 Bar. 29:4 (God has kept Leviathan and Behemoth "until that time" and "then they will be food for all who remain").

the Messiah and the survivors in 7:28b and 13:50 is substantially the same.[70] The Messiah makes the people rejoice by showing them the wonders they can enjoy in the paradisal period, but he is not said to reign. It is clear that 4 Ezra consistently avoids depicting the Messiah as a king. That office is reserved for God.

It is possible that 4 Ezra's stress on the fact that the Messiah does not wield weapons and has no army is related to the avoidance of language of kingship and rule (despite his Davidic descent: 12:32). The former was not an innovation, since it is part of the portrayal of the messianic king in Psalms of Solomon 17, but the figure in that text is emphatically a king. Behind 4 Ezra's stress on the nonmilitant character of the Messiah and the depiction of a Messiah who is a judge but not a king, there may be a desire to repudiate the militant messianism of the revolt of 66–70 CE, in which more than one militant leader claimed to be a king. Judgment is a royal function, but so is defeating enemies by leading armies in battle. By not calling the Messiah a king, 4 Ezra avoids the militant connotations of kingship. The Messiah's importance is strictly focused on his role of destroying the enemies of God by judicial condemnation and his liberation of the survivors. He will not be known until he is revealed, when he arrives, without an army, to confront and destroy the hostile nations. In 4 Ezra's time this would have been strongly opposed to the expectations that were to lead to the Bar Kokhba revolt.

Conclusion

In 4 Ezra the profile of the Messiah emerges gradually, reaching a climax in Episode 6, the vision of "the man from the sea." A crucial point of interpretation is that the figure in Daniel 7:13 is understood to be a man, a descendant of David, who lived on earth in the past, was exalted to heaven without dying, and has been preserved by God until the time when he is "revealed" and performs his eschatological role. Moreover, he is one of the several figures, such as Enoch and Elijah, who similarly did not die but are currently with him and will be revealed together with him in the last days. In the last episode, it emerges that Ezra himself is also one of this privileged group. There is no clue as to who this descendant of David was—whether an individual known from the Hebrew Bible or an otherwise unknown person. But the idea itself—of a man from the Davidic line, hidden by God and preserved for the end—made it possible for

---

70. Cf. 2 Bar. 29:6: "And those who have been hungry will rejoice; and also they will see wonders every day."

the author of 4 Ezra to apply key prophecies of the Davidic Messiah (Gen 49:9; 2 Sam 7:12; Ps 2; Isa 11) to the "one like a son of man" of Daniel 7:13. In fact, that text itself does not contribute much to the account of the Messiah other than the idea that there is a human figure who is being preserved by God for an important role in God's purpose in the future.

This Messiah is the one "through whom" God "visits" the world in judgment and delivers his people in the events that will bring the present course of history to its close. This is not the last judgment, the judgment of the dead, in which God alone is the judge, and which will follow the four-hundred-year messianic age and the new creation. The Messiah has no role in those events. But he is God's agent in the events in which the hostile nations will be judged and destroyed and the "survivors," the righteous remnant of Israel, will be delivered. These events (not the last judgment) are understood to be the subject matter of Daniel's vision in Daniel 7, as the allusion to Daniel 7:10 in 4 Ezra 6:20 shows. Daniel's fourth beast is understood to be the Roman Empire, pictured as an eagle in the vision in Episode 5, the details of which provide details of the history of the emperors going beyond what had been revealed to Daniel. The vision and its interpretation in Episode 5 focus on the Roman Empire and its condemnation and destruction by the Messiah, here pictured as a lion, with allusion to Genesis 49:9. The lion is a symbol of destructive power, but the Messiah exercises this power solely in a judicial capacity. He convicts the empire of all its evils, hauls its living representatives before his judgment seat, condemns them to death, and destroys them. (Only in Episode 6 does it become clear that his word of condemnation itself destroys them.) At this point there has been no allusion to Daniel 7:13 or to Psalm 2.

The same events are differently imagined in the vision in Episode 6,[71] which recasts the figure of Daniel 7:13 as "a man who comes up from the sea" and who flies with the clouds to the land of Israel. But, along with Daniel 2 and Isaiah 11, Psalm 2 is formative in this account of the Messiah. Here the enemies are not the Roman Empire but the innumerable multitude of the nations gathered from the four winds of heaven in order to make war on the Messiah, who in this vision is called by God "my Son" (echoing Ps 2:7). He takes his stand on Mount Zion,[72] not the present one but a new one, now revealed, understood to be the "stone"

---

71. It is possible that, while the enemy in Episode 5 is the Roman Empire, the nations who gather from the four winds of heaven in Episode 6 are the remoter nations, comparable with Gog and its allies in Ezek 38–39.

72. Presumably this is not just a mountain, though that is the relevant aspect in this vision, but the city, the new Jerusalem, of 7:26; 10:50–54.

of Daniel 2:45. To defeat and destroy the nations the Messiah uses no weapons, but only his word of reproof and condemnation (portrayed in the vision as fiery products of his mouth), in accordance with Isaiah 11:4. That this is the judgment and condemnation that God has already pronounced and the Messiah implements accounts for the elements of imagery in the vision that echo biblical metaphors relating to God acting in judgment (4 Ezra 13:3b–4, 10). They do not make the Messiah "divine." The vision depicts him consistently as "that man." This is coherent with the earlier revelation that, at the end of the messianic age, he, along with all other humans alive at that time, will die (7:29).

By destroying the hostile nations, the Messiah delivers the "survivors," the righteous remnant of Israel, who, because of their righteousness, are preserved by God through the horrors of the last days. This act of judgment and deliverance is part of what makes the role of the Messiah of key importance to the argument of the book. It vindicates the justice of God, which Ezra had queried in the early part of the book, by revealing how the wicked will not continue to flourish but will be judged, and how the righteous will be delivered and rewarded. But the Messiah performs another function crucial to the argument of the book. He gathers a "peaceable multitude." (That this is based on Isa 11:12 shows that the author did not read Isa 11:4 in isolation but as part of the whole chapter.) This turns out to be the exiles of the northern tribes who have been living in a distant land where they were able to remain faithful to the law of God. This element in the Messiah's activity is important because it vindicates the faithfulness of God to his covenant with Abraham, to whom he promised innumerable descendants. The people of God in the messianic age will comprise not only the righteous few who have truly kept the law among the Israelites in the land, but also the large numbers of the returning exiles of the northern tribes.

The Messiah will inaugurate the messianic age, in which the righteous who survive will enjoy the "wonders" God has prepared for them. This should not be called "the messianic kingdom," because the Messiah is not said to reign. He is never called "king" in 4 Ezra, and the only royal function he fulfills is judgment. The author of 4 Ezra is not interested in describing the messianic age but appeals to what he could presume would be known about its marvelous blessings. Its importance for him is solely that it constitutes the way the righteous are rewarded and compensated for the injustices they have endured hitherto. However, this reward is only for the "survivors" who are alive when the four hundred years commence, and it is strictly temporary. All, including the Messiah, must perish in the dissolution of the world into its primordial condition, out of which God creates a transformed world.

TABLE 1. *The Messiah in 4 Ezra*

Episode 1 (3:1–5:20)
Eschatological predictions (1):   5:1–13
(Messiah?):   5:6–7

Episode 2 (5:21–6:34)
Eschatological predictions (2):   6:18–28
Those who did not die: 6:26

Episode 3 (6:35–9:26)
Eschatological predictions (3):   7:26–44
Messiah + those with him: 7:28–29
Summary of predictions: 9:1–6

Episode 4 (9:27–10:59)
Vision (1):   9:38–10:4
Interpretation of vision: 10:38–54

Episode 5 (11:1–12:51)
Vision (2):   11:1–12:3
Messiah: 11:36–46
Interpretation of vision: 12:10–36
Messiah: 12:31–34

Episode 6 (13:1–58)
Vision (3):   13:2–13
Messiah: 13:3–13
Interpretation of vision: 13:20–55
Messiah: 13:25–52

Episode 7 (14:1–48)
Messiah + those like Ezra: 14:9

TABLE 2. *Biblical allusions in 4 Ezra 11–13*

4 Ezra 11
1	Dan 7:1, 3; Ezek 17:3
2	Dan 7:2
37	Gen 49:9
39	Dan 7:3–7
43	Isa 37:29

4 Ezra 12
3	Dan 7:11
11	Dan 7:7, 23
13	Dan 7:7
31	Gen 49:9
32	2 Sam 7:12
33	Dan 7:36?

4 Ezra 13
1	Dan 7:1
2	Dan 7:2
3	Dan 7:13; 7:3
	Ps 104:32; Hab 3:6
4	Mic 1:4; Ps 68:2; 97:5
5	Ps 2:1–2; Joel 3:9–11 [4:9–11]
6	Dan 2:34–35, 45
8	Ps 2:5
10–11	Isa 11:4; Ps 18:8[9]
12	Isa 11:12; Zech 10:8
13	Isa 66:20; 45:14
31	Dan 2:41; Isa 19:2
32	Ps 2:7
34	Ps 2:1–2
35	Ps 2:6
36	Dan 2:34, 45
37	Ps 2:7
38	Isa 11:4
40	2 Kgs 17:5–6
45	Deut 29:28

TABLE 3. *"Those who have not tasted death"*

4 Ezra

> 6:26: And they shall see the people who were taken up [*recepti sunt*], who from their birth have not tasted death.

> 7:28a: For my Messiah shall be revealed with those who are with him.

> 13:52: He said to me, "Just as no one can explore or know what is in the depths of the sea, so no one on earth can see my son or those who are with him, except in the time of his day."

> 14:9: For you [Ezra] will be taken up [*recipieris*] from among men, and henceforth you shall be with my son and those who are like you, until the times are ended.

> 14:50: At that time Ezra was caught up, and taken to the place of those who are like him, after he had written all these things.

LAB

> 48:1: At that time Phinehas was verging towards death, and the Lord said to him, "Behold you have passed the 120 years that have been established for every man. Now rise up and go from here and dwell in the desert on the mountain and dwell there many years. I will command my eagle, and he will nourish you there, and you will not come down again to mankind until the appointed time arrives and you will be tested at the appropriate time; and then you will shut up the heaven, and by your mouth it will be opened up. Afterward you will be raised up [*elevaberis*] to the place where those who were before you were raised up, and you will be there until I remember the world. Then I will bring you [pl.] [*vos*], and you [pl.] will get a taste of death [*gustabitis quod est mors*]."[a]

2 Baruch

> 13:3: Because you [Baruch] have been astonished at what has happened to Zion, you will surely be preserved to the end of times, that you may be a testimony.

> 25:1: You too will be preserved until that time, until [that] sign which the Most High will give for the inhabitants of the earth at the end of days.

48:30: For you will surely be taken up, as I told you before.

76:2: For you will surely depart from this world, yet it will not be unto death, but you will be kept unto the completion of the times.[b]

Cf. also 46:7.

Derekh Eretz Zuta

1:18: Nine have entered the Garden of Eden while living. They are: Enoch the son of Jared; Elijah; the Messiah; Eliezer the servant of Abraham; Hiram king of Tyre; Ebed-melech the Cushite; Jabez the son of Rabbi Judah the Prince; Bithiah the daughter of Pharaoh; and Serah the daughter of Asher. Some say also Rabbi Jehoshua ben Levi.[c]

Vocabulary

Enoch, Elijah, Ezra, Baruch, those who have not died
"be taken":	Gen 5:24; 2 Kgs 2:10; Jub. 4:23; 2 En. 36:2
"go up":	2 Kgs 2:11
"be taken up":	Sir 44:16; 48:9; 4 Ezra 6:26; 2 Bar. 46:7; 48:30
"be lifted up":	LAB 48:1; 1 En. 70:1–2
"be caught up":	4 Ezra 14:50; 1 En. 39:3
"be preserved/kept":	2 Bar. 13:3; 25:1; 76:2
"be revealed":	4 Ezra 7:28 (with Messiah)

Messianic Figure
"be preserved/kept":	4 Ezra 12:32; 13:26; 1 En. 62:7
"hidden":	1 En. 62:7; Isa 32:2 LXX;[d] Tg. Mic 4:8
"be revealed":	4 Ezra 7:28; 13:32; 2 Bar. 29:3 (cf. 39:7); Tg. Isa 66:7; Tg. Jer 30:21; Tg. Zech 3:8; 4:7; 6:12; Tg. 1 Chr 3:24; b. Sukkah 52b
"appear":	1 En. 69:29; Isa 32:2 LXX

[a] Translation from Jacobson, *Commentary on Pseudo-Philo's Liber Antiquitatum Biblicarum*, vol. 1, 172–73.

[b] Translation from Gurtner, *Second Baruch*, 45, 61, 85, 121.

[c] My translation.

[d] The LXX reading may be based on a Hebrew text different from MT.

CHAPTER 2.6

A Messiah from the Past in Rabbinic Traditions

Fourth Ezra reveals an understanding of the Davidic descent of the Messiah that may at first sight seem radically novel: that a descendant of David, born in the past, escaped death and is being preserved by God, waiting for the time when he will return to the world to fulfill the role of the Messiah son of David in the eschatological events. This idea of the Messiah results from combining the prophecies of an ideal Davidic king (such as Isa 11) with Daniel's vision of "one like a son of man." But it is unlikely that the author of 4 Ezra invented this understanding of the Messiah, since it seems to be taken for granted rather than explained. No indication is given of the time in which this figure lived on earth, and there is no hint of his specific identity. Fourth Ezra seems to presuppose an idea of which its readers will be aware.

Confirmation of this may be found in some traces of it in rabbinic literature. Probably the oldest of these is a tradition about the death of Rabbi Yohanan ben Zakkai, which appears in multiple sources, and in which his last words are said to have been the following (in two slightly divergent versions):

> Clear the house because of uncleanness[1] and give a chair for Hezekiah king of Judah. (y. Avod. Zar. 3:1)

> Clear out the vessels[2] and prepare a chair for Hezekiah who comes. (b. Ber. 28b)[3]

---

1. I.e., corpse impurity resulting from Yohanan's death.
2. Yohanan's death will render the vessels impure.
3. These translations are from Jacob Neusner, *Development of a Legend: Studies on the*

Jacob Neusner's careful examination of the traditions about Yohanan's death concludes that these dying words are the oldest element, which he attributes to the school of Rabbi Eliezer ben Hyrcanus in the Yavneh period (late first century).[4] Whether the words were actually spoken by Yohanan ben Zakkai need not concern us here, but the expectation that Hezekiah would come in the near future, obviously unfulfilled, is unlikely to have been attributed to Yohanan a long time after his death. So we are in touch here with a tradition about the Messiah that was current at the time when 4 Ezra was written.

There can be no doubt that, according to this saying, Yohanan expects the imminent coming of King Hezekiah as the Messiah.[5] His disciples are to prepare a throne for him. This identification of King Hezekiah as the Messiah who is to come is unique in rabbinic literature. Like all messianic expectation it must have had an exegetical basis, and we can with some confidence identify two texts that could have given rise to it. One is the statement that "there was no one like him among all the kings of Judah after him, or among those who were before him" (2 Kgs 18:5).[6] Not only does this make Hezekiah the most suitable of all the kings of Judah to be the Messiah. Strictly understood, it could require the Messiah to be Hezekiah. Since the Messiah will be a king of Judah and since no previous king of Judah could be greater than the Messiah, the statement that "there was no one like him among all the kings of Judah after him" excludes anyone except Hezekiah from being the Messiah.

The other text that may well have given rise to the expectation that the Messiah would be Hezekiah returning to the world is Isaiah 9:5-6[6-7]. This can readily be understood as an oracle of Isaiah about a child who has been born into the house of David. Especially if this passage is read in connection with 7:10-14, the child may easily be understood as King Ahaz's son Hezekiah. (In the history of interpretation many exegetes have identified the child as Hezekiah.) But the promise of an eternal reign of peace and justice in 9:5-6

Traditions Concerning Yoḥanan ben Zakkai, StPB 16 (Leiden: Brill, 1970) 222. Other versions of the tradition are in y. Sotah 9:16; Avot R. Nat. 25.

4. Neusner, *Development*, 88, 131, 136-37, 221-24, 282.

5. It has sometimes been suggested that the reference is to the Galilean bandit-chief Hezekiah, who was executed by Herod the Great early in his reign (Josephus, *War* 1.204; *Ant.* 14.159). But there is no evidence that this Hezekiah made messianic claims, and it is extremely unlikely that Yohanan ben Zakkai should be reported to have regarded him as the Messiah. See Martin Hengel, *The Zealots*, trans. D. Smith (Edinburgh: T&T Clark, 1989) 292 n. 340.

6. The explicit identification of Hezekiah as "king of Judah" in y. Avod. Zar. 3:1 may be a clue pointing to this source.

suggests, not the historical reign of Hezekiah, but the future ideal age of the Messiah. It follows that, for this promise to be fulfilled, Hezekiah himself must return as the Messiah.

In Justin Martyr's dialogue with the Jewish teacher Trypho, he attributes to Trypho and other Jewish teachers the view that Isaiah 7:14 refers to the birth of Hezekiah (*Dial.* 35; 67; 71; 77), but there is no indication that Trypho thought Hezekiah was the Messiah. It is Justin who insists that Isaiah 7:14 refers to the birth of the Messiah, whereas for Trypho the passage is not messianic. Rabbi Hillel II (mid-fourth century CE) is reported to have said, "There shall be no Messiah for Israel, because they have already enjoyed him in the days of Hezekiah," a remarkably radical view for which he was firmly reprimanded (b. Sanh. 98b–99a).[7] Hillel's view was probably based on Isaiah 7:14, 9:5–6, and 11:1–5, all read as prophecies fulfilled during the historical reign of Hezekiah. But the view that Hezekiah is the Messiah who is still to come is attributed in rabbinic literature only to Yohanan ben Zakkai. It seems to have been a view that did not survive beyond the time of Bar Kokhba, when any form of imminent expectation of the Messiah received a heavy blow. In view of the fact that this view is evidenced only for the period around the end of the first century, it is tempting to think that the author of 4 Ezra shared it. But we have seen that 4 Ezra seems to place the Messiah in the category of those who had not died, and the Hebrew Bible states clearly that Hezekiah died (2 Kgs 20:21; 2 Chr 32:33). His tomb could probably be seen in Jerusalem.

Another interpretation of Isaiah 9:5–6 could be that it refers not to the birth of Hezekiah himself but to the birth of a son of Hezekiah, who could be supposed not to have died. This probably explains the rabbinic tradition that the Messiah will be called Menahem the son of Hezekiah. In the catalogue of rabbinic opinions on the name of the Messiah in the Babylonian Talmud, this opinion is ascribed simply to "some." Like the others it is supported by a prooftext, in this case Lamentations 1:16, where the devastated city of Jerusalem laments, "A comforter [מנחם] is far from me" (b. Sanh. 98b). In the shorter parallel catalogue in the Yerushalmi (y. Ber. 2:4 [25b]), no prooftext is given, and the opinion is ascribed to Rabbi Yudan the son of Rabbi Aibo, but this is probably because the story about the birth of Menahem son of Hezekiah that follows is ascribed to Rabbi Yudan the son of Rabbi Aibo.[8] It is likely that the

---

7. This translation from Joseph Klausner, *The Messianic Idea in Israel from Its Beginnings to the Completion of the Mishnah*, trans. W. F. Stinespring (London: Allen & Unwin, 1956) 404.

8. Lam. Rab. 1:51 has "Rabbi Yudan in the name of Rabbi Aibo."

name Menahem was already suggested as the name of the Messiah before the story was devised. The name Menahem (which means "comforter") could be thought appropriate for the Messiah, not only because of the occurrence of the word in Lamentations 1:16, but also because of Isaiah's prophecies that the restoration of Jerusalem will occur when God "comforts" (נחם) his people (Isa 12:1; 40:1; 51:12; cf. Luke 2:25).[9]

Some scholars have tried to connect this tradition with Menahem the son (or grandson?) of Judas the Galilean, the Zealot leader during the early period of the First Revolt (Josephus, *War* 2.433), who probably claimed to be the royal Messiah.[10] The connection depends on the identification of his father Judas with Judas the son of Hezekiah, the bandit-leader, who is then regarded as the founder of a "dynasty" of rebel leaders.[11] But the name Judas was extremely common, and the identification is highly speculative. It seems in any case unlikely that later rabbis would think the true Messiah would be called Menahem because a failed and dead Messiah had been so called. More plausible would be the view that the Zealot Menahem was either given this name by his father or himself adopted the name because it was already said in tradition to be the name of the Davidic Messiah. But the name Menahem, though it occurs as a personal name only once in the Hebrew Bible, was a relatively common name in the late Second Temple period.[12] It may have been popular either for naming a child who brought "comfort" to a hitherto childless couple or as an expression of hope that God's "consolation of Israel" would occur in the child's lifetime.

So we cannot be at all sure when the tradition that the Davidic Messiah is to be called Menahem originated, but it is likely that the idea that he would be a son of King Hezekiah was based on Isaiah 9:5-6. A tradition to this effect may lie behind 4 Ezra's understanding of the Messiah as a Davidide from the past. Fourth Ezra itself does not allude to this passage of Isaiah,[13] but this is

---

9. Support for the name Menahem was also found in gematria, since the numerical value of the name is equal to that of the word צמח, "branch," used of the Messiah in Zech 6:12 (y. Ber. 2:4 [25b]; Lam. Rab. 1:51).

10. Hengel, *The Zealots*, 293-396. Arnold Goldberg, "Die Namen des Messias in der rabbinischen Traditionsliteratur: Ein Beitrag zur Messianologie des rabbinischen Judentums," in *Mystik und Theologie des rabbinischen Judentums: Gesammelte Studien*, vol. 1, ed. Margarete Schlütter and Peter Schäfer, TSAJ 61 (Tübingen: Mohr Siebeck, 1997) 208-74, here 230, rejects the connection.

11. See the reconstructed genealogy in Hengel, *The Zealots*, 332.

12. By my calculations, based on the data in Tal Ilan, *Lexicon of Jewish Names in Late Antiquity*, part 1, *Palestine 330 BCE-200 CE*, TSAJ 91 (Tübingen: Mohr Siebeck, 2002), we know of thirty-seven Palestinian Jews named Menahem in the period 50 BCE-135 CE.

13. But the reference to joy in 12:34 may allude to Isa 9:3.

not surprising in view of the fact that 4 Ezra seems to avoid portraying the Messiah as a king. We shall find that 2 Baruch does allude to Isaiah 9:5-6, suggesting that 2 Baruch's understanding of the Messiah as a Davidide from the past, parallel to 4 Ezra's, was dependent on that prophecy.

The name Menahem son of Hezekiah features in a story about the birth of the Messiah that is ascribed to Rabbi Yudan the son of Rabbi Aibo[14] (Palestine, c. 300). It relates how the Messiah was born in the royal palace in Bethlehem on the day when the temple was destroyed, but in his early infancy was snatched from his mother's arms by a wind or spirit that carried him away (presumably to paradise or heaven, though this is not said). The child's name was Menahem, and his father's name was Hezekiah (y. Ber. 2:4 [25b], with a parallel in Lam. Rab. 1.51). The temple in this story must be the first temple, but the chronology is highly implausible. A child born at the time of the fall of Jerusalem to the Babylonians could not be the son of king Hezekiah. The story is an artificial construction based on the messianic name Menahem son of Hezekiah and at least two biblical texts: Lamentations 1:16 and Micah 5:2, where Bethlehem is said to be the birthplace of a ruler of Israel whose "origin is of old, from ancient days." (I suggested in chapter 2.5 that this verse may lie behind the description of the Messiah in 4 Ezra 13:26 as "he whom the Most High has been keeping for many ages.")

Finally, there is a tradition that is of special interest in our present context because it relates to the interpretation of Daniel 7:13. This is the tradition that names Anani as the Davidic Messiah. Anani is the last name in the genealogy of the descendants of David in 1 Chronicles 3, the seventh of the seven sons of Elioenai (3:24). In the Targum to Chronicles his name is followed by the comment "He is the King Messiah who will be revealed."[15] It is possible that this identification was occasioned simply by the fact that Anani is the last descendant of David to be mentioned in the Hebrew Bible. But it is probable that behind this comment lies the fuller tradition about Anani that is preserved in Midrash Tanhuma-Yelamdenu. There are two recensions of this collection of homilies, which frequently diverge,[16] but the passage about Anani is closely similar in both.[17]

---

14. This is the reading in y. Ber. 2:4(25b), but the parallel in Lam. Rab. 1:51 has "Rabbi Yudan in the name of Rabbi Aibo," which may be correct.

15. J. Stanley McIvor, *The Targum of Chronicles*, in *The Targums of Ruth and Chronicles*, ArBib 19 (Edinburgh: T&T Clark, 1994) 57.

16. For introduction and discussion, see H. L. Strack and G. Stemberger, *Introduction to the Talmud and Midrash*, trans. Markus Bockmuehl (Edinburgh: T&T Clark, 1991) 329-33.

17. I am dependent on the translation of the Buber edition by John T. Townsend, *Midrash Tanhuma: Translated into English with Introduction, Indices, and Brief Notes* (S. Buber

In the context of a messianic interpretation of Zechariah 4:7, the midrash raises the question of the ancestry of the Messiah. He is said to be descended from Zerubbabel, who was descended from David. The text of 1 Chronicles 3:19–24 is quoted. The author asks, "Who is Anani?," and answers that he is the King-Messiah, as it is written in Daniel 7:13. Here Anani is identified with the Messiah, the "one like a son of man" of Daniel's vision, because his name (עֲנָנִי) is identical with the word for "clouds" in Daniel 7:13.[18] This is rather like the way Rabbi Aqiva is said to have identified Shimon bar Kosiva as the Messiah, by associating his name with the word "star" (*kokhav*) in Numbers 24:17. He decoded the text to find the name of the Messiah hidden in it (y. Ta'an. 4:8). The tradition about Anani does this better than Aqiva, who found only an approximation to Bar Kokhba's real name in the words of Balaam the prophet. In Anani's case the consonantal text of "clouds" in Daniel 7:13 is identical with his name.[19] The name of the Messiah is discovered in the very words of the Danielic vision.

How did the exegete who originated and those who passed on this tradition suppose that Anani could be the Messiah? Although the number of generations from Zerubbabel to Anani in 1 Chronicles 3 could be reckoned in more than one way, it is not conceivable that anyone in the rabbinic period could have supposed that Anani was still to be born in the future. They must have thought he had been born in the past (perhaps as the last member of the house of David in the royal line) and was now awaiting the time when he would be "revealed" (as the Targum to 1 Chr 3:24 says).[20] Identifying Anani with the

---

Recension), vol. 1, *Genesis* (Hoboken: Ktav, 1989) 167–68 (6.20), and the translation of the "ordinary" edition by Samuel A. Berman, *Midrash Tanhuma-Yelemmedenu* (Hoboken: Ktav, 1996) 182–83 (Genesis 6.14). The Hebrew text from Buber's edition is in Gregory R. Lanier, *Corpus Christologicum: Texts and Translations for the Study of Jewish Messianism and Early Christology* (Peabody, MA: Hendrickson, 2021) 597–98.

18. In the MT they are vocalized as עֲנָנִי (1 Chr 3:24) and עֲנָנֵי (Dan 7:13).

19. Maurice Casey, *Son of Man: The Interpretation and Influence of Daniel 7* (London: SPCK, 1979) 82–83, argues that, because the interpreted text of Daniel would read "with 'Anani of heaven one like a son of man was coming," the humanlike figure has to be understood here as a corporate symbol of Israel. Anani the Messiah comes with the people of Israel. But the Midrash is not really proposing a new translation of the Danielic text, reading "Anani" rather than "clouds." It is discerning additional meaning in the familiar text. The "one like a son of man" comes "with the clouds of heaven," and hidden in that phrase is his personal name Anani. Cf. Goldberg, "Die Namen," 235.

20. The word "revealed" need imply only that the Messiah is living unrecognized on earth. This appears to be the meaning in Tg. Jer 30:21 and may also be the meaning in Tg. Isa 66:7; Tg. Zech 3:8; 4:7; 6:12. But in the case of Tg. 1 Chr 3:24, it seems likely that the

figure in Daniel's vision who comes "with the clouds of heaven" would indicate that in the meantime he is in heaven. Thus Anani, in this interpretation, fits very well the role of the Messiah as it is depicted in 4 Ezra: a descendant of David, exempted from death, and being preserved by God for the time when he will come on the clouds as the eschatological judge.

The Targum to Chronicles and Midrash Tanhuma are late rabbinic works of uncertain date, while the traditions they transmit are doubtless older but impossible to date. I am not suggesting that the author of 4 Ezra knew the identification of Anani with the Messiah. But the examples we have discussed—Hezekiah, Menahem son of Hezekiah, and Anani—all show that rabbinic traditions over a long period were familiar with the idea that the Messiah son of David will be a descendant of David who was born in the distant past and has been preserved by God in readiness for his future coming at the end of days. There should be no difficulty in supposing that the author of 4 Ezra knew such a tradition and presupposed it in his depiction of the Messiah. As in the case of Anani, it meant that there would be nothing problematic about identifying the humanlike figure of Daniel 7:13 with the Davidic Messiah.

Targumist knows the tradition in the Midrash Tanhuma and thinks of the Messiah as being revealed from heaven when he comes on the clouds. See the parallels to this terminology listed in chapter 2.5, table 3.

CHAPTER 2.7

A Context for the Parables of Enoch

In chapter 1.6 I argued that the Parables of Enoch can be most plausibly dated in the late first or early second century CE, especially because of its resemblances to three apocalypses from the late first century: 4 Ezra, 2 Baruch, and the book of Revelation. Following the detailed study of 4 Ezra in the previous chapter, I am now able to pursue that argument in more detail.

THE MESSIANIC FIGURE IN 4 EZRA AND THE PARABLES OF ENOCH

Our analysis of these two texts shows that there are many close resemblances between them in their respective portrayals of the Messianic Figure, resemblances that have been ignored in the recent resurgence of interest in the Parables of Enoch and the scholarly trend toward dating the Parables in the early first century CE.

We may usefully begin with a striking resemblance that is not, however, unique to these two texts. This is the idea that Daniel 7:13 depicts a human person who had in the past lived on earth, had been taken up to heaven or paradise without dying, and is being preserved by God in order to be revealed on earth in the last days, when he will play a key role in the eschatological events. This interpretation of Daniel 7:13 is found in 4 Ezra (where this Messianic Figure is a Davidide), in the Parables of Enoch (where he is Enoch), in the fifth book of the Sibylline Oracles (where he is Joshua), and in Christian literature (where he is Jesus). In fact, no other interpretation of Daniel 7:13 is attested in this period. It was probably the view in 2 Baruch (where the Messiah exists in paradise/heaven before being revealed in the last days) and may have been the view in 4Q246, which is too fragmentary to be explicit on this point. At any rate, neither of these texts positively attests an interpretation of Daniel 7:13 other than the one I have described. There is no evidence of an interpretation of Daniel 7:13 as referring to a heavenly being, divine or angelic, who had never lived on earth. The "one like a son of man" was understood to be a visionary figure representing, in real life, a man. He might look like an angel, as a righteous man exalted to heaven would probably be expected to look, and he might be endowed with some superhuman qualities or powers for the sake of his messianic task, but he is human.

Also common to 4 Ezra and the Parables of Enoch but not unique to them is the idea that the Messianic Figure will destroy his enemies, not by military force or mere supernatural power, but by the force of his judicial condemnation of them. This idea, based on Isaiah 11:4, is found in the Psalms of Solomon 17 and in the book of Revelation (2:16; 19:15, 21).[1]

But there are important parallels unique to 4 Ezra and the Parables of Enoch:

(1) The only royal function attributed to the Messianic Figure is that of judgment (a function that kings regularly delegated to others). He will condemn and pronounce judicial sentence on the enemy, thereby destroying them. But he is not called a king or said to reign. This is especially remarkable in view of Daniel 7:14, which 4 Ezra ignores despite depending heavily on Daniel 7 in other ways, while in the Parables there is an allusion that speaks of "glory" and "might" but not of "dominion" or "kingship" (1 En. 49:2; cf. 51:3). This common feature of the portrayal of the Messianic Figure in both texts contrasts with all the other texts that identify the figure in Daniel 7:13 with the Messiah: 4Q246 (ii 5, 9), book 5 of the Sibyllines (108–109), 2 Baruch (40:3), and the book of Revelation (19:16; 20:4). It also contrasts with other portrayals of the Messiah that do not draw on Daniel 7: Psalms of Solomon 17 and Qumran sectarian texts about the Davidic Messiah or the "Prince of the Congregation" (1QpIsa^a 8–10 iii 21; 4Q252 v 1–5; 1QSb v 20–21, 27–28; CD 7:19). Moreover, it ignores not only Daniel 7:14 but also many passages in the Hebrew Bible that were commonly interpreted as referring to a royal Messiah (e.g., Gen 49:10; Num 24:17; 2 Sam 7:13-16; Jer 23:5-6; Ezek 37:24-25; Mic 5:2; Zech 9:9-10).[2] A Messiah who judges but does not reign seems to be unique to 4 Ezra and the Parables of Enoch.

(2) When the Messianic Figure is introduced in the vision in 4 Ezra, with allusion to Daniel 7:13, he is described as "something like the figure of a man"

---

1. Cf. also 4QpIsa^a 8–10 iii 18–19.
2. In the Targums and rabbinic literature, the Davidic Messiah is often called "the King Messiah" (e.g., Tg. Neof. Gen 49:10).

(13:3), while when he is introduced in the Parables of Enoch, again with allusion to Daniel 7:13, he is described as "another, whose face was like the appearance of a man" (46:1). Both descriptions expand on the phrase "one like a son of man" (Dan 7:13), probably drawing on Daniel 8:15 or 10:18.

(3) Both texts then refer back to this figure seen in the vision by the use of demonstratives or a specifying phrase. In 4 Ezra the figure is called "that man" (13:3, 12) or "the man who came up from the sea" (13:12; similarly 13:25, 32). In the Parables of Enoch he is "that son of man," meaning "that man" (46:2; 48:2; 62:5, 9, 14; 63:11; 69:26, 29; 70:1; 71:17) or "the son of man who has righteousness" (46:3; 71:17).

(4) Both texts imagine the Messianic Figure as presently with other righteous people in paradise or heaven. In 4 Ezra they are the people who had not died, while in the Parables they are the righteous dead. In both cases it seems the Messianic Figure is preeminent among these companions. Despite the difference as to the identity of the companions, the general similarity is significant because these are the only Jewish texts from the period that envisage the Messianic Figure among other humans in heaven or paradise, prior to his eschatological role. (There are some Christian texts that do so—e.g., Phil 1:23.)

(5) In both texts there is a vaguely expressed role for the Messianic Figure with the righteous after the judgment of the enemies and the deliverance of the righteous. According to the Parables they will eat with him (64:18). In 4 Ezra he will show them God's "wonders" and make them rejoice (13:50; 12:34). If the "wonders" are those described in 2 Baruch 29:3-8, as seems likely, they include eating. This correspondence coheres with the fact that in neither case is the Messianic Figure said to reign. He will be with the righteous, it seems, but not as a king. There is a difference in that in 4 Ezra this relates to the four-hundred-year period of the messianic age, while in the Parables it probably describes the new creation (cf. 45:5-6).

(6) There is a striking symmetry between the two texts in that in both cases the seer discovers, in the final part of the text, that he himself is to have a role in the eschatological events. In the Parables it is revealed to Enoch that he is "that son of man" (71:14), whereas in 4 Ezra, Ezra is told that he will not die but be one of the Messiah's companions, who are to be revealed with him when he comes to judge and deliver (14:9). There is considerable difference between actually being the Messianic Figure (Enoch) and being a companion (Ezra), but the similarity is significant, especially given the fact that both figures belong to the category of people who lived in the past but did not die and so will still be living in the last days and able to take part in the eschatological events.

Among these six features, (2), (3), and (6) seem to require not just a commonality of ideas but a *literary* connection between the two texts, whether that is a matter of direct dependence or of common dependence on a source.

Use of Scriptural Sources

It is the selection of scriptural sources that largely determines the particular profile of the Messianic Figure in any specific text. Table 1 shows the texts that have contributed significantly to the portrayals of the Messianic Figure in 4 Ezra and the Parables of Enoch. There are three key sources that they have in common: Daniel 7, Isaiah 11, and Psalm 2. For both, Daniel 7 as a whole (as the context of 7:13) and Isaiah 11:4 play a formative role. The detailed (verse by verse) comparison of their use of Isaiah 11 and Psalm 2 shows that, outside of verse 4, they draw on different parts of Isaiah 11, and that Psalm 2 is of considerably more significance in 4 Ezra than in the Parables. Beyond these three sources, the two texts diverge. Fourth Ezra alludes to two obviously Davidic prophecies (Gen 49:9–10; 2 Sam 7:13), which, not surprisingly, do not feature in the Parables. But most significant is the important role that the passages about the Isaianic servant play in the Parables of Enoch. Other Jewish literature from this period does not treat these passages as messianic. Their role in the Parables of Enoch accounts for much of the distinctiveness of the portrayal of the Messianic Figure in that text.

The designations of the Messiah in the two texts say something about the importance of their respective scriptural sources. In 4 Ezra, "the Messiah" and "my Son" are both drawn from Psalm 2. In the Parables, "his Messiah" (much the least frequent term) derives from Psalm 2, while "the Chosen One" is drawn from Isaiah 42:1. The two texts share a way of referring to the figure of Daniel 7:13 as "that man" or "that son of man."

A Hypothesis of Direct Literary Dependence

Postulating nonextant sources is often necessary in the study of ancient literature, but preference should be given to a direct literary relationship between the extant texts when this accounts for the data. I suggest that in this case dependence by the Parables of Enoch on 4 Ezra may be an adequate explanation of the features we have discussed. The Messianic Figure in 4 Ezra is a more traditional figure in that he is descended from David and is portrayed on the basis of scriptural sources already understood as messianic in 4Q246, other Qumran literature (such as 1QSb, 4QpIsa[a], and 4QTest), and the Psalms of

Solomon. The Parables of Enoch, on the other hand, seems innovatory in its use of Isaianic servant passages and its identification of the Messianic Figure with Enoch. This contrast establishes an initial probability that the direction of dependence is of the Parables of Enoch on 4 Ezra. But this hypothesis needs to be supported by more detailed consideration of how the portrayal of the Messianic Figure in the Parables could have been constructed with 4 Ezra as at least one of its sources.

The Parables of Enoch is a complex work to which a variety of sources must have contributed. I suggest that its portrayal of the Messianic Figure is partly inspired by 4 Ezra 13 and 14:9.[3] These parts of 4 Ezra account for the parallels listed above that are features unique to 4 Ezra and the Parables, including those that indicate a literary connection (nos. [2], [3], and [6]). Chapters 11–12 of 4 Ezra will have been less relevant to the author of the Parables, because there the opposition is between an empire, identified with Daniel's fourth beast, and a clearly Davidic Messiah. The Book of Parables always represents the enemies as plural ("the kings and the mighty and the exalted") and does not feature a single entity corresponding to Daniel's fourth beast. Chapter 13 of 4 Ezra does not refer to kings, but the enemies are plural—"all the nations" (13:33)—and nations can be presumed to have kings (as they do in Ps 2:1–2). Moreover, there is nothing necessarily Davidic about the Messiah in chapter 13. So 4 Ezra 13 could supply the author of the Parables with a Messianic Figure who destroys the enemies of God's people by judicial condemnation alone, not military might, along with exegetical sources for this figure in Daniel 7:13, Isaiah 11:4, and Psalm 2:1–2.

Fourth Ezra 14:9, promising Ezra that he "will be with my Son and with those who are like you, until the times are ended," could have been read by the author of the Parables as referring, not merely to those "who had not tasted death," but more generally to the righteous dead (cf. 1 En. 39:4–7), supplying the otherwise unique idea of the Messianic Figure awaiting the time of the end in company with the righteous whom he will vindicate when the time comes. At the same time, this revelation to Ezra could have suggested the idea of a revelation to the seer, withheld until the end of his visions, of his own future.

---

3. It is curious that Nickelsburg in George W. Nickelsburg and James C. VanderKam, *1 Enoch 2: A Commentary on the Book of 1 Enoch Chapters 37–82*, Hermeneia (Minneapolis: Fortress, 2012) 61, says that these "parallels indicate either that the 4 Ezra is dependent on the Parables or that the Parables and 4 Ezra are dependent on a common eschatological tradition." The fact that he does not consider dependence by the Parables on 4 Ezra is explicable only because he has already determined on other grounds that the Parables date from before 70 CE (cf. 60).

Ezra learns that he is to be taken up; Enoch, when he is taken up, learns that he himself is to be the Messianic Figure.

Of course, the author of the Parables makes his own use of the exegetical sources on which 4 Ezra depends in chapter 13. He does not depend on them purely at secondhand. No Jewish exegete would do so. He would be in any case familiar with those sources. But the fact that he makes recurrent and important allusions to Isaiah 11:2-5, despite the fact that Isaiah 11:1 identifies this figure rather obviously as a descendant of David's father Jesse, may be explicable from the role of Isaiah 11:4 in 4 Ezra 13. This verse is the key to the image of the Messiah destroying the enemies with what comes from his mouth, understood as judicial sentence, which is the most important motif the Parables derives from 4 Ezra 13. Isaiah 11:1-5 does not attribute royal functions to its subject other than those of a judge. The author of the Parables was prepared to ignore its Davidic character (perhaps he had an ingenious way of interpreting Isa 11:1 differently) because it exemplifies the Messiah as a judge who judges in favor of the oppressed and condemns their oppressors to death. We should note that none of his other scriptural sources is explicitly Davidic. Psalms 2 and 72 seem to most readers of the Hebrew Bible to refer to kings of the Davidic line and were generally understood in that way when applied in antiquity to the Messiah. But they do not make that explicit, and it was open to the author of the Parables to read them differently.

In expanding the range of his scriptural sources beyond those on which 4 Ezra 13 is based, the author of the Parables was especially guided by the verbal and thematic links he found between Isaiah 11:2-5, on the one hand, and, on the other, Isaiah 42:1-7, 49:1-7, and Psalm 72. In all these passages he found the judge who destroys the enemies by judicial condemnation, not military might, as portrayed in 4 Ezra 13. In addition he was concerned to portray the Messianic Figure as in solidarity with the oppressed "righteous and chosen ones," someone who would give judgment in their favor and deliver them from their powerful oppressors. So he privileged the title "my Chosen One" from Isaiah 42:1 (he never calls the Messianic Figure the servant of the Lord), closely associating "the Chosen One" with "the chosen ones" (a term from the Enoch tradition; see 1 En. 1:1-9). By alluding twice to "his Anointed One" in Psalm 2:2 (though making little other use of this psalm), he probably intended to retain a connection with the traditional expectations of a "Messiah," while also introducing his most innovatory contribution: the identity of the Messianic Figure with Enoch. For this purpose, Isaiah 52:13-15 was relevant, describing the Messianic Figure as someone exalted to the highest position, to the astonishment and dismay of the kings.

The Parables of Enoch, of course, devotes much more space to the Messianic Figure than 4 Ezra 13 (or even the whole of 4 Ezra) does, and so the use of Daniel 7 is much more extensive in the Parables, though broadly along the same lines. For 4 Ezra (as for book 5 of the Sibyllines) Daniel 7:13 portrays a human being who is with God prior to being revealed in the world as the eschatological judge described in Isaiah 11:4. This understanding of the Danielic text was also fundamental for the author of the Parables of Enoch, who gave the inevitable question, "Who is that man?," the novel answer: Enoch. Like 4 Ezra, he ignores the "kingdom" of "that son of man," developing instead his "glory" (Dan 7:14) as the judge to whom "the Head of Days" delegates the execution of his judgment. With allusion to Isaiah 24:21, he also clarified the scope of the Messianic Figure's judgment, including the heavenly host as well as humans on earth.

I suggest that this offers a plausible account of the way the author of the Parables of Enoch could have developed his portrayal of the Messianic Figure with 4 Ezra 13–14 as at least one of his starting points.

A Common Context for 4 Ezra and the Parables of Enoch

A purely textual explanation of the resemblances between 4 Ezra and the Parables, such as I have just given, is important but is probably not sufficient to explain the most remarkable of the parallels noted above: "The only royal function attributed to the Messianic Figure is that of judgment (a function that kings regularly delegated to others). He will condemn and pronounce judicial sentence on the enemy, thereby destroying them. But he is not called a king or said to reign." The clue to this may lie in the fact that kings lead armies and defeat enemies in battle.

We know of two rebel leaders during the Jewish War (66–73 CE) who gathered armies and had pretensions to kingship: Menahem son of Judas the Galilean and Simon son of Gioras. It is a reasonable supposition that they claimed to be Messiahs, appointed by God and fulfilling the prophetic expectations, though not necessarily of a Davidic nature.[4] Unfortunately, Josephus is virtually our only source of information, and it seems to have been a deliberate

---

4. Martin Hengel, *The Zealots*, trans. David Smith (Edinburgh: T&T Clark, 1989) 293-98; Richard A. Horsley and John S. Hanson, *Bandits, Prophets, and Messiahs: Popular Movements at the Time of Jesus* (San Francisco: Harper & Row, 1985) 118-27. Hengel, *The Zealots*, 331-33, was probably wrong to posit a family connection between Menahem and Judas the son of Hezekiah, and in relating him to the rabbinic tradition in which the Messiah is called Menahem the son of Hezekiah.

policy of Josephus to dissociate the Jewish revolt from any connection with authentic elements of the Jewish religion. If either or both of these rebel leaders claimed descent from David, Josephus is unlikely to have said so. He does not even say that they claimed God's authority for their aspirations to kingship, even though it is hardly conceivable that a Jewish rebel leader in that context at that time would not have done so.

However, Josephus does highlight an "ambiguous oracle" in the Jewish scriptures that "more than anything incited them to go to war." It

> revealed that at that time someone from their country would become ruler of the world. They took this to mean someone of their own race, and many of their scholars followed this wrong path of interpretation. In fact, the oracle was pointing to the principate of Vespasian, who was in Judaea when he was proclaimed emperor. (*War* 6.312–313)[5]

The application to Vespasian, of course, was Josephus's own original interpretation. Despite other suggestions, it is virtually certain that the oracle was Numbers 24:17, which speaks explicitly of a ruler *from the land of Israel* ("a star shall come out of Jacob, and a scepter shall rise out of Israel").[6] This is not said in Daniel 2:44–45 or in Daniel 7:13–14. Moreover, those texts speak of a kingdom that would succeed the fourth of Daniel's kingdoms. Josephus himself considered the Roman Empire to be Daniel's fourth kingdom,[7] and so could hardly have considered Vespasian its successor. Numbers 24:17 was one of the most, if not the most, popular messianic texts,[8] perhaps because of its great antiquity and the fact that it is written in the Torah, as well as its content, which predicts a ruler who would conquer Israel's enemies. It is noteworthy that neither the Parables of Enoch nor 4 Ezra alludes to it, whereas book 5 of the Sibyllines does.

It is surely very likely that Menahem son of Hezekiah and Simon son of Gioras claimed to fulfill this prophecy, if not others too. Josephus records that, when the temple had been burned to the ground by the Romans, Simon

---

5. Translation from Josephus, *The Jewish War*, trans. Martin Hammond (Oxford: Oxford University Press, 2017) 330.

6. Hengel, *The Zealots*, 237–40; Gerbert S. Oegema, *The Anointed and His People: Messianic Expectations from the Maccabees to Bar Kochba*, JSPSup 27 (Sheffield: Sheffield Academic, 1998) 137. See the fuller discussion of this passage of Josephus in chapter 2.10.

7. William Horbury, *Jewish War under Trajan and Hadrian* (Cambridge: Cambridge University Press, 2014) 145–46 and n. 171.

8. Oegema, *The Anointed*, 22.

dressed himself in white tunics and buckling over them a purple mantle arose out of the ground [from an underground tunnel] at the very spot where the temple formerly stood. (*War* 7.29, LCL)

Dressing in imperial purple was an obvious challenge to the Roman emperor himself and a claim to be the rightful ruler of the world. Josephus says Simon's intention was to "cheat the Romans by creating a scare" (*War* 7.29), but it could well be that he had a sincere conviction that God would intervene at that point and grant him a miraculous victory. In view of the location, he may well have had in mind Psalm 2:6: "I have set my king on Zion, my holy hill."

After the catastrophe of 70 CE, it could well have appeared to the authors of 4 Ezra and the Parables of Enoch that a kind of messianism that expected a king to lead an army to defeat the Romans was a tragic and culpable error. Faced with contemporaries who continued to advocate that sort of messianism, they focused on a Messianic Figure who would be revealed only at the time of God's choosing and who would be, not a warrior, but a judge, whose mere pronouncement of divine judgment would be effective.

Perhaps it could be argued that the Parables of Enoch was reacting against the royal pretenders (Judas son of Hezekiah, Simon the slave, and Athronges the shepherd) who led uprisings in the turbulent aftermath of the death of Herod the Great (*Ant.* 17.271–285). The evidence for attributing messianic claims to any of these is weaker,[9] but in any case their activities did not have catastrophic consequences for the Jewish people, like the destruction of the temple in 70 CE. A context in the late first century (or the very early second century) explains at the same time the literary relationship between the Parables and 4 Ezra and the fact that they agree in not calling their Messianic Figure a king.[10]

The Kings of the Parthians and the Medes

First Enoch 56:5–8 has often been thought to provide a clue to the date of the Parables of Enoch. Most often it has been seen as alluding to the Parthian invasion of Palestine in 40 BCE, described by Josephus (*War* 1.248–273; *Ant.* 14.330–393), though the Parthian campaign of Trajan in 113–117 CE has also

---

9. Hengel, *The Zealots*, 292–93; Horsley and Hanson, *Bandits*, 111–16.
10. The Davidic Messiah of Pss. Sol. 17 also destroys his enemies by judicial condemnation (17:22–25), reflecting Isa 11:4, but he is very emphatically a king.

been suggested.[11] The passage of the Parables, which is presented as a prophecy of what will happen in the last days, has been supposed to be a *vaticinium ex eventu* (prophecy after the event), presenting events that had already happened at the time of writing as future events from Enoch's perspective. *Vaticinia ex eventu* are common in Jewish and Christian apocalyptic literature, which can often be dated at the point at which historical events, described with relative historical accuracy, give way, in a sequence of eschatological predictions, to events that the author merely foresaw. However, we should note that in the Parables of Enoch this would be the only example of a *vaticinium ex eventu*, since there are no such predictions preceding it, and the passage that follows (57:1-3), though its meaning is debated,[12] is generally agreed not to refer to a known historical event. Yet the text ties them very closely together. The latter passage begins: "After that I saw *another host* of chariots . . ." (57:1, italics mine).

There are serious difficulties with the claim that 56:5-8 is a summary description of the events of 40 BCE. There are far too many discrepancies between it and the account of Josephus, even if one supposes the author of the Parables intended a "symbolic transfiguration of an historical event."[13] Most importantly, the outcome of the invasion is completely different in the two cases. In the Parables the kings of the Parthians and Medes fail to capture Jerusalem, and their forces destroy themselves in internecine warfare.[14] In Josephus's account the Parthians succeed in entering Jerusalem, at the invitation of Antigonus, and nothing at all like the self-destructive behavior described in the Parables occurs. In the Parables the Parthians fail in their goal and self-destruct. In Josephus they succeed in the goal of assisting one of the two Jewish factions involved.

---

11. See the history of scholarship in Nickelsburg, *1 Enoch 2*, 209-10. Darrell L. Bock, "Dating the *Parables of Enoch*: A *Forschungsbericht*," in *Parables of Enoch: A Paradigm Shift*, ed. Darrell L. Bock and James H. Charlesworth, JCT 11 (London: Bloomsbury, 2013) 58-113, is a history of scholarship from 1893 to 2011, taking note of all considerations relevant to the date of the Parables, but including views of 1 En. 56:5-8.

12. Nickelsburg, *1 Enoch 2*, 213-15.

13. Luca Arcari, "A Symbolic Transfiguration of a Historical Event: The Parthian Invasion in Josephus and the Parables of Enoch," in *Enoch and the Messiah Son of Man: Revisiting the Book of Parables*, ed. Gabriele Boccaccini (Grand Rapids: Eerdmans, 2007) 478-86.

14. Scholars trying to harmonize 1 En. 56:8 with the historical events sometimes take the reference to be to conflict between the kingdoms surrounding the Parthian Empire or between political factions. But, especially in view of the allusion to Ezek 38:21 or Hag 2:22, it is clear that what is intended is conflict among the Parthian troops when they are besieging Jerusalem, leading to large-scale slaughter.

Some scholars take the view that the text does allude to the events of 40 BCE, but only as the basis for a prediction of the future.[15] Darrell Bock, for example, thinks the author understood the Parthian invasion of 40 BCE as standing typologically for a similar but intensified event in the future.[16] In such a case, he argues, the historical event need not "be replicated in exact detail."[17] However, it seems implausible that a historical event in which the Parthian invasion was relatively successful would provide the basis for an eschatological event in which such an invasion ends in catastrophic defeat and annihilation. Other scholars have therefore argued that 1 Enoch 56:6-8 bears no relation to a historical event but is a general representation of the final battle that draws on biblical precedents and apocalyptic stereotypes.[18] This approach has been developed most systematically by Ted Erho, who finds the same general pattern of events in four other texts: Ezekiel 38-39; Sibylline Oracles 3:657-732; Revelation 20:7-15; 4 Ezra 13:5-11.[19] He certainly identifies some important common features among these passages, though it is not clear to me why other such passages are not included, such as Zechariah 12:1-6, which is actually echoed in 1 Enoch 56:7.[20]

As table 2 shows, 1 Enoch 56:5-8 does not just conform to a general pattern—an eschatological battle in which the hostile nations gather at Jerusalem and are defeated by God. The passage also echoes specific passages in the Hebrew Bible. In 56:7 "hindrance" (Ethiopic *māʿeqaf*) could be translated as "stumbling block."[21] The idea that the city will be "a stumbling block to their horses" can therefore be explained as a summary of Zechariah 12:3-4.[22] An explanation of these words by means of a historical event, implying that at the time Jerusalem had walls that would obstruct the Parthian cavalry,[23] is

15. Cf. Nickelsburg, *1 Enoch 2*, 210.
16. Bock, "Dating the *Parables*," 93-94, 101, 108, 112.
17. Bock, "Dating the *Parables*," 108.
18. E.g., Michael A. Knibb, *Essays on the Book of Enoch and Other Early Jewish Texts and Traditions*, SVTP 22 (Leiden: Brill, 2009) 155.
19. Ted M. Erho, "The Ahistorical Nature of *1 Enoch* 56:5-8 and Its Ramification upon the *Opinio Communis* on the Dating of the *Similitudes of Enoch*," *JSJ* 20 (2009) 23-54.
20. Cf. Matthew Black, *The Book of Enoch or 1 Enoch*, SVTP 7 (Leiden: Brill, 1985) 222: "a clear allusion to Zech. 12.3."
21. Nickelsburg, *1 Enoch 2*, 212.
22. MT has "stone of burden" in Zech 12:3, but the Targum, perhaps by analogy with Isa 8:14, has "stone of stumbling."
23. Gillian Bampfylde, "The Similitudes of Enoch: Historical Allusions," *JSJ* 15 (1984) 9-31, here 17, 27. It is true that the Parthians were famed for their cavalry (Ted W. Erho, "Historical-Allusional Dating and the Similitudes of Enoch," *JBL* 130 [2011] 493-511, here

completely redundant. Although Jeremiah 51:11 cannot explain the double reference to Parthians and Medes, it may explain why the Medes are, unusually, coupled with the Parthians (though the common expression "the Medes and the Persians" may also do so).

Biblical interpretation also explains what happens when the Parthian soldiers turn on each other and slaughter each other. This self-destructive behavior is prophesied in Ezekiel 38:21 and Haggai 2:22, but those texts do not explain why this happens. The key is in a proper reading of 1 Enoch 56:7. Whereas in Nickelsburg and VanderKam's translation "a man will not acknowledge his brother," Isaac has "a man shall not *recognize* his brother."[24] The author of the passage in the Parables has taken the "blindness" with which God strikes the horses of the peoples (Zech 12:4) to apply also to their riders. In their "madness" they will not be able to recognize each other and so will strike out at each other. This interpretation is confirmed by an interesting parallel in the *Biblical Antiquities* of Pseudo-Philo. In the account of Kenaz's great victory over the Amorites, we are told that the angel Ingethel "smote the Amorites with blindness so that, since each could not see his fellow, they thought they were his adversaries and they killed one another" (LAB 27:10).[25]

The self-destruction of enemies by internecine fighting is also a feature of the great victory over the Ammonites and Moabites in the reign of Jehoshaphat (2 Chr 20:23). It meant that victory was attributable to God alone (20:15–17). It was thus an ideal form of the holy war, like the paradigmatic event of the crossing of the sea at the time of the exodus, when the people had only to watch as God destroyed the enemy. This kind of event is what is envisaged in 1 Enoch 56:7, and it makes sense only as an apocalyptic portrayal of the final battle, not as any kind of historical allusion.

Erho's case focuses on a common pattern of apocalyptic depiction of a final battle rather than on the specific exegetical sources of 1 Enoch 56:5–8. But we have repeatedly seen, in studying the Parables of Enoch, that the text is frequently indebted to detailed exegetical work, bringing together allusions to a variety of biblical sources. In this particular case, the author may have

---

500–501), but in biblical prophecy so were the Medes (Jer 50:41–42) and all the nations allied with Gog (Ezek 38:15), while Zech 12:4 imagines all armies of all the nations attacking Jerusalem as equipped with cavalry.

24. Ephraim Isaac, "1 (Ethiopic Apocalypse of) Enoch," *OTP* 1:5–89, here 39. The continuation of this text ("nor a son, his mother" or "nor a son, his father or his mother") may be a gloss influenced by 1 En. 100:1–3.

25. Translation from Howard Jacobson, *A Commentary on Pseudo-Philo's Liber Antiquitatum Biblicarum*, vol. 1, AGJU 31 (Leiden: Brill, 1996) 140.

been aware of a kind of broad outline of how the eschatological events would be expected to unfold, but the specific contours of the account result from deliberate selection and combination of biblical sources. The same is true of the other postbiblical passages that Erho presents as parallels (Sib. Or. 3:657–732; Rev 20:7–15; 4 Ezra 13:5–11).

The weakness of Erho's case is its failure to explain why specifically the *Parthians* are the enemy. The other passages he studies refer very generally to "the nations" or "the kings" or invoke the near-mythical Gog and Magog (who, when localized, were more geographically remote than the Parthians and Medes).[26] For most Jewish literature from the early Roman period, the principal enemy was the Roman Empire. This is one reason why many scholars have continued to think there must be some sort of allusion to the Parthian invasion of 40 BCE, since this provides the only tangible evidence that the Parthians could have been seen as a threat to Judea and Jerusalem. The Parthian Empire was, of course, a recurrent threat to the Roman Empire, but in the Jewish circles in which apocalyptic literature was written and read, an enemy of Rome was likely to be viewed as a friend, not a foe. So, to explain the "Parthians and Medes" in 1 Enoch 56, it is not sufficient to suppose that it was written in a period when "Parthians were understood as the chief foreign threat."[27] In an occupied country, it is necessary to ask: Chief foreign threat to whom? Are we to imagine that the Parables of Enoch were written by Jewish friends of Rome—supporters of the Herods or members of the temple hierarchy? Since the opponents of the chosen and righteous ones are regularly portrayed in the Parables as "the kings and the mighty," this seems very implausible.

The question is, why would the author of a Jewish apocalypse portray the Parthians and Medes as the hostile nations in a version of the final assault of the nations against God's people and their city? Why Parthians, not Rome? The answer to this most puzzling of the issues concerning 1 Enoch 56:5–8 is to be found, I suggest, in the late first-century expectation of the return of the emperor Nero from the east. (Scholars customarily call this the Nero *redivivus* myth, but this is a misnomer. In almost all the evidence, Nero is believed not to have died but to have fled to the east, where he is in hiding and from where he will return. *Nero reditus* would be more appropriate.) This is the only context in Second Temple Jewish literature, apart from 1 Enoch 56, where the Parthians feature in Jewish eschatological expectations.

---

26. Erho, "The Ahistorical Nature," 46–47, attempts to associate the Parthians and the Medes in 1 En. 56 with Gog and Magog, but with limited success.

27. Erho, "The Ahistorical Nature," 53.

The hope or fear of the returning Nero was not a specifically Jewish expectation but a broadly popular one, especially in the eastern parts of the Roman Empire.[28] After Nero committed suicide, in somewhat clandestine circumstances, in 68 CE, there were rumors that he had not died but had fled secretly to the east, to the Parthian Empire, where he was well received because of his previously good relations with the Parthian kings, and stayed in hiding, awaiting the time when he would return to wreak his revenge on Rome. Three imposters who actually claimed to be the returning Nero appeared in 69, 80, and 88/89 CE, the last of whom actually had the support of the Parthian king Pacorus II and briefly posed a real threat to the Roman Empire. These unsuccessful pretenders, so far from discrediting the legend about Nero, seem to have helped keep it alive. Despite his reputation as a moral monster, Nero could be seen in the eastern regions of the empire as a potential savior from Roman domination. For Jews, however, he could not been seen in this light, if only because he had been responsible for the destruction of Jerusalem and the temple.

It was the authors of the Jewish Sibylline Oracles who adapted this popular expectation to a Jewish eschatological context. The returning Nero appears in books 3, 4, and 5 of the Sibyllines, though the interpretation of his role varies somewhat. In book 4, Nero crosses "the Euphrates with many myriads" and destroys Rome. This is Asia's revenge on Rome for Rome's domination and plundering of the east, but it is also God's retribution for the destruction of Jerusalem (Sib. Or. 4:119–148). The subject is given much more attention in the five passages about Nero in book 5 (5:28–34, 93–110, 137–154, 214–227, 361–380). The same idea of Nero's secret flight to the east is found, and his taking refuge with "the Medes and the Persians" is explained by his good relations with them during his reign (lines 147–149). In this treatment, Nero is so identified with Parthia (always called Persia in this book) and the traditional threat to the Roman Empire from the Parthians that he is actually called "the Persian" (line 93) and "the one who has obtained the land of the Persians" (line 101). The destructive war that he brings on the Roman Empire is seen as divine vengeance, especially for the destruction of Jerusalem (lines 225–227).

In the section of most importance in our present context (lines 93–109: see table 3), Nero brings destruction to the land of Italy and to Rome and rampages across the empire, massacring a third of humanity. Then, reaching the zenith of his audacity, he enters the land of Israel, "wishing to destroy the

---

28. For a detailed account, see Richard Bauckham, *The Climax of Prophecy: Studies on the Book of Revelation* (Edinburgh: T&T Clark, 1993) 407–23.

city of the blessed ones" (line 107). But the "king sent from God against him will destroy all the great kings and noble men" (lines 108–109). Two points are worthy of notice here. First, Nero is accompanied by "all the great kings," who must be the subordinate rulers and client kings of the Parthian Empire. Second, this passage envisages Jerusalem as a city that can be destroyed, despite the fact that the city had been sacked and the temple demolished by Titus (lines 397–413). What the returning Nero seeks to destroy cannot be the new Jerusalem that the king sent from God subsequently builds (lines 420–425; cf. 247–252). The author must have thought that the city survived or recovered to some degree after the events of 70 CE. Perhaps he was inclined to do so because the attack on Jerusalem by the nations was a traditional part of the eschatological scenario.

The book of Revelation, written toward the end of the first century CE, also makes its own distinctive use of this apocalyptic narrative of the return of Nero. Chapter 16 depicts a series of seven final judgments, represented as bowls full of the wrath of God, which angels pour out on the earth. The sixth angel pours his bowl on the river Euphrates, drying it up, in order to "prepare the way for the kings of the east" (16:12; see table 3). This is significantly parallel to 1 Enoch 56:5. Both passages suggest that the actions of angels, carrying out the divine purpose of judgment, lie behind the military excursion of the kings of the east across the Euphrates into the Roman Empire. Neither passage refers explicitly to a returning Nero figure in command of these kings, but in Revelation the kings certainly include Nero. At this point in the book, the scenario of invasion of the Roman Empire by kings from beyond the Euphrates is probably sufficient to evoke the expectation of Nero's return at the head of a Parthian army, at least for many contemporary readers. But Nero's role becomes clear in chapter 17, where, in the rather complex allegory of the beast that represents the Roman imperial power, Nero is one of the seven heads of the beast, who "was and is not" but will return, as an eighth (17:9–11). Ten kings, represented as ten horns, are his allies in his campaign to destroy the city of Rome, represented as Babylon, the great whore (17:12–13; 16:17). In Revelation's perspective, this is a kind of self-destruction by the Roman imperial power. The ten kings become horns of the beast when a Roman emperor, Nero, turning against Rome, recruits them to aid him in his destruction of Rome. As in the Sibyllines, this is both Nero's revenge on Rome and divine retribution on the evil city. Following the fall of Rome, the kings of the whole earth, instigated by the forces of evil, gather in the land of Israel (not in this case at Jerusalem) for the final battle (16:12) in which they are defeated by a warrior from heaven (as in Sib. Or. 5) who is Jesus Christ (19:11–16). Modern readers of Revelation do not find it easy to piece together this narrative, but the author could expect his original readers to be familiar enough with the story of Nero *reditus* to recognize his allusions to it.[29]

I suggest that 1 Enoch 56:5–8 is a streamlined version of a narrative something like Sibylline Oracles 5:93–109. It does not refer to Nero individually, but we could compare the way the fifth Sibylline represents Nero as completely assimilated to the Parthians (he is "the Persian" and "the one who has obtained the land of the Persians"). In effect, he is the Parthian king, supreme over the other rulers of the Parthians and Medes. We could also compare the way Revelation 16:12 refers to "the kings from the east," implicitly including but not naming Nero. It is perhaps more problematic that the passage in the Parables does not refer to Rome. There is no indication that the kings first sack the city of Rome and only then enter "the land of my chosen ones," intent on destroying Jerusalem. But there is a telltale clue that suggests the destruction of Rome was originally part of the tradition that has been abbreviated here. First Enoch 57:5 surely echoes Jeremiah 51:11:

> The LORD has stirred up the spirit of the kings of the Medes, because his purpose concerning Babylon is to destroy it, for that is the vengeance of the LORD, vengeance for his temple.

Especially after 70 CE, Jews regarded Babylon, the greatest evil city of the biblical period, as a precursor of Rome. The parallel was especially notable in that Babylon destroyed the first temple, Rome the second temple. The same kind of divine judgment might be expected for Rome as the one Babylon had suffered. In the fifth Sibylline, "Babylon" means Rome, the city from which Nero fled (line 143),[30] and biblical prophecies about Babylon (Isa 14:15; 47:8–9) are applied to Rome (lines 169, 173, 178). The book of Revelation calls Rome "Babylon" and makes many allusions to the biblical prophecies about Babylon, including Jeremiah's great oracle against Babylon (Jer 50–51).[31] The typological parallel between Babylon and Rome, brought to light by the events of 70 CE, is the basis for the fictional setting of both 4 Ezra and 2 Baruch. So the allusion to Jeremiah 51:11 in 1 Enoch 57:5 strongly suggests that in a fuller version of

---

29. On the use of the returning Nero traditions in Revelation, see Bauckham, *The Climax*, 423–31. Another brief echo of this tradition may be found in 2 Bar. 70:7 (see table 3).
30. But in 5:434–46 the old Babylon, the city on the Euphrates, is meant.
31. See especially Rev 18.

this tradition the kings of the Parthians and Medes destroyed Rome before they marched on Jerusalem.[32]

The author of 1 Enoch 56:5-8 may well have abbreviated his source because he wanted to focus on the final attack of the nations on Jerusalem. He is generally not interested in predictions of specific political events, focusing rather on the judgment by the Messianic Figure of "the kings and the mighty" in general. His telescoped version of the tradition about Nero and the Parthians served the purpose of adding a degree of specificity to his depiction of the future, making contact with other apocalyptic forecasts, but the abbreviated version sufficiently served this purpose. Because this passage is somewhat out of character with the rest of the Parables, it has sometimes been supposed to be a later interpolation in the text (along with 57:1-3), but the references to "my chosen ones" and "my righteous ones" (56:7-8) are characteristic of the Parables.[33] More likely is the suggestion that the author of the Parables has here adopted and adapted existing traditions. The otherwise surprising specificity of "the Parthians and Medes" is explicable if the underlying tradition was more obviously a version of the return of Nero with his Parthian myriads. This would date the Parables of Enoch in the late first century or the beginning of the second century CE. As Nickelsburg remarks, it would be hazardous to rely on any one passage for dating the whole book,[34] but my argument about 1 Enoch 56:5-8 coheres very well with my argument for the dependence of the Parables on 4 Ezra. Since 56:5-8 has so often been used to date the Parables in an earlier period, it has been important to show that it is fully explicable in the later period, when the return of Nero "the Persian" had become part of Jewish apocalyptic expectations, and probably more easily explicable in this period.

Finally, we should note that there are two rabbinic traditions, attributed to second-century rabbis, that reflect the survival of the notion of a Parthian invasion of the land of Israel which would precipitate the final events:

> There is not a single palm tree in Babylon to which a Persian horse will not be tied, and not a single coffin in the land of Israel from which a Median horse will not be eating hay. (Attributed to Rabbi Yose ben Qismah, second-generation Tanna, b. Sanh. 98a-b)

---

32. Possibly the image of the threshing floor (1 En. 56:6) originally applied to Babylon/Rome (see Jer 51:33).

33. Nickelsburg, *1 Enoch 2*, 99-100.

34. Nickelsburg, *1 Enoch 2*, 210.

When you see a Persian horse tethered in the land of Israel, then look for the footsteps of the Messiah. (Attributed to Rabbi Simeon ben Yoḥai, third-generation Tanna, Lam. Rab. 1:13 [41])[35]

Although "Babylon" in the first quotation presumably refers to Mesopotamia, as the reference to palm trees shows,[36] a Parthian invasion of the land of Israel must presuppose the defeat of Rome by the Parthians. So these two related sayings attest the survival of a tradition like that in 1 Enoch 56:5–8, in which an invasion by Persians (Parthians) and Medes is one of the last of the eschatological events before the coming of the Messiah and a prior conquest of the Roman Empire could be presupposed, though not explicitly mentioned.[37]

OTHER SHARED TRADITIONS

As well as the parallel between 1 Enoch 56:5–8 and Revelation 16:12–16, two other units of tradition in the Parables of Enoch have close parallels in literature from the late first or early second century CE: the three apocalypses (4 Ezra, 2 Baruch, and Revelation) and the *Biblical Antiquities* of Pseudo-Philo, which includes passages of eschatological prophecy. (See tables 4 and 5.) Close study of the texts of each of these units of tradition will show that the variations between the parallels cannot be adequately explained by any literary relationship between these four works. They seem to be units of tradition that were known to these authors independently of any literature known to us. I have discussed them at length elsewhere, and there is no need to repeat those discussions.[38] What is important in the present context is that none of these traditions can be found in earlier Jewish literature, though in the case of the tradition about resurrection (table 4) there are some less close parallels in later Jewish and Christian literature.[39] Moreover, these units of tradition do not have biblical sources.

---

35. Translations from Emil Schürer, *The History of the Jewish People in the Age of Jesus Christ (175 BC–AD 135)*, vol. 3/1, rev. and ed. Geza Vermes, Fergus Millar, and Martin Goodman (Edinburgh: T&T Clark, 1986) 259 n. 21. The version of Simeon ben Yoḥai's saying in Cant. Rab. 8.9.3 reads, "If you see a Persian horse tethered to a grave in the land of Israel, look out for the coming of the Messiah" (Soncino translation).
36. Palm trees have been introduced to Italy only in modern times.
37. It is possible that in the saying of Rabbi Yose ben Qismah, "Babylon" originally meant Rome and the trees were not originally palm trees.
38. Bauckham, *The Climax*, 48–70.
39. Bauckham, *The Climax*, 58–61.

It is possible that these units of tradition were known to the author of the Parables a century or more before they were taken up by other writers at the end of the first century CE, but it seems more likely that the Parables are a product of the same milieu of teaching and writing about eschatological matters to which the other four works belong.[40] This is not a conclusive argument for the date of the Parables, but it fits into place alongside the other considerations that point to the end of the first century CE as the most probable context for the composition of the Parables of Enoch.

---

40. I offered some suggestions and speculations about the transmission of such "units of tradition" in *The Climax*, 83–91.

TABLE 1. *Scriptural sources of the Messianic Figure: 4 Ezra and the Parables of Enoch compared*

4 Ezra	Parables of Enoch
Dan 7	Dan 7
Isa 11	Isa 11
Ps 2	Ps 2
Gen 49:9	
2 Sam 7:13	
Dan 2	
Ps 90:15–16	
	Isa 24:21
	Isa 41:11–12
	Isa 42:1–7
	Isa 49:1–7
	Isa 52:13, 15
	Ps 72
Isaiah 11	Isaiah 11
	11:2
11:4	11:4
	11:5
11:12	
Psalm 2	Psalm 2
2:1–2	2:2
2:5	
2:6	
2:7	
	2:8

TABLE 2. *1 Enoch 56:5–8 with scriptural sources*

⁵In those days, the angels will assemble themselves, and hurl themselves toward the east against the Parthians and Medes. They will stir up the kings, and a spirit of agitation shall come upon them, and they will shake them off their thrones.	The LORD has stirred up the spirit of the kings of the Medes. (Jer 51:11)
They will break out like lions from their lairs, and like hungry wolves in the midst of their flocks. ⁶They will go up and trample the land of my chosen ones, and the land of my chosen ones will be before them like a threshing floor and a (beaten) path; ⁷but the city of my righteous ones will be a hindrance to their horses. They will begin (to make) war among themselves, and their right hand will be strong against them(selves), a man will not acknowledge his brother, nor a son, his father or his mother. Until the number of corpses will be enough due to their slaughter, and their punishment will not be in vain.	On that day I will make Jerusalem a heavy stone for all the peoples; all who lift it shall grievously hurt themselves. And all the nations of the world shall come together against it. On that day, says the LORD, I will strike every horse with panic, and its rider with madness. But on the house of Judah I will keep a watchful eye, when I strike every horse of the peoples with blindness. (Zech 12:3–4) I will summon the sword against Gog in all my mountains, says the Lord GOD; the sword of every man will be against his brother. (Ezek 38:21) The horses and the riders shall fall, every one by the sword of his brother. (Hag 2:22; cf. 2 Chr 20:23)
⁸In those days Sheol will open its mouth, and they will sink into it. And their destruction will be at an end; Sheol will devour the sinners from the presence of the chosen.	Therefore Sheol has enlarged its appetite and opened its mouth beyond measure. (Isa 5:14) The earth opened its mouth and swallowed them up. . . . So they with all that belonged to them went down alive into Sheol; the earth closed over them and they perished from the midst of the assembly. (Num 16:32–33)

TABLE 3. *Kings from the east*

1 Enoch 57:5–7a

> In those days, the angels will assemble themselves,
> and hurl themselves toward the east against the Parthians and
> Medes.
> They will stir up the kings, and a spirit of agitation shall come
> upon them,
> and they will shake them off their thrones.
> They will break out like lions from their lairs,
> and like hungry wolves in the midst of their flocks.
> They will go up and trample the land of my chosen ones,
> and the land of my chosen ones will be before them like a
> threshing floor and a (beaten) path;
> but the city of my righteous ones will be a hindrance to their
> horses.

Revelation 16:12–14, 16

> The sixth angel poured his bowl on the great river Euphrates, and its water was dried up in order to prepare the way for the kings from the east. And I saw three foul spirits like frogs coming from the mouth of the dragon, from the mouth of the beast, and from the mouth of the false prophet. These are demonic spirits, performing signs, who go abroad to the kings of the whole world, to assemble them for battle on the great day of God the Almighty. . . . And they assembled them at the place that in Hebrew is called Harmagedon.

Sibylline Oracles 5:147–149

> He [Nero] will come to the Medes and to the kings of the Persians,
> those whom he first desired and to whom he gave glory,
> lurking with these evil ones against a true people.[a]

Sibylline Oracles 5:93–94, 101–103, 106–109

> For the Persian [Nero] will come onto your [Rome's] soil like hail,
> and he will destroy your land and evil-devising men. . . .
> But the one who obtained the land of the Persians will fight,
> and killing every man he will destroy all life
> so that a one-third portion will remain for wretched mortals. . . .
> But when he attains a formidable height and unseemly daring,
> he will also come, wishing to destroy the city of the blessed ones,
> and then a certain king sent from God against him
> will destroy all the great kings and noble men.

2 Baruch 70:7

> Then the Most High will disclose those people whom he has prepared before, and they will come and wage war with the rulers who will then be left.[b]

[a]Translation from Collins, "Sibylline Oracles," 396.
[b]Translation from Gurtner, *Second Baruch*, 115.

TABLE 4. *Resurrection*

1 Enoch 51:1

> In those days, the earth will give back what has been entrusted to it,
> and Sheol [*wasi'ol*] will give back what it has received,
> and Abaddon [*ḥagwal*] will give back what it owes.[a]

LAB 3:10

> I will give life to the dead and raise from the earth those who sleep,
> and Sheol [*infernus*] will give back what it owes,
> and Abaddon [*perditio*] will restore what has been entrusted to it.[b]

4 Ezra 7:32

> And the earth will give back those who sleep in it,
> and the dust those who dwell silently in it,
> and the treasuries will give back those who have been entrusted to them.[c]

Revelation 20:13a

> And the sea gave up the dead that were in it,
> Death and Hades gave up the dead that were in them.

2 Baruch 21:23b

> Let Sheol be sealed so that from now on it may not receive the dead,
> and let the treasuries of souls restore those who are enclosed in them.[d]

[a] Translation from Nickelsburg, *1 Enoch 2*, 180, 184. The textual variants are discussed on pp. 180–81. I have substituted "Abaddon" for "destruction" in Nickelsburg's translation. He thinks that אבדן was probably the Aramaic original (184).

[b] My translation.

[c] My translation.

[d] Translation from Gurtner, *Second Baruch*, 57.

TABLE 5. *The number of the righteous dead*

1 Enoch 47:1–4

    In those days there had arisen the prayer of the righteous,
        and the blood of the righteous one, from the earth into the
            presence of the Lord of Spirits.
    In these days the holy ones who dwell in the heights of heaven
        were uniting with one voice,
        and they were glorifying and praising and blessing the name of
            the Lord of Spirits,
    and were interceding and praying on behalf of the blood of the
        righteous that had been shed,
        and the prayer of the righteous, that it might not be in vain in
            the presence of the Lord of Spirits;
    that judgment might be executed for them,
        and endurance might not be their (lot) forever.
    In those days I saw the Head of Days as he took his seat on the
        throne of his glory,
        and all the books of the living were opened in his presence,
        and all his host, which was in the heights of heaven, and his
            court, were standing in his presence.
    And the hearts of the holy ones were filled with joy,
        for the number of the righteous was at hand;
        and the prayer of the righteous had been heard,
        and (a reckoning of) the blood of the righteous one had been
            required in the presence of the Lord of Spirits.

Revelation 6:9–11

    When he opened the fifth seal, I saw under the altar the souls of those who had been slaughtered for the word of God and for the testimony they had given; they cried out with a loud voice, "Sovereign Lord, holy and true, how long will it be before you judge and avenge our blood on the inhabitants of the earth?" They were each given a white robe and told to rest a little longer, until the number would be complete both of their fellow servants and of their brothers and sisters, who were soon to be killed as they themselves had been killed.

4 Ezra 4:33–37

Then I answered and said, "How long and when will these things be? For our years are few and evil." He answered me and said, "You do not hasten faster than the Most High, for your haste is for yourself, but Highest hastens on behalf of many. Did not the souls of the righteous in their treasuries ask about these matters, saying, 'How long are we to remain here? And when will come the harvest of our reward?' And Jeremiel the archangel answered them and said, 'When the number of those like yourselves is completed;
    for he has weighed the age in the balance,
    and measured the times by measure,
    and numbered the times by number;
    and he will not move or arouse until that measure is fulfilled.'"

2 Baruch 23:4–5a

For when Adam sinned and death was decreed against those who were to be born, then the number of those who would be born was set, and a place was prepared for that number where the living might dwell and the dead might be preserved. Therefore, no creature will live again until that number previously declared is achieved.[a]

[a] Translation from Gurtner, *Second Baruch*, 59.

CHAPTER 2.8

Interpretation of Daniel 7 in the Syriac Apocalypse of Baruch (2 Baruch)

Second Baruch survives only in the Syriac version, an Arabic version made from Syriac, a small fragment in Greek, and a quotation in Latin.[1] The Syriac version was very likely translated from Greek, but the evidence is insufficient to determine whether the work was originally written in Greek or in a Semitic language (Hebrew or Aramaic).[2] It was undoubtedly written between the two revolts but cannot be dated more precisely unless "the twenty-fifth year of Jeconiah" (1:1) is meant to give an indication of the real date of writing.[3] There is undoubtedly a close relationship between 2 Baruch and 4 Ezra, but the nature of that relationship is debated and hard to determine.[4]

---

1. For details see Daniel M. Gurtner, *Second Baruch: A Critical Edition of the Syriac Text*, JCT 5 (New York: T&T Clark, 2009) 6-8. Translations of 2 Baruch in this chapter, unless otherwise specified, are Gurtner's.

2. Gurtner, *Second Baruch*, 10-13.

3. This is argued by Daniel M. Gurtner, "The 'Twenty-Fifth Year of Jeconiah' and the Date of 2 Baruch," *JSP* 18 (2008) 23-32. Alternatively, the twenty-fifth year of Jeconiah is the fictional date of writing, and the number of years stated cryptically in 28:2 should be reckoned from it to produce the expected date of the end, which would be not far in the future from the author's actual time of writing. If 28:2 is understood as $2 \times (7 \times 7^2) = 686$ years, it probably indicates a date somewhere around the end of the first century CE, but it is impossible to know how long the author thought the period from the fall of the first temple to his own time was. His chronology would certainly have been different from ours. See Anttii Laato, *A Star Is Rising: The Historical Development of the Old Testament Royal Ideology and the Rise of the Jewish Messianic Expectation* (Atlanta: Scholars Press, 1997) 365-66.

4. See Matthias Henze, "4 Ezra and 2 Baruch: The *Status Quaestionis*," in Fourth Ezra *and* Second Baruch: *Reconstruction after the Fall*, ed. Matthias Henze and Gabriele Boccaccini, JSJSup 164 (Leiden: Brill, 2013) 3-27, here 12-15. For my own proposed understanding

PART 2 · INTERPRETATION OF DANIEL 7 IN SECOND TEMPLE-PERIOD JUDAISM

Second Baruch has a fictional setting in Jerusalem at the time of the fall of the city to the Babylonians. As in 4 Ezra, this destruction of Jerusalem functions as a type that enables the real author to reflect on the fall of Jerusalem in 70 CE. Baruch laments the fall of the city and the exile of the people, which he attributes to their sin. His urgent need is to know "what will happen at the end of days" (10:10), which God reveals to him in a series of prophecies, especially two prophetic visions. He also instructs the people and writes to the exiles, encouraging them to obey the law of Moses. For our present purposes, we can focus on the passages in which the Messiah features: chapters 29–30 and the two visions (with their interpretations).

Allusions to Daniel 7 in 2 Baruch are largely confined to the interpretation of the first vision (see table 1). It has been claimed that there are allusions to Daniel 7 in the second vision, but we shall see that that claim cannot be sustained. However, the accounts of the Messiah in chapters 29–30 and in the interpretation of the second vision are relevant to understanding how this author read Daniel 7:13–14 in relation to other messianic prophecies. All these passages will therefore be discussed.

The Messiah in Chapters 29–30

Second Baruch works with broadly the same eschatological scenario as 4 Ezra. The Messiah will destroy the last oppressive empire and deliver the righteous; there will be a temporary paradisal age, over which the Messiah will preside; the dead will rise and be judged; the new creation of the world will follow. Within this scheme there are differences. One is that 2 Baruch seems much more interested in the messianic age that will conclude the history of this world. It is described in much more detail (2 Bar. 29; 40:3; 73–74). In this first of the book's eschatological predictions, the full description of the blessings of the messianic age is probably designed to balance and surpass the evils of the end time catalogued in chapter 27. They are no doubt the wonders to which 4 Ezra only briefly alludes (4 Ezra 7:27).

The Messiah is mentioned on either side of the description: "the Messiah will then begin to be revealed" (2 Bar. 29:3); "when the time of the appearance[5] of the Messiah is fulfilled, he will return in glory" (30:1). This "return" of the Messiah

---

of the way that the author of 2 Baruch related his work to 4 Ezra, see Richard Bauckham, "Apocalypses," in *Justification and Variegated Nomism*, vol. 1, *The Complexities of Second Temple Judaism*, ed. Donald A. Carson, Peter T. O'Brien, and Mark A. Seifrid, WUNT 2/140 (Tübingen: Mohr Siebeck, 2001) 135–87, here 175–77.

5. *Me'tita* is commonly used in Syriac to translate the Greek παρουσία.

precedes the resurrection of the dead (30:1-2). It has been variously understood. R. H. Charles took it to be the Messiah's return to heaven, from where he had come at his revelation (29:3),[6] and Charles has been followed by several others.[7] But this interpretation makes it hard to make sense of the statement about the resurrection of the dead that immediately follows the Messiah's "return": "Then all who have fallen asleep in hope of him shall rise" (30:1b). If he has returned to heaven and plays no further part in the eschatological events, it is odd that these people should be described as having died "in hope of him."

Matthias Henze argues that, in 2 Baruch 29–30, two phases of the revelation of the Messiah are distinguished, one belonging to the last period of the history of this age, the second to the new creation, when the dead will be raised.[8] These chapters certainly do distinguish the temporary paradisal age from the age that begins with the resurrection of the dead. The question is whether the Messiah belongs to both ages or only to the first. If his "return" (30:1) is a return to earth, then it is odd that his previous absence has not been intimated. Moreover, there is no suggestion elsewhere in 2 Baruch that the Messiah will have any role in events following his reign at the end of this age. In 40:3, which somewhat resembles 30:1 ("until the aforementioned times are fulfilled"), there is reference only to the end of his reign when "the world of corruption will come to an end."

Henze allows that "we cannot rule out the possibility that 2Bar 30.1 or parts thereof, is a Christian gloss."[9] In my view, this is a probability.[10] We have the text of this part of 2 Baruch only in the Syriac version and only in one manuscript, which is, of course, a Christian one. The phrases "return in glory" (cf. Matt 24:30) and "all

---

6. R. H. Charles, *The Apocalypse of Baruch* (London: Black, 1896) 56.

7. L. H. Brockington, "The Syriac Apocalypse of Baruch," in *The Apocryphal Old Testament*, ed. H. F. D. Sparks (Oxford: Clarendon, 1984) 841–95, here 857, gives this interpretative translation: "And it shall come to pass after this, when the time of the presence of the Messiah *on earth* has run its course, that he will return in glory *to the heavens*." This is also the view of Pierre Bogaert, *Apocalypse de Baruch*, vol. 2, Sources chrétiennes 145 (Paris: Cerf, 1969) 65; John J. Collins, *The Apocalyptic Imagination* (New York: Crossroad, 1984) 175.

8. Matthias Henze, *Jewish Apocalypticism in Late First Century Israel*, TSAJ 142 (Tübingen: Mohr Siebeck, 2011) 294–98.

9. Henze, *Jewish Apocalypticism*, 297.

10. Scholars who take this view are listed in Rivka Nir, *The Destruction of Jerusalem and the Idea of Redemption in the* Syriac Apocalypse of Baruch, EJL 20 (Atlanta: Society of Biblical Literature, 2003) 152 n. 100. It is odd that, although Nir considers that 2 Baruch as a whole is a Christian composition, she thinks 30:1 refers to a return of the Messiah to heaven. But "he will return in glory," in a Christian composition, refers most naturally to the parousia, though 1 Tim 3:16 could support the idea of a return to heaven in glory. (The New Testament texts Nir cites here are a strangely assorted selection and do not include 1 Tim 3:16.)

who have fallen asleep in hope of him" (cf. 1 Cor 15:19) strongly suggest a Christian hand at work.[11] A Christian scribe would readily think the resurrection of the dead should be connected with the parousia (cf. 1 Thess 4:15–16). So it will be wise not to include 30:1 in the evidence for 2 Baruch's conception of the Messiah.

The statement that "the Messiah will then begin to be revealed" (29:3) is surprising. Elsewhere it is said that the Messiah will be revealed (4 Ezra 7:28; 13:32; 2 Thess 1:7), but the idea of a gradual revelation of the Messiah is not otherwise attested. The closest parallel in 2 Baruch is in 39:7: "Then the reign of my Messiah will be revealed."[12] Perhaps originally in 29:3 the reference was to the kingdom of the Messiah.[13] If it is the Messiah who is revealed, then the meaning is probably not that he is gradually revealed but that he is revealed and remains revealed until "the time of the appearance of the Messiah is fulfilled" (30:1).

That he will be revealed could imply that he will be living on earth among people but will not be recognized until his identity as the Messiah is disclosed. However, the next verse says that "Behemoth shall be revealed from his place, and Leviathan shall arise from the sea" (29:4). These two monsters were created on the fifth day of creation and have been preserved by God until this time (29:4; 4 Ezra 6:49–52). They have been in hidden places, on earth and in the sea respectively, and will be revealed at the end. The parallel implies that the Messiah too will be revealed "from his place," where God has been keeping him until this time (cf. 4 Ezra 12:32; 13:26). His place is likely to be paradise or heaven (cf. 2 Thess 1:7: "revealed from heaven"). There is no allusion here to Daniel 7:13, but this account of the Messiah is at least consistent with the interpretation of Daniel 7:13 that we have seen in 4 Ezra, whose eschatological ideas are so often very close to those of 2 Baruch.

The Vision of the Vine and the Forest (Chapters 36–40)[14]

Second Baruch contains two symbolic visions, of which the vision of the vine and the forest is the first. As we shall see, both visions are exegetically based

---

11. Charles, *The Apocalypse*, 56, states that the "words 'of him' cannot be original," but he explains them as a textual corruption, not a Christian gloss.

12. This translation represents an emendation of the text. The Syriac has "Then the beginning of my Messiah will be revealed." Bogaert, *Apocalypse de Baruch*, 2:74, suggests that the Greek had ἀρχή, which can mean either "beginning" or "rule." Perhaps a similar mistranslation underlies 29:3.

13. This is suggested by Charles, *The Apocalypse*, 52.

14. This section is adapted from my essay "The Messianic Interpretation of Isaiah 10:34" in Richard Bauckham, *The Jewish World around the New Testament: Collected Essays I*, WUNT 233 (Tübingen: Mohr Siebeck, 2008) 193–205, here 197–200.

in a somewhat similar way. Each is elaborated from a scriptural text that we could call the focal text and from a series of other scriptural texts that are linked to the focal text by verbal correspondences (utilizing the exegetical method known as gezera shava). In both cases, the interpretation of the vision does more than provide a key to the vision's symbols. It also fills out the vision with additional information. This is especially the case in the very long interpretation of the quite short second vision (chapters 53–74), but it is true also of this first vision.

In this vision of the vine and the forest, the Roman Empire is symbolized by a large forest surrounded by high mountains (40:2), while the Messiah and his kingdom are symbolized by a vine and a fountain (40:3; 39:7). The fountain comes to the forest and submerges it, uprooting all the trees and leveling the mountains (40:4–5). Only one cedar is left, which is felled and then brought to the vine, who denounces it for its evil rule and condemns it to be reduced to ashes like the rest of the forest (40:6–11). According to the interpretation, the cedar is the last ruler (i.e., the last Roman emperor), who, when his army is destroyed, will be bound and brought to the Messiah on Mount Zion. The Messiah will convict him of his wickedness and put him to death (39:8–40:2). The Messiah's peaceful and prosperous rule follows (37:1; 40:3).

The focal text is Isaiah 10:34 with its immediate context. The author has adopted a messianic interpretation of this text that is also attested in 4QpIsa[a] (4Q161) frag. 8–10 lines 2–9 and 4Q285 frag. 5.[15] In these Qumran texts, the forest, also called Lebanon, is understood as the enemies of Israel (the Kittim). The forest is felled by "a powerful one" (אדיר), who is understood to be the Davidic Messiah.

In Baruch's vision, the forest is the forest of Isaiah 10:33–34a. (See table 2, where the links between the focal text and other texts are indicated by the words that are italicized in the other texts.) When the account of the vision says that "the height of the forest became low" (2 Bar. 36:5), there is an echo of Isaiah 10:33b: "the tall in stature will be hewn down, and the lofty will be brought low" (my translation). The fact that the forest seems to be first uprooted (2 Bar. 36:4–6) and then burned to ashes (36:10) is probably because the phrase "the thickets of the forest" (סבכי היער) occurs not only in Isaiah 10:34a, where the thickets are said to be cut down, but also in Isaiah 9:18[17], where they are said to be burned. (The phrase is found nowhere else in the Hebrew Bible.) The fact that the emperor is portrayed in 2 Baruch as a cedar is because

---

15. Bauckham, "The Messianic Interpretation," 193–97.

he is understood to be the "Lebanon" to which Isaiah 10:34b refers.[16] The fact that the cedar is first thrown down (36:6), and then judged, sentenced, and executed by the vine (the Messiah), may well be due to a sequential interpretation of Isaiah 10:34a–11:4. First, Lebanon falls by the Messiah (Isa 10:34b); then the Messiah, acting as righteous judge (11:3–4), kills the wicked one (רשע) with the breath of his lips (11:4; note the stress on the cedar's wickedness in 2 Bar. 36:7–8; 40:1). The fact that the cedar is finally destroyed by burning (36:10; 37:1) may result from an exegetical link between the reference to Lebanon in Isaiah 10:34b and the prophecy that Lebanon will burn in Zechariah 11:1. Alternatively, it may derive from Daniel 7:11, since the cedar has been identified in the interpretation as "the fourth kingdom" (2 Bar. 39:5), which is the fourth beast in the vision of Daniel 7.[17] (In that case, this would be the only respect in which the vision itself, as distinct from the interpretation, has been influenced by Daniel.)

Other features of the vision can also be explained by exegetical links between Isaiah 10:33–11:1 and other passages of scripture. The vision symbolizes the Roman Empire not only as the forest that is thrown down but also as the high mountains that are leveled: "the height of the forest became low, and that top of the mountains became low" (2 Bar. 36:5). This is probably due to Isaiah 2:12–14:

> For the LORD of hosts has a day against all that is proud and lofty,
> against all that is lifted up and high;
> against all the cedars of Lebanon, lofty and lifted up; . . .
> against all the high mountains, and against all the lofty hills.
> (NRSV, modified)

Not only the reference to Lebanon links this with Isaiah 10:34, but also other verbal links associate it with Isaiah 10:33b: "and the tall in stature will be hewn down, and the lofty will become low." Isaiah 40:4 is similar: "every mountain and hill [shall] be made low."

The messianic shoot (חטר) or branch (נצר) of Isaiah 11:1 has been interpreted as a vine, perhaps under the influence of Psalm 80,[18] but more probably by association with Ezekiel 17:6–8, where the twig that symbolizes a scion of

---

16. Cf. the explicit reference to "the cedars of Lebanon" in the interpretation (39:5).

17. This point was suggested to me by George W. E. Nickelsburg.

18. Andrew Streett, *The Vine and the Son of Man: Eschatological Interpretation of Psalm 80 in Early Judaism* (Minneapolis: Fortress, 2014) 151–53, argues for a more significant role for Ps 80 in the vision, but I am not persuaded. In the sort of exegetical practice that underlies the vision, verbal links between passages are key, and Ezek 17:6–8 has striking verbal

the royal house of Judah is said to have "sprouted [ויצמח]] and become a vine" (17:6) and is later described as a "noble [אדיר] vine" (17:8). The use of אדיר links this vine with the messianic interpretation of Isaiah 10:34b (באדיר).

Finally, the use of a fountain to symbolize the royal power of the Messiah[19] was probably suggested by "the waters of Shiloah that flow gently" (Isa 8:6), interpreted with the aid of a messianic interpretation of Shiloh (Gen 49:10)[20] as a reference to the kingdom of the Messiah. The emphasis on the peace and tranquility of first the fountain (2 Bar. 36:3) and then the vine with the fountain (36:6), which might seem surprising in view of their destruction of the forest and the cedar, may be due not only to the statement that "the waters of Shiloah flow gently" but also to an association of the name Shiloah (שלח) with שלה (to be quiet, tranquil) or שלום (peace), as well as an allusion to Isaiah 11:9 (cf. 9:7).

DANIEL 7 IN THE INTERPRETATION OF THE VISION

The vision concerns the transition of power from the rule of the earthly empires to that of the Messiah, which will last until the end of this creation. Unlike the visions in 4 Ezra 12–13, which in many respects it resembles, this vision and especially its interpretation present the Messiah not only as a judge but also as a king. He defeats the last empire, condemns and executes the last emperor, and then reigns over his own kingdom. Despite the reference to the peacefulness of the vine and the fountain in the vision (2 Bar. 36:6), the Messiah's power prevails over the enemy by military force (40:1). The peace is doubtless the peace that his rule brings with it (cf. Isa 9:7; 11:9; 2 Bar. 73:1), not the manner of his victory. In contrast to 4 Ezra's Messiah, 2 Baruch's is a military leader who establishes his own kingdom.[21]

The fact that the interpretation of the vision refers to "my Messiah" (2 Bar. 39:7; 40:1), as well as to "Mount Zion" (40:1), indicates dependence on Psalm 2 (cf. Ps 2:2, 9), as in 4 Ezra 13:35. This is a scriptural allusion not to be found in the vision itself but introduced to assist the interpretation of the

---

links with both Isa 10:34 and Isa 11:1, which belong to the focal passage. This is much more than "a fairly thin verbal connection" (Streett, *The Vine*, 152 n. 116).

19. 2 Bar. 39:7 is not clear as to the distinction between the fountain and the vine, but from the whole account of the vision and its interpretation it is evident that the vine is the Messiah in person and most likely the fountain is his dominion or royal power.

20. This interpretation is attested in the Targums, rabbinic literature, and probably the OG.

21. This makes it plausible that 2 Baruch reflects ideas that led to the Bar Kokhba revolt. Cf. Gerbern S. Oegema, "*2 Baruch*, the Messiah, and the Bar Kochba Revolt," in *Apocalyptic Interpretation of the Bible*, JCT 13 (London: T&T Clark, 2012) 133–42.

vision. Similarly, the account of the four empires in 39:3–5 uses Daniel 7:4–8, 17–22, and 24–25 to interpret the forest of the vision as the fourth of these, the Roman Empire (cf. 4 Ezra 12:11). This use of Daniel 7 makes it virtually certain that the author understood Daniel 7:13 to refer to the Messiah whom he describes, but there is no allusion to that verse. It is possible that 40:3 ("his reign will last forever, until the world of corruption comes to an end") alludes to Daniel 7:14. The earthly kingdoms have been said to last for "times" (39:4–5), but the Messiah's reign will be forever. The "times" of the fourth kingdom (39:5) may echo the "time, times and half a time" of Daniel 7:25 (NIV). In that case the contrasted eternal kingdom of the Messiah echoes that of the humanlike figure in Daniel 7:14, 27. But Isaiah 9:7 is an alternative source, one that is probably echoed in 2 Baruch 73:1.

In conclusion, the overall concept of the Messiah's eternal kingdom succeeding the four earthly kingdoms by way of judgment reflects Daniel 7. In this respect the interpretation of the vision goes beyond the vision itself, which is based largely on Isaiah. But, as in 4 Ezra 12–13, the Danielic scheme is filled out with allusions to other messianic passages, Psalm 2 and Isaiah 11:4 in particular.

The Vision of the Black and Bright Waters (Chapters 53–74)

In the vision of the black and bright waters, Baruch sees a cloud, containing both black and white waters, rise from the sea. Above it is "something like great lightning" (53:1). The cloud covers the whole earth. It rains, first, a large quantity of black waters, then a small quantity of bright waters. In all it rains twelve times in succession, with black and bright waters alternating. Finally, there are darker black waters, mixed with fire, which bring great destruction on earth. The lightning then seizes the cloud and hurls it to the earth (53:8). Now the lightning lights up the whole earth and heals the lands that the last black waters had devastated. It assumes dominion over the earth (53:10). Twelve rivers then flow from the sea and surround and become subject to the lightning.

The subject of the vision is the sovereignty of God over the whole course of world history, symbolized by the cloud. As we learn from the interpretation, God at creation determined the whole history of the world (56:2–4), dividing it into twelve periods, dominated alternately by human evil and human righteousness, symbolized by the black and bright rain (69:2–3). The events belonging to these periods are narrated at length in the interpretation (56:5–68:8). The last black waters, darker than the others, symbolize the period of evils and judgments prior to the messianic age (69:5–70:10). A peculiarity of the interpretation is that it adds to the thirteen periods symbolized in the vision another rain of bright waters (72:1), which apparently begins with the advent of the Messiah. This corresponds to the period associated with the lightning in the vision (53:8-11). The lightning is not mentioned in the interpretation. Not surprisingly, scholars have thought it must symbolize the Messiah.[22] Charles went so far as to amend the text of 72:1 and 74:4 to read "bright lightning" instead of "bright waters."[23] The meaning of the lightning will be discussed after we have studied the exegetical composition of the vision.

Understanding how the symbols of the vision have been developed is essential to deciding the issue of whether the vision alludes to Daniel 7, as has been claimed. The method of composition is similar to that of the first vision (see table 3). There is a focal passage to which other scriptural texts are connected by verbal correspondences. In this case the focal passage is Jeremiah 10:12-13 (= 51:15-16), and the word "lightnings" (ברקים) is the point of connection to other passages, which are all in the Psalms (77:17-18[18-19]; 97:4; 135:7; 144:5-7).[24] The vision contains one near-verbatim allusion to these passages (2 Bar. 53:9; cf. Ps 77:18; 97:4).

Although it does not contribute to the symbolism of the vision, it is important to notice that the focal text begins with an emphatic (with three lines in parallel) statement that God made the whole world, earth and heaven (Jer 10:12). (There is very likely an allusion to this statement in 2 Bar. 56:3-4, at the beginning of the interpretation of the vision.)[25] What follows in Jeremiah illustrates God's supremacy over the world he has made. In 2 Baruch God created the world and at the same time determined its whole history (56:2-4). So the author has taken the meteorological imagery of Jeremiah 10:13 as symbolic of God's sovereignty over the whole of human history.

The focal text supplies all the key symbols of the vision: cloud, waters, lightning, rain. In Jeremiah 10:13 (and Ps 135:7) clouds "rise from the ends of the earth." It is not surprising that 2 Baruch changes this to "from the sea."[26]

---

22. Bogaert, *Apocalypse de Baruch*, 2:100; Henze, *Jewish Apocalypticism*, 270. But Collins, *The Apocalyptic Imagination*, 176, thinks the lightning symbolizes "the messianic age."

23. Charles, *The Apocalypse*, 114, 116.

24. In Pss 77, 97, and 135, the word is plural, as in Jer 10:13, while in 144:6 the cognate verb, ברק, "to flash lightning," is used.

25. The words "he took counsel to make the world" (56:3) plausibly allude to Jer 10:12, since in Jewish thought it was from his wisdom that God took counsel when he created the world (2 En. 33:4). In that case 56:3-4 picks up all three of the divine instruments of creation from Jer 10:12: wisdom, word, understanding.

26. Here Gurtner's translation (following Charles and Klijn) has "A cloud was coming

This is a more natural image, since in Palestine rain clouds do rise from the Mediterranean Sea. (Though there is not likely to be an allusion to 1 Kgs 18:44, the parallel language shows that this is an expected phenomenon.) The "multitude" (המון) of waters in the heavens (Jer 10:13) could easily suggest a variety of waters—that is, bright and different shades of black.

The key to understanding the symbol of the lightning is that lightning causes rain (Jer 10:13; Ps 135:7: "he makes the lightnings for rain"). It acts on the cloud to make the cloud release its waters as rain. It is above the cloud so as to act on it. It should be supposed to be active in causing the rain all through the thirteen periods of black and bright waters. Then, after the last dark waters that have wrought destruction on earth, the lightning apparently destroys the cloud (53:9). This may be inspired by Psalm 144:5-6, where God sends lightning to deliver the psalmist from "many waters." The removal of the cloud means that the lightning now shines on the whole earth, as in Psalm 77:17-18, where, after the clouds have poured out waters, "your lightnings lit up the world" (cf. Ps 97:4). This is then interpreted to mean that the lightning "seized the whole world and had dominion over it" (2 Bar. 53:10).

The final image of the vision—the twelve rivers that flow from the sea surround the lightning and become subject to it (53:11)—is obscure. As with the lightning, there is no explicit attempt to decode the rivers in the interpretation of the vision. They might represent the twelve tribes returning from exile and settling around the new Jerusalem temple. Although this is not mentioned in the interpretation, the use of the number twelve makes it more likely than that the rivers represent the nations who will come at the Messiah's call (72:2).

What does the lightning symbolize? Since it dominates the cloud throughout the whole history of the world from the creation onward, it must represent the divine sovereignty over history. It is responsible for both black and bright waters, as well as for the messianic age that concludes the history of this creation. It cannot represent the Messiah, since there is no indication in 2 Baruch or any other early Jewish literature that the Messiah is understood as the divine agent of all divine action in the world throughout history. The Messiah's role, which is explicit in the interpretation, is not directly symbolized in the vision. The fact that the rivers, whatever they symbolize, "surround"

---

out of the great sea." The adjective "great" could qualify either the cloud or the sea, but the parallel in 56:4 ("You saw a great cloud which came out from the sea") is decisive in favor of "a great cloud," not "the great sea," in 53:1. See Bogaert, *Apocalypse de Baruch*, 2:99. Brockington, "The Syriac Apocalypse," 872, correctly translates: "a very great cloud was coming up out of the sea."

the lightning suggests that the lightning is the power and presence of God, in heaven throughout the thirteen periods of rain, but on earth in the Jerusalem temple in the messianic age.

Two allusions to Daniel 7 in the account of the vision have been proposed. First, it is said that 2 Baruch 53:1 ("a very great cloud was coming up out of the sea")[27] alludes to Daniel 7:2–3.[28] But (1) Baruch's vision is not a vision in the night, unlike his first vision (36:1) and Daniel's. (2) The parallel looks closer if the adjective "great" is taken to qualify "sea" rather than "cloud," as it is in some translations of 53:1, but it is clear from 56:4 ("you saw a great cloud which came out from the sea") that it qualifies "cloud." (3) The image of the four beasts coming out of the sea is a fantastic one, whereas Baruch's is a naturalistic one, describing how clouds appear to rise from the Mediterranean Sea (cf. 1 Kgs 18:44). (4) Jeremiah 10:13 adequately accounts for 2 Baruch's image and language.

Second, it is alleged that the image of "something like great lightning" at the top of the cloud (2 Bar. 53:1) alludes to Daniel 7:13: "one like a human being coming with the clouds of heaven."[29] Of course, if the lightning symbolizes the Messiah, this connection might be attractive, but we have seen that that is not the case. The lightning is atop the cloud in order to activate rain. This is a very different image from the humanlike figure "coming with the clouds of heaven." Only in the Old Greek version of Daniel does the humanlike figure come "on" the clouds. (4 Ezra 13:3 follows the Aramaic: "with the clouds of heaven.") So there is no good reason to see allusions to Daniel in 2 Baruch 53:1.[30]

In the interpretation of the vision, the last period of the "corruptible world" is described as "the bright waters which came after the last dark waters" (74:3; cf. 72:1), although there are no such waters in the vision. Here the Messiah appears[31] in a role broadly similar to his role in the first vision: he slaughters the nations that have ruled over the people of Israel, but spares those that have not, who become subject to Israel (72:2–6). But there is no reference to empires (cf. also 70:2, which refers generally to the earth and "its rulers") and no final ruler condemned and executed by the Messiah. The Messiah is thus a military conqueror and subsequently a ruler, but he is not depicted as a judge.

---

27. Henze, *Jewish Apocalypticism*, 270.
28. This translation is from Brockington, "The Syriac Apocalypse," 872.
29. Charles, *The Apocalypse*, 88; Henze, *Jewish Apocalypticism*, 270.
30. Thus I disagree with Henze, *Jewish Apocalypticism*, 270: "All in all, the cumulative evidence strongly suggests that Daniel's vision stands in the background of Baruch's vision of the cloud."
31. He is first mentioned in 70:9 in a statement that anticipates his appearance in 72:2.

So there is no reason to think that Daniel 7 is the background to this account. His kingdom is described in 73:1 in terms drawn, not from Daniel 7, but from Isaiah 9:3–7 (see table 3).

Insofar as there are scriptural allusions in chapters 72–74, they seem all to be Isaianic (see table 4). Isaiah may also provide the explanation for the surprising introduction here of "the bright waters" after "the last black waters." The two references to these additional bright waters, which did not appear in the vision, frame 9:2: "The people who walked in darkness have seen a great light."[32] This whole account of the Messiah could be seen as based on the focal passage Isaiah 9:2–7, augmented by other Isaianic passages, especially Isaiah 11 and 65 (see table 4). Thus, whereas the messianic age was described in the vision in terms of scriptural references to lightning, this parallel account in the interpretation draws instead on Isaianic sources (entirely absent from the vision) to provide a much more detailed account. The technique is the same as in the case of the first vision, where the interpretation draws on Daniel (absent from the vision) in order to augment the content of the vision. But in the second vision the interpretation is even more independent of the vision. Practically no attempt is made to decode the symbolism of the vision.

Whence the Messiah?

It is nowhere said explicitly in 2 Baruch that the Messiah is descended from David, but the first vision is based on Isaiah 10:33–11:4 (see table 2), and the account of the Messiah in the interpretation of the second vision draws on Isaiah 11:1–10 and 9:2–4 (see table 4). The figure in these passages is unequivocally Davidic. It is true that in the Parables of Enoch, whose Messianic Figure is not a descendant of David (he is Enoch), Isaiah 11:2–5 contributes to his portrayal, but other scriptural prophecies that are not explicitly Davidic are as or more important (see chapter 1.2, table 2). In 2 Baruch the Davidic prophecies from Isaiah are much the most important sources for its accounts of the Messiah.

We have also seen that, when 2 Baruch says that the Messiah will be "revealed" (29:3), it probably means that he is being preserved by God in some special place, presumably paradise or heaven, until the last days. This would cohere with the probability that chapter 39 implies that the Messiah is the humanlike figure of Daniel 7:14. In these two respects 2 Baruch's Messiah resembles the Messiah of 4 Ezra, which is not surprising in view of the many other correspondences between the two books in their eschatological expectations.

32. There is a different interpretation of Isa 9:2 in 2 Bar. 59:2.

Interpretation of Daniel 7 in the Syriac Apocalypse of Baruch (2 Baruch) · 2.8

In chapter 2.5 I argued that 4 Ezra's Messiah, being both a Davidide and the humanlike figure of Daniel 7:13, is best understood as a human descendant of David, born in the distant past, but preserved in heaven or paradise for his messianic rule at the end. That 2 Baruch presupposes the same idea is corroborated by the importance of Isaiah 9:2–4 in chapter 73 of 2 Baruch (see table 4). As we have noted in chapter 2.6, the birth of a son who is to inherit the throne of David (Isa 9:6–7) could be understood as an oracle of Isaiah's about an offspring of the house of David born in his time. The author of 2 Baruch cannot have supposed that this was Hezekiah, because there is no hint of that in his own account of Hezekiah (chapter 63), but he could have thought that the future Messiah was a son of Hezekiah or another Davidide born in Isaiah's time and then removed from earth by God with a view to his future mission.

Conclusion

The Messiah in 2 Baruch is a king and military leader who defeats the oppressors of God's people Israel and reigns over the world from Jerusalem in an age of unprecedented peace and prosperity up to the resurrection of the dead and the new creation. Since the scriptural passages on which this portrayal of the Messiah is very largely based (Isa 9:2–7; 10:33–11:10) are Davidic, it appears that he is a descendant of David, although this is not explicitly stated. When he first appears at the time of the end, it is said that he will be "revealed" (2 Bar. 29:3), probably meaning that he will come from a place where God has been keeping him (paradise or heaven) since the time of his birth on earth in the past. He is thus "preexistent" in only the same sense as the Messiah in 4 Ezra is, not existing from eternity or from before creation, and not a heavenly or "divine" being by nature but a human being with a unique role in the eschatological purpose. Whereas 4 Ezra provides no clue as to his origin, other than implying that he is a Davidide from the distant past, the fact that 2 Baruch, unlike 4 Ezra, alludes to Isaiah 9:5–7 suggests that this passage refers to the birth of the Messiah into the royal line in the time of the prophet Isaiah.

Daniel 7 is less important than Isaianic prophecies in 2 Baruch's depiction of the Messiah, but it provides the broad framework for the future events symbolized and explained in the first vision and its interpretation. The last ruler, whom the Messiah defeats, judges, and executes, is the ruler of the fourth of Daniel's four kingdoms. The Messiah's own kingdom is the successor to all those empires and lasts forever—that is, until the end of this created world. There is no allusion to Daniel 7:13, but an identification of the Messiah as the humanlike figure of Daniel's vision is evidently presupposed. This vision and its interpretation are otherwise mostly dependent on Isaiah 10:33–11:4, with allusions also, in the interpretation, to Psalm 2. That God calls the Messiah "my Messiah" (2 Bar. 39:7; 40:1; also 72:2) reflects Psalm 2:2, which, as in the Parables of Enoch, is presumably the source of the title "Messiah" as used in 2 Baruch. Unlike the Parables of Enoch, 2 Baruch never calls the Messiah anything other than "the Messiah" (29:3; 30:1), "my Messiah" (39:7; 40:1; 72:2), or "my servant, the Messiah" (70:9), While the last phrase might reflect Isaiah 42:1, the fact that 2 Baruch nowhere else alludes to the Isaianic servant passages makes it much more likely to reflect Davidic passages (Ps 89:3, 20, 39).

In Baruch's second vision, the Messiah appears only in the interpretation. (The view that the lightning represents the Messiah has been shown to be mistaken.) The vision itself focuses on God's sovereignty over the whole course of history and God's own intervention to bring about a period of blessing at the end. Only in the interpretation do we learn that the Messiah is the agent of this divine intervention and that the period of unprecedented divine blessing is the Messiah's kingdom. In neither the vision nor the interpretation is there any dependence on Daniel 7, and accordingly it is not the ruler of the last world empire that the Messiah defeats, but "all the nations" (2 Bar. 72:2). (He destroys Israel's enemies but spares others.) The portrayal of the Messiah and his kingdom is here based largely on Isaianic prophecies, especially Isaiah 9:2–7.

In many ways 2 Baruch's account of the eschatological events and the Messiah's role in them resembles that of 4 Ezra. But whereas in 4 Ezra the Messiah is a judge, not a military leader or king, 2 Baruch (while including his judicial condemnation of the last ruler: 36:7–10; 40:1) foresees his victory over the enemies by military violence and understands the paradisal age as the kingdom over which the Messiah will rule from a throne (73:1; cf. Isa 9:7). Though dependent on many of the same scriptural sources as 4 Ezra, 2 Baruch does not appear to be reacting against militant messianism. In this respect 2 Baruch differs also from the Parables of Enoch.

TABLE 1. *Allusions to Daniel 7 in 2 Baruch*

2 Baruch	Daniel
21:6	7:9–10
24:1	7:10
39:3–5	7:4–8, 17–22, 24–25
39:7	7:14
40:3	7:14, 27

TABLE 2. *Biblical background to 2 Baruch 36–37*

Focal passage: Isaiah 10:33–11:1, 4b

Look, the sovereign, the LORD of hosts,
    will lop the boughs with terrifying power;
the tall in stature will be hewn down,
    and the lofty will be brought low,
The thickets of the forest will be cut down with an axe,
    and Lebanon by a powerful one[a] will fall.
A shoot shall come out from the stock of Jesse,
    and a branch shall grow out of his roots.
. . . .
He shall strike the earth with the rod of his mouth,
    and with the breath of his lips he shall kill the wicked.
    (NRSV, modified)

2 Baruch	Isaiah
A vine arises (36:3)	A shoot shall come out (11:1)
A fountain runs peacefully (36:3, cf. 6)	The waters of Shiloah that flow gently (8:5)
The fountain becomes great waves that submerge the forest (36:4)	The mighty flood waters of the river (8:7)
The height of the forest becomes low (36:5)	The tall in stature will be hewn down, and the lofty will be brought low (10:33)
	For the LORD of hosts has a day against all that is proud and *lofty*, against all that is lifted up; and it shall *become low* (2:12)
The top of the mountains becomes low (36:5)	Against all the *lofty* mountains, and against all the high trees (2:14)
	Every mountain and hill shall *become low* (40:4)
The fountain destroys and uproots the forest (36:4–6)	The thickets of the forest will be cut down with an axe (10:34)

2 Baruch	Isaiah
The fountain casts down the cedar (36:6)	Against all the cedars of *Lebanon, lofty and lifted up* (2:13) Lebanon by a powerful one will fall (10:34)
The vine condemns the cedar to destruction (36:7–10)	He shall strike the earth with the rod of his mouth, and with the breath of his lips he shall kill the wicked (11:4)
The forest and the cedar are burned to ashes (36:10)	For wickedness burned like a fire consuming briers and thorns; it kindled *the thickets of the forest*, and they swirled upwards in a column of smoke (9:18[17])

[a] NRSV translates באדיר as "with its majestic trees," but "by a powerful one" is the meaning presupposed in 4QpIsa[a] (4Q161) viii–x 2–9, where the interpretation paraphrases it as גדולו, "his great one"—that is, the Messiah.

309

TABLE 3. *Biblical background to 2 Baruch 53*

Focal passage: Jeremiah 10:12–13 = 51:15–16

It is he who made the earth by his power,
> who established the world by his wisdom,
> and by his understanding stretched out the heavens.

When he utters his voice, there is tumult [or: multitude][a] of waters in the heavens,
> and he makes the mist [or: clouds][b] rise from the ends of the earth.

He makes lightnings for the rain,
> and he brings out the wind from his storehouse.

2 Baruch	Biblical passages
Cloud rising from the Great Sea (53:1)	Look, a little cloud no bigger than a person's hand is rising from the sea. (1 Kgs 18:44)
	He makes the mist [or: clouds][c] rise from the ends of the earth. (Jer 10:13)
	He it is who makes the clouds rise at the end of the earth. (Ps 135:7)
Many waters (53:1)	When he utters his word there is a tumult [or: multitude][d] of waters in the heavens. (Jer 10:13 = 51:16)
Lightning causes rain	He makes lightnings for the rain. (Ps 135:7)
	He makes lightnings for the rain. (Jer 10:13 = 51:16)
Lightning delivers from the waters (53:8)	Bow your heavens, O LORD, and come down. . . . Make the lightning flash and scatter them. . . . Stretch out your hand from on high; set me free and rescue me from the mighty waters. (Ps 144:5–7)
Lightning lights up the whole earth (53:9)	The clouds poured out water; . . . your lightnings lit up the world. (Ps 77:17–18)
	His lightnings light up the world. (Ps 97:4)

a המון can mean "tumult" or "multitude."
b NRSV translates נשאים here as "mist" but as "clouds" in the parallel passage in Ps 135:7.
c See previous note.
d See note *a*.

TABLE 4. *Isaianic background to 2 Baruch 72–74*

2 Baruch	Isaiah
72:1: . . . concerning the bright waters which are to come at the end after these black (waters) . . . (cf. 74:4)	9:2: The people who walked in darkness have seen a great light
72:2: . . . he will call all the nations . . .	11:10: the root of Jesse shall stand as a signal to the peoples
73:1: . . . after he has brought low everything that is in the world,	2:11: the haughty eyes of people shall be brought low
	10:33: the lofty shall be brought low
and has sat down in eternal peace on the throne of his kingdom, then joy will be revealed,	9:7: His authority shall grow continually, and there shall be endless peace, for the throne of David and his kingdom.
	9:3: you have increased its joy; they rejoice before you as with joy at the harvest
and rest will appear.	9:4: For the yoke of their burden, and the bar across their shoulders, the rod of their oppressors, you have broken
73:2: . . . lamentation will pass from among men . . .	65:19: no more shall the sound of weeping be heard
73:3: And no one will again die when it is not his time . . .	65:20: No more shall there be . . . an old person who does not live out a lifetime
73:6: And wild beasts will come from the forest and serve men, and asps and dragons will come out of their holes to subject themselves to a child.	Cf. 11:6–7; 65:25
	11:8: The nursing child shall play over the hole of the asp, and the weaned child shall put its hand on the adder's den
74:1: . . . the reapers will not grow tired, nor will those who build be worn out from work.	Cf. 65:21–22

TABLE 5. *Exegetical sources of the Messianic Figure: 2 Baruch, 4 Ezra, and the Parables of Enoch compared*

2 Baruch	4 Ezra	Parables of Enoch
Dan 7	Dan 7	Dan 7
Isa 10:33–11:10	Isa 11:4, 12	Isa 11:2, 4–5
Ps 2:2, 6	Ps 2:1–2, 5–7	Ps 2:2, 8
Gen 49:10	Gen 49:9	
Isa 8:6		
Isa 9:2–7		
Isa 65:18–25		
Ezek 17:6–8		
	2 Sam 7:13	
	Dan 2	
	Ps 90:15–16	
		Isa 24:21
		Isa 41:11–12
		Isa 42:1–7
		Isa 49:1–7
		Isa 52:13, 15
		Ps 72

CHAPTER 2.9

Rabbi Aqiva on Daniel 7

Rabbi Aqiva[1] was one of the most prominent rabbis in the period after Yavneh, the early years of the second century CE. According to rabbinic traditions that are probably reliable to this extent, he supported the revolt of Bar Kokhba (132–135 CE), acclaiming Bar Kokhba to be the Messiah, and was executed by the Roman authorities after teaching Torah when this was prohibited.[2] There are two traditions purporting to report his interpretation of Daniel 7:9. Whether either or both are authentic is debatable. Some reasons for thinking that at least the first may derive from the time of Aqiva will be offered below. But our primary concern must be with the meaning of these two interpretations. Both are reported in a passage of the Babylonian Talmud:

> One passage says: His throne was fiery flames (Dan 7:9); and another passage says: [I watched] until thrones were set in place, and an Ancient of Days (*'atiq yomin*) took his seat! (Dan 7:9)—There is no contradiction: one (throne) for him [the Ancient of Days], and one throne for David: For it has been taught (in a baraita): one was for him, and the other was for David—these are the words of Rabbi Aqiva.
>
> Said Rabbi Yose the Galilean to him: Aqiva, how long will you treat the Shekinah as profane! Rather, one (throne) was for justice (*din*) and one (throne) was for mercy (*tzedakah*).

---

1. In English the name is often spelled Akiva or Akiba.
2. The perhaps rather too skeptical assessment of the rabbinic traditions by Peter Schäfer, "Rabbi Aqiva and Bar Kokhba," in *Approaches to Ancient Judaism*, vol. 2, ed. William Scott Green, Brown Judaic Studies 9 (Chico, CA: Scholars Press, 1980) 113–30, allows that Aqiva was associated with the revolt and was executed in connection with it.

Did he [Aqiva] accept this explanation from him [Yose], or did he not accept it?—Come and hear:[3] One (throne) for justice (*din*) and one (throne) was for mercy (*tzedakah*)—these are the words of Rabbi Aqiva.

Said Rabbi Eleazar ben Azariah to him: Aqiva, what have you to do with Haggadah? Cease your talk (about the Haggadah), and turn to (the laws concerning) Nega'im and Oholot! Rather, one (throne stands) for the throne and one (throne stands) for the footstool—a throne to sit upon and a footstool to rest his feet upon, as it is said: The heaven is my throne, and the earth is my footrest (Isa 66:1). (b. Hag. 14a)[4]

The discussion concerns an exegetical issue: how to interpret the "thrones" (plural) to which Daniel 7:9 refers.[5] Daniel describes the throne of the Ancient of Days and says that he sat on it. Who sat on the other throne(s)? The editor of this passage of the Bavli has brought together two baraitot in which Aqiva gives his opinion on the subject. (A baraita is a short unit of tradition, usually of Tannaitic origin.) In the first one, Aqiva assumes that there are no more than two thrones, and says that one is for God and the other for David. In the second baraita, Aqiva gives a quite different explanation. He relates the two thrones to the two divine attributes, justice and mercy. In both cases, Aqiva is roundly rebuked by another famous rabbi of his time.

The two interpretations of Daniel that Aqiva gives in the two baraitot are, of course, incompatible. But the editor has reconciled them, by assuming that Aqiva accepted the alternative view propounded by Rabbi Yose in the first baraita and made it his own, only to find himself contradicted now by Rabbi Eleazar ben Azariah, who insists on yet a third interpretation.

Aqiva's first interpretation probably means that he assigned the second throne to the humanlike figure described in Daniel 7:13. No other individual is available in the Danielic context. Moreover, as we have observed previously, Daniel 7:14, in which this figure is given dominion over all nations, virtually requires that he have a throne. Kings rule from thrones; a universal emperor surely requires a throne appropriate to his status. So it is not especially surprising that Aqiva should suppose that this figure will sit on the second throne that the plural "thrones" in 7:9 implies. At the same time, Aqiva is giving his own

---

3. The parallel in b. Sanh. 38b inserts here: "For it has been taught (in another baraita)."
4. This translation is from Peter Schäfer, *Two Gods in Heaven: Jewish Concepts of God in Antiquity*, trans. Allison Brown (Princeton, NJ: Princeton University Press, 2020) 81–82. The parallel passage in b. Sanh. 38b is almost identical.
5. In part 1 of this book we found that the author of the Parables of Enoch probably took them to be two, one for God and one for the humanlike figure of Dan 7:13.

answer to the exegetical question that Daniel 7:13-14 inevitably poses: Who is this "one like a son of man"? He is "David."

Almost all scholars who have commented on these words of Aqiva think that he is referring to the Messiah, the son of David. According to Peter Schäfer, "there can be no doubt that here David cannot mean the earthly King David—that is, the elevation of David into heaven after his death—but rather the Davidic Messiah-King, who through the reference back to the Book of Daniel is understood here as the Son of Man in Daniel."[6] Why can there be no such doubt? Similarly, William Horbury writes that a reference "to the historical David rather than the messiah . . . is implausible, especially when the messianism of the early second century is remembered, especially because of the messianic understanding of 'David' prominent already in the Old Testament."[7] Unlike Schäfer, who thinks this saying of Aqiva inauthentic and dating from a later period in Babylonia, not Palestine, Horbury assumes it is an authentic saying dating from the early second century.[8] The Old Testament passages to which he refers will be considered shortly. At this point we may note that Horbury poses an exclusive alternative: "the historical David rather than the messiah." Why not consider the possibility that Aqiva refers to the historical David *as* the Messiah? He may mean that the great King David has been elevated to heaven and will come in the future as the messianic ruler of all nations.

The only scholar, so far as I know, who has dissented from the general view is Maurice Casey, who takes Aqiva to mean that "the historical David will rise from the dead and take part in the final judgment, sitting on one of the thrones." But he does not think Aqiva means to identify the "one like a son of man" as "David," since "there is nothing inconsistent in holding that there were two thrones, that David or the Messiah sat on one of them, but that vs. 13 actually symbolizes the arrival of the people of Israel."[9] But it is highly unlikely that Aqiva understood Daniel 7:13 in this symbolic way, since such an

---

6. Schäfer, *Two Gods*, 85. `He makes the same point, equally emphatically, in Schäfer, *The Jewish Jesus: How Judaism and Christianity Shaped Each Other* (Princeton, NJ: Princeton University Press, 2012) 73.

7. William Horbury, *Messianism among Jews and Christians: Twelve Biblical and Historical Studies* (London: T&T Clark, 2003) 141.

8. See also William Horbury, *Jewish War under Trajan and Hadrian* (Cambridge: Cambridge University Press, 2014) 382, where he sees it as consistent with Aqiva's alleged application of the "star" prophecy of Num 24:17 to Bar Kokhba.

9. Maurice Casey, *Son of Man: The Interpretation and Influence of Daniel 7* (London: SPCK, 1979) 87. In *The Solution to the "Son of Man" Problem* (London: T&T Clark, 2007) 221, Casey says that when Aqiva assigned one throne to "David," "he may or may not have meant the Messiah."

interpretation is found nowhere in Second Temple–period Jewish literature or in rabbinic literature. If one throne is for "the historical David," then he must be the "one like a son of man."

Is it likely that Aqiva himself or the tradents of this saying intended to refer to a descendant of David rather than David himself? There are only two other passages in rabbinic literature (y. Ber. 2:4 [5a]; b. Sanh. 98b), which will be discussed shortly, in which the Messiah is called simply "David."[10] Elsewhere the Davidic Messiah is referred to as "the King Messiah" or "the Messiah son of David." It is true that there are a series of passages in the prophets that refer to the ideal ruler of the future as "David" (Jer 30:9; Ezek 34:23–24; 37:24; Hos 3:5), and these were often understood to refer to the Messiah son of David. The Targums to Jeremiah and Hosea interpret the texts in that way, but the Targum to Ezekiel renders the Hebrew literally. According to Samson Levey, this is consistent with this Targum's "non-messianic eschatology," but whether "David" here "means the Davidic dynasty or a David *redivivus* is not altogether certain."[11]

However, a David *redivivus* certainly is envisaged in a rabbinic comment on Hosea 3:5:

"Thus the children of Israel will repent, seek the Eternal, their God, and their king David" (Hosea 3:5). The Rebbis say: This king Messiah, if he is from the living, his name is David. If he is from the dead, his name is David. Rebbi Tanḥuma said: I am declaring the reason (Ps 18:51) "He gives kindness to His anointed, to David." (y. Ber. 2:4[5a])[12]

It is not clear which of the two opinions Rabbi Tanhuma (fourth century CE) supported. His scriptural citation merely supports the idea that the Messiah will be named David because it refers to "his anointed" (i.e., the Messiah; cf. Ps 2:2) in conjunction with the name David. The option that the Messiah might

---

10. Arnold Goldberg, "Die Namen des Messias in der rabbinischen Traditionsliteratur: Ein Beitrag zur Messianologie des rabbinischen Judentums," in *Mystik und Theologie des rabbinischen Judentums: Gesammelte Studien*, vol. 1, ed. Margarete Schlütter and Peter Schäfer, TSAJ 61 (Tübingen: Mohr Siebeck, 1997) 208–74, here 225–30.

11. Samson H. Levey, *The Targum of Ezekiel*, ArBib 13 (Edinburgh: T&T Clark, 1987) 99 n. 12.

12. Translation from Heinrich W. Guggenheimer, *The Jerusalem Talmud: First Order: Zeraim: Tractate Berakhot*, SJ 18 (Berlin: de Gruyter, 2000) 209–10. There is a parallel in Lam. Rab. 1:51, where the saying is attributed to Rabbi Judah ben Rabbi Simon speaking in the name of Rabbi Samuel bar Rabbi Isaac (Palestine, third century).

be someone raised from the dead must imply that the historical David himself will be raised and therefore his name will be David.

A divergent and expanded version of this tradition is found in the Bavli, where the texts discussed are Jeremiah 30:9 and Ezekiel 37:25 rather than Hosea 3:5. Here it is Rav Naḥman (c. 300 CE) who entertains the possibility that the Messiah will be someone risen from the dead, like Daniel (cf. Dan 12:13). But he does not refer to David. The compiler cites a comment by Rav (Abba Arika) (early third century), who takes Jeremiah 30:9 to refer to "another David," a king who will be called David. Then Rav Pappa (mid-third century) is quoted, arguing from Ezekiel 37:25 that David himself will be the messianic ruler. But this opinion is qualified by his contemporary Rabbi Abaye, who reasons that, since in Ezekiel 37:25 David is called "prince" (נשיא) rather than "king," he will not be the King-Messiah but the Messiah's deputy, "like an emperor and a viceroy" (b. Sanh. 98b).

In rabbinic literature, the notion that the Messiah will be called David is unique to these two closely related passages and seems to arise only when the meaning of three specific biblical texts that seem to say so is discussed. There were many other opinions on what the name of the Messiah would be,[13] but the name David never appears in other such contexts. Exceptional though they are, these traditions do show that the rabbis could at least entertain the idea that the Messiah might be King David himself, and, perhaps more interestingly, they highlight the possible exegetical bases for such an idea.

So it is a real possibility that this was Aqiva's view. In this book we have seen that, among Jewish sources from the Second Temple period in which an identification of the figure in Daniel 7:13–14 is clear, in every case the figure is understood to be a human person who had lived on earth in the past and is now in heaven (or some other otherworldly location) awaiting the eschatological moment when they will appear in the world to exercise judgment on God's behalf. In the Parables of Enoch, this is Enoch. In Sibylline Oracles book 5 it is Joshua. In 4 Ezra it is an unnamed descendant of David from the past. Aqiva, we should notice, was roughly contemporary with all three authors of these books. Moreover, in the Parables of Enoch, the Messianic Figure very likely occupies the second of the plural thrones (Dan 7:9), located on earth, and this may well also be the case in 4 Ezra (12:32). In this context Aqiva's opinion that the second throne is for David is easily intelligible, along with the probability

---

13. Joseph Klausner, *The Messianic Idea in Israel from Its Beginnings to the Completion of the Mishnah*, trans. W. F. Stinespring (London: Allen & Unwin, 1956) 460–65. See especially y. Ber. 2:4[5a]; Lam. Rab. 1:51; b. Sanh. 98b.

that Aqiva understood the judgment scene in Daniel 7:9–10 to be located on earth. Meanwhile David has been preserved by God, presumably in heaven. The fact that David unquestionably died (1 Kgs 2:10; cf. Acts 2:29) is evidently not an obstacle to this view, as we can see from the case of Joshua in book 5 of the Sibyllines. It is worth recalling that in precisely this period many people in the eastern part of the empire, including Jews, thought that the allegedly dead emperor Nero was merely in hiding and would return. A returning David would make a good match for a returning Nero.

How did Aqiva reach this identification of Daniel's humanlike figure as King David? There is an obvious exegetical explanation: the Messiah is called David in several messianic prophecies (Jer 30:9; Ezek 34:23–24; 37:24; Hos 3:5), which we have seen some later rabbis thought might refer to the historical David himself. If Aqiva shared what seems to have been the common view of the Danielic figure around 100 CE—that he was a human being who had lived in the past—what more appropriate person than David? The prophecies can thus be understood literally.

That the view attributed to Aqiva in the first of the two baraitot in b. Hagigah 14a fits so well into the period around 100 CE in which 4 Ezra, book 5 of the Sibyllines, and the Parables of Enoch were written is a good argument for the authenticity of the tradition. Normally a baraita in the Bavli is a tradition of Palestinian origin from tannaitic times (which does not prove its authenticity but at least makes it more likely to go back to its named source). Schäfer makes the point that "by no means all baraitot [are] genuine baraitot,"[14] and continues:

> The attribution of the baraita to Aqiva is particularly suspicious here, as the rabbinic approbation of Bar Kokhba, the leader in the Second Jewish Revolt against Rome in 132–35 CE, as the Messiah—whether historical or not—was forever linked to the name of Rabbi Aqiva. Thus it is also no coincidence that Aqiva's proclamation of Bar Kokhba as Messiah was just as emphatically rejected by his colleagues as his enthronement of the Messiah-King David in heaven [y. Ta'an. 4:8(68d)].[15]

Schäfer here assumes that by "David" Aqiva means the Messiah son of David. However, if Aqiva means the historical King David, Schäfer's argument loses its force. Since Aqiva was well known to have proclaimed Bar Kokhba as the

---

14. Schäfer, *Two Gods*, 85.
15. Schäfer, *Two Gods*, 85–86; see also Schäfer, *The Jewish Jesus*, 82.

Messiah, why should a saying be attributed to Aqiva in which he expresses the view that the Messiah will be the historical David, a view incompatible with Aqiva's identification of Bar Kokhba as Messiah? The fact that this saying expresses such an unusual opinion favors its authenticity.

If this saying of Aqiva is authentic, how can it be reconciled with the tradition that Aqiva hailed Bar Kokhba as the Messiah? Our information about Aqiva's involvement in the Second Revolt is so minimal that we probably do not have the means to answer this question. But it is entirely possible that Aqiva had earlier held that the Messiah would be King David, but abandoned this view when he was impressed by the early successes of Bar Kokhba in the war.[16] The only messianic prophecy that we know was applied to Bar Kokhba is Numbers 24:17 ("a star shall come out of Jacob"),[17] which was the basis for the nickname Bar Kokhba, "the son of the star," a wordplay on his real name Shimon bar Kosiva.[18] That prophecy does not specify that the "star" will be a son of David, and it seems likely that Bar Kokhba did not claim Davidic descent. So it is also possible that Aqiva thought he was to play a role in the inauguration of the messianic age different from that of the King-Messiah David. We can only speculate, but Aqiva's support for Bar Kokhba is not a sufficient reason to deny the authenticity of his "throne for David" saying.

To further support the plausibility of the claim that Aqiva identified the Messiah with the historical David, we shall now turn to two Jewish sources outside rabbinic literature that attest such a belief.

Songs of David (Genizah Psalms)

A manuscript from the Cairo Genizah, first published in 1902, contains a number of psalms (two complete, one almost complete, and a portion of another) that were evidently part of a larger collection. They have been called "Songs of David" because they appear to be attributed to David, who speaks of himself in the first person, though the first psalm speaks about him in the third person. David Flusser and Shmuel Safrai argue that they were part of the Qumran library,[19] a view that has been more recently accepted in a qualified way by

---

16. Cf. Klausner, *The Messianic Idea*, 395: "Bar Cochba's great spirit of heroism was sufficient *in itself* to make him Messiah in the eyes of" Aqiva (italics original).

17. Horbury, *Jewish War*, 385, thinks Isa 11:4 may also have been used.

18. On the interpretation of Num 24:17 attributed to Aqiva and its interpretation elsewhere in rabbinic literature, see Richard G. Marks, *The Image of Bar Kokhba in Traditional Jewish Literature* (University Park: Pennsylvania State University Press, 1994) 14–20.

19. David Flusser and Shmuel Safrai, "The Apocryphal Psalms of David," in *Judaism of*

Geert W. Lorein and Eveline van Staalduine-Sulman.[20] While not wishing to be so specific, David Stec concludes that these psalms "were composed in Palestine at about the same time as, or slightly later than, the literature of Qumran."[21] Of particular importance is his careful study of the Hebrew of the psalms, concluding that the language of the psalms "probably point[s] toward a date of composition of about the 1st century CE, and probably not later than the 2nd century."[22] Thus, although the arguments of Ezra Fleischer for a medieval date cannot be completely discounted,[23] we are justified in provisionally treating this text as dating from the late Second Temple or early rabbinic period.

For our present purposes, the interesting feature of these psalms is that they speak in the past tense of the historical David (Songs of David 1), but also in the future tense of a future role that far exceeds what could be said of the historical David. He is called "the root of Jesse" (1:15), a phrase that in Isaiah 11:10 refers to the Davidic Messiah as "a signal to the peoples," and "a light for the nations" (2:8; cf. Isa 42:6). It seems that, as in the Parables of Enoch, the Davidic ruler of Isaiah 11:1–10 is identified with the servant of the Lord in chapters 42–53 of Isaiah. In the Songs of David this identification is assisted by the fact that David is called "David your servant," as in Psalm 89:3 and many other places in the Hebrew Bible.[24] David is portrayed as the universal ruler, supreme over all the kings of the earth forever (1:23; cf. Ps 89:27). Whereas Psalm 89:28–29 promises that David's line will continue forever, in the Songs of David God makes David himself "king of all nations for ever" (1:23). This role is portrayed in very positive terms: he will bring the nations to know and worship the true God (2:8–16). The nations will never again serve idols (2:17–20; 3:18–19). The theme of judgment of nations is not absent (1:24–26) but is not a feature of David's future role, at least in the surviving text. The Songs of David provides another example of the way that a particular selection of biblical prophecies can produce a quite distinctive portrait of the Messiah.

---

the Second Temple Period, vol. 1, *Qumran and Apocalypticism*, by David Flusser, trans. Azzan Yadin (Grand Rapids: Eerdmans, 2007) 258–82.

20. Geert W. Lorein and Eveline van Staalduine-Sulman, "Songs of David," *OTPMNS* 1:257–71, here 259–62. Acknowledging differences from the Qumran scrolls as well as similarities, they suggest that these psalms were inspired by the apocryphal psalms (11Q5) and written in the last phase of the community's existence (262).

21. David Stec, *The Genizah Psalms: A Study of MS 798 of the Antonin Collection*, Cambridge Genizah Studies 5 (Leiden: Brill, 2013) 22.

22. Stec, *The Genizah Psalms*, 145.

23. Stec, *The Genizah Psalms*, 16–21, summarizes and responds to Fleischer's arguments.

24. On this terminology, see Stec, *The Genizah Psalms*, 13.

The Songs of David makes no allusion to Daniel 7, and there is no reason to think that its vision of the Messiah is much like Rabbi Aqiva's, but it does provide substantial evidence that the King-Messiah could be understood to be David himself, fulfilling in the messianic age the role that he accomplished only partially in his reign in the past.

Apocalypse of David

Arguably adopting the same view, but at a much later date is the so-called David Apocalypse, which is preserved in manuscripts of the Hekhalot literature, mostly of Hekhalot Rabbati, though it is an independent composition.[25] Although Anna Maria Schwemer has argued for a date around the time of the New Testament,[26] Schäfer convincingly dates it at "the very end of the Hekhalot tradition[,] due not least to the close relationship with the Third Book of Enoch."[27] Ulrike Hirschfelder's study documents abundantly this relationship with 3 Enoch,[28] whose portrayal of Enoch-Metatron's enthronement in heaven seems to be transferred to David in the Apocalypse of David. Because of the late date of this work, I shall treat it only briefly here. But it is worth noting that Gustaf Dalman thought it was inspired by Rabbi Aqiva's "throne for David" saying.[29]

Before the fall of Jerusalem, Rabbi Ishmael is permitted to see the future troubles of the Jewish people written in heaven but is also told that scheduled troubles are rescinded when people praise God in the synagogues. He then hears a prophecy of the destruction of Jerusalem and the desecration of the temple, including the prediction that "the sons of the king are destined for the death penalty."[30] Asking in despair whether there is any possibility of a "rem-

---

25. The text is in Peter Schäfer, Margarete Schlütter, and Hans-Georg von Mutius, *Synopse zur Hekhalot-Literatur*, TSAJ 2 (Tübingen: Mohr Siebeck, 1981) §§125–26. There is an English translation in Helen Spurling, "Hebrew Visions of Hell and Paradise," *OTPMNS* 1:699–753, here 751–53 (David Apocalypse). For discussion, see Anna Maria Schwemer, "Irdische und himmlische König: Beobachtungen zur sogennanten David-Apokalypse in Hekhalot-Rabbati §§ 122–126," in *Königsherrschaft Gottes um himmlische Kult im Judentum, Urchristentum und in der hellenistischen Welt*, ed. Martin Hengel and Anna Maria Schwemer, WUNT 55 (Tübingen: Mohr Siebeck, 1991) 309–59; Ulrike Hirschfelder, "The Liturgy of the Messiah: The Apocalypse of David in Hekhalot Literature," *Jewish Studies Quarterly* 12 (2005) 148–93; Schäfer, *The Jewish Jesus*, 85–94; Schäfer, *Two Gods*, 89–96.
26. Schwemer, "Irdische und himmlische König."
27. Schäfer, *Two Gods*, 89–96.
28. Hirschfelder, "The Liturgy," 164–66, 172, 174, 178.
29. Gustaf Dalman, *The Words of Jesus*, trans. D. M. Kay (Edinburgh: T&T Clark, 1902) 245.
30. My quotations are from the translation in Spurling, "Hebrew Visions," 751–53.

edy for Israel," Ishmael is taken by the angel Hadraniel to see "the treasuries of the consolations and salvations for Israel." These include a remarkable crown made for King David. He is then shown David in his glory, at the head of a procession of his royal descendants. David ascends to the heavenly temple and sits on a throne "opposite" the throne of God. There he leads the worship of all the heavenly beings and "the kings of the house of David," who proclaim the universal and eternal kingdom of God in scriptural quotations, culminating in the prophecy of the coming of the universal kingdom of the one and only God in Zechariah 14:9.[31]

Is David here portrayed as the Messiah? A point that scholars commenting on this work have not given the attention it probably deserves is that the prophecy of the fall of Jerusalem includes the information that the line of David's descendants will come to an end. The "sons of the king" will be put to death. This surely contributes to Ishmael's distress: the expectation of the Messiah son of David seems to have been canceled. This distress is met by the revelation that David, along with all the kings descended from him, is honored in heaven, where David is crowned and enthroned in near-godlike majesty. But Ishmael is surely not supposed to be content with this revelation of a kind of heavenly rule by David. David's main function seems to be to lead a liturgy that celebrates the absolute lordship of God. Given the earlier revelation that the praise of God in synagogues has power to avert troubles from Israel, it seems likely that this great heavenly liturgy, acknowledging God's kingship, will in some sense lead to the universal acknowledgment of God as king over all the earth (Zech 14:9). Is this the way in which David himself actually fulfills his messianic role? Or will the coming kingdom of God on earth include David's messianic rule on earth?

Whatever precisely is intended, this apocalypse seems to be indicating that the end of the line of David's descendants on earth should not put an end to messianic hope, because David himself, presently enthroned in heaven, will fulfill the messianic role. This medieval Jewish work cannot prove anything about Aqiva's "throne for David" saying, but it probably does represent a later

---

31. Schäfer, *The Jewish Jesus*, rightly affirms the eschatological goal of the narrative, whereas Hirschfelder, "The Liturgy," 177, seems to exclude it, stressing the experience of David's "celestial kingdom" in the corresponding heavenly and earthly liturgies. With the whole heavenly scene, there is a very interesting parallel with Rev 4–5, though not quite in the way that Schäfer, *Two Gods*, 95–96, envisages. See also 1 En. 61:6–13. I am not at all persuaded by the idea suggested by Schäfer, *Two Gods*, 95, "that the Messiah-King David and God . . . will at the end of days merge and become one: the Messiah is God and God is the Messiah."

variation on the idea that David himself, not a descendant, is to be the Messiah. It might also suggest a very speculative possibility: Did Jews at the end of the first century CE think that there were no longer any descendants of David, at least in the direct line of the kings of Judah? Might the belief that David himself would be the Messiah be a solution to that problem? Might Aqiva's endorsement of the non-Davidide Bar Kokhba also be related to such a belief?

The Objections and Alternatives to Aqiva's View

Before attempting to understand the way the other two eminent rabbis, Rabbi Yose the Galilean and Rabbi Eleazar ben Azariah, respond to Rabbi Aqiva in b. Hagigah 14a, it is worth repeating that in Jewish literature of the late Second Temple period the humanlike figure of Daniel 7:13 was not understood as "divine," a kind of second god alongside or even subordinate to the Ancient of Days. In every case for which we have good evidence, this figure was understood to be a human person who had lived on earth and would at the end execute judgment on God's behalf. If depicted in heaven, awaiting that role, he may be expected to be angelic in appearance (as in 1 En. 46:1), shining as all the myriad inhabitants of the heavenly realms were thought to be, but this does not make him a god. Daniel Boyarin's comment that, in the view attributed to Aqiva, "the Son of Man has become incarnate in the Davidic Messiah"[32] is grossly mistaken. Aqiva does not identify a divine figure ("the Son of Man") with David. He interprets Daniel to mean that David simply is the humanlike figure who comes on the clouds of heaven to the Ancient of Days.

It is similarly important to recall that Daniel 7:9–14 does not depict a state of affairs in heaven. It depicts the future moment of final judgment. It is then that the Ancient of Days will take his seat on this throne (as 1 En. 47:3 recognizes). Whether or not the throne is the same throne as the one on which God customarily sits in heaven, in this case "thrones were set in place, and the Ancient of Days took his seat" (Dan 7:9 NIV). In Jewish interpretation of Daniel 7, this moment lies in the future, and there is no reason to suppose that Rabbi Aqiva thought otherwise. He thinks David will, in the future, sit on a second throne. Finally, it is not clear in Daniel 7 whether this judgment takes place in heaven or on earth. Jewish interpretations evidently differed on this point. We do not know what Aqiva thought, but it is not justified simply to take for granted that he thought David will sit beside God's throne in heaven,

---

32. Daniel Boyarin, "Beyond Judaisms: Meṭaṭron and the Divine Polymorphy of Ancient Judaism," *JSJ* 41 (2010) 323–65, here 341.

as Peter Schäfer does, referring to Aqiva's "enthronement of the Messiah-King David in heaven."[33] Both Boyarin and Schäfer, much as they disagree, read Aqiva's saying too much in the light of the Christian view of Jesus seated at the right hand of God in heaven or of the enthronement of Metatron in heaven in 3 Enoch. The Christian view was based primarily on Psalm 110:1, which (at least in the Christian interpretation) indicates a period in which the Messiah is seated with God in heaven, awaiting his future victory. But there is no reason to think Aqiva had Psalm 110 in view at all, while in Daniel 7 there is no indication of a period of enthronement, any more than there is in the Parables of Enoch. In Aqiva's view, the enthronement need not be important for its own sake. It is the corollary of David's participation in the final judgment.

In that case, why does Aqiva's saying provoke Rabbi Yose's shocked response: "Aqiva, how long will you treat the Shekinah as profane (חול)?" He means that Aqiva is placing something profane (the man David) where only God has the right to be.[34] Probably he assumes the scene in Daniel 7:9-10 is set in heaven, where, almost without exception in Jewish tradition, only God sits enthroned. God's throne is the symbol of his uniquely supreme sovereignty over the whole creation.[35] It may well be that Yose has in mind the Christian claim that Jesus is seated at the right hand of God in heaven.[36] From the perspective of Jews who were not Christians, this was one of the most shocking of Christian claims about Jesus.[37]

In place of Aqiva's dangerous opinion, Rabbi Yose proposes a different interpretation of the two thrones in Daniel. (Like Aqiva he assumes there are no more than two, but unlike Aqiva he does not assume that one is for the "one like a son of man.") His interpretation is that "one (throne) was for justice (*din*) and one (throne) was for mercy (*tzedakah*)." This is Peter Schäfer's

---

33. Schäfer, *Two Gods*, 86; cf. Schäfer, *The Jewish Jesus*, 73: "the thrones emplaced in heaven."

34. Boyarin, "Beyond Judaisms," 341, strangely reads this to mean: "The second throne is for a second divine figure (the Shekinah) which Rabbi Akiva identifies as David."

35. Richard Bauckham, "The Throne of God and the Worship of Jesus," in *Jesus and the God of Israel: God Crucified and Other Studies on the New Testament's Christology of Divine Identity* (Grand Rapids: Eerdmans, 2008) 152-81; cf. also Timo Eskola, *Messiah and the Throne: Jewish Merkabah Mysticism and Early Christian Exaltation Discourse*, WUNT 2/142 (Tübingen: Mohr Siebeck, 2001) 65-157.

36. I do not understand why Schäfer, *The Jewish Jesus*, 83, thinks that a concern about this Christian claim requires that the tradition must derive from Babylonia at a late date rather than Palestine at an early date.

37. Note how Acts 7:56-8:1 portrays Paul's opposition to the Christian community as a consequence of Stephen's report of his vision of Jesus at the right hand of God (standing because he has stood up to pronounce judgment).

translation of b. Hagigah 14a, which I quoted above. But, by translating צדקה as "mercy," he is assimilating Yose's words to the pair of divine attributes that more commonly occur in rabbinic literature, where the word for the divine mercy or compassion is רחמים.[38] צדקה means "righteousness,"[39] and Yose is thinking of divine judgment. When God pronounces judgment (דין) on the wicked, he sits on one throne, and when, acting according to his righteousness (צדקה), he declares the righteous innocent, he sits on another.

According to the editor of the two baraitot, Aqiva accepted Yose's rebuke and adopted his interpretation. But when he propounded it himself, he was rebuked by Rabbi Eleazar ben Azariah, who said, "Aqiva, what have you to do with Haggadah? Cease your talk (about the Haggadah), and turn to (the laws concerning) Nega'im and Oholot!" (Nega'im and Oholot are the titles of tractates of the Mishna, referring to the laws dealing with the rather recondite matters of corpse impurity and skin disease.) Interpretation of Daniel is, of course, a matter of haggadah, not halakah. Aqiva is acknowledged to be expert in the latter, and his incompetent interpretation of Daniel shows that he should stick to it!

Eleazar thinks that the assigning of different aspects of God's judgment to two thrones could be understood as making a distinction in the divine and threaten the unity of God. So he proposes that there are not really two thrones at all. Daniel's plural refers to parts of the one throne: the throne itself and the footstool. He cites Isaiah 66:1 to prove that God's throne has both. With Eleazar's concern we come within sight of the famous rabbinic discussions of "two powers in heaven," but it is important to note that a concern with this issue appears only in this second of the two baraitot. Aqiva speaks only of the participation of the man David in God's activity of judgment. He does not think that the "one like a son of man" is some kind of second divine power, an interpretation that is nowhere found in Jewish literature. In response Rabbi Yose objects to this elevation of a human to occupy a throne beside God, which threatens the uniqueness of the divine sovereignty over all things. His interpretation leaves the "one like a son of man" out of consideration. Clearly he cannot occupy a throne in heaven, but Yose's view of the thrones in Daniel 7:9–10 need not affect the traditional view that the humanlike figure of 7:13–14 is a human figure from the past who will play an eschatological role in the future, as Elijah was expected to do. Rabbi Eleazar's view also leaves this view of the "one like a son of man" unaffected.

---

38. Schäfer, *The Jewish Jesus*, 71–72, 286 n. 8; cf. Alan F. Segal, *Two Powers in Heaven: Early Rabbinic Reports about Christianity and Gnosticism*, 2nd ed. (Leiden: Brill, 2002) 48 n. 24.

39. When used of humans, it can mean "charity," but this usage cannot apply to God.

The two baraitot featuring Rabbi Aqiva that an editor has combined into a whole are clearly a separate unit of tradition. This unit actually appears twice in the Bavli: at b. Hagigah 14a and b. Sanhedrin 38b. In both cases it is associated with discussions by later rabbis of passages of scripture that could be understood to speak of two divine powers, but this association is secondary, the work of the editor of this part of the Bavli. In b. Sanhedrin 38b our passage is tacked on to a short discussion of that kind, in which the interpretation of Daniel 7:9 arises (as one of several texts in which God acts in consultation with his council of angels). In b. Hagigah 14a our passage is attached to a quite different discussion, where the interpretation of Daniel 7:9 arises for a quite different reason (the portrayal of God as "ancient," whereas in other texts he is portrayed as a youthful man of war). In both cases the discussion of Daniel 7:9 prompts the editor to raise the question of the plural thrones and to introduce Aqiva's view as a solution to that issue, subsequently superseded by the opinions of Rabbi Yose and Rabbi Eleazar.[40]

The fact that the unit about Aqiva is linked with these other discussions in two different ways shows that it was an independent tradition, in which Aqiva's "throne for David" saying was neither an example of the "two powers" heresy nor designed to respond to that heresy. If we understand it in the context of the Jewish interpretations of Daniel 7 that we have from the late Second Temple period, it is a variation on the common view that a second throne, in a judgment scene set on earth, was occupied by the "one like a son of man," identified as a human born on earth, not a second divinity.

---

40. These opinions may represent a chronological progression, in which Aqiva's view, initially not perceived as objectionable, comes to seem so in the light of Christian claims about Jesus, and in turn Yose's opinion comes to seem dangerous in the light of the "two powers" heresy. The latter is beyond the scope of this book.

CHAPTER 2.10

The Significant Absence of Daniel 7 in the Works of Josephus

JOSEPHUS AND DANIEL

The book of Daniel was of considerable importance to Josephus. After the Torah, it was probably the part of the Jewish scriptures he most esteemed. The influence of Daniel on Josephus has been addressed by a number of Josephus scholars, especially in the 1990s, and can be said to be well established.[1] His treatment of Daniel stands right at the center of the *Antiquities*[2] and occupies a particularly generous amount of space.[3] But, as we shall see, Daniel's prophecies were already important to him in the *War*.

Daniel was important to Josephus for a number of reasons. It has been plausibly argued that, just as he saw himself as a second Jeremiah, counseling submission to the enemy during the siege of Jerusalem and being reviled for

---

1. David Daube, "Typology in Josephus," *JJS* 31 (1980) 18-36; F. F. Bruce, "Josephus and Daniel," in *A Mind for What Matters* (Grand Rapids: Eerdmans, 1990) 19-31 (this essay was first published in 1965); Geza Vermes, "Josephus' Treatment of the Book of Daniel," *JJS* 42 (1991) 149-66; Louis H. Feldman, "Josephus' Portrait of Daniel," *Henoch* 14 (1992) 37-96; Rebecca Gray, *Prophetic Figures in Late Second Temple Jewish Palestine: The Evidence from Josephus* (New York: Oxford University Press, 1993) 35-79; Christopher T. Begg, "Daniel and Josephus: Tracing Connections," in *The Book of Daniel in the Light of New Findings*, ed. A. S. van der Woude, Bibliotheca Ephemeridum Theologicarum Lovaniensium 106 (Leuven: Peeters/Leuven University Press, 1993) 539-45; Steve Mason, "Josephus, Daniel, and the Flavian House," in *Josephus and the History of the Greco-Roman Period: Studies in Memory of Morton Smith*, ed. Fausto Parente and Joseph Sievers, StPB 41 (Leiden: Brill, 1994) 161-91.

2. Mason, "Josephus," 171.

3. Feldman, "Josephus' Portrait," 40-41.

doing so,[4] so he saw himself as a second Daniel. The parallels between Daniel and him are more extensive than those between him and Jeremiah. Like Daniel, Josephus found himself, a similarly eminent member of the Jewish elite, in exile at the capital of the empire that had destroyed Jerusalem and the temple and ravaged his homeland. Like Daniel, he lived under the patronage of gentile emperors. Daniel provided a model for remaining a faithful Jew in such circumstances, loyal to his God and the Torah while also serving a pagan power, living peaceably with the non-Jewish elite without betraying his people. In the scriptural stories about Daniel, Josephus evidently saw his own situation, gifts, and virtues, as well as the dangers of such a situation and the skills required to negotiate them. He also saw the providence of God at work in the events of his life as it was in the events of Daniel's life.[5]

Above all and of most relevance to the argument of this chapter, Josephus saw himself as a prophet like Daniel. Unlike the book of Daniel, but like other Jews of his time, Josephus calls Daniel a prophet (*Ant.* 10.246, 249, 269) and devotes more space in the *Antiquities* to his prophecies than to those of Isaiah or Jeremiah. He saw some of them being fulfilled in the events of his own time. He considered Daniel superior to other prophets because he predicted the exact times when his prophecies would be fulfilled.[6] Daniel also foresaw the succession of the world empires under God's sovereign control, and his prophecies were given to kings as well as recorded for posterity.

Josephus saw himself as a prophet (while not using the word προφήτης),[7] skilled and inspired in the interpretation of dreams (as Daniel was) and of scriptural prophecies. The prophecy for which he became famous was delivered, not to the people, but to the Roman general Vespasian, who he predicted would become emperor. Daniel provided Josephus with a model and inspiration for his own vocation as a prophet and also a guide to the interpretation of history in his own work as a historian.[8]

---

4. Daube, "Typology"; Gray, *Prophetic Figures*, 72–74; Shaye J. D. Cohen, "Josephus, Jeremiah, and Polybius," *History and Theory* 21 (1982) 366–81, here 367–68, 371–77.

5. On these parallels, see Feldman, "Josephus' Portrait"; Gray, *Prophetic Figures*, 74–77; Begg, "Daniel and Josephus."

6. Josephus attributes this characteristic to his own prophetic power, in a minor way, when he claims that he accurately predicted that the siege of Jotapata would last exactly forty-seven days (*War* 3.406–407).

7. On Josephus's terminology for prophets and prophecy, see Gray, *Prophetic Figures*, 23–26, 37.

8. For a more detailed study, with many important insights, see Mason, "Josephus."

HISTORY AND PROPHECY

The key message of the book of Daniel is that the great empires rule by God's will alone. God alone is sovereign, and he gives sovereignty to whom he will. He may remove it in an instant, as he did in the case of Belshazzar. He may humiliate arrogant rulers until they acknowledge his sovereignty, as he did in the case of Nebuchadnezzar. All earthly rule is unstable; only God's rule endures eternally. In the end, all the pagan empires will perish and God will give sovereignty to his own people. All this has been decreed and announced in prophecies.

This message accorded well with Josephus's (and the general Jewish) belief that God oversees all earthly events, punishing the wicked and rewarding the righteous. But, of all the prophets, Daniel applies this the most precisely to the succession of the world empires. Already in the *War* Josephus echoes this Danielic theme when he writes:

> From every corner of the world fortune had passed to the Romans, and God, who transferred dominion from one nation to another, was now presiding over Italy. (*War* 5.367)[9]

The impact of the successive empires of the gentiles on the history of the Jewish people was a major theme of Josephus's account in the *Antiquities*. Josephus was consistently concerned to present the history of his own people as taking place on the stage of the history of the great nations, and to show the God of Israel to be no merely national deity but the Lord of history who governs all the nations with justice, while reserving Israel for his special favor. The important role of prophecy in his historical writing is to demonstrate this universal sovereignty of God. The course of history is predicted by Moses, Balaam, Isaiah, Ezekiel, and especially Daniel, partly because the dreams and visions in the book of Daniel chart the sequence of rulers and events, with detail and accuracy, down to Josephus's own time and beyond, as he believed. If his account of himself in the *War* is to be credited, during the Jewish War itself Josephus came to see how the catastrophic events of the revolt, the fall of Jerusalem and the destruction of the temple, fitted the pattern of the history of the Jews in relation to the great empires and also were specifically predicted in prophecy. This also had implications for the future, of which Josephus gives no indication in the *War* and only hints in the *Antiquities*, but the hints are

---

9. Translations are from Josephus, *The Jewish War*, trans. Martin Hammond (Oxford: Oxford University Press, 2017).

sufficient to provide at least a minimal indication of what he thought to be the divine purpose for the Jewish nation and the Roman Empire.

In such a context, we should expect chapter 7 of Daniel to have been important for Josephus. Our task in this chapter will be to establish whether that was indeed the case, but because Josephus, writing for a gentile audience, often leaves his allusions to scriptural prophecies obscure, we shall have to consider Daniel 7 in a wider context of prophecies Josephus took to refer to his own time and to the future.

JOSEPHUS AT JOTAPATA

In 67 CE the Galilean town of Jotapata, which Josephus, as the general of the Jewish forces in Galilee, was defending, fell to the army of the Roman general Vespasian. While much of the population was massacred, Josephus hid with others in a cave. Here, according to his own account, he reached the decision to surrender to Vespasian that determined the whole future course of his life. He

> found himself reliving those dreams he had at night, in which God had forewarned him of the disasters in store for the Jews and foretold the future of the Roman principate. The interpretation of dreams was one of his skills, and he was adept at deducing the true meaning of ambiguous divine communications: and as a priest himself descended from a line of priests, he was familiar with the prophecies in the sacred books. At that critical moment all this came clear to him in a flash of inspiration, and, drawing further on the terrifying images of his recent dreams, he offered up a prayer to God under his breath. "Since it is your will," he prayed, "to bring to its knees the Jewish nation which you created, since all good fortune [ἡ τύχη πᾶσα][10] has now passed over to the Romans, and since you have singled out my spirit to foretell what is to come, I now choose to surrender myself to the Romans, and to live: but I call you to witness that I go, not as a traitor, but as your servant." (*War* 3.351–354)

Here Josephus is unmistakably engaged in defending himself against the accusation of treachery that was not unnaturally directed against him after his

---

10. Josephus uses the term τύχη, which in the histories of Polybius has the sense of impersonal fate, as more or less equivalent to the providential activity of the God of Israel, which he calls πρόνοια. See Gray, *Prophetic Figures*, 38–41; Tessa Rajak, *Josephus: The Historian and His Society*, 2nd ed. (London: Duckworth, 2002) 101.

defection to the Roman side in the war.[11] This apologetic motif does not necessarily mean that his account may not reflect what he thought at the time. The decision to surrender was, of course, a decision to save his life, but it is not unlikely that this rather obvious motivation (open to interpretation as cowardice) was accompanied by a conviction that had already been growing in his mind that it was God's will that the Romans should win the war. At least in retrospect he understood this revelation as his prophetic vocation to predict the future.

It is hardly surprising that Josephus had had nightmares, but it is worth noticing that Daniel's dreams about the succession of the empires were also terrifying (Dan 7:15, 28; cf. 8:27). As a skilled interpreter of dreams, like Daniel, Josephus found meaning in the vivid images he saw in his dreams. But (since there can be no other reason for referring to his close knowledge of scriptural prophecies) the dreams seem to have come together with "prophecies in the sacred books" to lead him to the conclusion that God had determined to favor the Romans and to let his own people suffer defeat. Rebecca Gray argues that Josephus means he was aided by scriptural prophecies in his interpretation of his symbolic dreams.[12] Whatever the precise relationship between the dreams and the prophecies, evidently both came into play.

As well as predicting "the disasters in store for the Jews," Josephus's dreams—and presumably also the prophecies—"foretold the future of the Roman principate" (*War* 3.351). We learn more precisely what this means when Josephus eventually gets to speak to Vespasian. He tells him:

> I am come to tell you of your greater destiny. . . . You, Vespasian, will be Caesar and emperor, both you and your son here with us. . . . You, Caesar, are master not only of me, but of all land and sea and the whole human race. (3.401–402)

This specific prediction may have changed Josephus's life and certainly ensured for him a kind of fame. Whether he actually did make the prediction at this early date (rather than two years later, when the Flavians were obviously aspiring to control of the empire and other omens were bruited)[13] has been doubted,[14] but it would have been a brilliant strategy for ingratiating

---

11. Rajak, *Josephus*, 41–44. Both Gray and Rajak reject the view that Josephus's narrative is intended as propaganda for the Flavian dynasty.

12. Gray, *Prophetic Figures*, 52–53, 69–70.

13. William den Hollander, *Josephus, the Emperors, and the City of Rome: From Hostage to Historian*, AGJU 86 (Leiden: Brill, 2014) 94–100.

14. Rajak, *Josephus*, 187, notes the various views, as does Hollander, *Josephus*, 94–96.

himself, and the risk of it proving a false prophecy was surely, in the circumstances, worth taking. It is worth considering whether, in addition to this kind of self-interested motive, Josephus may not have convinced himself that the true interpretation of some scriptural prophecy indicated that Vespasian would become emperor.

The reference to "the prophecies in the sacred books" need not imply that more than one prophecy aided Josephus in interpreting his dreams.[15] It could be that Josephus points to his broad knowledge of such prophecies as the basis on which he was able to see the specific relevance of one prophecy in this case. There could have been several prophecies that elucidated the general content of his dreams ("the disasters in store for the Jews" and "the future of the Roman principate" [*War* 3.351]), but was there one in particular that concerned the future ascendancy of Vespasian? Not surprisingly, many scholars have connected this passage with one from book 6 of the *War* where Josephus refers to an "ambiguous oracle" that he, differing from the rebels, took to predict that Vespasian would become ruler of the world. But there is no reason why he should have had the same prophecy in mind in both cases.[16] The "ambiguous oracle" evidently spoke of a ruler who would come from Judea, and Josephus's rather forced interpretation seems required because the prophecy had been of great importance to the rebels (6.312–313). In the present case the "disasters in store for the Jews," as well as Vespasian's universal empire, seem to have been involved. I shall argue that two different prophecies are likely in view in the two passages. Finally, at this point we should note that some scholars have appealed to Daniel 7 in one or both of these cases.[17] For this reason, our inquiry into the identity of these prophecies needs to be pursued in some detail.

THE AMBIGUOUS ORACLE

We shall begin with the "ambiguous oracle" and return later to the prediction that Josephus claims to have made to Vespasian at Jotapata. Of the former he writes:

> But what more than anything else incited them to go to war was an ambiguous oracle also found in their holy scriptures, which revealed that at that

---

15. As Gray, *Prophetic Figures*, 70, supposes.
16. Gray, *Prophetic Figures*, 70, and Rajak, *Josephus*, 191, both distinguish the two.
17. E.g., Roger T. Beckwith, *Calendar and Chronology, Jewish and Christian*, AGJU 33 (Leiden: Brill, 1996) 266–67; Mason, "Josephus," 185–86.

time someone from their country would become ruler of the world. They took this to mean someone of their own race, and many of their scholars followed this wrong path of interpretation. In fact the oracle was pointing to the principate of Vespasian, who was in Judaea when he was proclaimed emperor. (*War* 6.312–313)

This famous passage comes at the conclusion of a series of portents or warning signs from God that presaged the destruction of the city and the temple (6.288–315). In Josephus's view, these were culpably ignored by the revolutionary leaders and the people they influenced or, worse, they were actually misinterpreted as indications that the revolt would succeed. They show that God watches over human affairs and provides signs that point people toward salvation, but the folly of the people themselves brings self-inflected destruction (6.310). Josephus is interested in vindicating the ways of God in this cataclysmic episode in Jewish history, as well as condemning the revolutionaries and the people they misled. At the same time, as someone skilled in understanding prophecies and portents, Josephus is engaged in showing that his own interpretation of the destruction of the city and the temple as God's judgment was justified all along. So, in referring to the "ambiguous oracle" (χρησμὸς ἀμφίβολος), Josephus recalls his claim to be "adept at deducing the true meaning of ambiguous divine communications [τὰ ἀμφιβόλως ὑπὸ τοῦ θείου λεγόμενα]" and, as a priest, "familiar with the prophecies in the sacred books" (3.352).

So this is not, as sometimes supposed, a passage of pro-Flavian propaganda, designed to show that Vespasian's rise to power was predicted in Jewish prophecy. Rather, Josephus is at the same time justifying both God and himself. God is not to blame for disaster because he gives warnings. The revolutionaries are to blame because they ignored or misunderstood the warnings. Josephus, with his special insight into the meanings of portents and prophecies, truly understood and can explain the ways of God.

The view that Josephus intended the passage to demonstrate divine approval for the Flavian dynasty has been encouraged by the closely parallel passages in the Roman historians Tacitus (*Hist.* 5.13) and Suetonius (*Vesp.* 4.5). But the verbal resemblances between these passages and Josephus make it very probable that they are dependent on Josephus.[18] There is nothing improbable in the idea that Tacitus read Josephus (while Suetonius probably depended on Tacitus). As Tessa Rajak says, at the end of Josephus's list of portents and

---

18. Mason, "Josephus," 185–87; Rajak, *Josephus*, 193–94.

prophecies "the reader's mind will remain with the delusions of the rebels and with the Temple in flames, not with Flavian claims. Josephus invokes prophecy not for Vespasian's sake, but because he is dealing with a grave moment in Jewish history. What is said about Vespasian plays a minor role. Only later was the motif transferred out of its Judaean context into one of Roman imperial history, and for that Josephus was scarcely responsible."[19]

If Josephus was right about the special importance of this particular "ambiguous oracle" in actually leading to the revolt in the first place, then it was especially important for him to be able to provide an alternative and true interpretation of it. He is not going to dismiss scriptural prophecies, as he claims some of the rebels did (*War* 4.385). It is very notable that this is the only place in the writings of Josephus in which he admits that there was what we would call "messianism" based on scripture among the Jews. Only here does he refer to a future Jewish ruler predicted in prophecy. In general he does not want to give gentiles any reason to suppose that the revolt had any roots in the Jewish scriptures, and so he avoids speaking even of alleged scriptural justifications for the actions of the rebels. That in this case alone he does refer to such a scriptural prophecy must be because it really was important in the ideology of the revolt, and so it was also very important for him to be able to refute the general interpretation. He even admits that many of "the wise" among the Jews—people skilled like him in scriptural interpretation—agreed with the rebels' interpretation of this prophecy. He does not quote the text or argue for his interpretation of it, since he did not expect gentiles to be interested in or to be able to follow a Jewish exegetical discussion, but we should not doubt that he could have propounded the kind of expert exegetical deductions that we find, for example, in the Qumran pesharim. He had been trained to do so and is very likely to have had to do so in this case in discussion with other Jews. So he is engaged here in more than just "rhetorical sleight of hand."[20]

For our purposes the most important issue is the identity of the oracle.[21] Josephus says clearly that it was in the Jewish scriptures.[22] There are two requirements that a plausible candidate must meet. First, the oracle must be one

---

19. Rajak, *Josephus*, 194.
20. Mason, "Josephus," 186.
21. N. T. Wright, *The New Testament and the People of God*, Christian Origins and the Question of God 1 (London: SPCK, 1992) 312–13, comments, "If there is one thing I wish Josephus had added to his entire corpus, it is the footnote to this text which would have told us for sure which biblical passage he had in mind"!
22. Elsewhere in the *War* Josephus uses χρησμός to refer to predictions by the biblical prophets (4.386; 6.109).

that the revolutionaries could interpret as predicting that a Jewish man would become ruler of the world and that Josephus could apply to Vespasian because, though not Jewish, he was in Judea when he was proclaimed emperor.[23] The second requirement is that the oracle should in some way indicate that this would happen "at that time" (κατὰ τὸν καιρὸν ἐκεῖνον).

The first requirement is convincingly met by Balaam's oracle in Numbers 24:17–19:

> A star shall come out of Jacob,
>   and a scepter shall rise out of Israel.
> ....
> One out of Jacob shall rule. (24:17b, 19a)

The obvious reference is to a ruler of Israelite descent, but Josephus took "Jacob" and "Israel" to refer to the land of Israel.[24] If this interpretation seems forced, it is no more so than many an actualizing of biblical prophecy in the Jewish literature of this period.

The oracle was well known: it is quoted several times in the Qumran scrolls (1QM xi 6–7; CD 7:19–21; 4Q175 [4QTest] i 9–13; 1QSb v 27–28),[25] and it inspired the supporters of Bar Kokhba ("the son of the star") in the Second Jewish Revolt (y. Ta'an. 68d [49]).[26] In chapter 2.4 we have seen that there is probably an allusion to Number 24:17, understood messianically, in Sibylline Oracles 5:155–159. A messianic interpretation is already attested in the OG version of Numbers 24:17, which reads "man" (ἄνθρωπος) rather than "scepter."[27] Philo twice quotes Numbers 24:7 (*Mos.* 1.297; *Praem.* 95),[28] which, in the OG

---

23. Vespasian was acclaimed emperor by the legions first in Alexandria, then in Judea.

24. Among those who take this view is Antti Laato, *A Star Is Rising: The Historical Development of the Old Testament Royal Ideology and the Rise of the Jewish Messianic Expectations* (Atlanta: Scholars Press, 1997) 357.

25. In at least the last three of these four, the interpretation is messianic; whether this is true in the case of the first is disputed. For a detailed study, see Libor Marek, *A Star from Jacob, a Sceptre from Israel: Balaam's Oracle as Rewritten Scripture in the Dead Sea Scrolls*, Hebrew Bible Monographs 88 (Sheffield: Sheffield Phoenix, 2020).

26. See Hillel I. Newman, "Stars of the Messiah," in *Tradition, Transmission, and Transformation from Second Temple Literature through Judaism and Christianity in Late Antiquity*, ed. Menahem Kister et al. (Leiden: Brill, 2015) 272–303, here 284–94.

27. Thomas Scott Caulley, "Balaam's 'Star' Oracle in Jewish and Christian Prophetic Tradition," *ResQ* 56 (2014) 28–40, here 29–31; William Horbury, *Messianism among Jews and Christians: Twelve Biblical and Historical Studies* (London: T&T Clark, 2003) 144–48.

28. In *Praem.* 95, Philo may be alluding to both Num 24:7 and 24:17–24.

The Significant Absence of Daniel 7 in the Works of Josephus · 2.10

unlike the MT, is given a very similar sense to 24:17 ("a man shall come forth from his [Israel's] offspring, and will rule over many nations").[29] The oracle probably had special prestige as a very ancient one and one that is found in the Torah.

That the predicted ruler will rule "the world" (τῆς οἰκουμένης), as Josephus says, could be deduced from the text in several ways. It could be correlated with related texts, especially Genesis 49:10, which shares the keyword "scepter" and speaks of "the obedience of the peoples" (cf. 1QSb v 27–29). The Onqelos Targum takes "all the sons of Seth" (Num 24:17) to refer to Seth the son of Adam and thus to mean "all humanity," since all humans since the flood descend from Seth. The enigmatic "city" (Num 24:19: "Ir" in NRSV) could plausibly be taken to be Rome (as in the Fragment Targum).[30] Edom (24:18) could be taken to represent the Roman Empire, as it was by the rabbis. Finally, if the whole of 24:17–24 is read as a unit related to the "star," the range of various nations named could seem to represent the whole world.

There is no other biblical text, to my knowledge, that could plausibly be interpreted both in the way that Josephus says the revolutionaries understood it and in the way that he says he did.[31] It is also worth noticing that when Josephus writes about Balaam's prophecies in the *Antiquities*, he does not give details of the final oracle (Num 24:16–24), but he does say that it contains predictions that have been fulfilled within Josephus's own memory (*Ant.* 4.125). It is not easy to see what these could be unless Josephus is referring to his own interpretation of the "ambiguous oracle."

Those who reject this identification of the oracle claim that it does not meet our second requirement: that the prophecy to which Josephus refers was to be fulfilled "at that time."[32] We should first note that Balaam's oracle does not lack some indications of when it would be fulfilled. In Numbers 24:16 Balaam indicates that the figure he foresees belongs to the distant future. In

---

29. The Targums attest a similar interpretation.

30. For the interpretation of this passage in the Targums, see Samson H. Levey, *The Messiah: An Aramaic Interpretation: The Messianic Exegesis of the Targums*, Monographs of the Hebrew Union College 11 (Cincinnati: Hebrew Union College, 1974) 20–27.

31. Cf. Martin Hengel, *The Zealots*, trans. David Smith (Edinburgh: T&T Clark, 1989) 240: "A high degree of probability can be obtained with Num 24.17." However, Hengel is mistaken in treating Tacitus and Suetonius as evidence for the oracle independent of Josephus.

32. E.g., Bruce, "Josephus and Daniel," 29. For this reason Bruce thinks that Num 24:17 could be the oracle to which Tacitus and Suetonius refer, but that "it must have come to be interpreted with the help of Daniel's oracle of the seventy heptads," which could supply the chronological precision to which Josephus refers with the phrase "at that time."

Numbers 24:14 he uses the phrase "at the end of days": the revolutionaries in 66 CE, along with many of their Jewish contemporaries, would certainly have thought that they were living in the climactic days of history to which that phrase refers. Greater precision could be found in Numbers 24:24. Since the Kittim were generally understood in the late Second Temple period to be the Romans (as in Dan 11:30), this prophecy would most obviously be understood to refer to the Roman conquest of Syria (= Asshur) and Judea (= Eber?) in 64–63 BCE. Would this be sufficient to account for Josephus's phrase "at that time"? If not, in the next section we shall discover another way in which the fulfillment of the oracle in Numbers 24:17 could have been expected to occur in precisely 66 CE.

The Ambiguous Oracle and the Comet

Josephus's account of the "ambiguous oracle" concludes his list of portents and prophecies that in his view presaged the destruction of the city and the temple. Scholars have not previously noticed the way in which this conclusion relates to the first of the series of portents. Because the oracle "more than anything else incited them to go to war" (*War* 6.312), chronologically it brings the list full circle, returning to the period immediately before the outbreak of the war when the first of the portents occurred. But the connection is more than chronological, as we shall see.

Josephus describes the first portent in this way (with my own translation):

> τοῦτο μὲν ὅτε ὑπὲρ τὴν πόλιν ἄστρον ἔστη ῥομφαίᾳ παραπλήσιον καὶ παρατείνας ἐπ' ἐνιαυτὸν κομήτης. (*War* 6.289)

> So it was when a star resembling a sword stood over the city, that is to say, a comet that remained for a year.

Previous translations distinguish two objects: a star and a comet. But in that case the sentence is grammatically awkward. The last five words are left hanging without a main verb, as in Thackeray's translation: "a star, resembling a sword, stood over the city, and a comet which continued for a year." Such a translation has also caused unnecessary difficulties in grasping what Josephus meant. The solution is to understand καὶ as epexegetical, meaning "that is to say."[33] A comet was considered a kind of star, but "comet" is the more precise

---

33. I am grateful to Simon Gathercole for pointing this out to me. It is worth noting that

term, and so it is intelligible that Josephus refers to a star and then specifies it further as a comet.

Josephus saw this comet himself, and so it is at first sight somewhat problematic that he exaggerates to the extent of saying that it remained over Jerusalem for a whole year. Comets are never visible to the naked eye for such a long period.[34] We know that Halley's Comet appeared in 66 CE. From Chinese records and from observations of Halley's comet in 1986, we can tell that in 66 it would have been visible for about seventy-one days from late January until early April or perhaps a little longer.[35] But from Chinese observations we also know that another comet appeared in 65, visible from the end of July until late September.[36] People could well have supposed that the comet seen in 65 reappeared early in 66. It could then have seemed that this comet's appearances lasted for much of a year.[37]

The appearance of a comet for such an extended period must have made a very strong impression on the people of Jerusalem. Since, unlike the fixed stars, comets appeared unpredictably, most people in the ancient world took them seriously as omens provided by the gods or by God. But they were as ambiguous as oracles. The famous comet that appeared after the death of Julius Caesar in 44 BCE was given at least four interpretations.[38] Though comets

---

this is evidently how the passage was understood in the paraphrastic Latin translation of Josephus's *War* known as Pseudo-Hegesippus: "For nearly a year a comet blazed above the temple itself. It bore a certain resemblance to a suspended sword" (translation from John T. Ramsey, *A Descriptive Catalogue of Greco-Roman Comets from 500 B.C. to A.D. 400*, Syllecta Classica 17 [Iowa City: The Classics Department at the University of Iowa, 2006] 155).

34. "The longest reliably attested period during which a comet has been visible to the naked eye is 260 days, a record set by the comet of 1811" (Ramsey, *A Descriptive Catalogue*, 150).

35. Ramsey, *A Descriptive Catalogue*, 148–50.

36. Ramsey, *A Descriptive Catalogue*, 150–51; John Williams, *Observations of Comets from 611 B.C. to A.D. 1640 Extracted from the Chinese Annals* (Hornchurch, Essex: Science and Technology Publishers, 1871) 12.

37. Ramsey, *A Descriptive Catalogue*, 165–67, provides a detailed reconstruction of the movements of the two comets as they would have been observed from Jerusalem in 65–66. In each case there was about a month in which the comet could be seen for nearly the whole night. The comet of 60 CE, which was visible for about 135 days, is said by Seneca (*Nat.* 7.21.3–4), a close observer of comets, to have appeared for six months.

38. Ramsey, *A Descriptive Catalogue*, 108. This comet was especially well known because it appeared on a denarius coin of Augustus: see Donald K. Yeomans, *Comets: A Chronological History of Observation, Science, Myth, and Folklore* (New York: Wiley, 1991) 13; Rafael Dy-Liacco, "Comet Halley of A.D. 66 and the Beast That Rises Out of the Sea (Revelation Ch. 13)," Academia.edu, 3–6, https://www.academia.edu/12856350/Comet_Halley_of_A_D_66_and_the_Beast_that_Rises_Out_of_the_Sea_Revelation_Ch_13_ (accessed January 31, 2022).

were generally thought to presage disaster of some sort, this was not always the case. After all, a change of political regime, a common interpretation of comets, could be bad news for some but good news for others.

A popular way of interpreting comets was to identify what they resembled. Pliny the Elder compiled a catalogue of types of comets, based on what they resembled (*Nat.* 2.22.89). The fact that he gives some of them Greek names suggests he derived them from a Greek source. To one category he gives the name Xiphias, derived from one of the Greek words for a sword: ξίφος. It has sometimes been claimed that when Josephus says that the comet of 66 resembled a sword, he is putting it into this category.[39] But the word Josephus uses is ῥομφαία. Whereas ξίφος refers to a two-edged dagger, ῥομφαία refers to a broad sword with one cutting edge.[40] Josephus's usage of the two words elsewhere seems to respect this difference. So it seems likely that he made his own observation of the shape of the comet. By the time he wrote the *War*, he thought it portended disaster—a war that would lead to the destruction of Jerusalem and its temple. Some people at the time may have thought this, in line with the prophecy of Jesus son of Ananias, who was continually announcing Jerusalem's doom (*War* 6.300–309). On the other hand, an impending war could be the messianic war in which Rome would be defeated and God's people liberated.

There is a good deal of subjectivity involved in recognizing the shape of a comet, especially as the appearance of a comet changes during its course. A comet that looked to some like a sword could very well look to others like a scepter. (An ancient royal scepter was a staff with a ball or similar decorated shape at the end.) To those familiar with Balaam's oracle (Num 24:17), it could mean that the time had arrived for the prophecy's fulfillment.[41] The scepter-shaped star had appeared in the sky, heralding the appearance on earth of the Israelite leader who was to rule the earth. This is surely how the revolutionaries knew it was "at that time" that the "ambiguous oracle" would be fulfilled (*War* 6.313). It was the oracle in combination with the unusually impressive comet that "more than anything else incited them to war" (6.132). The messianic expectation with which the war began would have seemed for a while to find its fulfillment in the figure of Menahem son of Judas, whom

---

39. Cf. Ramsey, *A Descriptive Catalogue*, 151.

40. Ramsey, *A Descriptive Catalogue*, 152, points out the difference, but I do not see the need for his further speculation about the significance of ῥομφαία.

41. Newman, "Stars of the Messiah," 277–84, finds eschatological significance in the coincidence of the star/comet with Passover, but surprisingly misses the connection with Num 24:17, to which he does refer in connection with Bar Kokhba (284).

Josephus clearly indicates claimed to be a king (2.433–434). So, when we put the "ambiguous oracle" together with the comet, we need look no further than Numbers 24:17 for the source of the prophecy.

THE AMBIGUOUS ORACLE AND DANIEL 7

Other scholars have found the source of the ambiguous oracle in Daniel 7. The identification of the oracle as Daniel 7:13–14 has been advocated quite frequently in the past,[42] and most recently by Roger Beckwith.[43] Beckwith's main reasons are that the figure described by Daniel is given universal dominion and that the "ambiguous oracle" was, according to Josephus, to be fulfilled at a stated time. Beckwith links this information, as others have done, with Josephus's comment in the *Antiquities* that Daniel not only predicted future events but also fixed the time when they would be fulfilled (10.267). Beckwith admits that the time for the fulfillment of Daniel 7:13–14 is given only rather generally: within the period of the fourth world empire, which the revolutionaries would have taken to be Rome. So Beckwith suggests that Daniel 7:13–14 could have been connected with the prophecy of the seventy weeks (Dan 9:24–27) and Daniel's humanlike figure identified with "the anointed one, the prince" of Daniel 9:25.[44] We shall return shortly to this latter prophecy, but a decisive objection to identifying the "ambiguous oracle" as Daniel 7:13–14 is that the dominion given to the humanlike figure is rather emphatically said to be everlasting. As we shall see, Josephus certainly did not regard the Roman Empire as destined to last forever.

Steve Mason, who makes this objection, proposes instead that Josephus is referring to the vision of the fourth beast in Daniel 7:3–8. He argues that Josephus, writing after 70 CE, would have identified the tenth horn of this beast as Vespasian. Counting from Julius Caesar, Vespasian was the tenth emperor. The three uprooted horns would be Galba, Otto, and Vitellius, uprooted to make way for Vespasian, the tenth. The additional "little horn" may then be Titus or Domitian.[45] According to Mason, "it is hard to see how a Jew living after 70 could have read this prophecy and *not* identified Vespasian as the tenth horn of the vision." Perhaps, though we should notice that the vision

42. See the list of scholars who have taken this view in Hengel, *The Zealots*, 238 n. 48.
43. Beckwith, *Calendar and Chronology*, 266–67; Roger T. Beckwith, *Calendar, Chronology and Worship: Studies in Ancient Judaism and Early Christianity*, AGJU 61 (Leiden: Brill, 2005) 141.
44. Beckwith, *Calendar and Chronology*, 266–67.
45. Mason, "Josephus," 185–86.

attributes no particular importance to the tenth horn: the focus is rather on the "little horn," who blasphemes the God of Israel and makes war on the people of Israel (Dan 7:21, 25).

However, there is a rather obvious reason why Daniel 7:3-8 cannot be Josephus's "ambiguous oracle": it is not ambiguous. Any Jewish interpreter would have understood the horns of this beast to be Roman emperors (cf. 4 Ezra 12:10-16). Nothing distinguishes the tenth horn from its predecessors. There is no way that the Jewish revolutionaries could have taken it to symbolize a Jewish ruler of the world. Mason's response to this difficulty is that Josephus "is engaging once again in rhetorical sleight of hand."[46] Josephus, he thinks, is merely *claiming* that the revolutionaries misinterpreted a biblical prophecy. But it is highly unlikely that Josephus has taken a prophecy that he himself understood to refer to Vespasian and pretended that it was ambiguous, such that the revolutionaries could interpret it in such an extremely implausible way, though he knew that actually they made no use of it at all. If that were the case, and if Josephus, as Mason says, "did not expect his Roman readers to look up the scripture,"[47] why need he have had an actual prophecy in mind at all? But we have no need to resort to this kind of explanation, given that Numbers 24:17, in conjunction with the comet, fits precisely what Josephus says about the oracle.

The Interpretation of Daniel's Seventy Heptads

The candidate for the "ambiguous oracle" we have not yet discussed is Daniel 9:26, which in the Hebrew text predicts that "the troops of the prince who is to come will destroy the city and the sanctuary." (OG: "a king of nations will demolish the city and the sanctuary along with the anointed one"; Theodotion: "it/he will destroy the city and the sanctuary along with the leader who is to come" [NETS].) It is easy to see how Josephus could have seen a reference to Vespasian here, but not easy to see how the rebels could have found a reference to a Jewish ruler. However, it is possible that the ambiguity attached to the "anointed prince" of 9:25. The main reason for identifying this passage as the "ambiguous oracle" is its chronological precision.[48] The main difficulty is that,

---

46. Mason, "Josephus," 186.
47. Mason, "Josephus," 186.
48. E.g., Lester L. Grabbe, "The 70-Week Prophecy (Daniel 9:24-27) in Early Jewish Interpretation," in *The Quest for Context and Meaning: Studies in Biblical Intertextuality in Honor of James A. Sanders*, ed. Craig A. Evans and Shemaryahu Talmon, Biblical Interpre-

if the "anointed prince" of 9:25 is the messianic king, there is no indication that he will rule the world. For this reason, those who associate the "ambiguous oracle" with this passage claim that it must have been connected with another prophecy, such as Genesis 49:10,[49] Daniel 7:13–14,[50] or Daniel 2:35, 44–45,[51] despite the fact that none of these could conceivably have been applied to Vespasian by Josephus.

Josephus clearly refers to a single oracle (χρησμός), not a combination of oracles or a book of prophecies (such as the book of Daniel).[52] Once again, we find that Numbers 24:17 fits the description better than any of the alternatives. But if Daniel 9:26 was not the "ambiguous oracle," it is very plausibly a passage that helped Josephus, in the cave at Jotapata, produce his original prediction that Vespasian was to become emperor. It is very likely that many people involved in the revolt thought about Daniel's prophecy of the seventy weeks, which could be calculated to end around this time,[53] and Josephus would have been among them. When he began to think that in his dreams God "had forewarned him of the disasters in store for the Jews," his mind could have turned to the obscure predictions of Daniel 9:24–27, which undoubtedly describe "disasters in store for the Jews." It now looked clear to Josephus that Vespasian, having effectively won the war in Galilee, would go on to capture Jerusalem. It looked like he was the "prince" (נגיד) of Daniel 9:26, whose troops would "destroy the city and the sanctuary." But Vespasian was not the emperor. So, in Josephus's interpretation of the text, Daniel 9:26 became a prophecy that he would *become* a "prince" (i.e., Roman emperor). The fact that Josephus's prophecy of Vespasian's accession to the principate was self-serving need not mean that he was not genuinely persuaded that it was soundly based on Daniel's predictions.

For Josephus, this may have become the key to a correct interpretation of the prophecy of the seventy weeks as a whole. There is good evidence for this. In the first place, in his treatment of Daniel in the *Antiquities*, while there is no explicit reference to Daniel 9, there are two probable allusions to it. One

---

tation 28 (Leiden: Brill, 1997) 595–611, here 607: "The only passage in the Old Testament likely to have been interpreted as a specific indication of time is Daniel 9."

49. Bruce, "Josephus and Daniel," 28–29. He thinks Josephus could also have had Num 24:17 in mind.

50. Beckwith, *Calendar and Chronology*, 266–67.

51. Wright, *The New Testament*, 312–14. He thinks that Dan 7 is also "implied by association."

52. Contrast *War* 4.386, where he refers to "the oracles [χρησμούς] of the prophets," probably referring to similar predictions made by both Jeremiah and Ezekiel.

53. Beckwith, *Calendar and Chronology*, 260–72; Beckwith, *Calendar, Chronology and Worship*, 142–43; Grabbe, "The 70-Week Prophecy."

is Josephus's statement that as a prophet Daniel was distinctive because "not only did he keep prophesying the future, like the other prophets, but he also determined the time when these things would come about" (*Ant.* 10.267).⁵⁴ Although there are a number of short periods of time in Daniel's prophecies (7:25; 8:14; 12:7, 11, 12),⁵⁵ the only prophecy that gives a long period of time with an identifiable starting point is the prophecy of the seventy weeks of years (9:24–27). This must be the main point of Josephus's statement, which he could hardly have made unless he himself had had an interpretation of the events and the time periods indicated in that passage.

The second probable allusion to the seventy weeks prophecy is Josephus's claim that "Daniel also wrote about the empire of the Romans and that it would be laid waste by them" (*Ant.* 10.276). Unfortunately neither the text nor the meaning of the last clause is certain, but the likely meaning is that the Jewish nation (mentioned earlier in 10.276) would be laid waste by the Romans.⁵⁶ Christopher Begg and Paul Spilsbury argue that the reference is to Daniel 11:30–33, citing Jerome's claim that the Jews saw this as a prophecy of the destruction of Jerusalem and the temple by Vespasian and Titus.⁵⁷ It is possible that Josephus read this passage (with its reference to Kittim, understood as the Romans, in 11:30) in that way. But the Roman Empire itself Josephus would certainly have seen predicted in Daniel 2:40 and 7:7, while the laying waste of the Jewish people (ἐρημωθήσεται) by the Romans could refer to Daniel 9:26 in accordance with his own interpretation of the "prince who is to come" as Vespasian. His war against the Jews is there said to end in "desolations" (שממות). It is possible that Josephus's words, "it would be laid waste by them," are intentionally ambiguous. Roman readers would assume the meaning to be that the Jewish nation will be laid waste by the Romans (as happened in 70–73 CE), but Jewish readers could suppose that the empire would be laid waste by the Jews, with a possible reference to the end of Daniel 9:27 ("until the decreed end is poured out upon the desolator").⁵⁸

Besides Josephus's interpretation of "the prince who is to come" (Dan 9:26) as Vespasian, it is possible to recover some other detailed elements of his interpretation of the prophecy of the seventy heptads. For one of these we can

---

54. Translations of *Antiquities* book 10 are taken from Christopher T. Begg and Paul Spilsbury, trans. and eds., *Flavius Josephus: Judean Antiquities Books 8–10*, vol. 5 of *Flavius Josephus: Translation and Commentary*, ed. Steve Mason (Leiden: Brill, 2005).
55. Josephus apparently alludes to some of these passages in *Ant.* 8.271, 275.
56. See Begg and Spilsbury, *Judean Antiquities*, 314 n. 1177.
57. Begg and Spilsbury, *Judean Antiquities*, 313–14 n. 1176.
58. See Begg and Spilsbury, *Judean Antiquities*, 314 n. 1177, citing J. Braverman.

return to the catalogue of omens and predictions that ended with the "ambiguous oracle." Immediately before discussing this prophetic oracle, Josephus refers to another oracle, this time one that the rebels unwittingly fulfilled:

ὅπου γε Ἰουδαῖοι καὶ τὸ ἱερὸν μετὰ τὴν καθαίρεσιν τῆς Ἀντωνίας τετράγωνον ἐποίησαν, ἀναγεγραμμένον ἐν τοῖς λογίοις ἔχοντες ἁλώσεσθαι τὴν πόλιν καὶ τὸν ναόν, ἐπειδὰν τὸ ἱερὸν γένηται τετράγωνον. (*War* 6.311)

So, for example, by demolishing the Antonia, the Jews made the temple a quadrangle, though they had it written in the oracles that the city and the sanctuary would be captured when the temple should become quadrangular. (my translation)[59]

Josephus is referring to the incident when rebels, in order to prevent Titus's troops from entering the temple from the Antonia Fortress, destroyed the connection between the Antonia and the porticoes at the northwest corner of the outer court of the temple (*War* 6.164–168). If the Antonia could have been previously considered part of the temple, severing the temple's connection with the Antonia reduced the temple to the rectangle formed by the outer court and its porticoes. But where did Josephus find a prophecy of this in the scriptures? The answer lies in Daniel 9:25b,[60] a passage whose obscurity is reflected in the even greater obscurity of the two Greek versions.[61] The relevant words with a literal translation are as follows:

תשוב ונבנתה רחוב וחרוץ

It shall be restored and built (as) a broad open space and a trench.

Josephus has probably taken verse 25a to mean that these events will take place after sixty-nine weeks. Unlike some of the English translations, the text refers to only one "broad open space." The word רחוב means a public space in a city, a plaza, which would normally be rectangular. I suggest that Josephus has, not unreasonably, thought this must refer to the outer court of the temple, easily

---

59. The translation "square" is misleading. Τετράγωνον means a shape with four angles, a rectangle, not a shape with four equal sides. The temple was quadrangular but never square.
60. This is suggested by Bruce, "Josephus and Daniel," 26; Grabbe, "The 70-Weeks Prophecy," 608. I hope I have improved on Bruce's explanation of Josephus's exegesis.
61. I assume that Josephus, a Jerusalem-educated priest, would treat the Hebrew text as the authoritative version of the oracle.

the largest open space in the Jerusalem of his day. So he takes the subject to be the temple and the prediction to mean that the temple will be restored to how it was before the building of the Antonia Fortress—that is, a large rectangular shape. This is an ingenious exegesis that presumably came to Josephus as he puzzled over the predictions in this very obscure passage and realized that this one could refer to the actions of the Jewish rebels during the final stage of Titus's capture of the city. His destruction of the city and the sanctuary is predicted, in the same last week of the seventy, in verse 26. Of course, it was entirely unreasonable of Josephus to suppose that the rebels could have understood the prophecy in this way, but Josephus is not concerned with being fair to them. After all, he believed in his own charismatic ability to discern the true meaning of obscure oracles (*War* 3.352). If the rebels had consulted him, they would not have brought disaster on the temple.

Another event that Daniel predicts will occur in the sixty-ninth week before the destruction of the city and the temple is this: "an anointed one shall be cut off" (Dan 9:26). It seems very likely that Josephus took this to refer to the sacrilegious murder of the high priest Ananus by the Idumeans,[62] which he regarded as a turning point in the history of the war:

> I would not be wrong to say that the fall of Jerusalem began with the death of Ananus, and that the overthrow of the walls and the destruction of the Jewish state date back to that day, when they saw their high priest, and the leader who could have saved them all, assassinated in the very centre of their city. (*War* 4.318)

Josephus believed that, had Ananus lived, he could either have reached a negotiated settlement with the Romans or, if the war had continued, have enabled the city to hold out much longer (*War* 4.321). This is coherent with the prominence of the death of "an anointed one" in Daniel's prediction of the end of the city.

With regard to some other details of the seventy weeks prophecy, we can make some reasonable guesses as to how Josephus would have interpreted them, though naturally, since he does not expound the text, they must remain guesses. At the beginning of the prophecy Gabriel announces the general themes of the whole:

> Seventy weeks are decreed for your people and your holy city: to finish the transgression, to put an end to sin, and to atone for iniquity, to bring in

---

62. Bruce, "Josephus and Daniel," 25, correctly notes that this was Josephus's source.

everlasting righteousness, to seal both vision and prophet, and to anoint a most holy place. (Dan 9:24)

Josephus was convinced that the destruction of Jerusalem and the temple was divine punishment for the sins of the revolutionary leaders in particular, but also of the people in general, whom they persuaded to follow their lead.[63] So he could easily have understood Gabriel's words to mean that by the end of the seventy weeks God would in this way bring an end to the sin of the people, somewhat in the manner announced in Isaiah 40:2. The destruction and its aftermath could therefore actually be the means by which God would inaugurate a new era of "everlasting righteousness." Crucially, for Josephus the priest, who always focused his understanding of the punishment on the destruction of the temple, God's rectification of the nation's life would culminate in anointing "a most holy place"—that is, consecrating a sanctuary in a restored temple. That Josephus did expect the temple to be restored we can be sure from the explicit prediction he attributes to Moses in *Antiquities* 4.314, which we shall discuss in due course. So whereas the prophecy in Daniel 9:24–27 concludes with the desolation of the sanctuary, followed by the destruction of the desolator, Josephus would have expected, on the basis of 9:24, that beyond that conclusion there was to be a restoration of the temple, implying also the restoration of the people, whose transgressions would by then have been sufficiently atoned.

Finally, we might wonder what Josephus would have made of the reference to "an anointed one, a prince" (משיח נגיד) in 9:25. He need not have identified this figure with "the prince who is to come," whom he took to be Vespasian. In fact, there are good reasons to think he would not have done so. Roman emperors were not anointed, and Josephus did not think Vespasian was the royal messianic figure of scriptural prophecy and Jewish expectation. In relation to Numbers 24:17, the "ambiguous oracle," what he claimed was that the rebels were wrong to see this as a prophecy of the expected Jewish Messiah. Rather, it referred to Vespasian, as did the reference to "the prince who is to come" (Dan 9:26). There is no reason why Josephus should not have shared, on the basis of other prophecies such as Isaiah 11, the general Jewish expectation of a Jewish Messiah to come in the future. Whether he did will be discussed in a later section of this chapter.

---

63. Jonathan Klawans, *Josephus and the Theologies of Ancient Judaism* (Oxford: Oxford University Press, 2012) 188–89. Josephus focused especially on bloodshed in or near the temple, and on civil strife.

THE INTERPRETATION OF NEBUCHADNEZZAR'S DREAM

Josephus's lengthy account of Nebuchadnezzar's dream and Daniel's interpretation of it (*Ant.* 10.203–210) is of special interest here because any reader of Daniel can easily recognize that in important respects Nebuchadnezzar's dream and its interpretation in chapter 2 parallel Daniel's vision and its interpretation in chapter 7. The imagery is different, but some of the substance is the same. In both cases there is a succession of four world empires, the fourth of which is especially strong and destructive. The four empires are destroyed and superseded by a world empire that will last forever. In both cases it is clear that this eternal kingdom is different in kind from its predecessors. Although God is sovereign over the whole succession of the empires, the eternal kingdom comes from God in a distinctive sense. In Daniel 2 this is indicated by the fact that the stone is cut from the mountain "not by (human) hands" (2:34, 45). Given these correspondences, chapter 7 provides much more detail, especially about the fourth empire, its last ruler, his conflict with the people of God, and the eternal kingdom that supervenes. Moreover, whereas in Daniel 2 there is no indication that the eternal kingdom is related to the nation of Israel, in Daniel 7 it is given to "the people of the holy ones of the Most High" (7:27). There are, as we shall see, good reasons why Josephus does not include the vision of Daniel 7 in his account of Daniel and his prophecies, but the correspondences between Daniel 2 and Daniel 7 make his reading of chapter 2, including his omissions, of special interest to us. It provides at least a minimal indication of what he must have made of chapter 7.

Some of the modifications that Josephus makes to the description of the statue and its interpretation in Daniel 2 function to make clear that in his view the four world empires are Babylon, Media-Persia, Alexander and the Hellenistic kingdoms, and Rome.[64] (He does not name them here, but the sequence is explicit in *Ant.* 15.385–387: Babylon, Persians, Macedonians, Romans.) Most ingenious is his interpretation of the two "hands and shoulders" of the statue as the two kings that will destroy the Babylonian Empire (*Ant.* 10.208)—that is, Cyrus the Persian and Darius the Mede (cf. 10.232). That the third kingdom is that of the Macedonians is made clear by the indication that it comes "from the west" (10.209), a detail that Josephus has drawn from Daniel 8:5. Here we see Josephus as the skilled interpreter of obscure oracles (*War* 3.352). Especially with these modifications, most readers would easily see that the fourth world empire is Rome.

---

64. For Rome seen as the fourth world empire in this period, see William Horbury, *Jewish War under Trajan and Hadrian* (Cambridge: Cambridge University Press, 2014) 142–46.

As well as these clarificatory additions to Daniel, there are even more significant omissions. In Daniel the legs of the statue are made of iron, but the feet and toes are partly of iron and partly of clay (2:34, 41–42). In Josephus's version the legs and feet are of iron and he omits all reference to clay (*Ant.* 10.206–209), perhaps because he wished to avoid any indication of weakness or division in the Roman Empire. It is also possible that Josephus is harmonizing the account with Daniel 7:7, which mentions only iron and gives the same impression of this empire's all-powerful domination of the world as Josephus's version of the statue and its interpretation gives.

The most significant omissions relate to the stone. Josephus omits the repeated "not by (human) hands" (Dan 2:34, 45) from Daniel's account. All that he really says about the stone corresponds closely to Daniel 2:35: the stone utterly destroyed any trace of the statue and "grew so large that the whole earth seemed to have been filled by it" (*Ant.* 10.207). Paul Spilsbury compares this passage with the prophecy of Balaam, in Josephus's version,[65] that

> there will be enough of you for the world to supply every land with inhabitants from your race. . . . The inhabited world lies before you as a dwelling place forever, and your multitude—as many as is the number of stars in heaven—will reside on islands and on the continent. (*Ant.* 4.115–116)[66]

But the parallel is not exact. Balaam speaks of the dispersion of the Jewish people throughout the world, but the stone in Nebuchadnezzar's dream is said to destroy the statue. Josephus describes that aspect of the dream graphically and emphatically (*Ant.* 10.207). The implication is surely clear that it represents a world empire that will destroy and succeed the others.

So readers of Josephus can assume that the stone is a worldwide empire, like its predecessors, but also somehow different in kind from them. However, when Josephus comes to Daniel's interpretation of the dream, he says that, although Daniel explained the stone, he will not do so:

> It seemed to me proper not to recount this, being obligated to record past events and things that have happened but not what is about to happen [τὰ μέλλοντα]. But if anyone, anxious for precision, will not be deterred from

---

65. Paul Spilsbury, "Flavius Josephus on the Rise and Fall of the Roman Empire," *JTS* 54 (2003) 1–24, here 19–20; see also Begg and Spilsbury, *Judean Antiquities*, 282 n. 884.

66. Translations of *Antiquities* book 4 are from Louis H. Feldman, *Flavius Josephus: Judean Antiquities 1–4* (Leiden: Brill, 2004).

being curious to the extent of even wishing to learn about the unexplained [τῶν ἀδήλων]—what is to happen [τί γενήσεται]—let him make the effort to read the book of Daniel. He will find it among the sacred writings. (*Ant.* 10.210)

Josephus's statement about his duty as a historian—to record the past and not to predict the future—is very largely true of his practice in the *Antiquities*. As we shall see, he provides no more than hints of the prophesied future, though some of these are significant hints. In his treatment of Daniel he ignores chapter 7, which adds to chapter 2 only future events, and chapter 12, with its explicitly eschatological material. As well as being defensible enough as the proper practice of a historian, there was doubtless an element of tact involved. Josephus did not want to offend his Roman readers. Yet, in this account of Nebuchadnezzar's dream, he leaves no doubt that the Roman Empire was destined to be destroyed. Evidently this in itself was not the sensitive point. It does contradict Roman propaganda about Rome's destiny to rule eternally (expressed, for example, in Virgil's *Aeneid*), but perhaps this was tolerable.[67] What Josephus withholds is the *identity of the empire* the stone represents.

That the Jewish people would destroy the Roman Empire and rule the world in its place is precisely the view that Josephus, in the passage about the "ambiguous oracle" in the *War*, attributed to the Jewish rebels in 66 CE. There he claimed that they misinterpreted a prophecy that actually spoke of Vespasian. Throughout his works Josephus carefully avoided any suggestion that the militant messianism that fueled the Jewish revolt had genuine roots in the Jewish religious tradition, specifically in the scriptures. His refusal to identify the stone is consistent with that.

Nevertheless, that does not seem sufficiently to explain this passage. After all, Josephus need not have recounted Nebuchadnezzar's dream at all. Or he could have played down the role of the stone. As it is, he draws attention to the stone in a way that seems actually to entice the reader's curiosity. Steve Mason argues that "his invitation to consult the book of Daniel also serves a rhetorical purpose. We know that Daniel does *not* materially clarify the meaning of the stone beyond what Josephus has said. It is therefore likely that Josephus does not expect his readers to consult the prophet (in Hebrew?).... He wants to leave the impression that the Jewish scriptures contain all sorts of oriental

---

67. Mason, "Josephus," 173, points out that "Scipio had reflected that Rome would one day fall as Carthage had done (Polybius 38.22.3)."

mysteries beyond what he as a historian can presently discuss."⁶⁸ But this is not convincing. Daniel 2 does clarify the meaning of the stone to the extent of predicting that "the God of heaven will set up a kingdom that shall never be destroyed, nor shall this kingdom be left to another people" (2:44).⁶⁹ But Josephus directs curious readers to "the book of Daniel." There is no reason why they should confine their attention to the passage in which Daniel explains Nebuchadnezzar's dream. They could go on to chapter 7, in which they would find a much fuller account of this eternal kingdom and the way in which, through the agency of the God of Israel, it will displace the Roman Empire.

Probably the average Roman reader would not be so curious as to do this, though Mason's query "in Hebrew?" is redundant. Daniel was available in Greek in many a Roman synagogue. But Josephus's hopes could well have exceeded probability, and, besides, he could very well have expected his readers to include gentile sympathizers, Romans who admired Jewish monotheism and ethics.⁷⁰ In fact, in a later essay, Mason makes a powerful case for the view that the intended audience of the *Antiquities* was a gentile audience in Rome that was keenly interested in Jewish matters.⁷¹

But why exactly would Josephus want to entice such readers to read Daniel? The clue to the answer may lie precisely in the Aramaic phrase that twice accompanies references to the stone in Daniel 2: "by no hands" (די־לא בידין), rendered in the Greek versions as ἄνευ χειρῶν. It means that the eternal king-

---

68. Mason, "Josephus," 173.

69. It has been supposed that Josephus understood the stone to symbolize the Messiah (Joachim Jeremias in *TDNT* 4:273). A messianic interpretation is attested in Luke 20:18 (but only here among the several New Testament passages that apply to Jesus various other scriptural references to a stone), in some rather late rabbinic sources (Num. Rab. 13:14, where it is linked with Dan 7:13–14; Tanhuma-Yelamdenu 6:14; 7:7), and in Christian interpreters from Jerome onward. But in 4 Ezra 13:6, 35–36, it is understood as the heavenly Mount Zion that will be revealed when the Messiah comes. Jerome says that "the Jews and the impious Porphyry" take the stone to be the Jewish people (John J. Collins, *Daniel*, Hermeneia [Minneapolis: Fortress, 1993] 171). This seems most likely to have been how Josephus understood it.

70. According to Feldman, "Josephus' Portrait," 68, who thinks in the *Antiquities* Josephus addressed two audiences—Roman and Jewish—"this would seem to be a hidden hint to Jews to read the Book of Daniel and to perceive the reference to the future downfall of Rome." But even Roman readers would have recognized that the dream portends the future downfall of Rome.

71. Steve Mason, "Should Any Wish to Enquire Further (*Ant.* 1.25): The Aim and Audience of Josephus's *Judean Antiquities/Life*," in *Understanding Josephus: Seven Perspectives*, ed. Steve Mason, JSPSup 32 (Sheffield: Sheffield Academic, 1998) 64–103.

dom will not be brought about by human agency but solely by divine agency. As Mason himself argues, Josephus found in Daniel an expectation of the kingdom of God that, though it certainly entailed the reign of the Jewish people over the world, was *not activist*. The God of Daniel is sovereign over the kingdoms of the world, which he removes and replaces at will. The "wise," among whom Josephus would surely have included both Daniel and himself, do not, as Mason puts it, "try to engineer change, which is God's prerogative."[72] This is how Josephus differed from the Jewish revolutionaries. Though he expected the end of the Roman Empire and its replacement by the empire of the people of Israel, this was entirely in the hands of God. So he could not be accused of sedition. This is what curious readers would find if they followed Josephus's invitation to them to read Daniel for themselves. The invitation is far from merely rhetorical. Josephus would genuinely like them to discover this.

The Interpretation of the Vision in Daniel 8

Following his suggestion that readers interested in what Daniel had predicted for the future should go to the book of Daniel itself, Josephus's account of Daniel keeps to his declared aim of recounting only the past, not the future. It retells the narratives in Daniel 3–6, passes over chapter 7 without comment, but then relates in detail Daniel's vision of the ram and the goat, along with its interpretation (*Ant.* 10.269–275). This is a prophecy that, unlike Nebuchadnezzar's dream, extended only as far as the time of Antiochus Epiphanes. It provided Josephus with a fine example of the precision with which Daniel predicted the future, extending to many generations after the prophet's own time (10.269, 276). Accordingly, he records the vision with some added details of his own, designed to make it correspond in more detail to the historical events it symbolized. He also rewrites the interpretation in the same way. In both the account of the vision and its interpretation, Josephus borrows some small details from the more detailed prophecy of the same period in chapters 10–11 of Daniel.[73] Josephus has reworked the text of Daniel 8 with extreme care, displaying his own expertise as a skilled interpreter of prophecies.

It is not difficult to understand why he has chosen this vision, rather than the prophecies of chapters 10–11, to show Daniel as a remarkably accurate prophet. Compared with the more straightforward and prosaic style of those

---

72. Mason, "Josephus," 164.
73. For the ways in which Josephus rewrites Dan 8, see the extensive notes in Begg and Spilsbury, *Judean Antiquities*, 309–13.

chapters, the vision in Daniel 8 makes for a more engaging reading experience. Readers are first intrigued by the vivid images and so made the more interested in the interpretation. In addition to these literary considerations, Josephus himself was attracted to and experienced in symbolic dreams and visions (*War* 3.352).[74] Moreover, chapters 10–11 present a seamless sequence of events that Josephus would probably have thought extended into the future of himself and his readers. The vision of chapter 8 had already been completely fulfilled. To make this especially clear, Josephus adds specific details to the accounts of the actions of Antiochus Epiphanes against the Jewish people in both the vision (*Ant.* 10.271: the little horn will "take the city by force") and the interpretation. In the latter he draws on 1 Maccabees (1:54; 4:52) for the time period for which the sacrifices were interrupted (three years), rather than the figure in days that he attributes to the vision (*Ant.* 10.271, 275).[75] He has Antiochus plunder the temple (10.275), as in 1 Maccabees (1:20–23) but not in Daniel.

All this warrants the conclusion:

> And our nation did indeed suffer these things under Antiochus Epiphanes just as Daniel saw and wrote they would happen many years beforehand. And in the same way [τὸν αὐτὸν δὲ τρόπον] Daniel also wrote about the empire of the Romans and that it would be laid waste by them. (*Ant.* 10.276)

By "in the same way" Josephus must mean that, just as Daniel foretold with remarkable accuracy what would happen to the Jewish nation in the time of Antiochus Epiphanes, so he foretold with equal accuracy what would happen to the Jewish nation at the hands of the Roman imperial power. As I have already argued, this must be a reference to Daniel 9:24–27 as Josephus interpreted it. The passage was much less suitable for explanation by Josephus in the context of the *Antiquities* than Daniel 8 was, and so the latter serves to make the point and the former is adduced simply as a parallel example. If, as I have argued, Josephus would have found still future events (the ruin of the Roman Empire, the rebuilding of the temple, and quite plausibly a Messiah) in the prophecy of the seventy weeks, that would be further reason not to enter into

---

74. See Gray, *Prophetic Figures*, 58–70. She usefully distinguishes between symbolic dreams/visions and message dreams/visions. Dan 10–12 belongs to the latter category.

75. The figure of 1,296 days (*Ant.* 10.271) is problematic because it does not correspond to the 2,300 evenings and mornings of Dan 8:14. It also differs from other similar time periods in Daniel (7:25; 9:27; 12:7, 11, 12). See the discussion in Begg and Spilsbury, *Judean Antiquities*, 311–12 n. 1158.

detail about it here. Unlike Daniel 8, it was not a prophecy that had already been entirely fulfilled.

Josephus treats Daniel's vision of the ram and the goat in detail because it demonstrates "the precise and unchangeable truth of his prophecies" (*Ant.* 10.269). No doubt, this serves Josephus's overall purpose of elevating the Jewish people and their religious tradition in the estimation of his readers. But, in the light of his invitation to curious readers who want to know what Daniel said about future events to see for themselves in the book of Daniel, is there not also a subtext? If Daniel's prophecies about events now past have been so exactly fulfilled, his prophecies about events still in the future can be expected to be equally accurate. Thus, while saying nothing about what Daniel predicted for the future, Josephus nevertheless contrives to encourage his curious readers to want to know. As he says elsewhere in connection with Jeremiah, "what [God] predicts must happen" (10.142).

INTIMATIONS OF THE FUTURE IN THE *ANTIQUITIES*: (1) BALAAM'S ORACLES

We are now in a position to gather those hints of the future that Josephus allows a few prophetic figures in his narrative to voice.[76] These are the minor transgressions of his claim to write only about the past, not the future.

First, there is Balaam, to whose story and predictions Josephus gives considerable space (*Ant.* 4.104–130). The fact that Balaam's oracles are embedded in a narrative, as Nebuchadnezzar's dream is, made them suitable for Josephus to include in the *Antiquities*. But they also serve exceptionally well his apologetic or propagandist purpose of exalting the Jewish people in the eyes of his readers. Balaam was not an Israelite, but, in spite of intending to curse the people of Israel, he found himself compelled by divine inspiration to recognize them as specially favored by God and to recount the blessings that would characterize their history.

There are some striking parallels between Josephus's accounts of Balaam and Daniel. They are the only seers[77] to whom Josephus in the *Antiquities* attributes extensive passages of prediction (paraphrases of the scriptural sources).

---

76. Among the opportunities offered by the biblical texts that Josephus passes up, see *Ant.* 2.194.

77. The term Josephus uses for Balaam is μάντις (*Ant.* 4.104). It is commonly thought he uses this term for non-Jewish diviners who predicted the future, while generally reserving προφήτης for the biblical prophets who were inspired to speak on God's behalf (see Feldman, *Flavius Josephus*, 366 n. 308). But Gray, *Prophetic Figures*, 108–9, argues that Josephus uses μάντις-terminology for "practitioners of types of prophecy that had a certain technical dimension—they required special training and skills" (109).

Moreover, the predictions of both contain some that were fulfilled in the past, others that have been fulfilled in Josephus's own lifetime, and others that have still to be fulfilled in the future (for Balaam, see *Ant.* 4.125). (This classification of prophecies into three categories was evidently standard, since Philo, *Mos.* 2.288, uses it of Moses's blessings of the tribes in Deut 32.) Finally, in Balaam's case Josephus makes explicit what I have argued is implicit in Daniel's: "From all the things that have attained the kind of end that he predicted, one might also draw conclusions as to what should also occur in the future" (*Ant.* 4.125).[78]

The first three of Balaam's oracles, according to the Torah's account (Num 23:7–24:9), are combined into one in Josephus's paraphrase (*Ant.* 4.114–117). The subject is the exceptional blessings God will lavish on the people of Israel, since he is their "ally and leader for eternity." Their numbers will increase to the extent that, not only will they fill the land of Canaan, which will always be subject to them, but the whole earth will become "a dwelling place" for them forever. They will always enjoy both the blessings of peace and victory in war (4.114–117). Notable in this vista of Israel's future is the stress on the fact that these blessings are for eternity. There is no hint here of punishments when the people go astray. In this respect Josephus is faithful to the scriptural form of the oracles.

Josephus combines the first three scriptural oracles of Balaam into one because he perceives them to have a common theme, but he keeps the last of the four scriptural oracles distinct and gives only a brief summary of it (4.125). This oracle, as he understands it, is evidently not about Israel but about gentile kings and cities. The scriptural source is full of the names of peoples of the biblical world (Num 24:15–24), but Josephus does not repeat these or translate them into contemporary equivalents. He says only that Balaam

> predicted what sufferings would befall kings and what (sufferings) would befall the most distinguished cities, of which it happened that some had not yet begun to be inhabited, and some things that have happened to people in previous times, through land and sea, within my memory. (*Ant.* 4.125)

The distinguished cities not yet founded must include Rome (see the discussion of the "ambiguous oracle" above), but it is not easy to tell which other cities Josephus might have identified in this prophecy. It is in any case clear that Josephus has not abandoned his interpretation of Numbers 24:17 as referring

---

78. Cf. Philo, *Mos.* 2.288: "Confidence in the future is assured by fulfilment in the past" (LCL).

to Vespasian, which meant that this oracle is not about Israel but concerns the gentile nations. He may well have taken much of the rest of the oracle to refer to Rome's wars and conquests under the Flavian dynasty. It must be almost certain that he would have taken the final lines of the oracle (24:24) to mean that the Romans (Kittim) "shall perish forever."

No such detailed interpretation of this oracle appears in his text. But it is to his brief summary of this oracle that he attaches the comment: "From all the things that have attained the kind of end that he predicted, one might also draw conclusions as to what should also occur in the future" (*Ant.* 4.125). As in the case of his comment about the stone in Nebuchadnezzar's dream, this seems designed to awaken curiosity. While not naming Rome, he must have expected that the words "the most distinguished cities, of which it happened that some had not yet begun to be inhabited" would bring Rome to mind. (How could "the most distinguished cities" not include Rome?) He could have expected that some readers, those who had some familiarity with the Jewish scriptures, might look up the original prophecy.

In addition to paraphrasing and summarizing the scriptural oracles of Balaam, Josephus adds a speech of Balaam in which the future sufferings of the people of Israel now come into view:

> Complete destruction will not befall the race of the Hebrews, neither in war nor in epidemic and famine and lack of the fruits of the earth, nor shall some other unexpected cause destroy it. For God's providence is theirs, to save them from every misfortune and to allow no such suffering to come upon them, by which all would perish. But some few sufferings may befall them and for a brief period of time, through which they will appear to be humbled; but then they will flourish and bring fear upon those who caused injury to them. (*Ant.* 4.127–128)

This is surely Josephus's own prophetic assessment of his nation's situation and prospects following the catastrophe of the fall of Jerusalem. He would have thought that the unqualified blessings pronounced by Balaam required that any sufferings that did come would be minor and brief (ὀλίγα τε καὶ πρὸς ὀλίγον).[79] The concluding words suggest that soon the tables will be turned and the Romans will fear the Jews.[80]

---

79. This phrase could be a paraphrase of βραχύ in Isa 57:17 OG, since βραχύ could mean "slightly" or "for a short time."

80. There is perhaps an echo of Esth 8:16; 9:2; cf. Josephus, *Ant.* 11.285.

If Josephus means that the "Jews will one day rise up to wreak vengeance on their enemies," the Romans, as Paul Spilsbury supposes,[81] this would fit with what Balaam has previously prophesied about the God-given victory of the nation when attacked by enemies (*Ant.* 4.116–117). But it would sit ill with Josephus's speech to the rebels in Jerusalem in the *War*, when he claimed that in their history the people of Israel had always been delivered from their enemies by God himself, not Israel's armies (*War* 5.376–390), concluding, "our fathers never triumphed by recourse to arms, and never failed to win through without warfare when they put their trust in God." It would not be a small inconsistency if Josephus now thought that, although the rebels were wrong because they did not have God on their side, there would come a time when God would bless an armed revolt against the empire. It may be that in fact Josephus is here speaking carefully when he says only that the Jews will "bring fear upon those who caused injury to them," not that they will fight and defeat them. He leaves unsaid that God will intervene on their behalf.

In the Jewish scriptures God is sometimes said to put fear of Israel on their enemies. This may be in the context of battles,[82] but the best-known case will have been in the Song of Moses, where God's guidance of his people from Egypt to the promised land is accompanied by terror on the part of all the nations Israel will encounter, not on account of anything Israel has done, but because of God's mighty act of delivering them from Egypt (Exod 15:14–16). Also, in the context of the exodus, the Egyptians are said to have been in dread of the Israelites because of the plagues sent by God (Ps 105:38). Given that the exodus was widely regarded as the model for God's liberation of his people at the end of days, this may be the background to Josephus's statement.

Both Mason and Spilsbury observe that, while Josephus expected the downfall of Rome, "his expectation was devoid of eschatological urgency."[83] The stone (in Nebuchadnezzar's dream) "is not expected immediately."[84] But the basis for their view is not apparent to me. The words of Balaam may indicate otherwise: the humiliation of the nation will be for only "a brief period of time" (*Ant.* 4.128). While this may not express "eschatological urgency," nor does it suggest that, when Josephus wrote the *Antiquities*, he thought there was still a long time to wait for the fall of Rome. Given his commitment to writing about the past rather than the future, we can hardly expect him to have said more.

---

81. Spilsbury, "Flavius Josephus," 19.
82. Deut 2:25; 11:25; 1 Chr 14:17. Cf. also Esth 8:16; 9:2; Josephus, *Ant.* 11.285.
83. Spilsbury, "Flavius Josephus," 16.
84. Mason, "Josephus," 173.

Intimations of the Future in the *Antiquities*:
(2) Moses's Prophecies

The second prophetic figure that Josephus allows to voice hints of the future in his narrative is Moses. Josephus gives a very short summary of Moses's last address to the people of Israel in Deuteronomy 29. If the people transgressed, they would suffer defeat by their enemies, "their cities would be razed to the ground; their Temple would be burnt down," and they would be sold into slavery. (Deuteronomy itself refers explicitly neither to cities nor to the temple, but Josephus has drawn these features from the earlier speech of Moses in Lev 25–26, specifically 26:31–35.) Moses, according to Josephus, continues:

> Although the God who created you will give back to your citizens both your cities and your Temple, the loss of these will occur not once but often. (*Ant.* 4.312–314)

This promise of restoration is broadly based on Leviticus 26:40–45, but neither in Deuteronomy nor in Leviticus is there reference to the restoration of the temple.

It is, of course, natural that Josephus, the aristocratic priest from Jerusalem, should add to Moses's words specific references to the temple. But probably he has not simply added them. As an expert exegete, he has found a textual basis for them in the reference to "sanctuaries" in Leviticus 26:31. The plural noun there explains how he could attribute to Moses predictions of more than one destruction and more than one restoration of the temple.[85] The effect of the phrase "not once but often" (οὐχ ἅπαξ ἀλλὰ πολλάκις) is perhaps intended to leave the number of times indefinite. Josephus might be thinking of more occasions than the fall of Jerusalem to the Babylonians and its fall to the Romans in 70 CE. Cities were destroyed when the Northern Kingdom fell to the Assyrians, and when Jerusalem and other cities were destroyed by the forces of Antiochus Epiphanes. As for temples, Josephus could be recalling Jeremiah 7:12–14, where the prophet cites the destruction of the temple at Shiloh as a precedent for God's abandoning the Jerusalem temple to destruction (cf. Jer 26:6, 9). As we shall see, this was a passage that Josephus applied to the destruction of Jerusalem by the Romans. Antiochus Epiphanes did not destroy the temple, but he put it out of action. So we need

---

85. I owe this suggestion to Klawans, *Josephus*, 300 n. 69.

not conclude that Josephus thought that after 70 CE the temple would not only be restored but also subsequently destroyed again. We can be sure he did not think the loss of the temple in 70 was final. We can see in this passage a kind of typological principle at work: God acts in the same way on similar occasions. If God allowed the temple to be destroyed, but then restored it, he would do the same again.

Josephus also refers to the "poem" (Deut 32:1–43) that Moses wrote,

> containing a prediction of what will be, in accordance with which everything has happened and is happening [καθ'ἥν (καὶ) γέγονε (τὰ) πάντα καὶ γίνεται], since he has not at all deviated from the truth. (*Ant.* 4.303)

This Song of Moses, together with his blessings on the tribes (Deut 33), which Josephus perhaps intends to include in the same "poem," constitutes the last words of Moses and had great prestige as a prophecy.[86] Josephus here probably means that it summarizes the whole history of Israel. It recounts God's care for Israel, Israel's disobedience, and God's punishment (Deut 32:10–35) in a sequence Josephus could well have regarded as a pattern to be repeated in history, in the same way as the repeated destruction and rebuilding of the temple (*Ant.* 4.314). But following punishment, when the people recognize that God is their only help, he will vindicate them and take vengeance on his enemies (Deut 32:36–43). Notably, the victory over the enemies is ascribed solely to God; no militant action by Israel is required.

Josephus will certainly have read this as predicting the events of 66–73 CE and the future downfall of the Roman Empire. His reference to this passage, although he says nothing about its content, confirms my proposed reading of the prophecy of Balaam in *Antiquities* 4.128. There is no armed uprising by Jewish people, only God's intervention on their behalf. Moreover, when Josephus speaks of everything that "has happened and is happening," he evidently expects no long interval of time before the final vindication of Israel and the end of the Roman Empire. We might even speak of eschatological imminence. None of this is explicit in what he writes, but he might have expected some knowledgeable readers to understand or to seek out the text.

---

86. David Lincicum, *Paul and the Early Jewish Encounter with Deuteronomy*, WUNT 2/284 (Tübingen: Mohr Siebeck, 2010) 86–99, 111–12. See also Josephus, *Ag. Ap.* 2.218, which Lincicum, *Paul*, 179, relates to Deut 32.

INTIMATIONS OF THE FUTURE IN THE *ANTIQUITIES*:
(3) JEREMIAH'S PROPHECIES[87]

Of Jeremiah, Josephus writes:

> This prophet proclaimed in advance the terrible things that awaited the city [Jerusalem]; he also left behind writings about its capture in our own time and the destruction of Babylon. (*Ant.* 10.79)[88]

From what he says in more detail about prophecies of the fall of Jerusalem to the Romans in the *War* (4.388), we can tell that Josephus very likely read at least chapter 7 of Jeremiah in this sense.[89] Since it is hard to believe that he took any of Jeremiah's predictions of the fall of the city and the temple to apply exclusively to the events of 66–70 CE and not to the capture of the city by the Babylonians, he presumably thought that chapter 7 applied to both occasions. This is a kind of typological reading not unlike the way 2 Baruch and 4 Ezra are fictionally situated in the context of the Babylonian destruction because these authors saw a parallel between it and the Roman destruction. Already in the *War*, Josephus frequently alluded to the parallels between the two destructions,[90] extending even to the fact that they occurred on the same day of the year (6.250, 267–268). Per Bilde has argued that the whole of the *Antiquities* is structured by this typology: books 1–10 tell the story of the first temple, including its destruction, while books 11–20 tell the story of the second temple and anticipate its destruction. The consequence of the fall of the first temple was the exile, in which the story of Daniel is set; the consequence of

---

87. From what Josephus says about the prophecies of Isaiah and the Twelve (*Ant.* 10.35), it is not possible to tell whether he thought some still awaited fulfillment in the future. On prophecies of Isaiah that were fulfilled long after Isaiah's own time, but in the past from Josephus's standpoint, see *Ant.* 9.276; 10.32; 11.5–6; 13.64, 68, 71; *War* 7.432. Note also that, according to Josephus's report, the prophecy of Jesus son of Ananias, predicting the downfall of Jerusalem and its temple, alludes clearly to Jer 7:34 (*War* 6.301).

88. Josephus goes on to say that Ezekiel wrote about the same matters, although there are actually no prophecies of the fall of Babylon in the canonical book of Ezekiel. It is possible that his reference to two books written by Ezekiel shows knowledge of the apocryphal Ezekiel that survives in fragments from Cave 4 at Qumran or to the Apocryphon of Ezekiel that was known to some of the church fathers. In connection with the profanation and destruction of the second temple, Josephus may well have thought of Ezek 7:22.

89. For the destruction of the temple by fire, see Jer 7:20; for the violent sedition (στάσις), see 7:11; for profanation of the temple precincts, see 7:30.

90. *War* 5.391–393, 411–412; 6.103, 435. See Klawans, *Josephus*, 192.

the fall of the second temple will be another exile, in which Josephus himself, with many other Jews, found himself at the time of writing.[91]

This makes it peculiarly interesting that, in this passage of the *Antiquities*, Josephus gives the topics of Jeremiah's predictions as the capture of Jerusalem by the Babylonians, the capture of the city by the Romans, and the destruction of Babylon (predicted in Jer 50–51). On the basis of the parallel between the two destructions of Jerusalem, the use of the nickname "Babylon" for Rome was probably already established in Jewish usage by the time Josephus wrote the *Antiquities*.[92] This passage about Jeremiah's prophecies surely implies that, just as the fall of Babylon was the consequence of the first destruction of the city, the analogy must be completed by the fall of Rome.[93] While the passage does not explicitly refer to the future downfall of Rome, well-informed readers might well see it implied.[94]

INTIMATIONS OF THE FUTURE IN THE *ANTIQUITIES*:
(4) DANIEL'S PROPHECIES

We have already considered the relevant passage in *Antiquities* 10.210, but we can now understand its role as the last of the series of hints of the future that Josephus has provided, more or less unobtrusively, in relation to the prophecies of Balaam, Moses, and Jeremiah. While Josephus has stated that Moses's and Jeremiah's prophecies of the future are written in their books, only now in the case of Daniel does he explicitly invite the reader who wishes to learn about the future to consult the source—the book of Daniel itself. When we add to this the lengths to which Josephus goes to establish the detailed accuracy with which Daniel predicted events long after his own time, it seems clear that for Josephus this prophet is the best guide to the future of the world empires and of the Jewish people. The implication is inescapable that Josephus is directing his

---

91. Per Bilde, *Flavius Josephus between Jerusalem and Rome*, JSPSup 2 (Sheffield: Sheffield Academic, 1988) 89–90.

92. Sib. Or. 5:143, 159. A typological relationship between Babylon and Rome is assumed in 4 Ezra and 2 Baruch.

93. According to *Ant.* 10.233, the immediate cause of the fall of Babylon to the Medes and Persians was Belshazzar's sacrilegious treatment of the vessels Nebuchadnezzar had taken from the Jerusalem temple. Would not a thoughtful reader be struck by the parallel with the removal of the temple vessels by the Romans and their exhibition in triumph in Rome?

94. See also Klawans, *Josephus*, 197, for the idea that, for Josephus and at least his Jewish readers, the events of the Babylonian destruction of Jerusalem and the subsequent restoration established a "script" that the events of his own time would follow.

readers, should they be interested, not only to the interpretation of Nebuchadnezzar's dream but also to the much fuller account of the same sequence of events in Daniel's vision in chapter 7. There they will read about the downfall of Rome and the vindication of the Jewish people, already predicted by Balaam, but more fully described by Daniel. This chapter of Daniel to which Josephus never explicitly alludes turns out to be, in his view, the most important series of scriptural predictions that were as yet unfulfilled.

Josephus and Messianism

It is remarkable that in all his voluminous works, his discussion of the "ambiguous oracle" is the only place where Josephus even hints that there was a Jewish expectation of a messianic figure based on scriptural prophecies. Even in that case it is a question of a single oracle that, according to Josephus, the rebels misinterpreted. Of course, he refers to a number of popular leaders of uprisings, both before and during the revolt, who claimed to be kings, but he does not say that they claimed to be fulfilling scriptural prophecies. Modern scholars infer that they did make such claims,[95] but Josephus evidently did not want his gentile readers to know that. In all his writings he only once uses the word χριστός as a substantive,[96] apart from in the highly contested passage about Jesus (*Ant.* 18.63), which I think very unlikely to be authentic in any form.[97] He does use the verb χρίω to describe the anointing of some of the kings of Israel (*Ant.* 6.83, 157, 159; 7.357, 382; 9.106, 149) and once to refer to the anointing by Moses of the priests and furniture of the tabernacle (*Ant.* 1.221), but not χριστός for an anointed one.

The one example of χριστός occurs when Josephus records the execution of "the brother of Jesus who is called Christ, James by name" (*Ant.* 20.200). Few have contested the genuineness of this reference. What is notable about it is that Josephus says nothing about a group of Jewish followers of Jesus in which James would have been the leader. If the others (τινας ἑτέρους) who were executed along with James were also followers of Jesus, he refrains from saying so. Given that Josephus needed to recount this incident in order to explain why the high priest Ananus was deposed (*Ant.* 20.201–203), he says as little as possible about James. His words need not even mean that James himself thought his brother

---

95. E.g., Hengel, *The Zealots*, 290–300.
96. The word also occurs in *Ant.* 8.137, where it means "painted."
97. There is a very thorough discussion of all the arguments in James Carleton Paget, "Some Observations on Josephus and Christianity," *JTS* 52 (2001) 539–624.

was the Messiah.[98] It is for his Roman readers that Josephus explains Jesus as "who is called Christ" (τοῦ λεγομένου Χριστοῦ), since they will have heard him called this by Roman Christians.[99] The phrase is no more than a common formula for noting a second name, which need not be understood as a title.[100] Most gentiles who were neither Christians nor Jews probably thought "Christ" was a name of some kind. For his gentile readers to know that it meant "the Messiah," Josephus would have had to explain it, as he does not. His own works could have given them no reason to think there was any such title used by Jews.

It is widely acknowledged that Josephus's apologetic approach to the Jewish War explains his silence about messianic beliefs. He did not want it thought that the revolt stemmed from any authentic elements in the Jewish religious tradition, such as scriptural prophecies of a Davidic king who would deliver the Jewish people from their enemies. While he has no difficulty ascribing royal pretensions to various popular leaders, he does not reveal that they claimed to fulfill prophecy or that they attracted support because people were expecting a prophesied deliverer. The "fourth philosophy" he explicitly describes as a complete novelty with no roots in Jewish traditions (*Ant.* 18.9–10).

The prophecies that with studied care he avoids mentioning were not only those that fed Jewish uprisings in the first century CE. They were also prophecies that Christians claimed were fulfilled in Jesus. Along with Josephus's silence about messianic belief goes his silence about Christianity.[101] The Jewish Christians were a significant enough group in Jerusalem in the decades immediately prior to the Jewish revolt for Josephus to have known a good deal about them. The argument that he had no occasion to refer to them, perhaps because they did not provoke uprisings against Rome, is not convincing, because, as

---

98. On this point I agree with Giorgio Jossa, "Jews, Romans and Christians: From the *Bellum Judaicum* to the *Antiquitates*," in *Josephus and Jewish History in Flavian Rome and Beyond*, ed. Joseph Sievers and Gaia Lembi, JSJSup 104 (Leiden: Brill, 2005) 331–542, here 340.

99. Thus this reference to Jesus does not presuppose that Josephus must previously have written something about Jesus. He assumes merely basic knowledge about Christian claims among his Roman readers. For the phrase τοῦ λεγομένου Χριστοῦ, there is a striking parallel in Matt 27:17, where Pilate asks the crowd whom they wanted released, "Jesus Barabbas or Jesus who is called Christ?" (Ἰησοῦν τὸν Βαραββᾶν ἢ Ἰησοῦν τὸν λεγόμενον χριστόν). Matthew is putting into Pilate's mouth what a Roman might say, and so Pilate uses "Christ" as a second name, not a meaningful title.

100. Gregory H. R. Horsley, "Names, Double," *ABD* 4:1011–17, here 1013.

101. See the cautious discussion in Paget, "Some Observations," 614–18. For an extended discussion of Josephus's silence about Christianity, see F. B. A. Asiedu, *Josephus, Paul, and the Fate of Early Christianity: History and Silence in the First Century* (Langham: Lexington Books/Fortress Academic, 2019).

we have seen, in relation to the death of James his narrative virtually demands some reference to them, whereas in fact he does not even acknowledge their existence. His silence about them must be a policy. To some extent this may be because, writing the *Antiquities* in Rome in the reign of Domitian, he did not want Christians to be associated with Judaism. His readers might not have been confusing Christianity and Judaism, as gentiles did at an earlier date,[102] but Josephus would not want to imply that Christianity had any kind of authentically Jewish root. The Christian claim that Jesus fulfilled the prophecies in the Jewish scriptures was best ignored. So Josephus's silence about any such prophecies or about expectations based on them may be partly explained by his deliberate exclusion of the Christians from his work.

None of this requires us to think that Josephus himself did not expect a messianic figure who would effect the succession from the Roman Empire to its prophesied Jewish successor. His silence about messianism was an apologetic necessity, not a matter of personal belief. Certainly the Messiah, if he expected one, would not lead a violent uprising against Rome. He would not be a figure who took it on himself to force the divine plan of history into its next phase. He would implement God's will at the moment determined by God. The most suitable such Messiah would seem to be one who came from heaven. This may be as near as we can get to Josephus's interpretation of Daniel 7:13–14.

Comparison with the Post-70 Jewish Apocalypses

Josephus's *Antiquities* is roughly contemporary with the apocalypses of 4 Ezra and 2 Baruch. The author of 4 Ezra may even have lived, like Josephus, in Rome (if that is implied in 3:1). But they are not commonly thought to have much in common. Of course, in genre and subject matter, they are very different. Josephus writes history with only, as we have seen, hints of what he thinks the scriptural prophecies predict for the future. The two apocalyptists are explicitly concerned with the eschatological future and depict it in prophetic words and visions. Yet Josephus was deeply interested in prophecy and its fulfillments in history, and Baruch's long vision surveys the whole of the history the *Antiquities* narrates before continuing it into the future. In their understanding of history and the divine plan of events, Josephus and the two apocalypses converge rather more than we might expect.[103]

---

102. This point is made by Paget, "Some Observations," 615.
103. This is recognized to some extent by Klawans, *Josephus*, 201. Also relevant is Per Bilde, "Josephus and Jewish Apocalypticism," in *Understanding Josephus*, ed. Steve Mason,

- All three authors presuppose that God is in sovereign control of all the events of history (e.g., 4 Ezra 13:48; 2 Bar. 56:2-4; Josephus, *Ant.* 1.20; 10.277-280).
- They all understand the fall of Jerusalem to the Romans by means of a typological relationship to the destruction of the temple and the city by the Babylonians (Josephus, *War* 6.250, 267-268; *Ant.* 10.79).[104]
- They see the fall of Jerusalem as divine punishment for sin (e.g., 4 Ezra 14:32; 2 Bar. 1:2-5; Josephus, *War* 5.566; *Ant.* 20.166).[105]
- Josephus and 2 Baruch believe that God abandoned the temple before it was destroyed (2 Bar. 8:2; Josephus *War* 5.19, 412; *Ant.* 20.166).
- Josephus and 2 Baruch believe that, as the first destruction of the temple was followed by its restoration, so the second temple will also be restored after destruction (2 Bar. 32:2-4; Josephus, *Ant.* 4.314; cf. 4 Ezra 7:26).
- All three authors adopt from Daniel (chapters 2 and 7) the sequence of four world empires, of which Rome is the fourth (4 Ezra 11:39-40; 2 Bar. 39:3-5; Josephus, *Ant.* 10.208-209, 276; cf. *War* 5.367). The empires are given their power to rule by God, who transfers it to the next after the allotted time of each.
- They all expect the downfall of the Roman Empire, through the action of God, and the vindication or liberation of the Jewish nation (4 Ezra 12:31-34; 2 Bar. 39:7-40:2; Josephus, *Ant.* 4.125, 128).
- For their understanding of God's ordering of history, they are all strongly influenced by the book of Daniel (though 2 Baruch less than the others).
- Symbolic dreams or visions, requiring interpretation, are important vehicles of divine revelation of the future in all three authors (2 Bar. 36-40, 53-74; 4 Ezra 9-13).[106] In Josephus these include his own symbolic dreams and his interpretation of them (*War* 3.351-353). Both he and 4 Ezra reinterpret symbolic dreams found in Daniel (*Ant.* 10.205-210, 269-276; 4 Ezra 11-13).

35-61, though he does not write specifically about the post-70 apocalypses or discuss the parallels I point out below.

104. In 4 Ezra and 2 Baruch the typology is implied by the fictional setting during or after the fall of Jerusalem to the Babylonians.

105. For this theme in Josephus, see especially Jonathan J. Price, "Josephus and the Dialogue on the Destruction of the Temple," in *Josephus und das Neue Testament*, ed. Christfried Böttrich and Jens Herzer, WUNT 209 (Tübingen: Mohr Siebeck, 2007) 181-94; Price, "Some Aspects of Josephus' Theological Interpretation of the Jewish War," in *"The Words of a Wise Man's Mouth Are Gracious" (Qoh 10,12): Festschrift for Gunter Stemberger*, ed. Mauro Perani, SJ 32 (Berlin: de Gruyter, 2005) 109-19. See also Klawans, *Josephus*, 188-89. In 2 Baruch and 4 Ezra, of course, the theme is applied to the fall of the first temple, but typologically readers must apply it also to the fall of the second temple.

106. For symbolic dreams in Josephus, see Gray, *Prophetic Figures*, 64-70.

Of course, there are major differences. The two apocalypses focus extensively on the future, including not only the downfall of Rome and the messianic age, but also the last judgment, the resurrection, and the new creation. But even in the interpretation of the present, there are differences. The two apocalypses severely condemn the Roman Empire for its violence, oppression, and pride (2 Bar. 36:7–10; 4 Ezra 11:40–43; 12:32). It deserves its fate. Josephus, of course, cannot say this. The closest he comes is when he has Balaam say that, after their humiliation, the Hebrews will "bring fear upon those who caused injury to them" (*Ant.* 4.128). The fact that God used Rome to punish his people does not free Rome of blame for their oppression of the Jews. But otherwise Josephus refrains from criticism of Rome and its empire, which, in view of his readership, is understandable. Yet, apart from his obligatory flattery of Vespasian and Titus,[107] he has little to say in praise of Rome. He might not have disagreed with the apocalypses were he to speak his mind freely.

A final point of convergence between Josephus and 4 Ezra has an important bearing on how Josephus may have interpreted Daniel 7 and in particular 7:13–14. Josephus opposed the rebels in the Jewish War both because of their attempt to bring about the liberation of the Jewish people by armed revolt and because they took it into their own hands to undertake this liberation instead of awaiting God's intervention at the time God decreed. As Jonathan Price puts it, referring both to Josephus's speech to the rebels in Jerusalem (*War* 5.376–419) and Agrippa II's speech (*War* 2.345–401), "The Jews need merely to wait out Roman rule . . . , [and] dominion and divine favor will eventually come round to them again. The Jewish historian held fast to his Jewish beliefs while in the City of Rome, and they shaped his historical outlook."[108]

The author of 4 Ezra seems also intent on repudiating the militant messianism of the revolt. So in the last two visions (4 Ezra 11–13), for which interpretation of Daniel 7 is foundational, the Messiah, identified as the humanlike figure of Daniel 7:13, acts alone, without an army, and destroys the enemy by judicial sentence alone. Moreover, he appears out of the sea, flying "with the clouds of heaven" (4 Ezra 13:3). The significance of the sea is explained at the end of the interpretation of the vision:

---

107. 4 Ezra's account of the Flavian emperors could hardly be more different (12:22–28). They rule more oppressively than all the previous emperors and bring the wickedness of the empire to a climax. No doubt, the activity of Vespasian and Titus in Jewish Palestine is largely responsible for this judgment.

108. Jonathan J. Price, "The Provincial Historian in Rome," in *Josephus and Jewish History*, ed. Sievers and Gaia, 101–18, here 117.

Just as no one can explore or know what is in the depths of the sea, so no one on earth can see my servant or those who are with him, except in the time of his day. (13:52)

As the last word spoken by God about the Messiah, this is clearly a firm rejection of any attempt to force God's hand by taking an initiative to achieve the messianic liberation. The Messiah will come, from beyond the earth, when God alone determines.

This non-activist messianism, a message of hope for those who faithfully await God's intervention without seeking to effect it, would surely appeal to Josephus. This was a form of messianism consistent not only with his own rejection of messianic militancy and policy of submitting to Roman power but also with his continued hope for the downfall of the Roman Empire and the liberation of the Jewish nation by divine intervention at a time that could be imminent but could not be anticipated. Daniel's visions were the main basis for this hope, as far as we can tell, though the prophecies of Moses and Balaam also played a part. It therefore seems likely that Josephus did expect a Messiah, found that Messiah depicted in Daniel 7:13–14, and interpreted the passage in a way similar to the interpretation we find in 4 Ezra 13.

Conclusion

Josephus did not suggest that Daniel 7:13–14 incited the Jewish revolt in 66 CE, nor did he himself propose that that prophecy referred to Vespasian's rise to be Roman emperor. He did not see Vespasian as a Messiah. His prediction that Vespasian would become emperor was probably based on Daniel 9:26, and he also applied Numbers 24:17, which was a key messianic text for the rebels, to Vespasian. His argument was that the rebels were wrong to understand that text as messianic, not that Vespasian was the Messiah the Jewish people expected. His understanding of Vespasian's rise to power with God's assistance fits coherently with his guiding concept, derived at least in part from Daniel, that God's providence directs the rise and fall of rulers, especially the great world empires. Rome's empire was the fourth world empire of Daniel's prophecies, destined to rule but subject to God's ultimate sovereignty. Like the other great world empires it would fall, at the time God had determined and by God's action. The rebels were wrong in supposing that time had come and in attempting to achieve liberation from Rome by militant action.

Josephus was deeply interested in prophecy, and in the *Antiquities* he was guided by the biblical prophets, especially Jeremiah and Daniel, in discerning the pattern in God's providential ordering of history, especially in the relationships of the people of Israel and the ruling powers of the gentiles. He allowed himself only hints of prophecies that remained to be fulfilled in the future, though when careful attention is given to them these hints turn out to be significant ones. The future downfall of Rome is quite clearly signaled, especially in Josephus's account of Nebuchadnezzar's dream. The information he withholds in that context is both that the empire due to succeed Rome, brought about purely by divine action, would be eternal and that it would belong to the Jewish people. But his invitation to readers curious to know about future events to consult the book of Daniel itself, the only such invitation in the *Antiquities*, is seriously meant. No one who took up the invitation could fail to see that the course of the world empires summarily revealed in Nebuchadnezzar's dream is more fully depicted in Daniel 7, a terrifying symbolic dream like those Josephus himself had experienced.

It is clear that for Josephus the prophecies of Daniel were the most important guide to future events. The detailed accuracy with which, as Josephus shows, Daniel's prophecies had already been fulfilled in the past was a firm basis for trusting the predictions yet to be fulfilled. Josephus contrives to point to the importance of Daniel 7 without ever referring to its content, other than in the claim that Daniel predicted the Roman Empire. He would doubtless have seen this vision as one of those obscure divine oracles that needed interpretation but which he was especially skilled in interpreting. How he understood the details of the transition of universal rule from Rome to the Jewish people we cannot tell, but the initiative and instrumentality of God would undoubtedly have featured in his reading of the chapter.

Josephus maintained a deliberate silence, throughout his works, about messianism, in the sense of a Jewish expectation of a ruler of Israel and the nations who was predicted in scriptural prophecies. This was undoubtedly because he did not want his gentile readers to think that the Jewish War came about as a result of any genuine feature of the Jewish religious tradition and sacred books. His account of the death of James the brother of Jesus suggests that, when he wrote the *Antiquities*, he also wanted to avoid allowing that Christianity had any genuine roots in the Jewish religious tradition. The prophecies that Christians applied to Jesus, like those to which messianic pretenders appealed in the period up to and including the Jewish War, were best ignored. However, none of this requires that the expectation of a Messiah had no place in Josephus's own understanding of scriptural prophecies yet to be fulfilled. He undoubtedly expected the downfall of the Roman Empire, the supremacy of the Jewish people, and the restoration of the temple. All this would take place by God's initiative and action. Would God deploy a human agent, a Messiah, in accomplishing this? It is plausible that Josephus found such a Messiah in Daniel 9:25, but the more significant question is whether he read Daniel 7:13–14 in a messianic way.

Josephus has much more in common than is usually recognized with the Jewish apocalypses of 2 Baruch and 4 Ezra that were written around the same time as his *Antiquities*, including the importance of Daniel's prophecies of the four world empires and the typological correspondence between the fall of Jerusalem to the Babylonians and the fall of Jerusalem to the Romans. They were writing of the future for Jewish readers; Josephus was writing about the past for gentile readers. Given those considerable differences of subject matter and audience, the correspondences are remarkable. In the vision of 4 Ezra 13, the humanlike figure of Daniel 7:13, understood as the Davidic Messiah, comes from beyond the world and destroys the enemies of God and God's people by judicial sentence alone. The imagery of war is interpreted as the action of a judge. This Messiah is emphatically not a military leader. His victory is achieved without assistance from the people he comes to liberate. Moreover, his coming depends on God's timing and initiative; it cannot be anticipated. The author of 4 Ezra is tacitly rejecting the kind of messianism that led to the catastrophe of the Jewish War, just as Josephus did. His interpretation of Daniel 7:13 is exactly the kind of messianic expectation that everything we know about Josephus's views would lead us to expect Josephus to hold.

Since Josephus never broke his strategic silence about a Messiah, the likelihood that he read Daniel 7:13–14 in the same way as his contemporary, the author of 4 Ezra, can be only an inference. It is at any rate clear that, despite his avowed policy of writing about the past, not the future, he succeeded in indicating that the most important place to look for as yet unfulfilled and highly reliable prophecies was in the book of Daniel. In that respect he belongs to a widely evidenced focus on Daniel's prophecies of the future in Jewish literature of the period after 70.

CHAPTER 2.11

Conclusions on Jewish Interpretations of Daniel 7

For the major sources discussed in the preceding chapters, the appeal of Daniel 7 was that it provided both the assurance that history is governed by the sovereignty of God and a scheme of world history within which the Jewish people could place themselves. The scheme outlines a sequence of four world empires and their supersession by the eternal kingdom of God. The sequence of world empires culminates in one that is more oppressive than any before and which fiercely persecutes the people of God. But there follows a great transition in which God deprives the empires of their power and sets up an eternal kingdom. He delegates rule over this kingdom to a figure who is described only, in the language of vision, as "one like a son of man." The people of God have pride of place in his kingdom, and all the nations are subservient to it.

It is very notable that not only the writers of apocalypses but also the Jewish historian Josephus found in this Danielic scheme of world history, presented in both chapters 2 and 7 of Daniel, the most important key to understanding their contemporary place in history from the perspective of Jewish belief in the sovereignty of the one God over all nations and their history, along with his special commitment to the Jewish people. Though Josephus wrote history with only hints of the future, while his contemporaries who wrote the great apocalypses took history into their purview but focused on expectations of the future, their estimate and understanding of Daniel's prophecies had much more in common than has usually been supposed. We can infer that they were widely accepted among the Jewish intellectual elite.

The precise way in which the prophetic narrative of Daniel 7 is interpreted in our sources varies to some extent. For 4Q246, owing to its relatively early date, the fourth world empire is still understood to be the Hellenistic empire of Alexander and his successors, but for Sibylline Oracles book 5, 4 Ezra, 2 Baruch, and Josephus it is Rome. Its last ruler is identified in Sibyllines 5 as Nero returning from the east. The Parables of Enoch, on the other hand, shows no interest in the sequence of the empires and has only an obscure reference to the returning Nero. Those who are judged and destroyed by the Messianic Figure are described generally as the ruling powers.

In none of the sources we have studied is Daniel 7 interpreted in isolation from other messianic and eschatological prophecies. Interpreters assume that the scriptures, read synthetically, provide a coherent picture of the last days. When Daniel 7 provides an overall structuring framework, as it does in 4Q246, 4 Ezra, and 2 Baruch, the framework is filled out from a variety of other scriptural sources. It was taken for granted, therefore, that the obscure figure of "one like a son of man" could be identified from other scriptural sources. In almost every case, these include key passages about the Davidic Messiah, such as Isaiah 11, Psalm 2, Psalm 72, and 2 Samiel 7:13–14. The Parables of Enoch draws on these passages, except the last, even though its Messianic Figure is not descended from David. Book 5 of the Sibyllines, whose Messianic Figure is also not descended from David, may nevertheless have drawn on 2 Samuel 7:13 as well as the non-Davidic prophecy in Numbers 24:17. Rabbi Aqiva probably had in mind other messianic prophecies in which the Messianic Figure is called David. Also important in some of these sources are prophecies about the Isaianic servant, which similarly are understood to add further information about the royal Messiah, not to portray a distinct figure.

Because the figure in Daniel 7:13 can be described in a variety of ways that draw on these other texts, the sources do not need to allude explicitly to Daniel 7:13. In 4Q246 and 2 Baruch it is clear from the use of the Danielic framework that the Messianic Figure described in other terms is the figure in Daniel 7:13. In all of our sources, the figure in Daniel 7:13 is undoubtedly understood to represent an individual, who can be identified with individual Messianic Figures in other prophecies. That the "one like a son of man" is an individual, not a symbol for "the holy ones of the Most High," is already clear in the Old Greek version of Daniel, which distinguishes, within the vision, between the holy ones and the "one like a son of man." A "corporate" understanding of the humanlike figure is similarly absent from these sources. He may act on behalf of the people of God, but they are not "incorporated" into his person.

Only three sources—4 Ezra, the Parables of Enoch, and book 5 of the Sibyllines—make explicit allusions to Daniel 7:13, and it is of interest (not least for the study of the New Testament) to observe carefully how they do so. The Parables of Enoch and 4 Ezra respect the fact that "one like a son of man" or "something like a man" is a description of a figure seen in vision. Both Enoch and Ezra see a humanlike figure in a vision who is quite evidently the same figure as the one in Daniel's vision. Enoch sees "another, whose face was like the appearance of a man" (1 En. 46:1), a description based on Daniel 8:15 or 10:18. Ezra sees "something like a figure of a man" (4 Ezra 13:3), also echoing Daniel 8:15 or 10:18. It is noteworthy that neither description directly alludes to Daniel 7:13 or uses the phrase "son of man," though in both cases the context makes clear that the figure in Daniel 7:13 is intended (in 1 En. 46:1 the figure accompanies "one who had a head of days," while in 4 Ezra 13:3 he flies "with the clouds of heaven"). But in the Parables subsequent references are to "that son of man" or "the son of man who . . . ," while in 4 Ezra he is "that man" or "the man who . . ." The terms "son of man" and "man" are identical in meaning. Neither is a title, and both belong within the context of visionary images and their interpretation. In the Parables this figure is entitled the Chosen One (drawn from Isa 42:1) and the Lord's Messiah (drawn from Ps 2), while in 4 Ezra he is "the Messiah" and "my Son" (both drawn from Ps 2). These are titles that could be used outside the visionary context, as they are in scripture, but "that man" is not.

In 4 Ezra reference to the figure of Daniel 7:13 is not made sufficiently clear by the description "something like a figure of a man" alone. The allusion is made unmistakable by the information that he "flew with the clouds of heaven." The phrase "with the clouds of heaven" is found nowhere in the Jewish scriptures besides Daniel 7:13. It is notable that the words "flew with the clouds of heaven" cannot refer to the humanlike one's coming to the Ancient of Days, as in Daniel 7:13, because in 4 Ezra he has clearly already received the authority given to him in Daniel 7:14 and is coming to execute judgment on earth. The author has presumed that, as he flew with the clouds to the Ancient of Days, so he continues to fly with the clouds when he comes to earth. But perhaps more importantly, he uses the phrase in order to make it clear that the figure is the one described in Daniel 7:13. "With the clouds of heaven" is an identifying description.

The author of book 5 of the Sibyllines adopts a somewhat similar way of referring to the figure of Daniel 7:13. He is not describing a vision and does not attempt to reproduce the phrase "one like a son of man" literally in Greek. He takes it to represent simply "a man." The allusion to Daniel 7:13 is conveyed by means of the word "heaven": the Messianic Figure is "a man from the sky" (line 256) or "a blessed man [who] came from the vault of heaven" (line 414). As in 4 Ezra, he comes to earth with the authority described in Daniel 7:14 already given to him (line 415). Although Sibylline prophecy does not make scriptural allusions with the same frequency and precision as apocalyptic literature does, in this case the scripturally literate reader would not miss the allusion to Daniel 7:13–14. No other scriptural passage associates a Messianic Figure with heaven.

In the text of Daniel 7, it is not said in so many words that the "one like a son of man" himself achieves the transition from the fourth empire to his eternal kingdom. But in the literature we have studied, it is assumed that he is given royal authority over the nations (7:14) so that he may implement it by judging and destroying the enemies of God and God's people. Here the actual role of the humanlike figure is determined by the other messianic passages associated with Daniel 7 by the interpreter. He may be portrayed either as a warrior who defeats the enemy in battle or as a judge who destroys the enemy by judicial sentence. In 4Q246, which draws on the Song at the Sea (Exod 15) as a precedent, it is God who wages war for him. In Sibyllines 5, where the precedent is the very different events of Joshua 10, he destroys all the cities and the wicked nations with fire. In 2 Baruch he defeats the army of the last emperor in battle and then passes judicial sentence on him and executes him. In 4 Ezra and the Parables of Enoch the Messianic Figure condemns and destroys the enemy by judicial sentence alone. As well as Daniel 7:26, Isaiah 11:4 has considerable influence on these portrayals. In most of the texts the Messianic Figure subsequently rules Israel and the nations, which seems a natural interpretation of Daniel 7, but in 4 Ezra and the Parables of Enoch the Messianic Figure is solely a judge. He exercises no other royal functions, is never called a king or said to rule. This surprising feature probably embodies a reaction against the militant messianism that could be considered to have led to the catastrophe of 70 CE. Such an attitude to the Jewish revolt is one of the features these apocalypses share with Josephus.

In all this literature the "one like a son of man," like the various messianic figures with whom he is identified, is unequivocally a man (a male human). The authors assume that a humanlike figure seen in a vision represents a man. Because he is understood to be a man who has been taken up to paradise or heaven, he may look like an angel (1 En. 46:1), but he is a glorified human, not an angel by nature. In just three very minor cases, there is a trace of "divine" language used of him, though only after he has been invested with authority (Dan 7:14). Both in the Parables of Enoch (56:2) and in 4 Ezra (13:3–4) some imagery used in scripture (outside Daniel) to characterize God's judgment is used of the Messianic Figure in his role as judge. In the Old Greek version of Daniel 7:14, the translator does not distinguish terminologically between the cultic worship of God and the political obeisance given to the Messianic

Figure, as the Parables of Enoch and the Theodotionic version of Daniel rather carefully do. These three instances of "divine" language reflect the office of the Messianic Figure who exercises judgment on God's behalf and rules over the kingdom that belongs to God. There is no suggestion that he is in any sense divine by nature (in 4 Ezra he is expected to die along with all other humans at the end). Even to speak of "functional divinity" would be to make far too much of these isolated instances in just three of the sources. Throughout the sources we have studied, the "one like a son of man" is treated as merely human, an eminent and exalted human, to be sure, but not an angel or a god.

The humanity of the "one like a son of man" relates to what is probably the most unexpected result of this study. It is that in all these sources, except 4Q246,[1] this figure is understood to be a human who had been born and lived on earth in the past and is now being preserved by God in paradise or heaven until the time of the end when he will fulfill the role of the Messiah described in Daniel 7 and other prophecies. Evidently, all these authors assumed that Daniel 7:13 portrays a man who is presently in heaven, not a preexistent heavenly being, and so asked the question, Who could this man be? In 4 Ezra we find the view, of which there also traces in later rabbinic traditions, that he is a descendant of David born in the past and removed from the earth by God. This is an obvious means of combining the Davidic figure of other messianic prophecies with the figure in Daniel 7:13. Second Baruch, whose messianic ideas are very close to 4 Ezra's, probably presupposes the same notion. Texts such as Isaiah 9:6–7 and Micah 5:2 likely played a part in the formation of this tradition. Rabbi Aqiva, discussing the "thrones" in Daniel 7:9, identified the figure in 7:13, who would occupy one of them, as King David himself. But there were also non-Davidic identifications. In the Parables of Enoch the figure in Daniel 7:13 is Enoch, while in book 5 of the Sibyllines he is Joshua. These authors, for their own very different reasons, evidently judged these eminent figures from the scriptural past to be the most suitable candidates for the role. In explaining the prevalence of this kind of interpretation of Daniel 7, we should recall that one great figure of the past was expected, already in scriptural prophecy, to return at the end time for a divinely preordained role: the prophet Elijah (Mal 4:5–6 [3:23–24]). That the Messiah himself should be another such figure must have seemed very appropriate.

Thus Daniel 7:13–14 was not, as has often been supposed, the source of a form of messianic expectation quite different from the Davidic hope: a heav-

---

1. The fragmentary condition of 4Q246 unfortunately makes it impossible to tell whether the Messianic Figure had been born and lived on earth at an earlier time.

enly (angelic or divine) figure coming from heaven, as opposed to an earthly, human king, born on earth. In the interpretations of Daniel 7 we have studied, the Messiah has been born on earth in the past and will come in the future from heaven. This is remarkably close to the way early Christians read Daniel 7, a comparison that will be explored in part 3 of this work.

By now it is surely needless to say that, on the evidence of the extant Jewish literature in which we find interpretations of Daniel 7, there was no Son of Man tradition or Son of Man concept in Second Temple Judaism. Daniel 7:13–14 was always interpreted in close connection with other messianic prophecies, often those that expected an ideal king in the line of David. Indeed, it is misleading to speak generally of "messianic concepts" in Second Temple Judaism, as though there were mutually exclusive versions of messianic expectation subsisting independently of the scriptural texts and their interpretation. It is better to think of traditions of exegesis. Any particular portrayal of the Messiah resulted from a particular selection of potentially messianic texts in the scriptures and the way they were associated and related to each other. Such portrayals differed, but they all overlapped because none drew uniquely on scriptural sources ignored by all others. In such configurations some authors drew on Daniel 7:13–14; others did not. For those who did, the Messiah would come as a man from heaven, but he did not originate from heaven. He was no more "divine" or less human than the Messiah as others portrayed him, not drawing on Daniel. In every case a Messiah ("the Lord's Anointed One") was expected to exercise judgment, authority, and rule on God's behalf, but on earth, as did King David and other agents of God in the Hebrew scriptures. He was not presently reigning from heaven, nor would he reign over the cosmos from the heavenly throne of God in the future. His eternal kingdom would be that of an earthly emperor.

Finally, it must be stressed that no Messianic Figure, even those whose portrayal relied most heavily on Daniel 7:13–14, was ever called "the Son of Man." Only within the context of the visions of Ezra and Enoch could "that man" or "that son of man" be used to refer back to a figure modeled on the "one like a son of man" in Daniel 7:13. It is hard to believe that anyone in late Second Temple times could have recognized the phrase "the Son of Man" as an allusion to Daniel 7:13.

Bibliography

Alexander, Philip S. "3 Enoch." Pages 223–316 in vol. 1 of Charlesworth, *The Old Testament Pseudepigrapha*.

Arcari, Luca. "A Symbolic Transfiguration of a Historical Event: The Parthian Invasion in Josephus and the Parables of Enoch." Pages 478–86 in Boccaccini, *Enoch and the Messiah Son of Man*.

Asale, Bruk Ayele. *1 Enoch as Christian Scripture*. Eugene, OR: Pickwick, 2020.

Asiedu, F. B. A. *Josephus, Paul, and the Fate of Early Christianity: History and Silence in the First Century*. Langham: Lexington Books/Fortress Academic, 2019.

Assefa, Daniel. "The Identity of the Son of Man in the Traditional Ethiopian Commentaries on 1 Enoch." Pages 24–31 in *Wisdom Poured Out like Water: Studies on Jewish and Christian Antiquity in Honor of Gabriele Boccaccini*. Edited by J. Harold Ellens, Isaac W. Oliver, Jason von Ehrenkrook, James A. Waddell, and Jason M. Zurawski. Deuterocanonical and Cognate Literature Studies 38. Berlin: de Gruyter, 2018.

Aviam, Mordechai. "The Book of Enoch and the Galilean Archaeology and Landscape." Pages 159–69 in Bock and Charlesworth, *Parables of Enoch*.

———. *Jews, Pagans and Christians in the Galilee: 25 Years of Archaeological Excavations and Surveys; Hellenistic to Byzantine Periods*. Rochester, NY: University of Rochester Press, 2004.

Aviam, Mordechai, and Richard Bauckham. "The Synagogue Stone." Pages 135–59 in Bauckham, *Magdala of Galilee*.

Bampfylde, Gillian. "The Similitudes of Enoch: Historical Allusions." *JSJ* 15 (1984) 9–31.

Barclay, John M. G. *Jews in the Mediterranean Diaspora: From Alexander to Trajan (323 BCE–117 CE)*. Edinburgh: T&T Clark, 1996.

Barrett, Charles Kingsley. *A Commentary on the First Epistle to the Corinthians.* Black's New Testament Commentary. London: Black, 1968.
Bartlett, John R. *1 Maccabees.* GAP. Sheffield: Sheffield Academic, 1998.
Bauckham, Richard. "Apocalypses." Pages 135–87 in *Justification and Variegated Nomism.* Vol. 1, *The Complexities of Second Temple Judaism.* Edited by Donald A. Carson, Peter O'Brien, and Mark A. Seifrid. WUNT 2/140. Tübingen: Mohr Siebeck, 2001.
———. *The Climax of Prophecy: Studies on the Book of Revelation.* Edinburgh: T&T Clark, 1993.
———. "Covenant, Law and Salvation in the Jewish Apocalypses." Pages 268–323 in *The Jewish World around the New Testament.*
———. *The Gospels for All Christians: Rethinking the Gospel Audiences.* Grand Rapids: Eerdmans, 1998.
———. *Jesus and the God of Israel: God Crucified and Other Studies on the New Testament's Christology of Divine Identity.* Grand Rapids: Eerdmans, 2008.
———. *The Jewish World around the New Testament: Collected Essays I.* WUNT 233. Tübingen: Mohr Siebeck, 2008. Reprint, Grand Rapids: Baker Academic, 2010.
———. "Magdala As We Now Know It: An Overview." Pages 1–67 in Bauckham, *Magdala of Galilee.*
———, ed. *Magdala of Galilee: A Jewish City in the Hellenistic and Roman Period.* Waco: Baylor University Press, 2018.
———. "The Martyrdom of Enoch and Elijah: Jewish or Christian?" Pages 3–25 in *The Jewish World around the New Testament.*
———. "The 'Most High' God and the Nature of Early Jewish Monotheism." Pages 107–26 in *Jesus and the God of Israel.*
———. "The Nine and a Half Tribes." Pages 346–59 in vol. 1 of Bauckham, Davila, and Panayotov, *Old Testament Pseudepigrapha.*
———. "The Throne of God and the Worship of Jesus." Pages 152–81 in *Jesus and the God of Israel.*
Bauckham, Richard, James R. Davila, and Alexander Panayotov, eds. *Old Testament Pseudepigrapha: More Noncanonical Scriptures.* Grand Rapids: Eerdmans, 2013.
Bauer, Walter, William F. Arndt, F. Wilbur Gingrich, and Frederick W. Danker. *Greek-English Lexicon of the New Testament and Other Early Christian Literature.* 2nd ed. Chicago: University of Chicago Press, 1979.
Beckwith, Roger T. *Calendar and Chronology, Jewish and Christian.* AGJU 33. Leiden: Brill, 1996.

———. *Calendar, Chronology and Worship: Studies in Ancient Judaism and Early Christianity*, AGJU 61. Leiden: Brill, 2005.

———. "The Significance of the Calendar for Interpreting Essene Chronology and Eschatology." *RQ* 10 (1980) 167–202.

Begg, Christopher T. "Daniel and Josephus: Tracing Connections." Pages 539–45 in *The Book of Daniel in the Light of New Findings*. Edited by A. S. van der Woude. Bibliotheca Ephemeridum Theologicarum Lovaniensium 106. Leuven: Peeters/Leuven University Press, 1993.

Begg, Christopher T., and Paul Spilsbury, trans. and eds. *Flavius Josephus: Judean Antiquities Books 8–10*. Vol. 5 of *Flavius Josephus: Translation and Commentary*. Edited by Steve Mason. Leiden: Brill, 2005.

Berman, Samuel. *Midrash Tanhuma-Yelammedenu: An English Translation of Genesis and Exodus from the Printed Version of Tanhuma-Yelammedenu with an Introduction, Notes, and Indexes*. Hoboken: Ktav, 1996.

Bertalotto, Pierpaolo. "The Enochic Son of Man, Psalm 45, and the Book of Watchers." *JSP* 19 (2010) 195–216.

———. "Qumran Messianism, Melchizedek, and the Son of Man." Pages 325–39 in vol. 1 of Lange, Tov, and Weigold, *The Dead Sea Scrolls in Context*.

Bilde, Per. *Flavius Josephus between Jerusalem and Rome*. JSPSup 2. Sheffield: Sheffield Academic, 1988.

———. "Josephus and Jewish Apocalypticism." Pages 35–61 in Mason, *Understanding Josephus*.

Black, Matthew. *The Book of Enoch or 1 Enoch*. SVTP 7. Leiden: Brill, 1985.

———. "The Messianism of the Parables of Enoch: Their Date and Contributions to Christological Origins." Pages 145–68 in Charlesworth, *The Messiah*.

Boccaccini, Gabriele, ed. *Enoch and the Messiah Son of Man: Revisiting the Book of Parables*. Grand Rapids: Eerdmans, 2007.

Boccaccini, Gabriele, and John J. Collins, eds. *The Early Enoch Literature*. JSJSup. Leiden: Brill, 2007.

Bock, Darrell L. "Dating the *Parables of Enoch*: A *Forschungsbericht*." Pages 58–113 in Bock and Charlesworth, *Parables of Enoch*.

Bock, Darrell L., and James H. Charlesworth, eds. *Parables of Enoch: A Paradigm Shift*. JCT 11. London: Bloomsbury, 2013.

Bogaert, Pierre. *Apocalypse de Baruch*. Vol. 2. Sources chrétiennes 145. Paris: Cerf, 1969.

Box, George H. *The Ezra-Apocalypse*. London: Pitman, 1912.

Boyarin, Daniel. "Beyond Judaisms: Meṭaṭron and the Divine Polymorphy of Ancient Judaism." *JSJ* 41 (2010) 323–65.

———. "How Enoch Can Teach Us about Jesus." *Early Christianity* 2 (2011) 51–76.

———. *The Jewish Gospels: The Story of the Jewish Christ.* New York: New Press, 2012.

———. "Two Powers in Heaven; or, the Making of a Heresy." Pages 331–70 in *The Idea of Biblical Interpretation: Essays in Honor of James L. Kugel.* Edited by Hindy Najman and Judith H. Newman. JSJSup 83. Leiden: Brill, 2003.

———. "Was the Book of Parables a Sectarian Document? A Brief Brief in Support of Pierluigi Piovanelli." Pages 380–85 in Boccaccini, *Enoch and the Messiah Son of Man.*

Brockington, L. H. "The Syriac Apocalypse of Baruch." Pages 841–95 in *The Apocryphal Old Testament.* Edited by H. F. D. Sparks. Oxford: Clarendon, 1984.

Broyles, Craig C. "The Redeeming King: Psalm 72's Contribution to the Messianic Ideal." In *Eschatology, Messianism and the Dead Sea Scrolls.* Grand Rapids: Eerdmans, 1997.

Bruce, F. F. "Josephus and Daniel." Pages 19–31 in *A Mind for What Matters.* Grand Rapids: Eerdmans, 1980.

Burkett, Delbert. *The Son of Man Debate: A History and Evaluation.* SNTSMS 107. Cambridge: Cambridge University Press, 1999.

Casey, Maurice. *The Solution to the "Son of Man" Problem.* LNTS. Edinburgh: T&T Clark, 2007.

———. *Son of Man: The Interpretation and Influence of Daniel 7.* London: SPCK, 1979.

———. "The Use of the Term 'Son of Man' in the Similitudes of Enoch." *JSJ* 7 (1976) 11–29.

Caulley, Thomas Scott. "Balaam's 'Star' Oracle in Jewish and Christian Prophetic Tradition." *Restoration Quarterly* 56 (2014) 28–40.

Charles, R. H. *The Apocalypse of Baruch.* London: Black, 1896.

———. *A Critical and Exegetical Commentary on the Book of Daniel.* Oxford: Clarendon, 1929.

Charlesworth, James H. "Can We Discern the Composition Date of the Parables of Enoch?" Pages 450–68 in Boccaccini, *Enoch and the Messiah Son of Man.*

———. "The Date and Provenience of the Parables of Enoch." Pages 37–57 in Bock and Charlesworth, *Parables of Enoch.*

———. "Did Jesus Know the Traditions in the Parables of Enoch? ΤΙΣ ΕΣΤΙΝ ΟΥΤΟΣ Ο ΥΙΟΣ ΤΟΥ ΑΝΘΡΩΠΟΥ; (Jn 12:34)." Pages 173–217 in Bock and Charlesworth, *Parables of Enoch.*

———, ed. *The Messiah: Developments in Earliest Judaism and Christianity.* Minneapolis: Fortress, 1992.

———, ed. *The Old Testament Pseudepigrapha.* London: Darton, Longman & Todd, 1983.

Chester, Andrew. *Messiah and Exaltation: Jewish Messianic and Visionary Traditions and New Testament Christology*. WUNT 207. Tübingen: Mohr Siebeck, 2007.

Chialà, Sabino. "The Son of Man: The Evolution of an Expression." Pages 153–78 in Boccaccini, *Enoch and the Messiah Son of Man*.

Cohen, Shayne J. D. "Josephus, Jeremiah, and Polybius." *History and Theory* 21 (1982) 366–81.

Collins, Adela Yarbro. "The 'Son of Man' Tradition and the Book of Revelation." Pages 571–97 in Charlesworth, *The Messiah*.

Collins, Adela Yarbro, and John J. Collins. *King and Messiah as Son of God: Divine, Human, and Angelic Messianic Figures in Biblical and Related Literature*. Grand Rapids: Eerdmans, 2008.

Collins, John J. *The Apocalyptic Imagination: An Introduction to the Jewish Matrix of Christianity*. New York: Crossroad, 1984.

———. *Daniel*. Hermeneia. Minneapolis: Fortress, 1993.

———. *The Scepter and the Star: The Messiahs of the Dead Sea Scrolls and Other Ancient Literature*. New York: Doubleday, 1996.

———. "Sibylline Oracles." Pages 317–472 in vol. 1 of Charlesworth, *The Old Testament Pseudepigrapha*.

Collins, John J., and Peter W. Flint, eds. *The Book of Daniel: Composition and Reception*. 2 vols. VTSup 83. Leiden: Brill, 2001.

Collins, John J., and Daniel C. Harlow, eds. *Dictionary of Early Judaism*. Grand Rapids: Eerdmans, 2010.

Dalman, Gustaf. *The Words of Jesus*. Translated by D. M. Kay. Edinburgh: T&T Clark, 1902.

Daniel, Andrew Glen. "The Translator's Tell: Translation Technique, Verbal Syntax, and the Myth of Old Greek Daniel's Alternative Semitic Vorlage." *JBL* 140 (2021) 723–49.

Daube, David. "Typology in Josephus." *JJS* 31 (1980) 18–36.

Davila, James R. "Aramaic Levi: A New Translation and Introduction." Pages 121–42 in vol. 1 of Bauckham, Davila, and Panayotov, *Old Testament Pseudepigrapha*.

———. "Melchizedek, Michael, and War in Heaven." Old Testament Pseudepigrapha, University of St. Andrews. https://otp.wp.st-andrews.ac.uk/divine-mediator-figures-course/melchizedek-michael-and-war-in-heaven/.

———. *The Provenance of the Pseudepigrapha: Jewish, Christian, or Other?* JSJSup 105. Leiden: Brill, 2005.

Davis, Kipp, et al. "Nine Dubious 'Dead Sea Scrolls' Fragments from the Twenty-First Century." *DSD* 24 (2017) 189–228.

Davis Bledsoe, Amanda M. "The Relationship of the Different Editions of Daniel: A History of Scholarship." *Currents in Biblical Research* 13 (2015) 175–90.

Di Lella, Alexander A. "The Textual History of Septuagint-Daniel and Theodotion-Daniel." Pages 586–607 in vol. 2 of Collins and Flint, *The Book of Daniel*.

DiTommaso, Lorenzo. "Dating the Eagle Vision of 4 Ezra: A New Look at an Old Theory." *JSP* 20 (1999) 3–38.

Dunn, James D. G. *Christology in the Making: An Inquiry into the Origins of the Doctrine of the Incarnation*. London: SCM, 1980.

———. "'Son of God' as 'Son of Man' in the Dead Sea Scrolls? A Response to John J. Collins on 4Q246." Pages 198–210 in *The Scrolls and the Scriptures: Qumran Fifty Years After*. Edited by Stanley E. Porter and Craig A. Evans. JSPSup 26; Roehampton Institute London Papers 3. Sheffield: Sheffield Academic, 1997.

Dy-Liacco, Rafael. "Comet Halley of A.D. 66 and the Beast That Rises Out of the Sea (Revelation Ch. 13)." Academia.edu. https://www.academia.edu/12856350/Comet_Halley_of_A_D_66_and_the_Beast_that_Rises_Out_of_the_Sea_Revelation_Ch_13_.

Ellens, J. Harold. "The Dead Sea Scrolls and the Son of Man in Daniel, 1 Enoch, and the New Testament Gospels: An Assessment of 11QMelch (11Q13)." Pages 341–63 in vol. 1 of Lange, Tov, and Weigold, *The Dead Sea Scrolls in Context*.

Erho, Ted M. "The Ahistorical Nature of *1 Enoch* 56:5–8 and Its Ramifications upon the *Opinio Communis* on the Dating of the *Similitudes of Enoch*." *JSJ* 40 (2009) 23–54.

———. "Historical-Allusional Dating and the Similitudes of Enoch." *JBL* 130 (2011) 493–511.

———. "Internal Dating Methodologies and the Problem Posed by the Similitudes of Enoch." *JSP* 20 (2010) 83–103.

Eshel, Esther, and Hanan Eshel. "A Fragment of a Samaritan Inscription from Yavne (Jamnia)." *Tarbiz* 73 (2004) 171–79.

———. "New Fragments from Qumran: 4QGen[f], 4QIsa[b], 4Q226, 8QGen, and XQpapEnoch." *DSD* 12 (2005) 134–57.

Eskola, Timo. *Messiah and the Throne: Jewish Merkabah Mysticism and Early Christian Exaltation Discourse*. WUNT 2/142. Tübingen: Mohr Siebeck, 2001.

Feldman, Louis H. "Josephus' Portrait of Daniel." *Henoch* 14 (1992) 37–96.

Ferda, Tucker S. "Naming the Messiah: A Contribution to the 4Q246 'Son of God' Debate." *DSD* 21 (2014) 150–75.

Fitzmyer, Joseph A. "The Contribution of Qumran Aramaic to the Study of the New Testament." *NTS* 20 (1973) 382–407.

———. *The Genesis Apocryphon of Qumran Cave 1 (1Q20): A Commentary*. 3rd ed. BibOr 18B. Rome: Pontifical Biblical Institute, 2004.

———. *The Gospel According to Luke I–IX*. AB 28A. New York: Doubleday, 1981.

Fletcher-Louis, Crispin. *Jesus Monotheism*. Vol. 1, *Christological Origins: The Emerging Consensus and Beyond*. Eugene, OR: Cascade, 2015.

———. "*The Similitudes of Enoch* (1 Enoch 37–71): The Son of Man, Apocalyptic Messianism and Political Theology." Pages 58–79 in *The Open Mind: Essays in Honour of Christopher Rowland*. Edited by Jonathan Knight and Kevin Sullivan. LNTS. London: Bloomsbury, 2015.

———. "The Worship of Divine Humanity as God's Image and the Worship of Jesus." Pages 112–28 in Newman, Davila, and Lewis, *The Jewish Roots of Christological Monotheism*.

Flint, Peter W. "The Daniel Tradition at Qumran." Pages 41–60 in *Eschatology, Messianism, and the Dead Sea Scrolls*. Edited by Craig A. Evans and Peter W. Flint. SDSSRL. Grand Rapids: Eerdmans, 1997.

———. "The Daniel Tradition at Qumran." Pages 329–67 in vol. 2 of Collins and Flint, *The Book of Daniel*.

———. "Papyri from Qumran Cave 7." Pages 1026–27 in Collins and Harlow, *Dictionary of Early Judaism*.

Flowers, Michael. "The Two Messiahs and Melchizedek in 11QMelchizedek." *Journal of Ancient Judaism* 7 (2016) 194–227.

Flusser, David. "Melchizedek and the Son of Man." Pages 186–92 in *Judaism and the Origins of Christianity*. Jerusalem: Magnes, 1988.

Flusser, David, and Shmuel Safrai. "The Apocryphal Psalms of David." Pages 258–82 in *Judaism of the Second Temple Period*. Vol. 1, *Qumran and Apocalypticism*. By David Flusser. Translated by Azzan Yadin. Grand Rapids: Eerdmans, 2007.

Frölich, Ida. "The Parables of Enoch and Qumran Literature." Pages 343–51 in Boccaccini, *Enoch and the Messiah Son of Man*.

García Martínez, Florentino, and Eibert J. C Tigchelaar, eds. *The Dead Sea Scrolls Study Edition*. Vol. 1. Leiden: Brill, 1997.

Geffcken, Johannes. *Die Oracula Sibyllina*. Die griechischen christlichen Schriftsteller der ersten [drei] Jahrhunderte 8. Leipzig: Hinrichs, 1902.

———. *Komposition und Entstehungszeit der Oracula Sibyllina*. Texte und Untersuchungen zur Geschichte der altchristlichen Literatur, neuen Folge 8.1. 1902. Reprint, Leipzig: Hinrichs, 1967.

Gershenzon, Rosalie, and Elieser Slomovic. "A Second Century Jewish-Gnostic Debate: Rabbi Jose Ben Halafta and the Matrona." *JSJ* 16 (1985) 1–41.

Gieschen, Charles A. "The Name of the Son of Man in the Parables of Enoch." Pages 238–49 in Boccaccini, *Enoch and the Messiah Son of Man*.

Ginzberg, Louis. *The Legends of the Jews*. 7 vols. Philadelphia: Jewish Publication Society, 1909–1946.

Goldberg, Arnold. "Die Namen des Messias in der rabbinischen Traditionsliteratur: Ein Beitrag zur Messianologie des rabbinischen Judentums." Pages 208–74 in vol. 1 of *Mystik und Theologie des rabbinischen Judentums: Gesammelte Studien*. Edited by Margarete Schlütter and Peter Schäfer. TSAJ 61. Tübingen: Mohr Siebeck, 1997.

Goldingay, John. *Daniel*. WBC 30. Dallas: Word, 1989.

Grabbe, Lester L. "The 70-Week Prophecy (Daniel 9:24–27) in Early Jewish Interpretation." Pages 595–611 in *The Quest for Context and Meaning: Studies in Biblical Intertextuality in Honor of James A. Sanders*. Edited by Craig A. Evans and Shemaryahu Talmon. Biblical Interpretation 28. Leiden: Brill, 1997.

———. "The Parables of Enoch in Second Temple Jewish Society." Pages 386–402 in Boccaccini, *Enoch and the Messiah Son of Man*.

Gray, Rebecca. *Prophetic Figures in Late Second Temple Jewish Palestine: The Evidence from Josephus*. New York: Oxford University Press, 1993.

Grelot, Pierre. "Les Versions Grecques de Daniel." *Bib* 47 (1966) 381–402.

Grossfeld, Bernard. *The Targum Onqelos to Genesis*. ArBib 6. Edinburgh: T&T Clark, 1988.

Guggenheimer, Heinrich W. *The Jerusalem Talmud: First Order: Zeraim: Tractate Berakhot*. SJ 18. Berlin: de Gruyter, 2000.

Gurtner, Daniel M. *Introducing the Pseudepigrapha of Second Temple Judaism*. Grand Rapids: Baker Academic, 2020.

———. *Second Baruch: A Critical Edition of the Syriac Text*. JCT 5. New York: T&T Clark, 2009.

———. "The 'Twenty-Fifth Year of Jeconiah' and the Date of 2 Baruch." *JSP* 18 (2008) 23–32.

Gwynn, John. "Theodotion." Pages 970–979 in vol. 4 of *Dictionary of Christian Biography*. Edited by W. Smith and H. Wace. London: Murray, 1877.

Halperin, David J. *The Faces of the Chariot: Early Jewish Responses to Ezekiel's Vision*. TSAJ 16. Tübingen: Mohr Siebeck, 1988.

Hannah, Darrell D. "The Chosen Son of Man of the Parables of Enoch." Pages 130–58 in Hurtado and Owen, *"Who Is This Son of Man?"*

———. *Michael and Christ: Michael Traditions and Angel Christology in Early Christianity*. WUNT 2/109. Tübingen: Mohr Siebeck, 1999.

———. "The Throne of His Glory: The Divine Throne and Heavenly Mediators in Revelation and the Similitudes of Enoch." *Zeitschrift für die alttestamentliche Wissenschaft* 94 (2003) 68–96.

Hartman, Louis S., and Alexander A. Di Lella. *The Book of Daniel*. AB 23. New York: Doubleday, 1978.

Hayward, Robert. "Phinehas—the Same Is Elijah." *JJS* 29 (1978) 22–34.

Hengel, Martin. *Studies in Early Christology*. Edinburgh: T&T Clark, 1995.

———. *The Zealots*. Translated by D. Smith. Edinburgh: T&T Clark, 1989.

Henze, Matthias. "*4 Ezra* and *2 Baruch*: The *Status Quaestionis*." Pages 3–27 in *Fourth Ezra and Second Baruch: Reconstruction after the Fall*. Edited by Matthias Henze and Gabriele Boccaccini. JSJSup 164. Leiden: Brill, 2013.

———. *Jewish Apocalypticism in Late First Century Israel*. TSAJ 142. Tübingen: Mohr Siebeck, 2011.

Himmelfarb, Martha. "The Mother of the Messiah in the Talmud Yerushalmi and Sefer Zerubbabel." Pages 369–89 in vol. 3 of *The Talmud Yerushalmi and Graeco-Roman Culture*. Edited by Peter Schäfer. TSAJ 93. Tübingen: Mohr Siebeck, 2002.

Hirschfelder, Ulrike. "The Liturgy of the Messiah: The Apocalypse of David in Hekhalot Literature." *Jewish Studies Quarterly* 12 (2005) 148–93.

Hofius, Otfried. "The Septuagint Version of Daniel 7:13–14: Deliberations on Form and Substance." Pages 508–22 in Reynolds, *The Son of Man Problem*.

Hollander, Willian den. *Josephus, the Emperors, and the City of Rome: From Hostage to Historian*. AGJU 86. Leiden: Brill, 2014.

Hooker, Morna D. *The Son of Man in Mark: A Study of the Background of the Term "Son of Man" and Its Use in St Mark's Gospel*. London: SPCK, 1967.

Horbury, William. *Jewish Messianism and the Cult of Christ*. London: SCM, 1998.

———. *Jewish War under Trajan and Hadrian*. Cambridge: Cambridge University Press, 2014.

———. *Messianism among Jews and Christians: Twelve Biblical and Historical Studies*. London: T&T Clark, 2003.

Horgan, Maurya P. *Pesharim: Qumran Interpretations of Biblical Books*. CBQMS 8. Washington, DC: Catholic Biblical Association of America, 1979.

Horsley, Gregory H. R. "Names, Double." *ABD* 4:1011–1017.

Horsley, Richard A., and John S. Hanson. *Bandits, Prophets, and Messiahs: Popular Movements at the Time of Jesus*. San Francisco: Harper & Row, 1985.

Hurtado, Larry W. *Ancient Jewish Monotheism and Early Christian Jesus-Devotion: The Context and Character of Early Christian Faith*. Library of Early Christology. Waco: Baylor University Press, 2017.

———. "The Binitarian Shape of Early Christian Worship." Pages 187–213 in Newman, Davila, and Lewis, *The Jewish Roots of Christological Monotheism*.

———. *Lord Jesus Christ: Devotion to Jesus in Earliest Christianity*. Grand Rapids: Eerdmans, 2003.

———. "Summary and Concluding Observations." Pages 159–77 in Hurtado and Owen, *"Who Is This Son of Man?"*

Hurtado, Larry W., and Paul L. Owen, eds. *"Who Is This Son of Man?" The Latest*

Scholarship on a Puzzling Expression of the Historical Jesus. LNTS. London: T&T Clark, 2011.

Ilan, Tal. *Lexicon of Jewish Names in Late Antiquity*. Part 1, *Palestine 330 BCE–200 CE*. TSAJ 91. Tübingen: Mohr Siebeck, 2002.

Instone-Brewer, David. *Techniques and Assumptions in Jewish Exegesis before 70 CE*. TSAJ 30. Tübingen: Mohr Siebeck, 1992.

Isaac, Ephraim. "1 (Ethiopic Apocalypse of) Enoch." Pages 5–89 in vol. 1 of Charlesworth, *The Old Testament Pseudepigrapha*.

Jacobson, Howard. *A Commentary on Pseudo-Philo's* Liber Antiquitatum Biblicarum. Vol. 1. AGJU 31. Leiden: Brill, 1996.

Johnson, Nathan C. "Rendering David a Servant in *Psalm of Solomon* 17.21." *JSP* 26 (2017) 235–50.

Josephus. *The Jewish War*. Translated by Martin Hammond. Oxford: Oxford University Press, 2017.

Jossa, Giorgio. "Jews, Romans and Christians: From the *Bellum Judaicum* to the *Antiquitates*." Pages 331–542 in Sievers and Lembi, *Josephus and Jewish History*.

Kim, Seyoon. *"The Son of Man" as the Son of God*. WUNT 30. Tübingen: Mohr Siebeck, 1983.

Klausner, Joseph. *The Messianic Idea in Israel from Its Beginnings to the Completion of the Mishnah*. Translated by W. F. Stinespring. London: Allen & Unwin, 1956.

Klawans, Jonathan. *Josephus and the Theologies of Ancient Judaism*. Oxford: Oxford University Press, 2012.

Klink, Edward W. *The Audience of the Gospels: The Origin and Function of the Gospels in Early Christianity*. LNTS 353. New York: T&T Clark, 2010.

Knibb, Michael A. "The Book of Enoch or Books of Enoch? The Textual Evidence for 1 Enoch." Pages 21–40 in Boccaccini and Collins, *The Early Enoch Literature*.

———. "The Date of the Parables of Enoch: A Critical Review." *NTS* 25 (1978) 345–59.

———. "Enoch, Similitudes of (1 Enoch 37–71)." Pages 585–87 in Collins and Harlow, *Dictionary of Early Judaism*.

———. *Essays on the Book of Enoch and Other Early Jewish Texts and Traditions*. SVTP 22. Leiden: Brill, 2009.

———. *The Ethiopic Book of Enoch: A New Edition in the Light of the Aramaic Dead Sea Fragments*. 2 vols. Oxford: Clarendon, 1978.

Kobelski, Paul J. *Melchizedek and Melchirešaʻ*. CBQMS 19. Washington, DC: Catholic Biblical Association of America, 1981.

Koch, Klaus. "Questions Regarding the So-Called Son of Man in the Parables of

Enoch: A Response to Sabino Chialà and Helge Kvanvig." Pages 228–37 in Boccaccini, *Enoch and the Messiah Son of Man*.

———. "Stages in the Canonization of the Book of Daniel." Pages 421–46 in vol. 1 of Collins and Flint, *The Book of Daniel*.

Kohler, Kaufmann. "The Pre-Talmudic Haggada I." *Jewish Quarterly Review* 5 (1893) 399–419.

Kugel, James L. *Traditions of the Bible: A Guide to the Bible As It Was at the Start of the Common Era*. Cambridge, MA: Harvard University Press, 1998.

Kugler, Robert A. *From Patriarch to Priest: The Levi Priestly Tradition from Aramaic Levi to Testament of Levi*. EJL 9. Atlanta: Scholars Press, 1996.

Kurfess, Alfons. *Sibyllinische Weissagungen*. Berlin: Heimeran, 1951.

Kvanvig, Helge S. "The Son of Man in the Parables of Enoch." Pages 81–99 in Boccaccini, *Enoch and the Messiah Son of Man*.

Laato, Antti. *A Star Is Rising: The Historical Development of the Old Testament Royal Ideology and the Rise of the Jewish Messianic Expectations*. Atlanta: Scholars Press, 1997.

Lacocque, André. "Allusions to Creation in Daniel 7." Pages 114–31 in vol. 1 of Collins and Flint, *The Book of Daniel*.

———. *The Book of Daniel*. Translated by David Pellauer. London: SPCK, 1979.

Lange, Armin, Emanuel Tov, and Matthias Weigold, eds. *The Dead Sea Scrolls in Context*. VTSup 140. Leiden: Brill, 2011.

Langlois, Michaël. *Le premier manuscrit du* Livre d'Hénoch: *Étude épigraphique et philologique des fragments araméens de 4Q201 à Qumrân*. Lectio Divina. Paris: Cerf, 2008.

Lanier, Gregory R. *Corpus Christologicum: Texts and Translations for the Study of Jewish Messianism and Early Christology*. Peabody, MA: Hendrickson, 2021.

Leibner, Uzi. *Settlement and History in Hellenistic, Roman, and Byzantine Galilee: An Archaeological Survey of the Eastern Galilee*. TSAJ. Tübingen: Mohr Siebeck, 2009.

Levey, Samson H. *The Messiah: An Aramaic Interpretation; The Messianic Exegesis of the Targums*. Monographs of the Hebrew Union College 11. Cincinnati: Hebrew Union College, 1974.

———. *The Targum of Ezekiel*. ArBib 13. Edinburgh: T&T Clark, 1987.

Lincicum, David. *Paul and the Early Jewish Encounter with Deuteronomy*. WUNT 2/284. Tübingen: Mohr Siebeck, 2010.

Lindars, Barnabas. *Jesus Son of Man: A Fresh Examination of the Son of Man Sayings in the Gospels in the Light of Recent Research*. London: SPCK, 1983.

———. "Re-enter the Apocalyptic Son of Man." Pages 377–98 in Reynolds, *The Son of Man Problem*.

Longenecker, Bruce W. *2 Esdras.* GAP 7. Sheffield: Sheffield Academic, 1995.

Loopik, Marcus van. *The Ways of the Sages and the Way of the World: The Minor Tractates of the Babylonian Talmud; Derekh 'Eretz Rabbah, Derekh 'Eretz Zuta, Pereq ha-Shalom.* TSAJ 26. Tübingen: Mohr Siebeck, 1991.

Lorein, Geert W., and Eveline van Staalduine-Sulman. "Songs of David." Pages 257–71 in vol. 1 of Bauckham, Davila, and Panayotov, *Old Testament Pseudepigrapha.*

Lozano, Ray M. *The Proskynesis of Jesus in the New Testament: A Study on the Significance of Jesus as an Object of προσκυνέω in the New Testament Writings.* LNTS 609. London: T&T Clark, 2020.

Lust, Johan. "Daniel 7,13 and the Septuagint." Pages 490–96 in Reynolds, *The Son of Man Problem.*

Macaskill, Grant. "Matthew and the *Parables of Enoch.*" Pages 218–30 in Charlesworth and Bock, *Parables of Enoch.*

Maher, Michael. *Targum Pseudo-Jonathan: Genesis.* ArBib 1B. Edinburgh: T&T Clark, 1992.

Marek, Libor. *A Star from Jacob, a Sceptre from Israel: Balaam's Oracle as Rewritten Scripture in the Dead Sea Scrolls.* Hebrew Bible Monographs 88. Sheffield: Sheffield Phoenix, 2020.

Marks, Richard G. *The Image of Bar Kokhba in Traditional Jewish Literature.* University Park: Pennsylvania State University Press, 1994.

Marshall, I. Howard. *The Gospel of Luke.* NIGTC 3. Exeter: Paternoster, 1978.

Mason, Steve. "Josephus, Daniel, and the Flavian House." Pages 161–91 in *Josephus and the History of the Greco-Roman Period: Studies in Memory of Morton Smith.* Edited by Fausto Parente and Joseph Sievers. StPB 41. Leiden: Brill, 1994.

———. "Should Any Wish to Enquire Further (*Ant.* 1.25): The Aim and Audience of Josephus's Judean Antiquities/Life." Pages 64–103 in Mason, *Understanding Josephus.*

———, ed. *Understanding Josephus: Seven Perspectives.* JSPSup 32. Sheffield: Sheffield Academic, 1998.

Mattila, Sharon Lea. "Two Contrasting Eschatologies at Qumran." *Bib* 75 (1994) 518–38.

McIvor, J. Stanley. *The Targum of Chronicles.* In *The Targums of Ruth and Chronicles.* ArBib 19. Edinburgh: T&T Clark, 1994.

McLay, R. Timothy. "Daniel: To the Reader." Pages 991–94 in *A New English Translation of the Septuagint.* Edited by Albert Pietersma and Benjamin G. Wright. New York: Oxford University Press, 2007.

———. *The OG and Th Versions of Daniel*. Septuagint and Cognate Studies 43. Atlanta: Scholars Press, 1996.

McNamara, Martin. *Targum Neofiti 1: Genesis*. ArBib 1A. Edinburgh: T&T Clark, 1992.

Meadowcroft, T. J. *Aramaic Daniel and Greek Daniel: A Literary Comparison*. Journal for the Study of the Old Testament Supplement Series 198. Sheffield: Sheffield Academic, 1995.

Mendels, Doron. "Baruch, Book of." *ABD* 1:618–620.

Michalak, Aleksander R. *Angels as Warriors in Late Second Temple Jewish Literature*. WUNT 2/230. Tübingen: Mohr Siebeck, 2012.

Milik, Józef T. *The Books of Enoch: Aramaic Fragments of Qumrân Cave 4*. Oxford: Clarendon, 1976.

———. "Problèmes de la littérature Hénochique à la lumière des fragments araméens de Qumran." *Harvard Theological Review* 64 (1971) 333–78.

Mitchell, David C. *Messiah ben Joseph*. Newton Mearns: Campbell, 2016.

Montanari, Franco. *The Brill Dictionary of Ancient Greek*. Edited by Madeleine Goh and Chad Schroeder. Leiden: Brill, 2015.

Montgomery, James A. *A Critical and Exegetical Commentary on the Book of Daniel*. ICC. Edinburgh: T&T Clark, 1927.

Moo, Jonathan. "A Messiah Whom 'the Many Do Not Know'? Rereading 4 Ezra 5:6–7." *JTS* 58 (2007) 525–36.

Moore, Carey A. *Daniel, Esther and Jeremiah: The Additions*. AB 44. New York: Doubleday, 1977.

Müller, Mogens. *The Expression "Son of Man" and the Development of Christology: A History of Interpretation*. London: Equinox, 2008.

Muraoka, Takamitsu. *A Greek-English Lexicon of the Septuagint*. Leuven: Peeters, 2009.

Myers, Jacob M. *I and II Esdras*. AB 42. New York: Doubleday, 1972.

Neusner, Jacob. *Development of a Legend: Studies on the Traditions Concerning Yoḥanan Ben Zakkai*. StPB 16. Leiden: Brill, 1970.

Newman, Carey C., James R. Davila, and Gladys S. Lewis, eds. *The Jewish Roots of Christological Monotheism: Papers from the St. Andrews Conference on the Historical Origins of the Worship of Jesus*. JSJSup 63. Leiden: Brill, 1999.

Newman, Hillel I. "Stars of the Messiah." Pages 272–303 in *Tradition, Transmission, and Transformation from Second Temple Literature through Judaism and Christianity in Late Antiquity*. Edited by Menahem Kister, Hillel I. Newman, Michael Segal, and Ruth A. Clements. Leiden: Brill, 2015.

Newsom, Carol A. *Songs of the Sabbath Sacrifice: A Critical Edition*. HSS 27. Atlanta: Scholars Press, 1985.

Nickelsburg, George W. E. *1 Enoch 1: A Commentary on the Book of 1 Enoch Chapters *1–36; 81–108*. Edited by Klaus Baltzer. Hermeneia. Minneapolis: Fortress, 2001.

———. "Discerning the Structure(s) of the Enochic Book of Parables." Pages 23–47 in Boccaccini, *Enoch and the Messiah Son of Man*.

———. "Enoch, Levi, and Peter: Recipients of Revelation in Upper Galilee." *JBL* 100 (1981) 575–600.

———. "The Greek Fragments of 1 Enoch from Qumran Cave 7: An Unproven Identification." *RQ* 21 (2004) 361–63.

———. *Resurrection, Immortality, and Eternal Life in Intertestamental Judaism*. Harvard Theological Studies. Cambridge, MA: Harvard University Press, 2007.

Nickelsburg, George W. E., and James C. VanderKam. *1 Enoch 2: A Commentary on the Book of 1 Enoch Chapters 37–82*. Edited by Klaus Baltzer. Hermeneia. Minneapolis: Fortress, 2012.

———. *1 Enoch: A New Translation; Based on the Hermeneia Commentary*. Minneapolis: Fortress, 2004.

———. *1 Enoch: The Hermeneia Translation*. 2nd ed. Hermeneia. Minneapolis: Fortress, 2012.

Nir, Rivka. *The Destruction of Jerusalem and the Idea of Redemption in the Syriac Apocalypse of Baruch*. EJL 20. Atlanta: Society of Biblical Literature, 2003.

Nolland, John. *The Gospel of Matthew*. NIGTC. Grand Rapids: Eerdmans, 2005.

———. *Luke 1–9:20*. WBC 35A. Waco: Word, 1989.

Oegema, Gerbert S. "*2 Baruch*, the Messiah, and the Bar Kochba Revolt." Pages 133–42 in Oegema, *Apocalyptic Interpretation of the Bible*. JCT 13. London: T&T Clark, 2012.

———. *The Anointed and His People: Messianic Expectations from the Maccabees to Bar Kochba*. JSPSup 27. Sheffield: Sheffield Academic, 1998.

Olson, Daniel C. *Enoch: A New Translation*. North Richland Hills, TX: BIBAL Press, 2004.

———. "Enoch and the Son of Man in the Epilogue of the Parables." *JSP* 9 (1998) 27–38.

———. "'Enoch and the Son of Man' Revisited: Further Reflections on the Text and Translation of 1 Enoch 70:1." *JSP* 18 (2009) 233–40.

Olyan, Saul M. *A Thousand Thousands Served Him: Exegesis and the Naming of Angels in Ancient Judaism*. TSAJ 36. Tübingen: Mohr Siebeck, 1993.

O'Neill, John C. "The Man from Heaven: *SibOr* 5.256–259." *JSP* 9 (1991) 87–102.

Orlov, Andrei A. *The Enoch-Metatron Tradition*. TSAJ 107. Tübingen: Mohr Siebeck, 2005.

———. *The Glory of the Invisible God: Two Powers in Heaven Traditions and Early Christology*. JCT 31. London: T&T Clark, 2019.

———. "Roles and Titles of the Seventh Antediluvian Hero in the Parables of Enoch: A Departure from the Traditional Pattern?" Pages 110–36 in Boccaccini, *Enoch and the Messiah Son of Man.*

Owen, Paul. "Aramaic and Greek Representations of the 'Son of Man' and the Importance of the Parables of Enoch." Pages 114–23 in Bock and Charlesworth, *Parables of Enoch.*

Pace Jeansonne, Sharon. *The Old Greek Translation of Daniel 7–12.* CBQMS 19. Washington, DC: Catholic Biblical Association of America, 1988.

Paget, James Carleton. "Some Observations on Josephus and Christianity." *JTS* 52 (2001) 539–624.

Piovanelli, Pierluigi. "Sitting by the 'Waters of Dan,' or the 'Tricky Business' of Tracing the Social Profile of the Communities That Produced the Earliest Enochic Texts." Pages 257–83 in Boccaccini and Collins, *The Early Enoch Literature.*

———. "'A Testimony for the Kings and the Mighty Who Possess the Earth': The Thirst for Justice and Peace in the Parables of Enoch." Pages 363–79 in Boccaccini, *Enoch and the Messiah Son of Man.*

Pomykala, Kenneth. *The Davidic Dynasty Tradition in Early Judaism.* EJL 7. Atlanta: Scholars Press, 1995.

Price, Jonathan J. "Josephus and the Dialogue on the Destruction of the Temple." Pages 181–94 in *Josephus und das Neue Testament.* Edited by Christfried Böttrich and Jens Herzer. WUNT 204. Tübingen: Mohr Siebeck, 2007.

———. "The Provincial Historian in Rome." Pages 101–18 in Sievers and Gaia, *Josephus and Jewish History.*

———. "Some Aspects of Josephus' Theological Interpretation of the Jewish War." Pages 109–19 in *"The Words of a Wise Man's Mouth Are Gracious" (Qoh 10,12): Festschrift for Gunter Stemberger.* Edited by Mauro Perani. SJ 32. Berlin: de Gruyter, 2005.

Puech, Émile. "4QApocryphe de Daniel Ar (Planche XI)." Pages 165–84 in *Qumran Cave 4: Parabiblical Texts, Part 3.* Edited by George J. Brooke, John J. Collins, Torleif Elgvin, et al. Discoveries in the Judaean Desert 22. Oxford: Clarendon, 1996.

Rajak, Tessa. *Josephus: The Historian and His Society.* 2nd ed. London: Duckworth, 2002.

Ramsey, John T. *A Descriptive Catalogue of Greco-Roman Comets from 500 B.C. to A.D. 400.* Syllecta Classica 17. Iowa City: The Classics Department at the University of Iowa, 2006.

Reeves, John C., and Annette Yoshiko Reed. *Enoch from Antiquity to the Middle*

Ages. Vol. 1, *Sources from Judaism, Christianity, and Islam*. Oxford: Oxford University Press, 2018.

Reynolds, Benjamin E. "The 'One Like a Son of Man' According to the Old Greek of Daniel 7:13." Pages 523–34 in Reynolds, *The Son of Man Problem*.

———, ed. *The Son of Man Problem: Critical Readings*. London: T&T Clark, 2015.

Reynolds, Bennie H., III. "Adjusting the Apocalypse: How the Apocryphon of Jeremiah C Updates the Book of Daniel." Pages 279–94 in vol. 1 of Lange, Tov, and Weigold, *The Dead Sea Scrolls in Context*.

Rowland, Christopher. *The Open Heaven: A Study of Apocalyptic in Judaism and Early Christianity*. London: SPCK, 1982.

Rzach, Aloisius. *ΧΡΗΣΜΟΙ ΣΙΒΥΛΛΙΑΚΟΙ: Oracula Sibyllina*. Leipzig: Freytag, 1891.

Sacchi, Paolo. "The 2005 Camaldoli Seminar on the Parables of Enoch: Summary and Prospects for Future Research." Pages 499–512 in Boccaccini, *Enoch and the Messiah Son of Man*.

Schäfer, Peter. *The Jewish Jesus: How Judaism and Christianity Shaped Each Other*. Princeton, NJ: Princeton University Press, 2012.

———. "Rabbi Aqiva and Bar Kokhba." Pages 113–30 in vol. 2 of *Approaches to Ancient Judaism*. Edited by William Scott Green. Brown Judaic Studies 9. Chico, CA: Scholars Press, 1980.

———. *Two Gods in Heaven: Jewish Concepts of God in Antiquity*. Translated by Allison Brown. Princeton, NJ: Princeton University Press, 2020.

Schäfer, Peter, Margerete Schlütter, and Hans-Georg von Mutius. *Synopse zur Hekhalot-Literatur*. TSAJ 2. Tübingen: Mohr Siebeck, 1981.

Schürer, Emil. *The History of the Jewish People in the Age of Jesus Christ (175 BC–AD 135)*. Vol. 3/1. Revised and edited by Geza Vermes, Fergus Millar, and Martin Goodman. Edinburgh: T&T Clark, 1986.

Schwemer, Maria. "Irdische und himmlische König: Beobachtungen zur sogennanten David-Apokalypse in Hekhalot-Rabbati §§ 122–126." Pages 309–59 in *Königsherrschaft Gottes um himmlische Kult im Judentum, Urchristentum und in der hellenistischen Welt*. Edited by Martin Hengel and Anna Maria Schwemer. WUNT 55. Tübingen: Mohr Siebeck, 1991.

Scott, R. B. Y. "Behold, He Cometh with Clouds." *NTS* 5 (1958) 127–32.

Scott, Steven Richard. "The Binitarian Nature of the Book of Similitudes." *JSP* 18 (2008) 55–78.

Segal, Alan F. *Two Powers in Heaven: Early Rabbinic Reports about Christianity and Gnosticism*. 2nd ed. Leiden: Brill, 2002.

Segal, Michael. "Who Is the 'Son of God' in 4Q246? An Overlooked Example of Early Biblical Interpretation." *DSD* 21 (2004) 289–312.

Sievers, Joseph, and Gaia Lembi, eds. *Josephus and Jewish History in Flavian Rome and Beyond*. JSJSup 104. Leiden: Brill, 2005.
Sjöberg, Erik. *Der Menschensohn im äthiopischen Henochsbuch*. Lund: Gleerup, 1946.
Spilsbury, Paul. "Flavius Josephus on the Rise and Fall of the Roman Empire." *JTS* 54 (2003) 1–24.
Spurling, Helen. "Hebrew Visions of Hell and Paradise." Pages 699–753 in vol. 1 of Bauckham, Davila, and Panayotov, *Old Testament Pseudepigrapha*.
Stec, David. *The Genizah Psalms: A Study of MS 798 of the Antonin Collection*. Cambridge Genizah Studies 5. Leiden: Brill, 2013.
Stökl Ben Ezra, Daniel. "Messianic Figures in the Aramaic Texts from Qumran." Pages 515–44 in *Aramaica Qumranica*. Edited by Katell Berthelot and Daniel Stökl Ben Ezra. Studies on the Texts of the Desert of Judah 94. Leiden: Brill, 2010.
Stone, Michael E. "Enoch's Date in Limbo or Some Considerations on David Suter's Analysis of the Book of Parables." Pages 444–49 in Boccaccini, *Enoch and the Messiah Son of Man*.
———. *Features of the Eschatology of IV Ezra*. HSS 35. Atlanta: Scholars Press, 1989.
———. *Fourth Ezra*. Hermeneia. Minneapolis: Fortress, 1990.
———. "The Question of the Messiah in 4 Ezra." *Judaisms and Their Messiahs at the Turn of the Christian Era*. Edited by Jacob Neusner, William S. Green, and Ernest Frerichs. Cambridge: Cambridge University Press, 1987.
Strack, H. L., and G. Stemberger. *Introduction to the Talmud and Midrash*. Translated by Markus Bockmuehl. Edinburgh: T&T Clark, 1991.
Streett, Andrew. *The Vine and the Son of Man: Eschatological Interpretation of Psalm 80 in Early Judaism*. Minneapolis: Fortress, 2014.
Stuckenbruck, Loren T. *The Book of Giants from Qumran: Texts, Translation, and Commentary*. TSAJ 63. Tübingen: Mohr Siebeck, 1997.
———. "The Building Blocks of Enoch as the Son of Man in the Early Enoch Tradition." Pages 315–28 in Bock and Charlesworth, *Parables of Enoch*.
———. "The Early Traditions Related to 1 Enoch from the Dead Sea Scrolls: An Overview and Assessment." Pages 41–63 in Boccaccini and Collins, *The Early Enoch Literature*.
———. "'One like a Son of Man as the Ancient of Days' in the Old Greek Recension of Daniel 7:13: Scribal Error or Theological Translation?" Pages 497–507 in Reynolds, *The Son of Man Problem*.
———. "The Parables of Enoch According to George Nickelsburg and Michael Knibb." Pages 65–71 in Boccaccini, *Enoch and the Messiah Son of Man*.
Stuckenbruck, Loren T., with Ted M. Erho. "The Book of Enoch and the Ethiopian

Manuscript Tradition: New Data." Pages 257–67 in *"Go Out and Study the Land" (Judges 18:2): Archaeological, Historical and Textual Studies in Honor of Hanan Eshel*. Edited by Aren M. Maeir, Jodi Magness, and Lawrence H. Schiffman. JSJSup. Leiden: Brill, 2012.

Suter, David W. "Enoch in Sheol: Updating the Dating of the Book of Parables." Pages 415–43 in Boccaccini, *Enoch and the Messiah Son of Man*.

———. *Tradition and Composition in the Parables of Enoch*. Society of Biblical Literature Dissertation Series 47. Missoula: Scholars Press, 1979.

———. "Weighed in the Balance: The Similitudes of Enoch in Recent Discussion." *Religious Studies Review* 7 (1981) 217–21.

Theisohn, Johannes. *Der Auserwählter Richter*. Studien zur Umwelt des Neuen Testaments 12. Göttingen: Vandenhoeck & Ruprecht, 1975.

Tigchelaar, Eibert J. C. "Remarks on Transmission and Traditions in the Parables of Enoch: A Response to James VanderKam." Pages 100–109 in Boccaccini, *Enoch and the Messiah Son of Man*.

Tiller, Patrick. *A Commentary on the Animal Apocalypse of 1 Enoch*. EJL 4. Atlanta: Scholars Press, 1993.

———. "The Sociological Settings of the Components of 1 Enoch." Pages 237–55 in Boccaccini and Collins, *The Early Enoch Literature*.

Tilling, Chris. *Paul's Divine Christology*. 2nd ed. Grand Rapids: Eerdmans, 2012.

Townsend, John T. *Midrash Tanḥuma: Translated into English with Introduction, Indices, and Brief Notes (S. Buber Recension)*. Vol. 1, *Genesis*. Hoboken: Ktav, 1989.

Tromp, Johannes. *The Assumption of Moses*. SVTP 10. Leiden: Brill, 1993.

Uemura, Shizuka. *Land or Earth: A Terminological Study of Hebrew 'ereṣ and Aramaic 'araʿ in the Graeco-Roman Period*. Library of Second Temple Studies 84. London: T&T Clark, 2012.

Ulrich, Eugene. "The Text of Daniel in the Qumran Scrolls." Pages 573–85 in vol. 1 of Collins and Flint, *The Book of Daniel*.

Urbach, Ephraim E. *The Sages: Their Concepts and Beliefs*. Translated by Israel Abrahams. Jerusalem: Magnes, 1979.

VanderKam, James C. "The Book of Parables within the Enoch Tradition." Pages 81–99 in Boccaccini, *Enoch and the Messiah Son of Man*.

———. *Enoch: A Man for All Generations*. Columbia: University of South Carolina Press, 1995.

———. "Righteous One, Messiah, Chosen One, and Son of Man in 1 Enoch 37–71." Pages 169–91 in Charlesworth, *The Messiah*.

Vermes, Geza. "Appendix E: The Use of בר נש/בר נשא in Jewish Aramaic." Pages

310–30 in *An Aramaic Approach to the Gospels and Acts*. By Matthew Black. 3rd ed. Oxford: Clarendon, 1967.

———. *Jesus the Jew: A Historian's Reading of the Gospels*. 2nd ed. London: Harper-Collins, 1973.

———. "Josephus' Treatment of the Book of Daniel." *JJS* 42 (1991) 149–66.

Waddell, James A. *The Messiah: A Comparative Study of the Enochic Son of Man and the Pauline Kyrios*. JCT 10. London: T&T Clark, 2011.

Walck, Leslie W. *The Son of Man in the Parables of Enoch and in Matthew*. JCT 9. London: T&T Clark, 2011.

———. "The Son of Man in the Parables of Enoch and the Gospels." Pages 298–337 in Boccaccini, *Enoch and the Messiah Son of Man*.

Williams, John. *Observations of Comets from 611 B.C. to A.D. 1640 Extracted from the Chinese Annals*. Hornchurch, Essex: Science and Technology Publishers, 1871.

Wright, N. T. *The New Testament and the People of God*. Christian Origins and the Question of God 1. London: SPCK, 1992.

Yeomans, Donald K. *Comets: A Chronological History of Observation, Science, Myth, and Folklore*. New York: Wiley, 1991.

Index of Authors

Abrahams, Israel, 70n
Albertz, Rainer, 149n
Alexander, Philip S., 95n
Arcari, Luca, 276n
Asale, Bruk Ayele, 7n, 12n
Asiedu, F. B. A., 363n
Assefa, Daniel, 73n
Aviam, Mordechai, 119–24, 127–30

Baltzer, Klaus, 10n, 59n, 84n, 102n, 121n
Bampfylde, Gillian, 277n
Barclay, John M. G., 201n
Barrett, Charles Kingsley, 37n
Bartlett, John R., 144n
Bauckham, Richard, 14n, 18n, 50n, 78n, 101n, 103n, 119n, 122n, 128n, 177–78n, 202n, 223n, 233n, 245n, 251n, 280n, 282n, 284n, 294n, 296n, 297n, 325n
Beckwith, Roger T., 139n, 333n, 341, 343n
Begg, Christopher T., 146n, 328n, 329n, 344, 349n, 352n, 353n
Berman, Samuel A., 265n
Bertalotto, Pierpaolo, 30n, 139n

Berthelot, Katell, 192n
Bilde, Per, 360–61, 364n
Black, Matthew, 20, 22n, 33n, 34n, 41–43, 81n, 105, 277n
Bledsoe, Davis, 148n
Boccaccini, Gabriele, 7n, 8n, 9n, 11n, 12n, 13n, 19n, 25–26, 32n, 33n, 36n, 41n, 65n, 72n, 81n, 113n, 121n, 124n, 276n, 293n
Bock, Darrell L., 9n, 19n, 23, 25n, 39n, 50n, 66n, 81n, 113, 119n, 120n, 121n, 276n, 277
Bogaert, Pierre, 295n, 296n, 301n, 302n
Böttrich, Christfried, 365n
Box, George H., 240n, 248n
Boyarin, Daniel, 23–24, 34, 72n, 124n, 324–25
Braverman, J., 344n
Brockington, L. H., 295n, 302n, 303n
Brooke, George, 173n
Brown, Allison, 237n, 315n
Broyles, Craig C., 71n
Bruce, F. F., 328n, 337n, 343n, 345n, 346n
Burkett, Delbert, 1, 21, 22n, 110n

397

INDEX OF AUTHORS

Carson, Donald A., 251n, 294n
Casey, Maurice, 22, 29n, 33, 34n, 35, 38n, 66n, 74n, 86, 87n, 139–40, 155n, 244n, 245n, 246n, 247, 248n, 265n, 316–17
Caulley, Thomas Scott, 336n
Charles, R. H., 83, 112, 179n, 295, 296n, 301
Charlesworth, James H., 9n, 19, 23, 25n, 38–39, 43n, 50n, 66n, 72n, 81n, 113, 119–21, 124–25, 127, 130–31, 155n, 276n
Chester, Andrew, 18, 201n, 205n, 209n, 211n
Chialà, Sabino, 65n
Cohen, Shaye J. D., 329n
Collins, Adela Yarbro, 41n, 155n, 156
Collins, John J., 8n, 9n, 13n, 37n, 41n, 66n, 72n, 86n, 121n, 136n, 137n, 138n, 140, 141n, 142n, 143, 173n, 179n, 182–83, 202, 205n, 207n, 211n, 212, 214, 216n, 227n, 243n, 246n, 289n, 295n, 301n, 351n

Dalman, Gustaf, 35n, 322
Daniel, Andrew Glenn, 150, 153
Daube, David, 328n, 329n
Davila, James R., 36n, 48n, 95n, 99n, 122n, 139n
Davis Bledsoe, Amanda M., 143
Di Lella, Alexander A., 66n, 142n, 143, 144, 147n, 148, 152, 179n
DiTommaso, Lorenzo, 244n
Dunn, James D. G., 21n, 179–81
Dy-Liaccio, Rafael, 339n

Elgvin, Torleif, 173n
Ellens, J. Harold, 73n, 139n
Erho, Ted M., 20, 112, 115–16, 277, 278–79
Eshel, Esther, 8n, 9

Eshel, Hanan, 8n, 9
Eskola, Timo, 66n, 325n
Evans, Craig A., 136n, 174n, 179n, 342n
Feldman, Louis H., 328n, 329n, 349n, 351n, 354n
Ferda, Tucker S., 176–77
Fitzmyer, Joseph A., 85n, 176n, 177n
Fleischer, Ezra, 321
Fletcher-Louis, Crispin, 19, 24–25, 36n, 88n, 89n, 95n, 100n, 154, 156n, 160n, 163n, 248n
Flint, Peter W., 8n, 136n, 137, 138n, 141n, 142n, 174n
Flowers, Michael, 138–39n
Flusser, David, 139n, 320–21
Frerichs, Ernest, 248n
Frölich, Ida, 11n, 13n

García Martínez, Florentino, 173n, 181n
Gathercole, Simon, 338n
Geffcken, Johannes, 202n, 211n
Gershenzon, Rosalie, 237n
Gieschen, Charles A., 36n, 88–89
Ginzburg, Louis, 237
Goh, Madeleine, 208n
Goldberg, Arnold, 263n, 265n, 317n
Goldingay, John, 66n, 159n, 161n, 179n
Goodman, Martin, 244n, 284n
Grabbe, Lester L., 124n, 342n, 343n, 345n
Gray, Rebecca, 215, 328n, 329n, 331n, 332–33, 353n, 354n, 365n
Green, William S., 248n, 314n
Grelot, Pierre, 147n
Grossfeld, Bernard, 238n
Guggenheimer, Heinrich W., 317n
Gurtner, Daniel M., 16n, 259n, 289n, 292n, 293n, 301n
Gwynn, John, 148

398

Index of Authors

Halperin, David J., 129n
Hammond, Martin, 274n, 330n
Hannah, Darrell D., 20, 33n, 35, 40n, 41n, 45, 46, 47n, 48, 49n, 72n, 73n, 83n, 97n, 141n
Hanson, John S., 273n, 275n
Harlow, Daniel C., 8n, 121n
Hartman, Louis F., 66n, 144, 152n, 179n
Hayward, Robert, 233n
Hengel, Martin, 75n, 157, 233n, 261n, 263n, 273n, 274n, 275n, 322n, 337n, 341n, 362n
Henze, Matthias, 293n, 295–96, 301n, 303n
Herzer, Jens, 365n
Hirschfelder, Ulrike, 322, 322n, 323n
Hofius, Otfried, 156n, 157, 158, 161n
Hollander, William den, 332n
Hooker, Morna D., 35n, 72n, 81n
Horbury, William, 37n, 201n, 207n, 209n, 210n, 274n, 316, 320n, 336n, 348n
Horgan, Maurya P., 48n
Horsley, Richard A., 273n, 275n, 363n
Hurtado, Larry W., 19n, 20n, 23–26, 35n, 38n, 41n, 72n, 94n, 99n

Ilan, Tal, 263n
Instone-Brewer, David, 190n
Isaac, Ephraim, 42n, 69n, 278

Jacobson, Howard, 259n, 278n
Jeremias, Joachim, 351n
Johnson, Nathan C., 243n
Jossa, Giorgio, 363n

Kay, D. M., 322n
Kim, Seyoon, 157
Kister, Menahem, 336n

Klausner, Joseph, 72n, 262n, 318n, 320n
Klawans, Jonathan, 347n, 358n, 360n, 361n, 364n, 365n
Klink, Edward W., 14n
Knibb, Michael A., 8n, 10, 12n, 20, 42, 72n, 74n, 83, 86n, 116, 121, 277n
Knight, Jonathan, 89n
Kobelski, Paul J., 139n
Koch, Klaus, 32n, 141
Kohler, Kaufmann, 237, 239n
Kugel, James, 70
Kugler, Robert A., 48n
Kurfess, Alfons, 202n, 214
Kvanvig, Helge S., 32n, 72n, 81n

Laato, Antti, 201n, 235n, 293n, 336n
Lacocque, André, 136n, 145
Lange, Armin, 138n, 139n
Langlois, Michaël, 8n, 10n
Lanier, Gregory R., 265n
Leibner, Uzi, 122n
Leivestad, Ragnar, 35n
Lembi, Gaia, 363n, 366n
Levey, Samson H., 317, 337n
Lewis, Gladys S., 36n, 99n
Lietzmann, Hans, 35n
Lincicum, David, 359n
Lindars, Barnabas, 35, 93n
Longenecker, Bruce W., 221n, 248n
Loopik, Marcus van, 236–37n, 238n, 239n
Lorein, Geert W., 321
Lozano, Ray M., 99n
Lust, Johan, 154, 158n

Macaskill, Grant, 50n
Maeir, Aren M., 20n
Magness, Jodi, 20n
Maher, Michael, 239n
Marek, Libor, 336n

399

INDEX OF AUTHORS

Marks, Richard G., 320n
Marshall, I. Howard, 177n
Mason, Steve, 146n, 328n, 329n, 333n, 334n, 335n, 341–42, 344n, 350–51, 352, 357, 364n
Mattila, Sharon Lea, 173n, 183n
McIvor, J. Stanley, 264n
McLay, R. Timothy, 146n, 147n, 149–53
McNamara, Martin, 238n
Meadowcroft, T. J., 158–61, 162n, 164n
Meadows, Timothy, 158
Mendels, Doron, 148n
Michalak, Aleksander R., 139n
Milik, Józef T., 11n, 21, 105n, 112
Millar, Fergus, 244n, 284n
Mitchell, David C., 211n
Montanari, Franco, 208n
Montgomery, James A., 140n, 144–45, 147, 148–49, 155n, 159n
Moo, Jonathan, 227
Moore, Carey A., 148n
Müller, Mogens, 1, 20–21, 35n
Muraoka, Takamitsu, 162n
Mutius, Hans-Georg von, 322n
Myers, Jacob M., 252n

Najman, Hindy, 24n
Neusner, Jacob, 248n, 260n, 261
Newman, Carey C., 36n, 99n
Newman, Hillel I., 336n, 340n
Newman, Judith H., 24n
Newsom, Carol, 44n
Nickelsburg, George W. E., 8n, 10n, 11n, 12, 14, 15n, 16n, 20, 27n, 28, 32n, 33–35, 36n, 41n, 42, 46–47, 58n, 62n, 63n, 69n, 71, 78n, 82n, 84, 87, 89n, 92, 95n, 97n, 98n, 99, 102n, 120–23, 125–27, 129n, 271n, 276n, 277n, 278, 283, 298n

Nir, Rivka, 295n
Nolland, John, 31n, 177n

O'Brien, Peter T., 251n, 294n
Oegema, Gerbert S., 274n, 299n
Olson, Daniel C., 20, 34, 40n, 41n, 42, 63n, 86n, 87
Olyan, Saul M., 129n
O'Neill, John C., 211, 214
Orlov, Andrei A., 41n, 72n, 81n
Owen, Paul L., 20n, 35n, 66n, 72n

Pace Jeansonne, Sharon, 142n, 143n, 144–46, 150–51, 154n, 155–56, 159, 160
Paget, James Carleton, 362n, 363n, 364n
Parente, Fausto, 328n
Pellauer, David, 145n
Perani, Mauro, 365n
Pietersma, Albert, 151n
Piovanelli, Pierluigi, 13n, 121
Pomykala, Kenneth E., 235n
Porter, Stanley E., 179n
Price, Jonathan J., 365n, 366
Puech, Émile, 173n, 182n, 185n, 188, 189n

Rajak, Tessa, 331n, 332n, 334–35
Ramsey, John T., 339n, 340n
Reed, Annette Yoshiko, 102n
Reeves, John C., 102n
Reynolds, Benjamin E., 93n, 138n, 154n, 156n, 157n, 158n, 164n
Rowland, Christopher, 66n, 157n
Rzach, Aloisius, 202n, 214

Saachi, Paolo, 114–16
Safrai, Shmuel, 320–21
Schäfer, Peter, 75n, 237n, 238, 263n, 314n, 315n, 316, 317n, 319–20, 322, 323n, 325–26

Index of Authors

Schiffman, Lawrence H., 20n
Schlütter, Margarete, 263n, 317n, 322n
Schroeder, Chad, 208n
Schürer, Emil, 244n, 284n
Schwemer, Anna Maria, 322
Scott, R. B. Y., 159n
Scott, Steven Richard, 88–90
Segal, Alan F., 326n
Segal, Michael, 179n
Seifrid, Mark A., 251n, 294n
Sievers, Joseph, 328n, 363n, 366n
Sjöberg, Erik, 34–35
Slomovic, Elieser, 237n
Smith, D., 75n, 233n, 261n, 273n, 337n
Smith, W., 148n
Sparks, H. F. D., 295n
Spilsbury, Paul, 146n, 344, 349, 352n, 353n, 357
Spurling, Helen, 322n
Staalduine-Sulman, Eveline van, 321
Stec, David, 321
Stemberger, G., 264n
Stinespring, W. F., 72n, 262n, 318n
Stökl Ben Ezra, Daniel, 192n
Stone, Michael Edward, 38n, 74n, 75n, 79, 112–13, 114, 221–22, 223n, 224n, 225n, 227n, 228–29, 235, 242–44, 245n, 246, 248n, 252
Strack, H. L., 264n
Streett, Andrew, 298–99n
Stuckenbruck, Loren, 7n, 9n, 10, 12n, 20, 67n, 68, 81n, 87, 103n, 156, 157n
Sullivan, Kevin, 89n
Suter, Daniel W., 21–22, 60n, 113n, 114, 116

Talmon, Shemaryahu, 342n
Theisohn, Johannes, 43, 50n
Tigchelaar, Eibert J. C., 12n, 173n, 181n
Tiller, Patrick A., 13n, 103n
Tilling, Chris, 18–19
Tov, Emanuel, 138n, 139n, 149n
Townsend, John T., 264n
Tromp, Johannes, 141n

Uemura, Shizuka, 125–26
Ulrich, Eugene, 136n
Urbach, Ephraim E., 70n

VanderKam, James C., 10n, 14n, 20n, 41n, 58n, 72n, 74n, 81, 82n, 84n, 85n, 86n, 92n, 102n, 237n, 238n, 271n, 278
Vermes, Geza, 22, 35, 146n, 244n, 284n, 328n

Wace, H., 148n
Waddell, James A., 20n, 36n, 81n, 88–90, 95n
Walck, Leslie W., 19n, 33n, 34n, 35, 41n, 42n, 45–46, 72n, 81n, 86n, 87n, 88, 90–92, 113n
Weigold, Matthias, 138n, 139n
Wellhausen, Julius, 35n
Williams, John, 339n
Woude, A. S. van der, 328n
Wright, Benjamin G., 151n, 343n
Wright, N. T., 335n

Yadin, Azzan, 321n
Yeomans, Donald K., 339n

Index of Themes and Subjects

"abomination of desolation" (βδέλυγμα ἐρημώσεως), 144–46, 167
"ambiguous oracle," 274, 333–47, 362
Ammonites, 278
Amorites, 213, 215, 217, 278
Ancient of Days, 28–29, 30–32, 37, 45, 63, 65–67, 91, 157–58, 163, 165, 189, 194, 203–4, 314–15, 324, 372
Apocalypse of David, 322–24
Apocalypse of Ezra (4 Ezra): biblical allusions (4 Ezra 11–13), 257; and Daniel 7, 221–59, 371–72, 373–74; divine characteristics of "the man," 248–50; the eagle as enemy (Roman Empire), 244–45, 254; eschatological predictions, 224–27, 229–32, 240–41, 256; Ethiopic and Georgian translations, 221–22, 228, 229, 246; exegetical sources of the Messianic Figure, 313; Ezra's three eschatological visions, 223–24; and Josephus's *Antiquities*, 364–66, 369; Latin translation, 221–22, 228, 242–43, 246; the lion as image of the Davidic Messiah, 244–45, 254; the man who came up from the sea, 245–53; the Messiah in, 224–55, 256, 260, 267–73, 286; the Messiah in Episode 1, 224–27, 256; the Messiah in Episode 2, 227–32, 256; the Messiah in Episode 3, 240–41, 256; the Messiah in Episode 4, 256; the Messiah in Episode 5, 234–35, 243, 244–45, 256; the Messiah in Episode 6, 235, 243–44, 245–55, 256; the Messiah in Episode 7, 256; the Messiah's appearance, 240–41; the Messiah's destruction of the enemy, 245, 250–53, 255; the Messiah's inauguration of a messianic age, 240–41, 255; the Messiah's titles ("my Son" or "my Servant"), 242–44; and the Parables of Enoch, 39–40, 74–76, 110, 116–17, 246–47, 249, 267–84, 286; plot and setting (Israel in the Babylonian exile), 222–23, 226; and the rabbinic tradition, 235–39, 240–41; the survivors ("those who have not tasted death"), 230–35, 239, 254, 255, 258–59; Syriac translation, 221–22, 228, 229, 242–43, 246; translations from the Greek, 221–22, 228, 229, 242–43, 246, 252

Index of Themes and Subjects

Aqiva, Rabbi, 314–27, 371, 374; on Daniel 7 and a Davidic Messiah, 314–27, 371, 374; identification of the historical David as Messiah, 316–24; objections and alternatives to view of, 314–15, 324–27; Rabbi Eleazar's objection, 315, 324, 326–27; Rabbi Yose's objection, 314–15, 324–27; regarding the thrones of Daniel 7:9, 314–20, 324–27, 374

Babylonian astronomy, 131
Babylonian exile, 222–23
Babylonian Talmud (Bavli), 235–39, 240–41, 262, 314–19, 327
Balaam's oracle, 15, 207–8, 336–38, 340, 349, 354–57, 366
Bar Kokhba revolt, 253, 262, 314, 319–20, 336
Baruch, Epistle of, 148–49
Baruch, Syriac Apocalypse of (2 Baruch), 293–313, 371, 373; allusions to Daniel 7, 299–300, 303–4, 305–6, 307; and book of Isaiah, 304, 306, 308–9, 312; date of, 293; Davidic Messiah, 304–5, 374; exegetical sources of the Messianic Figure, 313; fictional setting, 294; and Josephus's *Antiquities*, 364–65, 369; the Messiah's "return," 294–96; the Messiah will be "revealed," 294–96, 304–5; "those who have not tasted death," 232–35, 239, 258–59; vision of the black and bright waters (chapters 53–74), 300–304, 306; vision of the vine and the forest (chapters 36–40), 296–300
Biblical Antiquities of Pseudo-Philo, 153, 239, 258–59, 278, 284–85

Cairo Genizah, 47, 320–22
Canaanites, 136, 213, 217

"clouds of heaven," 158–61, 246, 248–49, 265–66, 303, 324, 366, 372
cultic worship. *See* worship, cultic

Daniel 7 (Greek versions), 142–72; "the abomination of desolation" (βδέλυγμα ἐρημώσεως), 146–49, 167; Codex Chisianus 88, 142, 154–55, 169–70, 172; date of OG-Daniel, 143–46, 165; date of Th-Daniel, 146–49, 165; different translation techniques, 150–53, 165; "the holy ones" (OG-Daniel 7:8b), 164, 168–70; hypothesis of a different *Vorlage*, 149–53, 165; MT-Daniel (Masoretic Hebrew/Aramaic), 136n, 143, 147–48, 149–53, 154–64, 167, 168, 171; and New Testament writings, 146, 147–48; Old Greek (OG-Daniel), 142–46, 149–66, 167, 168–70, 171–72, 371, 373–74; "on the clouds of heaven," 158–61, 265n; and Origen's Hexapla, 142, 154; Papyrus 967, 142, 154–55, 169, 171–72; "Proto-Masoretic" version, 142, 143; relationships between OG-Daniel, Th-Daniel, and MT-Daniel, 149–66; Syriac version (the Syrohexapla), 142, 154; Theodotion (Th-Daniel), 142–43, 146–53, 154–64, 165, 167, 171, 374; versions of Daniel 7:13–14, 153–64, 165–66, 168–70; versions of Daniel 7:27, 162, 171–72; the "worship" of the "one like a son of man" (פלח in 7:14b), 161–64, 166, 373–74
Derekh Eretz Zuta, 235–39, 259

Enoch. *See* Parables of Enoch; Parables of Enoch (the Messianic Figure in)
"Enochic Judaism," 13–14
Enoch Seminar (2005) on "Enoch and

403

the Messiah Son of Man: Revisiting the Book of Parables," 19, 22, 25, 112–18, 121
Ethiopian Orthodox Tewahedu church, 7
Ezra. *See* Apocalypse of Ezra (4 Ezra)

Flavian dynasty, 332–33, 334–56, 366n

Gabriel (archangel), 36, 91, 103n, 346–47
Genizah Psalms ("Songs of David"), 320–22
Gog and Magog, 216n, 279

Hadraniel (angel), 323
Halley's Comet, 339
Hasmonean period, 112, 122, 144
Hekhalot literature, 95, 322; Apocalypse of David, 322–24

Ingethel (angel), 278
Isaiah (servant passages), 27–29, 47n, 96, 100, 104–5, 190, 194, 200, 218, 270–71, 272, 306, 321, 371

Jerusalem, fall of, 119, 148, 215–16, 222–23, 251, 261–64, 280–83, 294, 322–23, 328–69
Jerusalem temple, 128–30, 201n, 209–10, 215, 216, 217, 224n, 264, 274–75, 281, 282, 293n, 302–3, 322–23, 360–61; first, 264, 282, 293n, 360–61, 365n; Josephus and, 329–34, 338–40, 344–47, 353, 358–61, 365, 368–69
Jewish revolts against Rome, 118, 273–75, 319, 336, 350, 363–64, 367, 373; Bar Kokhba revolt (Second Revolt), 253, 262, 314, 319–20, 336; First Jewish War (66–73 CE), 253, 263, 273–75, 359, 367; Josephus and, 273–75, 328–29, 330–69

Josephus, 328–69, 370; the "ambiguous oracle," 274, 333–47, 362; the *Antiquities* and OG-Daniel, 146; the *Antiquities* and the post-70 Jewish apocalypses, 364–67, 369; on Balaam's oracles, 336–38, 340, 349, 354–57, 366; and 2 Baruch, 364–65, 369; and Christianity (silence about), 363–64; and Daniel's prophecies, 329–31, 341, 342–47, 353–54, 361–62; and Daniel's prophecy of the seventy heptads (seventy weeks), 341, 342–47, 353–54; and 4 Ezra, 364–66, 369; historical writing and prophecy, 330–31, 367–68, 370; importance of the book of Daniel to, 328–29, 368; interpretation of Daniel's vision of the ram and goat (Dan. 8), 352–54; on Jeremiah's prophecies, 360–61; on Jesus, 362–63, 364; and the Jewish War, 273–75, 328–29, 330–69; and messianism (silence about), 335, 351n, 362–64, 367, 368–69; on Moses's prophecies, 358–59; on Nebuchadnezzar's dream, 348–52, 354, 356, 357, 362, 368; portent of the comet over the city of Jerusalem, 338–41; as prophet, 329–47, 367–68; prophetic dreams, 331–33; as a second Daniel, 329, 368; and siege of Jotapata, 329n, 331–33, 343

Macedonians, 140, 348
"man from the sea," 37–38, 74, 224, 245–53
Masoretic Hebrew/Aramaic version of Daniel (MT-Daniel), 136n, 143, 147–48, 149–53, 154–64, 167, 168, 171; Daniel 7:13–14, 154–64, 168; Daniel 7:27, 171

Index of Themes and Subjects

Medes, 275–84
Merkavah mysticism, 130
messianic naming tradition, 176–77
messianic war, 117–18, 251n, 340
Metatron (angel), 95–96, 238–39, 322, 325
Michael (archangel), 91, 94, 103n, 105, 138, 139, 141
Moabites, 278
"Most High, the," 29, 31, 53–55, 63, 67, 74–75, 91, 100, 104, 138, 141, 162, 164, 166, 171–72, 177, 179–81, 187, 196–97, 234–35, 247, 252, 348, 371

Nebuchadnezzar's dream, 174–75, 348–52, 354, 356, 357, 362, 368

Parables of Enoch, 7–16, 17–57, 58–79, 80–108, 109–11, 112–18, 119–31, 267–92, 371–72, 373–74; Animal Apocalypse, 13, 16, 67, 102, 103n, 123; Apocalypse of Weeks, 13, 16; and Aramaic fragments of Enoch literature at Qumran library, 8–10, 13, 21–22, 105, 123; Astronomical Book (Book of the Luminaries), 7–8, 13, 14n, 102; and the *Biblical Antiquities* of Pseudo-Philo, 278, 284–85; Book of the Parables of Enoch (chapters 37–71), 7, 8, 12–16, 80–81, 91; Book of Watchers, 7–9, 12–16, 27, 35, 44, 68, 75, 85–86, 92, 102, 104–5, 111, 120–24, 128–30; date of, 2, 9, 13, 22, 112–18, 119–20, 267, 275–76; Dream Visions of Enoch, 7–8, 13, 102; and the Enoch legend in the Hebrew Bible, 101–4; Epistle of Enoch, 7–9, 13, 15, 16, 105; Ethiopic version, 7–8, 10–12, 32–36, 43–45, 124–27; and 4 Ezra, 39–40, 74–76, 110, 116–17, 246–47, 249, 267–84, 286; Final Book of Enoch (chapter 108), 7; Greek fragments, 7–8, 9, 10–11, 12; and the kings of the Parthians and the Medes, 275–84, 288–89; Noachic passages (interpolations), 11–12, 29n, 32n, 35, 41n, 51–52, 74n, 88; place of composition, 112, 119–31; and rabbinic tradition, 237–39; recent studies of, 19–24; social context of the Enochic literary tradition, 13–14; and three apocalypses of the late first century (4 Ezra, 2 Baruch, and book of Revelation), 116–18, 284–85. *See also* Parables of Enoch (the Messianic Figure in)

Parables of Enoch (the Messianic Figure in), 2–3, 17–57, 58–79, 80–108, 109–11; as the Anointed One, 26, 29–30, 51–52, 53–54, 272; as the "Chosen One," 26–31, 33, 39, 41–43, 46–47, 51–52, 53–54, 57, 58–59, 63, 76–77, 82–84, 90, 94–95, 96, 98, 105–6, 108, 109–10, 193, 249, 270, 272, 372; the cosmic tour, 15–16, 58, 105–6; and cultic worship, 17–19, 89, 93–101, 107–8, 111, 163–64, 166; and early Christology, 20–26; Enoch's first vision of "that son of man," 84–85; Enoch's first vision of the Messianic Figure, 82–84; Enoch's genealogy, 81; Enoch's identification as, 12, 23, 80–108, 111, 194, 214–15, 374; Enoch's vision of the two heavenly figures, 59–60, 62–64; eschatological judgment, 16, 17–18, 26–27, 30–31, 39–40, 58–79, 104, 110–11; the eschatological narrative sequence, 58–79; exegetical sources, 313; as "Head of

405

INDEX OF THEMES AND SUBJECTS

Days," 28, 31–32, 35, 41, 51–52, 53–57, 59–69, 76, 82–83, 273; the Head of Days takes his seat for judgment, 60–61, 64–68, 82; the judgment of the kings and the mighty, 62, 77–79; and the Messianic Figure in 4 Ezra, 267–73, 286; and the Messianic Figure of Qumran's 4Q246 (4QAramaic Apocalypse), 193–94, 200; and the Messianic Figure of Sibylline Oracles (book 5), 217–18; the name of "that son of man," 87–93; question of preexistence before creation, 71–76; recent studies of, 19–24; righteousness as the defining characteristics of "that son of man," 85–86, 92; as the "Righteous One," 26, 51–52; and the scriptures (biblical allusions), 26–31, 39, 53–56, 116–17, 286, 287; the term "Son of Man," 2–3, 26, 28–29, 32–40, 90, 109–10; the "throne of glory," 40–50, 51–52, 57, 62, 77–79, 95, 110–11; "to fall down and worship," 70–71, 89, 93–94, 96–100

Parthian Empire, 275–84

Ptolemaic kings of Egypt, 174

Qumran library: Aramaic fragments of Enoch literature, 8–10, 13, 21–22, 105, 123; book of Daniel at, 136–40, 173–200, 370–71, 373; Book of Giants, 8–9, 67–68; Genizah Psalms ("Songs of David"), 320–21. *See also* Qumran library's 4Q246 (4QAramaic Apocalypse)

Qumran library's 4Q246 (4QAramaic Apocalypse), 137, 173–200, 370–71, 373; "all the deeps," 187–88; allusions to Daniel, 174–75, 195; close verbal resemblances to book of Daniel, 174–75; composition, 173–74; date of, 173–74; exegetical background of 4Q246 ii 4–9, 181–92, 199, 200; and Exodus's Song of the Sea, 185–88, 190, 194; God wages war, 185–87; homage, 184–85; and Parables of Enoch (the Messianic Figure in), 193–94, 200; parallels with Luke 1:32–33, 176–78, 196–97; parallels with 2 Samuel, Luke, and Isaiah, 196–97; peace of the coming kingdom, 183–84, 199; raising up of the people (the opening words), 188–90; righteous judgment, 181–83; scriptural allusions, 190, 195, 198; "the son of God," 176–78; the subject of 4Q246 ii 4–9, 178–81; theme of coming supersession of the pagan kingdom, 174–75; theme of the eternal kingdom, 174–75, 178–79, 181, 183–84, 186–87, 188, 190, 191–94, 199; theme of the eternal kingdom's rule over all nations, 191, 199; translations, 173, 178–83

rabbinic tradition: David Apocalypse, 322–24; Davidic Messiah, 260, 262–66, 273–75, 314–27, 371, 374; the Derekh Eretz Zuta, 235–39, 259; and Enoch, 237–39; Hekhalot literature, 95, 322; and the idea of a Messiah from the past, 260–66; and the Messiah in 4 Ezra, 235–39, 240–41; notion of a Parthian invasion of Israel that would precipitate final events, 283–84; Rabbi Aqiva on Daniel 7 and a Davidic Messiah, 314–27, 371, 374; tradition of Anani as the Davidic Messiah, 264–66; tradition of Isaiah

406

9:5–6 on Hezekiah or a son of Hezekiah, 261–64, 305; tradition of Menahem son of Hezekiah, 262–64, 266, 273–75; tradition of the death of Rabbi Yohanan ben Zakkai and imminent coming of King Hezekiah, 260–62; "two powers in heaven," 24, 326, 327; Yavneh period, 261, 314. *See also* Aqiva, Rabbi

Raphael (archangel), 27, 94, 103n

Sariel (archangel), 103n
Seleucid kings, 140, 174, 176
Sibylline Oracles Book 5, 201–20, 371, 372–73; allusions to persons, 219; biblical allusions to other scripture passages, 219, 220; the "holy ones," 203–4, 216; Joshua as the "man from heaven," 213–16, 217, 374; the Messianic Figure in Oracle A, 205–6, 219; the Messianic Figure in Oracle B, 204, 206–8, 219; the Messianic Figure in Oracle C, 202–4, 210–16, 219; the Messianic Figure in Oracle D (a Christian gloss), 204, 208–10, 219; and the Messianic Figure of the Parables of Enoch, 217–18; relationship of the four oracles with Daniel 7, 202–4, 216–17, 219; the return of Emperor Nero as eschatological figure, 202–4, 216, 219
Song at the Sea (Song of Moses), 185–88, 190, 192, 194, 357, 359, 373
Song of Miriam, 186
"Songs of David" (Genizah Psalms), 320–22
"Son of Man" concept, 1–3, 22, 110, 114, 191–92, 375; Jesus's "Son of Man" sayings in the Gospels, 1–2, 11, 22–23, 113; the phrase, 1–3; and Second Temple Judaism, 2–3, 191–92, 375

Syriac Apocalypse of Baruch. *See* Baruch, Syriac Apocalypse of (2 Baruch)

Testament of Moses, 140–41, 229
Tetragrammaton (YHWH), 89
Theodotion version of Daniel (Th-Daniel), 142–43, 146–53, 154–64, 165, 167, 374; Daniel 7:13–14, 154–64, 168–69; Daniel 7:27, 162, 171; date of, 146–49, 165; and the Epistle of Baruch, 148–49; and New Testament writers, 147–48; relationships to OG-Daniel and MT-Daniel, 149–66
"throne of glory," 40–50, 51–52, 57, 62, 77–79, 95, 110–11
"two powers in heaven" (rabbinic literature tradition), 24, 326, 327

Uriel (angel), 223, 224–25, 251

vaticinia ex eventu, 135, 276

worship, cultic: distinction between obeisance and, 89, 95–96, 98–101, 111, 163–64, 166, 193, 373–74; OG-Daniel and the "worship" of the "one like a son of man," 161–64, 166, 373–74; and the Parables of Enoch, 17–19, 89, 93–101, 107–8, 111, 163–64, 166; "to fall down and worship," 70–71, 89, 93–94, 96–100

Yavneh period, 261, 314

Zealots, 263

Index of Ancient People and Places

Aaron, 123, 232–33
Abaye, Rabbi, 318
Abbahu, Rabbi, 237
Abel-Mayyin, 121–22
Abraham, 222, 240, 255
Adam, 37, 81, 337
Ahaz, King, 261–62
Aibo, Rabbi, 262–63, 264
Aibu, Rabbi, 237
Alexander the Great, 140, 371
Alexandria, 336n
Anani, 264–66
Ananus, 346, 362
Antigonus, 276
Antiochus Epiphanes, 135, 140, 144–45, 352–53, 358–59
Antonia Fortress, 345, 346
Aqiva, Rabbi, 265, 314–27
Assyria, 174, 358
Athronges the shepherd, 275

Baal, 160n
Babylonia, 316, 325n
Babylonian Empire, 135, 138, 222, 225–26, 264, 281–84, 294, 316, 348, 360–61, 365, 369
Balaam the prophet, 15, 207–8, 265, 330, 336–38, 340, 349, 354–57, 359, 361–62, 366–67
Bar Kokhba (Shimon bar Kosiva), 265, 314, 319–20
Belshazzar, King, 137, 330, 361n
Ben Sira, 48
Bethlehem, 264
Bithia the daughter of Pharaoh, 233n, 236

Caesarea Philippi, 122
Capernaum, 125
Carthage, 350n
Cyrus, 69, 90
Cyrus the Persian, 348

Dan (Northern Israelite cult center), 122–23
Darius the Mede, 348
David, historical, 135, 316–20, 321, 374–75
Dead Sea, 121
Deborah, 233n

Index of Ancient People and Places

Domitian, 341, 364
Dosa ben Arḥinos, Rabbi, 240

Ebed-melech the Cushite, 236, 239–40n, 259
Eden. *See* Garden of Eden
Egypt, 140, 174, 201, 202, 240, 357
"Egyptian, the," 215
Eleazar ben Azariah, Rabbi, 315, 324, 326–27
Eliezer ben Hyrcanus, Rabbi, 240, 261
Eliezer the servant of Abraham, 233n, 236
Elijah, 75n, 103–4, 231, 232–34, 236, 239, 253, 374
Elioenai, 264
Enoch, 7–131, 193, 194, 214–15, 218, 231, 232–33, 236–37, 267, 272, 374
Ethiopia, 1, 12
Euphrates River, 225–26, 280–81, 288
Ezekiel, 129–30, 137, 158, 330, 360n

Galba, 341
Galilee, 23, 119–31; Magdala, 119, 121, 127–30; Upper Galilee, 120–24
Garden of Eden, 102, 105, 233n, 236–37, 259

Ḥama ben Rabbi Hoshaya, Rabbi, 237
Hermon, Mount, 85, 121–23
Herod the Great, 21, 113–15, 127, 261n, 275
Hezekiah, King, 260–63, 264, 266, 305
Hillel II, Rabbi, 262
Hiram the king of Tyre, 236, 237
Homer, 212
Hulah Valley, 121, 125

Idumeans, 346
Ishmael, Rabbi, 322–23

Israel, nation of, 141, 207, 222, 234, 251, 274, 336, 348, 357, 359
Italy, 280–81, 330

Jabez, 233n, 236
Jabin, King, 216
James the brother of Jesus, 362–63, 364, 368
Jared, 85, 259
Jeconiah, King, 293
Jehoshaphat, 278
Jeremiah, 72–73, 328–29, 343n, 360–61, 367–68
Jericho, 215
Jeroboam, King, 123
Jerome, 142, 344, 351n
Jesse, 272
Jesus, 1–2, 11, 17, 20, 22–25, 38–39, 50, 73, 92, 97–98, 113–14, 211, 214, 267, 325, 362–63, 364, 368
Jesus son of Ananias, 340
Josephus, 144, 146, 165, 215, 273–75, 328–69
Joshua, 141, 211–18, 233n, 267, 318
Joshua ben Levi, Rabbi, 236–37
Jotapata, siege of, 329n, 331–33, 343
Judah ha-Nasi, Rabbi, 236
Judas son of Hezekiah, 263, 275
Judas the Galilean, 263, 273, 340–41
Judea/Judah, 122, 123, 127, 217n, 261, 279, 333, 336, 336n, 338
Julius Caesar, 339–40, 341
Justin Martyr, 37, 262

Kallirrhoë, 120
Kenaz, 233n, 278
Kittim, 297, 338, 344, 356

Lamech, 85
Lebanon, 297–98, 308, 309

409

INDEX OF ANCIENT PEOPLE AND PLACES

Levi, 182n, 232n

Macedonia, 140, 348
Magdala, 119, 121, 127–30
Malachi, 103
Media-Persia, 348
Mediterranean Sea, 302, 303
Melchizedek, 138–39, 235n
Menahem son of Hezekiah, 262–64, 266, 273–75
Menahem son of Judas the Galilean, 273–74, 340–41
Mesopotamia, 284
Messiah ben Ephraim, 211n
Messiah ben Joseph, 211n
Methuselah, 85, 102
Migdal. *See* Magdala
Moses, 140–41, 186, 233n, 330, 347; Josephus on prophecies of, 358–59; Song at the Sea, 185–88, 190, 192, 194, 357, 359, 373
Mount of Olives, 215

Naḥman, Rav, 318
Nazareth, 122
Nebuchadnezzar, 174–75, 182, 206, 330, 348–52, 361n, 368; dream of, 174–75, 348–52, 354, 356, 357, 362, 368
Nero, 202–5, 216, 219, 227, 279–83, 319, 371
Noah, 11, 35, 85, 101, 102, 233n
Northern Kingdom, 358

Origen, 85n, 142, 154
Otto, 341

Palestine, Jewish, 22, 119, 127, 302, 316, 366n
Paneas (modern Banias), 123
Pappa, Rav, 318

Persia, 135, 138, 278, 280, 282–84, 348, 361n
Philo, 85, 336–37, 355
Phinehas, 232–34, 258
Pilate, 363n
Pliny the Elder, 340
Polybius, 331n
Pseudo-Hegesippus, 339n
Pseudo-Philo, 153, 232, 239, 278, 284

Qumran library, 8–10, 13–14, 21, 123, 136–40, 143, 173–200, 320–21, 360n

Rav (Abba Arika), 318
Rome, 138, 140, 202, 216, 225–26, 279–84, 337, 341, 348, 350–51, 355–56, 361, 371

Seleucia, 226
Sepphoris, 122
Serah the daughter of Asher, 233n
Seth, 337
Shiloh, 299, 358
Simeon ben Yoḥai, Rabbi, 284
Simon son of Gioras, 273, 274–75
Simon the slave, 275
Suetonius, 334, 337n
Syria, 338

Tacitus, 334, 337n
Tanhuma, Rabbi, 317
Theodotion, 143, 146–47
Titus, 206, 281, 341, 344–45, 346, 366
Trajan, 275–76
Trypho, 37, 262

Vespasian, 206, 274, 329, 331–36, 341–44, 347, 350, 356, 366, 367
Virgil, 350
Vitellius, 341

410

Index of Ancient People and Places

Yohanan ben Zakkai, Rabbi, 260–62
Yose, Rabbi, 237–38
Yose ben Qismah, Rabbi, 283
Yose the Galilean, Rabbi, 314–15, 324–27
Yudan, Rabbi (son of Rabbi Aibo), 262–63, 264

Zerubabbel, 210, 265
Zion, Mount, 78, 117, 254–55, 297, 299, 351n
Zoilos, 123

Index of Ancient Literature

Hebrew Bible

Genesis
1:9	126n
1:9–10	126
1:14–18	70
3:23–24	55, 200
5	101–2
5:21–24	101
5:23	238
5:24	55, 102, 237–39, 259
5:29	85
6:9	101
15:13	240, 241
24:48	100
32:29	176
49:9	244–45, 254, 257, 286, 313
49:9–10	110, 270
49:9–12	116
49:10	188–89, 245, 268, 299, 313, 337, 343

Exodus
4:9	126n
13:21–22	160
14–15	187
14:13	55, 198, 200
14:14	200
14:16	126n
14:22	126n
14:29	126n
15	373
15:1	186, 190, 198, 200
15:1–3	200
15:1–18	185, 190, 192, 199
15:2	185, 190, 198
15:3	186, 198
15:5	188
15:7	53, 200
15:8	188
15:10	53, 200
15:14	186
15:14–16	357
15:18	186
15:19	126n
15:21	186
40:34–35	160

Leviticus
16:2	160
25–26	358
26:31	358
26:31–35	358
26:40–45	358

Numbers
16:32–33	287
23:7	15
23:7–24:9	355
23:18	15
24:3	15
24:7	207n, 336n
24:14	338
24:15	15
24:15–24	355
24:16	337
24:16–24	337
24:17	207, 208, 217, 218, 219, 220, 265, 268, 274, 316n, 320, 336–38, 340–41, 343, 347, 355–56, 367, 371

Index of Ancient Literature

24:17–19	336
24:17–24	336n, 337
24:17b	207, 336
24:17c–24	208
24:18	337
24:19	337
24:19a	336
24:20	15
24:21	15
24:24	356
25:11–13	232n
25:12	232n, 233n

Deuteronomy

2:25	357n
11:25	357n
29	358
29:28	257
30:4	233n
32	355
32:1–43	359
32:10–35	359
32:36–43	359
32:43	53
33:23	84n

Joshua

4:22	126n
6	215
10	217, 373
10:12–14	212–13, 219
10:15	213n
10:40	213
10:43	213n
11:4	216, 219
24:30–31	215n

Judges

7:12	216

1 Samuel

2:8	47
13:5	216

2 Samuel

3:18	243n
7	178, 191, 210
7:5	243n
7:8	243n
7:9	177, 196, 198
7:9–16	177
7:12	245, 254, 257
7:13	210, 217, 220, 270, 286, 313, 371
7:13–14	191, 194, 199, 200, 371
7:13–14a	196
7:13–16	268
7:14	192, 198, 243
7:14a	177
7:16	196
22:9	249

1 Kings

2:10	319
8:10–11	160
12:25–33	123
18:44	302, 303, 310
19:10	232n

2 Kings

2:9–12	103, 233
2:10	259
2:11	259
2:11–12	55, 200
17:5–6	257
18:5	261
20:21	262

1 Chronicles

3	264
3:19–24	265
3:24	264–65
4:9–10	236n
4:10	239n
14:17	357n

2 Chronicles

3:6	102n
20:15–17	278
20:23	278, 287
29:28–30	100
32:33	262

Nehemiah

9:5	40n
9:11	126n

Esther

8:16	356n, 357n
9:2	356n, 357n

Job

7:18	61
14:2	54
33:26	84n

Psalms

2	29, 56, 74, 78, 109, 110, 116, 117, 218, 245, 254, 270, 272, 286, 371, 372
2:1–2	257, 271, 286, 313
2:2	29, 37, 53, 60, 76, 78, 90, 200, 244, 272, 286, 299, 306, 313, 317
2:5	257, 286
2:5–7	313

413

2:6	76, 78, 117, 257, 275, 286, 313	72:2	30, 182, 184	105:38	357
		72:4	53, 71	106:4	84n
2:6–7	110n	72:7	184	110	46
2:7	177, 197, 243, 244, 247, 254, 257, 286	72:7–11	184	110:1	17, 43n, 50, 325
		72:11	53, 70–71, 190, 198	114:4	54
2:8	29, 54, 200, 286, 313	72:13	71	118:14	185
2:8–9	209, 217, 220	72:17	53, 70n, 184	132:10	243n
2:9	29, 76, 299	72:17a	70–71	135	301n
3:7	53, 200	72:19	40n	135:7	301–2, 310
5:12	84n	77	301n	138:1–2	100
7:5	184	77:17–18	302, 310	144:5–6	302
9:12	53	77:17–18[18–19]	301	144:5–7	301, 310
16:11	53	77:18	301	144:6	301n
17:3	61	80	298	147:11	84n
17:22–25	251	82:6	179n	149:4	84n
18:8[9]	249, 250, 257	84:1–2	83		
18:10–11	160	86:9	94n, 100	**Proverbs**	
18:10–11[11–12]	160	89:3	243n, 306, 321	8:35	84n
18:51	317	89:17	84n	11:20	84n
21:5	50	89:20	243n, 306	12:2	84n
28:7	185	89:20–29	199	12:22	84n
30:7	84n	89:25	188	18:22	84n
30:10	84n	89:26	198, 200	22:21	183n
45:3	50	89:27	321		
47:9	40n	89:28–29	321	**Isaiah**	
50:1–6	66	89:39	306	1:12	257
51:18	84n	90:15	240–41	2:2–3	220
60:6	183n	90:15–16	286, 313	2:4	184, 198, 199, 200
66:4	100	90:16	241	2:11	312
66:6	126n	96:10–13	66	2:12	308
68	160n	97	301n	2:12–14	298
68:2	249, 257	97:2	160	2:13	309
68:4[5]	160	97:4	301, 302, 310	2:14	308
69:28	64	97:5	249, 257	3:8	40n
71:20	187	99:5	100	4:3	64, 176
72	30, 70–71, 109, 272, 286, 313, 371	99:9	100	5:14	287
		103:3 [104:3]	160	6:3	93n
72:1–11	199, 200	104:3	160	7:10–14	261
72:1–17	200	104:32	249, 257	7:14	262

414

8:5	308	11:1–9	199	22:23	47
8:6	299, 313	11:1–10	304, 321	24:17–23	60n
8:7	50, 308	11:2	28, 54, 77, 286, 313	24:21	60–61, 77, 200, 273, 286, 313
9	178	11:2–3	76		
9:2	304, 312	11:2–4	42, 54, 77	30:27	249
9:2–4	304–5	11:2–5	27–28, 29, 30, 31, 39, 56, 74–75, 78, 109, 200, 272, 304	32:2	259
9:2–7	304, 305–6, 313			32:16	53
9:3	263n, 312			34:5–6	55
9:3–7	304	11:3–4	298	36:6	298
9:4	312	11:3b	77	37:29	257
9:5	198	11:4	28, 29, 30, 31, 54, 78, 117, 190, 198, 200, 209n, 245, 249, 251, 255–56, 257, 268, 270, 271–73, 275n, 286, 298, 300, 309, 313, 320n, 373	40:1	263
9:5–6	200			40:2	347
9:5–6[6–7]	177, 178, 184, 194, 196, 261–64, 305			40:4	308
				41:11–12	200, 286, 313
				41:12	55
9:5–7	193n, 305			42	77
9:6	176, 198			42–43	105
9:6[5]	177, 184, 191			42–53	321
9:6–7	374	11:4–5	313	42:1	27, 28, 31n, 39, 53, 54, 76, 83, 104, 105, 110n, 270, 272, 306, 372
9:7	299, 300, 306, 312	11:4a	182–83		
9:18[17]	297–98, 309	11:4b	77, 250, 308		
10:33	308, 312	11:5	53, 286		
10:33–34a	297–98	11:6–7	312	42:1–7	27–28, 29, 56, 109, 116, 200, 272, 286, 313
10:33–11:1	298–99, 308–9	11:6–9	184		
10:33–11:4	304, 306	11:8	312		
10:33–11:10	305, 313	11:9	299	42:1a	77
10:33b	297, 298	11:10	50, 312, 321	42:1b	77
10:34	297–99, 308, 309	11:12	251, 255, 286, 313	42:6	30, 321
10:34a	297–98	11:14	185, 251	43:5–6	94
10:34a–11:4	298	12:1	263	44:3	126n
10:34b	298–99	12:2b	185	45:1	90
11	77, 191, 254, 260, 270, 286, 304, 371	13:8	55, 200	45:4	69, 90
		13:15–22	225–26	45:14	100, 111, 184, 257
11:1	28, 31, 272, 298–99, 308	13:19	50	47:1	48
		13:20	226	47:1–7	116
11:1–4	193n	14:15	282	47:6	187
11:1–5	31, 48, 78n, 110, 116, 117, 183, 262, 272	14:18	50	47:8–9	282
		19:1	160–61, 248, 249n	49:1	53, 90
		19:2	257		

415

INDEX OF ANCIENT LITERATURE

49:1–7	27–28, 29, 56, 109, 272, 286, 313	65:18–25	313	49:38	66
49:1–8	200	65:19	312	50–51	282, 361
49:1–62:3	29	65:20	312	50:41–42	278n
49:1b	71	65:21–22	312	51:11	54, 282–83, 287
49:2	28, 29, 55, 71n	65:25	312	51:33	283n
49:3	27, 90, 100	66:1	326		
49:6	53, 71, 96, 190, 194, 198, 199, 200	66:15	249, 250	**Lamentations**	
		66:15–16	249	1:16	262–64
		66:20	54, 257	3:44	160
49:6a	71	66:22	53		
49:6b	71	66:23	94, 100	**Ezekiel**	
49:7	53, 54, 55, 71, 96–97, 100, 111	66:24	55	1:4–28	129
				1:15–21	129
49:7b	71	**Jeremiah**		1:26	36, 44, 110
49:8	53	1:5	73	7:22	360n
49:23	184	4:25	226n	10:1–8	129
51:12	263	7:11	360n	10:9–22	129
52:1–2	55	7:12–14	358	11:19	232
52:13	28, 55, 200, 286, 313	7:20	360n	17:3	257
		7:30	360n	17:6	299
52:13–15	28, 47n, 272	7:34	360n	17:6–8	298–99, 313
52:13–53:12	46n	10:12	301	17:8	299
52:15	55, 200, 286, 313	10:12–13	301, 310	28:13	239n
53	116	10:13	301–2, 303, 310	34:23–24	243, 317, 319
55:1	53	13:18	50	36:26–27	232
57:17	356n	14:21	44	37:24	317, 319
59:19	220	17:12	44, 45	37:24–25	243, 268
60:1	220	23:5	205n, 210	37:24–28	210n
60:1–2	55	23:5–6	30, 268	37:25	318
60:4	94	26:6	358	38–39	254n, 277
60:9	94	26:9	358	38:15	278n
60:10	84n	29:52	149n	38:21	54, 276n, 278, 287
60:14	184	30:9	317–18, 319	40–47	129
60:17–18	220	33:15–16	30	43:1–9	129
60:19–20	220	33:21–22	243n	48:23–29	252
61:6	176	33:26	243n		
62:4	176	39:15–18	239n	**Daniel**	
65	304	45:5	240	1:2	187
65:17	53	46:10	55	1:4	158

1:5	158	3:18	99n, 161, 162	7	16, 29n, 30–32, 34,
1:13	158	3:26	177		39–40, 56, 61, 77,
1:22	158	3:28	99n, 161		78, 100, 110, 116,
1:26	158	3:28[95]	162		135–41, 142–72,
1:27	158	3:33	195, 198		173–200, 202–4,
1:28	158	3:33 [4:3]	174		216–17, 218,
2	175, 178, 286, 313	3:54	43n		221–59, 270, 286,
2–6	174	4–5	165		294, 299–300,
2–7	159, 174	4–6	149–50, 152–53		303–4, 313, 314–27,
2:4	195, 198	4:2 [3:32]	177		328–69, 370–75
2:31–35	245	4:3	163	7–12	150, 153
2:34	257, 348, 349	4:3 [3:33]	181	7:1	257
2:34–35	257	4:17	177	7:1–8	66
2:35	343, 349	4:23[20]	176	7:2	67, 248, 257
2:37	50	4:24	177	7:2–3	303
2:40	344	4:25	53, 177	7:2–14	164
2:41	176, 195, 257	4:26[23]	176	7:3	37n, 248, 257
2:41–42	349	4:30	50	7:3–7	257
2:43	155, 176	4:31	195, 198	7:3–8	341–42
2:44	163, 175, 189, 190,	4:31[34]	174	7:4–8	300, 307
	195, 198, 351	4:32	53, 177	7:7	257, 344, 349
2:44–45	199, 200,	4:33	155	7:7–8	140, 203n
	274, 343	4:34	162, 163, 177, 190,	7:8	140, 164, 166, 202–3,
2:45	185n, 195, 198, 255,		195, 198, 200		219, 220, 226
	257, 348, 349	4:34–37[31–34]	199	7:8a	203
2:45–47	185	4:34b	163n	7:8b	164
2:46	99n, 195	4:36	50	7:9	28–29, 30, 44, 53, 54,
2:47	182	4:37[34]	182		55, 56, 63, 64n,
3–6	352	5:6	195, 198		65, 66–67, 109,
3:5	99n	5:10	195, 198		128, 129, 158, 246,
3:6	99n	5:18	50		314–16, 318, 324,
3:7	99n	5:20	50		327, 374
3:9	195, 198	5:20–21	53, 94n	7:9–10	45, 53, 54, 64–68,
3:10	99n	5:23	148		307, 319, 325–26
3:11	99n	6:17	161, 162	7:9–14	45–46, 59–60,
3:12	99n, 161, 162	6:21	161, 162, 195, 198		324
3:14	99n, 161, 162	6:22	147	7:9–22	200
3:15	99n	6:26	163	7:9–27	29, 32, 109, 199
3:17	161, 162	6:27	162	7:9b–10	60

417

INDEX OF ANCIENT LITERATURE

7:10	64–65, 69, 195, 223, 230, 230n, 254, 307	7:13c	155–56, 168, 169–70		204, 219, 220, 300, 342, 344, 353n
7:10–13	69	7:13c–d	155–56	7:26	204, 373
7:11	209, 219, 220, 257, 298	7:13d	155, 168, 169–70	7:26–27	204
		7:14	45, 54, 55, 69n, 76, 77, 100, 104–5, 116–17, 141, 161–64, 174, 179, 186–87, 190–94, 195, 198, 205, 208–9, 220, 268, 273, 304, 307, 315, 372–74	7:27	29, 74n, 100, 138–39, 141, 146, 161–62, 171–72, 174, 175, 177, 179–81, 190–92, 195, 198, 204, 219, 220, 300, 307, 348
7:13	2, 3, 22, 28–29, 32, 35–40, 45, 53, 54, 63, 66n, 69, 74–75, 76, 78, 84, 91, 104, 109, 139, 146, 153–61, 166, 174, 175, 179, 192n, 193–94, 204, 205, 206, 208, 218, 219, 220, 223–24, 230, 238, 244, 246, 246n, 247–48, 253–55, 257, 264–66, 267–73, 296, 300, 303, 305, 315–17, 324, 369, 371–75			7:28	332
				7:36	257
		7:14a	154–55, 166, 168–70	8	352–54
				8:5	348
		7:14b	161, 166, 168–70	8:9	67
		7:14c	168–70	8:10	53
		7:14c–d	163	8:13	167
		7:14d	168–70	8:14	144n, 158, 344, 353n
		7:15	332		
		7:16	53	8:15	36, 53, 84, 110, 200, 246, 246n, 269, 372
		7:16–18	63		
		7:17–22	300, 307		
		7:18	138, 141, 177, 219, 220	8:23–25	203n, 226
7:13–14	24, 30–31, 54, 60, 104, 116–17, 135, 138, 140, 153–66, 168–70, 181, 187, 192–93, 210, 215, 219, 274, 294, 316, 318, 326, 341, 343, 351n, 364, 366–67, 369			8:27	332
		7:20	203, 219	9:1–19	141
		7:20–21	226	9:4–19	148–49
		7:20b–21	203	9:18	145n
		7:21	147, 164, 342	9:20–27	138n
		7:21–22	65, 104–5, 189, 219, 220	9:24	139n, 347
				9:24–27	341, 343–44, 353
		7:22	29, 31, 53, 55, 66, 67, 74n, 141, 164, 177, 192n, 204	9:25	138, 341, 342–43, 347, 369
7:13–27	200				
7:13a	168, 169–70	7:23	53, 163n, 174, 195, 198, 257	9:25a	345
7:13b	155, 157, 168, 169–70			9:25b	345
		7:24–25	300, 307	9:26	145n, 342–45, 346, 347, 367
7:13b–c	155–56, 158n	7:25	29, 54, 74n, 177,		

Index of Ancient Literature

9:27	145, 167, 344, 353n	**Joel**		8:3	176
10–11	352–53	3:2	66	9:9–10	199, 268
10–12	353n	3:9–11 [4:9–11]	257	9:10	184, 198, 200
10:5–6	36			9:13–15	185
10:16	158	**Jonah**		10:8	257
10:18	36, 84, 110, 158, 246, 246n, 269, 372	1:9	126n	11:1	298
		2:10	126n	12:1–6	277
				12:2–4	54
11:16	67	**Micah**		12:3–4	277–78, 287
11:26	144n	1:3	141	12:4	278
11:29–12:1	138	1:4	54, 200, 249, 257	14:9	323
11:30	338	4:3	184, 199, 200		
11:30–33	344	5	191	**Malachi**	
11:30–35	138n	5:2	235, 264, 268, 374	2:4–7	232n
11:31	144, 145–46, 167	5:2[1]	74	3:1	232n
11:32	137	5:3	177n, 198	3:16–18	64
11:40–12:3	141	5:3–4[2–3]	200	4:5–6	103
11:41	67	5:4[3]	177, 191, 197	4:5–6 [3:23–24]	232, 374
12:1	54, 64, 138, 139, 141	5:4–5[3–4]	199	4:6 [3:23]	233n
		5:5	184		
12:1–11	146n	**Habakkuk**		## Deutero-canonical Books	
12:3	141, 207	3:6	249, 257		
12:4	144n			**Judith**	
12:7	146n, 204, 344, 353n	**Zephaniah**		10:23	99
		1:18	54, 200	14:7	99
12:10	137	3:13	55, 200	16:15	249
12:11	145–46, 146n, 167, 344, 353n	**Haggai**		**Additions to Esther**	
12:12	344, 353n	2:22	276n, 278, 287	C 5–7	99
12:13	146n, 318				
		Zechariah		**Wisdom of Solomon**	
Hosea		3:8	210, 243n	2:10–20	47n
2:18[20]	184, 190	4:7	72n, 265	3:2	46
2:18–19[20–21]	199	6:1–6	128	4:10–11	46
2:20	198	6:5	128n	4:16	46–47
2:20–22	200	6:12	210, 263n	4:16–5:13	46–47
3:5	317, 318, 319	6:12–13	210, 217, 220	5:1–5	47

419

Index of Ancient Literature

9:10	44	**Old Testament Pseudepigrapha**		36:7–8	298
15:15	148			36:7–10	306, 309, 366
				36:10	297, 298, 309
Sirach		*Apocalypse of Abraham*		37:1	297, 298
44:46	259	30:8	230	39–40	78
45:23	232n			39:3–5	78n, 300, 307, 365
45:24	232n	*2 Baruch*	78, 116,	39:4–5	300
46:1	215		293–313	39:5	298, 300
47:11	47	1:1	293	39:7	259, 296, 297,
48:2	232n	1:2–5	365		299–300, 299n,
48:9	259	8:2	365		306, 307
48:10–11	103	10:10	294	39:7–40:2	118, 365
		13:3	235, 258, 259	39:7–40:3	37
Baruch		21:6	307	39:8–40:2	297
1:1–3:8	149n	21:23b	290	40:1	78, 298,
1:15–3:8	148–49	23:4–5a	292		299–300, 306
4:5–5:9	148	24:1	64n, 230n, 307	40:1–2	118
		25:1	235, 258, 259	40:2	252, 297
1 Maccabees		28:2	293n	40:3	268, 294, 295, 297,
1:9	144n	29	294		300, 307
1:18	144n	29–30	294–96	40:4–5	297
1:20–23	353	29:3	62n, 259, 294–96,	40:6–11	297
1:45–46	144		304, 305, 306	46:7	259
1:54	144, 167, 353	29:3–8	252, 269	48:30	259
2:26	232n	29:4	252, 296	53	310–11
2:54	232n	29:6	252n, 253n	53–74	297, 300–304
4:41	144n	30:1	294–96, 306	53:1	300, 302n,
4:43	144n	30:1–2	295		303, 310
4:52	353	30:1b	295	53:8	300, 310
5:14–24	122	32:2–4	365	53:8–11	301
9:73	183n	36–37	308–9	53:9	301, 302, 310
		36–40	78n, 193n,	53:10	300, 302
2 Maccabees			296–99, 365	53:11	302
2:8	160	36:1	303	56:2–4	300, 301, 365
3:26	85n	36:3	299, 308	56:3	301n
15:12–16	215n	36:4	308	56:3–4	301
		36:4–6	297, 308	56:4	302n, 303
4 Maccabees		36:5	297, 298, 308	56:5–68:8	300
18:12	232n	36:6	299, 308, 309	59:2	304n

Index of Ancient Literature

69:2–3	300	10:19	130	37:2	126n
69:5–70:10	300	10:21	35n	37:4	83
70:2	303	11:1	35n	37:5	15, 126n
70:7	282n, 289	12:1	35n	37:6	88
70:9	243n, 303n, 306	12:3	92	38:1	15, 126n
72–74	304, 312	12:4	86, 92n, 102n	38:1–6	15
72:1	301, 303, 312	12:4–5	95	38:1–44:1	15
72:2	302, 303n, 306, 312	13	122	38:2	26, 51, 90, 126n
		13:1	92n	38:4	36, 127
72:2–6	303	13:1–2	95	39–45	26
73–74	294	13:7	121	39:1	35, 109
73:1	299, 300, 304, 306, 312	13:9	123	39:1–2	13
		13:32	110n	39:2	92
73:2	312	13:35	110n	39:3	82, 126n, 259
73:3	312	13:37	110n	39:3–40:10	105–6
73:6	312	14	68	39:3–41:9	58–59
74:1	312	14:1–2	95	39:4	12, 82, 83
74:3	303	14:4–5	95	39:4–5	58
74:4	301, 312	14:8	160n	39:4–7	271
76:2	259	14:18	128	39:4–8	104
		14:18–19	128	39:5	35, 82, 109
1 Enoch		14:18–23	68	39:6	30, 33n, 35, 51, 90
1–5	15	14:20	40n	39:6–7	27, 83, 86
1–36	7, 27, 122	14:24	92n	39:6–8	82–84
1:1	27	15:1	86, 92n	39:7	30n, 83, 89n, 93, 96, 107
1:1–9	272	15:1–16:4	123		
1:2	12, 15, 74, 86	15:12	35n	39:7–8	106
1:3	15	17–36	12–13, 15	39:8	70n
1:3–9	66n, 68	17:36	102	39:8–9	69
1:3b–9	16	18:8	67n	39:9	83, 89n, 107
1:3b–5:9	15	19:3	92	39:9–10	93
1:4–5:9	104	24:4	130	39:10	93, 107
1:6	54, 249	25:3	67	39:12	69, 93, 107
1:8	27, 83, 105	25:4	67	39:12–40:1	76n
5:7	105	31:2	130	39:13	69, 89n, 93, 107
6–16	13, 15, 16, 123–24	32:4	130	39:14	36
6:6	85, 121, 122–23	37–71	7, 20, 21	40:1	29
9:4	44	37:1	81, 92	40:2–7	94
10:1	95	37:1–5	15, 88	40:3	107

421

INDEX OF ANCIENT LITERATURE

40:4	94, 107		51, 53, 63, 86, 90,	48:4–51:5	16
40:5	27, 33n, 51, 94, 108		92, 246, 269	48:4a	71
40:6	89n, 126n	46:2–3	34–35, 92	48:4b	71
40:7	126n	46:2–48:2	26	48:5	19, 53, 89–90,
41:1–2	58	46:3	29, 30, 32–34, 51,		96, 99, 100, 107,
41:2	89n, 90		53, 63, 85–86, 90,		108, 126n
41:3–9	59n		92, 246, 269	48:5a	70–71
41:7	93, 107	46:4	32–34, 51, 53	48:6	53, 71, 72, 73–74
41:8	89n	46:4–5	19	48:6–7a	73
41:9	58–59	46:4–6	30	48:7	30, 53, 89n, 91
42:1–2	72n	46:4–8	64, 71	48:7c	71
42:2	35, 109	46:5	53, 94n, 107	48:8	29, 53, 60, 126
42:3	59n	46:6	53, 89n	48:9	53
43:4	89n, 126n	46:7	29n, 53, 74n,	48:10	26, 29, 30, 51, 53,
45:1	15, 53, 89n		89n, 90		60, 89n, 90
45:1–6	15	46:8	89n	49:1	53
45:1–51:5	58, 59	47:1	53, 66, 69, 82	49:1–4	60, 76–77
45:1–57:3	15	47:1–2	58	49:2	33n, 51, 54, 69,
45:2	53, 89n, 90	47:1–4	45n, 60,		76, 268
45:3	27, 33n, 41, 51, 53,		64–68, 291	49:2–3	30
	57, 59, 60, 68, 89n	47:2	31, 53, 61n, 65–66,	49:2–4	63
45:3–5	27		69, 89n, 107	49:2–62:1	26
45:3–6	59, 77	47:3	16, 32, 41, 51, 53,	49:2b	76–77
45:4	51, 53, 59		57, 61n, 63, 64–65,	49:3	54, 77
45:4–6a	60		66, 69, 230n, 324	49:3–4a	76
45:5	27, 33n, 53, 59	47:4	53	49:4	27, 31, 33n, 51, 54,
45:5–6	269	48:1	53, 66n, 93n		69, 83
45:6	53, 69, 77, 126n	48:2	32–33, 51, 53, 60,	49:4a	77
45:6b	59, 60		68, 69, 71, 76, 88,	49:4b	76
46:1	32, 33, 35–36, 40,		246, 269	50:1	36
	53, 59, 62–63, 82,	48:2–3	89, 90	50:2	89n
	84–85, 109, 110,	48:2–6	30	50:3	89n
	246, 248, 269,	48:2–10	68–71	50:4	69
	324, 372, 373	48:3	53, 69–71, 72–73,	50:5	42
46:1–2	28		83, 88	51:1	290
46:1–3	106	48:3–7	71	51:1–3	42
46:1–8	62–64	48:4	53, 96, 98	51:2	42n, 54, 59, 64, 65
46:1–48:2	29	48:4–7	73–74	51:2–3	60, 68, 77
46:2	26, 32–33, 34, 39,	48:4–10	71	51:2–5	59

422

51:3	33n, 42, 51, 54, 57, 95n, 268	56:6	283n	61:7	107
51:3–5	27	56:7	277–78	61:8	31, 33n, 41–42, 43, 45n, 50, 51, 57, 61, 77–78, 95n, 98
51:3b	42, 77	56:7–8	283		
51:4	31n, 54, 59, 60	56:7a	54		
51:5	27, 33n, 42, 51, 54, 59	56:7b	54	61:8–9	98
		56:8	276n	61:8–13	60
51:5a	42n, 59n, 60	57:1	54, 276	61:8b	61
51:5b	59, 60	57:1–2	94	61:9	89n, 107
52:1–3	54	57:1–3	276, 283	61:9b	98
52:3	92n	57:3	93–94, 107	61:9b–12	95
52:4	26, 29, 51, 54, 76	57:3b	15	61:10	33n, 51, 61, 95, 126, 129
52:5	54, 92n	57:5	282–83		
52:6	33n, 51, 54, 249	57:5–7a	288	61:10–11	73n
52:6–9	193	58:1	15	61:11	89n, 93, 107
52:7	54	58:1–6	15	61:12	89n, 93, 107
52:8	54	58:1–69:29	15	61:13	89n, 98
52:9	29, 33n, 51, 54, 63, 69, 126n	58:4	89n	62–63	46n, 61–62
		58:6	69	62:1	27, 30, 31, 33n, 46, 51, 54, 65n, 77–78, 98, 126n, 127
53:1	126	59:2	126n		
53:2	126n	59:22	29n, 54		
53:4	92n	60:1	29n, 54, 74n	62:1–2	61
53:6	26, 51, 86, 89n	60:1–10	11	62:1–7	47, 74
53:9	126n	60:1–25	88	62:1–12	60, 77–79
54:1–6	61–62	60:2	35, 41, 51, 54	62:1–63:12	98
54:4	92n	60:5	126n	62:2	31, 42–43, 46, 50, 51, 54, 57, 77–78, 91, 98, 250
54:6	126n	60:6	89n		
54:7–55:2	11	60:9	126		
54:9	126n	60:10	32n, 35, 88	62:2–3	30, 86
55:1	51, 126n	60:22	74n, 126n	62:3	46, 52, 54, 57, 77, 124–25, 127
55:2	89n, 126n	60:24–25	11		
55:4	27, 33n, 41–42, 51, 57, 60, 62, 77, 89n, 126n	61	95	62:3–63:12	16
		61:1–5	105n	62:4	54
		61:2	92n, 117	62:5	28, 32–33, 41, 52, 55, 57, 246, 269
		61:3	89n		
56	279	61:4–5	27		
56:1–4	124n	61:5	33n, 51	62:5–9	30
56:2	54, 92n, 373	61:6–7	95n	62:5–71:14	26
56:5	281	61:6–13	98, 323n	62:5–71:17	29
56:5–8	115, 275–84, 287	61:6–63:12	58		

423

INDEX OF ANCIENT LITERATURE

62:6	31n, 55, 77, 94, 96n, 97–99, 108, 127	65:6	126n	70:1–71:17	88
		65:12	126n	70:2	55, 88
		65:26	11–12	70:3–4	105
62:6–7	19	66:1	126n	70:3–71:17	12
62:7	27, 29n, 32–34, 52, 55, 64, 72, 73–74, 74n, 91, 259	67:3	89n, 126n	71	80
		67:7	126n	71–72	235n
		67:8	89n, 126n	71:1	36, 55
62:8	27, 55, 91	67:8–10	115	71:1–4	105
62:9	19, 32–33, 52, 55, 77, 97, 98, 108, 126, 246, 269	67:12	127	71:2–4	55
		69:1	126n	71:5	55, 92–93
		69:2–5	62	71:5–8	68
62:9–11	98	69:7	126n	71:6	129
62:10–11	55	69:13–25	89	71:6–7	55
62:11	27	69:22–24	93n	71:7	41, 52, 57, 128–29
62:12	27, 55	69:24	89n	71:8	55, 61n
62:13	27, 55	69:26	32–33, 52, 55, 62, 77, 88–89, 91, 107, 246, 269	71:9	55
62:13–16	60			71:10	32, 52, 55
62:14	32–33, 52, 55, 246, 269			71:11	56, 107
		69:27	31, 32–34, 41, 52, 55, 57, 58, 77, 91, 126n	71:11–12	93
62:15	27, 55			71:12	32, 52, 56
62:16	55, 69			71:13	32, 52, 56
63:1	77, 93–94, 97, 107, 126	69:27–29	58, 62, 91	71:14	30, 32–34, 52, 56, 63, 72, 80, 81, 83, 86, 88, 91–93, 234, 246, 269
		69:27a–b	62		
63:1–6	96–97	69:28	55, 60, 62, 77, 126n		
63:1–10	55				
63:1–12	60, 98	69:29	32–33, 41, 52, 55, 57, 63, 88, 92, 246, 259, 269	71:14–15	106
63:2	94, 107			71:15	56
63:2–4	94			71:16	30, 56, 83
63:4	31n, 97, 107	69:29a	62	71:16–17	106
63:5	107	69:29a–b	62	71:17	32–33, 52, 56, 89n, 246, 269
63:6	94	69:29b	15, 62		
63:7	89n, 107	69:29c	62	72–82	7, 102
63:11	30, 32–33, 52, 55, 69, 246, 269	70–71	12, 105, 111	79:9–10	68
		70:1	32–33, 52, 55, 69, 86–88, 126n, 246, 269	83–90	7, 13
63:12	55, 58, 127			85–90	13, 67, 102
64:1–2	62			87:2	103n
64:2	11–12, 77, 92n	70:1–2	28, 64, 86–88, 259	87:3	102
64:18	269			89:51	123
65:1–69:25	11, 62	70:1–71:14	15	89:54–58	123

Index of Ancient Literature

89:61–64	103n	4:51	224, 234	6:52	252n
89:70–71	103n	4:52	224	7:26	365
89:76–77	103n	5:1	225	7:26–44	224, 231,
90:14–20	103n	5:1–2	232		240–41, 256
90:20	67	5:1–13	224, 227, 256	7:26b	241
90:22	103n	5:1–6:34	256	7:27	234, 241, 294
90:30	99, 100n, 184n	5:2	225	7:28	75, 75n, 227, 228,
90:31	102, 103n	5:3	225		231, 234, 240,
91–105	7	5:4	225		242–44, 245,
92:1	105	5:4–5	226		252–53, 259, 296
93:1	15	5:6	227	7:28–29	243–44, 256
93:3	15	5:6–7	256	7:28–30	233–34
93:11	35n	5:6–7a	226	7:28a	258
100:1–3	278n	5:7	225, 227	7:28b	253
101:1	35n	5:7b–9a	226	7:29	229, 233, 242, 255
102:3	68	5:9–11	232	7:30	233
103:8	233	5:12	225	7:30–31	229, 233
104:1	64	5:21–6:34	222	7:30–33	229
106–107	7, 85, 102	5:56	227–29	7:31–32	234
106:7	102, 104	5:56–6:1	252	7:31–44	228
106:7–8	105	5:56–6:6	229–30	7:32	290
106:8	102	5:56–6:10	227–32	7:70	228
		6:1	228, 229, 231	8:1	223
2 Enoch		6:1–6	228	9–13	365
20:1	129n	6:2–6	228–29	9:1–6	229, 256
33:4	301n	6:6	228	9:8	241
36:2	259	6:18–28	224,	9:27	223
71–72	235n		229–32, 256	9:27–10:59	222, 256
		6:20	223, 248, 254	9:38–10:4	256
4 Ezra		6:20b	230	10:25–27	241
3:1	222, 364	6:25	75, 230–31, 240	10:38–54	256
3:1–5:20	222, 256	6:26	75n, 231, 235, 256,	10:41–48	224n
3:2–3	222		258, 259	10:53–55	241
3:23	243	6:26a	231	11	257
4:21	225	6:26b	232	11–12	245, 271
4:26	224, 234	6:27–28	232	11–13	110, 257–59,
4:33–37	292	6:28	235		365, 366
4:39	225	6:35–9:26	222, 256	11:1	248
4:44–50	224	6:49–52	296	11:1–35	244

425

11:1–12:3	256	13:3b–10	255	13:57–58	223
11:1–12:51	222, 223, 256	13:4	227, 249, 250	14:1–48	222, 256
11:36–46	256	13:5	37, 110, 245, 246	14:9	75, 75n, 225, 231, 234, 242, 243, 248, 256, 258, 269, 271–72
11:37	158n	13:5–11	277, 279		
11:39–40	365	13:6	351n		
11:40	235	13:9–11	78		
11:40–43	366	13:10	209n, 249, 250	14:18	225
12	257	13:10–11	248–49	14:32	365
12–13	299, 300	13:11	249	14:50	258, 259
12:1	75	13:12	38, 110, 117, 246, 251, 269	15:50	231
12:10–16	342				
12:10–36	256	13:14–20	234n	**Genizah Psalms**	
12:11	223, 300	13:20–55	256	**(Songs of David)**	
12:11–12	244	13:25	246–47, 269	1	321
12:11–30	244	13:25–26	247	1:15	321
12:12	224	13:25–38	228	1:23	321
12:22–28	366n	13:25–52	256	1:24–26	321
12:31–32	247	13:26	38, 74, 229n, 235, 252, 264, 296	2:8	321
12:31–33	228			2:8–16	321
12:31–34	256, 365	13:27–38	78	2:17–20	321
12:32	38n, 75, 234, 242, 243, 245, 253, 259, 296, 318, 366	13:32	38, 242, 243, 246–47, 259, 269, 296	3:18–19	321
				Jubilees	
12:32–33	78	13:33	227, 271	4:23	102, 105, 233, 259
12:34	227, 228, 241, 245, 263n, 269	13:35	78, 299	4:24	102
		13:35–36	351n	10:17	86
13	37–38, 39, 75, 78, 110, 117, 243, 257, 271–72, 367, 369	13:36–37	249		
		13:37	38, 242, 243	**LAB (Pseudo-Philo's**	
		13:37–38	78, 117, 250	***Biblical Antiquities*)**	
13–14	273	13:39	117, 251	3:10	290
13:1–58	222, 256	13:39–47	251	27:10	278
13:2	248	13:47	117, 251	47:1	232n
13:2–13	256	13:48	241, 252, 365	48:1	103, 232–34, 258, 259
13:3	37, 38, 245–50, 269, 303, 366, 372	13:48–49	252–53		
		13:49–50	252–53		
13:3–4	248–49, 373	13:50	234, 241, 253, 269	**Psalms of Solomon**	
13:3–13	256	13:51	246	2:19	48
13:3a	110	13:52	75, 75n, 231, 234, 243, 248, 258, 367	17	253, 268, 275n
13:3b	110			17:22–25	275n
13:3b–4	250, 255	13:57	242	17:24	250

17:26	243	5:96–97	216	5:256	204, 205, 206, 212,
17:28	252	5:98	216n		214, 217n, 219, 372
17:29	183	5:99–100	216n	5:256–259	210–16, 219
17:35	183, 250	5:101	280	5:257	211, 214
		5:101–103	289	5:257–259	214
Sibylline Oracles		5:106	219	5:258–259	206, 211,
2:34–38	230	5:106–107	203		212–13, 214,
3:1–96	209n	5:106–109	289		217n, 219
3:49–50	209n	5:107	281	5:260–270	217n
3:288	206	5:108	205–6, 212	5:274	209
3:300–313	226	5:108–109	202, 205,	5:286–434	219
3:334	207		219, 268, 281	5:349	214
3:388–394	140	5:108–110	204	5:361–374	219
3:388–400	140	5:111–178	219	5:361–380	280
3:396–400	203n	5:118	209	5:367	216n
3:400	140	5:137–154	219, 280	5:369	209
3:419	206, 210n, 212	5:143	282, 361n	5:377–378	209
3:573	210n, 212	5:147–149	280, 288	5:381–385	217
3:652	205, 210	5:149	204	5:388	208
3:652–654	205, 206	5:150–155	204n	5:397	201n
3:657–732	277, 279	5:155	204, 207, 219	5:397–413	208, 281
3:669–670	227	5:155–159	206–7, 336	5:399	209
3:672–674	230	5:155–161	219	5:401	204, 219
3:776	211n	5:158	205, 207, 219	5:408	206
3:801–802	214	5:158–160	217	5:414	204, 205, 208,
4:119–148	280	5:159	209, 361n		213, 372
4:173–174	230	5:169	282	5:414–415	219
4:175	227, 230	5:173	282	5:414–416	37
5	201–20	5:177	209	5:414–419	211n
5:7	219	5:178	282	5:414–433	208, 220
5:28–34	280	5:179–285	219	5:414–434	202, 219
5:36	206	5:211–213	209	5:415	217, 219, 372
5:52–110	219	5:214–227	219, 280	5:415–416	209n, 217
5:52–434	202, 219	5:222–223	202–3, 219	5:416	209
5:88	216n	5:225–227	280	5:418–419	209, 213, 219
5:93	280	5:228–237	203	5:420–425	281
5:93–94	289	5:229–230	217n	5:420–427	209–10
5:93–107	219	5:237	206	5:432	204, 219
5:93–109	280–81, 282	5:244–245	217n	5:434–446	226, 282n
5:93–110	280	5:247–252	281	5:477–478	214

427

INDEX OF ANCIENT LITERATURE

Testament of Abraham		vi 6	138	4Q208	8
B8:5	49n	x 10	138		
B11:2–10	102	xi 6–7	336	4Q209	8
B11:3	102n	xii 5	138		
		xii 8	138, 139	4Q210	8
Testament of Levi		xii 16	138		
2–7	122	xv 1	138	4Q211	8
5:1	43n	xvi 1	138		
13:9	48n	xvii 6–7	138	4Q212(En^g)	8n
		xix 8	138		
Testament of Moses				4Q242 [4QPrNab]	
2:4	141	1QSb		frag. 1–3	177
4:1–5	141	v 20–21	268		
4:4	141	v 24–28	183	4Q242–245	174
8:1	141	v 27–28	268, 336		
10:1	141	v 27–29	337	4Q243–244	
10:2	141	v 29	244–45	(4QpsDan$^{a,\,b}$ ar)	137
10:3	141				
10:7	141	2Q26	9	4Q245 (4QpsDan^c ar)	
10:9	141				137n
		4Q174	243		
DEAD SEA SCROLLS				4Q246 (4QAramaic	
		4Q175 [4QTest]		Apocalypse)	137,
CD (Damascus		i 9–13	336		173–200
Document)				i 4–ii 9	175
7:19	268	4Q201(En^a)	8n	i 6	174
7:19–21	336			i 7	197
		4Q202(En^b)	8n	i 7–ii 2	191
1Q23	9			i 9–ii 1	176–78, 196–97
		4Q203	9	ii 1	173
1Q24	9			ii 1–2	175
		4Q204(En^c)	8n	ii 2	176
1QapGen (Genesis				ii 2–3	175
Apocryphon)		4Q205(En^d)	8n	ii 3	174
ii 1–26	102n			ii 4	175, 176, 178,
ii 20	85n	4Q206(En^e)	8n		183, 185, 189–90
				ii 4–9	178–92
1QM (War Rule)		4Q207(En^f)	8n	ii 5	174, 175, 178,
i 1–17	138				179, 181, 182, 268

Index of Ancient Literature

ii 5–6	181–83	4QDan[e]	136	7Q4	9
ii 5–7	184–85				
ii 5–9	179	4QEn[b]		7Q8	9
ii 6	183, 185	1 iii 15	44		
ii 7	184			7Q11–14	9
ii 7–9	185–87	4QEn[g]			
ii 8–9	185, 191	ii 22–23	105	11QMelchizedek (11Q13)	
ii 9	174, 175, 179, 268			ii 7–8	139n
		4QFlorilegium		ii 9	139
4Q252		1–3 ii 3–4c	137	ii 11	139
v 1–5	268			ii 18	138
v 3–4	188–90	4QJub[a]			
		ii 11	187	11Q17	44
4Q285					
frag. 5	297	4QLevi		11QT[a]	
		93	47–48	39:6	99
4Q383–390	138n				
		4QLevi[a] ar (4Q213)		XQpapEnoch	9
4Q405		6 i 18	48n		
20–21–22 ii 2	44n			**ANCIENT JEWISH**	
20–21–22 ii 6–9	98n	4QLevi[b] ar		**WRITERS**	
20–21–22 ii 9	44	1 i 12	182n		
23 i 3	43n			**Philo of Alexandria**	
		4QpHab		*Legatio ad Gaium*	
4Q530 (4QEnGiants[b])		v 4–5	31	114–116	99
ii 16–19	9, 67–68				
		4QpIsa[a] (4Q161)		*On Abraham*	
4Q531	9	8–10, lines 2–9	297, 309	17	85n
		8–10 iii 18–19	268n	*On Rewards and*	
4Q532	9	8–10 iii 20	48	*Punishments*	
		8–10 iii 21	268	95	336
4Q533	9	8–10 iii 21–22	183		
				On the Confusion	
4Q552–553 (4QFour				*of Tongues*	
Kingdoms [a, b] ar)	137–38	4QTob[b] [4Q197]		123	85n
		4 ii 2	182		
4Q588				*On the Life of Moses*	
i 2:4	103	6Q8	9	1.297	336
				2.288	355

INDEX OF ANCIENT LITERATURE

On the Posterity		10.79	360, 365	*Jewish War*	
of Cain and His Exile		10.203–210	348–52	1.204	261n
35	85n	10.205–210	365	1.248–273	275
41	85n	10.206–209	349	2.261–262	215n
		10.207	349	2.345–401	366
Josephus		10.208	348	2.433	263
Against Apion		10.208–209	365	2.433–434	341
2.218	359n	10.209	348	3.132	340
		10.210	350, 361	3.351	332, 333
Antiquities		10.232	348	3.351–353	365
1–10	360	10.233	361n	3.351–354	331
1.20	365	10.246	329	3.352	346, 348, 353
1.221	362	10.249	329	3.401–402	332
2.194	354n	10.267	341, 344	3.406–407	329n
4.104	354n	10.269	329, 352, 354	4.318	346
4.104–130	354	10.269–275	352	4.321	346
4.114–117	355	10.269–276	365	4.385	335
4.115–116	349	10.271	353	4.386	335n, 343n
4.116–117	357	10.275	353	4.388	360
4.125	337, 355–56, 365	10.276	344, 352, 353, 365	5.19	365
4.127–128	356	10.277–280	365	5.367	330, 365
4.128	357, 359, 365, 366	11–20	360	5.376–390	357
4.303	359	11.5–6	360n	5.376–419	366
4.312–314	358	11.285	356n, 357n	5.391–393	360n
4.314	347, 359, 365	13.64	360n	5.411–412	360n
6.83	362	13.68	360n	5.566	365
6.157	362	13.71	360n	6.103	360n
6.159	362	14.159	261n	6.109	335n
7.357	362	14.330–393	275	6.164–168	345
7.382	362	15.385–387	348	6.250	360, 365
8.137	362n	17.271–285	275	6.267–268	360, 365
8.271	344n	18.9–10	363	6.288–315	334
8.275	344n	18.63	362	6.289	338
9.106	362	20.166	365	6.300–309	340
9.149	362	20.169–171	215n	6.301	360n
9.276	360n	20.200	362	6.310	334
10.32	360n	20.201–203	362–63	6.311	345
10.35	360n			6.312	338

6.312–313	274, 333, 334
6.313	340
6.352	334
6.435	360n
7.29	275
7.432	360n

New Testament

Matthew
2:11	71n
4:8	49n, 50
5:34	49
6:29	49n, 50
16:13–19	122
16:14	215n
16:27	49
19:28	48–49
23:22	49
24:15	167
24:27	49
24:30	2, 49, 146, 295
25:31	48–49
26:64	2, 146
27:17	363n
28:18b–20	146

Mark
8:28	215n
8:38	49n
9:12	103
10:37	49n
13:1–27	146n
13:2–27	149
13:4	146n
13:14	146n, 167
13:26	2, 49n, 146
14:62	2, 146

Luke
1:17	103
1:32–33	176–78, 196, 197
1:35	177
1:78–79	210n
2:25	263
4:6	50
6:35	177
7:6	177
9:26	49n
20:18	351n
21:27	49n

John
5:27	31

Acts
2:29	319
6:15	36n
7:48	177
7:56	1
7:56–8:1	325n
12:20	156

1 Corinthians
15:19	296
15:47–49	37
15:48–49	38n

Philippians
1:23	269
3:20	37n

1 Thessalonians
1:10	37n
4:15–16	296

2 Thessalonians
1:7	296

1 Timothy
3:16	295n

Hebrews
11:33	147, 149

1 John
1:1	74n

Jude
14	81
14–15	124

Revelation
1:13	37
2:16	268
3:9	99
4–5	323n
4:5	158n
4:10	98n
5	95
5:5	244
5:13	95
6:9–11	291
8:8	158n
9:7	158n
9:20	148
11:2	204
11:3–13	233n
11:7	147
12:11	117
12:14	204
14:1	117
14:14	37
15:2	158n

Index of Ancient Literature

16	281	b. Nedarim		Targum Micah	
16:1–2	141n	39b	70n	4:8	259
16:12	281–82	b. Pesahim		5:1	72n
16:12–14	288	54a	70n	Targum Neofiti: Genesis	
16:12–16	284	b. Sanhedrin		49:10	268n
16:16	288	38b	315n, 327	Targum Pseudo-Jonathan: Exodus	
16:17	281	98a–b	283		
17	281	98b	262, 317–18	4:13	233n
17:9–11	281	98b–99a	262	6:18	233n
17:12–13	281	99a	240–41	40:10	233n
18	282n	b. Sukkah		40:11	211n
19:1	158n	52b	259	Targum Zechariah	
19:6	158n			3:8	259, 265n
19:11	251	**Jerusalem Talmud**		4:7	259, 265n
19:11–16	281	y. Avodah Zarah		6:12	259, 265n
19:11–21	117	3:1	260, 261n		
19:13	117	y. Berakhot		**Other Rabbinic Works**	
19:14	117	2:4	75n	Avot of Rabbi Nathan	
19:15	117, 251, 268	2:4[5a]	317, 318n	25	261n
19:16	268	2:4[25b]	262, 263n, 264	Canticles Rabbah	
19:21	268	2:5a	75n	8.9.3	284n
20:4	31, 268	y. Sotah		Derekh Eretz Zuta	
20:7–15	277, 279	9:16	261n	1–3	236
20:8	216n	y. Ta'anit		1:18	259
20:12	230n	4:8	265, 319	1:18–20	236
20:13a	290	68d [49]	336	1:20	236
22:8–9	99			Genesis Rabbah	
		Targumic Texts		25:1	237
Rabbinic Works		Targum 1 Chronicles		Lamentations Rabbah	
Babylonian Talmud		3:24	259, 265–66n	1–13[41]	284
b. Berakhot		Targum Isaiah		1:16	75n
28b	260	66:7	259, 265n	1:51	75n, 262n, 263n, 264, 317n, 318n
b. Hagigah		Targum Jeremiah		Numbers Rabbah	
14a	45n, 315, 319, 324, 326–27	30:21	259, 265n	13:5	75n
b. Ketubbot					
77b	237				

13:14	351n	
Pesiqta Rabbah		
1	240	
Pirqe Rabbi Eliezer		
29	232n	
Tanhuma-Yelambenu		
6:14	351n	
7:7	351n	

Early Christian Writings

Justin Martyr

Dialogue with Trypho

32.1	37
35	262
67	262
71	262

77	262

Martyrdom of Polycarp

12.1	85n

Greco-Roman Literature

Lucian

De luctu

24	208n

Philopsuedes

27	208n

Pliny the Elder

Natural History

2.22–89	340

Seneca

Naturales quaestiones

7.21.3–4	339n

Suetonius

Life of Vespasian

4.5	334

Tacitus

Histories

5.13	334

Papyri

Codex 88 (OG-Dan) 142, 154–55, 169–70, 172

Papyrus 967 (OG-Dan) 142, 154–55, 169, 171–72